AMERICAN CLASSICS

THE FOUNDATIONS OF AMERICAN NATIONALITY

Evarts Boutell Greene

FREDERICK UNGAR PUBLISHING CO.
NEW YORK

PREFACE

MORE than half a century ago, George Bancroft closed his *History of the United States* with the adoption of the Federal Constitution in 1789. It is with this period also that the present volume is concerned; but in the interval our conceptions of American Colonial and Revolutionary history have been radically changed. The developments of the last half century, both in our national experience and in the progress of historical scholarship, require a different perspective. Though it is impossible to allot to colonial history the time formerly given to it in introductory courses in the history of the United States, it remains true that the characteristic institutions and ideals of the American people cannot be fully understood without serious consideration not only of our colonial experience, but also of the Old-World society from which our pioneer settlers came.

It is equally certain that older interpretations of this formative period no longer satisfy the serious student. Such scholars as Channing, Turner, Osgood, Beer, Andrews, and many younger workers have exploited new materials, suggested new points of view, and made necessary the modification or abandonment of time-honored traditions. This was evident when the first edition of this book was published in 1922, and has since been emphasized by the publication of several important books, notably Professor Osgood's *American Colonies in the Eighteenth Century* and the first volume of *The Colonial Period of American History* by Professor Andrews. It is the purpose of this book to give the general reader, as well as the college student, the story of our early development as it appears in the light of such recent research and discus-

iii

sion. No survey of this kind can be definitive; but the author has tried to write, without bias, whether for or against traditional views, and with an open mind for new facts or theories of interpretation.

With the general tendency of recent historical literature toward fuller recognition of economic and social, as distinguished from strictly political, history, the author is in full sympathy; and the allotment of space has been planned accordingly. It is well known also that many phases of colonial history have been given new meaning by relating this development more closely to that of the great empire of which the colonies formed only a part, though an increasingly important part. With full recognition of this imperial background, the author has nevertheless felt justified in emphasizing those aspects of colonial experience which seem most significant for the subsequent development of the American nation.

The brief bibliographical notes at the end of each chapter have been prepared for readers rather than for investigators; the latter will necessarily search for additional material through the standard bibliographical aids and in the footnotes of secondary authorities dealing with special periods or topics. For every chapter some illustrative material from the sources is indicated; but, in general, the lists do not include extensive documentary publications, such as legislative journals or statutes. It is obviously impossible also to make more than a very limited selection from the great mass of monographic and periodical literature which has been published, especially during the present century. In this new edition the reference lists have been carefully revised. New titles have been added, somewhat more attention given to monographs and periodicals, and a few books which now seem antiquated or relatively unimportant have been omitted. Though the changes made in the text have been more limited, many of the new references will guide the reader in the study of topics which necessarily received only summary treatment in the narrative.

While assuming full responsibility for all errors, whether of fact or judgment, the author desires to express his special sense of obligation to three friends: To the late Professor Carl Russell Fish of the University of Wisconsin and to my former colleague, Professor Laurence M. Larson of the University of Illinois, I am indebted for helpful advice in the preparation of the first edition. In the task of revision, I have profited greatly by the suggestions of Professor Richard B. Morris of the College of the City of New York.

EVARTS B. GREENE

GENERAL REFERENCES

E. Channing, *A History of the United States*, vols. I–VII, N. Y., 1905–1912 (cited as Channing, *United States*), is still the best general narrative history, covering the American development to 1789.

The following coöperative histories are important for this period:

J. Winsor, editor, *Narrative and Critical History of America*, 8 vols., Boston, 1884–1889 (cited as Winsor, *America*). Deals mainly with the period before 1789. Written many years ago but still indispensable, especially as a guide to the sources, both printed and manuscript.

A. B. Hart, editor, *The American Nation: A History*, vols. I–X, N. Y., 1904–1905. Each volume has a separate author. Useful both for narrative and bibliography, emphasizing both political and institutional history. (Cited by individual authors.)

A. M. Schlesinger and D. R. Fox, editors, *A History of American Life*, vols. I–IV, N. Y., 1927. Reflects the new emphasis upon non-political and non-institutional matters in "social history."

The Chronicles of America (A. Johnson, editor, New Haven, 1918–1921) has some interesting volumes on the colonial pre-Revolutionary eras, and *The Pageant of America, A Pictorial History of the United States*, edited by R. H. Gabriel and others (15 vols., New Haven, 1926) is useful for illustrative material.

Invaluable for biographical information is the *Dictionary of American Biography*, edited by A. Johnson and D. Malone, N. Y., 1928–

Of the first importance for the institutional history of the pre-Revolutionary era are the two series by H. L. Osgood: *The American Colonies in the Seventeenth Century*, 3 vols., N. Y., 1904–

1907 (cited as Osgood, *17th Cent.*); and *The American Colonies in the Eighteenth Century*, 4 vols., N. Y., 1924 (cited as Osgood, *18th Cent.*). In 1934 appeared the first volume of *The Colonial Period of American History* by C. M. Andrews, an outstanding authority, who emphasizes the imperial setting of colonial society, and views American development from the vantage point of the center of the "old Empire" in England.

There is as yet no comprehensive work on the economic development of this formative period; but the subject is dealt with briefly in a number of manuals on the economic history of the United States. Among these may be mentioned the recent surveys by H. U. Faulkner, H. J. Carman, and E. C. Kirkland. A one-volume book on colonial history which emphasizes social and economic topics, with excellent reference lists, is M. W. Jernegan's *The American Colonies, 1492–1750*, N. Y., 1929.

Useful for the history of culture are M. C. Tyler, *History of American Literature, 1607–1765*, 2 vols., N. Y., 1879; his *Literary History of the American Revolution*, 2 vols., N. Y., 1897; and the *Cambridge History of American Literature*, vol. I, N. Y., 1917. Stimulating essays toward a synthesis of political and social history with the history of culture are C. A. and M. R. Beard, *Rise of American Civilization*, vol. I, N. Y., 1927 (cited as Beard and Beard); and V. L. Parrington, *The Colonial Mind*, N. Y., 1927.

The *American Historical Review* (cited as *A.H.R.*), with such regional journals as the *New England Quarterly* (*N.E.Q.*) and the *Mississippi Valley Historical Review* (*M.V.H.R.*), supply much supplementary material, some of which is indicated in the reference lists for successive chapters of this book. The best one-volume bibliographical guide is still the *Guide to the Study and Reading of American History* by E. Channing, A. B. Hart, and F. J. Turner, Boston, 1912. Clues to more recent publications may be sought in such guides as the annual bibliography, the *Writings on American History* (American Historical Association), and the annual and decennial indexes of the *American Historical Review*. Historical materials, both printed and manuscript, available in New York City are listed in E. B. Greene and R. B. Morris, *A Guide to the Principal Sources for Early American History (1600–1800) in the City of New York*, N. Y., 1929.

Convenient collections of sources are: H. S. Commager, *Documents of American History*, N. Y., 1934 (cited as Commager, *Documents*); W. Macdonald, *Select Charters Illustrative of American History, 1606–1775*, N. Y., 1904 (cited as *Select Charters*); T. C. Pease and A. S. Roberts, *Selected Readings in American History*, N. Y., 1928 (cited as Pease and Roberts, *Readings*); A. B. Hart, *American History Told by Contemporaries*, vols. I–III, N. Y., 1897–1900 (cited as Hart, *Contemporaries*). J. F. Jameson, editor, *Original Narratives of Early American History*, N. Y., 1906–1917, is a more extensive series for the first century of colonization.

The most comprehensive atlas for American history is C. O. Paullin, *Atlas of the Historical Geography of the United States*, N. Y., 1932.

Statistics of population for the colonial period have been compiled by E. B. Greene and V. D. Harrington in *American Population before the Federal Census of 1790*, N. Y., 1932.

CONTENTS

		PAGE
GENERAL REFERENCES	....	vii
CHAPTER		
I.	THE EUROPEAN INHERITANCE...................	1
II.	THE ENGLISH OUTLOOK ON AMERICA..............	20
III.	THE VIRGINIA PIONEERS........................	45
IV.	THE CHESAPEAKE COLONIES, 1632 to 1688.........	67
V.	NEW ENGLAND PIONEERS.......................	87
VI.	THE PURITAN COMMONWEALTHS, 1635 to 1676......	112
VII.	EXPANSION AND CONQUEST......................	130
VIII.	ENGLISH COLONIZATION OF THE HUDSON AND DELAWARE VALLEYS, 1664 to 1688...................	155
IX.	IMPERIALISM AND SELF-GOVERNMENT..............	178
X.	FRENCH AND SPANISH RIVALS, 1608 to 1713........	207
XI.	THE EMPIRE AND THE COLONIES..................	226
XII.	PROVINCIAL NEW ENGLAND......................	257
XIII.	EXPANSION IN THE MIDDLE PROVINCES............	281
XIV.	EXPANSION IN THE SOUTH......................	311
XV.	ENGLISH AND AMERICAN WAYS...................	338
XVI.	THE STRUGGLE FOR THE WEST AND THE PASSING OF NEW FRANCE.................................	357
XVII.	IMPERIAL PROBLEMS AND POLICIES, 1760 to 1766....	388
XVIII.	THE EVE OF REVOLUTION, 1766 to 1774............	414
XIX.	REVOLUTION, 1774 to 1776......................	437
XX.	THE OPPOSING FORCES..........................	459
XXI.	EUROPE AND AMERICA, 1776 to 1780..............	475
XXII.	INDEPENDENCE WON............................	496
XXIII.	REPUBLICAN DIPLOMACY, 1779 to 1784............	512
XXIV.	INDEPENDENT AMERICA..........................	526

xi

CHAPTER PAGE

XXV. REPUBLICAN PRINCIPLES IN RECONSTRUCTION....... 547

XXVI. FEDERAL PROBLEMS, 1783 to 1787................. 565

XXVII. THE GREAT CONVENTION.......................... 584

XXVIII. THE NEW UNION............................... 603

MAPS

Section of the "Wright-Hakluyt" Map (An English View of the North Atlantic World in 1600) 28, 29

Extension of Royal Governments 1683–1702.................. 188

North America and the Caribbean Region after the Treaty of Utrecht, 1713 225

Principal Sea Routes of Colonial Commerce, 1700–1750... 244, 245

International Frontiers, 1739–1755.......................... 366

Europe and America, 1775–1783........................ 476, 477

THE FOUNDATIONS OF
AMERICAN NATIONALITY

CHAPTER I

THE EUROPEAN INHERITANCE

THE development of the people now politically organized in the United States of America is in a very true sense a part of European history; for it is the record of European enterprise on American soil, of the transfer to a new environment of social habits and ideals which, though greatly changed by American conditions, are still essentially a phase of European civilization. The true starting point for the history of the United States is not, therefore, the study of aboriginal America, nor even the process by which America became known to Europeans; it is rather the European world from which the colonists came, the stock of traditions and prejudices which they inherited from their fathers, and the special characteristics of the age in which they lived. *The European background.*

More definitely still, we must first try to understand the England and the Englishmen of the early seventeenth century. It is indeed true, as Thomas Paine said in his *Common Sense*, that America is the child not of England only but of Europe; nevertheless, our earlier history is primarily concerned with the emigration, and adaptation to American life, of English men and English institutions. It was in 1606, three years after the death of Queen Elizabeth, that the founders of the first successful English colony in America set out from the mother country. The foundation of twelve of the thirteen colonies which afterwards formed the United States of America was mainly the work of men then living, *English origins.*

their children, and their grandchildren. The social experience of these three generations, in the country from which most of them came, determined to a large extent their outlook upon life and the institutions which they founded in the New World.

England in 1606.

To understand the England of 1606, we must get rid of many associations which gather about the British world power of the present day. When James I was crowned in 1603, the United Kingdom of Great Britain and Ireland did not exist. In the English Parliament of that day only England and Wales were included. Though James I, King of England, was also James VI, King of Scotland, the two kingdoms were distinct, and for a hundred years more Scotland was regarded by Englishmen as a foreign country. Ireland was a half-foreign dependency, with a subordinate parliament of its own but without representation in the English Parliament. Indeed Ireland was itself considered a proper field for colonization and in the seventeenth century the northern province of Ulster was settled by Scotchmen and Englishmen, partly displacing the native Irish. The Indian Empire of to-day was still undreamed of and there were no "dominions beyond the seas," except the shadowy claims to North America based upon the discoveries of the Cabots and a few unsuccessful attempts at settlement. In the British colony planting of the early seventeenth century, Scotchmen, Irishmen, and even Welshmen were of minor importance; for the pioneers of New England and the Chesapeake colonies alike, the mother country was England proper.

Supposed excess of population.

The population of England in 1606 was hardly five million, a small fraction of the present number. Even then, however, it was commonly believed that the country was overcrowded and needed an outlet for its surplus population. Sir George Peckham, a well-known promoter of colonization, declared that since England had for a long time enjoyed peace and freedom from serious pestilence, "there are at this day great numbers (God he knoweth) which live in such penurie and want, as they could be contented to hazard their lives, and to serve one yeare for meat, drinke, and apparell only, without wages, in hope thereby to mend their estates." During the latter part of the sixteenth century, the natural increase of population was reënforced by immigrants from the Continent, especially Protestants from the Netherlands who had been driven from home by the intolerance of Philip II.

The people of England in 1606 were divided quite distinctly into social classes. One contemporary writer names four of these classes. First come the "gentlemen," including not only the nobility of various grades but also "they that are simplie called gentlemen." Among the latter were counted the landed gentry, scholars, professional men, and military officers. It was one of the essential marks of a gentleman that he could live without manual labor. Second in order were the merchants, who had increased decidedly in numbers and importance during the Tudor period and were thought by the country people to be responsible for the higher cost of living. The third class were the yeomen or small farmers, who by good management often became prosperous, so that their sons at least might receive the benefits of university education, "live without labour," and so rise into the class of gentlemen. At the bottom of the social scale were the peasants in the country and the mechanics and smaller tradespeople in the towns. This last class did not count for much politically, having "neither voice nor authoritie in the commonwealth"; they were "to be ruled and not to rule over." Nevertheless, they were called upon to fill minor offices in towns and country parishes. *Social classes.*

England was still mainly an agricultural country, but it was passing through radical economic changes which affected almost every element of the population. In the southeastern *Economic interests.*

counties especially, from which many of the American colonists came, woolen manufactures were developing strongly; their growth and protection against undesirable competition was an important phase of British policy during the colonial era. Furthermore, the discovery of America, the increased supply of precious metals, and the constantly broadening opportunities for trade at home and abroad were developing a strong mercantile class who were not only able to live well but ready to invest their capital in profitable enterprises abroad as well as at home. The advantages of combination were already recognized and many joint-stock companies were chartered by Elizabeth and James I for the purpose of carrying on foreign trade.

Joint-stock companies. Among the companies so organized were the Muscovy Company, first chartered in 1555, a few years before the accession of Elizabeth, to carry on trade with Russia; the Eastland Company, chartered in 1579 for the Baltic trade; the Turkey Company in 1581; and the East India Company, which, beginning in 1600 as a trading company only, became a great political power in the next century and laid the foundations of the British empire in India. London was the chief commercial port, but Bristol, Plymouth, and many smaller towns now rarely heard of played a large part in the seagoing commerce of the time.

Economic changes. Economic expansion brought important changes in the relation of various classes to each other. In the towns, the guild system was breaking down and the distinction between the employer who furnished the capital and the employee who worked for wages was becoming more fixed. The new commercial spirit also affected the country. Through the buying up of confiscated monastery lands and in various other ways, country estates were coming into the hands of more aggressive and businesslike, but often unscrupulous landlords, recruited in part from the merchant class. Even when the ownership of these estates remained in the hands of an old family, the actual management was put into the hands of a new type of leasehold farmers who were naturally determined to make the business pay. These changes affected seriously the status of the agricultural population. Under the old manorial organization, the relation between landlord and tenant had been determined more by custom than by formal contract. Serfdom had practically disappeared and the tenant held his land chiefly on condition of certain customary payments; so long as these conditions were met, his rights in the soil were nearly as secure as those of the landlord himself. Furthermore there were on every manor considerable tracts of land, pasture and woodland for instance, in which all the tenants had common rights. To the new landlord, these customary arrangements often seemed to interfere with efficient and profitable management of the estate. So, as the expanding woolen industry increased the demand for raw wool, he began to inclose common lands for his exclusive use and sometimes to convert arable land into pasture. Sometimes also the old customary tenure was converted into leases which gave the landlord a better opportunity to drive hard bargains with his tenants and evict them when they failed to meet his terms. The result was a temporary lessening of the demand for agricultural labor, the depopulation of many communities, and the development of a large vagrant class. So the statesmen of the Tudor period were troubled by the problems of pauperism and the crime that naturally follows.

Landlord and tenant.

Thus in the economic changes of the sixteenth century, as in many others before and since, the advantages of progress were unequally shared. While the commercial middle class was gaining in wealth, others were growing poorer; and, as prices rose, men of moderate means, as well as the very poor, were troubled by the increasing cost of living. In conditions like these contemporary writers found some of their chief arguments for colony planting.

Inequalities.

King and
Parliament.

The Englishmen of 1606 lived under a monarchy and few of them thought any other form of government possible or desirable. At the head of the system stood the King, who came to his throne by right of hereditary descent and had the loyal support of nearly all his subjects. Nearly everyone, too, was willing to allow the King and his Council a freedom in the exercise of royal power quite impossible at the present day. Nevertheless, intelligent Englishmen generally believed that the King's power was not unlimited, that new taxes should not be laid nor important changes made in the law without the consent of Parliament. This Parliament was not, however, representative of all classes but chiefly of those described as "gentlemen." The House of Lords included the greater nobility and the bishops of the national church. The country members of the House of Commons were chosen by the freeholders, who included beside the gentry the more independent of the farmer class. In the boroughs, the merchants had some representation, but the number of voters was generally small.

Constitutional issues

Throughout the seventeenth century, Englishmen disagreed sharply as to the exact boundary between the King's prerogative and the authority of Parliament. Under the Tudor kings, the royal power was greatly increased, partly because such rulers as Henry VIII and Elizabeth were strong and, on the whole, popular leaders of the nation. The common man profited in many ways from a strong central government which could preserve order and restrain the violence and injustice of the landowning aristocracy. The commercial classes also profited by the growth of royal authority which was used in many ways to promote their interests. During the latter part of Elizabeth's reign, however, the so-called "country party," including both country gentlemen and members of the mercantile class, began to insist more strongly on the rights of the House of Commons. James I and his son Charles I met these rising demands with the theory of "divine right," asserting that the King received his crown independently of the national will and had certain "prerogative" rights which were above the law and could not be controlled by Parliament. These controversies, increasing in violence, combined with religious issues to bring on the great Civil War and the execution of Charles I. Finally the Revolution of 1688 established the sovereignty of Parliament as the foundation principle of English constitutional law.

An important part of the work of government was done by the national courts of justice, all of which, from the justices of the peace in the various counties to the great courts of the King's Bench and Common Pleas, were composed of judges appointed by the King and removable by him at his pleasure. Gradually during the Middle Ages the King's judges, going out into the country on their "circuits," had built up, on the foundation of ancient customs, the great fabric of national law, displacing in large part the special jurisdictions of the feudal lords and the church. In these national courts, criminal cases were tried and justice administered in civil suits according to certain well-recognized principles of the "common law," including the right of the defendant to a jury trial and the right of every individual not to be deprived of life, liberty, or property without due process of law. Though these principles were generally acknowledged, there were still great differences of opinion about their application. Englishmen were not always free from arbitrary arrest and imprisonment by order of the King; the King's influence over the judges was often so great as to prevent impartial justice; and there was much complaint about the irregular proceedings of the Star Chamber and other special courts which developed out of the King's Council. As a matter of fact, however, these irregular methods were sometimes used to protect the common man against his more powerful neighbor.

Courts of justice.

The "common law."

Local
government.

The county.

The parish.

Under the close supervision of the King's Council, a large share of the public business was done through the local governments, of which the most important were the county, the parish, and, for the urban areas, the boroughs. The most influential officers of the county government were the justices of the peace. These were appointed by the King and could be removed by him; but as a matter of fact they were usually the leading gentlemen of the county in wealth, social standing, and influence. Sitting together as a court of "quarter sessions" they not only tried judicial cases but also did much that is now done by American county boards, including the levy of county taxes. One important authority exercised by the justices was that of fixing wages; in this, as in other matters, they naturally kept in view the interests of their own landowning class. The chief executive officer of the county government for ordinary purposes was the sheriff, who, like the justices, was usually a man of some wealth and social standing. A more imposing personage was the lord lieutenant, a leading nobleman of the county, who commanded its military forces. The landowners of the county had an essential part in the system: they served as jurymen in the courts and they could also vote for the knights of the shire who represented them in the House of Commons.

For the country population the parish was important. This was originally an agency for church government, and its principal officers, the churchwardens and vestrymen, were elected in the parish meeting to take charge, with the clergyman, of the spiritual as well as the civil interests of the community. The ordinary police duties of the parish were performed by the constable, who was sometimes chosen by the parishioners, sometimes by the justices, and sometimes by the lord of the manor in which the village was included. Just before the colonial era began, the parish was given another task, that of caring for the poor within its limits. For all these purposes money was needed, and the parish rate, or tax, was collected from the inhabitants. An important factor in the life of almost every parish was the principal landowner, or lord of the manor, from whom the inhabitants held their land by various forms of tenure. The judicial authority of the manorial lord was gradually disappearing, but he was commonly a justice of the peace and his personal influence in the social and political life of the people was very great.

The people of the urban areas and even of some small country towns were organized in boroughs; these were based on royal charters, some of which went back to the early Middle Ages. There was no uniform system. Mayors and aldermen were chosen in different ways, sometimes by the taxpayers, sometimes by a restricted class of so-called "freemen"; in many places the governing group was a "close corporation," filling vacancies in its own membership. In general the borough governments were controlled by a comparatively small number of persons. The borough.

Thus whether we look at national government by King and Parliament, or local government by justices of the peace and borough corporations, the English people lived under a political system which was sharply aristocratic. Generally speaking, it was the business of noblemen, other gentlemen, and to a certain extent of the richer middle class, to govern the country; it was the business of others to be ruled. Even a revolutionary leader like Oliver Cromwell believed that the distinction between "gentle" and "simple," between the "gentleman" and the common man, was desirable and should be preserved. It was, in fact, carried over to the New World by the colonists of New England and Virginia alike. Distinct as were the social classes, the barriers between them were not impassable. The sons of yeomen and merchants might, and often did, as the result of their own achievements or those of their fathers, become gentle- Aristocracy. Class barriers not impassable.

men; on the other hand, the younger sons of the landed gentry sometimes became city merchants. In this respect, as in many others, English society was freer than that of France, Spain, or Germany. It must never be forgotten, either, that England was then the only important European nation with an efficient system of national representation.

The national church. An essential part of English life was the national church. In the Middle Ages, England had been united with the rest of western and central Europe in the great Catholic Church of which the Roman Pope was the visible head. Partly under the influence of the Protestant Reformation on the European continent, partly from personal and political motives on the part of the Tudor sovereigns and their ministers, and partly as the result of a nationalistic movement against foreign control, England had lately broken away from the Church of Rome and reorganized its ecclesiastical constitution on national lines. In theory at least, every man born in England inherited the duty of loyalty to the church as he did that of loyalty to King and Parliament. Church and state were now more closely united than ever before. The King was the "governor" of the church, under God; as such he appointed the bishops and other principal church officers. Parliament also had its share in the government of the church; for theological tests and forms of worship, though framed by the clergy, were formally embodied in statute law. The freedom of the church was thus restricted, but these limitations were offset by some important privileges. The bishops sat in the House of Lords, and, in addition to the tithes charged upon the land, there were parish rates which all subjects were obliged to pay. No other religious body had any legal standing. Those who professed other forms of religion were subjected to various legal disadvantages or penalties, and all men were required to attend the services of the established church.

Nearly everyone agreed that there should be a state church, that it was the business of the state to support and defend the true kind of Christianity. Englishmen differed widely, however, as to what true Christianity was and how the church ought to be governed. Generally speaking, the policy of the government and of those who controlled the church after the separation from Rome was to keep as far as possible the old usages. The church was to be governed as before by bishops and archbishops; there was to be as little change as possible in doctrine; and the forms of service, though now spoken in English instead of in Latin, were taken with some changes and additions from the service books of the medieval church.

There were, however, two classes of Englishmen who were not satisfied with these arrangements. Many conservative people still opposed the separation from Rome and regarded the Pope as the supreme head of the church. They looked back with affection to the imposing ceremonial of the old days and regretted the changes which had been made in ritual and in doctrine. At the opposite extreme were the radical Protestants, or Puritans, who had been much influenced by Calvin and other leaders of the Reformation on the Continent. To them the Roman Church seemed utterly corrupt and they believed that the Church of England ought to be made a thoroughly Protestant institution. Not all Puritans held the same opinions, but in general they stood for what they considered a simpler and more Biblical form of religion with fewer forms and ceremonies and more emphasis on preaching. Though still for the most part laymen or clergymen in the established church, they were usually not in sympathy with the existing episcopal system of government and wished either to reduce the power of the bishops or to abolish it altogether, substituting a representative system like that advocated by Calvin and the Presbyterians of Scotland.

The Anglican system. Episcopal government.

Roman Catholics.

Puritans.

Conformity enforced by the state.

In organizing the Church of England efforts were made to conciliate both these opposing parties and find a middle way in which all could walk together; but in the end everyone was expected to conform to the established system. When James I came to the throne there was some hope that he might show more sympathy with the Puritans; but these expectations were disappointed, and a severely repressive policy was adopted. Toward the Catholics, James was personally more conciliatory, partly because he wished to cultivate friendly relations with Spain, then the leading Catholic power. The discovery of a Catholic conspiracy, however, and the intense popular feeling against the Roman Church led to more or less fitful persecution of its members during the early years of American colonization.

Puritans and Separatists.

Though nearly all Englishmen believed in an established church, including most of the Puritans, who wished to transform the church or even to be let alone in it rather than to withdraw altogether, there were small Puritan congregations here and there which felt quite differently. They were soon divided into various sects, but in general they believed that the Church of England was so thoroughly corrupt that all truly Biblical Christians must separate from it. Instead of wishing to establish a national state church, they believed that each local congregation of true believers should be self-governing, choosing its own ministers and other officers. In 1606 this party was too small to exert much influence, but every measure which made it more difficult for Puritans to remain in the church without giving up their convictions increased the number and influence of the "Separatist" element.

English civilization in 1606.

The civilization of England at this period was in some respects lower and in some respects, perhaps, higher than that of the present time. In contrivances for controlling natural forces and increasing physical comfort, even the wealthiest classes were not able to command what is easily within the reach of the ordinary man to-day. Indeed, the seventeenth century was in this respect worse off than the later Roman Empire. Government was less careful then than now to protect the life and property of the citizen against arbitrary treatment. Distinctions of rank also interfered seriously with the progress of the humbler classes. The idea that the state was bound to provide free education Education. for all the children of the community would have seemed quite strange in that day, and the church was much more important in this field. Education was the privilege of a comparatively small group.

Nevertheless, it is easy to overemphasize these deficiencies. The great universities of Oxford and Cambridge, with their rich endowments built up by the gifts of liberal men and women through many generations, were on the whole well adapted to the training of churchmen, scholars, and statesmen. Endowments for schools were common during the Middle Ages, and interest was stimulated by the scholars of the Renaissance period. In the early years of the seventeenth century many parishes had schools of their own, supported by endowments or public contributions or by a combination of these methods, and the somewhat meager records at hand indicate a rapid decrease in the rate of illiteracy. Among the ruling classes there was, perhaps, a keener intel- Intellectual lectual life than at the present time. The great awakening life. which began with the Italian Renaissance reached its height in England at the close of the sixteenth century; the names of Bacon in science and Shakespeare in literature are hard to match in any time. The fact that Shakespeare was the most popular dramatist of his age suggests that the average playgoer may have stood on at least as high a level of taste and intelligence as his present-day successor.

During the Tudor period the international position of International England had been greatly strengthened. After the demoral- relations. izing and weakening Wars of the Roses, the resources and power of the kingdom had been gradually built up by the Tudor sovereigns, three of whom — Henry VII, Henry VIII, and Elizabeth — were rulers of exceptional ability. Under Henry VIII, England began again to take a prominent part in European politics, though not always successfully, for she had powerful rivals. Of all these rivals the most

Spain and England.

powerful was the Spanish monarchy, which was consolidated under Ferdinand and Isabella in the last quarter of the fifteenth century and gradually acquired a series of dependencies in central Europe, including the Netherlands. Through the discoveries and conquests of Columbus and his successors, the gold and silver of the New World were brought into the Spanish treasury, and the Spanish army and navy became the most powerful in Europe. During a large part of the sixteenth century the relations of England and Spain were friendly. Henry VIII's first queen was the Spanish princess, Catherine of Aragon. Their daughter, Queen Mary, was the wife of Philip II of Spain, who after her death proposed to marry her successor, Elizabeth. The proposal was rejected; but for many years afterwards the English government kept on tolerable terms with Spain, partly to protect itself against a possible combination of the French with Elizabeth's rival, Mary, Queen of Scots.

Gradually, however, the two countries drifted into war. One factor in this change was the rising feeling of Protestant England against the Catholic Spaniards who were more or less involved in the conspiracies against Queen Elizabeth. When the Dutch Protestants rebelled against the attempts of Philip II to enforce the Catholic system upon them, the English government, which has always been keenly interested in the Netherlands, intervened in favor of the

Anglo-Spanish rivalry in the New World.

Dutch, at first secretly and then more openly. Most important of all was the refusal of English seamen to acknowledge the Spanish monopoly of colonization and trade in the New World. Daring adventurers like John Hawkins and Francis Drake persisted in carrying on this forbidden trade and, when attacked by the Spaniards, began a sort of private war in which Spanish-American ports were plundered and Spanish treasure ships captured on the high seas. Though professing disapproval of these exploits, the Queen often connived at them and shared in the profits, until finally the pretense of peaceful relations had to be abandoned. In 1588, after years of preparation, Philip II sent his "Invincible Armada" against England; but the great seamen who were so largely responsible for bringing on the war also brought about the decisive defeat of the Armada. England's supremacy on the seas was not yet established, but its foundations were laid at this time. The war lingered on during the last years of Elizabeth's reign; but when James I came to the throne, a treaty of peace was made and the King afterwards tried to arrange an alliance through the marriage of his son with a Spanish princess. This marriage project failed, however, and the attitude of the average Englishman toward Spain became one of habitual antagonism and distrust. Meantime as a result of the temporary union of Spain with Portugal, the Portuguese possessions in Asia were also involved and Anglo-Spanish rivalry was extended to the Far East.

The Invincible Armada.

During this period, France was a much less serious rival than Spain. While Ferdinand and Isabella were consolidating the Spanish kingdom, a similar work was being done in France by the great Louis XI and his successors; but French progress toward unity was seriously checked by the so-called "religious wars," which, though originating in the conflict between Protestants and Catholics, were complicated by economic factors and by the desire of the nobles to recover something of their old independence. The English people sympathized with the Huguenots, or French Protestants, as they had with the Dutch; and from time to time Elizabeth

France and England.

supported them in a half-hearted way. By the end of her reign the Huguenot leader, Henry of Navarre, had become King of France (Henry IV), though at the price of changing his religion. Protestantism was to be tolerated, but the Catholic Church was recognized as the official church of France. Under Henry IV, France again began to go forward; but when he was assassinated in 1610, there was another period of disorder and weakness. At last, however, there came to the front in 1624, the great cardinal-statesman, Richelieu, who raised the power of the King and the central government to a higher point than ever before, thus enabling France to supersede Spain as the strongest nation in Europe.

Italy and Germany.

Across central Europe from south to north lay two countries, Italy and Germany, which, though taking the lead in the great intellectual movements of the Renaissance and exerting an important influence on the art and literature of other countries, were crippled politically by internal divisions. Italy had long been broken up into a number of petty states, almost constantly at odds with each other, and it was frequently the battleground of foreign armies. In Germany a reform party tried to secure a unified national government like those of England, Spain, and France; but the movement failed, partly because of the mutual jealousies of the various principalities, and partly because at a critical time the Germans were further divided by the Protestant Reformation into two great religious parties. In 1618, two years before the Pilgrim colonists sailed for America, this religious antagonism, complicated by sordid interests of various kinds,

Thirty Years' War.

flamed up in the terrible Thirty Years' War, which completed the demoralization of Germany. In medieval times, the German cities had played a great part in international trade; but they were now seriously handicapped in competition with other nations whose governments were better able to protect and advance the interests of their subjects. Thus hopelessly divided, neither Italy nor Germany was able to win territory in the New World. The unhappy condition of Germany contributed in a more positive way to American colonial history, since it led a large number of Germans during the next hundred years to become colonists under the British crown.

On the shores of the Baltic England had trade relations of some importance with Russia and the Scandinavian countries, upon which she depended especially for "naval stores," including lumber, pitch, and tar. Important as these articles were to the English navy and merchant marine, the trade was liable to disturbance by unfriendly regulations and the chances of war. Englishmen were therefore deeply interested in finding other sources of supply, as they presently did in the New World. The Scandinavian countries were now Protestant; both Denmark and Sweden took an active part in favor of the Protestant party in the Thirty Years' War. Besides their common sympathy with Protestantism, England and Denmark were at this time somewhat drawn together by the marriage of James I with a Danish princess. *The Baltic countries.*

The most serious trade competitors of the English were the Dutch. During the latter part of the sixteenth century, they secured not only independence of Spain but also important conquests in the Far East at the expense of Spain and Portugal, then temporarily united under Philip II. In their navy, their mercantile marine, and their business methods, the Dutch took the lead among the European peoples. Among their citizens in the seventeenth century were some of the leading scholars of Europe, including Hugo Grotius, sometimes called the father of international law; the Dutch school of painters, with such men as Hals and Rembrandt, was famous all over Europe. Politically the Dutch provinces were organized in a loose federal republic dominated by the wealthy merchants; but they generally chose as their military head a prince of the House of Orange. In religion the Dutch were for the most part *Holland.*

followers of Calvin and radical Protestants; though under the leadership of such men as William the Silent they allowed more religious liberty than any other European country.

Influence of the Dutch.

The relations of England with Holland were particularly close. During the period of Spanish rule, Dutch Protestants found refuge in England and helped to develop the manufactures of their adopted country. The sending of English troops to the Netherlands during the Dutch war for independence furnished military training to a number of officers who afterwards used their experience in the New World. Englishmen studied the business methods of the Dutch, and their portraits were painted by Dutch artists. In matters of religion, the English Puritans were much influenced by their neighbors; and when troubled by persecution many of them found refuge in the hospitable Dutch cities. Though the English and the Dutch were drawn together as Protestants by a common hostility to the Catholic power of Spain, their commercial interests tended to drive them apart. During the seventeenth century they were competitors for trade not only in Europe but in Asia, Africa, and America. Though nominally at peace with each other during the greater part of this century, and sometimes political allies, they now and then came to blows. Gradually the English gained on the Dutch, until by the end of the century the latter were left far behind in the race for commercial supremacy.

Chief rivals of England.

When the Englishmen of 1606 faced the great contest for the possession of North America, the Spaniards seemed their most formidable rivals. Then as the century advanced, Dutch competition was for a time the most serious. Gradually, however, Spain and Holland declined in relative importance, while France became not only the leading European power, but the chief competitor of England in the contest for world supremacy.

BIBLIOGRAPHICAL NOTES

(For general plan and abbreviation of titles most
frequently used, see pages vii–ix)

Cheyney, E. P., *European Background of American History*, especially chs. VII–XVI. Smith, P., *A History of Modern Culture*, I. Hayes, C. J. H., *Political and Cultural History of Europe*, revised ed., I. Abbott, W. C., *Expansion of Europe*, I, chs. XII–XVI. *European background. World politics.*

Lybyer, A. H., "The Ottoman Turks and the Routes of Oriental Trade," *Eng. Hist. Rev.* (1915), XXX, 577–588. Hamilton, E. J., "American Treasure and Andalusian Prices, 1503–1660," *Journal of Business and Eco. Hist.* (1928), I, 1–35. *World trade and finance.*

Cross, A. L., *History of England and Greater Britain*, chs. XXVI–XXXV, especially chs. XXVI ("Elizabethan England") and XXXV ("Puritan and Cavalier England"). *Cambridge Modern History*, II, ch. XVI; and III, chs. IX, X. Creighton, M., *Age of Elizabeth*. Cheyney, E. P., *Hist. of Eng.*, I, 309–459. Beard and Beard, *Rise of American Civilization*, I, ch. I. Seeley, J. R., *Growth of British Policy*, I, pts. I, II. *English background.*

Channing, *United States*, I, 143–150. Cunningham, W., *Growth of English Industry and Commerce in Modern Times*, I. Ashley, W. J., *English Economic History*, II, chs. III–V. Cheyney, E. P., *History of England (1588–1603)*, I, pt. III. Tawney, R. M., *Agrarian Problem in the 16th Century*. Gonner, E. C. K., "Enclosure during the 17th Century," *Eng. Hist. Rev.*, XXIII. *Economic problems: Enclosures*

Maitland, F. W., *Constitutional History of England*, Period II, 226–236 (Law) and Period III. *Cambridge Modern History*, III, ch. XXII, "Political Thought," by Figgis. Channing, *United States*, I, 421–426 (Local government). Adams, G. B., *Constitutional History of England*, chs. X ff. Smith, Sir T., *De Republica Anglorum* (ed. by L. Alston). *Government, law, political ideals.*

Jusserand, J. J., *Literary History of the English People*, II, bk. V, ch. I. Onions, C. T., editor, *Shakespeare's England*. Traill, *Social England*, III, ch. XII; and IV, ch. XIII. Salzman, L. E., *England in Tudor Times*. Cheyney, E. P., *Social Change in England in the 16th Century*. *Tudor society.*

CHAPTER II

THE ENGLISH OUTLOOK ON AMERICA

KEEPING the Old World background always in mind, we must now try to see the New World, not as we now know it, but as it appeared to a well-informed seventeenth-century Englishman.

Spain and the New World. More than a hundred years had passed since in 1493 Christopher Columbus came back from his heroic journey across the mysterious ocean to announce that he had found a new route around the world to the lands and people of the Far East. The later voyages of Columbus and his successors gradually made it clear that he had found not a new route to the Far East, but a new world. By a strange fate, this New World soon received not the name of its greatest pioneer, but that of one of his lesser contemporaries, Americus Vespucius, a Florentine navigator who explored much of the coast of South America, the first part of the New World that was recognized as a previously unknown continent. Columbus, like Americus Vespucius and so many other great explorers of his time, was an Italian; but his voyages had been made under the auspices of the Spanish government, which at once set up its claim to sovereignty in the Western Hemisphere. The voyages of

Portuguese enterprise. Columbus to "the Indies" aroused the jealousy of the Portuguese, whose daring seamen had made their way down the western coast of Africa and around the Cape of Good Hope to the Indian Ocean, and the Pope was called upon

The "Papal Meridian." to decide the dispute. This resulted in the "papal line of demarcation," first fixed in 1493 one hundred leagues west of

20

the Azores and Cape Verde Islands but changed in 1494 at Portugal's request to run three hundred and seventy leagues west of the Cape Verde Islands. The new line was found to cut across the western part of South America, and so Brazil became Portuguese rather than Spanish. The effect of the Pope's decision was to put the whole Western Hemisphere, excepting Brazil, within Spain's "sphere of influence." At that time all the nations of western and central Europe were loyal to the Pope, and the Spaniards thus gained a substantial advantage in the occupation of America. Excepting the Portuguese settlement in Brazil, the Spaniards had the only permanent colonies in America for more than a hundred years.

During those hundred years the Spaniards achieved some remarkable results. They began with the exploration and colonization of the West Indies — Cuba, Hispaniola (or Haiti), Puerto Rico, Jamaica, and some of the lesser islands. Then came settlements on and near the Isthmus of Panama, from which the daring adventurer, Balboa, caught in 1513 his first glimpse of the Pacific Ocean. Still searching, like Columbus, for the rich islands of eastern Asia, Magellan, a Portuguese sailor in the employ of Spain, sailed in 1519 down the coast of South America, through the Strait of Magellan, and out into the Pacific. Though Magellan himself was killed in the Philippines, one of his ships completed the first journey around the globe in 1522; and it was realized as never before that America was a new world. During the sixteenth century, the Spaniards explored not only the coasts of South and Central America, but pushed up the Pacific coast of North America as far as Oregon. On the Atlantic side, they explored the northern shore of the Gulf of Mexico, rounded the peninsula of Florida, and sailed up the North Atlantic coast as far as Nova Scotia. *Spanish achievements; exploration.*

Nor were the Spaniards explorers only. From the colonization of the West Indies, they passed on to the occupation *Spanish colonization.*

of the mainland. The conquests of Cortes in Mexico and Pizarro in Peru were both accomplished within fifty years after the first voyage of Columbus in 1492. These conquests enriched the adventurous conquerors and their followers, and made possible the great treasure fleets which in the days of Philip II crossed the ocean with gold and silver for the service of the Spanish crown. In 1574, there were in the New World about two hundred Spanish towns with a European population of more than a hundred and fifty thousand, ruling over perhaps five millions of civilized or partly civilized Indians, a large proportion of whom were practically serfs. Partly as a remedy for the evils of Indian slavery, negro slaves were imported from Africa in large numbers, especially for the West Indian Islands. Much has been said about the Spaniard's greed for gold and his cruelty to the Indians; but in the former respect, Frenchmen and Englishmen, though less successful in their search, were not far behind the Spaniard. In their treatment of the Indians, the Spanish conquerors, from Columbus down, were often cruel and treacherous; but in their efforts to give the natives some kind of Christian civilization, they were more persistent and successful than the French or the English. Unlike the English colonists, before whom the Indians gradually disappeared, the Spaniards established communities in which Europeans and Indians have for three and a half centuries been able to live in tolerable relations.

Fortunately for their English rivals, the Spaniards were so much occupied with exploiting the rich resources of Central and South America, that their colonization scarcely touched that part of North America which is now the United States. Nevertheless, some attempts were made both in the East and in the West. In 1521 the picturesque adventurer, Ponce de Leon, lost his life in an unsuccessful effort to found a colony in Florida, and in 1526 the Spaniards came near preëmpting the territory afterwards occupied by Virginia

Spanish America.

Spain's efforts in North America.

and North Carolina. In that year Ayllon, a Spanish officer from Santo Domingo, planted a colony called San Miguel on the Carolina coast. Ayllon died, however, and his colony was abandoned.

During the next fifteen years, two striking attempts were made to match in North America the brilliant achievements of Cortes in Mexico. One such attempt was made by Narvaez, an unsuccessful rival of Cortes; in 1527 he set out Narvaez. with a royal grant covering the northern coast of the Gulf. His purpose was conquest, but he carried with him a considerable number of colonists, including some women. The attempt at colonization failed completely. Narvaez with a section of his company made his way painfully along the coast, partly by land and partly by sea, toward Mexico. He finally perished somewhere on the coast of Texas and only a handful of his men were able to reach Mexico. A few years later (1539–1542) De Soto, who had distinguished De Soto. himself with Pizarro in Peru and had later been made governor of Cuba, repeated the unlucky enterprise of Narvaez with similar results. For three years he wandered about in the Gulf region. He saw "the great river," Mis- Discovery sissippi, now for the first time definitely described, crossed of the Mississippi it somewhere near the site of Memphis, Tennessee, and then River. marched across the plains of Arkansas. Worn out by constant Indian warfare and hardships of every kind, the high-spirited leader perished and was buried by his followers in the Mississippi. The survivors went down the river and then by sea to Mexico. The expeditions of Narvaez and De Soto make a stirring chapter of American adventure, and they did something to extend geographical knowledge; but they are of slight importance in the founding of the American nation.

Notwithstanding their lack of success in North America, the Spaniards maintained their claim to it and regarded all others as trespassers. This attitude is best illustrated by

Florida.

their treatment of a French Huguenot colony, begun in 1564 on the St. Johns River in northern Florida. It was attacked in 1565 by a Spanish force under Menendez and entirely destroyed. As a means of holding the country, Menendez built the fort of St. Augustine, out of which presently developed the feeble colony of Florida.

Spanish exploration in the Southwest.

In the southwest, the Spaniards fared somewhat better. Through the courage, energy, and constructive ability of Cortes, the Aztecs were conquered between 1519 and 1521, and Mexico became a Spanish province. From this vantage point, explorers, soldiers, and missionaries pushed out in various directions. One survivor of Narvaez's unlucky expedition made his way to Mexico and on the strength of stories told him by the Indians, gave his countrymen exaggerated ideas of rich northern cities. The Franciscan, Friar Marcos, who was sent by the viceroy to investigate, brought back a report which made a similar impression. So in 1540 a great expedition was sent out under Coronado which spent about two years exploring Arizona, New Mexico, and the great plains beyond as far as the present state of Kansas. Coronado's expedition was less tragic than that of De Soto, but its immediate results were not great. The

New Mexico and Texas.

serious colonization of New Mexico began about sixty years later; still later enterprises, especially those of Catholic missionaries, carried a measure of Spanish civilization beyond the Rio Grande into Texas. Two centuries passed, however, before those western outposts had any vital significance for English-speaking people.

France in North America.

Meantime, other European powers had not been entirely frightened off by the papal bull. Almost continuously during the sixteenth century, European fishermen of various

Breton fishermen.

nationalities, including Frenchmen from Brittany and Normandy, made voyages across the Atlantic to the fishing grounds off the coast of Newfoundland. In 1524 an Italian named Verrazano explored a considerable part of the Atlantic

seaboard of the United States, probably under the authority
of the French government, and French names began to
appear on the maps of North America. King Francis I of
France was a jealous rival of the Emperor Charles V, who
was also King of Spain; he was therefore not unwilling to
poach upon the latter's preserves. In 1534, he sent out
Jacques Cartier, of the same province of Brittany from Cartier.
which so many seamen had gone out to the Newfoundland
fisheries. Cartier entered the Gulf of St. Lawrence in 1534 The French
and in a second expedition of 1535 he followed the St. St.Lawrence.
Lawrence River to the Lachine Rapids just above the present
city of Montreal. In 1541–1542, the French made a serious
attempt to plant a colony on the St. Lawrence, with a nobleman named Roberval as viceroy and Cartier as commander
of the fleet. The two leaders failed to act harmoniously,
and the colony was soon abandoned.

After the death of Francis I, the religious dissensions in Carolina and
France grew more serious and some of the Protestant leaders, Acadia.
including Coligny, conceived the idea of a French colony
in America, partly as a patriotic enterprise and partly as
a refuge for Protestants. After an unlucky venture in
Brazil, two attempts were made on the North American
coast. The first in 1562, at Port Royal in what is now South
Carolina, was almost immediately abandoned; the destruction of the post on the St. Johns by the Spaniards has
already been mentioned. In 1606 the French hold on North
America was of the slightest sort. Besides the fishermen
who went back and forth from France to Newfoundland,
there was one struggling little colony which had been planted
in 1604 on St. Croix Island near the present boundary
between Canada and the United States, but was soon
transferred to Port Royal in Acadia, now Nova Scotia.

The obstacles to English occupation so far set up on the England's
Atlantic seaboard of North America were evidently few opportunity.
and weak. Over the whole continent Spain had posted a

warning against intruders and her European power still made her a formidable rival; but between the equally feeble colonies of Spain in Florida and the French in Acadia the continent was still open. In the meantime Englishmen, though backward, had already shown in various ways their appreciation of the opportunities which the New World offered.

The Cabot voyages.

Before his first voyage to America, Columbus had made some overtures to King Henry VII of England which came to nothing; but shortly after the discoveries of Columbus became known, Henry took an important step which became the foundation of England's claim to sovereignty in North America. In 1496, a Venetian navigator, John Cabot, applied to the King for authority to make discoveries in the eastern, western, and northern seas, partly at least in the hope of finding the Spice Islands of the Far East. Henry VII gave him the desired patent and in 1497 Cabot crossed the Atlantic, making land somewhere north of New England — just where has never been finally decided. The next year he made a second voyage, from which he probably never returned.

Bristol merchants.

These expeditions were followed by trading and colonizing charters to Bristol merchants, who seem to have gone on voyages to Newfoundland during the early years of the sixteenth century. No important results followed from these enterprises at the time, but for the next two centuries and a half the Cabot discoveries were made the starting point of almost every argument for English dominion in North America.

English interest in America.

For many years afterwards, English interest in America was kept alive chiefly by the fishermen who frequented the coast of Newfoundland. Gradually, however, other interests began to develop. One of the chronicles collected by the geographer Hakluyt tells of visits made to Brazil in the reign of Henry VIII by William Hawkins of Plymouth, "one of the principall sea Captaines in the West partes of

England in his time," who was "not contented with the short voyages commonly then made only to the knowen coastes of Europe." He brought with him on a return voyage an Indian chief who made a great impression on the King and all the nobility. Shortly before Elizabeth's accession to the throne, there appeared the first books printed in England on the American discoveries, and during the early years of her reign there was a great stirring of interest in American affairs.

One important factor in bringing about this result was the slave trade, and the most striking figure in the early development of that trade was Captain John Hawkins. Like other conspicuous seamen of that day, Hawkins was an ardent English patriot and Protestant, as well as a daring fighter. Though England and Spain were nominally at peace, he regarded the Catholic Spaniards in the New World as fair prey; and while genuinely religious, his conscience was not troubled by the traffic in human beings. The character of his enterprises may be illustrated by his own story of certain voyages made in 1567 and 1568. By various means he gathered on the Guinea coast of Africa a cargo of four or five hundred slaves with which he sailed to the Spanish colonies in the West Indies and on the southern shores of the Gulf of Mexico. It was the policy of Spain to keep the trade with her colonies strictly to herself, and orders to this effect had been given to the colonial officials. Nevertheless, many Spanish colonists were glad of a chance to buy from the English; and so in many places, Hawkins had "reasonable trade and courteous entertainment." Elsewhere he was less fortunate and the opportunity for trade had to be fought for. At last, at Vera Cruz, Mexico, he was attacked by a Spanish fleet and barely escaped after the loss of his famous ship, the *Jesus*.

An associate of Hawkins in this voyage was Francis Drake, the most famous of the Elizabethan sea dogs. Like

Elizabethan seamen.

Hawkins.

Francis Drake.

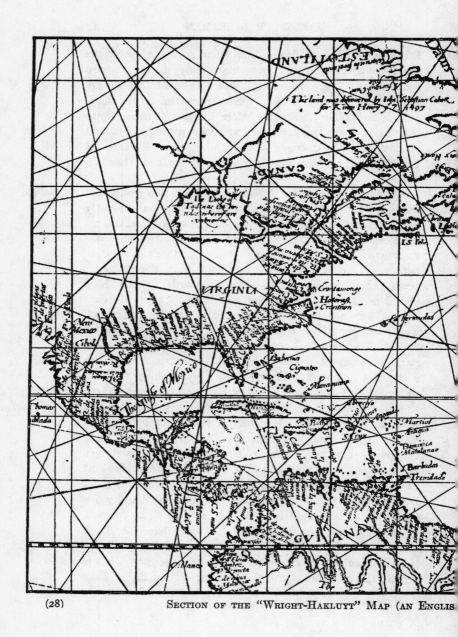

This land was discovered by John Sebastian Cabot
for Kinge Henry 7 1497

ESTOTILAND

CANADA

The Lacke of
Tadauac the bor
ders wherof are
vnknown

VIRGINIA

New
Mexico
Cibil

The Gulfe of Mexico

Crotamonge
Hotorask
Croaton

C. Hernudas

Bahama
Cignateo
Havaquinte

Abrecho

Martiol
Antigua
Dominica
Matalenao
Barbudas
Trenidade

S. Crux

GUIANA

C. Nanc

SECTION OF THE "WRIGHT-HAKLUYT" MAP (AN ENGLIS

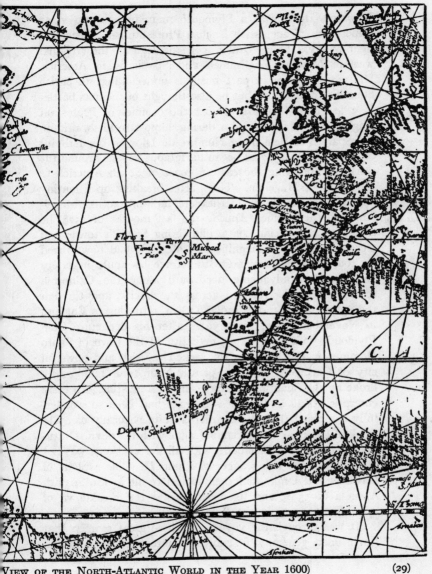

VIEW OF THE NORTH-ATLANTIC WORLD IN THE YEAR 1600)

(29)

Hawkins, Drake was a Plymouth man, brought up in an atmosphere of aggressive English Protestantism. After the fight at Vera Cruz, Drake took the lead in the irregular warfare between Englishmen and Spaniards in America. His voyages were in part business undertakings to enrich himself and his men; but he also thought of them as battles in a legitimate warfare against the enemies of Protestant England. In 1572 he led a daring, almost reckless, raid on the Spanish settlement of Nombre de Dios on the Isthmus of Panama. In 1577 he began his famous voyage around the world by following the eastern coast of South America to the Strait of Magellan. Then, after breaking up a mutiny by the execution of its chief leaders, he went on, like Magellan, into the Pacific. During the last months of 1578, he sailed up the Pacific coast, plundering Spanish towns and treasure ships on a magnificent scale. He had now stirred up too many hornets' nests to retrace his route in safety and so, after advancing northward along the California coast, he turned westward across the Pacific and through the Spice Islands to the Indian Ocean, returning to England in November, 1580, three years after his departure from Plymouth. Six years later, he captured the town of Santo Domingo in the West Indies, sacked the rich and powerful city of Cartagena on the Spanish Main, and temporarily broke up the Spanish settlement of St. Augustine. In these enterprises skill and reckless courage had been so wonderfully combined that the Spaniards quite naturally came to think of Drake as a magician in league with the devil. Naturally enough also, Elizabeth, with all her evasions, was not able to cool the rising anger of Philip II. The exploits of Hawkins and Drake had their logical result in the Spanish Armada of 1588, and its defeat meant the breakdown of Spanish monopoly in the New World.

Drake's voyages and the war with Spain.

It was through the voyages of these great seamen that Englishmen generally first became interested in America.

In the spirit of Drake and Hawkins, they thought of America as one of the great sources of Spanish power and the region where that power could most effectually be attacked. An important influence in spreading these ideas and keeping Englishmen informed about American affairs was Richard Hakluyt, a clergyman of the Anglican Church but best remembered as the leading geographer of Elizabethan England. From his boyhood up, he was an enthusiastic student of geography, and in 1582, two years after Drake's voyage around the world, he published a volume containing accounts of voyages to America. In 1589, the year after the defeat of the Armada, he published his great work, *The Principall Navigations, Voiages, and Discoveries of the English Nation*, which was issued in an enlarged edition in 1598–1600, and has ever since been a great storehouse of information on the achievements of the Elizabethan seamen and the beginnings of English expansion. Some copies of the later edition included the map here partly reproduced (pages 28, 29). In 1584, he wrote *A Discourse on Western Planting*, in which he argued that the establishment of English posts between Florida and Cape Breton would make it easier to attack Philip's fleets and menace his American power. "If you touche him in the Indies, you touch the apple of his eye; for take away his treasure, which is *nervus belli*, and which he hath almoste oute of his West Indies, his olde bandes of soldiers will soone be dissolved, his purposes defeated, his power and strengthe diminished, his pride abated, and his tyranie utterly suppressed."

Other motives, however, were at work to interest Englishmen in colonization. America was valued not only for itself but as a stage in the journey toward India and the Spice Islands of the farther East. This was the hope of Columbus, Cabot, and Magellan in the first period of American discovery; it was also prominent in the minds of English and French explorers in the seventeenth century.

Hakluyt, the geographer.

Motives of English colonization.

International rivalry.

America and the Indies.

The width of North America was not yet appreciated and there was constant searching for a passage through. At different times the St. Lawrence River, the Hudson, and Chesapeake Bay awakened hopes of a waterway to the Pacific, by means of which Englishmen might share in the rich trade of the East, which was dominated in succession by the Portuguese and the Dutch. Gradually, however, the American and East Indian enterprises were separated from each other and America was sought more largely for itself. The success of the Spaniards in finding gold and silver also made a great impression on Englishmen. Their seamen had enriched themselves by seizing the products of the Spanish mines, but they hoped also for mines of their own. The first American charters commonly assumed that gold and silver were likely to be found, and a fixed proportion, usually one fifth, was reserved to the King. Early colonial promoters were also quite insistent that mines should be found, but the actual yield was small.

The search for gold and silver.

The emphasis laid upon gold and silver was in accordance with the general economic theories of the time, which measured the wealth of a nation largely by its store of precious metals. It was desirable to own mines for this purpose; but if mines were not available, gold and silver might also be secured from the producing countries by a proper regulation of trade. If England could sell its own products to foreigners in return for gold and silver and could then get on with a comparatively small importation of goods from abroad, the national treasure might be largely increased. In the opinion of seventeenth-century thinkers, England was much too dependent upon other European nations for essential articles of trade. Her spices, for instance, came to her largely through foreign middlemen — at first the Portuguese and later the Dutch. There were important English fisheries, but much of the English supply was bought from foreign fishermen. Lumber, pitch, tar, and other naval

Theories of commerce and colonization.

stores were essential to the navy and merchant marine, but they were then secured largely from the Baltic countries.   Such imports might be cut off by war, blockade, or embargo, and involved payment of English money to foreign rivals.   If, how- *Desire for American trading posts.* ever, colonies, or perhaps better, trading posts, were founded in America this drain of the precious metals might be stopped. Fish might then be caught more largely by English fisher- men; naval stores might be bought from English colonists; and, instead of buying tropical products from continental rivals, England might even have a surplus for export.

It was expected that England's export trade would be *Export trade and shipping.* developed in other ways.   At first it was thought that the Indians were comparatively civilized people who would demand, for instance, large amounts of European textiles for their clothing; but this was soon seen to be a delusion. Later, as Englishmen settled in the New World, it was hoped that their prosperity would enable them to buy largely from the mother country, especially English manufactures.   Im- portant indirect advantages were also expected.   The At- lantic fisheries should prove a training school for the hardy sailors upon whom depended the sea power of the nation, while export and import trade with the colonies would em- ploy profitably an increasing amount of merchant shipping.

A common idea in the writings of that time was that of *Colonies as a safety valve.* colonization as a safety valve for undesirable population. The unemployed were to find employment; the unfortunate and criminal classes, who were burdensome and even danger- ous at home, were to take a fresh start in the New World. Probably few of these "submerged" people took the initiative in leaving home for America; they were more commonly sent by others as kidnaped children, indentured servants, and transported criminals.

Contemporary statements often emphasize the missionary *The missionary motive. Ad- venture.* motive.   It was frequently mentioned in the charters and though the results of English missionary activity were painfully slight, as compared with those accomplished by the Spaniards, there was after all some genuine feeling back of these plans; in every colony there were some men who did not forget their duty to the Indian. Naturally enough, however, the colonists failed to understand the natives, and in the pressure of self-interest and self-protection the missionary motive too often fell into the background. Simple love of adventure also played a large part, especially in the early stages of colonization.

Political and religious motives. In most of these arguments for colonization, the point of view is that of the national interest. In the main, they are not so much appeals to colonists as to colonizers. In 1606, few Englishmen looked upon America as a place where they themselves should personally engage in building up new commonwealths, where they could realize political and religious ideals not within reach at home. When, for instance, it was first suggested that Catholics might find a refuge from persecution in America, the proposal fell to the ground. Gradually, however, religious and political controversies created a discontented class which found its greatest opportunity in the Puritan colonies of New England.

Pioneer enterprises. With all the active interest in American affairs, not a single English colony was really established before the close of Elizabeth's reign. There had been, however, a few of those pioneer enterprises which, even in their failure, point the way to later and more successful ventures. The promoters of these enterprises were among the leaders in the national life — distinguished seamen, soldiers, and politicians. They were interested, of course, in their own personal profit, but they were also genuinely anxious to advance the welfare and prestige of the nation. Among these men, two stand out conspicuously, Sir Humphrey Gilbert and Sir Walter Raleigh.

Sir Humphrey Gilbert. Gilbert was a west-country gentleman, educated at Oxford, and an experienced soldier who had fought the

Spaniards in the Netherlands. Before his American ventures began, he had also been interested in the planting of Protestant colonies in Ireland. In his thinking about America the desire to find a northern passage to Asia played a prominent part, and with this in view, as well as the fisheries, he took a special interest in Newfoundland. At last in 1578 he received a patent from the Queen giving him the right to establish colonies in America and govern them, subject to the royal authority. After one unsuccessful voyage, Gilbert secured the coöperation of an association of merchants who took stock in the enterprise and were to share in the profits. He also worked out elaborate plans for the government of his proposed colony. After all these preparations, Gilbert set sail in 1583 for Newfoundland and landed his settlers; but the colony soon broke up, and on his return voyage he was lost at sea.

On Gilbert's death his enterprises were taken up by his half brother, Sir Walter Raleigh. Raleigh's personality, still more than that of Gilbert, brings the American movement into relation with the main currents of English national life. He was one of the most brilliant figures at the court of Queen Elizabeth and throughout his career a vigorous champion of the anti-Spanish party. In 1584 he also secured a patent for American colonization, and after sending an exploring expedition which landed on the coast of North Carolina he took up the work of actual settlement, sending out in 1585 a fleet with nearly two hundred prospective colonists.

Sir Walter Raleigh.

The commander of the fleet was Sir Richard Grenville, a daring sea-fighter whose heroic death six years later on the *Revenge*, in battle with the Spaniards against heavy odds, is one of the most stirring episodes in English naval history. Nearly three hundred years afterwards, Tennyson in his spirited ballad of *The Revenge* retold the story of the man who

Sir Richard Grenville.

> "had holden the power and glory of Spain so cheap
> That he dared her with one little ship and his English few."

The
Roanoke
colony.

This first Raleigh colony, having landed on Roanoke Island, spent there the autumn of 1585 and the winter and spring of 1586. Discouraged by the failure of their search for treasure, the hostility of the Indians, and the scarcity of food, the colonists returned to England in July, 1586, with one of Drake's returning fleets. They had hardly left Roanoke Island, when Grenville came back with supplies and new recruits who remained on the island after his departure. Undismayed by the first failure, Raleigh sent out a second expedition in 1587 which, after calling at Roanoke Island for the colonists there, was intended to settle in Chesapeake Bay. Before they arrived at the island, Grenville's settlers had disappeared, but in spite of Raleigh's directions the new colonists were kept at Roanoke. John White, the governor of this colony, soon returned to England, which he found on the eve of invasion by the Spanish Armada. In the strain and excitement of the next three years, the Roanoke colony, though not wholly forgotten by Raleigh, was left to its own devices, and in 1591, when White returned there, he found no trace of it. This was Raleigh's last important enterprise in North America. Under King James I he was condemned for alleged treason, imprisoned in the Tower of London for thirteen years, and finally executed. Though he had himself no part in the final settlement of Virginia, some of his associates kept alive the movement which had been so largely stimulated by him and carried it into effect before he died.

Increasing
knowledge
of North
America.

Besides the more striking undertakings of the Elizabethan period, there were several other voyages during the early seventeenth century which made the North American coast more familiar to Englishmen and especially directed attention to the northern section, which, as well as the southern, had ever since Raleigh's expeditions been included in the general name of Virginia, adopted in honor of the Queen. So in the century that followed the Cabot voyages, knowledge of America and its opportunities had, at first slowly and at the last more rapidly, increased among Englishmen. In spite of strange and inaccurate notions as to the "hinterland" of North America, the maps of the period show a roughly correct view of the coastline. Men still hoped for an easy passage through the continent, but the old notion of America as a mere appendage to Asia had passed away. Gradually also the Indians were changing in the popular mind from the rich and civilized people expected by Columbus to the half-naked savages which they really were. The value of colonies in the New World had been widely discussed, and, though many of the advantages expected were never realized, yet the idea of colonization had taken hold of some of the real leaders of the nation, who were especially stirred by the thought of successful competition with their Spanish rivals. Gradually, too, the merchant class and some of the nobility were being persuaded to invest their capital in American enterprises.

Public interest in colonization.

In 1603, Elizabeth was succeeded by James VI of Scotland, now become James I of England, and three years later the new King granted the famous Virginia charter which resulted in the planting of the first permanent English colony in America. The next fifty years of American colonization make up a period of extraordinary activity and substantial achievement in the history of the English-speaking people. The most familiar and the most important result of that half century was the planting of those colonies which were to prove the nucleus of the independent republic of the United States. Under the Virginia charter of 1606, two settlements were attempted. One of them, on the coast of Maine, failed utterly and was abandoned. The other, on the shores of Chesapeake Bay at Jamestown, seemed for a

Half a century of colonial enterprise.

time almost equally hopeless but finally survived to become
the colony or "Dominion" and later the state of Virginia.
In the territory carved out of Virginia by the royal charter
of 1632, Lord Baltimore planted his proprietary province
of Maryland. North of Maryland, English enterprise was
checked for a time by Dutch and Swedish settlements in
the Hudson and Delaware valleys; but beyond the Hudson
a great emigration of English Puritans made possible a
group of self-governing New England colonies. For Americans, at least, these are the outstanding events of those
fifty years; but they do not tell us the whole story of English achievement during that period; nor can they be rightly
understood unless we set them against the background of
other events which then appeared no less important.

Typical pro-
moters of
colonization.The promoters of English overseas expansion represented
many phases of the national life. Some were high officials
like Sir John Popham, Chief Justice of the Court of King's
Bench. No less influential were the merchants whose capital
was required to finance these activities. A conspicuous
Sir Thomas
Smith.figure in this group was Sir Thomas Smith, a kind of Pier-
pont Morgan in his day and generation, who was at one
time or another the chief executive officer of three great
corporations: the East India Company, which laid the foundations of the British Indian Empire; the Muscovy Company,
trading to Russia; and finally the Virginia Company.
Another conspicuous merchant of that day was Sir William
Courten, founder of the Barbados colony, whose enterprises
ranged from the West Indies to the Far East. Gentry and
nobility, too, of all degrees were deeply interested in
America. An especially attractive figure among them was
Sir Edwin Sandys, son of a famous Archbishop of York, a
leader of the "country party" in the House of Commons,
and for a time the most influential member of the Virginia
Company. In sharp contrast to Sandys in many ways was
Sir Ferdinando Gorges, governor of the port of Plymouth,

a soldier in the Continental wars, a lifelong promoter of trade and colonization especially in New England, a sturdy loyalist and antagonist of the Puritans on both sides of the Atlantic. There were also noblemen of higher rank: Sir George Calvert, first Lord Baltimore, Secretary of State under James I, an early member of the Virginia Company, and founder of Maryland; Robert Rich, Earl of Warwick, another leader in the Virginia Company and promoter of numerous other colonizing ventures, who became one of the great Puritan peers and on the outbreak of the English Civil War was created by the Long Parliament governor in chief of the colonies in America; the Earl of Carlisle, who in 1627 became proprietor of the Windward and Leeward Islands in the Caribbean Sea.

The business methods were not always the same. Sometimes, peers, gentry, and citizens united in a corporation to secure grants of land with rights of government, as in the Virginia charter of 1609 and the New England patent of 1620. Sometimes an individual nobleman persuaded the King to make him lord proprietor of a group of islands or a tract of land on the continent, as, for example, Lord Baltimore in Maryland and Sir Ferdinando Gorges in Maine. Except in New England, however, and at first even there, a colony was primarily the enterprise of promoters who remained in England, establishing for their own profit trading posts and settlements beyond the sea. Usually, also, the King was content to leave the government, as well as the title to the land, with the promoting corporation or proprietor. *Methods of promoting colonies.*

Before studying in detail the permanent colonies on the continent, it is worth while to take a rapid survey of what was accomplished elsewhere in this half century after the founding of Virginia. One of the most important results for England, and for the continental settlements as well, was the establishment of English colonies in the neighboring islands. This was, of course, poaching on the Spanish *Island colonies.*

preserves; but fortunately for the other nations there were many unoccupied islands and these were gradually taken up by French, Dutch, Danish, and English adventurers. The Bermudas were for a time attached to Virginia; but they were soon granted to a new company, under which they prospered until they came to support a population of about three thousand people. Between the Bermudas and the West Indies proper were the Bahamas; but these were not seriously occupied during this period.

The English West Indies. The two principal centers of English colonization in the West Indies before 1655 were St. Christopher, from which other small islands of the Leeward group were gradually settled, and Barbados. In 1627, when Charles I made the Earl of Carlisle Lord Proprietor of the Caribbean Islands, settlements had already been made on St. Christopher and Barbados. There were some conflicting claims; but these were disposed of by 1629 and, except for a brief period after the overthrow of the monarchy in England, the proprietor retained his rights until 1661, when the islands were brought under royal government. Beginning with tobacco as their chief product, the English West Indies gradually devoted themselves more and more to the production of sugar by means of slave labor. Much English capital was invested in these islands, and most English officials considered them at least as important as the continental colonies. By the middle of the century Barbados had a population, including negroes, larger than that of Virginia. The relation of these sugar colonies to those of the continent was extremely important. From the continent came the food supplies on which the islands were largely dependent and for which they paid by the sale of their sugar. They also kept up a brisk trade with some of their foreign neighbors, particularly with the Dutch.

Guiana. On the mainland south of Barbados was Guiana, where Raleigh made his last venture. While he was a prisoner in the Tower, attempts were made to establish settlements in this region; and in 1613 James I granted a patent for "all that part of Guiana or continent of America" between the Amazon and Essequibo to Robert Harcourt, who published "Notes" for the use of emigrants. In 1627 another Guiana patent was granted by Charles I to his favorite the Duke of Buckingham and certain associates, and two hundred colonists were sent over. This enterprise was soon abandoned; but some English settlements were subsequently made in Surinam, now Dutch Guiana. After 1650, this colony developed sufficiently to have a representative assembly, and in 1663 it was granted as a proprietary province to Lord Willoughby and Lawrence Hyde, the latter a son of the great Earl of Clarendon. On the coast of Honduras, also, the English had interests of some importance. In 1630 a Puritan company in which the Earl of Warwick and the parliamentary leader John Pym were prominent members founded a short-lived colony on the island of Providence, just off the Mosquito Coast. *Puritan enterprises in the Caribbean.*

In North America, too, there were some unsuccessful ventures which are worth remembering. In 1629, long before the final settlement of the Carolinas, a patent covering much the same territory was granted to Sir Robert Heath. Heath, who was then Attorney-General and shortly afterwards became Chief Justice of the Court of Common Pleas, had been a councillor of the Virginia Company and a member of the Council for New England; but this plan came to nothing. In New England, the only substantial achievements were those of self-governing Puritan colonies; but there were active efforts to establish colonies of a very different sort. An energetic promoter in this region was Sir Ferdinando Gorges, who had magnificent plans for a great principality of which he should be the head. He was obliged, however, to content himself with the comparatively modest proprietorship of Maine, and before long was *Unsuccessful ventures in North America.*

crowded out even there by the aggressive Puritans of Massachusetts.

Nova Scotia and New-foundland.

Even farther to the northward British enterprise was at work. In spite of the French colony in Acadia, the Scotch poet and politician, Sir William Alexander, Earl of Stirling, secured from King James a patent for Nova Scotia, which included much more than the territory now known by that name. Like Gorges, he took his work seriously and sent out colonists; but before he died in 1640 his province was abandoned to the French, and a real English province of Nova Scotia was not established until the beginning of the next century. Newfoundland, too, where thousands of Englishmen had engaged in fishing, seemed to offer an attractive field for the colonial promoter. Here Sir George Calvert, several years before the granting of his Maryland charter, tried to establish the province of Avalon; but he found the climate discouraging and gave it up.

English politics and American colonization.

Thus the first half century after the landing of the colonists at Jamestown was one of great and varied activity in colonial affairs. The air was full of American projects which interested many of the same men who were prominent in other great concerns of their country. In the political dissensions of the Stuart period and finally in the Civil War, many of them took sides, either like Gorges for the King or like Pym and the Earl of Warwick for the Parliament. These conflicts had important consequences for the American colonies. Many abortive projects would doubtless have failed in any case for other reasons; but some might have succeeded if their loyalist promoters had not been checked by the temporary defeat of their party in the Civil War. In some cases the failure of these attempts by distant speculators to transplant Old World institutions cleared the way for genuine colonization. During these stormy years thousands of real colonists, who in ordinary times could hardly have been tempted away from home, were led to cross the ocean. Some hoped to realize religious and political ideals for which there seemed to be little chance in England; others, like certain settlers of Barbados described by Clarendon, asked "only to be quiet." Through the embarrassment of English promoters and the growing number of substantial, self-reliant colonists, the center of gravity in colonial management was gradually shifted towards the American side of the Atlantic. This tendency was still further emphasized by the uncertain state of the sovereign government in England, which, alternately royal and republican, was for twenty years so much occupied with home problems that it could not develop a consistent American policy. Thus colonization came to be less and less an affair of merchants and noblemen in England and more and more the business of real settlers. *Development of colonial self-government.*

It is only by keeping in mind this background of projects, successful and unsuccessful, ranging all the way from Newfoundland at the north to Barbados and Guiana at the south, that one can hope to see in fair perspective the more familiar record of English colonization on Chesapeake Bay and the New England coast.

BIBLIOGRAPHICAL NOTES

Wright, J. K., *Geographical Lore of the Time of the Crusades.* Beazley, C. R., *Prince Henry the Navigator.* Jayne, K. G., *Vasco da Gama and his Successors.* Taylor, E. G. R., *Tudor Geography, 1485–1583.* *Geographical lore.*

Channing, *United States,* I, 1–16. Cawley, F. S., in *N.E.Q.* (1933), VI, 210–217. Quaife, M. M., "The Myth of the Kensington Rune Stone," *N.E.Q.* (1934), VII, 613–645. *Norsemen in America: fact and fiction.*

Brigham, A. P., *Geographical Influences,* pp. 76–104. Semple, E. C., *Amer. Hist. and Its Geographic Conditions,* ch. I. Farrand, L., *Basis of American History,* chs. I–IV. *Geography of North America.*

Winsor, J., *Christopher Columbus* (Harrisse's view). André, M., *Christopher Columbus* (Eng. tr., 1928) (Vignaud's view). Williamson, J. A., *Voyages of the Cabots.* *Columbus and the Cabots.*

Spanish
achievements

Bourne, E. G., *Spain in America*, chs. XIII, XIX, XX. Priestley, H. I., *Coming of the White Man*, chs. I–VI.

French
pioneers.

Brebner, J. B., *Explorers of North America, 1492–1806*. Munro, W. B., *Crusaders of New France*, chs. I, III. Parkman, F., *Pioneers of France*, and *The Struggle for a Continent* (a one-vol. condensation). Winsor, J., *Cartier to Frontenac*, chs. I–IV.

Native races.

Farrand, L., *Basis of Amer. Hist.*, chs. V–XVII. Wissler, *American Indian*. Huntington, E., *Red Man's Continent*.

Elizabethan
seamen.

Corbett, J., *Sir Francis Drake* (short biography by the author of *Drake and the Tudor Navy*, the standard work). Laughton, J. K., articles on Sir John Hawkins, Drake, and Raleigh in the English *Dictionary of National Biography*. Wood, W., *Elizabethan Seadogs*.

Readable
sources.

Burrage, H. S., *Early English and French Voyages*. Payne, E. J., *Voyages of the Elizabethan Seamen*, First and Second Series. Brief extracts in Hart, A. B., *Contemporaries*, I, nos. 28–32. Hakluyt's *Principall Navigations . . . of the English Nation* has been reprinted by the Hakluyt Society (1903–1905); abridged edition in *Everyman's Library*.

Raleigh and
Roanoke.

Andrews, C. M., *Our Earliest Colonial Settlements*, ch. I.

Trading
companies.

Scott, W. R., *Constitution and Finance of English, Scottish, and Irish Joint Stock Companies to 1720*. Biggar, H. P., *Trading Companies of New France*. Andrews, *Colonial Period of American History*, I, ch. II.

Colonial
policy.

Beer, G. L., *Origins of British Colonial Policy*, chs. I–III. Osgood, H. L., *American Colonies*, I, pt. I, ch. I. Schmoller, G., *The Mercantile System*.

West
Indies.

Lucas, C. P., *Historical Geography of the British Colonies*, II. Newton, A. P., *Colonizing Activities of the English Puritans*.

For the later history, see also Harlow, V. T., *A History of Barbados, 1625–1686*. Higham, C. S. S., *Development of the Leeward Islands, 1660–1688*. Whitson, A. M., *The Constitutional Development of Jamaica, 1660–1929*. Ragatz, L. J., *The Fall of the Planter Class in the British Caribbean, 1763–1833*.

CHAPTER III

THE VIRGINIA PIONEERS

THE first permanent English colony in America had its starting point in the royal charter granted by James I on April 10, 1606. The grantees were described in general as "knights, gentlemen, merchants, and other adventurers"; and they belonged to two principal groups, one having its center in London, and the other in the west-country port of Plymouth. Of the Londoners named in the charter, one was the geographical expert, Richard Hakluyt; the other three were soldiers who had fought the Spaniards and thus continued the tradition of Drake and Raleigh. The Plymouth group included Raleigh Gilbert, son of Sir Humphrey Gilbert and nephew of Sir Walter Raleigh; also a nephew of Chief-Justice Popham, who was probably the most important official supporter of the movement.

The Virginia charter of 1606.

According to this charter Virginia included all of North America between the thirty-fourth and forty-fifth parallels of latitude, that is, roughly, between Nova Scotia and the southern line of North Carolina. In claiming this vast area, James ignored not only the French claims to the north but also those of the Spaniards, with whom he had only two years before signed a treaty of friendship. Spanish jealousy was at once aroused, the progress of the colony closely watched, and every effort made to secure its abandonment by the English government. In most matters James was anxious to please the Spaniards; but on this point he stubbornly refused to yield.

International complications.

For the exploitation of this territory there were organ-

45

ized two "colonies" or companies: the London Company
was called the first colony, and the Plymouth Company,
the second colony. The London Company was entitled to
make a settlement anywhere between the thirty-fourth and
forty-first parallels. After having made its first settlement
it was entitled to all the land along the coast for fifty miles
north and fifty miles south of the point so occupied, with
an extent of one hundred miles into the interior. The Plymouth Company was given similar rights in northern Virginia,
from the thirty-eighth to the forty-fifth parallels. There
was therefore a zone of three degrees, extending roughly
from the mouth of the Potomac to the mouth of the Hudson,
which was open at the beginning to members of both companies; to prevent conflict, however, it was provided that
when one company had established its colony, the other
should not settle within a hundred miles of it.

The government of Virginia was to be under the close
control of the Crown; the affairs of each colony were to be
regulated by royal orders, under the general supervision of
a council appointed by the King. This superior council
appointed two subordinate councils, one to reside in each
colony and manage its local affairs. The colonists themselves were given no political rights; but the settlers and
their children should have the same "liberties, franchises,
and immunities" " as if they had been abiding and born
within this our realm of England." On the basis of this
clause and of similar provisions in other charters, the American
colonials in after years declared their right to share in those
fundamental personal and property rights which were embodied in the English common law. This principle was
afterwards reaffirmed by the legal advisers of the English
government, one of whom declared in words that have often
been quoted: "Let an Englishman go where he will, he carries
as much of law and liberty with him as the nature of things
will bear."

In 1607 both companies landed their first colonists in America, the London Company on Chesapeake Bay and the Plymouth Company at the mouth of the Kennebec River in Maine. The latter colony lived for only a few months; but the London Company, though at first almost equally unlucky, began what finally turned out to be a permanent American commonwealth. By December, 1606, three ships had been provided and 120 colonists were ready for the journey across the Atlantic. The instructions prepared for the colonists show that the promoters expected the establishment of a single fortified post near the coast as a basis for exploring and trading expeditions. The colonists were to cultivate the soil, to search for a passage through to the Pacific, to look for gold mines, and to develop trade with the Indians. The list of councilors was kept sealed until the end of the voyage; but the commander of the fleet was Christopher Newport, a thoroughly experienced seaman, who had commanded one of Raleigh's ships in the war with Spain.

Expedition of 1606.

In these days of transatlantic steamers, ocean cables, and wireless despatches, it is hard to realize what an ocean voyage meant three hundred years ago. For one thing, it was still painfully long; Newport's fleet sailed from London December 20, 1606, and entered Chesapeake Bay April 26, 1607, more than four months later. This voyage was delayed by storms and the fleet took a roundabout route, stopping at several of the West Indies; but even twenty years later, Winthrop, sailing directly from England to Massachusetts, took more than two months. These long voyages were taken in vessels which would now be regarded as small even for pleasure yachts. Newport's three vessels had a tonnage of one hundred, forty, and twenty respectively, in striking contrast with modern ocean liners whose tonnage is counted in thousands of tons. With passengers crowded together for months in badly ventilated quarters, supplied

Transatlantic travel.

with food which, without modern refrigerating processes, naturally grew worse as the voyage went on, and without water that was fit to drink, disease spread rapidly and the death rate was heavy; sixteen of the one hundred and twenty who sailed with Newport died on the voyage. When, to all these trials, there are added the chances of shipwreck in stormy weather and on unfamiliar coasts, the transatlantic voyage of 1606 may fairly be called an extra-hazardous undertaking, requiring strong bodies and stout hearts.

The Chesapeake country.

The physical characteristics of the region in which the American republic had its starting point had a lasting influence not only on the settlements there but on the whole course of American history. Fortunately there was among the first colonists an unusually keen observer in the person of Captain John Smith, whose *Description of Virginia* enables us in some measure to see the country as it appeared three hundred years ago. Chesapeake Bay at its entrance, between Cape Henry on the south and Cape Charles on the north, is about fifteen miles wide. From this entrance the tidal waters of the bay extend almost due northward for nearly two hundred miles, with a maximum width of about forty miles. Between the bay and the ocean stretches a narrow strip of low, sandy coast; but this "Eastern Shore" has not a single important ocean harbor. Much more important was the "Western Shore," opened up by a series of great rivers. Facing the entrance of the bay is the mouth of the James, on whose banks the first settlements were made; then in order to the northward come the York, the Rappahannock, the Potomac, the Patuxent, and at the head of the bay, the Susquehanna. Up these rivers the tide penetrates for considerable distances, and they are navigable still farther up for small vessels, the James for about a hundred miles and the Rappahannock and Potomac still farther. Each of these rivers has numerous tributaries,

The tidewater region.

so that the whole plain is intersected by waterways available for small craft.

During the seventeenth century the colonization of Virginia and Maryland was confined mainly to the low-lying region of the tidewater. From the beginning, however, traders and explorers made their way to the falls of the rivers among the low hills of the piedmont district. Still farther westward, in a region of which the first colonists had only a vague knowledge based upon the stories of the Indians, were the Blue Ridge and the Allegheny Plateau, with the "Great Valley of Virginia" lying between them; the settlement of this region had to wait for another century. The back country.

As to climate, Smith's statement seems pretty near the truth: "The temperature of this countrie doth agree well with English constitutions being once seasoned to the countrie." Nevertheless, the early colonists suffered severely during the "seasoning" period from malarial diseases. Nearly the whole tidewater country was covered with forest; the clearing of it for cultivation was difficult, but it furnished convenient building material. Game and fish were abundant and the soil was fertile. Wheat was unimportant until settlements advanced into the back country; but corn and tobacco were planted by the Indians and the colonists soon followed their example. Climate and resources.

The number of Indian inhabitants cannot be definitely stated; Smith thought there were some 5000 within sixty miles of Jamestown. Most of the Indians of this neighborhood, and indeed of the whole North Atlantic coast, belonged to the Algonquian family; but at the head of the bay were the Susquehannocks, who belonged to the same stock as the northern confederacy of the Iroquois. Most of the Indians of the southern Chesapeake region were united in a kind of confederacy under the leadership of the chief Powhatan, a name also applied to his tribe and to the confederacy. The primitive political organization of the Indian inhabitants. Political organization of the Indians.

Algonquian Indians was based largely on kinship. Families were grouped into clans and clans into tribes whose chiefs were usually chosen on the principle of hereditary succession in the female line; thus the successor of Powhatan was one of his brothers by the same mother. Sometimes, as in the case of the Chesapeake Indians, tribes were loosely united in a confederacy.

Indian customs. The strong ties of kinship which bound the Indians had important practical effects on their relations with the whites and made it harder for the two races to understand each other. As with other primitive peoples, the murder of a clansman by a member of some other clan was charged not merely against the individual who committed the crime, but against the clan or tribe to which he belonged. So the act of a single unscrupulous white man seemed to the Indian to justify retaliation against any of his associates. The relations of the white men with the Indians were also complicated by different ideas about property. Individual ownership hardly existed except in the most intimate personal articles, such as the warrior's weapons, which were commonly buried with him. The vague ideas held by the Indians regarding the ownership of land were the source of serious misunderstandings between them and the whites who claimed to have bought large tracts in exchange for more or less valuable goods.

Agriculture. Though in dress and other habits the Indians were distinctly savages, they had developed out of the purely nomadic stage and lived in more or less permanent villages, with clearings for the cultivation of tobacco, Indian corn, and vegetables. Thus the early white settlers were able to use the experience of the Indians and sometimes depended on them for food. In the hundred years of exploration that followed the discovery of America, the natives had had some trying experiences with white men, and the Virginia pioneers found them hostile or suspicious. On the

day that the fleet first entered Chesapeake Bay a landing
party was attacked by a party of "savages creeping upon
all foure, from the Hills like Beares, with their Bowes in their
mouthes." In the early history of Virginia, there were fre- Indian wars.
quent periods of open or secret warfare which interfered
seriously with the progress of the colony.

In locating their first establishment, the colonists had
the benefit of careful advice from the company. They were
to locate it on a navigable river, far enough up to avoid
attack from the sea and yet with sufficient depth of water
for vessels of fifty tons. Accordingly, they selected the spot The
on the northern bank of the James River, half island and Jamestown
half peninsula, where Jamestown was established. Un- settlement.
fortunately, however, they chose low ground close to a
marsh and covered with timber, which served as a cover
for hostile Indians. Here they presently built a palisaded
fort, placing within it a storehouse and a chapel. At this
remote outpost of civilization there were gathered in the
summer of 1607 about one hundred men and boys, no women
having been included among the first colonists; and during
the next two years about 180 additional settlers were brought.
More than a third of the pioneers were "gentlemen," but
there were also some artisans and agricultural laborers.
The spiritual and physical health of the colonists was cared
for by a clergyman of the Church of England and a doctor
of physic.

When the names of the first councilors were made public Government
it turned out that seven of the ships' company, including of the
Captain Newport, had been chosen and thus given almost colony.
absolute authority over the rest. From their own number
the councilors selected a president, but he could be deposed
by his associates and had little independent authority. The
first president was deposed within a few months after his
election and his successor was similarly disposed of not long
afterwards. Two other councilors were arrested at various

times and one of them condemned to death for mutiny.

Captain John Smith. Amid these mutual jealousies and bickerings, Captain John Smith stands out as more nearly qualified for leadership than any of the others. He was a man of marvelous adventures in the Old World and the New, and they certainly lost no picturesqueness in the telling. Having confidence in his own virtues and a low opinion of his associates, he was constantly quarreling and was twice arrested. Nevertheless his efficiency was finally recognized by his election as president of the council and for a short time he carried on a vigorously despotic government.

Apparent failure. Whether as a business investment or as the nucleus of a new community, the colony was for the first two years an almost absolute failure. It was kept alive partly by supplies from England and partly with corn bought from the Indians; but these resources were insufficient. Living in an unhealthful situation, constantly in fear of attack from the Indians, and half starved, the settlers succumbed in appalling numbers; out of nearly three hundred settlers sent to Virginia under the first charter only about sixty remained alive in May, 1610. Some had returned to England, but the great majority were dead. To the company in England the results bought at this fearful cost seemed small indeed. The James River and Chesapeake Bay had been explored, but there was no passage to the western sea; no gold mines had been discovered; and though some Virginia products had been carried back to England, the colony seemed likely to prove a source of expense rather than of profit to its promoters for some time to come.

Fortunately there were strong men among the promoters, who were not discouraged and who set themselves to the necessary work of reorganization. One of them was the **Sir Thomas Smith.** great merchant, Sir Thomas Smith, who brought to the service of Virginia, not only the expert knowledge of a financier, but also the influence of a conspicuous public

SIR THOMAS SMITH

53

man. Among the positions held by him were those of alderman and sheriff of the City of London, ambassador to Russia, and governor of the East India Company. In 1603 he was knighted and he afterwards became a member of Parliament. All in all he was probably the most distinguished capitalist and promoter of the period. As Smith stands for the rich and energetic London merchants of his day, so Sir Edwin Sandys represents the interest of the gentry in American affairs. He was a son of the Puritan Archbishop of York, an Oxford graduate with some experience abroad, and a writer of some reputation. Like Sir Thomas Smith, he was knighted by James I and had at first the confidence of the King. Later, however, he became a leader of the opposition, or "country party," in Parliament and in 1605 one of his books was burned by order of the High Commission. Though Smith and Sandys afterwards drifted apart, they coöperated for many years in the promotion of Virginia interests. Through the efforts of these men and their associates, the King was persuaded to issue, in 1609, a new Virginia charter.

Sir Edwin Sandys.

The new charter created a corporation, corresponding roughly to the London group, or "first colony," of 1606, called the "Treasurer and Company of Adventurers and Planters of the City of London for the first Colony in Virginia." This corporation received a definite extent of coast line, two hundred miles north and two hundred miles south of Old Point Comfort, with the interior country "up into the land, throughout from sea to sea, west and northwest." In the government of this territory the company was given a much freer hand than under the first charter; the treasurer and the first councilors were named by the King but their successors were to be chosen by the company. Virginia was thus placed almost completely under the control of a corporation having its "head office" in London. Nothing whatever was said about any right of the colonists to participate

The second charter.

in their own government; the company, acting through officers appointed in England, had "full and absolute power and authority to correct, punish, pardon, govern, and rule" all the King's subjects in Virginia. Three years later a third charter of 1612 made more definite provisions for quarterly meetings of all the stockholders and strengthened their control of the company's business, but left the status of the colonists unchanged. The treasurer, or chief executive, of the company was Sir Thomas Smith and whatever else may be said of him the fact remains that during his ten years' service the permanence of the colony was practically assured. *A third charter.*

The first problem of the new management was that of securing capital and in this they were strikingly successful. Among the charter members were fifty-six city companies of London, including the Goldsmiths' Company, the Mercers', the Drapers', and the Merchant Tailors'. Besides these corporations, there were 659 individuals, — merchants, peers, knights, and country gentlemen; one hundred or more were, at one time or another, members of Parliament. Public men like the Earl of Salisbury, the chief minister of James I, and Sir Francis Bacon saw in the company an opportunity to advance national power. Business men were looking for profitable trade, and religion was not forgotten. Here was a chance to convert the savages and save the New World for the Anglican, as distinguished from the Spanish, kind of Christianity. Popular interest was also keen; the Spanish Ambassador, Zuñiga, wrote that there was "no poor little man nor woman who is not willing to subscribe something for this enterprise." Then, as now, promoters were not always frank, and their optimistic accounts of life in Virginia resulted in serious disappointment for thousands of emigrants. *National interest in the enterprise.*

Another necessary task was that of reorganizing the government in Virginia. Government by a resident council

had apparently failed, and the company decided to choose
as governor a man of high standing and give him almost
absolute power. The man selected for this post was Lord
Delaware, but his actual residence in Virginia was short and
the government was carried on in succession by two military
men, Sir Thomas Gates, one of the grantees under the first
charter, and Sir Thomas Dale, who had lately been fighting
for the Dutch on the Continent; it is a striking illustra-
tion of the world-wide activities of Englishmen in those days
that Dale's last year was spent in the Far East, fighting
against the Dutch.

Virginia was now governed by a combination of military methods with those of a factory superintendent. It
was still primarily an investment proposition for the company and a large proportion of the settlers were bound to
service for a term of years. Colonists were furnished with
supplies by the company and expected to work for the common store. The promoters still emphasized the search for
gold and silver, and for some passage through the continent
to the rich trade of the Indies. The interests of religion were
also remembered. Ministers were sent out and one of the
first buildings was a chapel in which services were held according to the practice of the Anglican Church. The intolerance of the time is shown by the exclusion of Catholics
from the colony.

Still the colony did not prosper. Settlers came in large
numbers, but the "seasoning" process was still terribly
severe. In 1616, for instance, there were only about 350
survivors out of over 1600 who had been sent out. The visit
of a few Spaniards in 1611 caused some anxiety, though
they departed without doing any damage, leaving three
of their number as prisoners. There was constant complaint
also of arbitrary and extortionate conduct on the part of
the company's officials. The extravagant hopes of the early
promoters faded away and attempts to stimulate the pro-

duction of pitch, tar, silk, and wine were almost wholly unsuccessful.

During these trying years, however, the Virginians hit upon a product which was to become their chief article of export during the next century. The use of tobacco was common in England when the Virginia Company was chartered, but it was chiefly imported from the Spanish colonies and at first the Virginia product was not popular. By 1616, however, a method of curing was discovered which enabled the colonists to build up their export trade. Another step toward the foundation of a self-reliant community was the abandonment of the communal method of production. Settlement was stimulated by grants of land to individuals and the formation of subsidiary companies which received special privileges on condition of bringing over a certain number of colonists. Meantime, women were coming out and family life was taking root in new American homes.

As the colony developed out of a factory or trading station into a community of permanent settlers, the evils of the old arbitrary system were more keenly felt. Fortunately, there was a strong liberal element in the company and in 1618 a new governor was sent out with instructions which resulted in the first representative legislature ever held in America. This memorable assembly, which gathered in the little church at Jamestown on July 30, 1619, consisted of the governor and councilors appointed by the company, and "burgesses" chosen by the inhabitants. The speaker was a former member of the House of Commons. The members of this young legislature concerned themselves mainly with very simple and practical matters — how to prevent the one-sided development of the tobacco industry by encouraging the production of corn, wine, and even silk; how to discourage extravagance in dress and how to promote religion and morals, including church attendance and Sunday observance. In this modest fashion, the representative

Tobacco.

The colony taking root.

The first representative assembly in America.

idea which had hitherto found its highest expression in England was planted in the new soil of America, where it has had a development quite beyond the dreams of its original sponsors.

Internal troubles. Sandys and his opponents.

Meantime the Virginia Company was drifting into stormy waters. There were serious conflicts between opposing factions and finally Sir Thomas Smith gave up his position as treasurer of the enterprise. His successor, Sir Edwin Sandys, held office for only a year, but he was active in the affairs of the company until the charter was revoked in 1624. Sandys was not merely a radical politician, but a serious student of political philosophy and a sincere believer in popular government. In accordance with his views, the representative system in Virginia, which had been authorized while Smith was still treasurer, was presently embodied in a written constitution. Sandys also had plans for better support of the church and for the establishment of a college. None of these things, however, could be done without more revenue, and various projects for this purpose were discussed, including a plan to increase the profits of the company by giving it a monopoly in the importation of tobacco into England. It was not easy, however, to reach an agreement with the King, who disliked the political views of Sandys and his friends; they were also embarrassed by the attacks of their opponents in the company. Many of the charges made against them were doubtless false or exaggerated; but the results of the company's administration seemed after all hardly proportionate to the money expended and the efforts made. Thousands of settlers had been sent out, but the death rate was still abnormally high; and in 1624 there were only about 1200 people actually living in Virginia. In 1622 there was an Indian outbreak in which over three hundred whites were killed and this also was charged against the company's management.

Heavy losses.

Under these circumstances the company was unable to

defend itself successfully against the increasing hostility of
the King and his advisers. The Attorney-General brought
suit against the company and in 1624 the charter was annulled by an order in court. Virginia now became a royal
government, and though some of the settlers regretted the
change, real progress was probably made when the young
colony passed out of the control of a mercantile corporation
into direct relations with the English government.

The changes resulting from the forfeiture of the charter
were less radical than might be supposed. The ultimate
control of the colony was still in England; but the King,
through his ministers, now took the place of the company.
The head of the government in the colony was the governor,
appointed by the King to serve during the royal pleasure,
with powers and duties defined in his commission and instructions. Councilors, also appointed by the King, assisted the
governor and exercised a certain check upon him; usually
they were chosen from among the principal settlers. At
first it was not certain that the representative assembly
organized by the company would be continued, but before
long it was definitely recognized by the new King. As in
England the supreme lawmaking authority was exercised by
King, Lords, and Commons, so the Virginia legislature consisted of governor, councilors, and burgesses. According to
the English official theory, this and other colonial legislatures
were merely municipal corporations created by the government at home and wholly dependent upon it; but the American assemblies looked to the English House of Commons
as their model, insisting in particular that taxes should not
be levied by the executive without their consent. At first
governor, councilors, and burgesses sat together in one
house; but before long the two-house system of the English
Parliament, now a familiar feature of American state and
federal governments, was established, with the governor
exercising the right of veto.

The fall
of the
company.

Virginia as
a royal
province.

The repre-
sentative
principle.

The bi-
cameral
system.

The constitutional conflicts of the mother country were reproduced on a small scale in Virginia. Thus Captain John Harvey, appointed governor in 1629, soon quarreled with the assembly, which strenuously defended its exclusive right to levy taxes. The colonists finally expelled Harvey and, though the home government sent him back, a change was soon made. In 1641 the instructions to the new governor, Sir William Berkeley, recognized quite definitely the legislative power of the assembly. Little attention was paid, however, to that theory of the "separation of powers" which Americans later came to regard as so important. The governor and council not only had executive powers but also took part in the lawmaking process and heard appeals from the provincial courts of justice. The assembly itself was for many years the highest court of appeal.

The organization of local government was at first confused because of special political privileges given to companies or individuals who were prepared to bring over large numbers of settlers. Gradually, however, the Virginians reproduced the local institutions with which they had been familiar in England. County government was carried on by the justices of the peace assembled in the county courts; they administered justice, levied county taxes, and attended to various other kinds of local business. The Virginia justices were appointed by the governor; but, as in England, they were selected from the principal families of the county. The orders of the justices were executed by the sheriff and for purposes of military defense there was a county lieutenant corresponding roughly to the lord lieutenant of the English county. The English parish was also reproduced, though it often covered a very large area; sometimes, indeed, a whole county constituted a single parish. The parishioners were authorized by law to elect members of the governing body, or vestry, to sit with the parson; but before long, vacancies were quite generally filled by the surviving members, and the vestry thus became a "close corporation." Of these two divisions of local government, the county was much the more important. It was the election district for the choice of burgesses and about its courthouse centered not only the ordinary county business but many other political and social activities.

In the church, as in the civil government, Virginians were on the whole content to follow English practice, regarding the church and the state as two closely coördinated agencies for upholding morality and good order. While the company was in control, gifts were made to it for religious purposes by philanthropic persons in England and clergymen were employed by the company itself. When Virginia became a royal province, the governor was ordered to see that "God Almighty" was "devoutly and duly served," which meant that churches were to be managed and services conducted according to the Anglican form. The assembly also did its part by requiring the settlers in each parish to pay taxes for the support of the clergy. Having provided these religious advantages, the Virginia authorities expected the inhabitants to take advantage of them; laws were accordingly passed requiring church attendance and the proper observance of Sunday. The strictness of these regulations is noteworthy, because most of the Virginians were not in sympathy with the aggressive Puritan party in the mother country.

Church and state.

Under this civil and ecclesiastical government, Virginia society was evidently taking on a more permanent character. Having passed through the severe tests of the pioneer period, the survivors formed a well "seasoned" nucleus for future growth. A few of them lived on the eastern shore of Chesapeake Bay, but the majority were settled along the James River from its mouth to a little below the falls. During the first two decades of royal government, population grew slowly; the new settlers still found it hard to adjust

Expansion, 1624–1652.

themselves to the climatic conditions, and the death rate continued appallingly high. For some years after the massacre of 1622 there were no serious Indian troubles and the frontier was gradually pushed back to the north and west; but in 1644 there was another Indian outbreak, in which many settlers lost their lives. After the opening of the English Civil War, Virginia grew more rapidly; for the disappointed Cavaliers began to take refuge across the sea, especially after the defeat of the royal forces by the parliamentary armies. By 1652 there were perhaps 20,000 people in the province.

Social classes. This pioneer population was drawn from various classes. From the first there had been a fair proportion of the gentry and this element was strengthened by the coming of the Cavaliers; but there were also traders and a considerable number of workingmen. The latter were usually indentured servants, bound to labor for a term of years with the understanding that they should be supported during that time by their masters. Though their service was temporary, and their rights at law generally superior to those of slaves, they could be bought and sold like other property. Some white servants were criminals recruited from English jails, but such immigrants were regarded as undesirable and probably did not constitute a large proportion of the whole number. Many belonged simply to the class of the unfortunate poor and a surprising proportion were children, some of whom had been kidnaped. The best white servants were probably the political prisoners, sent over in considerable numbers during the second half of the seventeenth century as a result of the political dissensions at home. Until the last quarter of the seventeenth century, the Virginia planters depended mainly on white labor; the number of negro slaves, though slowly increasing, was still comparatively unimportant.

Land system. One of the decisive factors in the shaping of the "Old

Dominion" was its system of land tenure. According to the official theory, the title to all land within the territory claimed by the English was in the King, the Indian having no legal claims which white men and Christians were bound to respect. Actual practice was often better than the official theory; in many cases the Indians were paid for their land and the colonial assemblies sometimes took measures to protect the natives from unfair treatment. Nevertheless, in strict law, every valid title deed went back to the King. At first the rights of the King as supreme landlord were, in the main, transmitted to the Virginia Company; but after the revocation of the charter in 1624 all land not already granted to individuals or corporations reverted to the Crown.

The ordinary method by which this royal domain passed into the hands of private owners during the seventeenth century was the "head right" system, under which fifty acres of land were granted for each immigrant, the grant being made either to the immigrant himself or to the person who paid for his transportation. Thus a person who acquired one hundred "head rights" became entitled to five thousand acres of land. During the middle years of the seventeenth century the average size of a grant was under five hundred acres, only a portion of which was cultivable. The large plantations, in later years dominant, were still exceptional. Every grant of land was subject to certain general conditions. A part of it must be cleared and cultivated within a limited time and some sort of house built upon it. These requirements were not, however, strictly enforced and many planters acquired title to much more land than they were able to use. Later concentration of land in a few hands was naturally discouraging to new settlers and proved an important factor in the westward movement. Every holder of land was further required to pay an annual quitrent to the King. The amount demanded was small

The plantation system.

Quitrents.

and was commonly paid in tobacco; but it was collected with difficulty and caused much irritation.

Tobacco and the plantation system. The development of large estates was facilitated by the physical characteristics of the country, with its great rivers giving easy access to the interior; but it was also due to the fact that its chief product, tobacco, was peculiarly adapted to large-scale production by a servile class of workers. The people of Virginia were not of course exclusively occupied with the raising of tobacco; the normal plantation had also its corn, its live stock, and its orchards. Nevertheless tobacco was the one article which could be profitably exported to Europe in large quantities. Repeated efforts were made to encourage a more diversified industry by the planting of vines, the introduction of silk culture, and the establishment of iron works; but without much success.

This one-sided development had serious disadvantages. There were great fluctuations in the price of tobacco; and the problem was still further complicated when new tobacco-growing areas were settled, first in Maryland and then in North Carolina. Attempts were made to secure favorable Regulation of the tobacco trade. market conditions by regulating the quantity and quality of the product, but these regulations were always difficult to enforce. Naturally enough the Virginians and those English merchants who were interested in the Virginia trade desired to secure as complete control of the home market as possible, and in the end the English government discriminated in favor of their own colonists as against the Spaniards and other producers. The home government was even willing to prohibit tobacco production in England, though some experiments had been made there, the suppression of which caused considerable feeling. Virginians desired not only to keep the English market, but also to export their tobacco freely to foreign countries, especially to the Netherlands. On this point, British policy was fairly consistent; the general rule from the beginning was to require the shipment of colonial tobacco to England, and this was finally required by law in the Navigation Act of 1660.

Perhaps the most notable figure among the Virginians of this period was their governor, Sir William Berkeley. He came of a good Somersetshire family, studied at Oxford, traveled abroad, and tried his hand at playwriting. As a gentleman in waiting at the court of Charles I, his early manhood was spent in an atmosphere of loyalty to church and King. He was made governor of Virginia in 1641, when he was still a young man, and during the next decade he threw himself vigorously into the life of the province. Under his leadership the colony took a strong stand for the Church of England against various forms of religious dissent, with the result that many Puritans left Virginia, and took refuge in the new proprietary colony of Maryland. When the Civil War broke out in England, governor and assembly stood together for the King, and held their ground courageously even after the execution of Charles I. Yet the loyalty of these Virginians was not mere servility. In 1635 they had dared to send home a royal governor who offended them, and in the same spirit they asserted their rights against the victorious parliamentary party until, as will be seen in the next chapter, they finally yielded to superior force.

Sir William Berkeley.

The Virginia loyalists.

BIBLIOGRAPHICAL NOTES

Channing, *United States*, I, chs. VII, VIII. Andrews, C. M., *Colonial Period*, I, chs. V–X. *Earliest Colonial Settlements*, ch. II. Wissler, C., *et al.*, *Adventures in the Wilderness* (*Pageant of America*), ch. IX. Wertenbaker, T. J., *Virginia under the Stuarts*, pp. 1–94.

General accounts.

Brown, A., *First Republic in America;* his *Genesis of the United States* is the most comprehensive collection of material on the founding of Virginia. Kingsbury, S. M., *Records, of the Virginia Company* (introductory essay in vol. I). Craven, W. F., *Dissolu-*

Virginia Company.

tion of the Virginia Company. Scott, W. R., *English, Scottish, and Irish Joint-Stock Companies*, II, 246–289.

Economic factors: the land.
Beer, G. L., *Origins of the British Colonial System*, chs. IV–VII. Bruce, P. A., *Economic History of Virginia in the Seventeenth Century*, especially I, chs. I–V, VIII, IX. Wertenbaker, T. J., *Planters of Colonial Virginia.*

Institutions.
Bruce, P. A., *Institutional History of Virginia*, especially I, pt. I, ch. I; II, pt. V, chs. I–III (Government). Osgood, H. L., *American Colonies*, I, pt. I, chs. II–IV; III, chs. II, IV. Flippin, P. S., *Royal Government in Virginia* (very detailed).

Early society.
Bruce, P. A., *Social Life of Virginia in the Seventeenth Century*, chs. I–III. Stanard, M. N., *Colonial Virginia, Its People and Customs*, 118–165. Wertenbaker, T. J., *Patricians and Plebeians in Colonial Virginia*, and his *First Americans*, chs. XI, XII.

Berkeley.
Bruce, P. A., *Virginia Plutarch*, I, ch. VI.

Sources.
Charters of the Virginia Company in Brown's *Genesis*, I; extracts in Macdonald, W., *Select Charters*, nos. 1–3, and in Commager, H. S., *Documents*, 6–11. Hening, W. W., *Statutes of Virginia*, I (illustrating social as well as political conditions). L. G. Tyler, *Narratives of Early Virginia* (most convenient for the general reader). Brief extracts in Hart, *Contemporaries*, I, nos. 59–67, 82, 83.

CHAPTER IV

THE CHESAPEAKE COLONIES, 1632 TO 1688

WHILE Virginia was taking shape as a royal province, a different experiment was tried across the Potomac. The overthrow of the Virginia Company did not after all mean a complete change in English policy. In a long series of colonial charters, Charles I and Charles II gave away to private individuals or corporations the right to govern English subjects in the New World. Of the proprietary provinces thus established, one of the most important was Maryland, given in 1632 to Cecilius Calvert, second Lord Baltimore, who in that year secured by a royal charter certain rights already promised to his father. It was this father, George, first Lord Baltimore, who was the real originator of the Maryland colony.

Proprietary provinces.

The Maryland charter.

George Calvert was an Oxford graduate, a successful courtier, a member of the court party in Parliament, and finally in 1619 one of the King's "principal secretaries of state." His chance of a career in politics was closed later by his conversion to Catholicism, for the oath of supremacy administered to officeholders would have required him to renounce the authority of the Pope; but he found some compensation for this sacrifice in the continued good will of King Charles, who gave him a place in the Irish peerage as Baron Baltimore. Meantime he had shown in various ways his interest in trade and colonization, having been associated with the East India Company, the Virginia Company, and the Council for New England. After an unsuccessful attempt to establish a province of his own in

George Calvert, first Lord Baltimore.

Newfoundland, Lord Baltimore thought of settling in Virginia; but the Virginians kept him out by confronting him with that same oath of supremacy which blocked his career at home. In the end, however, his influence at court enabled him to get the better of his Virginia opponents. Before he died, the King had agreed to cut off from Virginia the territory north of the Potomac, and convert it into a separate province which was to be the hereditary possession of the Baltimore family.

Boundaries

The new province extended from the Potomac northward to the fortieth parallel, and from the ocean to the sources of the Potomac. Unlike Virginia, therefore, Maryland had a definite western boundary, a fact of some importance in the later history of the United States. The Virginians were much aggrieved by the loss of this territory, though the forfeiture of their charter in 1624 left them without any legal defense. Later, by a sort of poetic justice, the Baltimore family itself was made to realize the uncertainty of royal favors, when the northern part of Maryland (now southern Pennsylvania and Delaware) was given to William Penn.

Authority of the proprietor. The palatinate of Durham.

Within this territory, Lord Baltimore became not merely a landowner, but a feudal magnate with extensive political powers, explained in general terms as equal to those enjoyed by the English Bishop of Durham in the "county palatine of Durham." This palatinate of Durham, near the Scotch border, was one of those feudal principalities created in medieval times to guard the turbulent and sparsely settled frontiers of the kingdom against invaders. In return for this service, the nobleman or churchman who ruled the principality was given extraordinary powers and exempted to a large extent from the control of the central government. As the royal power increased, these jurisdictions tended to disappear; but the Bishop of Durham still kept his palatinate, though with greatly diminished authority. This nearly obsolete institution of medieval England was now given a new lease of life as the government of an American province. Like the palatinate of Durham in its palmiest days, Maryland and its proprietor occupied a very independent position. In recognition of the King's overlordship, the proprietor had to make an annual payment of two Indian arrows, with a fifth of all the gold and silver found. The laws of the province also had to be in harmony with those of England so far as possible. In most other respects, Lord Baltimore had a free hand. One medieval feature of the charter was the right of the proprietor to establish in Maryland the decadent manorial system of the mother country. In one important respect, however, this charter was more liberal than those granted to the Virginia Company; it recognized definitely the right of the settlers to share in the making of laws. *The proprietary system in Maryland.*

About two years after the Maryland charter was granted, Lord Baltimore's first settlers landed on the northern side of the Potomac. This second Lord Baltimore, who governed the colony at long range from England during the next forty years, seems to have been a hard-headed, practical business man, with a good deal of that tact and diplomatic skill which were sorely needed during these stormy years of English and American history. Having received from his father a great landed estate, he naturally wished to preserve and improve that estate and make it a source of profit. Like his father he desired, as a good Catholic, to promote the interests of his own church and provide a refuge for persecuted fellow Catholics. A good proportion of the early settlers and especially of the leading men did actually belong to this church; but the number of Catholic emigrants was too small to make possible the development of a strong colony. Most English Catholics preferred to take their chances with the English penal laws, which, though severe on paper were less so in practice, except in times of special excitement. *Early settlers.* *The Catholic element.*

Even if more Catholics had come over, it would still
have been difficult to make Maryland a strictly Catholic
colony; for the King to whom the province owed allegiance
was bound by his oath to defend the Church of England,
and the charter itself provided that the ecclesiastical laws
of England should be enforced.   Even under a friendly king,
Lord Baltimore had to keep in mind the Puritan party in
England, as well as his Virginia neighbors, who were only
too ready to find a pretext for attacking the new colony.
If, therefore, the province was to be prosperous and safe,
it could not pursue an exclusive religious policy but must
seek to attract Protestants and Catholics alike.   Whatever
Calvert's motives may have been, he undoubtedly adopted
a consistent policy of toleration and used his best efforts
to avoid religious dissensions among his colonists.   His
agents were warned at the outset to avoid giving the Protestants any just grounds for complaint in Virginia or in
England.

The early years of the new colony were much happier
than those of Virginia.   A healthful site was found for their
first settlement at St. Marys, near the mouth of the Potomac,
which the Jesuit, Father White, described as the "greatest
river I have seene, so that the Thames is but a little
finger to it."   Profiting perhaps by Virginia experience, the
early Maryland settlers escaped the heavy toll of human
life which was paid for the establishment of the older prov-

ince.   They were more fortunate, too, in their relations with
their savage neighbors.   The Indians about St. Marys were
less aggressive and the Jesuits were active in missionary
work among them.   So the Marylanders were saved from
serious border warfare until the growth of the colony brought
them into conflict with the more warlike Susquehannocks.

They had more trouble with the Virginians, and particularly
with one energetic and persistent individual named William
Claiborne, who had lately established a trading post on Kent

Island in Chesapeake Bay, within the limits of the Maryland grant. Lord Baltimore proposed that Claiborne should keep the land on condition of recognizing the proprietor's government; but the attempt failed and the two parties presently came to blows. In 1638, the English government settled the question for the time being in favor of Lord Baltimore, but Claiborne was not satisfied and a few years later took his revenge.

Meantime, the proprietor was fairly successful in getting settlers, both Protestant and Catholic, who were willing to take up lands on his own terms. These were liberal and not unlike those offered in Virginia. One peculiar feature of the Maryland system, however, was the plan for the establishment of manorial estates. An "adventurer" who took five men to Maryland, paid their transportation, and provided them with certain necessaries, might become a "lord of the manor," with an estate of a thousand acres, subject to an annual rent of twenty shillings. A few manors and manorial courts were actually established; but the institution was not adapted to American conditions and failed to take root.

Economic development; Maryland manors.

Here, as in Virginia, two classes stand out conspicuously in the early immigration: the "adventurers," or promoters, who not only came out themselves but brought others with them; and the indentured servants. Of the first two hundred colonists who settled at St. Marys, seventeen were classed as "adventurers"; two were brothers of the proprietor and several others were apparently persons of considerable social standing. In Maryland, the white servant remained an important feature of industrial life longer than in any other southern colony, but as each servant was entitled to fifty acres on the expiration of his term of service he sometimes rose considerably in the social scale. A contemporary pamphlet describes Maryland as very attractive for persons of this class. In the final outcome Maryland had a much

"Adventurers" and servants.

larger proportion of small proprietors than Virginia. For the first thirty years of Maryland history, the settlements were mainly on the west shore of Chesapeake Bay between the Potomac and the Patuxent; but there were outlying plantations on the upper part of the bay at Kent Island and at the mouth of the Severn River where some Virginia Puritans established a settlement called Providence, on the present site of Annapolis. The Marylanders, like the Virginians, devoted themselves largely to tobacco, until in 1666 it was said to be "the only solid staple commodity" of the province.

For most purposes the highest authority in the Maryland government was the proprietor. Cecilius Calvert never came to America, and the actual administration was therefore mainly in the hands of his agents, the lieutenant governor and the councilors. The proprietor accepted the principle, stated in the charter, that laws should be made with the consent of the freemen; but a true representative system was only gradually developed. At first all the freemen met, somewhat in the manner of a town meeting, to consider laws proposed by the proprietor. This worked fairly well when the colony was confined to the immediate neighborhood of St. Marys, but became inconvenient and unfair when new settlements were formed at a distance. For a time absentees were allowed to vote by proxy, much as they are in a modern corporation; but this method gave too much power to a comparatively few officeholders and other influential persons. So, in the end, a real representative assembly was established in which the people could speak through their elected representatives. The assembly was then divided into two houses, as in Virginia, the governor and council in one and the representatives in the other. At first the proprietor insisted that he alone could propose laws; all the assembly could do was to accept or reject his proposals. Finally, however, the representatives

Location of settlements.

Tobacco.

Beginnings of representative government.

made good their claim to an independent right of originating legislation. The result of this whole development was that the government of Maryland became much like that of Virginia, except that for most purposes the proprietor took the place of the King.

Religious conditions in the colony of Maryland were so different from those in Virginia that a radically different solution was necessary. Here was a Catholic proprietor, holding his title from a King who was himself the official head of the Anglican Church, and working under a charter which definitely recognized that church and no other. He knew also that he was jealously watched by the Puritans in England and his Protestant neighbors in Virginia. The colonists themselves were divided, the upper class being largely Catholic while the poorer element in the community was mainly Protestant or at least non-Catholic. Though the proprietor was anxious not to give offense, the Catholic element, and especially the Jesuit fathers, were very active in the early history of the colony. An account of Maryland, written in 1633, declared that the "first and most important design" of the colony should be not so much "planting fruits and trees in a land so fruitful," as "sowing the seeds of religion and piety." The Jesuits were anxious to Christianize the Indians, but they also felt responsible for the spiritual welfare of the Catholic colonists and the conversion of Protestants. According to the Jesuit *Annual Letter* of 1638, a majority of the Protestants who came out in that year were converted to the Catholic faith.

Problems of a Catholic proprietor.

The Jesuits.

Meantime, Lord Baltimore and his agents tried to deal fairly with both religious parties; and there are cases of Catholics being punished for annoying their Protestant neighbors. He was also a zealous defender of his own authority even against the clergy, insisting, for instance, that under the old English law of mortmain they could not acquire land from the Indians without his consent. The

Maryland Jesuits complained of Lord Baltimore's attitude, but the head of the order in England finally supported him.

Growth of the Protestant element. Under this liberal government, the proportion of Protestant settlers increased until they formed a clear majority. Some of them were ready to live quietly under the proprietary government. Others, however, were more aggressive, particularly the considerable group of Puritans who, having suffered persecution in Virginia, accepted Lord Baltimore's invitation to settle in Maryland but soon became his most bitter antagonists.

English Civil War. While the Virginians and Marylanders were struggling with their own American problems, their difficulties were increased by the outbreak of the great English Civil War. Ten years after the granting of the Maryland charter, Charles I was at war with the Long Parliament. Four years later his armies were defeated and dispersed and he himself was a prisoner. Then came three years of confusion and uncertainty until in 1649 the radical Puritan party tried to solve the problem by the execution of the King. From 1649 to 1660 England was a republic, about half the time under the Protectorate of the great Puritan soldier, Oliver Cromwell.

The Puritan Commonwealth. When this conflict broke out, a majority of the settlers in the Chesapeake colonies undoubtedly sympathized with the King. Virginia's governing class was defiantly loyalist even after the King's execution, although this stand was not popular with certain other elements. When, therefore, the Puritan party was well in the saddle, the position of these loyalist colonies became decidedly awkward. As early as 1643 the Long Parliament began to interest itself in the colonies and appointed a commission on the subject, headed by the same Earl of Warwick who had formerly been an active member of the Virginia Company, and had subsequently tried to establish a Puritan colony on the island of Providence.

For a time the parliamentary leaders were too busy to

pay much attention to America, but they did not forget the loyalist attitude of the Virginians. In 1650 an ordinance was passed prohibiting trade with that province and the island of Barbados, which had taken a similar stand. The next year Parliament passed a Navigation Act which prohibited the export of Virginia tobacco in foreign ships and also named five commissioners to secure the submission of the colonists to the revolutionary government. Three of the five commissioners were sent from England; but as two of them were lost at sea the control of the commission fell into the hands of two Virginians. One of them was William Claiborne, who had not forgotten his old quarrel with Lord Baltimore; the other was Richard Bennett, a Puritan who had been alienated by Berkeley's intolerant church policy. From such commissioners the existing governments of Virginia and Maryland could hardly hope for sympathetic treatment. When the commissioners reached Virginia in 1652, Berkeley and his loyalist friends saw that they could not resist and the colony agreed to recognize the sovereign authority of Parliament. Berkeley returned to private life and for the next eight years Virginia was almost an independent republic. Governors were elected by the colonial assembly, which now claimed sovereign authority on behalf of the people. There was some discontent over the Navigation Act of 1651, but on the whole this period was one of prosperity and rapid growth in population. Many of the newcomers were political prisoners sent over by the parliamentary government, or Cavaliers anxious to take refuge from the troubles at home.

Lord Baltimore's problem was even more complicated. Besides the hostility of the Puritans in England and his old enemies in Virginia, he had now a strong Puritan element in his own province. In order to avoid criticism he appointed a Protestant governor with instructions to continue the policy of toleration. At his suggestion also, the

Coercive measures.

Commonwealth government in Virginia.

assembly, composed partly of Catholics and partly of
Protestants, passed the Toleration Act of 1649, an important landmark in the history of religious liberty in America.
From a twentieth-century standpoint, it was not ideal;
there was no toleration except for Christians, and denial
of the doctrine of the Trinity was a capital offense. Nevertheless, in its quite impartial treatment of Catholics and
Protestants the law was unusually liberal. The prime
motive was one of practical statesmanship, because "the
inforcing of the conscience in matters of Religion hath frequently fallen out to be of dangerous consequence."

The Puritans, however, were still dissatisfied; and their
dissatisfaction increased when, during the temporary absence of the Protestant governor, his Catholic deputy
issued a proclamation declaring allegiance to King Charles
II. The proprietor was not responsible for this blunder, but
his enemies promptly took advantage of it. Under these circumstances, the same parliamentary commissioners who had
dealt with Virginia undertook to settle the affairs of Maryland as well. When they demanded of Governor Stone that
he should submit to the authority of the English Commonwealth, he agreed; but he was presently removed for refusing to substitute in the legal documents of the province the
title of the parliamentary government for that of the proprietor. Stone was later reinstated, but his troubles were
by no means over. The Puritan settlers soon organized a
strong anti-Catholic uprising. With the help of Claiborne
and his fellow commissioners, Stone was again deposed and
the government turned over to a revolutionary committee.
The insurgents now called a new assembly, which was controlled by the extreme Protestant party; it amended the
Toleration Act by excluding from its benefits practically
everybody except the Puritans.

Meantime, however, the so-called Rump Parliament in
England had been dissolved and, Cromwell having become

The Tolera-
tion Act of
Maryland.

Parliamen-
tary com-
missioners in
Maryland.

The Puritan
revolt.

head of the government as Lord Protector, Baltimore Reëstablishment of the proprietary government. assumed that the parliamentary commissioners in America no longer had any authority. He consequently instructed his officers to reëstablish his government in Maryland. The result was a pitched battle in which Governor Stone and his supporters were defeated and Stone himself became a prisoner. The Puritans remained in power during the next two years, but Cromwell failed to support them and Lord Baltimore soon recovered control. One of the fundamental conditions under which his government was restored in 1657 was the Toleration Act of 1649; but the friction between Protestants and Catholics continued to make the proprietor's position difficult and uncertain.

The year 1660 was one of great importance for America The Restoration. as well as for England. The English republican experiment came to an end and Charles II sat on the throne of his fathers, bringing back with him much of the old order in church and state — though some of the changes of the Puritan era had cut so deep that they could not be undone. The Restoration also had its echoes in America, especially in Virginia, where the loyalists once more had a free hand. The assembly having called Berkeley back from his retirement and elected him governor, the choice was soon legalized by the King's commission. The old constitution of governor, councilors, and burgesses was now in working order and the Anglican Church was restored to its accustomed place.

The population of Virginia was now growing rapidly. Growth of Virginia. In 1671, Berkeley reported over 40,000, of whom about 6000 were white servants; there were about 2000 negro slaves, or approximately one twentieth of the whole population. About 1500 white servants were said to be coming in annually, chiefly English, with a few Scotch and Irish.

In the next two decades the total population increased to about 60,000, with a much larger proportion of negroes, who were gradually displacing the white servants. Many

Development
of negro
slavery.

influences were at work to bring about this development of negro slavery, not only in Virginia but to a less extent in Maryland. English capitalists were more and more interested in the slave trade, and companies were organized to carry on the business. Some of the most influential men in the Restoration government were also involved, and in 1672 the Royal African Company was incorporated, with liberal privileges. Meantime, the Chesapeake planters came to believe that negro slaves were better suited to their conditions than the white servants. The important tobacco industry did not seem to demand more intelligence than could be secured from slave labor, which was more permanent than white service. The planter who bought a negro slave owned him for life and the children of a slave mother inherited her servile status, whereas white servants could be held only for a term of years. Besides, it was not thought necessary to spend so much money in providing food, shelter, and clothing for the negroes. Nevertheless, Virginia was nearly a century old before the plantation system was thoroughly established on the basis of negro slavery.

The prob-
lems of the
tobacco
growers.

The Virginians continued to feel the disadvantages of concentration in tobacco. They never knew what prices they would get in the English market, which was often depressed by excessive importations. Laws were passed to prevent overproduction, but it was hard to get coöperation among the tobacco-growing colonies. When legal regulation failed, illegal methods were sometimes used, as in the so-called tobacco-cutting riots. New attempts were made to establish other industries. Berkeley mentioned the beginning of silk culture and spoke somewhat less hopefully of small beginnings in the iron industry. Flax and hemp were also considered, but all this agitation brought comparatively slight results. Tobacco continued to be exported mainly in English vessels; there were some freighters from New England but few ships were actually built and owned in

Virginia. The planter generally shipped his tobacco to a merchant in England, who sold it for him and expended the proceeds in English goods, including clothing, furniture, and tools, together with such luxuries as the planter could afford. Being quite uncertain about London prices for the things he sold and bought, the planter rarely knew what his balance in London was.   Naturally, therefore, he often overdrew his account and got badly into debt.

The economic unit in Virginia society was the plantation. These plantations, which tended to increase in size, were scattered up and down the great rivers and the network of smaller streams which were the ordinary means of communication throughout the whole district. Perhaps the nature of this early plantation life can be understood best by studying the career of an individual planter whose letters have been preserved. William Fitzhugh, like many other Virginia gentlemen, belonged to an English merchant family with connections in London and Bristol. About 1670 he came out to practice law in Virginia and after some early struggles became very prosperous. By 1686, his holdings of land were large, including the thousand-acre plantation on which he lived and three other tracts, amounting in all to 23,000 acres. A large part of his home plantation was still covered with timber, but about three hundred acres were in "good hearty plantable land." Besides his comfortably furnished dwelling house, there were on this part of his estate negro quarters with accommodations for twenty-nine slaves. Tobacco was his chief crop, but there were also cornfields, an orchard of 2500 apple trees, and stocks of cattle and hogs. Like his fellow-planters, he put his new capital largely into land and slaves; when he made his will in 1700 he had about 54,000 acres. From England, he imported clothing and other household goods, as well as an occasional white servant. At one time he asked his agent for a good housewife and the next year he announced

Virginia plantations.

William Fitzhugh, a large planter.

that he would pay "something extraordinary" for a good bricklayer or carpenter. Business had its ups and downs. Sometimes Fitzhugh was "utterly discouraged" by the low prices of tobacco, though not without hope that the "tobacco-cutting" riots might bring prices up again.

The early westward movement.

While the older settlements were outgrowing the primitive conditions of pioneer life, those early trials were being reproduced among the people who were moving on from the coast plain up the rivers to a new frontier. In the middle years of the seventeenth century, a few Virginians at any rate were anxious to satisfy their curiosity about the country back of the narrow fringe of coast settlements.

Abraham Wood.

One such adventurous spirit was Captain Abraham Wood, and in 1671 a party sent out by him found their way through the Blue Ridge to one of the tributaries of the Ohio River. The chief motive which led men toward the west was the fur trade. During this period important trading expeditions were sent westward, and southwestward into the Cherokee country of western Carolina. It was largely through this Indian trade that

William Byrd.

William Byrd and other leading Virginians of the time built up fortunes which they later invested in land and slaves. After these explorers and traders came the more permanent pioneer farmers, who found on the edge of the wilderness the free land which was no longer available in the tidewater.

Virginia grievances.

With all these evidences of a vigorous and healthy development, the Virginia of the Restoration period was far from being a contented or harmonious community, and the prevailing discontent finally took shape in Bacon's Rebellion, the first really important popular uprising in American history. This discontent was due in part perhaps to the Navigation Acts, which to the great disgust of the Chesapeake planters were continued and developed by the royalist parliaments after the Restoration. Not only must the colonial trade be carried on in English shipping; but certain enumerated articles, including tobacco, could not be sent to Europe except by way of English ports. Vigorous, though unsuccessful, protests were made against this policy by Governor Berkeley and by John Bland, a London merchant who had relatives in Virginia. Gradually, however, the Virginians adjusted themselves to the new situation. They were more seriously disturbed by the lavish grants of land made by Charles II to some of his courtiers. While still in exile, he had granted the "Northern Neck," between the Potomac and the Rappahannock, to some of his loyal followers. After his restoration to the throne the grant was renewed and it was proposed to establish a special jurisdiction in this district, subject, however, to the general authority of the government of Virginia. In 1672 two noblemen, Lord Arlington and Lord Culpeper, were made proprietary landlords for the whole of Virginia for thirty-one years; but the colonists protested so vigorously that this grant was withdrawn. Measures of this kind kept the Virginians in a state of constant anxiety for fear that they might be transferred from the direct jurisdiction of the Crown to the irresponsible control of mercenary courtiers. *Grants to favorites.*

Though the colonists preferred to remain under the royal government, they were much dissatisfied with the existing administration. Many of them were convinced that affairs were being mismanaged by a political "machine," through which Governor Berkeley and his friends were promoting the special interests of their class. Berkeley seems to have been at first a rather successful and popular governor; but as he grew older his conservatism became more extreme and even his integrity was questioned. Similar charges were made against the councilors, a group of well-to-do planters who kept a firm grip on the important offices and managed the land system in such a way as to give themselves more than their fair share of the best lands. Even the House *Dissatisfaction with Berkeley's government.*

of Burgesses was distrusted; sixteen years passed without a new election and the members got out of touch with their constituents.   Taxation was said to be excessive and unfairly distributed.   This burden was especially resented because money appropriated for defense and other public purposes seemed to be spent without tangible results.   To a certain extent these divisions were on sectional lines.   The frontiersmen believed that the government and the tidewater planters were doing little to protect them against the savages and that the governor in particular was unwilling to punish outrages for fear of lessening his profits in the Indian trade.

Sectionalism; tidewater and back country.

These discontented elements found a leader in Nathaniel Bacon, a young man who came to the colony about 1674 and soon took up some land near the frontier.   Having unusual ability and a vigorous personality, with influential connections both in England and in Virginia, Bacon soon became a member of the governor's council; but the exposed situation of his estate on the upper James and the killing of one of his servants by the Indians led him to sympathize with the back-country people in their complaints against Governor Berkeley.   Impatient of delay, Bacon organized an independent expedition against the Indians, which was immediately condemned by the governor as an unauthorized and rebellious proceeding.   A popular uprising, however, compelled the governor to dissolve the old assembly and call a new one for the purpose of instituting reforms and dealing with problems of defense.   The new assembly passed a series of bills intended to give the government a more representative character.   It tried, for instance, to make the county and parish governments more democratic by putting them in the hands of officers elected by the people.

Bacon and Berkeley.

The meeting of this reform assembly, did not, however, solve the problem.   When Bacon came up to attend the

Bacon's Rebellion.

session, the governor had him arrested, and though he was released on declaring his submission to the authorities, the antagonism between the two men continued. Bacon then left Jamestown, only to return later at the head of an armed force which compelled the governor to commission him as its leader in an expedition against the Indians. Having yielded only under pressure, Berkeley soon issued a new proclamation denouncing Bacon as a rebel, and a small civil war followed, in which the governor was defeated and compelled to leave the capital. It is hard to say just how far Bacon meant to go in his revolutionary measures. He was charged with being ready to resist even the King's forces if they were sent out against him; there seemed to be some danger also of his being supported by rebellious elements in the neighboring provinces, particularly in North Carolina. In his own proclamations, however, Bacon insisted that he was merely defending the people of Virginia against the corrupt conduct of the governor and his associates. Whatever his plans may have been, they were cut short by his sudden death and there was no other leader who could hold his followers together. Berkeley now recovered his authority. The rebels were tried by military process. Thirty-seven were executed. Many more were condemned to heavy fines, banishment, or imprisonment, and still others took to flight. *Bacon's death.* *Collapse of the rebellion.*

Meantime, the home government, several thousand miles away from the scene of action, and receiving news only at long intervals, had to act very much in the dark; but commissioners were sent over to enforce the King's authority and report on the causes of the rebellion. They discovered on their arrival that the rebellion had been suppressed and that their first business must be to check the arbitrary proceedings of the governor. Berkeley was recalled to England, where he died soon afterwards, and one of the commissioners was put in charge of the government. In *Recall of Berkeley.*

accordance with the King's instructions, a careful investiga-
tion followed, in which the colonists were given a chance to
state their grievances.   The commissioners finally reported,
condemning the rebels but recognizing the justice of some
of their complaints.   Perhaps their most important work
was the establishment of satisfactory relations with the
Indians.

Failure of
the reform
movement.

On the whole the popular movement led by Bacon was
a failure.   Reform measures passed by the assembly of
1676 were repealed; in other respects too the hopes of
the Virginians were disappointed.   When the rebellion broke
out a serious effort was being made to secure a new charter
protecting the constitutional rights and economic interests
of the province.   A so-called charter was actually issued,
but it proved to be of slight importance.   The rebellion
had also failed to weaken seriously the control of government by a comparatively small officeholding class, and
Berkeley's successors, Lord Culpeper and Lord Howard
of Effingham, were not less arbitrary or corrupt than the
old Cavalier governor.   Berkeley, with all his faults, was
a real Virginian, with a permanent interest in the province;
the new men were courtiers, chiefly concerned with their
own personal fortunes.   For a time it looked as if the
privileges of the assembly would be seriously impaired,
though in the end this attempt was given up and the representative principle was preserved.

The
Chesapeake
colonies
in 1688.

At the close of the first quarter century after the Restoration the political situation on both sides of the Potomac
was unstable.   In Virginia there was much discontent not
only with the royal governors but also with the large planters,
who sat in the council, held other important provincial
offices, and controlled the local administration.   The people
of Maryland had similar grievances against their government, which was largely in the hands of the proprietor and
his little group of officeholders; but here there were

other complications. The proprietor who was responsible for the government of the colonists was also their landlord, with private interests often opposed to theirs. Religious differences also interfered with mutual understanding. On the whole, the proprietors tried to deal fairly with the Protestant settlers, who now formed a large majority of the population; but the latter complained that offices were too largely filled by Catholics, and this jealousy, whether reasonable or not, was a standing menace to the proprietary government.

The details of these political controversies are often confused and uninteresting. Yet, if we try to see them in proper perspective, one really important fact stands out. After about three quarters of a century of colonizing effort, there were now two vigorous English commonwealths, with a combined population of perhaps 80,000, facing each other across the Potomac. Their institutions were largely modeled on those of the mother country; but they were also well rooted in the American soil and quite capable of making trouble for royal officials who failed to respect the colonial point of view.

New English commonwealths.

BIBLIOGRAPHICAL NOTES

Channing, *United States*, I, chs. IX, XVIII; and II, 63–65, 79–93. Wissler, C., *et al.*, *Adventures in the Wilderness*, ch. XIII. Andrews, C. M., *Colonial Self-Government*, chs. XIII–XV. *General accounts.*

Browne, W. H., *Maryland a Palatinate*, chs. I–VIII, and his *George and Cecilius Calvert*. Andrews, C. M., *Earliest Colonial Settlements*, ch. VI. Andrews, M. P., *The Founding of Maryland*. Articles by B. C. Steiner in *Johns Hopkins Studies*, XXI, XXIV, XXV (detailed narrative of early years). Shea, J. G., *Catholic Church in Colonial Days*, 1–85 (scholarly account by a Catholic historian). Institutional development may be studied in Mereness, N. D., *Maryland as a Proprietary Province;* and Osgood, *17th Cent.*, II, 8–11, 58–94. *Founding of Maryland.*

Maryland sources.
Charter in Hall, C. C., *Narratives of Early Maryland*, 101–112; extracts in Macdonald, *Select Charters*, no. 12. Descriptive material in Hall, *Narratives*, and Hart, *Contemporaries*, I, nos. 72–77, 84 (Toleration Act; extract also in Macdonald, no. 21, and in Commager, *Documents*, 31).

Labor.
Ballagh, J. C., *White Servitude in Virginia* (*J. H. Studies*, XIII). McCormac, E. I., *White Servitude in Maryland*. Phillips, U. B., *American Negro Slavery*, chs. I–VI. *Life and Labor in the Old South*, chs. I–III. Smith, A. E., "Transportation of Convicts to American Colonies in the 17th Century," *A.H.R.* (1934), XXXIX, 232–249. Jernegan, M. W., *Laboring and Dependent Classes*, chs. I, II.

Tobacco and the land.
Craven, A. O., *Soil Exhaustion as a Factor in the Agricultural History of Virginia and Maryland, 1606–1860* (U. of Ill., *Studies*, XIII). Jacobstein, M., *Tobacco Industry in the U. S.*, chs. I–III. See also works of Bruce, cited in ch. III, and Bassett, J. S., *Writings of William Byrd*, pp. IX–XL.

Bacon's Rebellion.
Wertenbaker, T. J., *Virginia under the Stuarts*, chs. IV–VIII. Osgood, *17th Cent.*, III, ch. VIII.

Virginia sources.
Extracts in Hart, *Contemporaries*, I, nos. 68–71, 85–88, especially no. 70 (Berkeley's report, 1671). Andrews, C. M., *Narratives of the Insurrections*, 11–141 (Bacon's Rebellion). Interesting Fitzhugh letters illustrating social life, in *Virginia Magazine of History and Biography*, I, II.

CHAPTER V

NEW ENGLAND PIONEERS

IN most of the English colonies in America, the chief Promoters
and
colonists. promoters did not themselves become permanent colonists, but contented themselves with furnishing capital, sending out settlers, managing affairs from England, and drawing such profits as they could from their investments. This was at first true even in the case of New England. In the end, however, that section was left open for enterprises of a different kind, in which the leaders actually crossed the sea with their followers to build new homes and commonwealths.

The New England seaboard was fairly well known to Early plans
for New
England. English seamen by the beginning of the seventeenth century and a number of exploring voyages during the next few years helped to stimulate interest in it, especially as a profitable base for the fur trade and the fisheries. Out of this interest grew the Plymouth Company, which, under the first Virginia charter, made an unsuccessful attempt to plant a colony at the mouth of the Kennebec River. An important event in the development of English knowledge about New England was John Smith's voyage of 1614, in which he explored the seaboard with considerable care. In a book published shortly afterwards, he set forth in glowing terms the possibilities of this region. After Smith's voyage, Sir Ferdinando Gorges and some of the other men who had been interested in the old Plymouth Company determined to take advantage of these opportunities. Accordingly they secured from the King a charter which incorporated

The Council for New England. them as the Council for New England with the right to colonize and govern the vast territory lying between the fortieth and forty-eighth parallels of latitude and stretching across the continent to the Pacific. This was done in complete disregard of the Dutch traders on the Hudson as well as the struggling French settlements of Acadia and the St. Lawrence valley. This patent was surrendered fifteen years later, but during that time it had a marked influence on New England history.

Sir Ferdinando Gorges. The most conspicuous and active member of the New England Council was Gorges. His ideal seems to have been the organization of a great dominion of New England, with subordinate proprietary governments controlled by individuals or trading companies. Another important figure in the Council, as well as in national politics, was Robert, Earl of Warwick, who, like several other members of the Council, had been actively associated with the Virginia Company; he was soon taking a keen interest in various plans for Puritan colonization. From time to time the Council made grants to individuals and companies for the establishment of trading and fishing stations; in two instances proprietary governments were seriously undertaken, one in Maine by Gorges himself, and the other in New **Failure of proprietary government.** Hampshire by Captain John Mason. Both these enterprises failed, but other grants proved to be of lasting importance, notably those which gave the Puritan pioneers of Plymouth and Massachusetts their first legal titles to the land they occupied and enabled them to begin a unique series of experiments in colonial self-government.

Economic and religious motives. In the founding of these self-governing Puritan colonies, economic motives cannot, of course, be ignored. New England, like Virginia, could not have developed as it did if large numbers of people had not believed that they could make an easier, or a better, living for themselves in America. Yet, when all is said, it cannot be denied that religion, in the form of Puritanism, played a greater part there than in any other English colonies, with the possible exception of Pennsylvania. To understand New England, therefore, it is necessary to begin with some study of seventeenth-century Puritanism.

Definitions of Puritanism are numerous and generally unsatisfactory. Many things commonly called Puritan are not peculiar to Puritans; others are characteristic of particular kinds of Puritans, but not of all. It is safe to begin, however, by saying that Puritans were radical Protestants. Whatever their differences on other points, they were all dissatisfied with the "middle way," taken by the Church of England, between communion with the Roman Church on the one side and thoroughgoing Protestantism on the other. By thoroughgoing Protestantism they meant, above all, getting back from the traditional practices and ideas of the medieval church to what they considered a more completely Biblical Christianity. For them the final authority in religion was the Bible, rather than the clergy or the church as a whole.

Puritanism.

In their interpretation of the Bible, the Puritans were influenced by certain great teachers, of whom the most important was the French reformer, John Calvin. Under the guidance of these teachers, they concluded that Biblical Christianity required simpler forms of worship than those of the Roman and Anglican communions. The use of art to symbolize religious truth seemed to them full of danger, likely to obscure rather than reveal spiritual truth. They believed in the sacraments of baptism and the communion, but laid special stress on preaching. The Puritans held that church organization also needed to be simplified; they found no warrant in the Bible for the authority then exercised by the English bishops; some of the radicals wished to abolish that office altogether, though others were content with lessening its powers. Like most Protestants, they

Calvinism.

emphasized the principle of salvation by faith rather than by compliance with ecclesiastical forms and they accepted Calvin's doctrine that saving faith came only to those who had been divinely chosen or "elected." The English Puritans of the sixteenth and seventeenth centuries felt bound to protest against lax standards of morality, and many of them were doubtless excessively severe in their judgments of themselves and of other people, often condemning, as sinful, enjoyments which seemed to others quite innocent. This state of mind, however, is not peculiar to Puritans strictly so called; it has been characteristic of many intensely religious persons, regardless of the particular creed they happen to profess. A more distinctive characteristic of the English Puritans was their insistence on strict obedience to Old Testament precepts about Sabbath observance.

Puritan morality.

Agreeing fairly well in these fundamental matters, the Puritans were much divided among themselves about details of doctrine, modes of worship, and ideas of church government; and out of these differences there developed finally a large number of sects. At the beginning of the colonial era, the most important line of cleavage among these people was on the question of their relation to the national church — between the Puritans of various shades who wished to stay in the church and try to mold it in accordance with their own views and those who considered it so hopelessly wrong that all Christians should withdraw from it. This Separatist group became the pioneers of Puritan colonization in New England and though very few in numbers exerted an important influence on those who followed.

Different kinds of Puritans.

The distinguishing characteristic of the Separatists was their conception of the church. They rejected wholly the idea of a national church. To them a church was an association of the true Christian believers who lived in any particular community, a carefully sifted group of those

The Separatists.

who were divinely "elected" to be saved. Instead of an episcopal system of government, they believed in a "congregational" organization in which the minister and other church officers were chosen by the members. At the end of Elizabeth's reign the Separatist groups were few and weak; there were some scholars and gentry among them but on the whole they came from the less influential classes. The government regarded their doctrines as dangerous to good order in church and state, and they were condemned even by many of the Puritans. On the whole, they were strongest in the eastern counties and in such towns as Norwich, where there had been a considerable immigration of radical Protestants from the Netherlands. During the early years of James I, the Separatists were reinforced by a number of clergy and laymen who were disappointed by his unfriendly attitude toward Puritan elements in the national church; but they continued to be a small and persecuted group, forced to meet in secret or to take refuge abroad. In Holland they found an asylum among the Dutch Calvinists and formed a few churches of their own.

One little Separatist community, destined to play a notable part in American history, was formed at Scrooby Manor, in Nottinghamshire near where it joins the counties of York and Lincoln. Curiously enough, the manor house in which these people met belonged to the Archbishop of York; one of the archbishops of this province during Elizabeth's reign was the father of Sir Edwin Sandys, the liberal leader in the Virginia Company, and both father and son were sympathetic toward the Puritans. Most of the members of this little congregation were obscure people, but there were two interesting men among them. William Brewster, who kept the manor house, was then a postmaster. Brewster had studied at Cambridge University and was a considerable collector of books on politics and theology. One of their teachers, John Robinson, was a man of real intel-

The Scrooby congregation.

lectual distinction. He held for a time a fellowship at Cambridge University; but his heretical opinions shut him out from a career in the university or in the church, and he became instead a prolific and able writer on Calvinistic theology and the congregational theory of church government.

The Pilgrims in Holland.

With others of their faith, several members of the Scrooby congregation took refuge in Holland, and finally settled in the city of Leyden, where for twelve years they engaged in various trades and industries, while Robinson became a member of the Leyden University and took part in the theological controversies of the time. It soon became

Reasons for leaving Holland.

evident, however, that it would be difficult for these "Pilgrims" to preserve their separate community life, their English nationality, and their distinctive religious ideals. It was not easy, either, to make a satisfactory living under these conditions. To all these trials there was added the disturbing prospect of a reopening of the war between the Dutch and the Spaniards. It was not strange, therefore, that the thoughts of the Pilgrims turned to the New World in the hope of beginning there a new life under more favorable conditions. They hoped also, to use the words of one of their leaders, that they might lay a foundation "for the propagating and advancing the gospell of the Kingdom of Christ in those remote parts of the world; yea though they should be but even as stepping stones unto others for the performing of so great a work." The decision to go to America was made only after much debate, in which the hardships and dangers of the enterprise were pointed out; but the braver spirits insisted that "all great and honorable actions are accompanied with great difficulties," and must be "enterprised and overcome with answerable courages."

Organization of the enterprise.

Some difficult business problems had to be solved before the project could be carried into effect. For the land on which the settlement was to be made, the Pilgrims turned to the Virginia Company, which, under the leadership of Sandys, wanted settlers and was not unfriendly to the Puritans. A grant was finally secured, and their next task was to reach an understanding with the English government. In the effort to secure the King's approval, they took pains to declare their loyalty to the Crown and stated their religious opinions in such a way as to cause the least possible offense. They were so far successful that James I agreed to " connive at them " as long as they behaved peaceably. A most serious problem was that of getting capital and it was finally solved by a partnership between the Pilgrims and a group of London business men. As in the case of Virginia, a joint-stock company was formed, with shares divided between the emigrants and the London partners. A Virginia precedent was followed also in setting up for the first seven years a communal system in which all the land was held and worked for the company.

Finally all these difficulties were overcome and on September 6, 1620, the *Mayflower* sailed from Plymouth. Its company consisted partly of members of the Leyden congregation, many of whom, however, including Robinson himself, were left behind; some of the rest were Separatists also, but others were merely employees of the company. After a stormy voyage of more than two months the *Mayflower* made land in what is now Provincetown harbor, on Cape Cod; another month passed before they finally selected as the place of their settlement the harbor of Plymouth. December was a bad season for beginning a new settlement on the New England coast, and for the first year the death rate of the Plymouth people was comparable with that at Jamestown. The Pilgrims fortunately established friendly relations with some of their Indian neighbors — relations which were maintained for more than fifty years. As compared with Virginia, the period of extreme hardship was short. Though there was a scarcity of food for some time, the worst was over by the end of the first year.

The founding of New Plymouth.

Economic basis of the colony.

Here at Plymouth the Pilgrims were outside the jurisdiction of the Virginia Company and simply squatters on land which belonged to the Council for New England. With the help of influential friends, however, they secured in 1621 a grant from the council. This was enlarged in 1630 in favor of some of the principal settlers; and subsequently transferred to the colony as a whole. After a few years of unsatisfactory experience, the communal plan was abandoned and the land was allotted to individuals, first temporarily and then permanently. The colonists were also able before long to buy out the London partners and thus secure complete control of their own business affairs. Under these conditions, "New Plymouth" developed into a community of small farmers with some interest in the fisheries and a fairly prosperous trade in furs, not only with the Indians in their immediate neighborhood but in places as far away as the Maine coast and the Connecticut valley.

The political status of the colony.

The political status of Plymouth was always precarious; the colonists never received a charter from the King, and the Council for New England probably had no right to authorize their government. Left as they were without strictly legal authority, they proceeded to organize a prac-

The Mayflower Compact.

tically republican system. The famous "Mayflower Compact" which they adopted just before landing was not a constitution, but simply an agreement to abide by the will of the majority. For the business of a small community like this only the simplest kind of organization was necessary, and that was all they had. They chose a governor every year to handle some necessary business and represent them in their relations with the outside world; later, as the business developed, assistants were similarly elected. Necessary regulations or laws were made by the settlers at a general meeting. For a time the town of Plymouth and the colony of New Plymouth were practically identical; but as new

towns were established the general assembly of all the freemen was replaced by a gathering of representatives from the
towns.   Much of the success of this simple but practical
government was doubtless due to its governor, William   William
Bradford, who was first chosen a few months after the land-   Bradford.
ing and reëlected year after year. He was not only an efficient leader but something of a scholar as well; his history
of the colony is likely always to stand as a classic of early
American literature.

The Pilgrims were now free to carry out their ideals of   Influence
religious worship and church government. The congrega-   of the
                                                          Plymouth
tional church system which they established embodied the   colony.
same principle of democratic self-government as the civil
order which they built upon the Mayflower Compact, and
it had a definite influence upon the later Puritan colonies.
In this as in other respects, Plymouth is important primarily
as the pioneer in a new movement. Always small and comparatively poor, it was soon overshadowed, and finally
annexed, by the younger and more prosperous Massachusetts
Bay Colony. Nevertheless, the Plymouth Pilgrims will
always be remembered as having pointed the way which
was followed by others to far greater achievements; they
had truly been "as a stepping stone unto others."

Besides the colony of New Plymouth, which occupied   Early settle-
only a small area in the southeastern corner of the present   ments on
                                                            Massachu-
state of Massachusetts, there were by 1630 a number of   setts Bay.
small settlements around the shores of Massachusetts Bay,
based upon grants by the Council for New England. None
of these grants, however, has any lasting importance for
American history, except one; that is the one made by the
council in 1628 to the Massachusetts Bay Company. On
the basis of this grant, confirmed the next year by a royal
charter, there was established the strongest of all the Puritan commonwealths, and, indeed, the strongest colony
planted up to that time by the English in any part of America.

This new Puritan emigration, unlike that of the Pilgrims, stood in the closest relation to the central issues of English national life. Its leaders were members of a great national party, some of whom fought the battles of parliamentary government and the Puritan faith in England, while others saw their best opportunity for attaining their ideals in the founding of new commonwealths in America.

The
Puritan
outlook
in 1629.
To the typical Puritan of 1629, the European prospect seemed very dark. After more than a decade of fighting in Germany, the Protestants seemed to be badly beaten there. In France the uprisings of Huguenot nobles and cities had been crushed by the great cardinal-statesman, Richelieu, notwithstanding a badly managed English intervention in their behalf. At home Charles I and Bishop Laud, his chief ecclesiastical adviser, were suspected by the Puritans of desiring to undo the results of the Reformation. Laud had little more sympathy with the papacy than the Puritans, but he and his "high church" associates were undoubtedly trying to restore some of the old ceremonial; and that meant, from a Puritan point of view, a return to Rome. It also seemed to the Puritans that Laud and his friends were getting away from orthodox views in theology, more particularly from the Calvinistic teaching about "election" which for a time had a strong hold even among the Anglican bishops.

Mutual
intolerance.
Neither side was really tolerant. Laud wanted to make everyone conform to his ideas of ceremonial, and episcopal authority; the Puritans, while claiming their own right to vary from the prescribed services of the church, were fiercely intolerant of any departures from Calvinistic orthodoxy and denounced the King for his encouragement of Sunday sports. The Puritans, for the most part, did not wish to leave the church; but rather to reform and control it. For the present, however, the King and the "high church" men seemed to be having their own way. Nonconforming clergymen were

suffering persecution, and the members of Laud's party were receiving the important appointments in the church.

In politics, conditions seemed equally discouraging, for most Puritans believed that the cause of Protestantism was closely bound up with that of free parliamentary government. In 1628, the House of Commons forced King Charles to accept the Petition of Right, forbidding various forms of taxation without consent of Parliament and also forbidding the arbitrary imprisonment of accused persons without due process of law. Questions arose, however, as to the interpretation of the Petition, and the parliamentary party charged the King with breaking his word. In the Parliament of 1629, the illegal acts of the King and the so-called "popish" measures of Laud were violently attacked, with the result that the King dissolved Parliament, imprisoned some of his opponents, and got on for ten years without any parliament at all. The King's principal advisers during this period of autocratic rule were Laud and the very able, though sometimes high-handed, statesman, Sir Thomas Wentworth, better known by his later title as the Earl of Strafford. With this gloomy outlook in the Old World, it seemed to many Puritans that the best way of preparing for a brighter day was to leave Europe to its fate for the present and try to build up in America "a bulwark against the Kingdom of Anti-Christ." There they trusted the Lord would "create a new heaven and a new earth, " "new churches and a new commonwealth together."

The Puritan view of English politics.

"A bulwark against . . . Anti-Christ."

Puritan ideals are not at all apparent, however, in the businesslike document by which the Council for New England gave to the Massachusetts Bay Company the territory extending from three miles north of the Merrimac to three miles south of the Charles River, with a westward extension to the Pacific. The main object proposed was to make money out of the fisheries and the fur trade and to send out colonists who would engage in these industries. Presently such

The Massachusetts Bay Company.

a colony was sent out to Salem on the north shore of Massachusetts Bay under a governor appointed by the company.

The charter of 1629.

The royal charter of 1629 which gave the company legal authority to govern its colonists seems equally innocent of any Puritan design. On its face, it is like many other colonial charters giving English corporations the right to govern the people whom they sent across the sea; but the absence of any clause fixing the head office of the company in London made possible the transfer of control from mere promoters at home to actual colonists in America.[1] Thus the charter of a commercial corporation became the constitution of a self-governing commonwealth — the means of carrying on a radical experiment in church and state.

The Cambridge Agreement and the great migration.

By 1629 a number of Puritan gentlemen were ready to take advantage of such an opportunity as this charter offered; and in August twelve of them, only six of whom were original members of the company, signed the "Cambridge Agreement," promising to migrate to New England not later than March, 1630, provided the government of the company, with the charter itself, should be entrusted to those members who became actual colonists. Shortly afterwards, this condition was met; new officers were elected and John Winthrop, one of the signers of the agreement, was chosen governor. Preparations were vigorously pushed, and by March, 1630, Winthrop set sail for New England with a company of emigrants large enough to require eleven ships. Thus began the great migration, which in ten years took something like twenty thousand people to New England.

Signers of the Cambridge Agreement.

Some idea of the leaders in this movement can be gained by studying the signatures to the Cambridge Agreement. Two of the signers had married sisters of the Earl of Lincoln, a Puritan leader of the parliamentary party; with them was Thomas Dudley, who had been a steward of the Earl's

---

[1] It has been inferred from a later statement by Winthrop that friends of the colony procured this omission; but Andrews regards it as accidental.

estate. Another notable figure was Sir Richard Saltonstall;
though he did not settle permanently in New England, he
had a long line of New England descendants and was himself an active promoter of Puritan policies on both sides of
the Atlantic. There were other men of force and ability
among the early leaders; but, on the whole, the man who
best represented the character and ideals of the colony was
Governor Winthrop.

John Winthrop belonged to a substantial family of
country gentlemen, from whom he inherited the manor of
Groton in Suffolk, one of the "eastern counties" which
played an important part in the Civil War on the Puritan
side and from which a large proportion of the Massachusetts
emigrants came. Winthrop was born in the year of the
Spanish Armada and was, therefore, about forty-two when
he began his American career. He studied for a short time
at Cambridge University, but an early marriage took him
away from his studies. He did, however, study law afterwards; and as lord of the manor, justice of the peace, and
attorney in the Court of Wards, he was accustomed to
legal business. His desire to migrate probably came in part
from economic causes; though he had a fairly good estate,
the demands on his income were heavy, including the education of his sons at Dublin and Cambridge Universities.
Nevertheless, the serious reader of Winthrop's family letters
must feel that the religious motive was uppermost in his
mind — that he hoped to bear his part in the establishment
of an ideal Christian community.

An important part in the new enterprise was taken by a
group of Puritan clergymen, who were consulted in England
and who accompanied the emigrants to their new home.
They were generally university graduates, ordained in the
Church of England but unwilling to conform to the Anglican system as interpreted by Laud. The ablest of these
ministers was John Cotton, a fellow of Emmanuel College,

John Winthrop.

Puritan clergy.

John Cotton.

Cambridge, and afterwards the popular vicar of an Anglican parish in the seaport town of Boston, England, a name soon to be made more famous by the younger and greater Boston in Massachusetts. After trying for many years to reconcile Puritan ideas and practices with his position in the established church, Cotton was cited before the High Commission and forced to take refuge in Massachusetts. There he was much admired and had the satisfaction of seeing his ideals of church and state to a large extent realized.

Mingling of religious and economic motives.

It is not so easy to tell what were the thoughts and purposes of the many thousand obscure emigrants who followed the more conspicuous clergy and gentry. Some undoubtedly sympathized heartily with the hopes of their leaders. One of these "plain people," Edward Johnson, left behind him a book called *The Wonder-Working Providence of Sion's Saviour in New England*, whose very title suggests the strong religious feeling which inspired him to do his modest part in the establishment of a new Christian state. Besides these ardent Puritans, there were many others — yeomen, tenant farmers, mechanics, and small tradesmen, who were attracted to the New World chiefly by the desire for land and better homes. In the eastern and midland counties, particularly, this was a period of serious economic unrest.

Rapid development.

The early development of Massachusetts was much more rapid than that of the Chesapeake colonies. Virginia after seventeen years of strenuous effort had only about 1200 inhabitants; Massachusetts after thirteen years had more than 16,000. The new colony did not escape altogether the tragic features of pioneering; two hundred settlers died during the first year. After that, however, there was nothing to compare with the terrible mortality which for nearly twenty years seemed to carry off the Virginia settlers almost as fast as the company could send them out. The rapid growth of Massachusetts is all the more striking because many of the first settlers went out within the first ten years to found other colonies, which soon developed a vigorous, independent life of their own.

The early history of Massachusetts is associated almost entirely with a small area around the shores of Massachusetts Bay. On the south, it did not include more than the present suburban area of Boston; to the northward, there was the company's first settlement at Salem, and a few little villages beyond Cape Ann. The whole stretch of coast line may be covered to-day in a motor trip of a few hours. From the point of view of a farmer accustomed to the rich lands of the Mississippi valley, the region has few attractions. The ground close to the shore is hilly, with outcropping rock almost everywhere, and the New England farmer, except in the comparatively fertile valley of the Connecticut River, has had to work hard for meager returns. The Massachusetts seaboard also lacked great, hospitable, tidal rivers like those of Virginia to furnish easy transportation through the country. So the settlements tended to cling more closely to the sea, which was the main highway of colonial commerce. Nevertheless, in New England as elsewhere, farming was the essential foundation of community life. Upon the farmers with their Indian corn and their wheat rested the more distinctive and conspicuous New England activities of commerce and the fisheries. This was not a kind of agriculture which could thrive on ignorant labor and easy-going methods; it required intelligent individual industry working on lines of community coöperation. Here land was farmed not in large plantations with half-savage negro slaves, but mainly by small proprietors with the help of a few "hired men." *Geographic factors.*

One matter in which these settlers were deeply interested was the system of land tenure; here Massachusetts, and New England in general, stood out in sharp contrast to the other colonies. The original title was, as elsewhere, considered to be in the King, though the colonists generally recognized the Indian title also and often acquired it by *New England land system*

peaceful purchase. From the King, through the Council
for New England, the legal title passed to the General Court
of the Massachusetts Bay Company, which after the transfer
of the charter became practically the legislature of the
colony. The actual settlement of a particular neighborhood
ordinarily began with a grant by the General Court to a
group of proprietors, who proceeded to lay out a town and
make allotments to individual settlers. The holders of these
allotments became real owners, with no feudal services and
no quitrents. These freehold lands were, however, held
subject to the welfare of the community as a whole; and,
as in England, there were common lands — meadow, pasture,
or woodland — in which the inhabitants had a joint interest.
Community spirit was emphasized by the fact that many
New England settlements were made by church congregations, whose members, sometimes led by their pastors, had
emigrated together and wished to live together in their
new homes. Out of these conditions developed also a certain exclusiveness; the early New England towns were
extremely careful about the admission of new settlers, sometimes insisting that no one should acquire land without the
consent of the town.

Community spirit.

Generally speaking, New England agriculture could not
do much more than supply the local market; there was no
agricultural product like tobacco to exchange in large quantities for European goods. Indeed, Massachusetts ultimately came to depend for some of its wheat and flour upon
New York and the colonies farther south. New England
soil did, however, furnish one important article of export:
the forests provided abundant supplies of timber, sometimes made up into ships which were occasionally sold
abroad, and sometimes cut into various kinds of lumber for
export to the West Indies and even to Europe. The sea
itself, moreover, furnished the New Englanders with another
important staple. There were the small-scale fisheries near

Lumber and fish. New England commerce.

their own shores, and the cod fisheries on the Banks of New-foundland, reached by more venturesome voyages. For New England, as for old England, the fisheries were indeed a "nursery of seamen," and seamen of a particularly hardy breed. The uses of fish were varied: it furnished food for the people, fertilizer for farms, and an essential article of trade, especially to the island colonies. Thus Massachusetts like Virginia had its staple exports, but while the Virginians depended mainly on European shipping and carried on their trade almost entirely with England, the New Englanders built their own ships and soon developed an important foreign trade. A certain independence was, therefore, a characteristic feature of New England commerce.

Puritans, like other men, had to face economic facts; and before long they had won from the land and from the sea a good deal more than a bare living. Meantime their leaders, at least, were quite sure that man does not "live by bread alone." While the farmers were planting corn and the fishermen were going down to the sea in ships, some among them were working hard on the foundations of that "Bible Commonwealth" which they hoped would serve not only themselves and their children, but perhaps also the troubled peoples of the Old World.

Economic prosperity and a "Bible Commonwealth."

The legal basis of the whole experiment was the royal charter. By this document, which Winthrop and his associates brought over with them, almost unlimited authority for the management of colony business was put in the hands of the stockholders, or "freemen," of the company. The decisions of the freemen in the "General Court," or stockholders' meeting, were to be carried into effect by the governor and assistants, who corresponded roughly to the president and directors of a present-day corporation. These executive officers were to be chosen annually by the freemen and had little independent authority. Almost the only limitation on the powers of the General Court, other

Government under the first charter.

than a general acknowledgment of allegiance to the King, was the requirement that colonial laws must not be in conflict with the laws of England. It was this businesslike charter which the founders of Massachusetts developed into the constitution of a practically republican government.

The first problem was to decide what people in the colony should exercise these liberal powers. Only a few members of the company had crossed the ocean, and if all of them had come they would still have been only an insignificant fraction of the whole population. Certainly this handful of people could not long impose their will upon the thousands of incoming settlers. Nevertheless, the leaders were determined to keep the power in the hands of men who sympathized with the main object for which the colony was founded, namely, the establishment of a distinctly Puritan commonwealth. Though a considerable number of new freemen were soon admitted, it was agreed that no one should henceforth receive this privilege and become a fully qualified voter unless he were a member of some church in the colony. No congregation was, of course, approved unless it conformed to the orthodox Puritan standards in theology, manner of worship, and church government.

Church membership a qualification for voters, 1631.

The Puritan oligarchy.

Even the church-membership qualification was not sufficient from the point of view of the ruling group. For the first four years, the governor and the assistants kept the powers almost entirely in their own hands, sometimes even such important matters as the election of the governor and the levying of taxes. This course, however, provoked great discontent and, in 1634, Winthrop and his associates were compelled to accept a representative system, by which the freemen in each town, instead of coming up in person to meetings of the General Court, should send their deputies. This was quite as much at variance with the charter as the arbitrary methods of the governor and assistants; but it was obviously impossible for all the freemen to transact business in a general meeting.

The establishment of the representative system by no means ended the conflict between the little group of leaders and those who wished a wider distribution of political power. When the General Court met, with the governor, the assistants, and the deputies sitting together, the governor and assistants frequently took one side and a majority of the deputies ranged themselves in opposition. In such cases, the assistants were likely to be outvoted by the deputies, who were much more numerous. The assistants now claimed that no measure could be passed without a majority for it in each group. This claim, which meant that the assistants could veto any action desired by the deputies, was strenuously resisted; but the assistants finally had their way and the Massachusetts legislature thus developed into a two-house system. The victory of the assistants was made possible in part by the attitude of influential ministers, like Cotton, who felt that the smaller group of leaders could be better trusted to carry through the ideal of a Bible Commonwealth; some of the ministers even talked of allowing colonial officers to serve for life. In short, this early Massachusetts government, though practically republican in the sense that final authority rested with the qualified voters, was not democratic. The church members, who alone could vote, were only a small minority, and even within this minority a still smaller group generally controlled the policies of the colony.

The Bible Commonwealth idea influenced the system of law as well as the form of government. Though the charter required that colonial laws should conform as nearly as practicable to those of England, yet in the actual administration of justice, common-law precedents were frequently set aside in favor of principles derived from the Old Testament, especially from the Mosaic code. This led to much

Assistants and deputies.

The bicameral system.

Puritanism and the common law.

uncertainty about the law to be applied in any given case; and seemed to give the magistrates too much discretion. So there came a demand for a definite code of laws in order that the individual might know what his rights and duties were. For a time the leaders objected to such a code, but they finally gave way and in 1641 the so-called Body of Liberties was adopted. This code, based in the main on the common law, follows Biblical precedent in its sections dealing with crimes, servants, and descent and distribution.[1] Some of its provisions now seem harsh and narrow; but others show a distinct advance in liberality and humanity over the theory and practice of the old country.

The Body of Liberties.

County government in Massachusetts followed roughly the old English model with its justices of the peace and its sheriff. In the matter of town government, however, the New Englanders varied considerably from English local government. This was partly because of economic conditions, which led to compact settlements and emphasized the need of coöperation; but religion also had an important influence, since the prevailing congregational system of church organization tended to strengthen the spirit of local self-government. The organization of town governments was simple; some features of the English parish were retained and the most vital institution was the town meeting, composed of all the qualified voters. Here all important business was transacted, including the choice of the selectmen, who formed a kind of executive committee. The town was responsible for preserving order within its limits, and for the care of its own poor; it could also adopt by-laws regulating other local affairs and vote the taxes necessary for their various purposes. The vigor and self-reliance of the New England towns have rightly been emphasized; but they were not completely independent. Their by-laws had to be approved by the

Local government.

The town meeting.

---

[1] A number of years earlier John Cotton had proposed a code, known as "Moses his Judicialls," based entirely on Biblical law.

county justices, and they were subject to the higher authority of the General Court. For failure to perform duties assigned to them by law, the towns could be and actually were punished by fine or otherwise. On the other hand, it was the town which elected representatives to the General Court or assembly; it was also the unit for purposes of taxation, each town being assigned its quota of the colony tax which it was expected to collect from the inhabitants.

From the point of view of the thoroughgoing Puritans, the chief object of all their institutions was to establish what they believed to be the true Christian faith and worship. Though the early leaders, both clergy and laymen, generally regarded themselves as members of the Anglican Church and at the time of their emigration professed a real affection for it in spite of its "corruptions," they took a much more radical stand on their arrival in New England. They refused to permit the use of the English prayer book and, with some help from their neighbors at Plymouth, they organized their churches on the congregational basis. The plan of church government which was gradually developed under the leadership of John Cotton was a compromise between the two systems now known as Congregational and Presbyterian. Theoretically each congregation was a self-governing unit, choosing its own ministers. Actually, however, the local church was not always free from interference; the minister and elders also had more power than was quite consistent with the strictly congregational theory. This new organization gave the Puritans a free hand to carry out their ideas of a severely simple service, with preaching as its principal feature. *Organization of the church.*

This system of faith and worship having been set up in the church, it was considered the duty of the state to support it. Consequently the inhabitants, whether church members or not, were taxed to support Puritan ministers and required to attend their services. Other religious duties *Union of church and state.*

were enforced by law, including the strictest kind of Sabbath observance. Heretics were not only dismissed from the church but banished from the colony. In this close association of church and state, the New Englanders were, like the Virginians, following Old World precedents. Nevertheless, Massachusetts applied the principle in a more thorough fashion than Virginia, because religious motives had played a larger part in the Puritan migration. The clergy also had greater influence in New England than in any other English colony. They were generally men of superior education, whose advice was frequently asked for in secular as well as in religious matters. Under the influence of such leaders, public opinion was accustomed to the idea that the community should act together in religion as well as in other respects. Only a very independent or stubborn individual could hold out against this social pressure.

The place of the church in the community.

The conditions of life on the edge of the wilderness helped to emphasize the place of religion in the community. To-day the church as an educational and social agency has many competitors — newspapers, periodicals, places of public amusement, and an infinite variety of social organizations. Practically none of these things existed in the early years of the Massachusetts colony. The church was the central institution in each town for intellectual stimulus and social intercourse, as well as for religious worship. Such a system, intensified for many by the hardships and dangers which surrounded them, worked both for good and for evil. In the best men and women, it developed a strong spirit of idealism, a high sense of public and private duty; even such people, however, did not escape a common tendency toward intolerance and morbid types of religious feeling.

Education.

For the perpetuation of its ideals, every community must depend largely upon its schools. In this work church and state were both deeply interested, and provision for

public education was made almost immediately. A college
was established in 1636 by vote of the General Court, principally for the purpose of training ministers to continue the Harvard
work of those who had been educated in the English uni- College.
versities. Shortly afterwards, John Harvard, a young minister, died, leaving a considerable gift to the college, which
was thenceforth called by his name. Before long it began
to turn out influential leaders of the community, in civil
life as well as in the church. During the same decade, ele- Elementary
mentary schools were established in various places. The schools.
towns commonly helped to support them by grants of land
and otherwise; but the meager salary of the schoolmaster
had to be supplemented by fees from the parents of his pupils.
His status was often quite modest; in one case he was obliged
to combine his school duties with the care of the town herd.
In 1647, the colony tried to establish a general system of
education by requiring every town of fifty householders
to support an elementary school; a town with one hundred
householders was to maintain a grammar school where boys
could be prepared for college. A town which failed to observe this law was subject to a fine. Undoubtedly the act
was not fully enforced, but it does at least express the ideals
of the colony.

In almost every phase of this early Massachusetts his- Practical
tory, the dominant note was "self-determination." The independence
of the home
Puritan colonists were Englishmen with a real attachment government.
to certain English ideas of civil liberty; but they had their
special point of view and they were determined to solve
their own problems in their own way, whether those problems
related to commerce, politics, religion, or education. This
independent position was, however, seriously threatened
almost from the beginning. As early as 1634, when the Puritan migration had become so large as to cause anxiety
in England, Charles I appointed a commission consisting
of Archbishop Laud and other important dignitaries, giving

them a general authority over the colonies in America. Gorges, also, kept up a constant fire of hostile criticism. In 1635, the English government ordered the surrender of the charter. This was an anxious time; the ministers favored resisting any "general governor" who might be sent from England. But the troubles at home became so serious that the King and his advisers had little time for American affairs. So for half a century this Puritan experiment in government was carried on with little interference.

Dissent.

The enemies of this Bible Commonwealth were not all in England. The dissenting spirit which brought the Puritans to Massachusetts could not be kept within the limits set by a small ruling class. Some individuals and groups of people carried their dissent farther still, so that they again became exiles and founders of new colonies in which they were able to develop more freely their own theories.

BIBLIOGRAPHICAL NOTES

General accounts.

Andrews, C. M., *Fathers of New England*, chs. I, II, IV. Morison, S. E., *Builders of the Bay Colony*. Channing, *United States*, I, chs. X–XII. Adams, J. T., *Founding of New England*, chs. I–VII. Palfrey, J. G., *History of New England* (very detailed).

Puritanism in the Old World.

Cheyney, E. P., *European Background*, ch. XII. *Cambridge Modern History*, II, 342–376. Walker, W., *Calvin*, especially chs. XIV, XV. Gardiner, S. R., *Puritan Revolution*, 1–6, chs. IV, V. (His *History of England, 1603–1642*, is useful for reference; see especially I, 16–41). For the special religious background in England, see Burrage, C., *Early English Dissenters (1550–1641)*, I, and Hall, T. C., *The Religious Background of American Culture*.

Economic interpretation of Calvinism.

Tawney, R. H., *Religion and the Rise of Capitalism*. Weber, M., *The Protestant Ethic and the Spirit of Capitalism*. Troeltsch, *The Social Teaching of the Christian Churches*. Harkness, G., *John Calvin, The Man and His Ethics*, 137–191.

The Pilgrims.

Winsor, *America*, III, ch. VIII. Dexter, M., *Story of the Pilgrims*. Dexter, H. M., and M., *England and Holland of the Pilgrims*. Andrews, C. M., *Colonial Period*, I, chs. XIII–XIV.

Plooij, D., *Pilgrim Fathers from a Dutch Point of View*. Usher, R. G., *The Pilgrims and Their History*.

Bradford, W., *Plymouth Plantation* (various editions). Arber, E., *Story of the Pilgrim Fathers*. Masefield, J., *Chronicles of the Pilgrim Fathers* (*Everyman's Library*). Hart, *Contemporaries*, I, nos. 97–103. Macdonald, *Select Charters*, no. 5. — Sources.

Adams, C. F., *Three Episodes of Massachusetts History*, I. Ellis, G. E., *Puritan Age and Rule in Massachusetts Bay*, chs. I–VII. Winsor, J., *Memorial History of Boston*, I, *Colonial Period*, chs. I, II, XVI, XVII. Twitchell, J. H., *John Winthrop*. Andrews, C. M., *Colonial Period*, I, chs. XVII–XXI. Hart, A. B., ed., *Commonwealth History of Massachusetts*, I. — Massachusetts Bay.

Hart, *Contemporaries*, I, nos. 105–110. Macdonald, *Select Charters*, nos. 8, 17. Commager, *Documents*, 16, 17, 28, 29. Winthrop, J., *History of New England* (editions by Savage and Hosmer). Winthrop, R. C., *Life and Letters of John Winthrop*. Winthrop's "Little Speech," in *History* (Hosmer ed.), II, 237–239; in *Life and Letters*, II, 339–342; and in *Old South Leaflets*, no. 66. Johnson, *Wonder-Working Providence* (ed. by J. F. Jameson). — Massachusetts sources.

Crouse, N. M., "Causes of the Great Migration, 1630–1640," *N.E.Q.* (1932), V, 3–36. Morison, S. E., *Builders of the Bay Colony*, appendix, and review by J. T. Adams, *N.E.Q.* (1930), III, 741–746. — Economic and religious influences.

Sly, J. F., *Town Government in Massachusetts, 1620–1930*. Osgood, *17th Cent.*, I, pt. II, especially chs. I, II. — Political institutions.

Osgood, *17th Cent.*, I, pt. II, ch. 3. Walker, W., *Congregational Churches*, chs. I–IV, VII. Miller, P., *Orthodoxy in Massachusetts, 1630–1650*. Earle, A. M., *Sabbath in Puritan New England*. Hutchinson, T., *History of Massachusetts*, I, ch. IV. — Religion.

Morison, S. E., *The Tercentennial History of Harvard College*, I. Wright, T. G., *Literary Culture in Colonial New England*. — Education and letters.

Day, C. H., "Capitalistic and Socialistic Tendencies in the Puritan Colonies," Amer. Hist. Assoc., *Annual Report*, 1920, 225–235. Articles by E. A. J. Johnson in *N.E.Q.* I, 371–395; III, 235–250. Weeden, W. B., *History of New England*, I, chs. I–VI. — Business theories and practices.

Morris, R. B., "Massachusetts and the Common Law," *A.H.R.* (1926), XXXI, 443–453. Chafee, Z., Introduction to "Records of Suffolk County Court," Col. Soc. of Mass., *Publications*, XXIX, pp. xvii–xciv. — Early law.

CHAPTER VI

THE PURITAN COMMONWEALTHS, 1635 TO 1676

THE religious controversies which embittered the early history of Massachusetts have perhaps had more attention than they deserve. Most of the issues then debated have lost interest except for specialists, and few of the men who fought over them can claim any conspicuous place in history. One notable exception to this statement is Roger Williams, who illustrates admirably the spirit of thorough-going individualism in early American life. Though on the whole kindly and generous, he was not easy to get on with. He had not been long in Massachusetts before he began to promulgate certain ideas which disturbed the colonial authorities. Some of these views were of a kind to make trouble for the colony with the English government, as, for instance, when he denied the right of the King to give legal titles to Indian lands; or when, taking the extreme Separatist position, he insisted that the Church of England was so corrupt that every good Christian ought to repent of ever having been a member of it. When the Boston church refused to accept this latter theory Williams refused to associate himself with it. The Puritans generally disliked the use of the cross as a religious symbol; but when one of their leaders, apparently under Williams's influence, cut this emblem out of the royal ensign they felt that this was going too far. There were plenty of enemies in England who would be only too glad to make capital out of such occurrences.

From a modern standpoint, Williams was putting too much

energy into small disputes but he did identify himself with one
really big issue. Though himself a man of intense and often
narrow convictions, he made up his mind that religious errors
must be fought exclusively with spiritual or intellectual
weapons. The use of governmental authority to enforce
a man's religious obligations he condemned as contrary
both to reason and to Christian teaching. The magistrate,
he said, or in modern language the state, had a right to punish men's offenses against each other, but duties toward
God must be left to the individual conscience. Unfortunately,
the real importance of this issue was clouded by applying
it to a matter in which practical considerations even now
seem to most men more important than theory. He insisted, among other things, that the state had no right to
require an oath because it was essentially a religious act.
Whatever may be thought about this particular detail,
the fact remains that Williams had started an irrepressi-
ble conflict. If he was right in saying that the state had
nothing to do with religion, then the whole Massachusetts idea of a Bible Commonwealth was wrong. It is
hardly strange, then, that the Massachusetts authorities took
up the gauntlet which Williams had thrown down. In 1635
the General Court ordered his expulsion, and in the following winter he left Massachusetts to begin a new settlement
at the head of Narragansett Bay.

Williams was hardly disposed of before another ecclesiastical storm came up, and this time the leading figure
was a woman, Anne Hutchinson. In his journal for 1636
John Winthrop makes the following entry: "One Mrs.
Hutchinson, a woman of a ready wit and a bold spirit,
brought over with her two dangerous errors.... From these
two grew many branches." It is hardly possible and perhaps
not important now to state exactly what Mrs. Hutchinson's
theological opinions were. The essential fact is that she took
an active interest in criticizing some of the ministers, main-

Williams's attack on the union of church and state.

Banishment of Williams.

Anne Hutchinson.

The Anti-nomians.

taining that they laid too much stress on good works, rather than on divine grace. Many conservatives thought they found in Mrs. Hutchinson's doctrine traces of the ancient heresy that a truly religious person need pay no attention to the moral law. She and her associates, though probably guiltless of this particular offense, were therefore branded as Antinomians, and nearly all the ministers and church members were drawn into the controversy on one side or the other.

Among those who, for a time at least, showed more or less sympathy with Mrs. Hutchinson were John Cotton and young Henry Vane, son of a well-known English official and himself destined to become one of the leaders in the Puritan Revolution. Vane, who had been only a few months in the colony, made such a deep impression that he was promptly chosen governor and held that office while the Hutchinson controversy was at its height. In the hope of settling the matter, the churches of the colony held a synod, which condemned a number of doctrines held, or supposed to be held, by the Antinomians. In the midst of this excitement there was an election in which the conservatives were victorious,

Banishment of the Antinomians. and Winthrop once more became governor. Anne Hutchinson was now tried before the General Court, which was much disturbed by her claim to have had a direct revelation from the Holy Spirit. Convinced that she was a dangerous character, the Court sent her also into exile. With her went, under compulsion or voluntarily, many of her followers.

Other dissenters. The same policy of repressing dissenters was followed consistently during the next two decades. The teaching of certain Baptist doctrines was made a penal offense and in 1646 an attempt to induce the English Parliament, then dominated by the Presbyterians, to support that form of Puritanism in Massachusetts was promptly suppressed. The signers of a petition to this effect were brought into court and fined. The most tragic episode, however, in this whole period was the persecution of the Quakers.

The Society of Friends, better known as the Quakers, seemed to most men at that time almost the last word in religious radicalism. As against the Roman Catholics and many of the Anglicans, who emphasized the authority of the church in matters of faith, and the thoroughgoing Protestants who regarded the Bible as their ultimate authority, the Quakers declared that the final court of appeal was the individual conscience enlightened by the Holy Spirit. The Quakers also considered unnecessary the sacraments of the church, even baptism and the Lord's Supper, which were accepted in some form by practically all other Christians. To these radicals, Catholic priests and Puritan ministers were alike "hirelings." Instead of formal services conducted by a salaried clergy, they had only simple meetings of believers, at which each man or woman spoke as the Spirit moved. To most men of that generation this teaching seemed quite anarchistic, and the violent language used by some of the Quaker preachers intensified this feeling. Though most of them meant to be and were law-abiding citizens, some of their doctrines and practices seemed to show lack of respect for constituted authority. They rejected conventional forms of courtesy like removing the hat, objected to oaths even in court, and refused military service.

Almost everywhere Quakerism was regarded as a perni- cious infection and its adherents were severely persecuted. Nowhere, however, was their treatment so drastic as in Massachusetts. When two Quaker women arrived at Boston in 1656, they were dealt with somewhat as modern health authorities would deal with contagious diseases. The obnoxious visitors were isolated and as soon as possible deported. During the next two years three laws were made in the hope of stopping this "Quaker invasion." The last and harshest of all provided that Quakers who persistently returned after being deported should be hanged. Doubtless the advocates of this law believed that the death penalty would never have to be applied. Some of the Quakers, however, now considered it more than ever their duty to return in order to testify against the iniquity of their persecutors, and four of them, three men and one woman, were actually hanged. Such harshness naturally caused a reaction and the death penalty was given up; but that did not end the persecution. In 1661, the General Court, having expressed its desire to be as "lenient" as possible, indicated the prevailing idea of leniency by ordering that anyone found to be a Quaker should be tied to a cart's tail, and whipped from town to town until he was out of the jurisdiction of the colony.

The theory of persecution.

It is not for the historian to defend or palliate measures of this kind. All he can do is to explain how they came about and relate them to the prevailing standards of the time. The Puritans believed that they were working out an experiment of great importance to mankind and, therefore, had a right to keep their particular corner of the world exclusively for those who would coöperate in this great adventure. Unquestionably the Puritans were intolerant and cruel; but they lived in an age when only a handful of advanced thinkers anywhere believed that religion could safely be left to the individual conscience, and when even petty offenses were punished in the most barbarous fashion.

The new Puritan colonies.

So in New England, as in old England, those who could not find comfortable places for themselves in the existing social order became in their turn exiles and founders of new commonwealths. For the most part, however, the differences of the Puritans among themselves were less radical than those which separated them all from the party of King Charles and Archbishop Laud. To a large extent, therefore, the social and political institutions of the later New England colonies followed the Massachusetts model. Of these later Puritan colonies, there were three distinct groups. Those of the first group, settled at various points in and about Narragansett Bay, were finally combined in the col-

ony of Rhode Island and Providence Plantations. About
the same time the two colonies of Connecticut and New
Haven were planted on the Connecticut River and on the
shore of Long Island Sound. Finally, in Maine and New
Hampshire, Puritan emigrants from Massachusetts invaded
territory claimed by the two non-Puritan promoters, Gorges
and Mason, becoming, in time, the dominant element in
the population. The last of these three groups proved to be
of minor importance in the colonial era. By 1643 the New
Hampshire towns had been gradually absorbed by Massachusetts, and a few years later the same aggressive colony
annexed the scattered settlements in Maine.

The founders of the first group were mainly dissenters   Narragansett
from Massachusetts; it was these Narragansett settlements, settlements.
therefore, which departed most radically from the Massachusetts model. Small as Rhode Island is, this little colony was formed by the union of four distinct units. The
first was Roger Williams's own colony of Providence at   Providence.
the head of Narragansett Bay. Here, he and his associates
bought land from the natives and presently adopted a
"plantation covenant" agreeing to abide by the will of the
majority, but "only in civil things." Even in secular matters, government was reduced to its lowest terms. This
rudimentary government had, of course, no legal authority
which anyone either in England or America was bound to
respect. The second and third of these political atoms
came out of the Antinomian troubles in Massachusetts.
A number of Anne Hutchinson's followers took refuge   Portsmouth.
on the island in Narragansett Bay then called Aquidneck,
but better known as Rhode Island. The first settlers organized at Portsmouth a government which, notwithstanding their difficulties in Massachusetts, was strongly Puritan in spirit. Following Biblical precedents, they called
their elected officers, judge and elders rather than governor and assistants. The same vigorous individualism

which had exiled them from the "Bay" soon made trouble in their new home, and presently the island settlement split into two independent units, one at Portsmouth and the **Newport.** other at Newport, near the southern end of the island. The fourth of the Narragansett colonies was founded by an able, picturesque, and combative person by the name of Samuel Gorton. Gorton had strong religious convictions and expressed them after the fashion of his time with more vigor than tact. Having lived at one time or another in Massachusetts, Plymouth, and the Antinomian settlement at Portsmouth, he was nearly everywhere at odds with his neighbors; even Roger Williams was unwilling to have him as a fellow colonist. So he also sought freedom in a **Warwick.** new colony on the western shore of Narragansett Bay, to which he later gave the name of Warwick in honor of the great Puritan promoter.

The movement toward union. With all their differences the Narragansett settlements had much in common. Their governments were all republican; they were all at first without legal title either for their lands or their governments; and they were all in constant fear of being absorbed by their stronger neighbors, who considered them little better than anarchists. Under these circumstances they soon realized that individualism might easily be carried so far as to defeat its own objects. Unless they could bring themselves to some workable compromise between liberty and union, they were likely to lose their independence altogether. So the political atoms gradually began to unite. In 1640, the two island settlements were combined in what its founders called a "democrat or popular government." After the outbreak of the Civil War in England, Roger Williams went over for a conference with the Puritan parliamentary government; and in 1644, he secured a document authorizing the Narragansett settlers to organize a general government. On the strength of this parliamentary patent, representatives from the various towns came together in 1647 and organized a kind of federal union. The new government was to be republican; the president and the assistants, as well as the representatives of the towns in the assembly, were to be elected annually. So far, the political system was not unlike those of Plymouth and Massachusetts; but at two points the Rhode Islanders took an independent course. The rights of the towns were jealously guarded, and acts of the colonial assembly had to be submitted to a kind of referendum in each community. More notable still was the separation of church and state. No church-membership qualification was required for voters and every man was to be protected in the "peaceful and quiet enjoyment of lawfull right and liberty," "notwithstanding our different consciences touching the truth as it is in Jesus." *The Union of 1647.*

Unfortunately the new constitution did not end the troubles of the young colony. In 1651 the union was temporarily broken up and though it was reorganized in 1654, the next few years were an anxious period in Rhode Island history. Its territory was still claimed by neighboring colonies and the Restoration government of Charles II could hardly be expected to recognize a patent issued by the rebellious Long Parliament. Once more, however, the Rhode Islanders found a skillful agent to represent them in England, and in 1663 they secured their first royal charter. Under this constitution, whose legality no one could question, the qualified voters were enabled to carry on a practically republican government, closely resembling that of Massachusetts. Though in general the laws of the colony had to conform to those of England, there was an exception in favor of religious liberty. The charter declared that no person should be "any wise molested, punished, disquieted, or called in question for any differences in opinion in matters of religion," provided that he did not disturb the "civil peace." Fortunately, Roger Williams, the ardent *Rhode Island and Providence Plantations.* *The charter of 1663.* *Religious liberty.*

young radical of 1635, was still living to see his principle of "soul liberty" incorporated in the constitutional law of an American commonwealth. A few years earlier, when the Quakers visited Rhode Island, Williams's fidelity to this ideal had been severely tested. No one could use stronger language in denunciation of the Quakers than he did; but when asked to coöperate with other colonies in measures of persecution, Rhode Island under his leadership steadily refused.

The founding of Connecticut.

The founding of Connecticut and New Haven is quite another story in which religious differences were less important. Less than five years after the founding of Massachusetts Bay, some of its people discovered that in the Connecticut valley the land was more productive than any in the neighborhood of Boston. This region was already known to the Dutch, who came in from the Hudson valley and established their "House of Hope" near the present site of Hartford; there were also a few English pioneers from Plymouth. These facts did not, however, prevent conflicting plans being made in Massachusetts, where the Dutch were regarded as mere intruders on land properly belonging to the English. Besides the economic motive for emigration there was a certain amount of political and social discontent.

Thomas Hooker.

The chief promoters of the new project were Thomas Hooker, minister of the church at Newtown, now Cambridge, and John Haynes, an influential leader who had served one term as governor of Massachusetts. Hooker was of course somewhat liberal in his views and dissatisfied with the group of men who controlled the policies of Massachusetts; but he was obviously not a radical of the Roger Williams type. It is certainly difficult to regard Haynes as a very progressive person, since he was ready to criticize Winthrop for being too lenient. These founders of Connecticut were not exiles; the Massachusetts government at first refused them permission to emigrate and finally gave its consent reluctantly.

In 1635 the emigration began in earnest and before long members of three Puritan congregations near Boston had found new homes on the Connecticut. By 1636 there were about 800 settlers in the three river towns of Hartford, Wethersfield, and Windsor; a few miles to the north was another pioneer settlement at Springfield, which later turned out to be within the jurisdiction of Massachusetts. These newcomers crowded out the earlier settlers from Plymouth, and though they did not quite venture to expel the Dutch, they took up land close to the "House of Hope." Like the first settlers of Plymouth and Rhode Island, the Connecticut pioneers were squatters with no legal title to hold land or carry on a government. At the mouth of the Connecticut, there was the post of Saybrook, established by John Winthrop, Jr., son of the Massachusetts governor, under a grant made by the Council for New England to some of its Puritan members. An understanding was, however, reached between these rival interests, which allowed the colonists up the river to develop their settlements without interference. *Connecticut River towns.*

In 1639 representatives from the river towns met at Hartford and formed a constitution called the Fundamental Orders. This government also followed the Massachusetts model, with governor, deputy governor, and assistants all chosen annually by the freemen. The differences, which were not very important, are interesting chiefly as showing a desire to prevent the officers of the colony from gaining too much power; the governor, for instance, was not allowed to serve two years in succession. Evidently the framers of this constitution had no fundamental objection to the union of church and state; they declared, indeed, that it was one of their chief objects to preserve "the discipline of the Churches, which according to the truth of the said Gospel is now practised amongst us." In other words, the state was expected to maintain the Puritan system. The *The Fundamental Orders.*

governor was required to be a member of some approved congregation, and though no general law required that voters should be church members, most of the towns probably did not admit as "freemen" and voters persons who were not in sympathy with the religious aims set forth in the **Growth of** constitution. Under this government the colony grew and **the colony.** prospered; new towns were planted along the river and eastward toward Narragansett Bay. The Dutch in the Hudson valley were much impressed by the success of the English, contrasting it with the slow progress of New Netherland. Against possible attacks from that quarter, the Connecticut farmers depended partly on the English fort at the mouth of the river; but their best protection was a rapid growth in population with which the Dutch could not compete.

Connecticut was hardly established before New England Puritanism set its stakes still farther westward on Long **New Haven.** Island Sound, at New Haven. The promoters of this colony were well-to-do London Puritans, led by their minister, John Davenport, and an influential merchant named Theophilus Eaton. They came to Massachusetts in 1637, and, being thoroughly orthodox Puritans, were urged to stay in Massachusetts. They had more ambitious plans, however, and presently moved to New Haven, which they hoped to make an important trading center. They also proposed to make this new colony an even more thoroughgoing Bible Commonwealth than Massachusetts. Their hope of commercial development on a large scale was disappointed; but during the next six years, they succeeded in establishing another little Puritan republic which finally included, besides New Haven, several other towns, extending westward along the Sound almost as far as the present eastern boundary of New York.

For almost twenty-five years, Connecticut and New Haven continued as separate colonies. Though quite agreed on the fundamental tenets of Puritanism, they were not altogether congenial and the New Haven people prided themselves on the peculiar strictness of their church system. Both colonies were, however, at a disadvantage because they had no royal charter and therefore no legal security against outside interference. So long as the Puritan party kept control in England, they were fairly safe; but when the Stuart monarchy came back under Charles II, the Connecticut people, especially, were anxious for royal recognition. Through the skillful management of John Winthrop, Jr., who had been governor of Connecticut for several years, a royal charter was secured in 1662. Connecticut and New Haven, the latter much against its will, were now combined in a single colony. As in Rhode Island, political power was placed almost completely in the hands of the qualified voters; the charter proved so satisfactory to the people who lived under it that they used it as their state constitution for more than forty years after the Declaration of Independence.

Union of Connecticut and New Haven. The charter of 1662.

The westward movement of the New Englanders into the Connecticut valley brought the first serious conflict in this region between the whites and the Indians. The tribes most seriously disturbed by this white invasion were the Pequots, who, living in the eastern part of the present state of Connecticut, were hemmed in between the Narragansetts on the east and the Mohegans on the west. The trouble began with the usual misunderstandings between the races, followed by Indian attacks upon individual settlers, and finally by a real war. For a time the Connecticut frontiersmen were in grave danger, isolated as they were from the older settlements in Massachusetts; but they soon organized an effective defense and before long received reënforcements from Massachusetts and from the friendly Indians, so that they could take the offensive. By 1637 the Pequots were completely crushed. Unfortunately the record was

The Pequot War.

stained by wholesale slaughter and enslavement of the Indians, including many women and children.

Results of Puritan enterprise.

Within twenty-five years after the founding of the Pilgrim colony at Plymouth, the Puritan colonists had pre-empted nearly the whole New England seaboard from the Maine-New Hampshire border almost to the present suburban area of the City of New York.   Here for about half a century they were almost entirely free to carry out their religious, economic, and political experiments.   Before this period of practical independence came to an end, the ideas of the Puritan founders were so thoroughly impressed on New England society that they persisted with surprisingly little change through all the vicissitudes of the next hundred years.   This was in itself a great achievement, but it is not the whole story of Puritan enterprise, for it leaves out of account the aggressive Puritan minorities which made their influence felt in the Dutch territory of New Netherland, in the Chesapeake colonies, and even in the West Indies.

New England and the English Commonwealth.

Notwithstanding this remarkable record of expansion, the New England horizon was not altogether unclouded. The growing power of the Puritans in old England checked immigration and there was even some backward flow to the mother country. This falling off in immigration checked also the flow of capital into the colony, and severe financial depression led many to talk of deserting the enterprise. During the English Civil War, the New Englanders naturally sympathized with the parliamentary party as against the King; but their principal desire was to be let alone and they could never be quite sure about the final outcome. As they said later, it was their policy "only to act a passive part throughout these late vicissitudes and successive overturnings of state."

The Indian problem.

The Indians were another source of anxiety. The settlers had generally tried to be fair, usually paying the Indians

for their land and trying to settle justly the inevitable disputes between individuals of the two races. Some progress
was also made in missionary work, especially by the
Massachusetts minister, John Eliot. Yet there were
also many acts of injustice, some quite inexcusable but
others due to the fact that neither race could quite understand the other. So the danger of Indian uprisings could
never be forgotten and even the short Pequot War showed
how hard it was to get the scattered colonies to act together when a crisis did arise. There were white neighbors, French
too, who were not friendly. Along the Maine coast, New and Dutch
Englanders competed with Frenchmen for the Indian trade; neighbors.
and in 1643 the Massachusetts authorities were more or
or less involved in a conflict between two rival French leaders
in Acadia. The Dutch in New Netherland did not enjoy
the westward expansion of New England, which was steadily
going forward with little regard for their feelings. These
conflicting claims might well lead to war. Doubtless some
New Englanders could remember the massacre of Amboina
in the Spice Islands of the East Indies, which showed that
the Dutch could sometimes strike hard and ruthlessly in
defending their commercial interests against English competition. Even within the Puritan circle, everything did not go
quite smoothly. Massachusetts quarreled with Plymouth
about boundaries and Indian trade, while the radicals of
Narragansett Bay were disliked by nearly all their neighbors.

All these difficulties emphasized the need of coöperation.
On the whole, too, the interests which divided the New
Englanders were less fundamental than those which drew New Eng-
them together. They had a common inheritance of language land con-
and of law; they had all worked out practically repub- federation.
lican forms of government; and most of them agreed on the
fundamental Puritan ideas of religion and church government. The idea of forming a federation first came up in
1637, the year of the Pequot War, and was discussed at

intervals for the next six years. At last, the leaders were ready to act and in 1643 they organized the United Colonies of New England with four members: Massachusetts, Plymouth, Connecticut, and New Haven. The unpopular radicals of Narragansett Bay were left out and also the struggling Maine villages, soon to be absorbed by Massachusetts. In the articles of union stress was laid on the common religious interests which the new federation was to promote; but the spirit of independence was scarcely less strong and the federation was, therefore, organized on a "state rights" basis. The management of its business was entrusted to eight commissioners, the little colonies of Plymouth and New Haven receiving exactly the same representation as Massachusetts, which had a larger population than all the others combined. Each colony was also guaranteed complete independence except for the very few matters entrusted to the confederation, which was organized primarily for military defense. Among other matters provided for in the articles were the extradition of criminals and of fugitive servants and a plan for the settlement of intercolonial disputes.

Working of the confederation. The confederation had a short and troubled career. Usually the commissioners were content to make recommendations to the various colonial governments. They recommended, for instance, legislation requiring each man to keep himself supplied with arms; also that the judicial proceedings of one colony should receive full recognition by all the others, thus anticipating a familiar clause in the present Constitution of the United States. From time to time they discussed Indian affairs, deciding on one occasion that the Mohegan chieftain, Uncas, might lawfully put to death a captive Narragansett chief. The Dutch furnished another series of problems. In 1643, John Winthrop, the first president of the confederation, was instructed to demand satisfaction for damage done to English traders in the Delaware valley by the Dutch and the Swedes. Ten years later, however, when Connecticut and New Haven were eager for war against the Dutch, Massachusetts, which would have had to make the heaviest contribution in men and money, strongly opposed the proposition and when outvoted refused to coöperate. This was not the first case of this kind. A few years before, after it was regularly decided that Connecticut had the right to levy a tax on goods coming down the river from Massachusetts, that government held out against it and voted a retaliatory tax against the other members of the union. There was a still more serious breach of the constitution when, in 1662, New Haven was annexed to Connecticut notwithstanding a clause in the articles guaranteeing the independence of every member of the league.

The confederation had now about outlived its usefulness, though in 1675 it helped to put down the formidable Indian uprising known as King Philip's War. Compared with modern federal governments, the New England confederation was a feeble affair; nevertheless it may fairly claim an honorable place in the series of American experiments out of which has come the most successful federation in history.

The "golden age" of New England Puritanism ended with the passing of the first generation of colonists. By 1660 Winthrop and Cotton, the most trusted leaders in the state and in the church, and many of their associates were gone; their places were now taken by younger and usually smaller men. It was also becoming more difficult for the New Englanders to keep their independent position. The fall of the Commonwealth in England and the restoration of the Stuarts meant that the British government was passing into the hands of men who were not at all friendly to the Puritan communities across the sea. This dislike was increased when some of the "regicides," who were responsible for the execution of Charles I, found refuge in New

New England and the home government.

England. The Massachusetts authorities tried to ward off
the danger by sending over extremely polite, not to say
effusive, letters protesting their loyalty to the King but
quite firmly insisting on their right to manage their own
affairs. When the King demanded that property holders
should be allowed to vote, whether they were church members
or not, the Massachusetts General Court complied formally
with this requirement, but practically left the matter much
as it was before. In 1664, when the English government sent
over commissioners to investigate, the Massachusetts people,
particularly, obstructed their proceedings as much as they
could. These incidents convinced the English officials
that the aims of Massachusetts were quite inconsistent
with its obligations to the home government. The friction
became more serious when Parliament passed a series of
acts regulating colonial trade, only to find that the elected
governors of New England could not be trusted to enforce
them. For a time, Massachusetts was able to prevent
effective intervention, but the authorities at home
were getting more and more exasperated. Before many
years the colony was forcibly reminded that it was still
a part of the English dominions and must adjust its theories
and practices to that fact.

King
Philip's
War.

While these clouds were gathering on the political horizon, the New Englanders had to pass through the most
serious of all their Indian troubles. "King Philip's War"
was a natural result of the steady pressure of colonial population upon the Indian country. There was constant friction and the Indians were often unjustly treated. In 1675
the rising discontent of the savages found a leader in "King
Philip," the son of a chief, Massasoit, who had long
kept the peace between his own people and their English
neighbors. The serious fighting lasted until the summer
of 1676, when King Philip was killed. The final victory of
the English was inevitable, but before it came the war had

taken a fearful toll in life and property. At one time or another nearly half the settled towns were attacked and seriously injured; several were totally destroyed. It was a tragic experience whose depressing influence was felt for many years. For the student of history, however, the war is important chiefly because it was the last serious challenge offered by the Indians to the white occupation of New England.

BIBLIOGRAPHICAL NOTES

Beard and Beard, I ch. II. Channing, *United States*, I, 356–437, 485–495; II, 65–79. Adams, *Founding of New England*, chs. VII–XIV. *General accounts.*

Macdonald, *Select Charters*, nos. 14, 16, 18, 19, 24, 27. Hart, *Contemporaries*, I, nos. 108, 112; chs. XVII–XXI. *Collected sources.*

Osgood, *17th Cent.*, I, pt. II, chs. IV, V. Miller, P., *Orthodoxy in Massachusetts, 1630–1650*. Adams, B., *Emancipation of Massachusetts*, chs. II–V. Adams, C. F., *Massachusetts, Its Historians and Its History*, 1–64, and his *Three Episodes of Massachusetts History*, I, 362–532; II, 533–578. (The Adamses are sharply critical of the Puritans.) Jones, R. M., *Quakers in the American Colonies*, I, chs. I–V. Morison, S. E., *Builders of the Bay Colony* ("Robert Child"). Rugg, W. K., *Unafraid: a Life of Anne Hutchinson.* *Massachusetts and the dissenters.*

Osgood, *17th Cent.*, I, chs. IV, VIII. Parrington, V. L., *Main Currents*, I, 62–75. Ernst, J. E., *Political Thought of Roger Williams*. Parkes, H. B., "John Cotton and Roger Williams Debate Toleration, 1644–1652," *N.E.Q.* (1931), IV, 735–756. Writings of Williams in Narragansett Club, *Publications*. Richman, I. B., *Rhode Island, Its Making and Meaning*, 2 vols. *Roger Williams and Rhode Island.*

Andrews, C. M., *River Towns of Connecticut* (*Johns Hopkins Studies*, VII). Walker, G. L., *Thomas Hooker*. *Connecticut.*

Osgood, *17th Cent.*, I, pt. II, ch. X. Articles in Macdonald, *Select Charters*, no. 19; also in Hart and Channing, *Amer. Hist. Leaflets*, no. 7. *New England Confederation.*

Lincoln, C. H., *Narratives of the Indian Wars*, 7–167. Osgood, *17th Cent.*, I, pt. II, ch. XIV. *King Philip's War.*

CHAPTER VII

EXPANSION AND CONQUEST

The English colonies in 1660.

THE first half century of English colonization closed with three groups of settlements securely established in the New World. Farthest south were the island plantations of the West Indies, — Barbados, the Leeward Islands, and, by conquest just at the end of this period, the Spanish colony of Jamaica. Next came the tobacco-planting colonies of Chesapeake Bay; and, finally, with another long interval, the self-governing Puritan commonwealths of New England. Leaving Jamaica out of account for a moment, all these colonies had certain common characteristics. All were the result of real colonization, the taking up of land not previously occupied by Europeans. In the island colonies and to a slight extent on Chesapeake Bay, negro slaves had been brought in; otherwise the population was almost exclusively English. In the two southern groups, except for a short time during the English Puritan Revolution, established institutions and prevailing ideals followed closely those of the mother country. In each of these little dependent states, there was a governor representing the monarchical principle but also an assembly claiming the privileges of the English House of Commons. Justices of the peace and vestrymen regulated the affairs of lesser people much as they did in England. These people were also, for the most part, content with the religious system to which they had been accustomed in the old home. Except in Maryland, they believed that God Almighty should be "devoutly and duly served", in the orthodox Anglican manner. With the New Englanders, it was somewhat different. They, too, were Englishmen and clung to many of the old English ways; they also had their representative assemblies, their justices and constables, and their established churches which everybody had to support. They were Englishmen, however, of a special kind with some ideas opposed to those which finally prevailed at home. Left much more to themselves than the southern colonies, they became practically republican, and they preferred to serve God in a different fashion from that approved by English law and custom.

The second half century of the colonial era has a different story to tell. There were still settlements on virgin soil, but much of the newly occupied territory was taken by conquest from European rivals. Englishmen continued to cross the ocean, but in nearly all the new provinces they were soon living side by side with men of other nationalities; into the south the African negroes came in ever increasing numbers. Foreign elements and political experimentation brought new variations from the English standard; the forces which were finally to create a new and different national type were already at work. *New phases of colonization.*

The background for all these new phases of colonial expansion is the period known in English history as the Restoration. Strictly speaking, it begins with the accession of Charles II, but some of its most characteristic tendencies may be seen in the days of Oliver Cromwell. The Restoration era has not had a particularly good name with American readers of English history. It means to them, for one thing, the breakdown of the great English experiment in republican government and the return of a Stuart king who went as far as he dared in the direction of absolute monarchy. It was also a period of intolerance in religious matters. Even moderate Puritan ministers were excluded from the national church, and dissenters, as well *The era of the Restoration.*

as Catholics, were persecuted in various ways. Even more familiar is the sharp reaction from Puritan morality, in which the court of Charles II undoubtedly set the worst possible example. Not the least discreditable feature of the King's policy was his willingness at times to sacrifice the national interest in order to secure political and financial support from the French King.

Constructive forces.

Notwithstanding these facts, the Restoration was not, on the whole, a period of decadence; it was rather one of unusual national vigor. Even the decline in religion and morals has been exaggerated. There were dissolute princes and courtiers; but the number of new churches built after the great London fire of 1666 indicates that religion was not dead even in the Church of England. Among the dissenters were such great leaders as John Bunyan, George Fox, and William Penn. Natural science made great gains, and the new Royal Society helped to stimulate interest in that branch of knowledge. There were great names also in philosophy and political theory — Thomas Hobbes, Algernon Sidney, and John Locke. One subject in which thinkers and business men were almost equally interested was economics, more particularly the problem of developing British trade and making it contribute more effectively to the national wealth.

Commerce and sea power.

Interest in commercial expansion was not a new thing; but it was greatly stimulated after the Civil War. One of the most important elements on the side of Parliament as against the King, was the merchant class, which, after the defeat of the royalists, had a good chance to secure friendly legislation. The merchants were fortunate also in getting the support of Cromwell; and his vigorous administration did much to restore British prestige abroad. He was keenly interested in the navy, in the merchant marine, and in the expansion of English trade throughout the world. In all these matters the Restoration made less difference than might have been expected. Many of the merchants and officials who furnished expert advice to Cromwell were equally ready to coöperate with the King, and they continued to exert a strong influence upon the commercial policy of the government. Much is commonly said about the humiliating reverses of the royal navy at the hands of the Dutch; but the Restoration period as a whole shows a great development of the navy, and the merchant marine was doubled between 1660 and 1688.

Closely connected with this enthusiasm for commercial expansion was a renewed interest in colonization as one of the best means of promoting trade. This revival also had its beginning under the Puritan Commonwealth, when England competed vigorously with other European states for trade and colonial empire. During the short five-year period of Cromwell's protectorate, expeditions were organized against the Dutch in New Netherland, the French in Acadia, and the Spaniards in the West Indies. The first was still hanging fire when the home government decided to make peace with the Dutch; the second was successful and Acadia became for a few years the British province of Nova Scotia; the attack on the Spanish colonies was not wholly successful, but Jamaica was conquered and this rich sugar-planting island became a permanent part of the British Empire. *Colonial expansion.*

After the Restoration, many factors contributed to keep alive the interest in colonial expansion. Charles II himself, though self-indulgent and unprincipled, was an able man and really anxious to promote the economic welfare of his country — partly no doubt because increasing wealth for the nation meant more money for the royal treasury. He was interested in colonies because of the profits they might bring to himself and his friends, as well as to the nation at large. So, ignoring his previous promise to the Spaniards, he decided to keep Jamaica and when shortly afterwards *Personal interest of the Stuart family.*

Charles II.

he married a Portuguese princess he secured as a part of her dowry the African post of Tangier and the city and island of Bombay, in India, one of the nuclei about which the British Indian Empire has since developed. Charles was also directly concerned in other overseas enterprises, including the African slave trade. Other members of the royal family had similar interests. The King's uncle, Prince Rupert, also invested in the slave trade and took a leading part in the formation of the Hudson's Bay Company, one of the most powerful and picturesque trading monopolies ever established in the New World. Of all the members of the royal family, the most significant for American colonial history was the King's brother James, Duke of York, afterwards King James II. As Lord High Admiral, he had a substantial part in the development of the navy, though he owed much to expert advisers like the famous diarist, Samuel Pepys. He is chiefly remembered as the founder of the English province of New York; but he also included among his numerous ventures the African slave trade, the Hudson Bay fur trade, and the East India Company.

James, Duke of York.

Several of the King's ministers were also seriously concerned with American affairs: the Puritan general, Monk, who as a reward for bringing the army over to the King's side was made Duke of Albemarle and Master of the King's Horse; Lord Ashley, later Earl of Shaftesbury, who began his career as a Puritan politician; and Edward Hyde, Earl of Clarendon, the King's chief adviser during his exile and in the early years of his reign. All three of these men became proprietors of the new province of Carolina. Both Clarendon and Ashley were strongly convinced of the importance of colonies as sources of national wealth and did what they could to impress these views upon the King. About these larger figures gathered many lesser personages — soldiers, courtiers, and adventurers — who saw in the New World

Politicians, courtiers, and merchants.

an opportunity to mend broken fortunes or build new ones. Finally, in close touch with some of the politicians and courtiers, were the merchants who were engaged in the American trade and had ideas about the best means of making the plantations useful to the mother country.

The kind of colonization desired by these politicians and "big business men" was something quite different from the self-sufficient commonwealths of New England. They wanted rather plantations for the production of articles which would otherwise have to be bought from England's rivals. Since they regarded colonies primarily as a means of developing trade, they were generally not much interested in sending out large numbers of emigrants from England. Economists no longer talked about disposing of surplus population; on the contrary they encouraged the immigration of Protestant refugees from the Continent as a means of increasing the national wealth. Under these circumstances, the African slave trade was naturally favored since it furnished labor to the plantations without drawing man power from home industries. Accordingly organizations were formed for this purpose, of which the most important was the Royal African Company of 1672. Encouraged by the home government and by the increasing demand for labor in the plantations, there was soon a great increase in the importation of negroes into the southern and insular colonies. *Colonial policies of the Restoration.* *The slave trade.*

Though the government was not anxious to encourage large-scale emigration, it did nevertheless give many people good reasons for leaving home. The continued harsh treatment of dissenters sent thousands of Quakers and other religious radicals to the older American settlements and to the new Quaker colonies of West Jersey and Pennsylvania. The Quaker colonists included a considerable number from Ireland and Wales, as well as from England; the government itself encouraged the sending of servants from Scotland and Ireland. Besides these emigrants and the Protestant refugees *The new colonists.*

from Europe, some desirable material for the new settlements was drawn from the older colonies of New England, Virginia, and Barbados.

The new proprietary provinces.

The two main results of the new expansionist policy were the founding of Carolina, which pushed the English frontier farther to the southward, and the conquest of the Hudson and Delaware valleys, which filled in the great gap between the Chesapeake colonies and New England. In this forward movement, the government still depended mainly on private initiative. The new colonies of the Restoration period all began as proprietary provinces not under the direct control of the Crown.

Carolina.

The territory of Carolina had long been claimed by the English and much of it had been included in earlier charters. The first Virginia charter had implied an English claim to the whole South Atlantic coast as far as the thirty-fourth parallel; and the second Virginia charter put the southern boundary two hundred miles south of Old Point Comfort, far enough to include a large part of what is now North Carolina. In 1629, after this charter was revoked, Charles I went still farther in his disregard of Spanish claims by giving to his attorney-general, Sir Robert Heath, the territory between the thirty-sixth and thirty-first parallels, thus cutting off a slice of southern Virginia, and at the other end claiming the coast line as far south as the present boundary of Florida. Efforts to settle this region having proved unsuccessful, Heath's charter was forfeited, and

The charters of 1663 and 1665.

in 1663 this region was given to a group of eight proprietors. Three of these grantees were the great ministers of state already mentioned, Clarendon, Ashley, and Albemarle. Then came three Cavaliers, Lord Craven, Sir George Carteret, and Lord Berkeley, loyal followers of the King in the dark days of his exile, who now claimed their reward. Lastly, there were two men of long experience in colonial affairs, Governor Berkeley of Virginia and Sir John Colleton, a prominent planter of Barbados, whose influence with Ashley probably had much to do with the starting of this enterprise. The territory given in the first charter was the same as that granted to Heath; but a few "squatters" from Virginia had already settled near the northern boundary and in 1665 that line was pushed up to 36° 30'. With extraordinary audacity the southern boundary was now fixed at 29°, that is, south of the old Spanish settlement of St. Augustine, a claim which neither the government nor the proprietors were able to make good.

The authority of the proprietors in their new province was similar to that of Lord Baltimore in Maryland. Like him, they were authorized to establish a palatinate, or feudal principality, almost entirely free from royal control. Both charters provided for large estates under the manorial system and for titles of nobility. Lord Baltimore had not used this latter privilege, but the Carolina proprietors presently established two orders of nobility, taking the title "Landgrave" from the Germans and that of "Cacique" from the Indians. The right of the people to share in the making of laws was also recognized in both charters. In the matter of religion, however, there was an important difference. Though Lord Baltimore had adopted a policy of toleration, he had no warrant for it in his charter. The Carolina proprietors, on the contrary, were definitely authorized to tolerate dissenters if they saw fit. This is remarkable because some of these proprietors were members of a government which was making life miserable for English dissenters. In this case, as in the Rhode Island charter issued about the same time, it was explained that the colony was so far away that religious concessions there would not interfere with uniformity at home. The motive is evident; the proprietors wished to attract settlers who could not be secured under an exclusive ecclesiastical system. The Anglican Church was, however, recognized as the official

Governmental provisions.

church; complete religious liberty was not expected, but only toleration.

**A planta-
tion colony.**

What the Carolina promoters wished to do was to establish a plantation colony, somewhat like those of the West Indies. They hoped it would produce tropical or semitropical articles, like silk, wine, and olive oil, which ordinarily came to England from the Mediterranean countries or the Far East. Sugar and tobacco were provided for in other colonies and need not be encouraged in Carolina. The outcome, however, was quite different from that expected.

**Northern
settlements.**

The first settlers were Virginia frontiersmen who had begun moving south even before the proprietors set up their government. These pioneers of North Carolina led a lonely existence about the shores of Albemarle Sound, where they were cut off from their Virginia neighbors by great stretches of swamp land and where the shifting sands of the coast made access by sea difficult except to small vessels. Left largely to themselves at first, they raised the tobacco to which they had become accustomed in Virginia, with corn and live stock sufficient to meet their own requirements. Before long, however, they were sending some provisions to the West Indies. Such commerce as they had with the outside world was largely in small ships from New England, which exchanged manufactured goods of various kinds for tobacco and provisions.

**Frontier
conditions in
northern
Carolina.**

So there grew up in northern Carolina a community of self-reliant frontiersmen whom the proprietors could not easily control. From time to time governors were sent out who, with the representatives of the colonists, passed a few laws; but in general the proprietors paid little attention to this northern settlement, which from their point of view was an unprofitable affair. Attempts to restrain the settlers made trouble. In 1677, for instance, when customs officials tried to enforce English trade regulations, hitherto almost

wholly ignored by the colonists and the New England traders, the inhabitants rose in revolt and imprisoned the unpopular officials. For about a year the rebels had complete control
of the government. A few years later, a proprietary governor was arrested by the colonists and banished. For many
years, North Carolina had a bad reputation not only with
the home authorities but among its neighbors. It was
supposed to be a favorite resort for undesirable characters
from Virginia and for the pirates who infested the whole
Atlantic seaboard. The inhabitants were also said to have
little regard for religion. Though the Church of England
was officially recognized in the charter, no regular services
were maintained here for many years; almost the only
religious teaching then available was furnished by Quaker
preachers. Probably some contemporary criticism of these
settlers by unsympathetic neighbors should be discounted;
they doubtless had the characteristic virtues and vices of
frontier people as shown in various stages of the American
westward movement.

While the Albemarle settlements were gradually de- Plans for
veloping into the colony of North Carolina, the proprietors southern
were much more interested in the southern part of their
province. In the development of plans for this region some
of the Barbadian planters took an active interest. The
growth of the large slaveholding plantations was making
their island less attractive to small planters and white servants, who might, therefore, be persuaded to try the new
colony. Some of these Barbadians were promised land in
Carolina on favorable terms. The government was also to
be liberal, with elected assemblies and religious toleration.
The outcome of this movement was a colony on the Cape
Fear River, in what is now North Carolina; it seemed fairly
prosperous for a time but later met with reverses and had to
be abandoned. Six years after the first charter was issued, the
proprietors had little to show for all their troubles, except

the unmanageable tobacco growers and cattlemen on Albemarle Sound.

Lord Ashley.

The proprietors were not discouraged, however, and for a time they had an able leader in the person of Ashley, now Earl of Shaftesbury. He was an active politician and, being more liberal in his views than Clarendon, is generally regarded as one of the founders of the Whig party. He managed also to find time for American affairs and the serious study of colonial problems, though some of his ideas did not stand the test of practical experience. Perhaps the most serious blunder made by the proprietors during this period was their attempt to substitute for the comparatively simple governments at first proposed an intricate scheme called the

The Fundamental Constitutions.

Fundamental Constitutions. This document carried to an absurd extreme the feudal system anticipated by the charter, with a landed aristocracy occupying a place in the government similar to that of the English House of Lords. Even in the representative house, every member had to have at least five hundred acres of land. The Fundamental Constitutions caused general dissatisfaction from the beginning. They were repeatedly amended by the proprietors during the next thirty years, and in the end gave way to a comparatively simple system not unlike the other royal and proprietary governments.

Beginnings of South Carolina.

More important than this eccentric constitution making was the planting of a permanent colony in what is now South Carolina. For several years the proprietors had been advertising the attractions of their province for different types of settlers. Younger sons of the English gentry were offered a chance to build up large estates, thus becoming the founders of a new American aristocracy. For poorer people the life of a servant in the colony was optimistically described. The proprietors also counted largely on their ability to draw people from the older colonies. The colonists further north were promised a pleasanter climate and the people of the sugar islands better opportunities for acquiring land. At last in 1669 a small fleet was sent out from England with instructions to stop at Barbados for additional colonists. In 1670, this company was landed on the south side of the Ashley River, just above the point where it joins the Cooper River to form Charleston harbor.

Within two years this new settlement in and about "Charles Town" numbered about 400 people and within the next ten years the population increased to about 1200. From the beginning, South Carolina had a less homogeneous population than the older colonies. Of the Englishmen, some were Anglicans, but others were dissenters attracted by the promise of toleration. Ireland and New England both furnished settlers, and emigrants from the West Indies, especially from Barbados, formed an influential group. Among the most interesting of the early colonists were the French Protestants, or Huguenots, whose descendants have always played a conspicuous part in the social and political life of South Carolina. Here, as in Virginia, the early planters generally had white servants; but negro slaves were soon imported on a large scale and in a few years outnumbered the whites. This comparatively early establishment of the plantation system, on the basis of slave labor, was doubtless due in part to the example of Barbados. *Early population.* *Racial and religious elements.*

The economic development of South Carolina was disappointing to the proprietors. For the first few years the colonists naturally had to devote most of their energies to the problem of food supply, planting corn and wheat and raising cattle and hogs. Of these products, they soon had enough to export considerable quantities to the West Indies, with which they kept up a close connection throughout the colonial era — much closer in fact than with the colonies to the northward. Some pitch, tar, lumber, and furs were exported also; but it was some years before the South Carolinians developed an important staple for the European *Economic development.*

trade. Unlike their neighbors in North Carolina, they had
an excellent harbor. Ten years after the colony was founded,
the Charles Town settlement — later called Charleston —
was transferred to its present beautiful site between the
Ashley and Cooper rivers, where for about a century it
was the one important seaport in all the southern colonies.
Though plantations spread along the coast, northward and
southward, and up the rivers into the interior, many of the
well-to-do planters spent much of their time in Charleston,
which consequently became the economic, social, and political center of the colony, to an extent not equaled in any
other English province on the continent.

The institutional life of South Carolina developed in an
orderly way. Provision was soon made for the services of
the Anglican Church, to which most of the influential emigrants from England and Barbados belonged. Though the
Church of England had a preferred position, there was toleration for other churches, and there were soon houses of
worship for Congregationalists, Huguenots, and Scotch
Presbyterians.

The proprietors set out with the idea of a central government for the whole of Carolina; but the theory could not
be made to work, since the northern and southern settlements were too far apart. During the early years, there was
generally a governor commissioned for the whole province,
who lived at Charleston, while the actual government of
the northern settlements, so far as there was any, was usually
left to a deputy governor. In each of these divisions, forms
of government developed similar to those in Maryland,
though some peculiar features of the Fundamental Constitutions persisted for several years. In each colony, the governor
or deputy governor and the council represented the proprietors, while the lower house, or "Common House of
Assembly," as it was called in South Carolina, represented
the inhabitants. In South Carolina the tone of social and

Importance of Charleston.

Religion.

The government of Carolina

political life was distinctly aristocratic. In North Carolina
the spirit was more democratic.

The early history of South Carolina was much influenced
by its position as the southern outpost of the English empire
on the American continent. From the Spanish point of view
the English colonists were simply trespassers. Though the
Spaniards did not then occupy any territory within the
present limits of South Carolina, they kept a jealous eye on
the colony and occasionally made trouble, as in 1686, when
they destroyed an isolated Scotch settlement at Port Royal.
The province was now too thoroughly established to be
broken up by such attacks on outlying points; but for several
decades it was kept in dread of similar expeditions and of
Spanish intrigues among the Indians. It was evident, too,
that in case of a sudden attack South Carolina would have
to take care of itself with little help from others.

The Anglo-
Spanish
frontier.

More important than the extension of the English frontier
to the southward was the conquest of the Hudson and Delaware valleys from the Dutch. Here was a block of territory
under alien control which divided the English continental
colonies into two isolated sections. Within this stretch of
coast line were two great waterways into the interior, on
which have since developed the two richest and most populous cities of the Atlantic seaboard. The full value of the
region was not, of course, recognized at the time; the Dutch
had so far made only the slightest use of the Hudson valley
and still less of the Delaware country. Yet the strategic
importance of the section and its possibilities for the fur
trade were appreciated by the English, who denied that the
Dutch had any just claim.

The Hudson
and Dela-
ware valleys.

The starting point of the English argument was the Cabot
voyages, on the basis of which the middle region was included
in the Virginia charter of 1606 and the New England patent
of 1620. Between the last two dates, however, the Dutch
established a counter claim, through the exploration of the

The Dutch
claim. Henry
Hudson.

Hudson by the famous seaman from whom it takes its name. Henry Hudson was an Englishman and spent most of his active life under the English flag; but at this moment in his career he was a captain in the employ of the Dutch East India Company, which had engaged him to find a passage from Europe to China through the northern seas, in order to circumvent the Portuguese, who were still trying to monopolize the southern route around the Cape of Good Hope. One such attempt having failed, Hudson tried to find a passage through North America at about the fortieth parallel. So it came about that in 1609 he entered New York Bay and followed the great river as far as the present city of Albany. Then he sailed back to Europe and presently left the service of the Dutch company. His last voyage to Hudson Bay, on which he lost his life, was in command of an English ship. Meantime, however, the reports of this voyage proved convenient in subsequent controversies with the English and served to stimulate interest in the valley, particularly in its possibilities for the fur trade. During the next ten years, there was no real colonization; but the river and the adjoining coast were frequented by Dutch traders who made their headquarters on Manhattan Island.

Beginnings of colonization. The Dutch West India Company. The first serious move toward colonization was made in 1621, when the great mercantile interests of the Netherlands secured from their federal congress, the States-General, the charter of a new corporation known as the Dutch West India Company. The promoters of this organization hoped to make it a powerful agency for promoting national interests throughout the western seas, just as the Dutch East India Company was gradually breaking down the Portuguese monopoly in the Indian Ocean and the Far East. The scope of the new company included not only the Western Hemisphere but also the West African coast, with all its possibilities for the slave trade. In this ambitious program, the colonization of the Hudson valley was only one item, perhaps less important than the conflict with the Portuguese in Brazil. Nevertheless, it was this company which founded New Netherland, sending out its first settlers in 1624. It is characteristic of the whole subsequent history of this region, that these pioneer settlers of New Amsterdam on Manhattan Island were not all of one nationality. Less than half were Dutchmen, the majority being French-speaking Walloons from the provinces then held by Spain but now a part of Belgium.

By 1629, it became evident that the colony was not making much progress and that fresh efforts were necessary if it was to live and prosper. Accordingly, in 1629 the company adopted the so-called Charter of Freedoms and Exemptions, an elaborate plan for stimulating emigration and enlisting the capital of the wealthy Dutch merchants. Every investor who transported fifty adult colonists to New Netherland within four years was to become a patroon, or manorial lord, receiving a great landed estate on one of the two great rivers of the colony. On this estate, he would not only receive rents from his tenants but also exercise civil and criminal jurisdiction, though the tenant could appeal to the provincial government at New Amsterdam. Some provision was also made for smaller landowners who could not afford to make such large investments. Meanwhile the company reserved the control of Manhattan Island and a partial monopoly of the fur trade. *Charter of Freedoms and Exemptions.*

The new plan did not work well, partly because of unfair dealing by some of the directors, who used their inside information to secure much of the best land. The best known of the patroonships actually established was that founded in the neighborhood of Fort Orange (Albany) by Killian Van Rensselaer, an Amsterdam jeweler. The company's attempt to monopolize the fur trade also checked the progress of the settlement. So the company was soon obliged to make *Slow progress.*

concessions; some of the trade restrictions were removed and small freeholders settling in villages were promised a limited amount of self-government. These measures attracted some colonists; but as compared with New England, the growth of New Netherland was insignificant. In 1650, the Dutch had hardly 3000 people in all their settlements as against about ten times that number in the Puritan colonies alone.

Distribution of population.

This meager population was scattered over a vast area, extending from Fort Orange on the upper Hudson, and the "House of Hope" on the Connecticut to a few straggling posts on the Delaware. The greater part of the colonists lived on Manhattan and a few villages in the immediate neighborhood, on Long Island, Staten Island, and the west side of the Hudson. New Netherland was never a purely Dutch colony in the sense that Virginia and New England were English. Besides the French-speaking Walloons already mentioned, there were many English, chiefly on Long Island but some on Manhattan itself. The Jews, who have ever since played an important part in the life of the city, came to New Netherland in sufficient numbers to trouble the Dutch Reformed clergy.

Racial elements.

The fur trade.

The chief business of New Netherland was the fur trade, which the company tried to maintain exclusively for itself. The principal base for this trade was Fort Orange (Albany), from which expeditions were made into the Iroquois country along the Mohawk valley. There was some exchange of goods with the English colonies and the West Indies; but various causes, including the restrictions imposed by the company and its agents, prevented New Netherland from making any adequate use of its magnificent situation. Though agriculture was neglected, there were a few farmers at work, enough to produce a small surplus for export.

Political development was extremely backward as compared with that of Virginia or New England. The ultimate source of all authority was the States-General, or federal congress of the Netherlands; but for most purposes the actual control of the colony was vested in the West India Company, whose powers were similar to those of the London Company in Virginia. The company transacted its business mainly through a board of directors in Holland and a director and council in New Netherland. The managers at home were too far away to keep a close check on affairs in America, and the resident councilors were usually under the thumb of the director. The actual government of New Netherland was therefore thoroughly autocratic during most of its history. The secretary of the province wrote in 1650: "The burghers upon the island of Manhattan and thereabouts must know that nobody comes or is admitted to New Netherland (being a conquest) except upon this condition, that he shall have nothing to say, and shall acknowledge himself under the sovereignty of Their High Mightinesses the States General and the Lord Managers, as his lords and patrons, and shall be obedient to the Director and Council for the time being as good subjects are bound to be." During the last seventeen years of the Dutch rule the director, or governor, was Peter Stuyvesant, who came to this post from the West Indian island of Curaçao. Stuyvesant was an aggressive, self-confident person, determined to magnify his office and resentful of any attempts to appeal from his decisions. His efforts to regulate the religion and morals of his people suggest a somewhat Puritan point of view; but he was charged with being corrupt as well as despotic.

Before Stuyvesant's arrival, discontent with his predecessors had led the colonists to try some experiments with a kind of advisory council and at different times temporary groups, called the "Twelve Men" and the "Eight Men," were chosen by the inhabitants. There was, however, no regular representative assembly as in the English colonies. Early in Stuyvesant's administration he proposed a tax

Government of New Netherland

Peter Stuyvesant.

No adequate system of representation.

for purposes of defense; but to meet objections, he permitted the colonists to nominate eighteen persons, of whom nine were chosen by him as a sort of advisory board. Though this was a more permanent institution than the "Twelve Men" and the "Eight Men," it was not truly representative, since after the first election vacancies were filled by the board itself and the governor. Besides, the "Nine Men" had no real legislative authority. As the English population of the province increased, especially on Long Island, discontent with this autocratic system became more serious and in 1653 a convention from the various towns and villages insisted on the right of the people to share in the making of laws. The proposal was rejected by Stuyvesant; but, at the very end of the Dutch rule, he was forced to call another assembly, which for the first time really represented all parts of the colony. This gathering, however, ended in a deadlock so that New Netherland came to an end without having evolved a permanent system of representation.

Local governments. In the matter of local government, the Dutch had a better record. Though there was no such general development of town life as in New England, the little Dutch villages enjoyed a limited amount of local self-government; they had the right to nominate candidates for local offices, the final selection being made by the director and council. The English villages on Long Island, accustomed as they were to the New England system of town government, had to be given more freedom. New Amsterdam, as the capital of the province, had for a time no distinct municipal government, and even after such a government was established Stuyvesant kept the choice of municipal officers largely in his own hands.

Religious elements. The Dutch colonists, like the English, were accustomed to a religious establishment. The Dutch Reformed Church, whose ideas of doctrine and government were like those of

the Scottish and English Presbyterians, was established by
law in the mother country and officially recognized in New
Netherland. Every patroon was asked to support a minister, and several of the Dutch Reformed clergy came
out under the supervision of the *Classis*, or presbytery, of
Amsterdam. Notwithstanding the existence of a state
church, the Dutch government was unusually liberal in religious matters and for the most part a similar attitude was
taken in New Netherland, where religious sects were even
more numerous than the racial elements in the population.
Conspicuous among them were the Lutherans and the
Congregationalists, the latter being especially strong
among the New England settlers of Long Island. During
Stuyvesant's administration, however, there was some
persecution and ordinances were passed prohibiting public
services other than those of the established church. The
Quakers came in for specially harsh treatment, but
others also suffered. A Baptist preacher was expelled
from the colony and even the Lutherans complained of
unfair treatment. Stuyvesant's measures were, however,
finally disapproved by the company, which was particularly
anxious not to hamper the economic development of the
colony by discouraging settlers.

> Church and state.

The Dutch had an enviable reputation in the matter of
public education, and the obligation to provide such education
was also recognized in New Netherland. Along with the minister, each patroon was expected to support a schoolmaster.
The practice did not, however, quite conform to the theory;
and one of the chief complaints made by the colonists was
that the schools were neglected. In 1657, nearly thirty
years after the Charter of Freedoms and Exemptions, it was
reported to the church authorities in Holland that only
three places in the colony maintained schools. There was
some progress afterwards and the company itself sent over
a man to take charge of the Latin School in New Amster-

> Public education.

dam. Some of the schoolmasters evidently had to work hard for their meager salaries; the magistrates of Breuckelen (Brooklyn), for instance, wanted help in paying the salary of a general-utility man, to "conduct the service of the church, and to sing on Sunday; to take charge of the school, to dig graves, etc., ring the bell, and perform whatever else may be required."

Indian relations. Throughout its history New Netherland was surrounded by unfriendly neighbors. Though the Dutch adopted the policy of buying land from the Indians, there was a good deal of trouble with the tribes settled about Manhattan and up the river. The most serious Indian warfare was between 1640 and 1646, when settlers were killed and property destroyed even on Manhattan Island. Even as late as 1655, New Amsterdam was attacked by the Indians. Selling firearms to the Indians was a dangerous business, but it was not effectually regulated because the profits were too **The Iroquois.** tempting. In their relations with the Iroquois confederacy, or Five Nations, who occupied the region on both sides of the Mohawk Valley, the Dutch were more fortunate. This friendly understanding and the trade which developed with it were valued by the Iroquois as a support against the French in the North and also against their Indian rivals in the fur trade. Notwithstanding their alliance with the Iroquois, the Dutch managed to keep on fairly good terms with the French.

International rivalry. New Sweden. On the Delaware River, the Dutch had to meet both Swedish and English competition. New Sweden grew out of an elaborate plan for colonization which looked to the coöperation of the Swedes with the Protestants of Germany; one of its chief promoters was Willem Usselinx, the founder of the Dutch West India Company. The actual result of all this planning was disappointing; but in 1638 a Swedish fort was established on the present site of Wilmington, Delaware, and during the next seventeen years a few hundred settlers — Swedes, Finns, and Dutchmen — came out to farm and trade under Swedish protection. When the first Swedish colonists arrived, the Dutch had no substantial settlements on the river, though they still claimed jurisdiction over this region. During the Thirty Years War, the common interest of these two Protestant nations helped to prevent a break between the rival colonies; but the Dutch always regarded the Swedes as interlopers and were annoyed by their competition in the fur trade. When the peace of Westphalia brought the long war to an end, the two colonies naturally clashed. The Swedes won a short-lived advantage by taking the Dutch post of Fort Casimir on the lower Delaware; but in 1655 the Dutch retaliated, the Swedes were overpowered, and New Sweden was absorbed in New Netherland.

Conquest of New Sweden.

It was much easier for Stuyvesant to deal with the Swedes than with the English. The latter were aggressive, their numbers were increasing, and they had behind them a government which, if not always successful in European politics, was a keen competitor in everything connected with overseas commerce. While Stuyvesant was denouncing the Swedes as trespassers, the English were equally sure that the Dutch had no business on the Hudson. Especially dangerous was the westward advance of the New Englanders; from Connecticut and New Haven they were steadily moving along the northern shore of Long Island Sound toward the Hudson, and establishing settlements on Long Island itself. Yet, as in the Dutch-Swedish rivalry on the Delaware, the common interests of two Protestant powers restrained the rival colonists for a time and the Dutch did a good deal of trading with the Virginians and New Englanders. In 1650 Stuyvesant negotiated a boundary agreement with his New England neighbors which, though never ratified by the English government, was actually observed for a time. It was agreed that Long Island should be divided,

Anglo-Dutch rivalry.

the English keeping the eastern part while the western settlements, English as well as Dutch, were included in New Netherland.

In 1652 the old commercial jealousy between England and Holland broke out in actual warfare and New Netherland found itself in a dangerous position. The Connecticut and New Haven people were eager for an attack on the Dutch and in 1654 Cromwell sent out a fleet for that purpose under the command of New England officers. Massachusetts, however, was not so zealous. Before the expedition was ready, the European war came to an end and New Netherland was saved for the time being. Nevertheless, the commercial rivalry between the two nations could not be so easily settled. On the African coast Dutch slave traders were trying to drive out their English competitors and in the Far East old jealousies continued. More important still, Parliament was making a determined effort to dislodge the Dutch from their dominant position in the European carrying trade and also to break up their commerce with the English colonies by limiting such trade to English ships. One great obstacle to success in this policy, and a most convenient base for illegal trade, was the Dutch colony on the Hudson.

Thus English opinion on both sides of the water was gradually prepared for aggressive action. In 1664, while England and Holland were still nominally at peace, Charles II gave to his brother James, Duke of York, a patent making him proprietor of a new English province extending from the Connecticut to the Delaware, thus corresponding roughly with New Netherland. In the same year, while this territory was still in the possession of the Dutch, James appointed a governor, Richard Nicolls, to represent him in the management of his new province. In August, 1664, Stuyvesant was confronted by an English fleet and a military force too strong for him to resist, especially in view of the discontent among his own people. Accordingly he accepted the terms offered by Nicolls, and New Netherland became New York. Three years later the conquest was confirmed by the treaty of Breda (1667), and though, as the result of a new Anglo-Dutch War, the Dutch held the territory again for a few months in 1673–74, they soon had to give it up. Henceforth English control of the Atlantic seaboard extended without a break, so far as foreign rivals were concerned, from Maine to South Carolina. In the great series of events which have established the supremacy of English-speaking people in North America, this conquest of New Netherland and the Delaware valley ranks in importance with the conquest of Canada in 1760 and the Louisiana Purchase of 1803.

BIBLIOGRAPHICAL NOTES

Channing, *United States*, I, chs. XVI, XVII; II, 1–37. Andrews, C. M., *Colonial Self-Government*, chs. V, IX–X.
General works.

Beer, G. L., *Origins of the British Colonial System*, 1578–1660, 78–175, and his *Old Colonial System* (economic factors emphasized). Abbott, W. C., *Expansion of Europe*, II, chs. XXIII–XXVI. *Cambridge Modern History*, IV, ch. XXV; V, chs. V, VIII, IX. Shepherd, W. R., "The Expansion of Europe," *Political Science Qly.*, XXXIV (1919), nos. 1–3. Seeley, J. R., *Expansion of England*, especially Lecture VI. *Cambridge History of the British Empire*, ch. VII. Blok, P. J., *History of the People of the Netherlands*, III, ch. III; IV, 34–41, 186–219, 302–310, 317–338. Dodd, W. E., "The Emergence of the First Social Order in the U. S.," *A.H.R.* (1935), XL, 217–231.
Background of European imperialism.

Traill, H. D., *Social England*, IV, ch. XV. Trotter, E., *17th Century Life in the Country Parish*. James, M., *Social Problems and Policy during the Puritan Revolution*. Bernstein, E., *Cromwell and Communism*. Lipson, E., *The Economic History of England*, II, III. Nef, J. U., *Rise of the English Coal Industry*. Clark, G. N., *The Seventeenth Century*.
Contemporary English life.

Osgood, *17th Cent.*, II, chs. IX, X. Ashe, S. A., *North Carolina*, I, chs. VI–XII. Saunders, W. L., *Colonial Records of North Caro-*
Carolina beginnings.

lina, I, "Prefatory Notes," pp. ix–xxv. McCrady, E., *South Carolina*, 1670–1719, chs. I–XV. Ravenel, *Charleston, the Place and the People*, chs. I–III.

Sources.   Salley, A. S., *Narratives of Early Carolina*. Hart, *Contemporaries*, I, nos. 78–81; II, 34. Charters and Fundamental Constitutions in Macdonald, *Select Charters*, nos. 26, 32, 33.

New Sweden.   Ward, C., *Dutch and Swedes on the Delaware*. Jameson, J. F., "Willem Usselinx," Amer. Hist. Assoc., *Papers*, II, no. 3.

New Netherland and its conquest.   Flick, A. C., editor, *History of the State of New York*, I, chs. VI–VIII. Janvier, *Dutch Founding of New York*. Innes, J. H., *New Amsterdam*. Tuckerman, B., *Peter Stuyvesant*. Van Rensselaer, Mrs. S., *History of the City of New York*, especially ch. XIV. For institutional beginnings, see Osgood, *17th Cent.*, II, chs. V, VII; Van Laer, A. J. F., "The Patroon System under the Colony of Rensselaerswyck," N. Y. Hist. Assoc., *Proceedings*, VIII, 222–243.

Sources.   Macdonald, *Select Charters*, no. 9. Hart, *Contemporaries*, I, 150–155, 169–171. Jameson, J. F., *Narratives of New Netherland*. Fernow, B., *Records of New Amsterdam*. See also source materials in Stokes, I.N.P., *Iconography of Manhattan Island*, 6 vols., N. Y., 1915, 1928. Shepherd, W. R., *Story of New Amsterdam*.

CHAPTER VIII

ENGLISH COLONIZATION OF THE HUDSON AND DELAWARE VALLEYS, 1664 TO 1688

THE conquest of New Netherland and the outlying posts on the Delaware was comparatively easy, but the new problem of governing the country and developing its resources was far more difficult. The territory which the Duke of York secured by the royal patent was not only extensive but awkwardly distributed. Its central division was the long, narrow strip lying between the Connecticut and Delaware rivers, extending northward to the French colonies in the St. Lawrence valley. A second division included certain islands along the coast of southern New England — Long Island, Nantucket, Marthas Vineyard, and a few others. A third entirely detached section included the northeastern part of Maine, between the St. Croix and Kennebec rivers. Besides all this territory definitely granted by the patent, the Duke also claimed the Dutch and Swedish settlements on the western side of the Delaware on the ground that they were dependencies of New Netherland.

Almost every part of this area bristled with controversial questions, some of which were debated for more than a century, with the result that the territory of New York at the close of the colonial era was quite different from that described in the charter. So far as Maine, Nantucket, and Marthas Vineyard were concerned, the Duke's paper claim was soon disposed of and they became a part of Massachusetts. Before long, by the action of the Duke himself and that of the King, the southern territory on both sides of the Delaware was taken to form the new provinces of New Jersey

New York in 1664.

Territorial problems.

and Pennsylvania. After much wrangling, Long Island was brought under the control of New York; but even in the central division, something had to be given up. The Duke could not hold the territory so far east as the Connecticut without bringing on a serious conflict with the colony of that name, the most important part of which lay west of that river. Connecticut could also claim a royal charter issued only two years before the New York patent. Farther up the river was the conflicting claim of Massachusetts. Within a few years the controversy with Connecticut was substantially settled by a compromise which drew the line where it now is, a few miles east of the Hudson. The province of New York was thus reduced to two long and narrow strips, pivoting, so to speak, on Manhattan Island; one of these, Long Island, paralleled the New England coast in a north-easterly direction and the other extended northward on both banks of the Hudson, toward the French frontier. Fortunately for the future state of New York, the early English governors were able to bring the Iroquois country into an English "sphere of influence," thus opening a gateway for westward expansion.

Heterogeneous population. Problem of assimilation. The inhabitants of the conquered province, with their different racial origins, special interests, and religious traditions, required careful handling. For many years, the Dutch continued to form the principal element in the population. Most of them lived within a comparatively small circle, centering at New Amsterdam and including a group of villages at the western end of Long Island. Up the river at Fort Orange were a few settlers whose strategic position with reference to the Iroquois trade gave them an importance out of proportion to their numbers. Though the Dutch had enjoyed comparatively little self-government before the English conquest, they had certain local customs which they desired to preserve, some of which were guaranteed to them by Nicolls when he received the surrender of the province. Not less difficult to manage were the English villages on Long Island, which were deeply imbued with New England ideas about self-government and quite unwilling to accept quietly the rôle of subjects in a conquered province.

The government established over these people differed in important respects from the proprietary systems of Maryland and Carolina. It was not thought necessary, in a conquered country, to secure the consent of the people either in making laws or in levying taxes. ·Consequently there was no provision at first for a representative assembly, and the proprietor had almost absolute authority. The one important safeguard was the right of the colonists to appeal from the provincial courts to the Privy Council in England. In addition, the Dutch inhabitants of New Netherland had been promised certain privileges in relation to property, religious liberty, and local self-government. The Duke of York never visited his colony and his autocratic powers were therefore delegated, for the most part, to his governor, assisted by a council also appointed by the proprietor. *Autocratic government.*

James was fortunate in the man whom he chose for this important trust. Richard Nicolls, the first English governor of New York, was one of those loyal Cavaliers who fought for Charles I, and then went into exile with the King's son. Nicolls was a soldier but he understood better than most soldiers how to deal with civilians. Under the provisions of the patent and of his instructions, he had despotic powers; but his despotism was generally benevolent, and skillful diplomacy made it tolerable for the various kinds of people whom he governed. First of all, he set out to Anglicize the province. English place names were substituted for Dutch in many cases. So New Netherland and New Amsterdam became New York, and Fort Orange became Albany. The English county organization was introduced, with sheriffs *Governor Richard Nicolls.*

Establishment of English institutions.

and justices of the peace, who held court within their respective districts and also met once a year with the governor and council in a "court of assizes." Through this court, Nicolls put into effect a code known as the Duke's Laws, based partly on English law and partly on the practice of the New England colonies. After a short interval most of the old Dutch officers gave way to English constables and overseers, though the frontiersmen at Albany were allowed to go on for a time in the old ways. For the English settlers on Long Island, these new arrangements meant less political liberty than they had previously enjoyed, and there was considerable discontent among them, though Nicolls managed to avoid a serious break.

The Duke's Laws.

In 1674, after the temporary loss of the province to the Dutch, the proprietor sent out as governor a man who occupied a conspicuous place in American history for the next quarter century. This was Edmund Andros, another army officer, with influential family connections at the English court. Though less skillful than Nicolls in the art of managing men, Andros was an energetic official, honestly trying to carry out the policies assigned to him and loyal to his "King and country." During his administration, popular feeling against the unrepresentative character of the government increased, especially among the English settlers, and in 1681 some of the merchants refused to pay certain duties on the ground that they had never been legally authorized. Even the justices of the peace, themselves nominees of the governor, urged the establishment of a representative assembly.

Governor Andros.

The Duke was reluctant to call an assembly; but the difficulty of getting revenue without it finally convinced him that it was necessary. In 1683 he sent out a new governor with instructions providing that hereafter the laws of the province should be made by a legislature consisting, as in Virginia, of the governor, the council, and

Representation given and withdrawn.

representatives of the freeholders, subject to veto by the proprietor himself. The New Yorkers were much elated and the new assembly showed a decided tendency to magnify its office. Among other things, they adopted the so-called Charter of Liberties and Privileges which set forth emphatically the rights of the "people" and their representatives. Offensive as such language was to a Stuart prince, James was apparently ready to accept the charter; just at this time, however, Charles II died, James, Duke of York, became James II, King of England, and New York became a royal province. There were now great plans on foot for a radical reorganization of the colonial governments and James decided to keep a free hand by rejecting the Charter of Liberties and abolishing the assembly.

New York a royal province.

The religious situation was also difficult. The Dutch Reformed Church no longer received special recognition from the government, but it was still the strongest religious organization in the province and in some towns its ministers were supported by public taxation. Next in numbers and influence came the English Puritans, who were able to provide similar support for their Congregational churches in several of the Long Island towns. The Church of England was very small in New York, but it was now the official church and Anglican services were held in the fort on Manhattan. The situation was still further complicated by the fact that the proprietor himself was a Roman Catholic. Under these circumstances, the only possible policy was one of toleration, which was actually adopted. This did not, however, prevent bitter feeling on the part of the Protestants toward the small Catholic minority, which included a few officeholders. Unjust as this feeling was, it was partly due to the international situation. The New Yorkers felt keenly their exposed position on the Anglo-French frontier and were impressed by the influence of the Catholic French missionaries among the Indians. It was not difficult, therefore,

Problems of church and state.

to excite religious prejudice by suggesting that a good Catholic could not be a loyal English subject.

Economic development.

Notwithstanding these differences in religion and politics, New York was moderately prosperous during the early years of English rule. Some of the thrifty Dutch burghers found it possible to make money and acquire land at least as rapidly as under their old government. Dutch families like the Phillipses and Van Cortlandts were soon represented in the provincial council, where they met the new landowners of Scotch or English descent. The English governors made lavish grants of land to influential personages and there developed along the Hudson a number of large manorial estates, on which the life of the English gentry and their tenants was perhaps more nearly reproduced than anywhere else in America. Negro slaves had been introduced by the Dutch, and their numbers increased after the English conquest, though not on any such scale as in Virginia and South Carolina. Side by side with the great landowners and their tenantry there were small farmers, Dutch and English, the former most numerous on the Hudson and the latter on Long Island. During most of the colonial era, however, a small number of well-to-do families closely related to each other by intermarriage as well as by business interests, dominated the society and politics of the province.

The commerce of New York.

The New York farmers of this period were producing enough to enable them to export foodstuffs in considerable quantities. In 1678 Governor Andros reported that 60,000 bushels of wheat were exported annually, besides beef, pork, and other farm products. These were, for the most part, sent southward by sea, especially to the West Indies. Some of this trade was carried on in New York ships, but ship-building was less developed than in New England. In one branch of commerce, New York distinctly took the lead for the next half century. This was the fur trade, which had long been the chief attraction of this region to the competing European traders, and which after the English conquest became the great bone of contention between the New Yorkers and their French rivals on the St. Lawrence.

During the Dutch period, the fur trade was largely in the hands of a group of officials and traders at Albany, who succeeded in establishing close relations with the Iroquois. At first the furs which the Iroquois sold to their white neighbors were largely taken on their own hunting grounds, but as these fields were gradually exhausted, they became more and more middlemen between the Albany traders and the tribes of the Lake region. After the English conquest, the business was left as before in the hands of the Albany settlers, still mainly Dutchmen but now reënforced by a few British. Among these Albany traders two families stand out conspicuously, the Dutch Schuylers and the Scotch Livingstons. The chief articles used in the fur trade were firearms, coarse cloths, and rum, for all of which there was a steady demand among the Indians. The Iroquois valued their connection with the English, partly because the latter could sell goods cheaper than the French, and partly because the French, having important trade routes farther to the north, were less dependent on the Iroquois. So there was formed a close commercial and political alliance which the English used effectively during the next hundred years.

The English governor who saw most clearly the strategic possibilities of the New York frontier, whether for trade or politics, was not an Englishman at all, but the Irish Catholic, Thomas Dongan. In an era of intense religious partisanship, when the loyalty of Catholics was sharply questioned, this Catholic governor was probably the most persistent and aggressive defender of British interests in North America. In the face of vigorous protests from the French governor at Quebec, Dongan worked steadily to strengthen British influence over the Iroquois, and in 1684 persuaded some of the chiefs to put themselves definitely under English pro-

The fur trade and the Iroquois.

Thomas Dongan.

tection. He had even more ambitious plans, including the establishment of trading posts on the Lakes, but these were not realized.

Beginnings of New Jersey.   While the Anglo-Dutch farmers and fur traders of New York were strengthening their hold on the Hudson-Mohawk gateway to the West, a very different development was taking place in New Jersey. This province, included in the original grant to the Duke of York but almost immediately given away to his Cavalier friends, Berkeley and Carteret, had one advantage over most of the other English colonies. Except for the short northern line, drawn from the Hudson a few miles above Manhattan northwestward to the Delaware, its boundaries were all marked by obvious physical features. On the east were the Hudson and the Atlantic ocean; on the south and west, Delaware Bay and River. This, however, is about the only simple and clean-cut feature of early New Jersey history.

Political status.   The political status of the territory was confused from the beginning. From a purely legal point of view, the proprietors were probably landlords only, without the right to establish a government. Consequently when they sent out governors and other agents, these officials were confronted by the conflicting claims of the Duke's governors at New York. The most aggressive of the New York governors in this respect was Andros, who undertook to appoint officials in various parts of New Jersey and collect customs duties from vessels bound to New Jersey ports. In 1679, he even arrested Governor Carteret, a relative of Sir George, the proprietor, and took him to New York for trial. In the end, the Duke of York and the King practically recognized the governmental rights of the proprietors; but in the meantime these opposing claims had seriously complicated the relations of the provincial authorities with the incoming colonists.

As compared with other English colonies, New Jersey

had a long coast line, but it was deficient in good harbors. Geographic factors. Consequently there were only two good points of approach for the occupation of the territory. One was from the side of New York Bay, and it was here in the lowland region, much of which is now practically within the metropolitan or suburban area of the City of New York, that the chief settlements were made during the first ten years of the English occupation. The other natural approach was by way of the Delaware, and another series of settlements was soon established on or near the eastern bank of that river, extending from the bay to a point considerably above the present site of Philadelphia. The rough, hilly country of northwestern New Jersey remained practically unoccupied until a much later period.

The earliest occupants of this territory were a few Dutch Early settlers. on the west side of the Hudson, and a handful of Dutch and Swedes on the Delaware. Immediately after Nicolls took control at New York, he agreed with some New England Immigrants from New England. Puritans to give them lands south of New York Bay, where they could reproduce the characteristic features of New England town life. From the point of view of the New Jersey proprietors, these people had no legal rights; but they held their ground and for a time helped to make life strenuous, if not miserable, for the proprietary governor. Meantime the proprietors themselves were making a strong bid for more New England settlers. In 1665, they issued a "Conces- Concession and Agreement, 1665. sion and Agreement," providing for a governor and council appointed by themselves and a house of representatives chosen by the freemen; land was offered on liberal terms and a special appeal was made to prospective Puritan settlers by promising them not only toleration but grants of land to support ministers of their own choice. Under these condi- tions, the next ten years showed a considerable influx of settlers, partly from the old country but quite largely from New England. The promises of the proprietors were fairly kept, but they did not satisfy the aggressive Puritan settlers; there was constant bickering about titles and the quit-rents reserved by the proprietors.

About ten years after the original grant to Berkeley and Carteret, the situation was complicated still further. So far, the whole province had been held by the two proprietors jointly; but in 1674 Berkeley sold his rights to two Quakers named Fenwick and Byllinge, who made a bargain with Carteret by which the province was divided into two parts, known thereafter as East New Jersey and West New Jersey. Carteret's share included the new settlements in the northern region; but the western, or southern, part along the Delaware became the scene of the first important Quaker experiment in government. After a great deal of controversy between Byllinge and Fenwick, West New Jersey came into the hands of a large number of Quaker proprietors, among whom the leading spirit was William Penn, soon to become more famous as the founder of Pennsylvania. These new proprietors set up a constitution more liberal than any then existing outside of New England. Under this arrangement several towns and villages were established along the Delaware, of which the most important were Burlington, above the site of Philadelphia, and Salem, near the head of Delaware Bay. Thus by a curious irony of fate, the efforts of two Cavalier proprietors had resulted chiefly in giving new homes to New England Puritans and making possible for a few years a kind of Quaker Commonwealth.

Division of the province.

West New Jersey.

East New Jersey.

West New Jersey was hardly under way, before Sir George Carteret died and the holders of his title sold their interest in East New Jersey to another group of Quakers. William Penn, who had just secured his Pennsylvania charter, was also one of the new proprietors of East New Jersey and his influence may be seen in the elaborate constitution now prepared for the latter colony, but never actually put in operation. The original Quaker purchasers almost immediately took in other partners of different religious affiliations; several of them were not Englishmen at all but Scotchmen. Under the influence especially of the new partners, many Scottish immigrants, largely Presbyterians, now found their way to East New Jersey. Their relations with the New England Puritans who were the leading element in these northern towns may not have been altogether happy at first; but in the end these two Calvinistic groups combined with still later immigrants from the north of Ireland to make Presbyterianism the dominant religious force in this region. Neither of the Jerseys, however, had any established church corresponding to those set up in Massachusetts and Virginia.

At the end of their first quarter century, the Jerseys probably had a total population between ten and fifteen thousand. About two thirds of them lived in the northern province of East Jersey, where the economic and social development was similar to that in the rural sections of New England. The inhabitants were largely farmers with moderate holdings, living together in fairly compact settlements. Some effort was made to develop Perth Amboy into an important port, but without much success, and throughout the colonial era this region was commercially dependent on New York. In West New Jersey, there were a few large holdings, comparable with those in the southern colonies, and there were some negro slaves. *Social and economic conditions.*

Meantime, across the Delaware, one of the Quaker promoters just mentioned had begun the most important colonizing enterprise of the whole Restoration period. In the personality and career of William Penn, the founder of Pennsylvania, there was a curious meeting of the two quite different forces which contributed most largely to British colonial expansion in the later seventeenth century. By birth and family connections he belonged to that ruling class *William Penn.*

in England which was eager to exploit the economic resources of the New World, for themselves as well as for their country. Yet by his own choice Penn was also associated with a group of radical enthusiasts, quite outside that ruling circle, who looked to America as a refuge from intolerable conditions at home and as the scene of a hopeful experiment in religion and government.

Penn's early associations and education. Penn's early surroundings seemed adapted to the making of a successful politician and courtier, rather than a religious leader and social reformer. His father, Sir William Penn, was, like some of the Carolina proprietors, a servant of the Puritan Commonwealth who managed to keep and improve his political fortunes under the King. An admiral in Cromwell's time, he became one of the chief personages in the royal navy under the Duke of York. The official and court circles in which he moved included many of the people who were promoting the colonization of New York, the Jerseys, and the Carolinas, or investing their funds in the Hudson Bay and Royal African companies. In order to fit the younger Penn for a creditable part in this society, he was sent to Oxford. When, under the spell of a Quaker preacher, the boy developed unconventional religious ideas, he was given the benefit of the "grand tour" on the Continent and came back, as Pepys said, quite a "modish" youth. When the admiral died, his more worldly contemporaries must have thought that he had done very well by his son. He had given the young man the education of a gentleman, access to court circles, and a considerable fortune, not to mention a claim of £16,000 against the King. With all these advantages, the younger Penn might have gone far in English politics, or, if he figured in American history at all, it might have been as an ordinary plantation promoter. As a matter of fact he did make good use of his assets in property, education, and social training; but for purposes quite different from those which might have been expected.

The turning point in Penn's career came a few years before his father died, when with romantic enthusiasm he threw in his lot with a persecuted sect, called by themselves the Society of Friends, but better known to the outside world as the Quakers. About twenty years before Penn's conversion, George Fox, the founder of the society, began to preach his gospel of a purely spiritual Christianity, independent of external forms and deriving its authority solely from the voice of God speaking to the individual conscience. As Penn himself put it, the "right way to peace with God," which they believed "others had been vainly seeking *without*, with much pains and cost, they by this ministry found *within*." Forms and ceremonies, priesthoods, and temples built with human hands — all these had served their purposes in times gone by; but they were only "signs, types, and shadows" destined to disappear. So the Quakers rejected not only the Catholic and Anglican priesthoods, but formally ordained ministers of any kind. Even the sacraments of baptism and the Lord's supper seemed to them quite unnecessary; their preachers were not to pray or preach at fixed times, but only when moved by the spirit, for which they waited in silence. Rejecting a paid ministry for themselves, they refused to pay tithes for the support of any other clergy, whether in England or in a Puritan colony. They also claimed exemption from certain traditional duties to the state, including military service and the taking of an oath in a court of justice. Both these things they regarded as contrary to Christian teaching. In other respects the Quakers were generally law-abiding and they condemned the idea of resistance by force even to a tyrannical government. Though democratic and, in theory, highly individualistic, they developed an organization of weekly, monthly, and yearly "meetings," which they used effectively for mutual protection, supervising the personal conduct of members, and spreading the faith. The center of this organization was the London yearly meeting, at which regular reports were received from Friends throughout the world.

Persecution of the Quakers.

People holding such opinions could hardly escape persecution at the hands of the Restoration government. All dissenters were penalized by the legislation of that time, but the authorities were especially drastic in their treatment of radical sects like the Baptists and the Quakers. The latter were made more conspicuous in the public eye by superficial peculiarities, like their refusal to use the pronoun *you* in speaking to a single person and their habit of keeping their hats on even in the presence of official superiors. So the Quakers were frequently imprisoned for holding illegal meetings and many died in prison. Notwithstanding his social connections, young Penn had his share in these experiences and was deeply impressed, not only with the iniquity of persecution for conscience's sake, but almost equally with the unfairness of the judges, which seemed to ignore the

Penn's defense of religious liberty.

fundamental English traditions of personal liberty. In 1670 he set forth his theories in a notable book, *The Great Case of Liberty of Conscience.*

If England was a discouraging place for conscientious Quakers, the older American settlements were not much better. Massachusetts was the only colony which actually enforced the death penalty, but almost everywhere there was some hostile legislation. It was not strange, therefore,

Quaker projects of colonization.

that George Fox and other Friends began to think of establishing a colony of their own. For a time West New Jersey seemed to offer the desired opportunity; but to make the Quaker experiment a thorough success there must be better security against interference, and that required a royal charter. Fortunately, Penn's early encounters with magistrates and jailers did not prevent his becoming intimate with the highest personages, including the two royal brothers, Charles and James. Neither of the latter really sympathized with the Quakers, but James's conversion to Catholicism and his brother's secret sympathy with it led them to favor toleration, primarily for Catholics but incidentally also for Protestant dissenters. This intimacy damaged Penn's reputation among Anglicans and Puritans; but out of it came, first, the royal charter giving him a great tract of land along the Delaware; and, second, the Duke of York's grant of the "territories" occupied by the early Dutch and Swedish settlements west of the Delaware River, which he claimed as a dependency of New Netherland.

The Pennsylvania charter of 1681.

The boundaries of Pennsylvania were more definite than those of some other colonies, but there was plenty of room for differences of interpretation and these led to some of the most persistent and disagreeable boundary disputes of colonial times. The eastern boundary was the Delaware, and instead of the indefinite sea-to-sea grants of Virginia, Massachusetts, and Connecticut, Pennsylvania was to extend only five degrees westward. There was some question later just how that western line should be drawn; but for the next half century, the chief difficulties arose about the northern and southern boundaries. The northern line of the forty-third parallel finally had to be given up on account of the conflicting claims of New York to the Iroquois country, and the present line of the forty-second degree was accepted by the Pennsylvanians as "the beginning of the forty-third degree."

Boundaries of Pennsylvania.

Much more troublesome was the southern boundary, which was to begin on the Delaware twelve miles above Newcastle and follow the curve of a circle, drawn with the same twelve-mile radius, until that circle intersected the "beginning of the fortieth degree." There were several difficulties about this statement. To begin with, the proposed circle about Newcastle was too far south to intersect the fortieth parallel. Then came Lord Baltimore with a reminder that all the territory south of that parallel belonged to him under the charter of 1632. Unfortunately, his claim

The controversy with Maryland.

was not supported by actual occupation; and Penn, who was determined to have the line drawn far enough south to give him a good port for seagoing commerce, maintained that the phrase, "beginning of the fortieth degree," included the whole zone between the thirty-ninth and fortieth parallels. This controversy and that about the so-called "territories" farther down the river, which were not included in the Pennsylvania charter but had been secured from the Duke of York, were not completely settled in Penn's lifetime, and they embittered the relations of Pennsylvania and Maryland until the middle of the eighteenth century. Penn did not make good his extreme claim, but he kept the strip lying between the Newcastle "circle" and the fortieth parallel and was able to build upon its water front a city which soon became one of the chief commercial ports of North America. He also established his claim to the "territories" now included in the state of Delaware. Evidently Penn was quite capable of looking after his own interests and knew how to use his political influence to good advantage.

The government of Pennsylvania.

Penn's authority over his new province was in many respects similar to that of the earlier proprietors. Executive power was to be exercised by him directly or through his agents, but the settlers had to be consulted in the making of laws. The chief differences between Penn's charter and those of Maryland and Carolina were due not so much to his own personal views, as to a change in the colonial policy of the English government. In the older colonies, the proprietary governments were surprisingly independent of the Crown; but by 1681 the authorities in England were convinced that this arrangement was not satisfactory. Parliament had recently passed a series of Navigation Acts regulating American commerce, which depended for their enforcement upon the coöperation of the colonial governments. In the chartered colonies, however, colonial officials were chosen either by the inhabitants or by the proprietors and

Imperial control.

were not much interested in suppressing profitable trade, even when it happened to conflict with an act of Parliament. So the King, though willing to oblige Penn in general, saw to it that imperial interests were better protected than in the earlier charters. The laws of Pennsylvania had to be sent to England for approval or veto; anyone who was dissatisfied with the decision of a provincial court could appeal to the Privy Council; and in order to make sure that the acts of trade were strictly enforced, Penn had to keep an agent in England who could be called to account for violations of the law. One interesting clause of the charter implied the right of Parliament to tax the colonists; taxes were to be laid only with the consent of the colonial assembly, "*or by Act of Parliament in England.*" Nothing in the charter indicated that this was to be a Quaker colony, but there was a clause recognizing the right of the Bishop of London to send out "preachers" of the Anglican Church who were to be protected in the exercise of their duties.

Some of the restrictions imposed by the royal charter caused Penn and his successors considerable inconvenience in after years; but at first he had a fairly free hand and the Stuart government was as friendly as could reasonably be expected. For Penn, as for other colonial promoters, the first essential was to attract settlers, and the methods which he adopted were not altogether different from those of his predecessors, though his plan had some unique features. In working it out, he kept two quite distinct considerations in view. Penn certainly desired to carry out a "holy experiment," which he believed would be of great value to mankind; but at the same time he wanted fair returns on his investment, — a legitimate expectation which, nevertheless, led to some disparagement of his philanthropic purposes. *Penn's "holy experiment."*

His first inducement to settlers was the chance to take up land on easy terms, either in large tracts for a lump sum, with an annual quitrent reserved to the proprietor, or in smaller *Land policy.*

quantities at the modest rental of a penny an acre. Indentured servants were to receive fifty acres each on the expiration of their terms of service. Here were opportunities for almost everyone—artisans whose labor would bring much larger returns in America than they could expect at home, and prosperous middle-class people, of whom the Quakers were coming to have at least their fair share, who were glad to become landowners on a considerable scale. Penn also appealed to men who felt in themselves a special capacity for leadership, "men of universal spirits . . . that both understand and delight to promote good discipline and just government among a plain and well intending people." Such persons, Penn thought, though not of "much use or service to great Nations under settled customs," might "find room in colonies for their good counsel and contrivance."

Penn also provided a liberal government, which had been worked out in consultation with some of the more influential among the prospective settlers. In 1682 he issued his first "Frame of Government," whose complicated machinery shows the influence of contemporary political speculation; it also reminds one of the unlucky Fundamental Constitutions of Carolina. The document brings out clearly Penn's sincere desire to establish the principles of English liberty as he understood them. The governorship was to be held either by Penn himself or, in his absence, by his agent, or deputy; but the councilors and assemblymen were to be chosen by the "freemen," or landowners. He proposed also to simplify and humanize the administration of justice. This first "Frame of Government" proved too complicated and was almost immediately replaced by a second, which in turn gave way in practice to much simpler forms, partly because of popular dissatisfaction but partly also because Penn's own opinions changed. In 1701, on Penn's second visit to America, he came to an understanding with the colonists which was embodied in a "Charter of Privileges." By this time, the peculiar and unworkable features of the system. had been pretty well sloughed off, and the government had come to be much like that of an ordinary royal province, but with these important exceptions: the governor and council were appointed by the proprietor instead of by the King; the council, no longer an upper house, became merely an administrative body; the assembly, a unicameral body down to the Revolution, comprised the legislative branch. In all these arrangements, Pennsylvania and Delaware were at first treated as a single province; but in the charter of 1701 Penn agreed that the Delaware "territories" should have an assembly of their own, if they desired it, a privilege of which they soon took advantage.

No part of Penn's program was better advertised or more attractive than his promise of religious freedom. Though his new colony was meant to be a "Quaker experiment in government," he had no intention of limiting its opportunities to those of his own faith. Before his first visit to Pennsylvania, he agreed with some of his principal associates upon a guaranty of religious liberty, which was subsequently adopted by the colonial assembly. This guaranty included freedom of worship for all law-abiding persons who "acknowledged one Almighty and Eternal God to be the Creator, Upholder, and Ruler of the world." This meant liberty not only for all Protestant Christians but also for Catholics and Jews. Officeholding was limited to Christians, but this limitation was unimportant in the early years of the colony, since the number of persons excluded by it was negligible. The later record of the colony was not so satisfactory. Under pressure from the home government, Catholics also were excluded from office. Nevertheless the outstanding fact is that a great variety of religious sects, persecuted in the Old World, found in Pennsylvania a refuge where they could work out their theories without interference.

Religious freedom.

Rapid
growth of
population.

All these advantages, economic, political, and religious, were advertised throughout the British Isles and on the Continent as well, especially in Germany, which was still suffering from the terrible experiences of the Thirty Years' War. At Frankfort, which Penn had visited a few years before, a land company was organized to take advantage of the opportunities offered. The results of this advertising were soon evident. At the beginning of 1682, there were perhaps a thousand white people in Pennsylvania and Delaware, chiefly Swedes, Finns, and Dutch. Then the tide of immigration set in strongly; Penn himself came out that year, and by the end of 1683 he reported a population of 4000. In 1685 he estimated that in about three years ninety ships had come over with a total of over 7000 passengers; there was also some immigration from the neighboring English colonies. By 1689 the total population of Pennsylvania and Delaware was probably about 12,000, and this was only the beginning of a remarkable growth which finally gave Pennsylvania the largest white population of any English colony. Penn took great satisfaction in avoiding many mishaps and disasters of the older colonies. He declared that during the first three years not one ship bound for Pennsylvania had miscarried and also that, because of the healthy situation, there was no such terrible mortality as in early Virginia and New England. An important factor in the prospects of Pennsylvania was the skill and fairness with which Penn dealt with the Indians. About these matters a good deal of legend has grown up, but his methods certainly won the confidence of the Indians and saved the colony from serious troubles.

Indian
policy.

The new
settlers.
Racial
elements.

The new settlers represented a great variety of social, racial, and religious elements. Among the Englishmen who came over were some well-to-do merchants who acquired large tracts of land and were able to bring servants with them. Then there were many artisans, small farmers, and agricultural laborers coming out, either at their own expense or by making agreements to serve for a term of years, after which they could acquire land and become free citizens. According to Penn's estimate in 1685, only about half the population were English. Of the rest, many came from other parts of the British Isles. Welsh immigration has left its mark in the names of many places in the vicinity of Philadelphia, such as Merion, Radnor, and Bryn Mawr; there were also some Irish Quakers. From the Continent came a few French Protestants and Hollanders. More important *German immigrants.* were the Germans, led by the agent of the Frankfort Land Company, Francis Daniel Pastorius, a notable personage, *Pastorius.* who laid out the settlement of Germantown, and also deserves to be remembered for one of the best early descriptions of the province. The Germans showed some tendency to develop a separate community life, and Pastorius speaks in one of his early letters of having secured land in order that "we High Germans may maintain a separate little province, and thus feel secure from all oppression." The German immigration was not large, however, until about thirty years later; and on the whole these German pioneers got on harmoniously with their Quaker neighbors.

Of the English, Welsh, and Irish settlers, the majority *Religious elements.* were Quakers. There was, however, a small but aggressive Anglican element, encouraged by royal officials, which was quite out of sympathy with the "holy experiment." Among the German settlers the Lutherans were numerous; but Pennsylvania also proved attractive to certain radical sects which had broken away from the state churches of Germany and suffered persecution for doing so. Conspicuous among them, at first, were the Mennonites, who, like the Quakers, emphasized the "inner light."

In Penn's advertisements, much was said about the wealth *Economic resources.* of the soil and especially the opportunities for wheat growing. With these generous resources, the province almost immediately became self-supporting. Before long, wheat, flour, beef and pork were being exported, especially to the West Indies. Penn also did what he could to stimulate manufactures and it was partly for this reason that he welcomed the Germans, who began in a small way the manufacture of woolen and linen goods. Especially dear to his

Philadelphia. heart was the idea of making Philadelphia into an important commercial city. Placed just above the junction of the Delaware and Schuylkill rivers, with a good frontage for seagoing vessels on either side, it was planned more systematically than any other colonial town. Within four years after Penn received his charter, there were said to be about 600 houses in Philadelphia, some of them substantially built of brick. The fisheries were developed early and the abundant timber was soon used for shipbuilding. In short, Pennsylvania had from the beginning a varied and healthy economic development.

Trials and achievements. With this general prosperity, there were naturally some less pleasing features. After a stay of about two years, Penn went back to England and thereafter, with the exception of a second visit of about the same length (1699–1701), he was an absentee landlord and governor, with all the opportunities for misunderstanding and friction which naturally go with such a position. It seemed to Penn that the colonists often showed little appreciation of his services. Equally serious friction developed between the proprietary government and those royal officials whose special duty it was to enforce the Navigation Acts. They claimed that Penn's agents were not maintaining an orderly government, that illegal trade was permitted, and that the colony was much too hospitable to pirates. Fortunately, during the first critical years, Penn's influence at court was sufficient to ward off serious attacks. He had still many trials to undergo; and, from the point of view of personal profit, the results in his lifetime were disappointing. These, however, are small matters. The really important fact is that he had succeeded in his "holy experiment," the establishment of a new commonwealth on the principles of civil and religious liberty.

BIBLIOGRAPHICAL NOTES

Andrews, C. M., *Colonial Self-Government*, VI–VIII, XI–XII; later chapters *passim*. Channing, *United States*, II, 37–60, 142–151 and ch. IV. General accounts.

Best accounts by Andrews and Channing as above. For institutional developments see Osgood, *17th Cent.*, II. For New York as a frontier province, see McIlwain, C. H., *Wraxall's Abridgment of the Indian Records*, Introduction, especially xxxv–lxii. Fisher, S. G., *Quaker Colonies*, chs. VIII–X. New York and New Jersey.

Morris, R. B., *Select Cases of the Mayor's Court of New York City, 1674–1784 (American Legal Records*, II), 1–62. Flick, A. C., ed., *History of the State of New York*, III, 1–45. Borough and common law in New York.

Duke of York's Charter in Macdonald, *Select Charters*, no. 29; New Jersey documents, *ibid.*, nos. 30, 31, 35–37, 39. Hart, *Contemporaries*, I, nos. 156, 164–168. James, B. B., and Jameson, J. F., *Journal of Jasper Danckaerts*. Sources.

Hodgkin, T., *George Fox*. (Fox's Journal in various editions.) Hodges, G., *William Penn* (good brief account). Fuller narrative, in Janney, S. M., *William Penn;* Buck, W. J., *William Penn in America;* and Brailsford, M. R., *The Making of William Penn*. George Fox and William Penn.

Fisher, S. G., *Quaker Colonies*, chs. I–V, XII. Wissler, C., *et al.*, *Adventures in the Wilderness*, ch. XIV. Sharpless, I., *Quaker Experiment in Government*, pt. 1, esp. chs. I–III. Jones, R. M., *The Quakers in the American Colonies*. Institutional beginnings described in Osgood, *American Colonies*, II, especially ch. XI, and Shepherd, W. R., *Proprietary Government in Pennsylvania (Columbia Studies)*. Pennsylvania and Delaware.

Macdonald, *Select Charters*, nos. 38 (Royal charter), 40–41 (Penn's "Frames"), 46 ("Charter of Privileges"). Myers, A. C., *Narratives of Early Pennsylvania, West New Jersey and Delaware*. Hart, *Contemporaries*, I, nos. 161–163; II, no. 25. Sources.

CHAPTER IX

IMPERIALISM AND SELF-GOVERNMENT

England's overseas empire.
DURING the first two thirds of the seventeenth century, England had acquired, in more or less haphazard fashion, a great overseas empire, chiefly in America though with important commercial interests in Africa and the East Indies. During the greater part of that period, the novelty of the experience and the long conflicts between King and Parliament prevented the working out of any real imperial plan. There were certain general ideas about the economic function of colonies, but little was done to give those ideas any practical effect. By the time of the Restoration a new spirit was clearly at work; there was a good deal of fumbling still, but there was evidently a serious and fairly consistent policy taking shape whose purpose was to weld the scattered parts of the empire into an effective union. Though the driving force of this seventeenth-century imperialism was economic, it could not be carried through without political reorganization, the substitution of a uniform system of colonial government for the hit-or-miss methods of earlier times.

The mercantile theory.
The economic principles of the old English imperialism were embodied in the so-called Navigation Acts or "acts of trade." These, however, cannot be understood without some knowledge of seventeenth-century economics and of the prevailing ideas about the purposes for which colonies were established. According to the orthodox, or mercantile, theory, which emphasized the control of individual enterprise in the national interest, the wealth and power of a nation were

measured largely by its stock of money and precious metals. A given branch of trade was, therefore, considered good or bad according as it increased or diminished this public treasure. So far as possible, Englishmen should be relieved from the necessity of buying foreign goods and so sending English money out of the country. Conversely, any industry which produced articles for export was considered desirable because it brought foreign money into England and helped to create a "favorable balance of trade."

According to the mercantile theory, there were three chief services which colonies ought to render to the mother country. They were expected, first, to employ English shipping, thus not only bringing profits to shipowners and merchants but also contributing indirectly to the growth of England's naval power, the merchant marine and the fisheries being regarded as feeders for the royal navy. Colonies were expected, secondly, to produce articles which England would otherwise have to buy either from continental Europe or from the colonies of other European nations. Some of these articles were tropical or semi-tropical products, such as oil, silk, wine, and sugar. " Naval stores " also, such as lumber, pitch, tar, were desirable because their production by the colonists would make the English navy and merchant marine more independent of the Baltic countries. Lastly, it was hoped that the colonies would furnish expanding markets for English manufacturers. This consideration was less important at first than the other two, but indications of foreign or colonial competition in manufactures were jealously watched.

Economic functions of the colonies.

Though these theories were not applied to the colonies systematically until the Restoration period, they were acted upon in a partial and fitful fashion from the beginning of the colonial era. The Virginians were encouraged to produce silk, olive oil, and wine to take the place of imports from foreign countries. When tobacco, at first frowned upon

Beginnings of colonial policy.

by the King, became an important article of export, the Virginians were forbidden to send it directly to continental Europe; by requiring it to go first to England, English merchants were enabled to share in the profits of the trade. Colonial interests were not quite forgotten, for Virginia tobacco was protected against Spanish competition, and tobacco growing in England was forbidden. All these measures were merely orders of the King and for about forty years after the founding of Virginia, Parliament did not legislate regarding colonial trade. The King considered the colonies as his special preserve and expected Parliament to keep its hands off.

Colonial policy before 1660. Then came the Civil War and the temporary overthrow of the monarchy. For a time, Parliament had the whole field to itself, and it began to take a hand in the management of colonial affairs. Its first task was to suppress the royalist elements in the Chesapeake colonies and the West Indies. This was not very difficult; but in the meantime, the offending colonies were punished by restricting their trade. More important still was the growing influence of the merchant class, which had, on the whole, taken the side of Parliament as against the King and was now anxious to secure legislation for its own advantage. Just at this time, too, English jealousy of Dutch competition in the carrying trade was becoming more intense; the trade of England and her colonies at least must be kept in English hands. The **Navigation Act of 1651.** outcome of the discussion was the Navigation Act of 1651, requiring all colonial exports to England to be carried in ships owned and operated by Englishmen; European products were to be taken to the colonies only in English ships or in ships of the exporting country. This act was intended especially to destroy the Dutch predominance in the carrying trade and it helped to bring on the Anglo-Dutch war, which Cromwell brought to a victorious close in 1654. The law was not, however, strictly enforced as against the Dutch traders in Virginia, and, though Cromwell was interested in commercial expansion, there was no important legislation on colonial trade during his protectorate.

The most important result up to the accession of Charles II was not any particular piece of legislation, but the growth of an influential group of merchants who knew what they wanted and a group of politicians with similar ideas about commercial policy. Whether from motives of patriotism or from a regard to their own fortunes, these men adjusted themselves easily to the political changes of the Restoration. Several of them sat in the Convention Parliament of 1660 which reëstablished the monarchy. The work of these men was not spectacular, but they laid the foundations of an American policy which lasted until the colonies became independent. Two men especially prominent among the experts consulted by the government were Martin Noell and Thomas Povey, both hard-headed business men, chiefly interested in the West Indies. Among the politicians who took special interest in commercial and colonial policy, one of the most influential was Sir George Downing, a nephew of John Winthrop and a graduate of Harvard. From New England, Downing found his way back to England by way of the West Indies and before long was holding responsible positions in Cromwell's government, including that of ambassador to Holland. This last appointment he managed to keep after the Restoration and he also distinguished himself by betraying some of his old Puritan associates. Notwithstanding this unpleasant business, he was certainly able and efficient, whether in executive business or in shaping legislation. Among the men "higher up" who were interested in trade expansion were Lord Clarendon, Lord Ashley, and the King himself.

Almost immediately after the King's return a committee of the Privy Council was set to work on American problems. A few weeks later, the House of Commons appointed

Makers of colonial policy. Merchants and politicians.

a committee of its own, headed by Downing, "to consider
of encouraging and regulating the manufacture, both of
new and old wool, and navigations in English bottoms."
Among the other members were several prominent politicians, "all the merchants," and all the representatives
from the seaport towns. The committee worked rapidly and
in a little more than a month after its appointment, the
Navigation Act of 1660 had been passed by both houses
and approved by the King. This seems like hasty work,
but it was really the ripe fruit of a discussion which had
been going on for many years. This first statute was soon
followed up by others, of which the most important were
the Staple Act of 1663 and the Colonial Duty Act of 1673.
During the next hundred years, this legislation was developed in detail, modified at certain points, and systematized;
but the fundamental principles were worked out by the
merchants, economists, and statesmen of the Restoration.

The margin note: **The acts of trade, 1660–1673.**

The first essential principle was that colonial trade,
both import and export, was henceforth to be reserved exclusively for English ships; in order to be considered English,
a ship must be English built, English owned, and manned
by a crew of which the master and three fourths of the men
were English. The purpose of this regulation was to ex-
clude foreign competition; the English colonists shared
in this monopoly of trade, as did also the Irish; Scotch ships
were, however, regarded as foreign; though, under the common
law as interpreted by the courts, Scotch seamen might be
counted as English because they also were subjects of the
English King.

Margin note: **Colonial trade in English ships.**

The second principle embodied in the acts of trade was
that of making England the distributing point for certain
colonial products. These "enumerated articles," of which
the most important were tobacco and sugar, were not to be
sent directly to continental Europe, but were first to be
landed in a British port, from which, after the payment of

Margin notes: **Colonial exports.** **"Enumerated articles."**

customs duties, they could be reshipped to the Continent. The law did not prevent the shipment of any of these articles from one English colony to another, and this left the way open for a good deal of illegal trading. New England shippers, for instance, would take Virginia tobacco to New England; and, with the connivance of easy-going officials, reship it directly to continental Europe, escaping the payment of English duties and underbidding the English merchant. To check this practice and incidentally to secure some revenue, Parliament passed in 1673 an act requiring shippers of tobacco and other enumerated articles from one colony to another to pay a small export duty. The list of enumerated articles was short at first and affected only the Chesapeake colonies and the West Indies. No New England products were then included. During the next hundred years, however, the list was considerably extended.

Having shut out foreign ships from the colonial trade and required certain colonial exports to go through English ports, Parliament next undertook, through the Staple Act of 1663, to regulate the importation of European goods into the colonies, thus securing an enlarged market for English manufactures, or, in case of goods produced in continental Europe, giving the middleman's profits to English merchants. All goods of European production, with a few exceptions, had to be shipped to the colonies from English ports. The exceptions are, however, of some interest because they show that while the government was restricting colonial enterprise in some directions, it was willing to encourage it in others. One such exception was salt for the fisheries of New England and Newfoundland; and though Ireland was, under this act, treated much like a foreign country, provisions, horses, and servants, all much needed in the plantation colonies, could be sent directly from Irish ports.

Staple Act of 1663.

Colonial imports.

The pro-
tective
principle.

Taken as a whole, the acts of trade may be best understood as an application to the English empire of what is now called the protective principle, that is, the protection of English subjects against foreign competition. The empire was treated as an economic whole, so far as possible independent of the outside world, in which each part had its particular function to perform. In the case of shipping the protective principle was applied impartially to Englishmen on both sides of the Atlantic. In other cases there was a kind of give and take. The Virginians, for instance, had to send all their tobacco to England, or to some other English colony; but in return they were protected against competition in the English market. If England as a distributing center levied toll on the colonial trade, there was some compensation in the protection afforded by the English navy. On the other hand, these acts caused freight rates to rise, restricted the market for tobacco, with a consequent rapid drop in price, and increased the costs of manufactured goods in the colonies.

The problem
of enforce-
ment.

It was one thing to put this legislation on the statute books and quite another really to enforce it. It was assumed at first that the existing colonial governments would do this work; but the results were disappointing. Even royal governors hesitated to enforce unpopular laws; proprietary governors were still less satisfactory; worst of all, from the imperialist point of view, were the New England governors, who, being elected annually by the colonists, were much more anxious to please their constituents than to satisfy a government three thousand miles away. A few far-seeing men realized these difficulties from the beginning and advocated a thorough reorganization of the colonial governments; but this was not easy at a time when the granting of proprietary provinces seemed a comparatively cheap way of satisfying the King's friends. Meantime, Parliament took an important step toward the enforcing of the

Navigation Acts in America by providing, in the Colonial Duty Act of 1673, for colonial collectors directly responsible to the commissioners of customs in England.

The new collectors, however, soon reported that they were not supported by the local authorities. The most aggressive of these imperial officials was Edward Randolph, who was specially responsible for New England. From his own point of view, Randolph was simply a zealous servant of the Crown, trying to enforce the plain provisions of the law. The New Englanders, however, regarded him as a busybody, interfering in affairs which did not concern him and transmitting ill-natured and unjust reports to his superiors. There was similar friction in Maryland, Virginia, and North Carolina. The statements of Randolph and other collectors naturally strengthened the aggressive imperialists who were working for a reconstruction of the colonial governments. Before long the new policy began to take effect, chiefly through the recommendations of a series of governmental committees, beginning with the "Council for Foreign Plantations" appointed by Charles II in the first year of his reign and continued after 1674 by a permanent committee of the Privy Council for "Trade and Foreign Plantations."

Some results of the new policy may be seen by comparing the earlier colonial charters of Charles II with those issued during the later years of his reign. A good example of the first group is the Carolina charter, which gave that government almost unlimited authority within the colony. The new charters of Connecticut and Rhode Island also gave to those colonies for the first time a legal basis for their practically republican governments. Soon, however, the influence of more imperialistic ideas begins to be seen. In the New York charter, for instance, the King reserved the right of appeal from provincial courts to the Privy Council; in the Pennsylvania charter of 1681, issued not long after the new customs officials began sending in their reports,

Imperial collectors.

Privy Council committees.

Development of imperial control.

there was a whole series of reservations, —appeals from colonial courts, a royal veto on colonial laws, an agency in England to answer for the enforcement of the Navigation Acts, and a definite statement that failure to enforce those acts might result in the withdrawal of proprietary rights. Evidently the framers of this document meant that Pennsylvania was to be an integral part of a real empire. To the thoroughgoing imperialists, however, these reservations seemed nothing better than half way measures. Such men could see no excuse for chartered colonies of any kind, proprietary or republican; the executive power at least should always be in the hands of a governor appointed by, and directly responsible to, the government in England.

Imperial control applied to New England.

Nowhere was imperial control considered more necessary than in New England. The King naturally thought of the New England Puritans as the American branch of the party which had cut off his father's head and kept himself in exile for many years. Nor was it difficult to prove that some of the Massachusetts leaders were claiming practical independence. The economic development of New England also seemed of little real advantage to the mother country. These enterprising colonists were building their own ships instead of employing those of England; they absorbed a large part of the intercolonial trade; they sent no important staple to England for the profit of English merchants; and they were generally believed to carry on their business with little regard for the Navigation Acts. Massachusetts tried to make up for these deficiencies by ardent protestations of loyalty but carefully avoided giving up any substantial rights. When, in 1664, the King sent out commissioners to investigate the situation, they accomplished little except to add new items to the formidable indictment which English officials were making up against Massachusetts. A few years later the Committee on Trade and Plantations decided to institute legal proceedings against the Massachusetts Bay Company for the forfeiture of the charter, and when the case came to trial the correspondence of Randolph furnished the government lawyers with a mass of damaging evidence. For a time Massachusetts was able to delay action, but in 1684 the charter was annulled by an order in the Court of Chancery. *Massachusetts charter annulled.*

For the Massachusetts leaders the revocation of the charter was a real tragedy. On this foundation they had built up a social structure quite distinct from that of the mother country and to a large extent antagonistic to it. Now the whole fabric was threatened with destruction. From the imperial point of view, however, the overthrow of the old Massachusetts government was only one move in the working out of a great constructive policy. The essential features of this policy were: (1) the establishment wherever possible of royal governments, in place of the prevailing system of chartered colonies; (2) the combination of small and weak colonies into one or more large provinces; (3) the strengthening of the executive power, represented by royal governors and councilors, at the expense of the representative assemblies. It was believed that these changes would insure greater efficiency both in the enforcement of imperial regulations and in the defense of the colonies against foreign enemies. *Imperialist principles.*

The revocation of the Massachusetts charter offered an excellent opportunity for carrying this policy into effect. A few years before, New Hampshire, previously a part of Massachusetts, had been made a distinct royal government; but in 1685 it was again united with Massachusetts and Maine in the province of New England. A temporary government was then provided for this new province with Joseph Dudley as president. Dudley was the son of one of the early Puritan leaders, but his willingness to aid in carrying out the new program made him scarcely less obnoxious than an outsider would have been. One of his associates *Extension of imperial policy 1685–1688.* *The "Greater New England."*

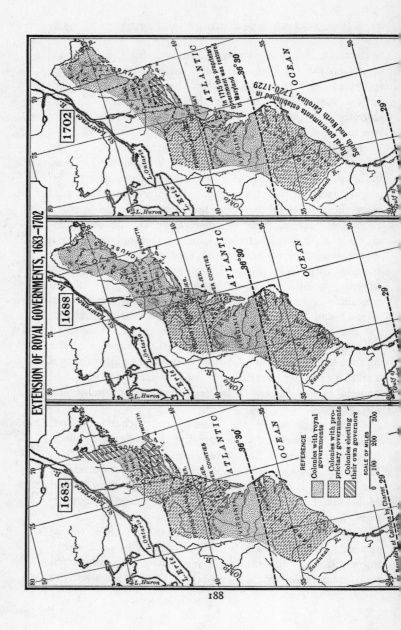

EXTENSION OF ROYAL GOVERNMENTS, 1683–1702

REFERENCE

Colonies with royal governments

Colonies with proprietary governments

Colonies electing their own governors

SCALE OF MILES
0   100   200   300

was the equally unpopular Edward Randolph. In 1686 the system was developed still further. "New England" was expanded by taking in Plymouth, and Sir Edmund Andros, the former governor of New York, was placed at the head. The new commission and instructions put practically all power, legislative and executive, in the hands of the governor and council, all of whom were appointed by the King. Even this was not the end. Legal proceedings were begun for annulling the charters of several other colonies, including Connecticut, Rhode Island, East New Jersey, and West New Jersey. In 1688 Andros received a second commission as governor of the "Territory and Dominion of New England," now defined so as to include, besides New England proper, New York and the Jerseys. Within four years the boundaries of eight distinct colonies had been wiped off the slate and a single royal government established over them. This compulsory union of more or less uncongenial elements was bad enough in itself; even more objectionable was the abolition of the colonial assemblies. After being accustomed to practically complete control of their own affairs, the New Englanders were now asked to adjust themselves to a system in which every department was controlled, directly or indirectly, by a government three thousand miles away. This was a real revolution and its natural effect was to provoke a counter-revolution in the colonies.

Perhaps an exceptionally tactful personage at the head of the new "Dominion" might have partly reconciled the colonies to the loss of their privileges. Unfortunately Andros, though honest and in some respects efficient, especially in the matter of military defense, was not exactly a diplomatist. Neither was his previous experience, as an army officer and as the governor of a conquered province, likely to help him much in dealing with stubbornly independent people like the Massachusetts Puritans. He cannot be blamed

Sir Edmund Andros.

for the main policies of his administration, which were determined by others; but he was at times offensive in his way of asserting his own prerogatives and those of the King. Even among his associates in the council, he was often overbearing and so alienated men who might otherwise have helped him. Andros was not, of course, the only unpopular member of the council. No language was too strong to express the popular detestation of Randolph and the "renegade" Dudley.

Problems
of defense.

The problem which interested Andros most was that of defense. On the northern borders of the Dominion, especially in New York and in Maine, there were many signs of an approaching conflict with the French and the Indians. To meet this danger, Andros held a conference with the Indians at Albany and also visited the frontier posts in Maine. Garrisons were strengthened and steps taken to counteract French emissaries among the Indians. This work was on the whole well done, though the governor's long absence from Massachusetts gave his enemies a chance to spread malicious gossip, including the charge that he was a papist and had a secret understanding with the French. Unfortunately this willingness to believe the worst about Andros was partly the result of his own tactless handling of a delicate situation.

New England land
system
attacked.

One of the first things Andros did was to attack the New England land system. The titles by which these colonial farmers held their land were questioned and they were told that new deeds would be necessary. The land was not necessarily to be taken away, but fees were required for new deeds and the owners were to pay quitrents as in other colonies. In carrying out this policy there was some unnecessarily rough talking, as when a Massachusetts landowner was told that his Indian deed was worth no more than "a scratch with a bear's paw." Popular feeling was increased by the fact that some of the leading councilors were trying to get land for themselves from the town commons. Doubtless the Massachusetts method of allotting land through the town organizations was not technically legal; but the general exasperation of the landowning population was a high price to pay for insisting on this point.

No less offensive was the attempt to collect taxes without the consent of any representative body. The home government was of course primarily responsible since it had provided no legislative assembly except the governor and council. Andros apparently interpreted his instructions to mean that the payment of taxes should continue under the old colony law, even though the period for which they were levied had expired. Instructions were accordingly issued to this effect, without a formal vote of the council. Then the trouble began; for the Massachusetts revenue system required the coöperation of the towns. Some of the towns submitted; but the people of Ipswich, under the leadership of their minister, John Wise, won a conspicuous place in American history by refusing to take the part expected of them. For this defiance of the government, Wise and some of his associates were arrested, fined, and disqualified from holding office. This incident helped to convince the government that the town meetings should be curbed; and in March, 1688, the council forbade the calling of them except for the annual election of town officers. The machinery for collecting taxes was also changed so as to make the government more independent of the towns. In this matter, as in the land dispute, opposition on principle was apparently intensified by undiplomatic language. It was said, for instance, that Dudley, who presided at the trial of the Ipswich men, had told the prisoners that the laws of England on which they relied against arbitrary measures were not supposed to follow them to the ends of the earth.

In their sensitiveness about land titles and taxes, the Massachusetts people were like other Englishmen the world

Taxation without representation.

Disregard of Puritan traditions.

over; but they had special grievances of their own. No one thing about the Andros *régime* kept their nerves more on edge than its disregard of Puritan traditions. They objected, for instance, to kissing the Bible when taking the oath in court. They disliked the lax observance of the Sabbath and were scarcely less annoyed by the Anglican celebration of Christmas, which they regarded as "popish." The established Puritan churches were allowed to go on as before, but the new government was expected to encourage the Anglican services. Accordingly, one of the Boston churches had to allow the use of its meetinghouse at certain times for the Episcopal service, until the new Anglican church could be built. To the ruling element in Massachusetts, the use of the prayer book in one of their churches seemed nothing short of a scandal.

Appeal to England; Increase Mather.

After all these controversies, serious and trivial, the year 1689 began with New England, and especially Massachusetts, in a deeply resentful state of mind. In the previous spring, the opposition leaders had sent Increase Mather, minister of one of the Boston churches and perhaps the ablest man in the colony, to England in the hope that he might get some relief. Mather had some conferences with prominent dissenters, and even with King James II, who was then inclined to favor a general policy of toleration in order to save his Catholic subjects from the disabilities imposed upon them by the English law. James was unwilling, or unable, to do anything for the New Englanders; but, fortunately for Mather, the whole situation was soon radically changed by the Revolution in England.

The Revolution of 1688.

The "glorious Revolution" of 1688 was the result not of a really democratic movement but rather of a conflict between two parties in a comparatively small ruling class, a conflict in which politics and religion both played important parts. The political, or constitutional, issue developed from the effort of James II to secure for himself a posi-

tion more or less independent of Parliament. This policy
was much like that followed by Charles II, but it aroused
more serious opposition because James was less popular
than his brother and less skillful as a politician. Possibly,
however, the loyalty of the nation as a whole to the reigning house would have kept the King on his throne if the
constitutional controversy had not been complicated by
religious issues. It was certainly awkward for the Anglican Church that the King, who was by law the "supreme
governor" of that church, actually belonged himself to the
Roman communion. As a loyal Catholic, James could
hardly be blamed for trying to increase the influence of his
own faith and free his fellow Catholics from the harsh legislation against them. Unfortunately for him, he could not
secure these results by legal methods, and therefore undertook by his own authority to suspend the laws excluding
Catholics and other dissenters from public office. This
action combined against him various elements which could
hardly have been brought together in any other way. Believers in constitutional government and the supremacy
of the law were alarmed by the King's claim that he could
set aside acts of Parliament. Anglican churchmen who had
strenuously asserted the "divine right" of the monarchy,
now turned against him because he was attacking the privileged position of their church. Even the Protestant dissenters, whom James tried to attract by his promise of
religious toleration, generally agreed that they must save
Protestantism by uniting, for the time being at any rate,
with their old opponents of the high-church party.

So, by the autumn of 1688, the King was almost iso- Results of
lated and unable to make a stand against his Dutch son- the Revolu-
in-law, William of Orange, whom his rebellious subjects England.
tion in
had invited to become their leader. Before the year ended,
James was an exile and the Revolution was practically
accomplished. In 1689, William and his Stuart wife, the

Princess Mary, were proclaimed jointly King and Queen of England — William III and Mary II — with the express understanding that they were to rule as constitutional monarchs, recognizing the sovereignty of Parliament and certain fundamental "rights of Englishmen." These understandings were presently embodied in the famous Bill of Rights and a few years later in the Act of Settlement (1701). The Revolution had important consequences in religion as well as in politics. The Church of England retained its privileged position and to hold important offices in the local and central governments it was necessary to take the communion in that church. This qualification ruled out both Catholics and Protestant dissenters. The Toleration Act of 1689 gave freedom of worship, in the strict sense of that word, to nearly all Protestants, but the Catholics were refused even this grudging kind of toleration.

The Revolution in America.

The effects of this comparatively peaceful revolution were scarcely less important for America than for England. A little less than a century later the political philosophy which was used to justify the expulsion of James II was used effectively by the leaders of the American revolt against George III. The doctrine that government was founded upon compact or agreement and that rulers who violated the terms of the compact could be set aside was soon well known to Americans through Locke's *Two Treatises of Government* and it was echoed in the Declaration of Independence. These consequences, however, no one could have foreseen at the time. For the present, the chief practical result on the American side was the temporary breakdown of the new imperial policy and the permanent abandonment of its most objectionable features. On both sides of the Atlantic, the rallying cry was much the same. The colonists claimed to be defending representative institutions against arbitrary government, and Protestantism against the supposed Catholic menace. Unrest was general from

New England to Carolina; and in a few cases the revolutionary movement threatened to go farther than the new English government was willing to approve.

First in order came the sudden collapse of the great "Dominion of New England." By March, 1689, when it was known in Boston that James had been deposed, New England was ripe for revolt; and on April 18 a carefully prepared uprising came to a head in Boston. By the end of that day Andros was a prisoner in the hands of the insurgents, together with Randolph and a few other officials. Two days later a temporary government was organized with some of the older Puritan leaders in control. These men hesitated at first; but, after consulting a convention of delegates from the towns, they decided to go on with the government as it was under the old charter. According to their theory, the charter had never been legally revoked and the Andros government was a mere usurpation. The other New England colonies soon followed the lead of Massachusetts. It was comparatively easy for Connecticut and Rhode Island to resume their governments, for the legal proceedings against them had not been completed. Plymouth had no charter, but it went back to the simple republican government established by Bradford and his associates half a century before. All these measures were taken by the colonists on their own responsibility, but they now sought the approval of the new government in England. They felt that they had a strong case. As one contemporary writer put it, "no man does really approve of the Revolution in England but must justifie that in New England also." Andros and his associates, they said, were "King James's Creatures who had invaded both the Liberty and Property of English protestants after such a manner as perhaps the like was never known in any part of the World where the English nation has any government."

From New England the revolution spread to New York.

The Revolution in New England.

Discontent in New York.

The people of that province had no well-established traditions of self-government like those of their Puritan neighbors, but they had not forgotten the short-lived assembly of 1683. Dissatisfaction with arbitrary government was complicated by class feeling. The principal officials formed an aristocratic class which had made money in trade and used it to build up great landed estates. Conspicuous among them were Nicholas Bayard, a nephew of old Peter Stuyvesant; Stephen Van Cortlandt, mayor of New York; and Peter Schuyler, Van Cortlandt's brother-in-law, who was mayor of Albany and the most conspicuous figure in the Indian trade. Against this ruling group there was now formed an opposition party, made up partly of the poorer element but headed by Jacob Leisler, an immigrant from Germany, whose energy and success in business had given him an influential position. Religious feeling was more serious than might have been expected in a colony which had long been accustomed to a great variety of sects. The Catholics were comparatively few in number and certainly the Catholic governor Dongan had fairly earned the confidence of his people by his zealous defense of their interests against the French. Gradually, however, the intense anti-Catholic spirit which had shown itself in England and New England was worked up in New York; here also fear of the French and their Catholic missionaries strengthened popular suspicion of the few Catholics who held office under Governor Andros and his New York deputy, Lieutenant-Governor Nicholson.

Leisler's revolt.

In the midst of this excitement over dangers, real and imaginary, the New Yorkers got word of the English revolution and later of the developments in New England. Nicholson, as acting governor, tried to reassure the people and strengthen the defenses of the city against a possible French invasion. Popular excitement continued, however, and on May 31, 1689, there was a clash between the colonial

militia and a few English regulars acting under Nicholson's
orders. The latter now weakened and sailed back to England after giving up the fort on Manhattan to the muti-
nous militia. Thereupon the insurgents organized a provisional government with Leisler at the head. They claimed
to be merely defending the people against arbitrary
power, and declared that they would give up their authority only to a Protestant governor sent out by the new
King. To strengthen his position, Leisler called a convention at New York; but its members represented only
a section of the province, while Albany and other settlements
held aloof. This convention now appointed a committee
of safety, which authorized Leisler to act as commander in
chief with practically absolute authority. A few months
later, Leisler tried to legalize his position by accepting,
as for himself, certain orders from the home government
which were addressed to the lieutenant governor of the
province "and in his absence to such as for the time being
take care for the preserving the peace and administering
the laws."

In the management of his revolutionary government, Leisler's
Leisler showed some energy and ability. War had now problems.
broken out between France and England, and Leisler did
what he could to unite his own people with the neighboring
colonies in vigorous measures, both defensive and offensive; among other things they worked out an elaborate
plan for a land-and-sea attack on Quebec. His personality,
however, was unfortunate. Though probably honest and
well meaning, he lacked education and was constantly making
enemies by his violent methods. In the north, the Albany
settlers with Peter Schuyler as their leader held out against
Leisler until the destruction of the neighboring post at
Schenectady by the French and Indians made evident the
need of coöperation against the common enemy. Under
the old Charter of Liberties, the people were now called

on to elect representatives to a provincial assembly; but the elections were not fairly representative of the province as a whole.

The fall of Leisler. The new royal government.

With his own people badly divided, Leisler drifted into a serious conflict with the home government. Though a new royal governor had been commissioned in 1689, more than a year elapsed before he was sent out to his province with a few soldiers to support him. The soldiers made their appearance early in 1691, but Leisler refused to recognize the authority of their commander and some fighting took place between the two opposing parties. A few weeks later, Governor Slaughter himself arrived, and Leisler finally saw the necessity of yielding, though he hesitated long enough to strengthen the case of his enemies. He and some of his associates were now tried by a special court which was strongly prejudiced against him, with the result that Leisler and his son-in-law, Milborne, were found guilty and sentenced to death. They appealed to the home government, but before their case could be presented the governor yielded to pressure and the two revolutionary leaders were hanged. For a time, order seemed to be restored, but for the next ten years the mutual hatred of Leislerians and anti-Leislerians gave to the politics of New York a peculiarly venomous character.

Unrest in the South.

The revolutionary spirit which had upset the Andros *régime* in the northern colonies was also felt in the South. In Virginia royal officials noted some unrest among the people, though there was no serious outbreak. In North Carolina the year 1689 was marked by one of the numerous insurrections which were so characteristic of the early history of that province. It was only in Maryland, however, that the popular discontent resulted in any change of permanent importance, and there the revolutionary movement was directed not against royal officials but against an unpopular proprietor.

As compared with the northern colonists, Maryland seemed to have less cause for complaint. While the New Englanders had seen practically independent commonwealths suddenly merged in a single autocratic administration, Maryland was living under a government not essentially different from that established half a century before. The colony was not deprived of its representative assembly, but after 1670 the government became increasingly arbitrary, suppressing opposition by strong-arm methods. The popular party objected, for instance, to the governor's claim that he could fix the number of representatives to be elected in each county and to his refusal to allow an increase in the number. The colonists also complained that they were refused certain benefits of the English statute law. Probably the most serious charge made against Baltimore was that he treated the province too much like a piece of property, filling the principal offices with his own relatives or other personal connections. Religious animosity also made trouble. The policy of toleration was still observed; but the Protestants alleged that the Catholics got more than their share of the offices. Here, too, the religious issue was made more serious by the impending war with the French.

When the news of the English Revolution reached Mary- land, Lord Baltimore's government was in the hands of the council with a comparatively inexperienced man at its head. Though the proprietor, who was then in England, promptly ordered the proclamation of the new King and Queen, official notice was not received in Maryland until much later. This delay played into the hands of the anti-Catholic leaders, who by this time had worked up a strong revolutionary organization, known as the Protestant Association. The most conspicuous insurgent leader was an agitator named John Coode, but associated with him were more responsible men, among them the royal collector of customs. Supported by a majority of the Protestant inhabitants, the insurgents soon got control of the provincial government and issued a proclamation, explaining their grievances and emphasizing the need of a Protestant government on the eve of war with a great Catholic power. A clever appeal was made for royal support by mentioning the ill treatment of royal officials by the proprietor's agents and declaring the purpose of the association to assert the sovereign rights of the English Crown. A convention was then held, made up of partisans of the Protestant Association, and in April, 1690, this convention appointed a committee with Coode at its head to carry on the government until a royal governor could be appointed.

The problems of reconstruction.

Thus within a few months after the deposition of King James, the existing colonial governments, from the Canadian border to the Potomac, with the exception of Penn's colonies on the Delaware, had been swept away. All the colonial leaders professed entire loyalty to the Revolution government in England; but they differed widely from each other and from the authorities at home about the new order to be established. William III and his advisers were therefore confronted with serious problems of reconstruction in which the aspirations of the colonists had somehow to be adjusted to the interests of the mother country and of the empire as a whole. It seemed to the New Englanders, especially, that the overthrow of the Stuart government ought to carry with it the complete reversal of Stuart policies on both sides of the Atlantic; not merely the restoration of representative assemblies, but the return of the colonial charters. To most British officials, it seemed equally clear that the old arrangements should not be restored. In one respect, however, the home government recognized the justice of the American claims. The government of William and Mary, itself founded on the principle of parliamentary sovereignty, could not well deny some sort of representative government to Englishmen in America. It was there-

Representative assemblies.

fore agreed that each colony should have its own elected assembly.

Though the worst feature of the Stuart *régime* in America was thus abandoned, no radical departure was made in other respects from the policies of the Restoration era. Several of the men who had influenced the colonial measures of Charles II and James II held office also under the Revolution government, and William III himself was a strong believer in the royal prerogative. Though he was much occupied with European problems and not able to give much personal attention to American affairs, his influence was distinctly on the side of imperial control. The war with France, which covered the greater part of his reign, naturally emphasized the need of unity in colonial administration. Along the whole seaboard, from Hudson Bay and Newfoundland to the West Indies, English interests had to be defended against the French and their Indian allies. Already the confused condition of New England after the overthrow of Andros had weakened the English defense and shown the disadvantage of distributing authority among several weak governments only slightly controlled by the Crown. The military arguments for centralization were reënforced by those of the merchants and financiers. The principles of the Navigation Acts were as popular as ever and the commercial interests were determined that they should be strictly enforced. It was believed that if the New Englanders recovered their charters, they would use their freedom to make the acts of trade little more than a dead letter.

Imperial control under the new government.

The natural outcome of this discussion was a series of compromises which satisfied neither side, but worked fairly well for the next seventy years. The colonists were given a considerable measure of self-government, through their assemblies; but, through the appointment of royal governors and councilors, the executive power was kept so far as possible under the control of the Crown. Practical reasons

Compromises.

of various kinds prevented the full application of this policy, but the principle was not forgotten and the aggressive imperialists were always looking for opportunities to apply it.

New York and the Jerseys.

The Maryland revolution was most satisfactory to the home government. Its avowed object was in accord with the colonial policy in London, namely, the overthrow of proprietary authority and the establishment of a royal government. It was agreed on both sides of the Atlantic that at this crisis it was desirable to have a Protestant governor. So, with the help of a legal opinion from Chief-Justice Holt, it was decided that, though the proprietor might keep his property rights, the King could establish his own government in the province. Accordingly a royal governor was appointed, who began his administration in 1692. In New York also the question of policy was comparatively simple. The strategic importance of the province seemed to make a royal government essential; but the uncongenial union with New England was given up, and with the royal governor there was to be an assembly chosen by the freeholders. East and West New Jersey were comparatively unimportant and for a few years were left to their respective proprietors.

The New England problem.

The New England problem was more complicated. The Massachusetts agents, ably led by Increase Mather and supported by influential English dissenters, worked hard to get back the old charter of 1629; but the odds were against them. An attempt to include the colonies in a general act of Parliament, restoring charters which had been annulled under the last two Stuarts, also failed. Accordingly, Mather decided that half a loaf was better than no bread and set out to get the best charter possible. Early in the discussion, the King himself decided that there must be a royal governor with a veto on colonial laws. This was a keen disappointment to the Massachusetts people, though it was a natural decision for a soldier-statesman in those troubled times. After this question was settled, it took several months to work out the details, but in September, 1691, the new charter was authorized.

Like other features of the Revolution settlement, this charter of 1691 was distinctly a compromise. No attempt was made to restore the "Dominion of New England." The separation of New York and the Jerseys was already settled and the little colonies of Connecticut and Rhode Island were allowed to resume their charters. The Massachusetts leaders tried to unite the rest of New England under one government; but here the English authorities abandoned their own principle of concentration and decided to make New Hampshire a separate royal province. Even with this reduction, however, the territory of Massachusetts Bay, with Maine, Plymouth, and the temporary conquest of Nova Scotia from the French, was a large province. The governmental provisions of the charter show a similar give and take between opposing principles. Imperial interests were protected by the royal governor with his veto power; even bills which he approved had to be sent to England and might be annulled by the Privy Council. That body was also to take appeals from provincial courts and so could decide in specific cases whether a colonial law was in harmony with the laws of England. Property instead of church membership was hereafter to be the qualification for voting. Disappointing as some of these changes were, the Massachusetts people were much better off than their neighbors in other royal provinces. They had a permanent constitution, which could not be changed arbitrarily by a simple modification of the governor's commission and instructions. They could choose a new house of representatives every year; and these representatives had unusual power, including a share in the annual election of councilors and the right to choose some of the more important provincial officers. The old system of local government remained practically unchanged, and with it the privileged position of the Congregational

The charter of 1691 a compromise.

churches. On the whole, therefore, the policy of the English government was liberal. Imperial control was thought necessary for defense and for the enforcement of the acts of trade; but local traditions were generally respected and a good deal of self-government conceded.

Pennsylvania.

So far the English authorities had been concerned chiefly with the reconstruction of colonial governments disorganized by the Revolution; but presently they turned their attention to Pennsylvania. Penn's friendship with the Stuarts and his comparatively new charter had saved the colony from interference before the Revolution; but now these associations seemed suspicious. In his own colony too, the royalist and Anglican group was keeping up a fire against him, claiming that his government failed to preserve order, disregarded the acts of trade, and even sheltered pirates. Furthermore, the empire was now at war and the refusal of the Quakers to bear arms naturally provoked criticism from officials who felt the responsibility for national defense. All these hostile influences came to a head in 1692, when Penn's government was temporarily taken from him and intrusted to the royal governor of New York. Penn was more fortunate, however, than Lord Baltimore; for in two years he cleared himself sufficiently to recover control of his province, which his family held until the Revolution.

New Jersey.

For the Jerseys, the next decade was one of confusion and uncertainty. The proprietors were nominally in control but their position was so much weakened by doubts about their authority and by internal disputes that the proprietors had little to lose by giving up their political claims. In 1702, an agreement was reached by which East and West New Jersey were united in a single royal province. For many years afterwards the governorship of New Jersey was held by the governor of New York, though the two provinces were otherwise distinct.

The English Revolution of 1688 evidently affected colonial policy much less than the colonists had hoped. The new government did, indeed, give up the idea of abolishing or crippling the colonial assemblies and showed in general more respect than its predecessors for local practices and traditions; but the Stuart policy of concentrating authority in a few royal governments was not forgotten. The acts of trade were not relaxed; on the contrary, new machinery was created for their enforcement. Parliament, emerging victorious from its long conflict with royal prerogative, was more ready than ever to assert its authority over all parts of the empire. Thus the Revolution of 1688 has a logical connection with that of 1776; for it was the sweeping assertion of this principle of parliamentary sovereignty in the case of the colonies, which brought on the American Revolution. For the time being, however, the colonists were thinking not so much about the danger of parliamentary tyranny as about certain principles of political liberty which triumphed in the English Revolution and seemed equally applicable in America. The Bill of Rights, with its guarantees of individual liberty against arbitrary government, strengthened the determination of Americans to claim the same rights for themselves. The English Toleration Act of 1689 helped forward somewhat, though indirectly, the cause of religious freedom in America. Finally, the increasing power of the House of Commons encouraged the colonial assemblies to take a more decided stand against the royal governor and his councilors.

Significance of the English Revolution in American history.

BIBLIOGRAPHICAL NOTES

Andrews, *Colonial Period*, ch. V (*Home University Library;* brief but suggestive), and *Colonial Self-Government*, chs. I–IV, XVI, XVII. Channing, *United States*, I, 485–495; II, 5–13, 155–230. More extended treatment in Osgood, *17th Cent.*, II, chs. V–VII, X, XIII–XVI, and "Conclusion."

General accounts.

English background.

Cambridge Modern History, V, ch. X (1). Lodge, R., *Political History of England, 1660–1702*. Trevelyan, G. M., *England under the Stuarts*, chs. XI–XIV.

Colonial policy. The acts of trade.

Andrews, C. M., in *Cambridge Hist. of British Empire*, I, ch. IX. Ashley, W. J., *Surveys Historic and Economic*, 309–335 (English view). Beer, G. L., *Origins of British Colonial Policy*, chs. XI–XII, with his *Old Colonial System*, I, chs. I–V. Egerton, H. E., *British Colonial Policy*, Bk. II, chs. I–IV.

Administration.

Andrews, C. M., *Committees*, etc., *of Trade and Plantations* (*Johns Hopkins Studies*, XXVI). Root, W. T., "Lords of Trade and Plantations" (*A.H.R.*, XXIII, 20–41). Crump, H. J., *Colonial Admiralty Jurisdiction in the 17th Century*.

Documents.

Extracts from the acts of trade in Macdonald, *Select Charters*, nos. 22, 23, 25, 28, 34; Commager, *Documents*, 32, 38.

English political thought and the Revolution.

Laski, H. J., *Political Thought in England from Locke to Bentham*. Figgis, J., *Divine Right of Kings*. Borgeaud, C., *Rise of Modern Democracy in Old and New England*, trans. by B. Hill. Gooch, G. P., *English Democratic Ideas in the 17th Century*.

The Andros régime in New England and its overthrow.

Barnes, V., *Dominion of New England*. Parrington, V. L., *Main Currents*, I ("John Wise"), 118–130. Murdock, K. B., *Increase Mather*. Andrews, C. M., *Fathers of New England*, chs. IX–XI. Adams, J. T. *Founding of New England*, chs. XII, XIII, XV–XVII. Kimball, E., *Joseph Dudley*, chs. I–III.

Leisler's revolt.

Van Rensselaer, S., *Hist. of City of N. Y.*, chs. XXIV–XXIX. Brodhead, J. R., *History of New York*, II, 502–649.

Revolution in Maryland.

Sparks, E. E., *Causes of the Revolution of 1689* (*Johns Hopkins Studies*, XIV, 477–578).

Sources for the colonial revolutions.

Andrews, C. M., *Narratives of the Insurrections*. *Andros Tracts*, 3 vols. (Prince Society, *Publications*).

CHAPTER X

FRENCH AND SPANISH RIVALS, 1608 TO 1713

THE imperial policies described in the last chapter were largely influenced by the desire of English leaders, at home and in the colonies, to organize the national forces more effectively for the impending struggle with France, now recognized as England's chief rival for primacy in North America. Spain also had to be considered; but her power was declining and for the present her American possessions touched those of the English only in the Caribbean islands and on the Carolina-Florida frontiers. England and France, on the contrary, were both rising powers and in North America their interests clashed all along the line from Hudson Bay to the lower Mississippi and the West Indies.

The problem of imperial defense.

The main base of French enterprise in North America was then in the St. Lawrence valley. This colony of New France began in 1608, when the explorer, Samuel de Champlain, under the patronage of Henry IV, laid the foundations of Quebec and made it the starting point of a notable series of westward ventures in exploration, trade, and missions. Two years later, Henry IV was assassinated and the internal troubles which followed discouraged great national undertakings on either side of the Atlantic. By 1624, however, another great figure came to the front. Cardinal Richelieu, the real ruler of France for the next eighteen years, was an active promoter of American colonization whether on the mainland or in the West Indies. He organized for New France a company called the "Hundred Associates," with commercial and political privileges not wholly unlike

Beginnings of New France.

those of the English Virginia Company. The development of the colony was interrupted in 1629 by a short war with England, during which Quebec was captured by an English fleet; but in 1632 the colony was given back to France and, under the skillful leadership of the veteran Champlain, was able to make a fresh start. A few farmers and fur traders settled in the neighborhood of Quebec, westward exploration was pushed as far as the western shore of Lake Michigan, and the Jesuits began their heroic service as missionaries among the Indians.

New France and Louis XIV.

The middle years of the century brought fresh difficulties and discouragements. With not more than five hundred fighting men, New France barely escaped destruction at the hands of the Iroquois, who disliked French competition in the western fur trade and were supplied with firearms by the Dutch settlers on the Hudson. Before long, however, a new period of prosperity set in. The young King, Louis XIV, began to gather about him a group of able men, under whose leadership France advanced rapidly to a predominant position among the European powers. A spirit of national expansion was awakened, which soon made itself felt across the Atlantic.

Colonial policy of Colbert.

Louis XIV was himself seriously interested in his American possessions, but during the early years of his reign the man who had most to do with French colonial policy was the finance minister, Jean Baptiste Colbert. Like his English contemporaries, Colbert desired a favorable balance of trade which would bring money into the kingdom and swell the revenues of the Crown. So he tried to organize French industry and commerce on a national basis, protecting them so far as possible against foreign competition. Manufactures were stimulated by tariff duties and government aid of other sorts. Great commercial companies were organized under royal patronage to exploit the slave trade in Africa, open up commerce with the East Indies, and develop the

American colonies. In the West Indies, the French islands
were brought into closer relations with the mother country;
with a steadily expanding population of negro slaves, they
were soon to become formidable competitors of the British
sugar planters in Jamaica and Barbados.

In these far-reaching plans for commercial and colonial
expansion, Canada was not forgotten. The old company of the
"Hundred Associates" had been weighed in the balance
and found wanting. After thirty years of effort, New France
had less than 2500 inhabitants. Agriculture had made little
progress and the colony even depended in part on the mother
country for its food supplies. Its only important business
was the fur trade and even this was precarious on account
of the hostility of the Iroquois. So the old company was
dissolved, and although another short-lived company was
organized, the King decided to keep the government of the
colony in his own hands. This government resembled that
of a province in France. At its head was the governor, usually a nobleman and sometimes a man of considerable
importance. The greatest colonial governor of this period
was Count Frontenac, a soldier with an excellent military
record who could adapt himself to the peculiar problems of
a frontier province. Such a governor could make the office
one of much greater importance than it was in the hands of
a provincial governor at home. Second in dignity, and sometimes superior in real power, was the intendant, usually not
a nobleman or a soldier but a civilian official of the middle
class, trained in the law. He was the head of the judicial
system, issued ordinances regulating the conduct of the
inhabitants, and was expected to serve as a check on the
governor. The highest authority in the province was vested
not in any one official but in the Superior Council, which
included, besides the intendant, who presided, the governor,
the bishop, and some other members appointed by the King.
A proposal to establish a representative assembly was con-

*Reorganiza-
tion of New
France.*

1663.

*Provincial
government.*

sidered and deliberately rejected.   As the English provinces
reflected in their governments the constitutional system of
the mother country, so New France reproduced the autocratic institutions of the age of Louis XIV.

Expansion

Under this paternalistic government, Canada made
substantial progress.   Immigration began on a larger
scale, though still insignificant when compared with the
growth of the English colonies.   By the close of Colbert's
administration, the population had increased to about 10,000,
four times the total for 1663.   Economic development was
also more encouraging.   The cultivated area was increased,
the fur trade expanded, and New France reached across
the Great Lakes to establish French sovereignty in the
Mississippi valley.

The
westward
movement.

The French statesmen who dreamed of their growing
empire in America were ably supported by their countrymen
in the colony.   One of the ablest of these colonial officials
was the intendant, Jean Talon, a hard-working administrator but also a man of imagination, under whose leadership
New France resumed its advance into the Great West.
In 1671, Talon's agent, St. Lusson, staged an imposing ceremony at Sault Ste. Marie, taking formal possession for France
of the whole region surrounding the Great Lakes.   For years
French missionaries and traders had been moving toward
the discovery of the upper Mississippi, and the work was
crowned in 1673, when the trader, Joliet, acting for the government at Quebec and accompanied by the Jesuit missionary Marquette, made his way from Green Bay by way of the
Fox and Wisconsin rivers to the Mississippi.   They followed
the great river as far as its junction with the Arkansas and
gave the world for the first time accurate knowledge about
the general course of the stream.

Frontenac
and La Salle.

Talon left New France before the great discovery was
accomplished, and for the next decade the chief inspiration
to western trade and exploration came from the new gov-

ernor, Count Frontenac, who served from 1672 to 1682.
A strenuous personality and a hard fighter, who made many
enemies among his associates in the government and in the
church, he was also a constant and aggressive defender of
French interests against the English and, when necessary,
their Indian allies, the Iroquois. Like Talon he appreciated
the importance of the West and did more than any other
single official to promote French interests in the Mississippi
valley. Inspired and supported by Frontenac, the great
adventurer, La Salle, began a series of explorations, cul-
minating in his voyage of 1682 down the Mississippi to the
Gulf, where, with another dramatic ceremony, he took
possession of the great valley in the name of his sovereign
Louis XIV.

Exploration was followed by occupation. Marquette
inaugurated a mission among the Illinois Indians and for
the next hundred years Catholic Christianity was brought to
the Indians and the incoming French settlers in the upper
Mississippi valley by a long series of missionaries, chiefly
of the Jesuit order. With the missionaries came the fur traders, some of them official agents like Joliet and La Salle;
others were trading without license from the authorities and in
defiance of official rules. La Salle did not despise the profits
of the fur trade, but his imagination was stirred by the vision
of a new empire which should redound to the glory of the
French King and nation. About his famous Fort St. Louis,
at Starved Rock on the Illinois River, he proposed to gather
the friendly Indians as a bulwark against the Iroquois and
the intrusion of English interests, already making themselves felt in the Indian trade between the Alleghenies and
the Mississippi. His last journey, from which he never returned, was an unsuccessful effort to establish a military post
on the Gulf to hold the lower gateway of the great valley.
A few years later, La Salle's work was carried forward by
the Canadian adventurer, Le Moyne d'Iberville, who in 1699

*French
occupation
of the
Mississippi
valley.*

established at Biloxi the first French settlement on the Gulf of Mexico.

The missionary and the trader.

The missionary and the trader each rendered important service in opening up the West, but they did not always see eye to eye. The Jesuits would have liked to keep the Indian converts free from the contaminating influence of the lawless elements among the traders, and especially denounced the brandy trade. Both sides had friends in Quebec and at the King's court, where the question was argued back and forth. The evils of drunkenness were acknowledged; but the traders declared that if the Indians could not get their brandy from the French, they would simply go to the English heretics for rum and be still worse off from a religious point of view. The result was a vacillating policy, and a large amount of illegal and demoralizing trade.

French expansion, north, south, and east.

French colonial expansion was not limited to the West. The growth of the sugar islands has already been mentioned; they were not only important commercially but also convenient bases for naval and privateering expeditions. In the remote wilderness about Hudson Bay, adventurous French traders were competing with equally adventurous English rivals in the employ of the Hudson's Bay Company. There were new settlements on the Newfoundland coasts, which had long been a resort of French fishermen. About Port Royal in Acadia the little colony of fishermen and farmers took on a more permanent character.

Strength and weakness of French colonial policy.

In all these enterprises, the French showed not only energy and courage, but keen appreciation of strategic positions. The territory which they could fairly claim by occupation was immense, perhaps greater than could reasonably be claimed for the English on the same basis. Measured, however, in terms of solid colonization, the comparison works out quite differently. When Andros became governor of the Greater New England in 1687, he was probably responsible for about ten times as many white people as were to be found in the whole of New France. This was partly, no doubt, because the average Frenchman preferred to stay in France, while the French Protestant dissenters who suffered persecution at home were not, like the English, allowed to take refuge in the colonies. So far as the Huguenots came to America at all, they were forced to settle under a foreign flag. The French were certainly less fortunate, also, in having their principal base so far north, in a region less adapted for agriculture than the more temperate areas occupied by the English. Taking the period of Louis XIV as a whole, the French colonists could hardly complain of neglect by the home government. Certainly, during his reign in France, no one of the four sovereigns who ruled England gave as much time and thought to colonial business as the "Grand Monarch," and it would be hard to name any one English statesman of the time who was the equal in this respect of Colbert. This paternal supervision secured to the colonists a moderately efficient government, but it failed to develop self-reliant communities like those which grew up under the comparatively easy-going policy of the English government.

In the life of New France, the church had an important influence. The bishop sat in the provincial council and took an active part in public business, sometimes in coöperation with the civil authorities, sometimes, as in the case of the brandy trade, in outspoken opposition. Under his direction were the parish clergy, a faithful, hard-working body of men who had great influence over their peasant flocks. Besides these "secular clergy," there were several religious orders, both of men and women, among whom the Jesuits were the most conspicuous. The very limited amount of education available in the province was furnished mainly by the members of these orders. The church was supported partly by tithes from the inhabitants, partly by grants of land, and partly by royal grants.

Influence of the church.

The economic and social organization of New France was based on the modified feudalism of the old country, now modified still further to meet the conditions of American life. The unit in this system was the *seigneurie*, corresponding roughly to the English manor and varying from a few thousand acres to 75 square miles. The lord, or *seigneur*, of this estate held his title from the King on condition of rendering fealty to the King's representative at Quebec. He was to give military service when required, but above all to see that his land was occupied by settlers and made productive. During the administration of Talon, officers and men from one of the King's famous regiments received lands extending southward from the St. Lawrence, along the Richelieu River. Here they formed a kind of military colony, somewhat after the old Roman fashion, which in time of war furnished effective leaders for Indian raids against the English settlements. The peasants, or *habitants*, received their holdings from the *seigneur* on condition of certain annual payments and a few customary services, which were not as a rule very burdensome. Some *seigneurs* had courts of their own; but not all of them cared to exercise this privilege, and in any case there was the right of appeal to the government at Quebec. Under the paternal supervision of the King's government, generally used to protect the *habitants* in their customary rights, Canadian feudalism seems on the whole to have worked fairly well. Perhaps the most serious obstacle to the development of a thoroughly prosperous agriculture was the superior fascination of the fur trade, which drew some of the most vigorous young men away from the hard work of the farm to the adventurous life of the forest.

For three quarters of a century French and English colonies developed with surprisingly little friction, partly because they were separated by great stretches of wilderness within which each nationality could develop its own sphere of

influence. Gradually, however, the intervening spaces began to narrow down and the more enterprising representatives of the rival nations began to find traces of each other
in the debatable "No man's land." French and English
rivalry turned not so much on territory, for both sides had
room to grow in without crowding each other, but primarily
on the rich profits of the fur trade. The advance of white
settlements naturally pushed this trade farther and farther
back into the wilderness. Every year a great fur flotilla,
marshaled by the French *coureurs de bois*, made its way
from the Lake region to Montreal. English contact with the
Indians of the Northwest was comparatively slight at this
time; their part of this trade was carried on largely through
the Iroquois, whose fighting spirit made them a power throughout the West. Notwithstanding the enterprise of the French
traders, they could not usually offer quite such good bargains as the English. In connection with the fur trade of
this central region, it is important to keep in mind the competition farther north in the basin of Hudson Bay, and also
in the South. In the latter region, bounded by the Appalachians, the Ohio, the Mississippi, and the Gulf of Mexico,
the Indians were coming in contact with traders from all
three of the great Western nations — Frenchmen from the
St. Lawrence and the Mississippi, Spaniards from Florida,
and Englishmen, chiefly from Virginia and the Carolinas.
Back of the frontier traders stood the merchants of the
seaboard colonies, and behind the colonial merchants were
the promoters and investors of the Old World.

International significance of the fur trade.

In the decade preceding the Revolution of 1688, both
sides were making strenuous efforts to strengthen their positions. The French tried to win over the Iroquois through
their missionaries and to overawe them by military expeditions. Frontenac did something during his first governorship to improve French prestige, but his successors were
less successful, and on the whole the English more than held

Preparing for war.

their ground.   In 1684, Governor Dongan persuaded the Iroquois to set up the English arms in their villages and all the efforts of the French failed to win over more than a small minority in the confederacy.   In the summer of 1689, the Iroquois invaded French territory and massacred the settlers of La Chine, within a few miles of Montreal.

Influence of European politics.

The condition of European politics had so far tended to postpone a decisive conflict between France and England in the New World.   There were some clashes during the earlier part of the seventeenth century, as when Captain Argall of the Virginia Company broke up the French Jesuit colony on the Maine coast and later attacked the French settlement at Port Royal.   There was another breach of the peace in 1629, when for a short time the English held Quebec.   For the most part, however, the rulers of England from the accession of Charles I to the expulsion of James II, including Cromwell himself, were inclined to cultivate friendly relations with France, and the last two Stuart kings accepted pensions from Louis XIV.   This does not mean that Charles II and James II were wholly forgetful of English interests;   they refused to acknowledge the justice of the French claims in America and supported Dongan in his controversy with the governors of New France. Nevertheless, the close relations between the two royal families did help for a time to keep the peace in America. By 1689 the international situation had radically changed. Already the growing fear of French predominance in Europe and English anxiety about French conquests in the Netherlands, had been shown by the short-lived Triple Alliance of 1668, in which England combined with the Swedes and the Dutch to protect the Spanish Netherlands against Louis XIV.   Now in 1689 this rising jealousy of France was given free play.   The new King of England, William III, was already the ruler of Holland and the organizer of a great coalition which was trying to defend the balance of power against

France. War became inevitable when Louis XIV defied the English people by trying to put James II back on the throne.

What with revolutions on both sides of the water and the outbreak of war with France, the summer and autumn of 1689 were a troubled time for the English colonies. Rumors flew thick and fast — dangers of attack on the fishing fleets or on the seaboard towns by privateers, and wild talk about English or Irish Catholics combining with the French and Indians against their Protestant neighbors. The temporary disorganization of several colonial governments aggravated the general confusion and panic. The mother country was asked for help, but English control of the sea was by no means secure and during the next eight years the home government was chiefly occupied with the European conflict. For two years there was a hard fight between James and William for the control of Ireland, ending in William's triumph. Then there was a series of campaigns, on a large scale for those days, in the Netherlands and on the Rhine frontier. Most important of all, perhaps, was the struggle of the French and English fleets for the command of European waters. Problems like these required most of the attention of William and his ministers, and nearly all the money and the fighting men that the nation was willing to furnish. So the colonial "King William's War" seemed to contemporaries a mere incident of the greater European conflict.

The British did not altogether neglect the protection of their interests in America. The merchant fleets, which carried home the great colonial staples — sugar, tobacco, and furs — taking back English goods in exchange, were guarded by convoys of warships. Special naval protection was also given in the West Indies. Land operations in America were mainly left to the colonists, though a few regulars were kept at New York and some munitions were sent out in response to appeals from the colonies. Louis XIV also

War between England and France. King William's War.

The conflict in America.

was pressed too hard in Europe to send much help to his American subjects. He did, however, give them a really effective leader — something that the English colonists did not have at any time during the war.   In the late summer of

Count Frontenac.

1689, the inhabitants of Quebec welcomed back with enthusiasm their old governor, Count Frontenac, called home a few years before because of quarrels with his associates but now seen to be the right man for a difficult, almost desperate, situation. On the English side, there was overwhelming superiority in numbers but a much looser political organization, with a dozen different governments each absorbed in its own special interests and often painfully indifferent to the needs of its neighbors. Of the English governors, Benjamin Fletcher of New York was perhaps as efficient as any, though in other respects he had a bad name. Peter Schuyler, the Dutch trader at Albany, also deserves to be remembered for his work in keeping the Iroquois in line for the English. Neither of these men, however, can be compared with Frontenac.

Frontenac's policy.

With all his ability and his command of the situation, Frontenac's resources were too meager for any ambitious military plans; there was talk of large enterprises like the capture of Boston and New York, but nothing came of them. In the main, what the French did was to defend themselves against English attacks and try to overawe the enemy by border raids. Frontenac was also successful in restoring some of the prestige among the Indians which the French had lost under the last two governors. For his policy of border warfare, he had instruments ready to hand among the Indian allies; and the Canadian *seigneurs* furnished daring and ruthless leaders.   In 1689 and 1690, New England was appalled by destructive raids on the borders of New Hampshire and Maine. The most terrible affair of the latter year was the massacre of the Dutch and English settlers at Schenectady, a few miles west of

Albany, on the Mohawk River. Meantime New England fisheries and commerce suffered considerably from French privateers.

By the spring of 1690, the English colonists were thoroughly aroused and ready to retaliate. In May a new fleet under the command of Sir William Phips, a Maine sea captain, easily captured Port Royal in Acadia and converted that territory temporarily into an English province. Flushed by this success, the New Englanders and New Yorkers worked out an ambitious scheme for the conquest of Quebec. A land force was to move northward from Albany while a fleet under the command of Phips sailed up the St. Lawrence. The land force did not get beyond Lake Champlain. Phips's fleet reached Quebec; but its amateur commander was no match for a veteran like Frontenac, and after some futile cannonading sailed away without accomplishing anything. The next year the French recovered Acadia and so the New Englanders had nothing to show for two expensive operations. Then followed six years of petty warfare, in which the French were on the whole more effective. In 1696, an expedition under the personal command of Frontenac attacked the Iroquois country and did enough damage to strengthen French prestige in the West. Neither side, however, could claim a decisive victory, whether in Europe or America. So the peace of Ryswick, in 1697, closed the war with vital issues still unsettled.

Hostilities in America, 1690–1697.

On both sides of the water, international issues were complicated by the problem of the Spanish succession. The feeble King of Spain was childless, and the two leading claimants to the throne were a French Bourbon and an Austrian Hapsburg, representing the two great continental powers. Neither rival government was willing to let the other carry off the prize, which included among other things the trade and empire of Spanish America. Various plans of partition were discussed and finally one was apparently agreed

The Spanish succession.

upon between Louis XIV and William III; but the Spaniards objected to this division of their empire, and when their King died his whole inheritance was left to Philip of Anjou, a grandson of Louis XIV. Louis could not resist this temptation; the young French prince now became King Philip V of Spain.

The War of the Spanish Succession

To statesmen like William III, who had been working hard to preserve the balance of power, this new bond between the reigning houses of France and Spain seemed a great calamity; but he could not prevent it. Neither the Dutch nor the English nation was much interested in a family quarrel between Hapsburgs and Bourbons; even the balance of power argument did not make much impression at first. Before long, however, it was clear that something more than mere dynastic rivalry was involved. French soldiers appeared in the border provinces of the Spanish Netherlands, and in 1701, when James II died, Louis XIV once more challenged the independent spirit of the English nation by recognizing the Stuart pretender (the son of James II) as King of England. Finally, the English merchants began to see a danger for their own commerce in certain new regulations adopted by the Spanish government under French influence. So by the end of 1701 public opinion in England and Holland turned toward war with France. William III did not live to see the actual outbreak of hostilities, but one of the first acts of his successor, Queen Anne, was the formal declaration which opened the War of the Spanish Succession, commonly known on the American side as Queen Anne's War.

American issues. 1697–1701.

In America also a good deal had happened since the treaty of Ryswick. Both the French and the English were reaching out to control the mouth of the Mississippi. In August, 1699, a British vessel sent out by Daniel Coxe, a famous promoter, entered the river, but it was too late. A few months earlier the French commander, Iberville, had established

his fort at Biloxi and so begun the new colony of Louisiana.
Yet even now the French did not have a clear field; for
Virginia and Carolina traders were active in the Tennessee valley. In the North also the French gained some advantages.
Notwithstanding the English claim to a protectorate over
the Five Nations of Iroquois, those Indians were induced in
1701 to make a separate treaty with the Quebec government.
In the same year, the settlement of Detroit by Cadillac
strengthened still further French influence in the Lake
region.

The outcome of Queen Anne's War was determined
largely by events in Europe. During the first half of the
war, England and her allies had the best of it. Under their
great generals, the Duke of Marlborough and Prince Eugene,
they gave Louis XIV the severest check he had yet received.
On the American side during the same period results were
quite indecisive. For the first time, the English colonies
had to face a combination of the two Latin powers, France
and Spain, which had hitherto been about as jealous of
each other as each had been of the English. The British
West Indies now had to be guarded not only against the
French in Guadeloupe and Martinique but also against the
Spaniards of Cuba, Santo Domingo, and Porto Rico. Even
Charleston, on the southern frontier of the continental
colonies, was exposed to naval attacks from the same quarter.
In general this war, like that of King William, was made up
of petty operations, though the total amount of damage
done was considerable, especially in New England. Once
more there were border raids against the lonely settlements
of Maine, New Hampshire, and western Massachusetts,
with now and then some daring stroke within a few
miles of Boston. An awkward feature of the situation was
the quasi-neutral attitude of the New Yorkers. In order
to keep the Five Nations out of the war, the French were
willing to refrain from attacking New York, and the in-

Early phases of the war in Europe and America.

habitants of that province were ready to promote their trade interests by keeping aloof from their hard-pressed neighbors in New England. Meantime French privateers from Port Royal and the West Indies made commerce unsafe all along the seaboard, convoys were again provided by the British navy, and merchant ships had to go armed. British men-of-war and privateers were, of course, also active in commerce-destroying.

The frontiers of New England and Carolina. There were two New England expeditions against Acadia; but, as in the previous war, they lacked expert leadership and were unsuccessful. On the southern border, results were equally indecisive. South Carolina, separated from her nearest English neighbor by an almost impassable wilderness, suffered as New England had done from Indian raids, often led by white officers. There was a Spanish-Indian invasion of South Carolina in 1702, and English invasions of Florida both in that year and in the winter of 1703–1704. Considerable damage was done in each case, particularly when the English in their expeditions of 1702 ravaged the settlement of St. Augustine. Neither side was able, however, to hold any of the enemy's territory. The most striking incident of the war in the South occurred in 1706, when the South Carolinians under the lead of their energetic governor, Sir Nathaniel Johnson, repulsed a formidable attack by the French and Spanish fleets.

Up to 1709, the English colonies had little to show for their military efforts and the home government had not taken a very active part in the American campaigns. In that year, however, the British authorities, partly at the suggestion of Samuel Vetch, a Scotch merchant of Boston, planned an expedition against Quebec and Montreal. A British fleet and some regular troops were to work with militia from the northern colonies. The plan aroused much enthusiasm. Though Quaker influence in Pennsylvania and New Jersey caused some difficulty, even the New York-

ers, hitherto somewhat lukewarm, agreed to coöperate and
to use their influence with the Iroquois. At the last moment,
however, the home government decided that it could not spare
the necessary forces from the European campaigns and so
the plan fell through. Next year, however, New England
found some consolation in the conquest of Acadia by their   The conquest
own militia, supported by British men-of-war and a few   of Acadia.
marines, and in 1711 the new Tory ministry in England,
though trying to make peace in Europe, showed real interest
in a possible conquest of Canada. They took up the old plan
of a combined sea-and-land campaign and a strong fleet
actually sailed up the St. Lawrence. The prospects of success were good even after the loss of some transports in   Failure
the river; but the British commanders were discouraged,   on the St.
and turned back without reaching Quebec, much to the dis-   Lawrence.
gust of the New Englanders.

Meantime events in Europe were moving toward a com-   A compro-
promise peace. The allies were the stronger, and France   mise peace.
was feeling the strain of the long war; but the prevailing
sentiment both in France and Spain was against accepting
the extreme terms demanded by the allies. The Spaniards
in particular were showing a good deal of national feeling
in favor of the Bourbon Philip as against an Austrian prince
imposed upon them by foreign troops. The English Tories
were also anxious to bring the "Whig War" to a close.
So in 1713 Great Britain and France accepted the treaty of
Utrecht.

Though the English demands were not fully met, the   The treaty of
treaty is an important landmark in the expansion of Eng-   Utrecht.
land's commercial and colonial empire. The acquisition of
Gibraltar materially strengthened British sea power in the
Mediterranean. British merchants received new commercial privileges in Spanish America, including a monopoly
in the business of supplying negro slaves. In the West
Indies, the French lost their part of the little island of

St. Christopher, but the more important islands were
saved. In North America, the Anglo-Spanish frontier remained unchanged, but elsewhere the British gains were very
great. The English fur-trading interest gained a great victory by the abandonment of the French posts in the Hudson Bay region. A corresponding advantage was gained for
the fisheries of New England and the mother country when
Newfoundland was definitely recognized as a British possession, though certain rights were reserved to French fishermen. Acadia now became the British province of Nova
Scotia, though most of the inhabitants continued to be French
at heart and embarrassed their new governors by keeping up
relations with their Canadian neighbors. Of special importance for the westward movement was the clause in the
treaty by which France recognized the British protectorate
over the Iroquois.

*Primacy
in North
America
unsettled.*

Notwithstanding these solid gains, the fundamental issue
of primacy in North America remained unsettled. The
conquest of Canada, which seemed almost within reach in
1711, was postponed for half a century and the struggle for
the Great West was still in its early stages.

BIBLIOGRAPHICAL NOTES

*General
references.*

Bolton and Marshall, *North America*, chs. IV, XIII, XIV.
Channing, *United States*, I, 100–110; II, 131–154, 527–533.
Thwaites, R. G., *France in America*, 1–80, with Greene, E. B.,
Provincial America, chs. VII–X. Winsor, *America*, III, chs.
III–VII; V, 1–6, 13–25. Wissler, C., *et al.*, *Adventures in the
Wilderness*, ch. XVII.

New France.

Wrong, G. M., *Rise and Fall of New France*, 2 vols. Munro,
W. B., *Crusaders of New France*, chs. III–XI. Lucas, C. P.,
Historical Geography of the British Colonies. Canada, I, chs. II–V.
Colby, C. W., *Canadian Types of the Old Régime*. Selections from
Francis Parkman's series on *France and England in America* in
Edgar, P., *Struggle for a Continent*, 88–286. *Chronicles of Canada*,
especially volumes by Colby, *Founding of New France* and *The*

Fighting Governor; Munro, *Seigneurs of Old Canada;* T. Chapais, *The Great Intendant* (Jean Talon). Lives of Champlain by Dionne, and Frontenac by Le Sueur, in *Makers of Canada* series.

Parkman, *La Salle.* Heawood, E., *Geographical Discovery in the Seventeenth and Eighteenth Centuries,* ch. IV. Alvord, C. W., *Centennial History of Illinois,* chs. III–VII. Thwaites, R. G., *Marquette.* Winsor, J., *Cartier to Frontenac.* — The West.

Grant, W. L., *Voyages of Champlain (Original Narratives series).* Kellogg, L. P., *Early Narratives of the Northwest.* Hart, *Contemporaries,* I, nos. 39–43. Thwaites, editor, *Jesuit Relations.* — Readable sources.

Cambridge Modern History, V, chs. I, II. Lavisse, *Histoire de France,* VII, bk. II and bk. III, ch. III; VIII, bks. I, II. Mims, S. L., *Colbert's West Indian Policy.* — The age of Louis XIV and French colonial policy.

Andrews, C. M., "Anglo-French Commercial Rivalry, 1700–1750," *A.H.R.,* XX, 539–556, 761–780. *Cambridge Modern History,* V, chs. XIII, XIV. Mahan, A. T., *Influence of Sea Power on History, 1660–1783,* chs. IV, V. Seeley, J. R., *Expansion of England,* Lecture VII. — World politics and war, 1689–1713.

Parkman, *Frontenac and New France.* Wrong, G. M., *Conquest of New France,* chs. I–III. Drake, S. A., *Border Wars of New England.* McCrady, E., *South Carolina, 1670–1719,* chs. XVI–XVII (Anglo-Spanish War). Crane, V., *Southern Frontier.* Lauber, A. W., *Indian Slavery in Colonial Times.* McIlwain, C. H., *Wraxall's Abridgment,* pp. liii–lxv (New York frontier). Morgan, W. T., "The Five Nations and Queen Anne," *M.V.H.R.,* XIII, 169–190. Sources in Lincoln, C. H., *Narratives of the Indian Wars,* and Colden, C., *Five Indian Nations (Trailmaker Series).* Hart, *Contemporaries,* II, ch. XIX. — Border warfare in America.

Brebner, J. B., *New England's Outpost: Acadia before the Conquest of Canada.* Barnes, V. F., "Rise of William Phips," *N.E.Q.* (1928), I, 271–294, 532–553. — New England's outpost.

Channing, *United States,* II, 153–154. Macdonald, *Select Charters,* nos. 45, 47. — The treaties.

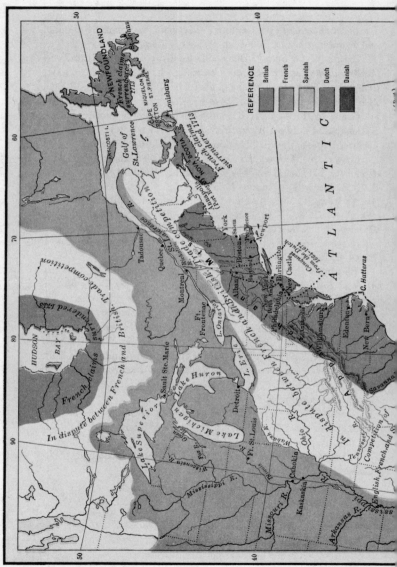

REFERENCE

British
French
Spanish
Dutch
Danish

NEWFOUNDLAND
French claims surrendered 1713
Fortune

ANTICOSTI I.
Gulf of St.Lawrence
MIQUELON
ST.PIERRE
CAPE BRETON
Louisburg

French claims surrendered 1713
NOVA SCOTIA
Port Royal (Annapolis)

Trade competition
In dispute between French and British
French claims
Surrendered 1713

HUDSON BAY

Tadousac
Quebec
Montreal
Lake Superior
Sault Ste.Marie
Detroit
Lake Huron
Lake Michigan
Ft. St.Louis
Wisconsin R.
Fox R.
Green Bay
Chicago
Kaskaskia
Cahokia
Missouri R.
Mississippi R.
Arkansas R.
Wabash R.
Ohio
Tennessee R.

Fox R.
Ft. Frontenac
L. Ontario
L. Erie

York
Salem
Boston
Providence
Newport
Albany
Hartford
New York
Perth Amboy
Philadelphia
Burlington
New Castle
Annapolis
Williamsburg
Edenton
New Bern
C. Hatteras
Savannah

Conquered by Dutch from the English 1667

A T L A N T I C

In dispute between English, French and Spanish

ATLANTIC

Following 224

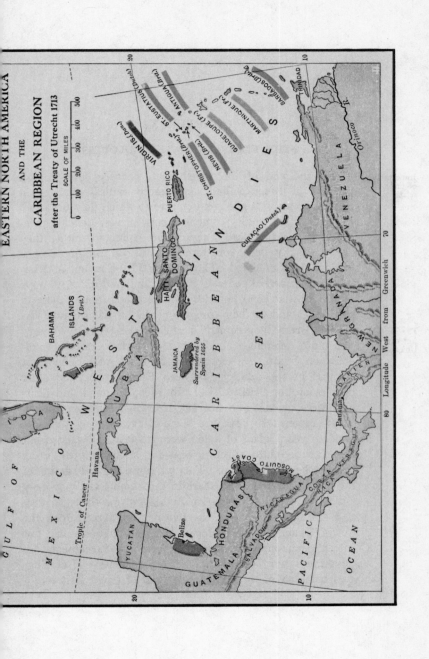

EASTERN NORTH AMERICA
AND THE
CARIBBEAN REGION
after the Treaty of Utrecht 1713

SCALE OF MILES

0   100   200   300   400   500

GULF OF MEXICO

Tropic of Cancer

Havana

CUBA

WEST

BAHAMA

ISLANDS
(Brit.)

JAMAICA

Surrendered by
Spain 1655

HAITI

SANTO
DOMINGO

PUERTO RICO

VIRGIN ISL (Dan.)

ST. EUSTATIUS (Dutch)

ANTIGUA (Brit.)

ST. CHRISTOPHER (Brit.)

NEVIS (Brit.)

GUADELOUPE (Fr.)

MARTINIQUE (Fr.)

INDIES

CURAÇAO (Dutch)

CARIBBEAN SEA

BARBADOS (Brit.)

TRINIDAD

VENEZUELA

Orinoco R.

NEW GRANADA

DARIEN

Panama

COSTA RICA VERAGUA

NICARAGUA

MOSQUITO COAST

HONDURAS

SALVADOR

GUATEMALA

Belize

YUCATAN

PACIFIC

OCEAN

Longitude   West   from   Greenwich

20

10

80

70

20

10

90

CHAPTER XI

THE EMPIRE AND THE COLONIES

Importance of imperial relations.

By the end of the seventeenth century, the English colonies in America had experienced radical changes in their relations with the great empire to which they belonged. Beginning as trading-company settlements, feudal principalities, or practically republican commonwealths, they had gradually been transformed into real provinces of a world-wide dominion. They were still self-reliant and impatient of external control; but in a hundred different ways their lives were conditioned by the ties which bound them to each other and to their common center in the British Isles.

The British Act of Union, 1707.

The British government of the early eighteenth century was quite different from what it was when American colonization began. There were, to begin with, important changes in the relations between England and the other peoples of the British Isles. In 1606, England and Scotland were distinct and not very friendly kingdoms, though they happened to have the same King. During the next hundred years, plans of union were frequently discussed but never carried into effect, except for a short time during Cromwell's protectorate. Finally, however, the desire of the Scotch merchants to share in the commercial monopoly established by the Navigation Acts overcame their jealousy of the English. In 1707 the two nations agreed upon the Act of Union, and thenceforth the two kingdoms had not only a common King but also a common Parliament. So the American provinces became dependencies not of England only but of the United Kingdom of Great Britain.

Meantime Ireland remained, as before, a dependent principality, and the constitutional changes in England which increased the power of Parliament only emphasized the subjection of Irish to English interests. The Irish parliament was closely checked by the English government, which in turn was responsible only to the Parliament of England, in which Irishmen were not represented. After 1707, there was the same control by the British Parliament, in which Ireland was still unrepresented. Though the overwhelming majority of the Irish were Catholics, the Anglican Church was established by law and the unsuccessful stand of the Catholic Irish for James II against William and Mary made their position harder than ever. The Protestant Irish of the North were better off, but they also had their trials. As dissenters from the established church, they were subject to various disabilities and the development of their manufactures was jealously watched by the English mercantile interest, through whose influence Parliament passed in 1699 a bill prohibiting the export of Irish woolens. The colonies profited by this illiberal policy through the great Scotch-Irish immigration of the eighteenth century, but England paid the penalty in the loss of a sturdy population and in the anti-English feeling of the emigrants and their descendants.

Ireland.

The Scotch-Irish.

Of primary importance for the Americans of the provincial era were the changes which took place in the government of England itself. The Revolution of 1688 disposed of the King's claim to a prerogative above the law; but it did not establish the exact relation between the legislative power of Parliament and the executive power of the Crown. William III was no figurehead; though he took advice from his ministers and chose them partly because of their influence in Parliament, he made personally many important decisions, including some relating to colonial business. His conception of the kingship was that of a reai ruler, not altogether unlike the

Constitutional changes in England.

American President. So long as he lived, William was fairly successful in carrying out his theory. With his successors, it was quite different. Under Queen Anne, and still more under the first two German Kings, George I and George II, whose ignorance of the English language and English politics made them quite dependent on their advisers, the ministers came more and more to the front while the personal opinions of the King grew less important. The Georges held the throne by act of Parliament, and if they wished to keep it they had to act in accordance with public opinion. Thus the ministry became practically an executive committee of the House of Commons, or rather of the majority party in that house, responsible to it both in shaping legislation and in the decision of executive policies.

Parliamentary government.

Parliamentary government did not mean democracy. Though the House of Lords had lost some of its power, the landed aristocracy was able through its family connections, its wealth, and its social prestige to keep a strong hold on the House of Commons, many of whose members were, in spite of the forms of popular election, practically chosen by influential noblemen. Even when there were real elections, only a small fraction of the population could vote, and bribery was general. To make matters worse, the successful candidates were frequently tied up with the ministry which happened to be in power, by means of sinecure offices and pensions. The men who shaped national policy spoke, therefore, not for the whole people but for a comparatively small group made up of the landed aristocracy and, to an increasing extent, of the great mercantile interests. Among the latter were some absentee landlords with large estates in the sugar islands of the West Indies, a fact which sometimes proved inconvenient for the continental colonists.

Unrepresentative character of Parliament.

The highest executive authority for both Great Britain and the colonies was the Privy Council, or the "King in

The Privy Council; the cabinet.

Council." The final action or "order in council" was usually a formal matter, the real decisions being made by committees and more and more by the little group of ministers known as the cabinet, who were also the leaders of the House of Commons. During this period the unity of the cabinet was strengthened by the recognition of its leader as the prime minister. The most important holder of this position during the first half of the eighteenth century was Sir Robert Walpole, who by sheer ability, as well as by parliamentary corruption, was for twenty years the real head of the government. While larger questions of policy were determined by the cabinet, actual administration was left to various executive departments managed by single heads or by administrative boards, such as the Treasury Board, the Commissioners of Customs, and the Board of Admiralty, which had charge of the royal navy. There had been some improvements in business methods, but the organization was still loose and wasteful. In few departments was there any effective concentration of responsibility, and offices dealing with closely related or overlapping subjects were often located at inconvenient distances from each other. These conditions led to long delays and confusion of authority, which were especially serious in colonial administration.

Of the great ministers, those most closely concerned with the colonies were the "principal secretaries of state," of whom there were in this period sometimes two and sometimes three. At first there was no clear distribution of authority among these secretaries, who dealt with a great variety of matters, domestic, foreign, and colonial, including the absorbing problems of "practical" party politics. The situation was somewhat improved later by dividing the secretaryships between the "Northern" and "Southern" departments, and the secretary of state for the Southern department was made specifically responsible, among other

The "principal secretaries of state."

things, for colonial affairs. The chief holder of this office in the second quarter of the eighteenth century was the Duke of Newcastle, an influential figure in party politics. About the best that can be said of him as a colonial administrator is that as a rule he avoided disturbing questions; his inefficiency and ignorance may have been exaggerated, but they were bad enough at best.

The Board of Trade.

Not until the eve of the American Revolution was there a real colonial secretary with a real colonial office. The nearest approach to such an office was that of the Lords Commissioners for Trade and Plantations, better known as the Board of Trade. This board, organized in 1696, took the place of the former Privy Council Committee on Trade and Plantations. It included, first, as *ex-officio* members, certain ministers, of whom the most important for this purpose were the secretaries of state; and, secondly, a small group of salaried members. These latter were expected to furnish expert service and actually did most of the business, though one or more of the *ex-officio* members commonly attended the meetings. The Board of Trade was, as its name suggests, primarily concerned with the promotion of commerce. The supervision of colonial government was only one of several duties imposed upon it; this function being considered important not so much as an end in itself, but because of its relation to the protection and expansion of trade. Accordingly, the board was expected to study the resources and industries of the colonies, encouraging those which were thought useful to the mother country and discouraging those which competed, or threatened to compete, with British trade and manufactures. Keeping these objects always in view, the board drafted commissions and instructions for the royal governors and corresponded with them after their appointment; it examined colonial laws and recommended approval or rejection; it also inquired into the administration of justice.

The usefulness and influence of the Board of Trade varied greatly at different times. In the early years, there were a few members who were as nearly expert in colonial business as could be expected of men who had never been in America. One of them was John Locke, the political scientist and philosopher, whose connection with American affairs began more than twenty-five years before his appointment to the board. Another was William Blathwayt, for many years secretary to the old Committee on Trade and Plantations. Membership changed with the exigencies of party politics, and in the second quarter of the eighteenth century men of inferior or mediocre ability were generally appointed. A certain continuity in routine business and in more important matters was kept up by the permanent secretary of the board. In the first sixty years after the board was organized there were only three changes in this important office; the first appointee was succeeded in turn by his son and grandson, and the last of these four secretaries managed to hold his position for over twenty years. Of the presidents of the board before 1760, only one deserves an important place in American colonial history; this was George Dunk, Earl of Halifax, whose administration, beginning in 1748, was marked by a serious and partly successful effort to improve the management of colonial business.

As a "colonial office" the board was never satisfactory, largely because it had little real authority. It could recommend policies but could not always secure their adoption, and even when measures were approved by the government no effective means were provided for their execution. The board did not control the appointment or removal of colonial governors and often was not even consulted. Secretaries of state instead of helping to secure colonial officials who would coöperate efficiently with the board often preferred to use such offices to reward personal or partisan services. Important branches of colonial business were handled by

Membership of the Board.

John Locke.

Lord Halifax.

Defects of the system.

entirely independent boards. The Admiralty was responsible for the naval defense of the colonies and of their commerce; decisions on questions of trade and revenue were made by the Commissioners of Customs and the Treasury Board. These boards often worked harmoniously enough, but bad organization caused delay and there was always danger of friction. It must be remembered also that the Board of Trade could not give itself up to colonial business. Much of its time was taken up with such topics as the improvement of British manufactures, the expansion of European trade, and the problems of poor relief.

The English judicial system.
The development of the English judicial system during this period had a certain influence on American history. The independence of the courts was one of the great issues fought out in the seventeenth century, and the Act of Settlement (1701) protected the judges from interference by establishing the principle of service during good behavior rather than during the King's pleasure. The colonists believed that colonial judges should be similarly independent and were much aggrieved when the home government refused to make them so. The judicial authority exercised by the Privy Council in the Tudor and early Stuart periods was for the most part swept away, but a part of it survived, including the right to pass on appeals from colonial courts, the real decision being left to a committee. In one respect, the English courts had perhaps lost ground during the seventeenth century. Whatever right they might have had in earlier times to set aside acts of Parliament as unconstitutional was now clearly eliminated. The whole idea of a fundamental law binding even upon Parliament passed out of English jurisprudence. In the colonies, on the contrary, it gained ground and became one of the characteristic features of American political philosophy.

No part of the governmental machinery just described was constructed primarily for colonial business. It was first and foremost the government of England, and (after 1707) of Great Britain. Incidentally, however, not to say accidentally, it had to serve the purposes of government for an expanding empire overseas. Of this overseas empire, the American continental colonies were only a part and a far less important part than present-day Americans can easily realize. For a century England had been developing her commerce in Asia, chiefly through the great East India Company, whose original charter was granted by Queen Elizabeth a few years before the founding of Virginia. This company had not as yet much territory; but it had many trading posts in India and monopoly rights in the China trade, and in the direction of these distant activities the company exercised many of the rights of a sovereign government. Far away as these interests were from America, they have their place in American history. It was partly the desire of the British government to promote the trade of the East India Company which brought on the Boston Tea Party of 1773. More closely related to America were the trading stations of the African coast, where slaves were bought from native traders and shipped to America for the use of Spanish or English planters. In this trade, the Royal African Company took the lead for many years, though the larger part of the business finally went to independent traders, including some Americans. Here and there along the African coast were British forts for the protection of trade, though there was no serious attempt to hold territory. *Overseas interests outside of America.*

The constitutional relations of the American colonies to the home government were as varied as their climates and their economic resources. Even to-day, it can hardly be said that the British Empire has anything that can properly be called a constitution; certainly no really imperial constitution had been worked out in the colonial period of American history. From some points of view, the colonies were a part of the British realm; in other respects they were *Lack of an imperial constitution.*

mere appendages of it. According to the charters and the opinions of the highest legal authorities, the rights of the colonists, except perhaps in conquered territory, were protected by the common law and statutes declaratory of the common law which had been enacted when the colonies were founded, so far as these were applicable to colonial conditions. Later statutes did not take effect overseas unless the colonies were specifically mentioned.

English and American points of view.

Englishmen and Americans differed widely about the relation between Parliament and the colonial legislatures. English lawyers generally regarded the American assemblies as municipal corporations and their legislation as nothing more than municipal by-laws which Parliament could set aside as it saw fit. This theory may have been technically correct but it was almost certain in the end to provoke a conflict with the universal desire of the colonists for the largest possible measure of self-government. Most American politicians regarded the colonial assembly as a miniature parliament, having within its own sphere an authority similar to that of the Parliament at Westminster. For the present, however, these questions were not brought to a sharp issue, though the authority of Parliament was at times exercised to a far-reaching extent and in ways which the colonists found more or less inconvenient.

Colonial legislation of Parliament.

Nearly everybody recognized the necessity of some one authority to regulate the commercial relations of the British Empire with the outside world, and of its various parts with each other. It was equally clear that the only authority available for this purpose was the British Parliament. In this matter of commercial policy the pioneer work had already been done and the main principles determined; but during the half century following the Revolution of 1688 the system was considerably developed. The Navigation Act of 1696 remedied defects in administration which had

been pointed out by English merchants and colonial offi-   Navigation Act of 1696.
cials. It also established a system of registration for Eng-
lish vessels, whether owned in England or in the colonies.
In order to insure imperial control of the chartered colonies, all governors not directly appointed by the King had
to be approved by him. This requirement was enforced
in the proprietary provinces though it was in conflict with
their charters. In those colonies where the governors were
elected annually, the rule was of course impracticable.
All governors had to take oath to enforce the Navigation
Acts; negligence in this respect made them liable to heavy
fines and dismissal from office. Finally all colonial laws
at variance with the acts of trade were declared null and
void.

Later statutes developed the commercial system in   Later statutes; the Molasses Act of 1733.
other ways, as, for instance, by extending the list of enumer-
ated articles which could be shipped to Europe only through
English ports. Among the additions to this list were rice,
molasses, naval stores, and ship timber; in certain cases
trees were reserved for the royal navy, though this reservation could not be strictly enforced. The most unpopular attempt by Parliament to regulate colonial commerce,
during this period, was the Molasses Act of 1733. This
law attempted to break up one of the most profitable branches
of trade carried on by the continental colonies, namely, that
of the foreign West Indies. During the preceding quarter
century, the colonies from Maryland northward to New
England discovered that the British West Indies could not
give them as good bargains in sugar and molasses as the
French and other foreign islands. The provisions, lumber,
and horses of the continental colonies also demanded a
larger market than the British islands could give. So the
trade of the North American continent with the foreign islands
grew steadily until the powerful West Indian lobby in London appealed to Parliament for the protection of their spe-

cial interests. In the face of protests from the continental colonies, Parliament imposed prohibitive duties on sugar and molasses imported into those colonies from the foreign West Indies. This act was, however, so directly in conflict with the natural course of trade that it was generally disregarded. If strictly enforced it would have been disastrous to New England and the "bread colonies" of the middle region. Perhaps the chief interest of the Molasses Act is that it shows the peculiar importance of the sugar islands in the estimation of British statesmen. More than any other colonies, they lived up to the orthodox theory that a colony should devote itself to producing staples for the mother country.

Regulation of American industry.

English manufacturing interests were steadily growing, and under their influence Parliament watched closely any colonial industries which might possibly compete with them. In 1699 the manufacture of woolens in the colonies was discouraged by prohibiting their export from one colony to another. In 1732 the London Company of Felt Merchants induced Parliament to limit the number of apprentices who could be employed by colonial hat makers. In the iron industry, the colonists were encouraged to ship iron ore; but a law of 1750 prohibited all but the more rudimentary forms of iron manufacture. This did not, however, prevent notable progress in the colonial iron industry.[1] Meantime, Parliament, while checking some industries, was ready to encourage others. The production of naval stores, for instance, was encouraged by bounties; and regulations which caused hardship were sometimes repealed or modified. South Carolina rice, for example, though placed on the list of "enumerated articles" in 1750, was subsequently taken off to the extent of allowing it to be shipped to southern Europe.

From commerce and manufactures, Parliament ex-

[1] By 1775, the American colonies had more blast furnaces and forges than England and Wales combined.

tended its control to colonial coinage, currency, and bank- Coinage,
ing, on the ground that imperial, as well as local, interests currency,
were involved, more particularly those of British merchants. and banking.
The coinage act of 1707 enacted into law the provisions of
a previous royal proclamation, fixing the rates at which
foreign coins should be accepted in terms of English money,
thus establishing a uniform rule in place of the conflicting
action of the various colonies. When English merchants
complained of the inflation of the colonial currency by successive issues of paper money, the home government first tried
to remedy the evil by instructions to the governors and by
disapproving colonial laws; later, Parliament took the matter
up and in 1751 forbade the issue of paper money by the
New England assemblies except under certain conditions.
A few years earlier, Parliament legislated out of existence
the so-called "land bank" of Massachusetts, a scheme for
the issue of notes based on mortgages. Another measure
passed at the suggestion of British merchants was the act
of 1732 to facilitate the collection of debts due by Americans
to British creditors. Parliament also promoted the interests
of colonial commerce by establishing a general post office
in America and passing a law for the suppression of piracy
in American waters.

Parliament was, therefore, a real legislature for the Limits of
whole empire. Yet there were some important things which parlia-
Parliament refrained from doing. Customs duties in Amer- mentary
legislation.
ica were left mainly to the colonial legislatures, which, unlike our present state legislatures, could levy duties on both
exports and imports. Now and then some zealous official
in England or America proposed to raise a larger revenue
in the colonies by means of parliamentary duties or a stamp
tax, but the cautious Whig statesmanship of Walpole, Newcastle, and their associates prevented any such action.
The Post Office Act of 1710 did indeed refer to the raising
of revenue, and some objection was made to it on that

account, but the colonists did not generally consider it as a revenue measure. Parliament was equally cautious about elaborate schemes for remodeling the colonial governments. Though many influential officials favored the complete elimination of the charters, and bills for this purpose were repeatedly introduced, none was actually put through.

Restrictions on colonial legislation. Royal instructions.

Meantime the executive department of the British government was limiting considerably the lawmaking of the American assemblies. Royal instructions to the governors guided them in the exercise of their veto power; provincial laws were disallowed by the Privy Council, which also declared invalid colonial statutes held to be contrary to the principles of English law. The governor's instructions about legislation were numerous. He was forbidden, for example, to approve finally any laws which diminished the King's prerogative, made paper money a legal tender, discriminated in favor of colonial as against English shipping, or interfered with the importation of convicts and slaves. Some bills the governor was not allowed to approve at all; others he could pass only with a "suspending clause," providing that they should not take effect until approved by the Crown. These instructions were not always obeyed, but on the whole they did seriously limit the freedom of the colonial assemblies and caused much discontent.

Disallowance of colonial statutes.

A bill once signed by the governor, without a "suspending clause," became law; but a copy had to be sent to England, where it was examined by the Board of Trade, which, after getting advice from the law officers of the Crown or their own special counsel, prepared its recommendation to the Privy Council, either for or against the law. In the latter case, the law was generally disallowed, or repealed; and this actually happened in hundreds of cases. In recommending the disallowance of colonial laws the Board of Trade usually acted on carefully considered principles. Generally speaking, laws were repealed because they were not in harmony with the English law or with the royal prerogative, because they affected unfavorably the economic interests of the mother country, or because they conflicted with fundamental imperial policies in administration. A few examples will show how these principles were applied. Acts providing for triennial or biennial elections were rejected because they took from the governor his freedom to summon and dissolve assemblies as he saw fit. Other laws were disallowed because they interfered with the King's revenue from quitrents, discriminated in favor of the shipping of a particular province, or authorized excessive issue of paper money. Often the action of the board seems quite reasonable, as when it condemned intolerant legislation against the Quakers, or prevented attempts by one colony to regulate trade without due regard to the interests of its neighbors. At other times, the board showed little appreciation of American conditions and so aroused a spirit of resentment, which was expressed later in several clauses of the Declaration of Independence.

Closely connected with the disallowance of colonial laws was the judicial action of the Privy Council while sitting as a court of appeal in colonial cases. These appeals came not only from the royal provinces but also from the chartered colonies, whose charters expressly declared that legislation must, so far as possible, be in harmony with English law. Colonial laws were sometimes set aside on the ground that they were in conflict with the laws of England and therefore null and void. In other words, the Privy Council was acting somewhat as the United States Supreme Court now does when a state law is declared unconstitutional. *Judicial action of the Privy Council.*

In the present system of the United States, the federal government is not confined to the District of Columbia but operates through its agents in the individual states. In a similar way, the British imperial government was made up partly of officials in London and partly of imperial *Imperial agents in the colonies.*

Royal
governors.

agents in the colonies. The comparison does not, however, hold good completely, because most of the colonial governors were themselves representatives of the central government rather than of the people whom they governed. By 1702 all the West Indian and continental colonies had royal governors except Connecticut, Rhode Island, Penn's colonies on the Delaware, and the Carolinas. During the next half century, the Baltimore family recovered its control of Maryland; but this departure from imperial policy was offset by the transformation of the Carolina proprietorship into the two royal provinces of North and South Carolina. When Nova Scotia was finally conquered it was at once made a royal province. In 1732 Georgia was given temporarily to a philanthropic corporation, the "Trustees," but with the definite understanding that after twenty-one years it was to come under the direct control of the Crown. In all these provincial governments, the governor was primarily an agent of the Crown; the councilors also were royal officials, except in Massachusetts. Even proprietary governors had become imperial agents, since they had to be approved by the Crown and give security for the due performance of the duties imposed on them by Parliament.

The presence of royal governors and councilors meant not only control of executive policies but also a check on lawmaking and the administration of justice. Every law passed by the representatives had to be approved by the councilors as well as by the governor. The judges were appointed by the King, either directly or through the governor acting with the advice and consent of the council. Governor and council together also acted as a court of appeal in civil cases. Every one of these officials was ultimately dependent on the Crown for his continuance in office.

Colonial
control of
imperial
agents.

Nevertheless, even officials appointed by the imperial government were influenced by public opinion in the provinces which they governed. Most councilors and judges

were permanent residents in their respective colonies and
so bound by many ties of sympathy and interest with their
neighbors. This was true also of some governors, and there
were few even of the adventurer type who were quite indifferent about popular approval. The acknowledged right
of the assembly to grant or refuse money gave it another
hold on the governor which he could not well shake off.
This was especially true when, as in a majority of the colonies, the governor's salary was granted only for a limited
term of years, sometimes for one year only. Many a governor
was puzzled to choose between the home government,
the "master" who gave him his commission, and his second "master," the provincial assembly, which gave him
his pay. Even the most conscientious governor might
hesitate to oppose an assembly which controlled the appropriations necessary for the ordinary conduct of government
or for military defense. The result of all this pressure was
that a good deal of executive authority was taken from the
governor and transferred to officers and committees appointed
by the assembly. The control of provincial funds, for instance, was often intrusted to treasurers named either by
act of assembly or by the lower house alone.

This weakening of the prerogative element in the provincial governments emphasized the need of other imperial agents less affected by local interests. So in each colony
there developed side by side two groups of officials, corresponding roughly to the state and federal officers of the present day. In Massachusetts, for instance, the governor had
certain responsibilities in connection with the Navigation
Acts; but the home government depended primarily upon
a royal collector, appointed by the Commissioners of Customs
in England and working under the supervision of an imperial surveyor-general. Again, since provincial courts with
local juries could not be trusted to convict illegal traders,
imperial courts of admiralty were created to try such cases.

Special imperial agencies.

Imperial piracy courts were also organized to deal with a serious evil about which colonial opinion was sometimes very lax.

Difficulties of overseas administration.

It is hard to say how efficient this imperial machinery was as compared with corresponding agencies at the present time, because difficulties of communication were then inconceivably greater. To-day a question may be sent by a subordinate officer to his chief several thousand miles away and an answer given in the course of a single day. Two hundred years ago, the British government had to wait several months for information about conditions in Virginia or Massachusetts. Before a decision could be sent to the colony, on the basis of this information, all the conditions might have been radically changed. Until 1755 there was no regular mail service and no one could tell when letters would arrive at their destination. Besides the ordinary chances of wind and weather, there was always the possibility of loss by shipwreck, enemy privateers, or pirates. Doubtless many officials were incompetent, lazy, or corrupt; but any fair judgment must take into account these physical handicaps which no body of men, however efficient, could hope to overcome. It is on the whole remarkable that this colonial system of the eighteenth century should have worked as well as it did.

Colonial agents.

While imperial interests in America were safeguarded by royal officials, the colonists also had their spokesmen in London. These colonial agents were generally appointed by formal acts of assembly, requiring the consent of the governor and council, as well as the representatives; but in any case they usually reflected public opinion in the colony. Though not entitled to a seat in Parliament, like the territorial delegates in the present American Congress, a colonial agent could, and frequently did, present the claims of his constituents in formal hearings before the Board of Trade. It was also his business to watch the proceedings in Parliament

and use his influence against legislation which seemed likely
to injure the interests of his colony. These agents were
often surprisingly successful in their efforts to influence the
action of the home government. It was in the work of a
colonial agent that Benjamin Franklin received some of
his early training.

The political ties which bound the colonists to the mother
country were certainly very important, but there were other
connections scarcely less significant which linked the Old
World with the New. Especially far reaching was the
influence of commerce. The closest economic relations of
the colonies, other than those which they developed with
each other, were naturally with England. First of all, it
was from England that they received the greater part of
their manufactured goods. This was not merely because
the acts of trade required all European products, with few
exceptions, to be shipped from English ports. It was largely
the result of natural forces, — a common language, personal
associations, the relatively high development of English
manufactures, and the favorable situation of England as
a base for transatlantic commerce. The development of
domestic manufactures for the household and the local
market was fairly general; but they would probably not
have advanced very far in this period, even if there had
been no restrictive acts of Parliament. Trade and agriculture seemed to offer greater incentives for the investment
of capital.

Undoubtedly there was much smuggling, in America as
elsewhere, and the products of continental Europe, such as
dry goods and wines, were frequently brought in without
entering them at English ports. European goods were also
smuggled in from the foreign West Indies. We shall never
know just how large this irregular trade was; but the bulk
of the manufactures imported probably came from England
in the regular way.

*The com-
merce of the
empire.*

*Colonial
commerce
with
England.*

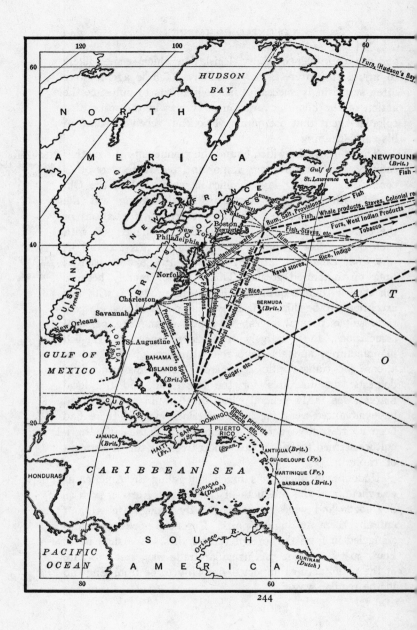

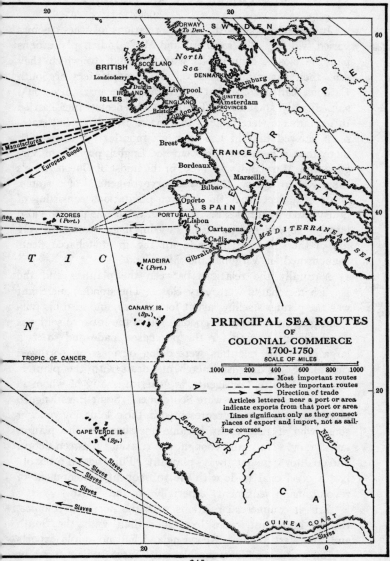

PRINCIPAL SEA ROUTES
OF
COLONIAL COMMERCE
1700-1750
SCALE OF MILES

1000   200   400   600   800   1000

— — — Most important routes
— — — Other important routes
→ ← Direction of trade
Articles lettered near a port or area
indicate exports from that port or area
Lines significant only as they connect
places of export and import, not as sail-
ing courses.

Commerce
of the
plantation
colonies.

In other respects the trade relations of the colonies varied widely. The southern and West Indian plantations had the closest connections with England, to which they sent their sugar and tobacco; the rice planters of South Carolina had a somewhat wider range because they could ship directly to southern Europe. The fleets which carried this commerce were large. In 1692, a British official statement showed that in less than six months 136 ships with more than 2000 seamen had entered English ports from Virginia and Maryland. In 1706, in the midst of Queen Anne's War, Robert Quary, the royal surveyor-general of customs, wrote of a fleet from the tobacco plantations consisting of nearly three hundred sail. The plantation colonies were also largely dependent on English shipping; comparatively few of the ships which made up the great tobacco fleets were owned in Virginia and Maryland.

English
merchants
and
American
planters.

Naturally the relations between the planters and the English merchants were very close. The London merchant was the planter's selling agent for tobacco, and also his purchasing agent for English goods. Often the tobacco sold was not sufficient to pay for the purchases made and so to a large extent the planters were doing business on borrowed capital. Some English merchants dealt with the planters through "factors," or agents, in America, many of whom in the eighteenth century were Scotchmen. Sometimes English merchant families were represented in the colonies by younger sons, who if prosperous became members of the planter aristocracy. Naturally enough, the relations between debtor and creditor were not always pleasant. This friction probably had a good deal to do with the subsequent development of revolutionary sentiment, especially in the South.

Trade
of the
northern
colonies.
New
England.

British commercial relations with the northern colonies, though important, were less close than with the South and the West Indies. New England had no staple exports to England at all comparable with West Indian sugar or

Virginia tobacco. Her fish and lumber were marketed largely elsewhere, chiefly in the West Indies but also in other English colonies, in the Azores, and in southern Europe. From the American point of view the British government ought to have encouraged the trade with the foreign West Indies instead of trying to check it by the Molasses Act. It was through this trade, Americans said, that they were able to pay for English manufactures. The English authorities were, however, less impressed by this argument than by the smuggled European goods which came in through this "back door." Before, as well as after, the passage of the Molasses Act, sugar and molasses from the foreign West Indies continued to supply the distilleries of New England, whence rum was sent out for use in the Indian trade and in the purchase of African slaves. In this latter trade, Boston and especially Newport merchants competed with those of the mother country. In trade relations the middle region, The "bread with its grain, flour, and provisions, shipped largely to the colonies." West Indies, resembled New England more than the South, though there was a heavy export of furs to England, especially from New York. New York and Pennsylvania, like Massachusetts, depended largely on the profits of the West India trade to settle their balances with English merchants.

The financial relations of the colonies with England were somewhat like those developed in the nineteenth century between the western farmers and the "Wall Street" interests. In each case the new settlements naturally depended on the older communities for capital. The inevi- British table friction between debtor and creditor was complicated American by unbusinesslike methods and the ocean barrier, which made debtors. mutual understanding more difficult. In many respects the interests of British merchants coincided with those of the colonies; if the latter did not prosper, British trade would suffer. Yet on certain matters there was sharp difference of opinion, as, for instance, in the matter of paper money,

regarding which the American farmers of 1750 felt much as
the Greenbackers and Populists did in the next century.
Americans also resented the British tendency to undervalue
the northern colonies as against the West Indian plantations.

The
Anglican
outlook
on the
colonies.

While British statesmen and merchants were working
for a politically unified and economically self-sufficient empire, some English churchmen hoped to accomplish a similar
result in ecclesiastical organization.   This idea of extending
the Church of England was most nearly realized in Virginia
and the West Indian plantations, where the Anglican system
was recognized by law and supported by public taxation.
Most of the continental colonies, however, were founded
either by opponents of the Anglican Church, like the Catholic Baltimore family in Maryland, the Puritans of New England, and the Quakers in Pennsylvania; or, as in New Jersey
and the Carolinas, by proprietors who, though Anglicans
themselves, thought it good policy to attract dissenters
by offering religious toleration.   So a decided majority of
the English in America were outside the Anglican fold.

Church es-
tablishments.

At the end of the seventeenth century, vigorous efforts
were made to strengthen the Anglican position. In New
England, the Puritans were forced to give the Episcopal
Church at least a bare toleration. In New York an act of
assembly for the support of a Protestant ministry was so
interpreted by the royal governors as to give the Anglican
Church an establishment in certain counties. About the
same time the overthrow of Lord Baltimore's government
paved the way for an Anglican state church in Maryland.
In the first years of the eighteenth century, with the backing of the proprietors, similar legislation was secured in the
Carolinas, though it was not fully enforced in South Carolina and was almost a dead letter in the northern province.
Elsewhere, also, ardent churchmen were hopeful that much
could be done through the influence of the royal governors,
who were definitely instructed to promote Anglican interests.

The officer chiefly responsible for keeping up the connection between the Anglican Church and its members in America was the Bishop of London, whose authority was definitely recognized in the instructions to the royal governors. Without his certificate, no clergyman could regularly take a position in the colonies. The Bishop of London.

The exercise of episcopal jurisdiction over people three thousand miles away was of course difficult. The rite of confirmation, normally required for communion in the Anglican Church, could not be performed in America because no bishops were there to administer it. Similarly candidates for the ministry had to go to England for episcopal ordination. Various abuses resulted from this absentee system. Many parishes refused to have ministers inducted in the regular way and preferred to "hire" them from year to year. The Bishop of London tried to overcome some of these difficulties by appointing commissaries, but they could not perform the rites of confirmation and ordination and their influence was limited. The most logical method of dealing with the problem, from the Anglican point of view, was to establish resident bishops in America, and during the last years of Queen Anne, it looked as if this plan might be adopted; but when the Queen died, the Whigs came into power and they decided that an American bishop might make trouble with the dissenters on both sides of the water, including some who were fairly influential. Though much could be said for the measure on religious grounds, the dissenters were afraid an American bishop might not be content with promoting the spiritual welfare of his own flock. American bishops proposed.

The most active promoters of an American episcopate were the members of a new missionary organization, known as the Society for Propagating the Gospel in Foreign Parts, often referred to more briefly as the S.P.G., which was chartered by William III in 1701. Its founders were leaders in religious and philanthropic work and its first head was Society for Propagating the Gospel.

Thomas Tenison, Archbishop of Canterbury; the Bishop of London was also an active member. Money was raised to send missionaries to America, and some pains were taken to select good men; but these efforts were not always successful and the church never gave the movement proper financial support. Though the S.P.G. missionaries strengthened considerably the influence of their church in New England, the middle colonies, and the Carolinas, they could not overcome the preponderance of the dissenting elements in those colonies. The comparative weakness of the Anglican Church at the close of the colonial era was unfortunate from the imperial point of view, for the Anglican clergy were usually active supporters of the royal prerogative against political radicalism.

Other ecclesiastical relations.

In most of the other churches, the connection between the European and American organizations was much less close. The New England Congregationalists, for example, had no organic relation with the Independent or Congregational churches of the old country. Their ministers also, instead of bringing over the traditions of the English universities, as the Anglican clergy did, were generally trained in the colonial colleges. There was some correspondence, however, between the Puritan clergy in America and their sympathizers in England. The theological writings of such men as Richard Baxter in England and the Mathers in America were read on both sides of the Atlantic. Prominent English dissenters made gifts to Harvard College and were frequently helpful in staving off undesirable interference by the home government in New England affairs.

The American Quakers.

For the American Quakers, the English connection was more important. For protection against the intolerance of their Puritan and Anglican neighbors they relied largely on their influential friends in England. The English organization, represented chiefly in such matters by the London Yearly Meeting and the "Meeting for Sufferings," corresponded constantly with Friends in all the colonies from New England to the Carolinas and the West Indies, securing information about their grievances and then taking up these complaints with the authorities in London. Contact between English and American Friends was also kept up by traveling missionaries, who made extended tours through the colonies.

Meanwhile there was an increasing number of settlers whose closest ecclesiastical associations were not with England but with other European countries. The Presbyterians, who were comparatively weak in 1700 but increased rapidly in numbers and influence during the next half century, owed their inspiration to Scotland and Ireland. Their first notable leader was Francis Makemie, a native of Ireland but of Scottish parentage and education, who made numerous preaching tours through the colonies. A few years later the great stream of Scotch-Irish immigration set in, bringing many Presbyterian clergy from Ulster, and a few directly from Scotland. These early ministers had been ordained by Scottish or Irish presbyteries, but before long they were organizing presbyteries of their own. Other denominations maintained more or less formal connections with the Protestants of continental Europe. The Dutch Reformed churches of New York continued long after the English conquest to receive ministers from the mother church of the Netherlands. There were also several German sects — Calvinists, Lutherans, Mennonites, Moravians, and others, each representing some contribution of Old World thought and feeling to American life. The French had a number of Huguenot churches, but many of the French were drawn into the Church of England.

The status of the Catholic Church was quite different from that of any of the Protestant bodies. Except in the early years of the Maryland colony, the immigration of English Catholics was small. In the eighteenth century

Scotch and Irish Presbyterians.

Other Protestants.

The Catholic Church.

some Catholics came from Ireland, but this immigration was not large before the Revolutionary era. The Catholics were almost everywhere regarded with suspicion by their Protestant neighbors and suffered from legal disabilities of one kind or another. This was true even in Maryland, where their public worship was actually forbidden by law. Under these conditions, the Catholics could not build up a normal organization until after the Revolution, though a few churches were built, including one in Philadelphia where John Adams attended a service in 1774.

Thus religion, as well as politics and commerce, established associations which counteracted somewhat the effects of physical separation and the American environment, and helped to keep these colonial communities in contact with the European world. It is worth remembering in this connection that the religious revival known as "The Great Awakening," the one movement of its kind, before the middle of the eighteenth century which affected the English colonies as a whole, owed much of its success to the visiting English preacher, George Whitefield, and to the evangelistic fervor of Presbyterian ministers who had recently come over from Ireland.

Intellectual relations.

The educated, or reading, class was comparatively small on both sides of the Atlantic, but the influence of English literary and intellectual movements can be plainly seen in provincial America. Some of the royal governors were men of education and literary taste, who gathered about them other people of their own kind. Most of the Anglican, and some of the Presbyterian, clergy had been trained in British universities and contributed largely to the development of education, especially in the southern and middle colonies. There were many others, too, in all the colonies who had spent more or less time in Europe. New England was probably more satisfied with its own intellectual resources than any other region in America, but some of its most representative men had seen a good deal of the Old World. In Massachusetts, for example, any list of outstanding personalities in 1702 should include Joseph Dudley, member of an old colonial family but just appointed royal governor; Increase Mather, the ablest representative of the Puritan clergy; and Samuel Sewall, judge, councilor, and typical Puritan layman. All these men had spent more or less time in England. Dudley had been abroad three times, once for nine years; he had served as deputy governor of the Isle of Wight and as a member of Parliament. Among his friends and correspondents was the famous English essayist, Richard Steele. Increase Mather supplemented his course at Harvard by going to Trinity College, Dublin, where he took his M.A. degree, and later spent three years in London as colonial agent. Sewall's diary records a six months' visit to England in which he showed himself a careful observer of men and manners. In the southern and middle colonies, educational contact with the mother country was closer. In the South, the sending of sons or even daughters to England was fairly common, and associations thus formed in youth and early manhood were often kept up in later years.

A number of Americans belonged to the Royal Society, or were among its correspondents, including such men as the Puritan minister, Cotton Mather; an eighteenth-century Winthrop, who was a professor in Harvard College; William Byrd, a rich Virginia planter and councilor; the physician, John Lining, of South Carolina; and, last but not least, Benjamin Franklin. One striking feature of American life in the first half of the eighteenth century was the development of the legal profession, and a fair number of the leading lawyers were trained in the English Inns of Court, from which they brought back not only a better knowledge of the common law but some understanding of Old World thought and manners.

The Royal Society and the Inns of Court.

English
literature in
America.

The influence of contemporary English literature can be traced in various ways. The colonial newspapers of Boston, Philadelphia, Williamsburg, and Charleston show considerable interest in the work of such writers as Addison and Pope. The *Spectator* essays of Addison and Steele furnished models for ambitious young writers in America and were reprinted in colonial papers. Pope was perhaps the most admired poet and received, like Addison, the compliment of imitation. Mather Byles, a Boston clergyman, was acclaimed by his admirers as one "who bids fair to rise and sing and rival Pope." In 1727 Byles sent some of his poems to Pope, "to let you see a little of the reputation you bear in these unknown climates." No one illustrates better than Franklin the effort of intelligent Americans to keep up with European thought. In his brother's newspaper office in Boston, he read Addison and deliberately formed his style on this model. Moving to Philadelphia, he became a bookseller as well as a journalist and politician, advertising in his paper, *The Pennsylvania Gazette*, the works of Dryden, Defoe, Swift, Addison, Steele, and Locke. A few years after his arrival in Philadelphia he established a Library Society, which offered its members not only books of the kind just mentioned but even such foreign classics as the works of Voltaire.

European
philosophy.

By the middle of the eighteenth century some of the young men who were to become the political leaders of independent America, had come under the influence of European and especially English philosophy. The great idealist, Berkeley, visited Rhode Island and made an ardent disciple of young Samuel Johnson, a graduate of Yale, who afterwards became president of King's College (now Columbia). Johnson tried to popularize his master's teaching, but Berkeleian idealism did not make much headway with the matter-of-fact Americans of that generation. More widely read and influential with young men of a radical turn of mind were the principal rationalistic and deistic writers, and above all such political philosophers as Algernon Sidney and John Locke. It was largely on books of this kind that Franklin, John Adams, and Thomas Jefferson sharpened their wits for the controversies of the next epoch.

BIBLIOGRAPHICAL NOTES

Adams, J. T., *Provincial Society*. Andrews, *Colonial Period*, chs. VI–IX. Greene, *Provincial America*, chs. III–VI, XI, XVII, XVIII and pp. 194–200. Channing, *United States*, II, chs. VIII–XVIII. Osgood, *18th Cent.*, I–IV. *[General accounts.]*

Hearnshaw, F. J. C., *Social and Political Ideas of Some English Thinkers of the Augustan Age*. Morgan, W. T., *English Political Parties and Leaders in the Reign of Queen Anne*. Botsford, J. B., *English Society in the 18th Century*. George, M. D., *London Life in the 18th Century*. *[Contemporary English life.]*

Andrews, C. M., in *Cambridge Hist. of British Empire*, I, ch. XIV. Beer, G. L., *Commercial Policy of England toward the Colonies*, chs. III–VII. Guttridge, G. H., *The Colonial Policy of William III in America and the West Indies*. Clarke, M. P., "Board of Trade at Work," *A.H.R.*, XVII, 17–43. Dickerson, O. M., *American Colonial Government* (deals with the Board of Trade). Basye, A. H., *The Lords Commissioners of Trade and Plantations*. Hertz, G. B., *Old Colonial System*, chs. II, III. Kellogg, L. P., "American Colonial Charter," Amer. Hist. Assoc., *Report*, 1903, 187–341. Root, W. T., *Relations of Pennsylvania with the British Government*, especially chs. I–VI. *[Colonial policy and governmental relations.]*

Labaree, L. W., *Royal Government in America*. Greene, E. B., *Provincial Governor*, especially chs. VIII–X. Pownal, T., *Administration of the Colonies* (by a liberal provincial governor). *[The governor.]*

Russell, R. B., *Review of American Colonial Legislation by the King in Council*. Washburn, G. A., *Imperial Control of the Administration of Justice*. *[Disallowance and appeal.]*

Andrews, "Colonial Commerce," *A.H.R.*, XX, 43–63. Bell, H. C., "West India Trade," *ibid.*, XXII, 272–287. Nettels, C., "Markets in the Old Colonial System," *N.E.Q.* (1933), VI, 495–512. McClellan, W. S., *Smuggling in the American Colonies*. *[Colonial commerce.]*

West Indian commercial lobby.

Pitman, F. W., *British West Indies*, especially chs. IX–XII; Penson, L. M., "London Merchant's West Indian Interests," *Eng. Hist. Rev.*, XXVI, 373–392.

Lumber and naval stores.

Albion, R. G., *Forests and Sea Power*. Osgood, *18th Cent.*, I, ch. XV.

Industrial growth.

Nettels, C., "Menace of Colonial Manufacturing, 1690–1720," *N.E.Q.* (1931), IV, 230–269. Clark, V. S., *History of Manufactures in the U. S.*, chs. I–VIII. Bining, A. C., *British Regulation of the Colonial Iron Industry*. Cole, A. H., *American Wool Manufacture*, I, chs. I–III. Lord, E. L., *Industrial Experiments in the British Colonies*. Tryon, R. H., *Household Manufactures*, chs. I–III.

Currency.

Nettels, C., *Money Supply of the American Colonies before 1720*.

Sources on business and trade relations.

Bogart, E. L., and Thompson, C. M., *Readings in Economic History of the U. S.*, 69–81 and ch. IV. Callender, G. S., *Selections from Economic History of the U. S.*, chs. II, III. Hart, *Contemporaries*, II, nos. 45–54, 65–68, 73–74. Macdonald, *Select Charters*, nos. 43, 50.

Ecclesiastical relations.

Cross, A. L., *Anglican Episcopate in the American Colonies*, chs. I–IV. Greene, E. B., "Anglican Outlook," *A.H.R.*, XX, 64–85. Ford, H. J., *Scotch-Irish in America*, especially chs. XIII, XVI. Jones, R., *Quakers in America*, especially bk. V, ch. VIII.

Intellectual relations.

Parrington, V. L., *Main Currents*, I. *Cambridge History of American Literature*, I, bk. I. Cook, E. C., *Literary Influences in Colonial Newspapers*. Richardson, L. N., *A History of Early American Magazines, 1741–1789*. Tyler, M. C., *American Literature*, II. Riley, I. W., *American Philosophy, The Early Schools*, bks. II–III. Morais, H. M., *Deism in 18th Century America*. For the European background, see Smith, P., *Rise of Modern Culture*, II; Stephen, Sir L., *History of English Thought in the 18th Century*, 2 vols. See also bibliographical notes to chs. XII–XIV.

Women, marriage, and family life.

Calhoun, *Social History of the American Family*, I. Howard, G. E., *History of Matrimonial Institutions*, II. Morris, R. B., *Studies in the History of American Law*, ch. III. Dexter, E. A., *Colonial Women of Affairs*. Woody, W. T., *History of Women's Education in U. S.*

CHAPTER XII

PROVINCIAL NEW ENGLAND

WITHIN the framework of the British Empire, each colony or group of colonies had its own peculiar problems, its special customs and points of view.   In the provincial America of the eighteenth century, New England had a peculiarly clean-cut sectional individuality which was recognized by friends and enemies alike.   Radical politicians found it convenient to use New England precedents, while royal governors complained of the spread of "Boston principles" which threatened to undermine the foundations of imperial authority.

In the last decade of the seventeenth century, the settled area of New England was only a small fraction of that now occupied by this group of states.   Vermont was still virgin soil, and Maine, then a part of Massachusetts, was scarcely less so; only three of its towns were thought important enough in 1694 to be listed for purposes of taxation, and these were all on the coast within thirty miles of the New Hampshire line.   For practical purposes, New Hampshire meant as yet little more than its short ocean frontage and a back country hardly twenty-five miles deep. The upper Merrimac valley was still in dispute between Massachusetts and New Hampshire and actually occupied by neither.   From the Merrimac southward and westward around the coast, the colonists were still nearly all within fifty miles of the sea, though a slender line of settlement went up the Connecticut River across Massachusetts, growing very thin at its northern end.   Central Massachusetts, as well as the Berkshire country and the adjoining section

257

of Connecticut, was still waiting for a new generation of New England pioneers. In 1695 the Massachusetts legislature mentioned eleven frontier towns as requiring special protection against the Indians. Three of these towns were in Maine and one in the Connecticut valley; the others were within fifty miles of Boston.

Population. The rough guesses available for this period indicate a population of about eighty thousand whites in the whole of New England — more than half of them in Massachusetts. The regions which counted for most in population and wealth were the district about Cape Ann, including Salem and Ipswich; the basin of Boston harbor; the shores of Narragansett Bay and Long Island Sound; and the lower end of the Connecticut valley. In Massachusetts, nearly half the province taxes were paid by towns within the present municipal and suburban area of Boston.

Growth checked by war. For more than three decades after the outbreak of King William's War in 1689, the expansion of New England was seriously checked by border warfare. Even after the treaty of Utrecht, there were some destructive Indian raids, especially on the Maine frontier. During the next quarter century, conditions were more favorable; but Thomas Hutchinson, the governor and historian of Massachusetts, estimated at the close of the provincial period that the population of New England would have been larger by 200,000 "if the French had been driven from Canada an hundred years ago." This was not the only reason for the **Small immigration.** comparatively modest growth of New England. To the farmer-immigrants of the eighteenth century, it offered no such agricultural opportunities as a colony like Pennsylvania. The exclusive spirit of New England Puritanism also had some effect in discouraging immigration. For a time it seemed as if there might be a fairly large influx of Scotch-Irish settlers, and several hundred of them did actually settle in Massachusetts, New Hampshire, and Maine;

but the great majority turned southward to Pennsylvania
and beyond. To a larger extent than any other section,
the New England of 1760 was inhabited by descendants of
the first colonial generation.

In spite of all these handicaps, the population of these Expansion of New England.
four colonies had increased by 1760 to some point between
400,000 and half a million. Much of this increase was in
the seaboard towns. Boston with about 20,000 inhabitants
was still much the largest place in New England; but other
towns also profited by the growth of seagoing commerce:
Portsmouth, in New Hampshire; Salem, in Massachusetts; Newport and later Providence in Rhode Island; New
London and New Haven on the Connecticut side of Long
Island Sound. Equally important was the movement of
population toward new frontiers, westward, northward, and
eastward. The descendants of the Puritan pioneers were
now founding new communities, still largely on the old
models, in the central counties of Massachusetts and beyond
the Connecticut River in the Housatonic valley. Connecticut and Massachusetts people predominated in this Berkshire region, but they met here a few Dutch families from
the Hudson valley. Land speculation helped to stimulate
the pioneering movement. With the encouragement of
their government, Boston and Salem capitalists began to
invest in "wild lands," not only within the acknowledged
limits of Massachusetts but farther north in territory claimed
by New Hampshire. Along with the old type of settlement
by organized groups, there came a more individualistic
kind of pioneering. The settled area of New Hampshire
was now gradually pushed northward, especially in the
Merrimac and Connecticut valleys. By the middle.of the
eighteenth century there were even a few outposts in what
is now Vermont. In Maine, which had actually lost ground
during the Indian wars, the advance was resumed, though
progress was slow.

**Maritime
enterprise.
The
fisheries.**

The pioneer spirit was not limited to the men who went in search of new lands. It was scarcely less evident in those who manned the fishing fleets, developed shipbuilding, and sailed on distant voyages. Like other New England interests, the fisheries suffered severely from the colonial wars, as well as from French competition in time of peace; but the middle years of the eighteenth century brought a new prosperity. It was estimated in 1731 that five or six thousand men were employed in this industry. In 1713, a Gloucester sea captain devised a new type of ship, the schooner, which gave the deep-sea fishermen more efficient service than anything they had had before. The mackerel fishery took on a new importance, especially for the West Indian trade, and whaling developed from small beginnings into an immense and profitable industry. At first, whales were taken by comparatively small boats along the coast; but the European demand for illuminating oil, whalebone, and other products of this fishery increased rapidly and the development of deep-sea whaling was a natural result. Many places shared in the profits of the business, but the Nantucket sea captains were conspicuously successful. Before long they and others of their kind were sailing as far north as Davis Strait on the Arctic Circle.

Shipbuilding.

Shipbuilding also made great progress — so much so that the first third of the eighteenth century has been called the "golden age" of this industry. It was carried on not only in a few centers but all along the coast. Ships were built largely for use by New Englanders; but they were also sold in other colonies, in England, and in the Mediterranean countries. By 1724 some British builders found this colonial competition so formidable that they tried to have it checked; but the imperial government was too thoroughly committed to the policy of encouraging English shipping on both sides of the Atlantic. The later development of the industry was less rapid; with the clearing of the forests about the older settlements, lumbering and shipbuilding naturally moved northward and the shipyards of the Piscataqua region became more important.

The shipbuilders were, of course, meeting the demands Trade. of an expanding commerce, and the Boston shipping lists indicate the character of this trade. During the summer quarter of 1714, 103 ships were cleared for various ports: sixty-one of these were owned in Boston and over two thirds of the whole number belonged to New England ports; ten belonged to other continental colonies, four to the West Indies, one to Ireland, ten to London, and the rest to minor English ports. All but two of these ships had been built in America. There was much more variety in the ports to which they were bound: a little less than a third were going to continental English colonies, most of them south of the Potomac; another third, approximately, were bound for various ports of the British West Indies and Honduras (Barbados and Jamaica were the islands most frequently named); eight were bound for Newfoundland; eight sailed for the Dutch colonies of Surinam and Curaçao; the rest were crossing the Atlantic, the majority to English ports, but a few to Portugal and the Portuguese islands. The vessels which embarked on these long voyages were nearly all very small. Less than one tenth had a tonnage of 100 or over; the largest tonnage was 310 and the next only 200.

The cargoes were as varied as the ports of destination. Varied To the mother country, the New Englanders shipped partly cargoes. their own products — staves, oil, whalebone; partly also the products of other colonies, such as rice and sugar. Lumber, fish, and horses bulked large in the cargoes shipped to the West Indies. The big items in the trade with the continental colonies were rum and "European goods," with a miscellany of such merchandise as wooden ware, pewter, iron pots, and frying pans. Lists of ships entering port show what was coming into Boston from other parts of the world, either for New England consumption or for distribution elsewhere. In 1718, for instance, the lists showed European goods from England, including both English manufactures and imports from the Continent; wine from the Azores and the Madeiras; grain, flour, and other provisions from the middle colonies; sugar, molasses, rum, and cotton from the West Indies. From Ireland came linen, some provisions, and servants.

Newport.

Next to Boston among the New England ports was Newport. In the early years of this period, it attracted the attention of royal officials as a favorite resort for pirates and privateers, the two employments tending to shade into each other. In time of war the privateer had a legal warrant for preying on commerce, and when peace came, such craft sometimes found ordinary trade too tame. In

The slave trade.

the first half of the eighteenth century, Newport became the chief base in North America for the African slave trade. The round of this trade began with rum manufactured from West Indian molasses. What followed may be illustrated from the correspondence of some of these Newport merchants. In 1755, for instance, the firm of Wilkinson and Ayrault sent Captain David Lindsay to the African coast, where he was to exchange his cargo for gold and slaves. With this human freight he was to sail for Barbados or St. Christopher, where the slaves were to be sold, provided he could get an average price of twenty-seven pounds for them all, "great and small." If satisfactory bargains could not be made at the first mentioned islands he could try Jamaica. The captain did this business on commission, getting among other things five slaves for his own share. A letter written from the Guinea coast several years earlier shows how lively the competition sometimes was. The shipmaster reported to his Newport employer that there never had been "so much Rum on the coast at one time before," but "slaves is very scarce," so much so that the "rum men" were "ready to devour one another." Newport was also, like Boston, deeply involved in the foreign sugar trade.

The profits of this trade, legal and illegal, were building up at Boston, Newport, Salem, and elsewhere a rich merchant class of decidedly cosmopolitan interests. A fairly typical Boston merchant of this period was Thomas Amory. Born in Ireland of English parents, he spent his childhood in South Carolina, where his father was a prominent merchant and politician. The boy was then sent to England for formal schooling and some practical business training from a French merchant in London. He then went to the Azores, and finally set up in business there for himself, incidentally serving as consul for the English, French, and Dutch. While still a young man, he moved to Boston, where he interested himself largely in the trade with the Carolinas and the West Indies. Another prominent colonial merchant was Peter Faneuil. Born in New York of Huguenot stock, he went into business in Boston, becoming a shipowner, importer, and commission merchant, with correspondents in England, France, Portugal, and Spain. He believed in his right to "fair trade," even if it happened to be in violation of the Navigation Acts; there was also the slave trade, in which he had a considerable interest. He was public-spirited, however, and gave to his fellow citizens the famous Faneuil Hall. Such men as these inevitably changed the tone of Boston society, though the old families were still in the majority.

The merchant group at Newport was more heterogeneous than that of Boston. Among its wealthy and prominent families there were not only English but West Indians, Irish, Scotch, French (Huguenots), Germans, and Jews from Spain and Portugal. The Redwood family illustrates some interesting aspects of Newport society.

Typical Boston merchants.

Amory.

Faneuil

The Newport group.

Abraham Redwood, senior, was born in England; but he was interested in the West Indian trade and later became a sugar planter in Antigua, one of the Leeward Islands. About 1715 he came to New England, settling first at Salem and then at Newport. When he died, in 1729, his son inherited not only his father's commercial interests but also his sugar plantation with its numerous slaves. His correspondence shows the usual exchange of lumber, horses, and miscellaneous goods, chiefly for sugar; now and then negro servants are mentioned. His London agents, some of them influential in colonial politics as well as in trade, sold his sugar and filled, or tried to fill, his orders for various articles of use and luxury. He also showed some public spirit. The famous Redwood Library in Newport began with a gift from him and a building site for it was given by another liberal citizen.

New England industry.

The intercolonial wars at the beginning of this period stimulated manufactures somewhat, too much so according to some overzealous officials. Even the Woolens Act of 1699, intended to protect English manufactures, did not wholly discourage these New England enterprises. When peace came, however, most people there, as in other colonies, depended mainly upon England for the better grades of manufactured goods. The two manufactures of prime importance which got much beyond local markets were ships, with their accessories, and rum. Some industries were encouraged by colonial assemblies; but most of the available capital found more attractive outlets in foreign and intercolonial trade.

The currency problem. Paper money.

These developing communities found the currency problem a difficult one. One reason why they were so sensitive about the West Indian trade was because they depended on it so largely for Spanish money, the "pieces of eight," which they used in their own business and in settling accounts with the English merchants. Experiments with paper money were general during the provincial period. Sometimes, as in the case of the first Massachusetts issue of 1690, the policy was adopted to meet specially heavy war expenditures. Beginning in a fairly conservative way, successive assemblies became more and more reckless until in 1748 it took eleven or twelve Massachusetts shillings in paper to make one in English sterling. Rhode Island was even worse off.

The evils of inflation were felt not only by British creditors but also by many of the New England merchants. In 1749, this conservative party, taking advantage of a grant made to Massachusetts in compensation for its outlay in "King George's War," and in spite of opposition from the farmers and small traders, induced the General Court to redeem the paper in specie. In 1731, the governor of Rhode Island stretched his authority by attempting to veto a paper-money bill, but he was overruled and lost his place in the next election. One of his successors declared optimistically that "if this colony be in any respect happy and flourishing, it is paper money and a right application of it that hath rendered us so"; but the situation finally became so serious that the leading business men of the colony signed a petition asking the home government to intervene. In 1751, Parliament restricted the issue of paper bills by the New England governments; such bills were not to be made a legal tender. This paper-money discussion brought out clearly the division of the colonists themselves on certain economic issues. The conservative merchant class, though none too scrupulous about obeying the acts of trade, sometimes found in the home government a convenient protection against radical majorities.

The growing wealth of the towns showed itself in more comfortable ways of living. Some of the best colonial architecture dates from the latter part of this period. Even the better houses were still generally of wood, but some sub-

Opposition to inflation.

Parliamentary intervention, 1751.

Wealth shown in ways of living.

stantial brick houses were built, especially in Boston. English models were followed to a considerable extent both in private and public buildings. Furniture became more pretentious, and costume, imitating the English fashions, was often luxurious, as may be seen from contemporary portraits of New England dignitaries. Governor Belcher, a Massachusetts man by birth, ordered from London a suit of "very good silk" "trimmed rich." Fashionable families expected to have their servants dressed in style. One runaway "English manservant," described in the Boston *Newsletter* of 1742, wore a blue coat with black velvet buttons, a silk jacket, and "a fine white shirt with ruffles." An English traveler wrote of Boston in 1740 that both "ladies and gentlemen dress and appear as gay, in common, as courtiers in England on a coronation or birthday."

Economic classes.

Such luxuries were of course confined to a comparatively small class, chiefly in the towns, though the " Narragansett planters" of Rhode Island had also a reputation for generous living. The owners of the older farms were struggling ·hard, with a soil none too good to begin with and now losing its fertility after a century of hard use. For the frontiersman, conditions were more hopeful, but luxuries were generally beyond his reach. In the towns, too, there were all grades of society — prosperous merchants and lawyers, small tradesmen, mechanics, and domestic servants. Indentured servants came in from England and Ireland, though not in such numbers as in the colonies farther

Slavery.

south. Prosperous families, especially in the larger towns, often had one or more negro slaves and there was no general feeling against the practice, though a few protests were heard. Rhode Island had the largest proportion of negroes and the Narragansett planters used slave labor more than any other part of rural New England. Generally speaking, the small farmers of New England could not use negro slaves to much purpose.

In their political problems, all the New England colo- nies had some experiences in common. They all had to adjust themselves more fully than before to the principle of imperial control. Whether they kept their old charters or had to accept royal governors, they were all vitally concerned with such unpleasant phenomena as acts of trade, royal customs collectors, and occasional appeals from their courts to the Privy Council. To officials in London, New England seemed the bad child of the imperial family, keeping up irregular habits acquired in the earlier years of lax discipline and straying willfully from the course of legitimate commerce, when there was a fair chance of not being caught. Meanwhile, New Englanders complained of unintelligent interference with the natural course of trade. Why should Parliament try to force their West Indian trade into the narrow limits of the British sugar islands when better markets could be had elsewhere? Why, if their own representatives considered paper money a proper remedy for local troubles, should Privy Council and Parliament meddle with matters much better understood by people on the ground? Questions like these entered into all New England politics, from New Hampshire to Connecticut. All these colonies also carried over from the seventeenth century the essential framework of local government. Their town meetings continued as before to manage those interests which came nearest to the average man, and they followed much the same old paths of law and custom.

In other respects, the New England colonies did not stand on an equal footing. In Connecticut and Rhode Island, which kept their old charters, self-government was not limited to the towns. The property holders continued to elect every year their own governors, assistants, and representatives in the assembly or lower house. Other executive and judicial officers were appointed by the assembly. The governor had little formal authority; he could not, for instance, veto bills passed by the colonial legislature. Nevertheless, these little republics often showed remarkable steadiness in supporting leaders whom they trusted. Connecticut, with its comparatively homogeneous and mainly rural population, had only two governors between 1707 and 1741. One was an influential Congregational minister; the other had been thoroughly tested as selectman, justice of the peace, representative, assistant, judge of the Superior Court, and deputy governor. Rhode Island society was more complex and its politics less steady, but even here one governor served continuously for twenty-eight years. This man, Samuel Cranston, had to steer the ship of state through troubled waters in the face of severe criticism by the home government; but he evidently satisfied his constituents better than most present-day politicians are able to do.

Attacks on the charters.
The independence of these chartered colonies was repeatedly threatened. In 1701, the Board of Trade drew a long indictment against the chartered colonies, giving special attention to Rhode Island, with its bad reputation for illegal trade and even piracy. The remedy proposed was an act of Parliament revoking the charters. Bills for this purpose were introduced more than once, and in 1721 the **Dummer's defense.** board took the matter up again. In 1721 Jeremiah Dummer, the agent of Massachusetts, published a skillful defense of the New England charters against the usual charges of arbitrary government, lack of interest in the national defense, and disregard of English law. He insisted that the New Englanders were not aiming at independence, that their prosperity depended on their free governments, and that a generous policy would also be best for the mother country. Doubtless, he said, Parliament had the "power" to revoke the charters, but this was a question of "right." "And shall not the Supream Judicature of all the Nation do right?" Whether these particular arguments were effective

or not, both Rhode Island and Connecticut weathered the storm and kept their charters.

In Massachusetts and New Hampshire conditions were quite different, since they both had royal governors. The problem which the Massachusetts leaders, especially, now set themselves to solve was how far they could manage, within the forms of their monarchical constitution, to keep the substance of power. Even the second charter gave Massachusetts a decided advantage over the ordinary royal government. The members of the council, which was also the upper house of the legislature, had been suggested in the first place by the friends of the colony in London and were chosen thereafter by the two houses of the legislature on a joint ballot. Since the lower house, chosen by the voters in the towns, was more numerous than the council, the former had a decided advantage in the choice of new councilors; the election was, however, subject to the governor's veto. The charter also deferred to the old traditions of the colony by requiring annual elections to the General Court, or legislature, and giving it the right to elect a number of officers, including the province treasurer.

Massachusetts under the second charter.

Even in the appointment of royal governors, the British government was often willing to consider local conditions. Sir William Phips, the first governor appointed under the new charter, was a native of the province who had been suggested by the provincial agents themselves. Then after a few years under the administration of a lieutenant governor who belonged to one of the old Massachusetts families, the province was put in charge of a prominent British nobleman of liberal principles, who was willing to denounce the Stuart kings as vigorously as any New Englander and even attended the Thursday lectures of the Puritan clergy. In 1702, Joseph Dudley, another Massachusetts man, was selected. Though extremely unpopular during the Andros régime, he was now able to secure testimonials from the

The royal governors.

Puritan clergy of London and even from such an influential personage as Cotton Mather, minister of the Second
Church of Boston. Dudley's first successor was an English colonel whose grandfather was a Puritan minister;
the second was the liberal son of a liberal bishop; the third
was a wealthy Massachusetts merchant who had several
times been elected councilor and at the time of his appointment was the London agent of the House of Representatives;
the fourth was a lawyer who had lived several years in Massachusetts and won public confidence to the extent of being
appointed counsel for the province in a boundary dispute.
In short, most, if not all, of these men took office with something in their experience or point of view which should have
helped them to understand local problems.

Constitu-
tional con-
flicts. The
salary
question
The comparative care with which the Massachusetts
governors were chosen did not save them from frequent
conflicts with their assemblies. This was due partly,
no doubt, to the personal peculiarities of individual governors, but chiefly to the fact that as agents of the Crown
they were obliged to oppose policies which the popular leaders were equally determined to carry through. Perhaps the
most significant of these issues was the question of temporary or permanent appropriations for the governor's salary.
The leaders in the House of Representatives were determined
that, having lost the power to choose their own governor,
they would keep him in check by determining his salary
at short intervals. The controversy reached its climax in
1728, when Governor William Burnet, acting strictly in
accordance with his instructions, refused to accept the temporary grant which the legislature was willing to make,
insisting that only a permanent settlement was consistent
with his dignity and independence. This independence
was just what the popular party did not mean to give him,
and he presently died without getting any salary at all.
His successor brought with him equally positive instruc-

tions, but the assembly was stubborn. Finally the home government yielded and the governor was allowed to accept annual grants. Other governmental expenditures were similarly met by detailed appropriations from year to year, though the effort of the lower house to control the issue of warrants drawn under these appropriations was finally given up.

The popular party was not always successful. Suc- **Governor and councilors.** ceeding governors repeatedly exercised the right to veto the election of councilors. In this way radical leaders were kept out of the council, which was fairly conservative during most of the provincial era. The problem for the councilor who wanted to keep his place was how to be popular enough to win the votes of the representatives without being so aggressive as to offend the governor. The system naturally tended to keep men of vigorous and independent personality out of the council. Governor Dudley also asserted his right **The speakership question.** to approve or disapprove the election of a speaker duly chosen by the house. The claim was based partly on the old English custom of presenting the speaker to the King for his approval, and partly on an interpretation of the charter, which gave the governor a veto on all acts of the General Court. The English practice had become a mere formality, both in England and in most of the royal provinces; but Dudley and his successor both used their veto, and the home government settled the point in their favor by the "explanatory charter" of 1725. The assembly, being then afraid of more drastic action, submitted with as good grace as possible.

Questions of military policy also made trouble between **Control of military policy.** the governor and the representatives. The governors were instructed, for instance, to maintain a fort at Pemaquid on the Maine coast. To the assembly, however, this fort seemed too far beyond the existing settlements to be of much value. The necessary appropriations were, therefore,

refused.   Later governors sometimes found that the only way
to get money for military purposes was to leave much of
the management in the hands of legislative committees.
Thus, in spite of royal governors and imperial vetoes, the
Massachusetts people did actually to a large extent control
their own affairs.

New Hampshire politics.

Some of the questions which disturbed New Hampshire
politics were similar to those in Massachusetts. The smaller
province was, however, at a disadvantage in not having
a royal charter.   For more than forty years it was unequally
yoked with Massachusetts, whose governor was also the
chief executive of New Hampshire and was suspected of
neglecting the interests of the weaker colony.   The actual
administration in New Hampshire was generally in the hands
of a lieutenant governor, more or less successfully directed
by his superior in Boston.   In 1741 this personal union of
the two provinces was given up and a separate governor
appointed for New Hampshire.

Party politics in Massachusetts.

The most permanent line of division in the Massachusetts assembly was doubtless between the "friends of government" and the popular or "country" party; but during
the middle years of the eighteenth century, the question
of banks and paper money proved no less interesting
than the governor's salary.   To the average man it seemed
an easy matter for the government to make money by the
issue of paper bills, or to relieve debtors by forming a "land
bank" which would lend notes on the security of real estate; but as business developed, the mercantile interests
came to realize the damage done by an inflated and depreciat-
ing currency.   So when Governor Belcher set himself to
fight the "land bank" he made himself unpopular with the
majority of his fellow citizens, but still had the backing
of many influential people.   With this support he was able
to secure action by Parliament, putting an end to this ill-
considered enterprise.   This same conservative group con-

tinued throughout the provincial era and later became the nucleus of the loyalist party in the Revolution. These men of "competent estates" had their own grievances against the home government, but they nevertheless depended on it for support against their radical neighbors.

Religion still played a large part in New England life. Everywhere except in Rhode Island orthodox Puritanism was the dominant influence and the church had the support of the state to a greater or less extent. When Massachusetts and New Hampshire became royal provinces, they found it necessary to tolerate Episcopalians and other dissenters; but, except in a large town like Boston, where there were several congregations, each supporting its own pastor, the inhabitants generally had to help pay the salaries of the Congregational ministers. Quakers, Episcopalians, and Baptists protested, but for many years without success. Similar conditions existed in Connecticut, where the old church order was even more strongly intrenched, with no royal governor to interfere. *Puritan church establishments.*

Nevertheless, many influences were at work to weaken the Puritan system. The growth of commerce increased the indifferent element, which had always existed in the colony. Even before the old Massachusetts charter was revoked, representative clergymen were lamenting the decline of religious enthusiasm. In order to keep their hold on people who inherited Puritan traditions, but shrank from the severe personal tests required for full communion, the so-called Half-Way Covenant was adopted, permitting such persons to share in certain privileges, including the baptism of their children, by professing a kind of formal orthodoxy and "owning the covenant," without being examined as to their spiritual experience. So besides the large number of people who had no formal membership in the established churches, there were many "Half-Way" members who could not be counted on to fight vigorously for the old order. It must *Weakening of the Puritan tradition.* *Half-Way Covenant, 1662.*

be remembered also that the qualification for voting was now property, rather than church membership.

Salem witchcraft. While the Puritan clergy were trying to adjust themselves to the new provincial government, there occurred the strange tragedy of the Salem witchcraft, in which nineteen men and women were hanged by authority of a special court on the charge that they had conspired with the devil to bewitch their neighbors. This was no new thing in the world. Thousands of supposed witches had been executed in England alone during the sixteenth and seventeenth centuries, and the belief in the reality of witchcraft was general among all kinds of orthodox Christians. The Massachusetts epidemic came, however, at a time when liberal-minded men were turning away from this particular kind of superstition. Before long there was a sharp reaction and a few years later the provincial legislature voted a public fast in recognition of the wrong that had been done. Incidentally there was sharp criticism of the Puritan leaders who were held responsible for this outbreak of the mob spirit. Just how far the whole affair served to discredit the old *régime* is hard to say; but the discussion which followed seems to have made for more humane and liberal thinking.

Conservatives and liberals. The Mathers. By the end of the seventeenth century, there were some spirited contests between conservative and liberal elements in the Massachusetts churches. The conservatives were led by Increase Mather and his son Cotton, both ministers of the principal church in Boston. The older Mather was probably the ablest man in the province; his scholarship and his numerous services to church and state gave him a right to be heard with respect. His son was also a man of ability, but his learning though enormous was pedantic and uncritical, as may be seen in his extraordinary book called the *Magnalia Christi*, a series of essays on New England history. Both men were steeped in the theocratic traditions of the Bay Colony, which they felt bound to preserve for future generations. Their opponents would not have seemed especially liberal half a century later, but they proposed certain innovations which the Mathers regarded as dangerous. A church was organized to promote these ideas, and a few years later the "liberals" got control of Harvard College.

To combat these and other undesirable tendencies, the Mathers favored a closer organization of the local churches under something like a Presbyterian constitution. Thereupon a strong party in the colony attacked the new proposals as contrary to Congregational principles and undemocratic. This view was ably set forth by John Wise, the same minister who had resisted Andros twenty years before. He argued for Congregationalism not only because it was believed to be Scriptural but because democracy was the kind of government which harmonized best with reason and "the light of nature." "Power," he said, "is originally in the people." No wonder that Wise's books were reprinted half a century later on the eve of the American Revolution. For the moment the Mathers were probably more influential than Wise and their plan might have been adopted if Massachusetts had been free to settle such matters for herself. When, however, it was proposed to call a synod for the purpose of determining church policies, the British government refused its consent.

John Wise on democracy.

In Connecticut the situation was quite different. There the Puritan leaders were in complete control and at the critical moment the governor himself happened to be a Congregational minister. So with church and state working harmoniously together a plan of "Consociation" similar to that advocated by the Mathers was adopted.

"Consociation" in Connecticut.

The same combination of local opposition with imperial intervention which had defeated the hopes of the Mathers, finally brought the dissenters not only freedom of worship, but also relief from the payment of taxes to support the

Concessions to the dissenters.

Congregational clergy. Neither the Quakers nor the Anglicans were numerous in New England, though the latter were slowly gaining strength, partly through official encouragement and partly through the efforts of the S.P.G. (page 249). Both, however, were constantly sending complaints to England, and the unpopularity of the Puritan colonies in official quarters helped these "conscientious objectors" to get a hearing. Under this double pressure, both Massachusetts and Connecticut passed laws providing that church taxes paid by dissenters might be given to ministers of their own kind. This was an important step toward the separation of church and state, but it took about a century more to complete the process.

The "Great Awakening."

The outstanding event in the religious history of provincial New England was the "Great Awakening," an extraordinary religious revival which affected all the English colonies on the continent. For New England, it began in 1734 with the preaching of Jonathan Edwards in the little town of Northampton, Massachusetts. A few years later, his work was reënforced by the great Methodist preacher, George Whitefield, who, though still a clergyman of the Church of England, showed little regard for the conventions of that church. Edwards, who has been generally recognized as one of the greatest minds America ever produced, was first of all a thinker, trying to restate the prevailing Calvinistic theology in such a way as to combine the old tenets of divine sovereignty and predestination with a new emphasis on personal accountability and a more passionate zeal for communion with God. Highly intellectual as his preaching was, it had also an intensely emotional effect on his audiences. The less intellectual but more popular eloquence of Whitefield reached a still wider circle of hearers. Both tried to draw men from the surface aspects of traditional doctrine and formal observance to an inner spiritual experience. As the revival proceeded, differences of opinion

Edwards and Whitefield.

developed. The violence of some preachers, including Whitefield, provoked a sharp reaction. The faculties of Harvard
and Yale protested and were supported by many ministers.
Gradually the movement spent its force. Edwards was
dismissed by his congregation and threw himself into missionary work among the Indians, finding leisure, however,
to do some of his most important writing.

Aside from a certain lethargy which naturally followed   Effects of
this intense emotionalism, the Great Awakening brought   the Great
out two important tendencies in religious thought, both   Awakening.
working against the old ecclesiastical system. One group
of enthusiasts carried their dissatisfaction with the formal-
ism of the established churches so far that they broke
away from them altogether. These "New Lights"
offered a fruitful field for such popular churches as the
Baptists, especially in rural communities and frontier
districts. The other movement had its greatest strength   Beginnings
in the more sophisticated society of the older towns.   of Uni-
It was intellectual rather than emotional and represented tarianism.
above all a sharp reaction against some of the main tenets
of orthodox Calvinism,—original sin, predestination, and,
finally, even the doctrine of the Trinity. The full consequences of this so-called "Arminian" teaching, which was
much influenced by the writings of contemporary English rationalists, were not realized until the Unitarian movement took shape after the Revolution. Long before that
time, however, many churches in eastern Massachusetts
had traveled far from the old Puritan orthodoxy.

In education, New England made some progress during   Education.
its second century. Connecticut developed sufficiently to   Harvard
have a college of its own; Yale was founded in 1701, much and Yale.
to the satisfaction of the Mathers and their friends, who hoped
it would offset the less orthodox tendencies developing at
Harvard. There was one anxious moment when President
Timothy Cutler announced his conversion to Anglican

principles and carried a few followers with him; but he was promptly dismissed and precautions taken to prevent "Arminian and Prelatical Corruptions" in the future. With the help of generous benefactors among the English dissenters, Harvard was able to take some forward steps. Two professorships were established, one in divinity and one in natural philosophy, the latter held during this period by John Winthrop, a true scientist and a member of the Royal Society. Elementary education was not yet free in the present sense of that term, but fair opportunities for schooling were offered under the Massachusetts and Connecticut laws. Rhode Island had several schools but as yet no public educational system.

Literature.   The atmosphere of provincial New England was not favorable to art or literature. The writings of Cotton Mather, the leading author of his day, have little interest now except for the special student of history or literature. Jonathan Edwards, who belongs to the next generation, was an infinitely greater man and some of his work has a distinctly poetic quality; but it is so involved in a subtle system of metaphysical theology that it can appeal only to a select few. Probably the most significant literary development of the time was the establishment of weekly newspapers, beginning with the *Boston Newsletter* of 1704. These publications offered opportunities for literary expression on other subjects besides theology and gave the younger generation some experience in political writing.

Provincialism.   The spiritual expansion of New England hardly kept pace with the growth of its population, the forward movement of its frontier, or the broadening scope of its commerce. In politics, the Puritan colonies knew how to think freely and vigorously; but their intellectual life was distinctly provincial. Rhode Island profited somewhat by its tradition of religious liberty and the two years' visit of Dean Berkeley, the great idealist philosopher, helped to stimulate intellectual interest, at least in a little group of choice spirits. On the eve of the Revolution Newport had perhaps the most liberal society in New England.

BIBLIOGRAPHICAL NOTES

Adams, J. T., *Revolutionary New England*, chs. II–V. Osgood, *18th Cent.*, II, pt. I, ch. XII; pt. II, 295–299; III, pt. II, chs. XII–XVI. Hutchinson, *History of Mass.*, II (partly contemporary). Palfrey, *New England*, IV, V (comprehensive; too detailed for most readers). Selections from the sources in Hart, *Contemporaries*, II, ch. III, and nos. 47, 48, 78–80, 84, 90–93, 95. *(General references.)*

Matthews, L. K., *Expansion of New England*, chs. III, IV. Turner, F. J., *Frontier in American History*, chs. II, III (especially 69–79). *(Expansion.)*

Akagi, R. H., *Town Proprietors of the New England Colonies*. Bidwell, P. W., and Falconer, J. I., *History of Agriculture in the Northern U. S., 1620–1860*. *(Town proprietors, non-commoners, and farming.)*

Weeden, *New England*, chs. IX–XV. Peabody, R. E., *Merchant Venturers of Old Salem*. Interesting letters in *Commerce of Rhode Island* (Mass. Hist. Soc., *Collections*, LXIX). Morison, S. E., *Maritime Hist. of Massachusetts*, chs. I, II. *(Commercial development.)*

Du Bois, W. E. B., *Suppression of the Slave Trade*. Phillips, U. B., *American Negro Slavery*, chs. I–III. *(New England and the slave trade.)*

Capen, E. N., *Poor Laws of Connecticut*. Kelso, R. W., *Public Poor Relief in Massachusetts*. Jernegan, M. W., *Laboring and Dependent Classes*, 189–210. *(Poverty and poor relief.)*

Kittredge, G. L., *Witchcraft in Old and New England*. Notestein, W., *Witchcraft in England*. Taylor, J. M., *Witchcraft Delusion in N. E.* Burr, G. L., ed., *Witchcraft Cases*. *(Witchcraft delusion.)*

Miller, P., *Orthodoxy in Massachusetts*. Reed, S. M., *Church and State in Massachusetts, 1691–1740*. Meyer, J. C., *Church and State in Massachusetts*. Earle, A. M., *Sabbath in Puritan New England*. Greene, M. L., *Religious Liberty in Connecticut*, chs. V–XI. Walker, W., *Congregational Churches*, chs. VI–VIII. Adams, B., *Emancipation of Massachusetts*, chs. VII–X, and Adams, C. F., *Massachusetts, Historians and History*, 65–107, are sharply critical. *(Religious life.)*

Education. Morison, S. E., *History of Harvard College*, I. Jernegan, M. W., *Laboring and Dependent Classes*, 59–130. Littlefield, G. E., *Early Schools and School Books of N. E.* Fleming, S., *Children and Puritanism*.

The press. Duniway, C. A., *Freedom of the Press in Massachusetts*, chs. V–VII. Cook, E. C., *Literary Influences in Colonial Newspapers*, chs. I, II. Tyler, M. C., *American Literature*, II, chs. XI–XIV. Weeks, L. H., and Bacon, E. M., *Historical Digest of the Provincial Press*, I (issues of the *Boston Newsletter*).

"Great Awakening" Parrington, V. L., *Main Currents*, I, 148–163. Schneider, H., *Puritan Mind*. "Jonathan Edwards" in *Dictionary of American Biography*. McGiffert, A. C., Jr., *Jonathan Edwards*. Osgood, *18th Cent.*, III, pt. III, ch. I.

Typical New Englanders. *Diary* of Samuel Sewall (Mass. Hist. Soc., *Collections*). Van Doren, M., *Samuel Sewall's Diary* (selections). Murdock, K. B., *Increase Mather*. Parrington, *Main Currents*, I. Murdock, K. B., *Selections from Cotton Mather*. Kimball, E., *Joseph Dudley*. Mayo, L. S., *John Wentworth*. Wendell, B., *Cotton Mather*. Diary of John Adams in *Works*, II. Letters of Governor Belcher (in Mass. Hist. Soc., *Collections*, Sixth Series, VI, VII). G. S. Kimball, *Correspondence of Colonial Governors of Rhode Island; Talcott Papers* (Conn. Hist. Soc., *Collections*, IV, V).

Music and Puritanism. Sonneck, O. G., *Early Concert Life in America*. Scholes, P. A., *The Puritans and Music in England and New England*.

Travels. Knight, S. K., *Travels* (1704; new edition, 1921; available in Stedman and Hutchinson, *Library of American Literature*, II, 248–264). Burnaby, A., *Travels* (1759–60; in various editions and in Pinkerton, *Voyages*, XIII). Hamilton, A., *Itinerarium* (ed. by A. B. Hart, 1907).

CHAPTER XIII

EXPANSION IN THE MIDDLE PROVINCES

AFTER the reunion of the two Jerseys in 1701, there The middle colonies in 1689. were four provinces between New England and Maryland. New York and New Jersey were royal governments while Pennsylvania and Delaware were governed by William Penn. The population of these colonies was still very small. In 1689, there were perhaps 40,000 in all, of whom about half were in New York. Leaving the political boundaries out of account for a moment, these early settlements fell mainly within two circles, each with a radius of about fifty miles. One circle, with the southern tip of Manhattan as its center, included most of the inhabitants of New York and East New Jersey. The other, similarly drawn from the junction of the Delaware and Schuylkill rivers, took in most of the settlers in Pennsylvania, West New Jersey, and Delaware. Outside of these two circles, centering about New York city and Philadelphia respectively, the chief outposts were Albany on the Hudson, the eastern part of Long Island, which had much in common with New England, and a few settlements on Delaware Bay.

During the first half of the eighteenth century, this Rapid expansion. section grew faster than any other, until in 1760 the total was about 400,000, ten times the figure for 1689. Pennsylvania forged rapidly ahead of New York and now stood with Massachusetts and Virginia as one of the three largest continental colonies. The two central regions about the cities of New York and Philadelphia still had a large proportion

281

of the population, but the settled area had expanded rapidly.   In the north there was not much actual occupation above Albany, but a thin broken strip of settlements extended westward along the Mohawk. On the southern edge of this strip there were a few pioneers in the Schoharie valley and about the sources of the Susquehanna.   South of the Catskills, prosperous farming communities were established some distance back from the Hudson and some settlements were made in the highlands of northern New Jersey. Even yet, however, there were considerable gaps between the settlements adjoining New York and those about Philadelphia.

Expansion of Pennsylvania.

The expansion of the settled area was most important in Pennsylvania. From its original nucleus about the junction of the Delaware and the Schuylkill, it moved northward up both these rivers and westward to the eastern slopes of the Appalachians and their intersecting valleys. Perhaps the most notable development was in the valleys of the lower Susquehanna and its tributaries. By 1750, there were well established towns in this country, of which Lancaster was the most important. Farther back were the pioneer farms of the Scotch-Irish and other recent immigrants. The rapidly growing population of this southern border was politically within the limits of Pennsylvania, but it soon formed scarcely less important social and economic relations with the Marylanders of the upper Chesapeake region. Beside the old New York and Philadelphia "spheres of influence," a third was gradually developed, without much regard to provincial boundaries, about the new port of Baltimore.

Land policies.

The land policies of the provincial governments had much to do with the direction of this advance, checking it in some directions and stimulating it in others. The land systems of the middle provinces were, of course, radically different from those of New England. From the Hudson valley southward the landholder was everywhere a tenant, either of the King or of some proprietor or group of proprietors, and the chief outward sign of this landlord-tenant relation was the quitrent. The amounts charged varied in the different provinces, and at different times in the same province; but though never large, they were difficult to collect and a continual cause of friction. The most serious disturbances of this kind occurred in eastern New Jersey between 1745 and 1755, when the riots amounted almost to civil war. On the borders of Pennsylvania, large numbers of squatters questioned the right of the proprietors to interfere with their taking up wild lands as they saw fit. If cases were taken into the courts, juries were likely to side with delinquent tenants. So the trouble resulting was out of all proportion to the collections made.

Quitrents.

The quitrent problem existed in all these provinces, but some features of land administration varied from one province to another. New York suffered most from the concentration of land in a few hands. This evil began in the Dutch period, continued under the Duke of York, and was made worse by the lavish grants of the early royal governors. Four families controlled about two hundred square miles of the best land on Long Island; and in Westchester County, adjoining Manhattan, more than half the land belonged to six manorial estates. These conditions were not inviting to the immigrant who hoped to become a small freeholder and they help to explain why New York grew so slowly. In New Jersey the proprietors kept their rights as landlords after they gave up the government to the Crown, and were active in provincial politics. In East Jersey especially, the situation was complicated by the conflicting grants of earlier years and the New England traditions which the settlers brought with them from their old homes. In Pennsylvania, the Penn family were landlords as well as rulers and were frequently accused of thinking more of their property rights than of the welfare of the province.

Problems of land administration.

Especially did the colonists object when the proprietors claimed that their reserved lands and quitrents should be exempt from taxation. On the whole, however, Penn's land policy was much more liberal than that of New York and especially favorable to purchasers of moderate freehold estates. This fact and his tolerant religious policy explain in large part the turning of immigration from New York to Pennsylvania.

Diversity of racial elements.   In sharp contrast to New England, the middle region showed the same diversity of racial and religious elements which had characterized it from the beginning. Again, however, the developments in New York and Pennsylvania were quite different. In New York, the fusion of Dutch and English went on, with the Dutch language steadily losing ground, though in the middle of the eighteenth century it still predominated in certain localities, especially about Albany. Lawyers complained that in some counties it was hard to get men who knew enough English to serve on juries. The intermingling of racial elements was especially marked in the wealthy landowning and mercantile families. Dutch Schuylers and Van Rensselaers intermarried with English Morrises, Scotch Livingstons, and French De Lanceys, so that the leaders of New York politics and society were a decidedly mixed stock. Nevertheless, in the vital matters of language, law, and political institutions, the English strain prevailed. In Pennsylvania, large-scale immigration left the descendants of the seventeenth-century pioneers in a decided minority and increased materially the proportion of non-English people. Philadelphia was now the main gateway through which Europeans found their way to the opportunities of American life; and the two countries from which most of them came were Germany, with the German cantons of Switzerland, and Ireland.

Perhaps no nation in modern times has been so severely tried as were the German people during the century which began with the outbreak of the Thirty Years' War. That war was in itself one of the most destructive in history. An appalling proportion of the population was swept away, — in battle, by the wanton cruelty of a brutal soldiery, by privation and disease. There was also widespread demoralization in agriculture, industry, and commerce. Politically, the war almost completed the disruption of the old "Holy Roman Empire of the German Nation." On its ruins, a few states were expanding and developing a separate national consciousness; but the greater part of Germany was divided into petty principalities, exploited by petty despots, wasted by dynastic conflicts, and exposed to foreign invasion. Recovery from the effects of war was slow, and in western Germany, especially, the healing process was interrupted repeatedly during the next half century. A new generation had not come of age after the peace of Westphalia, before Louis XIV began the wars of conquest which continued with comparatively short intervals for nearly fifty years. In these wars the German states were often involved on opposite sides, considerable territory was taken from the old empire, and the western border was usually within the war zone. No region suffered more seriously in this way than the territory in the upper Rhine valley, known as the Palatinate, which was repeatedly invaded by the French armies.

Germany in the seventeenth and eighteenth centuries.

For most of the German emigrants, the principal motive was doubtless economic, the desire for a country where they could work on their own land, free from the burdensome dues imposed by feudal lords and petty princes, free also from constant wars and rumors of wars. The neighboring cantons of German Switzerland were saved from the worst of these experiences. Yet even in these little republics there were feudal dues, services required by the lords, and tithes for the support of the state churches. Another serious grievance of the Swiss was the selling of their military

Motives for German emigration.

service to foreign princes. Both in Germany and in Switzerland, economic motives were reënforced for many people by religious troubles. The treaty of Westphalia marked some advance in toleration; but Catholic and Protestant princes could still restrict seriously the religious freedom of their subjects, while neither Catholics nor Protestants could be counted on to respect the rights of the smaller dissenting groups. The Calvinists suffered from certain Catholic governments in Germany; but in some of the Swiss cantons which the Protestants controlled, dissenting sects like the Mennonites were harshly treated, partly because they objected to military service.

English interest in German colonists. Political, economic, and religious discontent made a fertile soil for colonial promoters to work in; but Germany was too disorganized to have colonies of its own and so the distressed and discontented had to look elsewhere. It happened at this particular time, that English economists and statesmen felt the importance of increasing population. Protestant refugees from France, the Netherlands, and Germany had done much for English industry, and the hard-working peasantry of the Continent would make excellent material for the colonies. One result of this feeling was an act of Parliament passed in 1709 for the naturalization of foreign Protestants. Ever since Penn began to plan his colony the advantages of America as a home for German colonists had been persistently advertised, and in the early years of the eighteenth century many thousand peasants had come to think of America as a promised land of freedom, peace, and prosperity.

The great migration. It was not, however, until 1709, that emigration from Germany and Switzerland began on a large scale. In that year there was published a new edition of a book by Joshua Kocherthal, a German Protestant pastor, describing in glowing terms the advantages of Carolina and suggesting the possibility of assistance from the English government. It happened also that the winter of 1708-1709 was unusually severe and caused widespread distress. The result of all these things and of the activities of English agents was the exodus of many thousand Germans from the Palatinate and other parts of the Rhineland to England. Whatever the British government may have done to stimulate this movement, it was certainly perplexed by the enormous number of refugees whom it was expected to take care of. For several months they were encamped near London and generous private contributions were made for their support; the expenses of the government itself were also large.

Obviously such conditions could not continue indefinitely. Several hundred refugees who were Catholics and therefore could not take the oath required of them by the new naturalization act, were sent back to Germany. Of the rest, many remained in England, some settled in Ireland, a few hundred joined a group of Swiss emigrants to North Carolina; and especially notable are the three thousand refugees sent to New York in 1710. Acting on the advice of Robert Hunter, the newly appointed governor of New York, it was decided to send these unfortunate people to that province and set them to making naval stores in the forests of the Hudson valley. Hunter doubtless meant well but the affair was bungled and finally the project had to be given up. Meantime, the Germans undertook to buy land from the Indians without authority from the government and got into more difficulties in consequence. A few finally got satisfactory titles and formed the nucleus of a somewhat important German element in the Mohawk valley; but the chief effect of this episode was to convince the immigrants and their friends that New York was not the right place for them. A few years later a number of them made their way from the Mohawk valley to the upper Susquehanna and down that river into Berks

Palatinate Germans in New York.

County, Pennsylvania. Even this colony had its problems; but on the whole it proved much more congenial to the foreign colonists. So the main stream of German immigration for the next fifty years was diverted to Pennsylvania.

German and Swiss migration to Pennsylvania.

The same year, 1710, which brought Hunter and the "Palatines" to New York, was marked by the beginning of an important settlement of Swiss Mennonites in the region about Lancaster, Pennsylvania, which soon became one of the chief centers of German and Swiss population. The annual average of German immigrants from 1727 to 1754 inclusive seems to have been about 2000, the high point being reached in the last six years of this period. Some of them settled in New Jersey, and others, especially in the middle years of the century, moved southward into Maryland and Virginia; but the largest number remained in Pennsylvania, where on the eve of the Revolution they formed about one third of the total population. With remarkable skill, the Germans picked the best farming lands in the limestone valleys, and they were not afraid to break away from the river courses to clear the forests of the back country. Many immigrants, however, were so poor that they had to get their transportation and support by selling their services for a term of years. These "redemptioners" suffered many hardships but many of them earned before long an honorable status as independent farmers.

Influence of the German element.

This "mass-immigration" of the Germans caused some anxiety. Provincial officials complained that "being ignorant of our language and laws" they formed "a distinct people from his Majesty's subjects." Even so liberal a man as Benjamin Franklin feared that the Germans might be able to establish their language to the exclusion of the English. An effort was made to avert the danger by restricting immigration, but the proprietary governors usually opposed such legislation and it generally failed.

Meantime the Germans were establishing their own churches schools, printing presses, and newspapers, becoming more and more a factor to be reckoned with; though their foreign language kept them for many years comparatively inactive in politics.

Irish emigration also was the result of unfortunate conditions at home. Most of these early Irish emigrants, however, came not from the Catholic population of the south and west, but from those northern counties of Ulster whose bitter opposition to "Home Rule" has resulted in recent years in the political separation of Ulster and the Free State. In 1718, when this emigration first became important, the Scottish colony in Ireland was about a century old. At the beginning of the seventeenth century, the English attitude toward Ireland was in some respects like that taken toward America. A large part of the native population, mainly Catholics, was to be dispossessed and the land turned over to the King's Protestant subjects. Great tracts were granted to English promoters, much as Virginia and New England were then being given away to corporations of a similar kind. Of the actual colonists in Ulster, however, the great majority were Scottish rather than English.

These "Scotch-Irish" had some trying experiences. There was constant friction both with the native Irish and with the English government. After the Revolution of 1688 they supported the cause of William of Orange (William III) and the Protestant succession, as against the Catholic Irish, who generally favored James II. The Orangemen were victorious but the struggle left behind a bitterness of feeling between them and their Catholic neighbors which is still painfully evident. Nevertheless, the colony was now securely rooted. They were hard-working, thrifty farmers, and good business men; they also developed promising woolen and linen manufactures.

Emigration from Ireland. The Scotch-Irish.

Conditions in Ulster.

Economic
grievances.

Unfortunately the British government of that period pursued a narrow policy which checked the prosperity of Ireland in general and of Ulster in particular. In order to check Irish competition in English, colonial, and foreign markets, restrictions were imposed on Irish exports, including live stock and woolen manufactures. The Woolens Act of 1699 applied to Ireland as well as to the colonies and practically destroyed that promising industry. In order to divert Irish interest from woolen manufactures, the government promised to encourage the production of linen, which became an important Ulster industry; but even this trade suffered at times from discouraging regulations. Agrarian troubles also caused unrest. There were unfortunate restrictions on tillage, and landlords were charged with raising rents unfairly. The Anglican Archbishop of Dublin declared in 1719 that these economic grievances were the chief reasons for the Irish emigration. "Your Parliament," he wrote a little earlier to the Archbishop of Canterbury, "is destroying the little trade that is left us. These and other discouragements are driving away the few Protestants that are amongst us."

Religious
grievances.

Religious grievances were probably not the chief cause of Scotch-Irish emigration, but they also had something to do with it. From their old homes, these people had brought with them the strenuous Protestant spirit of Scotch Presbyterianism, and they soon had a strong organization with an able and aggressive clergy, many of whom had been trained in the Scotch universities. The Presbyterians were, however, obliged to pay tithes for the support of the Church of Ireland, an Anglican organization which represented only a small minority of the Irish people. Some concessions were made to Protestant dissenters after the Revolution of 1688, but they were still at a serious disadvantage.

Discouraged and exasperated by these experiences, many of the Ulster people began to look for new homes across the sea. At first some were attracted to New England, where they formed pioneer settlements in central Massachusetts, Maine, and New Hampshire. They did not always mix well, however, with the New England variety of Puritanism, and after 1720 most of the Scotch-Irish went to other colonies. In New York they helped to develop the prosperous farming counties of Ulster and Orange, and on the eve of the Revolution there were also a few frontier settlements about the upper Susquehanna, just above the Pennsylvania line. Scotch-Irish in New England and New York.

Like the Germans, the Scotch-Irish found Pennsylvania more attractive. Before 1720 comparatively few had gone to that province, but after that, their numbers rapidly increased until they rivaled the Germans. In 1724, James Logan, secretary of the province, complained of the "bold and indigent strangers" from Ireland who had squatted on lands then in dispute between Pennsylvania and Maryland. When, in 1729, over five thousand of these people came in, Logan wrote in alarm: "It looks as if Ireland is to send all its inhabitants hither." By the middle of the century the Irish pioneers had pushed well up the Delaware River, but their principal settlements during this period were in the Susquehanna valley, following its course northwesterly to the neighborhood of Harrisburg and then turning southwest across the river into the Cumberland valley. A little later they moved up the Juniata, one of the principal tributaries of the Susquehanna. Here on the edge of the wilderness the Scotch-Irish with the Germans were forming buffer communities, bearing the brunt of Indian attacks and taking views of their savage neighbors quite different from those held in the older settlements. Scotch-Irish in Pennsylvania.

Unlike the Germans, the Scotch-Irish had no serious language barrier to isolate them from their neighbors. With some dialectic peculiarities, they were English speaking; nevertheless they proved on the whole more difficult for Relations with the government.

the provincial authorities to deal with than the Germans. When charged with occupying land without legal titles, they declared it was "against the laws of God and Nature, that so much land should be idle while so many Christians wanted it to labour on." Such people were almost certain to oppose a system of land tenure under which quitrents had to be paid by settlers to absentee landlords.

The great majority of the immigrants of this period in the four middle provinces were indentured servants, free laborers, or workers on their own farms. In the first class were voluntary apprentices, who served a term of years in order to learn a trade or craft, and involuntary servants, pauper children, debtors, and transported convicts whose terms were likely to be longer. Free laborers were relatively scarce and wages somewhat higher than in England. The number of negro slaves was comparatively small, New York having much the largest number. In the city of New York and on some of the large estates in that vicinity, they were numerous enough to cause some anxiety. The "negro plots" of 1712 and 1741, of slight importance in themselves, produced a state of hysterical excitement even more tragic than the witchcraft panic in Massachusetts. In 1741, fourteen negroes were burned at the stake in New York and eighteen more were hanged; there were similar disturbances in New Jersey. In Pennsylvania some Quakers owned slaves; but the evident need of intelligent white labor on the wheat farms combined with ethical motives to keep slavery down. There was a striking difference in this respect between Pennsylvania and its nearest neighbor to the southward.

The chief business of this whole middle section was farming. Here were the "bread colonies" of England's American empire, exporting wheat and flour in large quantities. New York had only begun to use her agricultural resources; but by the middle of the century she was shipping flour at the rate of 80,000 barrels a year, the product of her own farms and those of northern New Jersey. The chief granary of the continent was Pennsylvania, where the Germans took the lead in intelligent farm management. Governor Pownall, who visited the German and Swiss settlements about Lancaster in 1754, found "some of the finest farms one can conceive, and in the highest state of culture." Primitive log huts gradually gave way to more pretentious houses of brick and stone. Travelers were especially impressed by the immense stone barns of the more prosperous German farmers. Hardly less picturesque were the great wagons in which wheat, flour, and vegetables were carried to the Philadelphia market. Before long, however, some of these settlements began to find their best outlet across the Maryland line through Chesapeake Bay.

For New York the fur trade was still a prime interest. To hold it against French competition, the post of Oswego was founded on Lake Ontario and strenuous efforts were made with some success to establish direct connections with the western Indians. Under the influence of Governor Burnet and his advisers, the assembly tried to check the export of English goods to Canada, in the hope that the Indians, who preferred English goods, might be drawn away from the French. This legislation failed, however, because too many New Yorkers were interested in the trade with Canada. As the German and Scotch-Irish pioneers moved on to the frontiers of Pennsylvania, this colony also acquired an increasing interest in the western fur trade. The sturdy backwoodsmen, led by such famous guides as the German Conrad Weiser and the Irish George Croghan, dealt directly with the Indians, while Philadelphia merchants supplied capital and made large profits in the trade. *The fur trade.*

Shipbuilding and ocean commerce were both growing interests. New York and Philadelphia, like Boston, found their most valuable market in the West Indies and were *Shipbuilding and ocean commerce.*

similarly annoyed by the Molasses Act. They also sent provisions and lumber to Spain, Portugal, and the Portuguese islands. Philadelphia developed much faster than either New York or Boston and before the Revolution stood first among the cities of the English seaboard. In the Jerseys some trade, legal and illegal, went on at Perth Amboy in the north and Burlington on the Delaware River; but as Governor Franklin said, just before the Revolution, New York and Philadelphia were "the commercial capitals of East and West New Jersey." Both in New York and in Philadelphia, society was dominated by rich merchant families, — Dutch, French, Scotch, and English in the former; in the latter, the old Quaker families still held the lead. Both towns impressed foreign travelers as comfortable and prosperous. Before the Revolution, New Yorkers were building "spacious, genteel houses" of stone and brick, some of them four or five stories high. Philadelphia was more uniformly, not to say monotonously, built of brick. The English Burnaby and the Swedish Kalm both spoke of it with enthusiasm. The latter wrote of "its fine appearance, good regulations, agreeable situation, natural advantages, trade, riches, and power."

New York and Philadelphia society.

In the history of colonial manufactures, Pennsylvania and New Jersey have an honorable place, partly because the foreign immigration, especially from Germany, brought many skilled workmen. In a wheat-growing region, milling was important and before the Revolution the best flour mills of this region were probably equal to any in Europe. Though the coal resources of Pennsylvania were practically unused for industrial purposes, the Delaware colonies were active in manufactures of iron, textiles, paper, and glass. Philadelphia had a remarkable variety of skilled mechanics. Two other Pennsylvania towns also were noted for their manufactures. At Germantown, according to the Swedish traveler Kalm, "most of the inhabitants are manufacturers,

Manufactures.

and make almost everything in such quantity and perfection, that, in a short time, this province will lack very little from England, its mother country." Lancaster, the largest inland town in the English colonies, was another considerable center for weavers and metal workers. The printing business was well developed both by the English and by the Germans. William Bradford and Benjamin Franklin were perhaps the most successful among the former; it was Franklin also who printed the first German book in America. Conspicuous among the Germans was Christopher Sauer, who established his press in 1738. Five years later he published his quarto edition of the German Bible.

In the history of the middle provinces, economic and **Politics.** social evolution seems more important than politics. Most of the important political issues of the period are like those already noted in other royal and proprietary colonies. So far as local conditions produced issues of a more distinctive kind, they were usually characteristic of particular provinces rather than of the section as a whole. Expansion did, however, bring some problems of intercolonial politics. Boundary questions, for instance, became more urgent **Boundary** as settlers moved into the disputed regions. On the New **controversies.** England border, New York's dispute with Connecticut was most easily disposed of; a similar one with Massachusetts dragged on through the whole of this period and the conflict with New Hampshire was just becoming serious on the eve of the Revolution. About the middle of the century, Connecticut tried to colonize the Wyoming country (part of the Susquehanna valley) in Pennsylvania on the strength of her sea-to-sea charter. There were also disputes between New York and New Jersey, decided just before the Revolution, and between New York and Pennsylvania, though in the latter case the slow progress of settlement prevented a really serious conflict. The most famous and acrimonious of all the intercolonial boundary disputes was ended by the fixing of "Mason and Dixon's line," in 1769, between Pennsylvania and Maryland.

Some political connections cut across provincial boundaries. From 1702 to 1738, New Jersey had to get on with a governor who was also responsible for New York and spent most of his time there. The New Jersey people naturally objected and in 1738 got a separate governor of their own. Several prominent politicians owned land or had business interests in more than one province. Some of the New Jersey councilors lived in New York or Philadelphia and one of them was for a time chief justice of New York. Quaker traditions affected politics on both sides of the Delaware and one New Jersey governor complained that his people were too much influenced by the Pennsylvanians. In the famous Zenger libel case, one of the best-known politicians and lawyers of Pennsylvania was called in by the New Yorkers to defend the liberty of the press.

New York continued to have a political importance out of proportion to its population. Leaving out of account the detached trading stations of the Hudson's Bay Company, it was the chief base for the northern fur trade, and the northwestern outpost of the British dominions. Within its sphere of influence was the most powerful of the Indian confederacies, on whose attitude depended to a large extent the outcome of the great Anglo-French struggle for supremacy in North America. As Governor Bellomont said in 1699, New York "ought to be looked upon as the capital Province or the Cittadel to all the others; for secure but this and you secure all the English Colonies, not only against the French but also against any insurrections or rebellions against the Crown of England, if any such should happen, which God forbid." From this imperial point of view, the actual development of New York politics was disappointing. Though the New Yorkers were among the last to receive a representative assembly, they were soon conspicuous for their encroachments on the King's prerogative and that of his governor.

This fight for autonomy was carried on, during most of this period, not by or for the great body of the colonists, but in the interest of a privileged class. In New York and Albany merchants and artisans could vote as freemen of the corporation, admission to which could be gained by inheritance, by serving an apprenticeship, or by payment of a relatively low fee. Elsewhere the suffrage was limited to freeholders of land worth at least forty pounds. This excluded a majority of the adult male population. Apart from the municipalities, which were comparatively democratic, politics was, therefore, largely controlled by a few leading families. This aristocracy, however, had its factions, each striving to control the government for its own purposes. Succeeding governors usually played for the support of one or more of these factions; the other factions tended to join the opposition. In all this there was not much real democratic feeling; but as time went on the opposition leaders tried to win popular support by laying more stress upon genuine constitutional principles and the rights of the common man. *New York politics.*

Here, as elsewhere, constitutional conflicts turned largely on the control of the purse. The official theory was that, while taxes had to be levied by the assembly, the government should be made stable by permanent grants for its support; that appropriations should be general, leaving specific expenditures to be determined by the governor and council; and that the assembly should have no further control except the right of examining and criticizing the accounts. Before long, this view was challenged by the assembly, partly because of the misconduct of the early governors, especially the notorious misappropriation of public funds by Lord Cornbury, a cousin of Queen Anne and the degener- *Constitutional issues. Control of the purse.*

ate grandson of the great Earl of Clarendon. Bit by bit, a policy was adopted which almost revolutionized the provincial government, shifting the center of gravity decidedly from the governor to the assembly. In spite of vigorous protests by successive governors and by the Board of Trade, appropriations, including the governor's salary, were made only for limited terms, first for five years, but finally only for one. The representatives also decided that the money raised by taxes should be kept by the provincial treasurer, an officer of their own choosing who could be depended upon to carry out their policies. When the council, acting as an upper house, objected to these policies, the house of representatives took a leaf out of the practice of the English House of Commons and denied the right of the council to amend money bills at all.

New York and the home government. In 1751 the Board of Trade made an elaborate report on New York and called for drastic action; but the hard fact was that the assembly, having the right either to give or refuse money, could fix its own conditions and the governor could not prevent it. The only remedy which might have been effective was the raising of revenue by act of Parliament, and as early as 1711 this was actually proposed by Robert Hunter, perhaps the ablest of the New York governors. Similar suggestions were made later, but the home government shrank from such extreme action. Thus, in spite of its early "strong government" traditions, the merchants and landowners of New York were surprisingly successful in their fight for self-government.

The assembly and public opinion. It has already been suggested that even the assembly did not adequately represent the people. A skillful governor could indeed so distribute his favors as to build up a party for himself among the representatives. To lessen this danger and keep the assembly in closer touch with public opinion, the assembly passed a law requiring triennial elections; but it was disallowed by the English Privy Council, which called it "a very high infringement upon the prerogative of the Crown." Under these circumstances, free discussion in the public press was essential if there was to be any real popular control of the government. Fortunately for New York, and for other colonies as well, this principle of a free press won a notable victory in the famous Zenger case of 1735.

Shortly before this time, the chief justice of New York had been removed because Governor Cosby objected to his stand in a case in which the latter was personally interested. Sharp criticism of the governor naturally followed and some of it was printed in the *New York Weekly Journal*, published by a German immigrant named John Peter Zenger. The governor then caused the prosecution of Zenger for criminal libel. The new chief justice who presided at the trial showed a strong bias against the defendant, but Zenger's supporters were fortunate in securing the services of Andrew Hamilton, a leading lawyer and politician of Pennsylvania. By a skillful appeal to the jurymen he persuaded them to disregard the ruling of the court, which was that they had nothing to do but decide whether Zenger had, or had not, published the articles in question. This theory would have allowed the judges alone to decide whether the articles were really libelous; but Hamilton argued that the jury had a right to decide whether a publication was actually false, malicious, and so libelous. Moved by Hamilton's eloquent plea for free public discussion, the jury acquitted Zenger and established a new landmark in the history of a free press.

The Zenger case.

Pennsylvania, too, had its perennial conflicts between governor and assembly, the former defending his own prerogative and the rights of his superiors in England, and the latter representing the desire of the ruling class among the colonists to manage their business with the least possible interference. Here also the assembly got the better in these

Pennsylvania politics. Demands of the assembly.

encounters. The Pennsylvanians had a certain advantage in Penn's liberal charter of 1701, which gave them annually elected assemblies. Before long, they went a step further and denied the governor's right to dissolve or prorogue the house. "We sit," said Speaker Andrew Hamilton in 1739, "upon our own adjournments, when we please, and as long as we think necessary." In using their grip on the purse strings to extort political concessions, there was little to choose between the "topping" Quakers and their northern neighbors. Governors were kept in hand by making their salaries a matter of annual or semiannual votes, and treasurers, chosen by the assembly and subject to its orders, kept the province funds. The governor's appointing power was also seriously curtailed in other ways.

Conflicting interests.

In certain other respects, Pennsylvania was quite different from New York. In the Quaker colony, politics was a triangular game, with King, proprietor, and colonists—all standing for special interests of their own. The governor had to think not only of the proprietor, who appointed him, and the assembly, without whose coöperation the public business would stop, but also of the British government, which expected him to enforce the acts of trade and raise funds for military purposes. The Penn family were responsible for the civil government and for the welfare of the people who lived under it; but they were also the principal landowners, claiming quitrents from their tenants and holding on their own account great areas of improved and unimproved land. This complicated relationship made trouble even in the lifetime of William Penn, when proprietor and people had a common interest in the realization of Quaker ideals. There was still more trouble under his sons and grandsons, who gave up the Quaker faith and whose interests in the province were scarcely different from those of any other absentee landlord.

For many years, the assembly refrained from taxing the

proprietary estates or their quitrents; but during the last French wars, tax bills were held up because the assembly insisted on what the proprietors considered unfair charges upon their estates. With the home government urging appropriations for defense and the assembly determined not to give them without the obnoxious taxes, the governor was in a hard place. Finally the assembly practically bribed him into a violation of his instructions. The irritation caused by these controversies was so great that in 1764 a strong party, with Benjamin Franklin as one of its principal leaders, tried to have the proprietary government overthrown and a royal government established, though this project was finally given up.

Taxing of the proprietary estates.

As a Quaker colony, Pennsylvania found it hard to adjust its institutions and ideals to the demands of the home government. This was especially serious because, under the royal charter, the province was more closely controlled by the home government than were the other proprietary colonies. Its laws had to be sent to England for approval and the whole experiment was jealously watched by unfriendly critics on both sides of the Atlantic. Many of the early laws were disallowed by the home government on the ground that they were contrary to the laws of England. Penn was so much harassed by these complaints, as well as by the apparently ungrateful attitude of his own people, that he came near giving up his government altogether.

Pennsylvania and the English government.

Among the controversies which arose between Pennsylvania and the British government, two were closely connected with the peculiar teaching of the Society of Friends. One was the question of oaths, and the other that of military service. On the first question, the Quakers stood for a law allowing in all cases the substitution of a solemn affirmation in place of an oath. To secure this privilege for themselves in their own colony seemed reasonable enough; even the British Parliament allowed Quakers in certain cases to affirm

The question of judicial oaths.

instead of swearing.   In England, however, oaths were required of all jurymen, witnesses in criminal cases, and officials generally.   The early Pennsylvania practice naturally went farther and allowed affirmations in all cases.   It also failed to provide adequately for administering oaths to persons who preferred to use that form.   So one provincial law after another was passed only to be disallowed by the home government.   The long deadlock was ended by two acts of the Pennsylvania assembly, one in 1718, and one in 1724, both approved by the King;   taken together they extended to Pennsylvania a considerable part of the English penal code, but relieved the Quakers from the obligation of taking oaths.   Since, however, judges were obliged to administer the oath to any person who desired it, a strict Quaker could hardly hold that office.

The question of military service caused even more trouble. Though some Quakers were less strict than others, most of them agreed that a Friend should not bear arms himself and that a Quaker legislator should not vote for strictly military appropriations.   Since the assembly was generally controlled by the Quakers, such appropriations were frequently refused.   Some of the Quakers, however, realized the difficulty of the situation and grants were sometimes made in such terms that they could be used, directly or indirectly, for military purposes, as for instance for the relief of friendly Indians or "for the Queen's use."   During the period of peace between 1713 and 1739, this issue fell into the background;   but when the Anglo-Spanish war broke out, in 1739, followed shortly afterwards by war with France, Pennsylvania was naturally asked to do her part in the common defense.   Meantime, the relations of the Pennsylvanians with their Indian neighbors had changed decidedly for the worse.   Unfair practices of unscrupulous officials weakened the old friendly feeling and few of the new frontiersmen had any sympathy with Quaker ideas;

The question of military service.

The problem of defense, 1739–1763.

the Scotch-Irish were especially pugnacious. So the Quakers were in a trying position. They were still unwilling to vote for militia laws and military appropriations, but they were under severe pressure both from the British government and from their own frontier settlers. They finally found a way out of this dilemma by giving up enough seats in the assembly to relieve themselves temporarily of the responsibility for carrying on the government.

Until the crisis of the French War, the old Quaker families were fairly successful in their control of provincial politics. This was true long after they had lost their numerical majority, because they got on fairly well with the earlier German immigrants, who, being unfamiliar with the English language and English political methods, were willing to leave the government in the hands of the old ruling class. With the Scotch-Irish and many of the German frontiersmen the case was quite different. As against the conservatism of the seaboard there gradually developed an aggressive frontier democracy, which demanded more energetic measures for defense. It also denounced the political system which kept down the representation of the western counties and enabled a minority in the older settlements to control the policies of the province. *Quaker control in politics.*

Perhaps the most striking characteristic of society in the middle provinces was the way in which men of different religious traditions were learning to live together. Except in New York, no serious efforts were made to establish any one church, and even there the attempt failed almost completely. Though the New York law of 1693 providing for the support of a Protestant clergy was for a time used by Anglican governors to give their church a privileged position, this policy had to be given up because the great majority of the inhabitants belonged to other churches. Popular prejudice against the Catholics led to some harsh legislation against them in New York. The instructions *Religion in the middle colonies; toleration.*

to the royal governors requiring them to respect liberty of conscience made an exception of "papists," who were excluded from office even in Pennsylvania. In the latter colony, however, Catholic worship was not interfered with and mass was publicly celebrated in Philadelphia. In New York the Jews had a regular place for public worship. William Smith, the contemporary historian of New York, though speaking of his own province, probably expressed the prevailing opinion in this whole section when he said that the "body of the people" were "for an equal, universal toleration of Protestants, and averse to any kind of ecclesiastical establishment."

Anglican Church.

Of the principal religious groups in the middle colonies, the Anglicans were more conspicuous for their prestige and political influence than for their numbers. Through the work of the Society for Propagating the Gospel and the active support of some royal officials, this church made substantial progress and there were fairly strong parishes in Philadelphia, Burlington, and New York. Because of the close relation between the Anglican clergy and the office-holding group, the other denominations were always afraid that the Church of England might gain some unfair advantage.

Developments among the Quakers.

The Quakers held their ground fairly well in Pennsylvania and West New Jersey, though at the beginning of this period they suffered from the propaganda of a former Friend, George Keith, who first formed a group of his own called the "Keithian" Quakers and then led some of his followers into the Anglican Church. Within the Society, there were differences of opinion between those who emphasized the mystical aspects of Quaker teaching and those who were more rationalistic and practical. Many of the younger generation lacked the enthusiasm of the founders; but the Society was fairly consistent in upholding Quaker principles in the matter of oaths and military service. The Quakers also came to take a more definite antislavery position, though there were a number of slaveowners among them. In 1758 the Yearly Meeting resolved that Friends should set their slaves "at liberty, making a Christian provision for them"; and a committee was appointed to confer with slave-owning members.

The Germans and Swiss brought a great variety of religious denominations. The Lutherans and the Calvinists were the most numerous; but the smaller sects, being more picturesque, have attracted more attention. Some of them were strongly mystical and formed communities in which they withdrew from the distractions of the world to lead a strictly religious life. Conspicuous among the minor groups were the peace-loving Mennonites and Moravians; the latter were especially devoted missionaries to the Indians. There were Lutherans on the Delaware even before Penn's time and their numbers grew rapidly with the German migration of the eighteenth century. At first they had no efficient organization, but in 1741 they found an able leader in the person of Heinrich Mühlenberg. He came to Pennsylvania from Halle, in Saxony, and he represented the pietistic element in the Lutheran Church, which was trying to get below formalities to a deeper spiritual life. In 1748 was organized at Philadelphia the first American synod of the Lutheran Church. Similar work was done for the German Reformed churches by another able man, the Rev. Michael Schlatter.

German and Swiss churches.

The Lutherans.

Taking the middle colonies as a whole, the most important religious element was probably the group of denominations which accepted the teaching of John Calvin. This group included the Dutch Reformed Church of New Netherland and New York, which still kept up some connection with the established church of Holland; the Puritan emigrants from New England, chiefly in New York and New Jersey; the Scotch-Irish Presbyterians; and the German Reformed churches. Before long many of the English-speaking Cal-

The Calvinistic churches. Presbyterianism.

vinists came together in a new Presbyterian organization. The first American presbytery was organized at Philadelphia in 1706, by the Scotch-Irish preacher, Francis Makemie, and the church grew rapidly after the Scotch-Irish migration set in. The Great Awakening was responsible for some dissensions among the Presbyterians; but they furnished some of its principal leaders and were on the whole stimulated by it. Presbyterianism was also reënforced by some Dutch Calvinists who had become accustomed to the English language. By 1758, the various presbyteries were united in the synod of New York and Philadelphia, and on the eve of the Revolution this church was a powerful factor in politics as well as in religion. Unlike the Anglicans and the peace-loving Quakers, the Presbyterians inclined toward a somewhat aggressive democracy.

Problems of education. In an age when religion and education were closely associated, the heterogeneous population of the middle provinces naturally found it difficult to establish efficient public-school systems. In New York a small beginning was made by the Dutch; but after the English conquest, the two races failed to get together on any effective program of public education, and a contemporary writer says that the New York schools were "in the lowest order." One of the early Pennsylvania laws required parents to see that their children learned to read and write, and were taught "some useful trade or skill." For the most part, the responsibility for education was assumed by families, religious societies, and other private organizations. The Anglican missionary work included the maintenance of church schools, and the Quakers, while neglecting higher education, founded a number of elementary and secondary schools. The various German sects were also active and they had some highly educated men among their clergy. An Anglican churchman wrote in 1763 that they seemed to be "abundantly well provided in teachers of one kind or another." The Presbyterian ministers also emphasized general education as well as theological training.

Higher education naturally came much later here than in New England, but about the middle of the century three colleges were founded. The College of New Jersey, now Princeton University, was chartered in 1746 and graduated its first class in 1748. Its chief promoters were Presbyterian clergy of Irish, Scotch, or New England stock, and like the other Puritan colleges, it laid special stress on the training of ministers. Princeton became more and more the chief intellectual center of the Scotch-Irish population in the middle region and in the South. Some prominent New Yorkers were trained at Yale; but in 1754, King's College was chartered in the city of New York. The dominant influence in this college was Anglican, with some representation of other elements in the governing board. Its first president was that energetic Anglican churchman and writer, Samuel Johnson. A little earlier, Benjamin Franklin and a few other liberal-minded citizens founded the "Academy" in Philadelphia, which later developed into the University of Pennsylvania. Unlike its predecessors, it was not controlled by a religious denomination and gave more attention to modern subjects like English and the sciences.

Colleges. Princeton.

King's College.

University of Pennsylvania.

The middle region had its fair share of active-minded men who contributed to the education of their contemporaries. The royal governors, for instance, were not all rakes or adventurers. One of them, Robert Hunter, was a friend of Addison and Swift, and his letters show his interest in natural science. His successor, Burnet, was a Cambridge University man, with some reputation as a collector and reader of books. A *protégé* of both these governors was Cadwallader Colden, one of the most interesting personalities of provincial New York. A graduate in medicine of the University of Edinburgh, he came to America, spent a few years in business and medical practice at Philadelphia, and

The intellectual class.

Cadwallader Colden.

then attracted the attention of Governor Hunter, who made him surveyor-general of New York. Becoming interested in Indian relations, Colden wrote a well-known *History of the Five Indian Nations.* He was also the author of numerous philosophical and scientific papers, some of which were important enough to give him a recognized place in the history of American thought.

The list of Colden's Pennsylvania correspondents shows how the thinking men of these provinces were keeping in touch with one another. Three of them deserve special notice. **James Logan.** James Logan was a liberal-minded Scotch-Irish Quaker who came to Pennsylvania as William Penn's secretary. Though a successful business man, politician, and judge, he kept up his scientific interests, contributing to the *Transactions* of the British Royal Society articles on mathematics, physics, and botany. In his old age Franklin printed for him a translation of Cicero's *De Senectute.* Another interesting figure **John Bartram.** was John Bartram, the botanist, whom a well-known contemporary scientist in England characterized as a "wonderful natural genius."

Benjamin Franklin. The outstanding figure in this Pennsylvania group was of course Benjamin Franklin. A Yankee by birth, his naturally free and tolerant spirit found in Philadelphia congenial and stimulating associations. Beginning as a printer's apprentice, he edited the principal newspaper of Pennsylvania and then turned naturally to politics. A leader first in his own province, his influence reached out into intercolonial and even imperial affairs. Better than any other American he was fitted to mediate between his countrymen and the British government. He represented the latter as the head of the postal service in America and he became later the chief interpreter in England of the American point of view. Through his newspaper and his *Poor Richard's Almanac,* he partly expressed and partly molded the popular "common-sense" philosophy of his fellow citizens. **He**

was full of plans for improving the life of his neighbors, — inventing improved fireplaces, devising protection against fires, and organizing an academy of sciences. Years before the Revolution, his wide acquaintance with men of distinction in other colonies and in Europe, together with his researches in electricity and other branches of science, made him a really international figure.

Philadelphia also illustrated the debt of American science to the physicians, some of whom were active in Franklin's Philosophical Society. From a modern standpoint, colonial practice was still primitive; but a few ambitious young men went abroad for training, commonly at Edinburgh and London. One of them, Dr. John Morgan, was the principal founder of the medical department in the College of Philadelphia (1765); another, Samuel Bard, helped to establish the medical faculty of King's College in New York (1767). *Medical science.*

BIBLIOGRAPHICAL NOTES

Becker, C. L., *Political Parties in N. Y.*, ch. I. Osgood, *18th Cent.*, II, pt. I, chs. XVIII, XIX; pt. II, ch. IV; IV, ch. X. Flick, A. C., *Hist. of State of N. Y.*, II, chs. VIII, IX; III, chs. I, II, IV, V. Good contemporary account in Smith, W., *History of New York* (various editions, including N. Y. Hist. Soc., *Collections*, 1st ser., IV, V). Governors' letters in *Documents relating to the Colonial Hist. of N. Y.*, especially V. Colden's letters in N. Y. Hist. Soc., *Collections*, L, LVI. *New York.* *Sources.*

Osgood, *18th Cent.*, II, pt. I, ch. XXIV; pt. II, ch. VII; IV, ch. VI. Channing, *United States*, II, ch. XI. Root, W. T., *Relations of Pennsylvania with the British Government.* Sharpless, *Quaker Government*, I, and his *Political Leaders of Provincial Pennsylvania.* Biographies of Franklin by P. L. Ford, S. G. Fisher, W. C. Bruce, and B. Faÿ. *Penn-Logan Correspondence* (Penn. Hist. Soc., *Memoirs*). Franklin's *Autobiography.* *Pennsylvania.* *Readable sources.*

Special students of constitutional history are referred to monographs by Shepherd (Pennsylvania), Fisher and Tanner (New Jersey), and Spencer (New York). *Political institutions.*

Immigration.   Osgood, *18th Cent.*, II, pt. II, ch. VI. Jernegan, M. W., *American Colonies*, ch. XII. Channing, *United States*, II, ch. XIV. Report of American Council of Learned Societies, Amer. Hist. Assoc., *Annual Report*, 1931, I, 103–408. Bolton, C. K., *Scotch-Irish Pioneers*, chs. III–VIII, XIV. Ford, H. J., *Scotch-Irish in America*, chs. I–XVI. O'Brien, M. J., *A Hidden Phase of American History* (the Irish; cf. review in *A.H.R.*, XXVI). Faust, A. B., *German Element in the United States*, 3d ed., 1927, especially I, chs. III–V. Kuhns, O., *German and Swiss Settlements of Colonial Pennsylvania*. Mellick, A. D., *Story of an Old Farm*, especially chs. III–VII, XI, XII (immigrant experiences).

Sources.   Penn. German Society, *Proceedings*, XVIII (immigrant's diary). Rush, B., *Manners of the German Inhabitants* (*ibid.*, XIX).

The frontier and its problems.   Osgood, *18th Cent.*, I, ch. XIV; III, pt. II, ch. XVIII. Turner, *Frontier in American History*, ch. III. Halsey, F. W., *Old New York Frontier*, and his *Tour of Four Great Rivers*. Walton, J. S., *Conrad Weiser*. McIlwain, *Wraxall's Abridgment*, pp. lxiv ff. Higgins, R. L., *Expansion in N. Y.* Pound, A., *Johnson of the Mohawks*. Volwiler, A. T., *George Croghan and the Westward Movement*. Cribbs, G. A., *Frontier Policy of Pennsylvania*.

Religious elements.   Jones, R., *Quakers in America*, bks. IV, V. Vols. in *American Church History Series* on Episcopal, Lutheran, Presbyterian, Dutch Reformed, German Reformed, and Moravian Churches. Maxson, C. H., *Great Awakening in the Middle Colonies*.

Labor.   Herrick, C. A., *White Servitude in Penn.* Seybolt, R. F., *Apprenticeship in Col. N. Y. and N. E.* McKee, S., *Labor in Col. N. Y.*

New York and Philadelphia merchants.   Nettels, C., "Economic Relations of Boston, Phila., and N. Y., 1680–1715," *Journal of Bus. and Eco. Hist.* (1930), III, 185–215. Harrington, V. L., *New York Merchant on the Eve of the Revolution*. Kraus, M., *Intercolonial Aspects of American Culture*, ch. I.

The press.   Hildeburn, C. R., *Sketches of Printers and Printing in Colonial N. Y.* Zenger episode: Osgood, *18th Cent.*, II, pt. II, ch. V. Rutherford, L. A., *Zenger*. Cook, E. C., *Literary Influences in Colonial Newspapers*, chs. III–V. Oberholtzer, E. P., *Literary Hist. of Phila.*, chs. I, II. Oswald, J. C., *Benjamin Franklin, Printer*.

Education.   Kilpatrick, W. H., *Dutch Schools in New Netherland and N. Y.* Kemp, W. W., *Support of Schools in Colonial N. Y.* Brown, E. E., *Making of Our Middle Schools*.

CHAPTER XIV

EXPANSION IN THE SOUTH

IN the last decade of the seventeenth century, the *Different stages of development.* southern colonies were in various stages of development. On Chesapeake Bay, Maryland and Virginia were securely established, — both for the time being under royal governments. In the tidewater section of these provinces, the colonial experience of three generations had taken shape in institutions, economic, political, and religious, whose main features were fairly well fixed. Half a century of remarkable growth was to follow, but largely on lines already indicated. With the struggling and isolated settlements to the southward, it was quite another story. Thirty years after the Carolina proprietors secured their first charter, this great province was only slightly developed. On its northern edge, a few frontiersmen were raising corn, tobacco, and live stock, with slight regard to the authority of the proprietors. Separated from these settlements by a long stretch of unoccupied coast line was Charleston, the nucleus of a somewhat more orderly community. This southern settlement, though favored by the proprietors, had hardly yet found itself economically or politically. In 1689, the Carolinas hardly numbered more than five thousand inhabitants between them. With two separate assemblies and no effective general government, their future political relations were still uncertain. Nominally Carolina extended to the twenty-ninth parallel; forty years passed, however, before the founding of Georgia definitely established British sovereignty beyond the Savannah.

Political re-
adjustment.

Gradually the political geography was readjusted. The Revolution of 1688 had upset Lord Baltimore's authority and put a royal government in its place; but in 1715 a Protestant Calvert reclaimed the family inheritance and Maryland again became a proprietary province. This relaxation of imperial control was, however, soon offset by the overthrow of proprietary government in the Carolinas. In 1732, the British government went back to seventeenth century practice and entrusted the new colony of Georgia to a private corporation; but this government was recognized as temporary, and definite provision made for its reversion to the Crown. When, in 1754, royal government was established in Georgia, the political subdivision of the coast line was complete from Delaware Bay to the Altamaha River. Beyond that point was the "no-man's land" of the Anglo-Spanish frontier. On the eve of the Revolution, the machinery of royal government was set up in every province south of the Potomac.

Opposition
to the
Carolina
proprietors.

The South Carolina uprising of 1719, which overthrew the proprietary governments, was the culmination of influences at work for many years. The proprietary rights, originally held by some of the chief personages in English politics, gradually passed to men of inferior caliber less able to defend themselves against criticism; and of such criticism there was plenty on both sides of the Atlantic.

Complaints
of the home
government.

Contrary to early expectations, Carolina did not send to England any staple comparable with West Indian sugar. North Carolina had little commercial connection with England, and even the early development of rice culture about Charleston was still a small affair compared with the highly colored statements of fifty years before. Meantime royal agents were busy with reports of illegal trade and even more objectionable practices. No other province except perhaps the Bahamas had so bad a reputation for piracy as the Carolinas; even provincial officials were suspected of a criminal interest in the business. There were other evidences of poor management. North Carolina, for instance, attracted attention chiefly by a series of insurrections and small civil wars unparalleled in the history of any other province. During Queen Anne's War, both the home government and the colonists felt that the proprietors had failed to do their part in defending the southern frontier. Then came two serious Indian wars, with the Tuscaroras in the north and the Yemassees in the south, and again the proprietors were found wanting.

Notwithstanding this unsatisfactory record, the proprietors had enough influence at court to save their chartered privileges until the South Carolina people finally took matters into their own hands. By 1719, the proprietors had gradually alienated almost every influential element in that province. The dissenters were exasperated by the Church Acts of 1704, put through by the high-church party under the governor's leadership. These acts not only obliged them to pay church taxes but made them ineligible for membership in the assembly. Despairing of relief from the proprietors, they sent a mission to England which won over the Bishop of London by pointing out a clause in the law which interfered with his jurisdiction. The House of Lords finally took the matter up in an address to the Queen and there was serious talk of revoking the charter; but the proprietors were allowed to keep the government, with the understanding that the obnoxious laws were to be repealed, which was done shortly afterwards. Meantime the colonists had learned the possibility of appealing over the heads of the proprietors to the imperial government.

Unrest in South Carolina.

Church Acts of 1704.

Before long, new issues united most of the colonists in opposition, without regard to religious affiliations. In 1719 it was announced that the proprietors had disallowed some popular laws, including one regulating elections to the assembly. Until 1716 all these elections had been con-

The revolution of 1719.

centrated in Charleston, an arrangement which became increasingly inconvenient as the colony developed, besides giving too much influence to the officeholders. So in 1716 the assembly ordered that representatives should be chosen by elections in their respective districts. Unfortunately after one election had been held under the new law, the proprietors rejected it and ordered another election in Charleston on the old plan. New representatives were chosen accordingly; but they presently organized themselves into a revolutionary convention and, with the help of militia assembled to meet a threatened Spanish invasion, they upset the proprietary government, choosing a new governor to act temporarily in the King's name.

Royal government in South and North Carolina

The home government promptly took advantage of this revolution and sent a provisional royal governor to Charleston. The proprietary government held on in North Carolina, thus emphasizing still further the division of the old province; but most of the proprietors saw the futility of trying to keep their control and in 1728 agreed to a bargain by which the government was given up. All the proprietors but one also transferred their rights in the soil to the Crown. This bargain was confirmed by Parliament in 1729 and permanent royal governments were set up in North and South Carolina. For twenty years the two provinces had had almost nothing in common except their common subjection to the proprietors. Now the separation was complete.

Southern expansion; population and settled area.

Even more significant than these political changes was the steady expansion of the settlements. In 1689, the whole region south of Pennsylvania probably had less than 90,000 inhabitants. By 1760 this population had increased some seven or eight times, to about 700,000. About two thirds of these people still lived in the old Chesapeake provinces, but the rate of increase was naturally much faster in the younger colonies. For every colonist south of Virginia in

1689, there were probably at least forty in 1760. North Carolina lagged behind for a time, but in the middle years of the eighteenth century it grew faster than any of its neighbors. At first the increase was largely in the tide-water region. In Virginia and Maryland, the strip between the coast line and the falls of the rivers had been fairly well occupied in the seventeenth century; but during the next fifty years the settlements became more compact. In the Carolinas, the occupation even of the lowland country was delayed by great areas of swamp land and by the "pine barren" strip which lay only a short distance back from the sea. There were a number of new settlements on the coast like Wilmington in North Carolina and Georgetown in South Carolina, but considerable stretches of coast line were still unoccupied. Meantime, the founding of Georgia pushed the international boundary southward beyond the Savannah River.

A variety of motives worked together when James Oglethorpe and his fellow trustees secured their charter from the King in 1732. Oglethorpe was really interested in giving poor but honest debtors a fresh chance in the New World. At the same time there was a good deal of sympathy for the German Protestants who had suffered persecution in the ecclesiastical principality of Salzburg and now sought refuge under the British flag. Imperialistic motives were also at work. The English fur traders had long been pushing through the mountains and around the southern end of the Appalachian system and the fate of the whole Southwest, from the mountains to the Mississippi, hung in the balance. Spaniards, Frenchmen, and English-men were engaged in a triangular competition for trade with the Indians and for political influence as a means of extending that trade. Georgia was thus expected to com-bine the advantages of a philanthropic establishment, a military garrison against the Spaniards, and a base for the

The founding of Georgia.

western fur trade. For such a colony something different from the older plantation settlements was needed. Regu· lations were therefore made to keep the land distributed among small proprietors capable of defending themselves against hostile neighbors, and slavery was prohibited because a colony so near the frontier could not run the risk of slave insurrections.

The expectations of the proprietors were not realized. A few debtors and foreign Protestants settled in the province, and Georgia traders began to compete successfully with those of Carolina; but the growth of the colony was painfully slow and opposition to the policy of the trustees finally became too strong to be resisted. Before long Georgia began to reproduce on a small scale the economic system of the South Carolina tidewater, with its large plantations, its rice culture, and its negro slaves.

Development of negro slavery. The slave trade.

So far as the southern tidewater is concerned, the increase in population came largely through the involuntary immigration of African negroes. During the seventeenth century the southern planters, having experimented with different systems of labor, decided that negro slavery was best suited for their purposes. Meantime British merchants and their government were organizing as never before for the exploitation of the slave trade. The prosperity of the Royal African Company stimulated competition, and before long "separate traders" from England and America broke down the company's monopoly. In 1713 the British slave-traders gained a great advantage over Dutch and French rivals by the Asiento agreement, giving them the privilege of supplying slaves to the Spanish colonial market. There are no comprehensive statistics; but in 1734 it was estimated that about 70,000 slaves annually were exported from Africa to the New World.

The responsibility for slavery in the English colonies must be widely distributed. British merchants, the imperial government, which defeated efforts on the part of colonial assemblies to check the trade, New England traders, and Southern planters, — each group must take its share. At any rate, the main results are quite clear. In 1689 slavery was just beginning to count largely in the industrial life of Virginia; elsewhere on the continent slaves were few. Even in Virginia, the proportion of slaves to white men was probably less than one in ten. All this was radically changed in the next seventy years. Except in Maryland, the white servant class gave way rapidly before the negroes, until in 1760 the blacks formed about two fifths of the whole southern population. In South Carolina, where labor on the hot, low-lying rice plantations was almost impossible for Europeans, there were more than twice as many negroes as white men. In Virginia nearly half the population was black, and in the tidewater district of that province more than half. In Maryland, where white service still continued on a large scale, the proportion of slaves was smaller; and in North Carolina it was least of all, the development of the lowland plantation district being overshadowed by the migration of small farmers into the back country.

Growth of negro population 1689-1760.

There was, of course, some additional white immigration on the seaboard. Virginia had a few hundred French Protestant immigrants at the beginning of the century, most of whom were soon thoroughly assimilated. A few Germans also came in a little later, some of whom settled at Germanna near the Rapidan River. Some of the Palatine emigrants of 1709 settled with a few Swiss in North Carolina, though the growth of this settlement was checked by Indian troubles. South Carolina had a sprinkling of non-English elements from the start, of whom the Huguenots were perhaps the most important. Between 1730 and 1750, new groups of non-English settlers took up land in this province, some in the lowlands and others in the piedmont area. Among them

European immigration.

were Swiss, Germans, Scotch, Scotch-Irish, and Welsh. The sum total of this later white immigration to the southern lowlands was small, however, as compared with the great mass of negro immigrants, and the white society of the tidewater was still dominated by people of English descent. It is this "old South" with its plantations and its numerous slaves whose doings are most prominent in southern history for the first half of the eighteenth century.

Colonization of the uplands.
Meantime, however, a "new South" was developing, sometimes in contact with the older society and shading into it, but often separated from it by great tracts of wilderness. This new colonization of the uplands came in part by expansion from the seaboard, where the best lands were being concentrated in a comparatively few hands, making it necessary for less fortunate people to turn elsewhere. Small farmers who could not compete with slaveholding planters, servants hoping to set up for themselves when their service expired, well-to-do land speculators, — all helped in the settlement of the piedmont district. As these settlements grew older, some of the characteristics of tidewater society were reproduced. Here also there were a few large plantations worked by negro slaves whose owners maintained the social traditions of the seaboard people. On the whole, however, the small farm rather than the large plantation was the characteristic feature of this region, and the number of negroes was comparatively small.

Immigrants from the North.
More important was the colonization of the interior by immigrants from the North. By the second quarter of the eighteenth century, many of the immigrants who came into Pennsylvania began to move southward along the eastern slopes of the Blue Ridge and through the Great Valley of the Appalachian system. As the price of land rose in Pennsylvania, the Chesapeake colonies began to attract immigrants by offering more favorable terms. This was done not only by the colonial governments, but also by speculators

who had secured immense tracts which they were willing to lease or sell on easy terms. Concessions were also made in the direction of greater religious liberty. So the Germans and Scotch-Irish came in steadily increasing numbers from Pennsylvania into Maryland and Virginia. In 1738 Virginia created two new counties west of the Blue Ridge, to provide for the new population; and in the fifties and sixties of that century thousands of these northern immigrants moved into the back country of North Carolina, transforming that colony from one of the smallest on the continent into one of the largest. A somewhat smaller number passed on into South Carolina.

As a result, then, of two great migrations, the South of the eighteenth century became quite different from that of the seventeenth. During the earlier period, it had been colonized almost entirely by white men, nearly all of whom were English. Now almost, if not quite, half the tidewater people were blacks, and in the back country, where negroes were comparatively few, the old English stock was outnumbered by a combination of Scotch-Irish, Germans, and other minor elements. The "new South" and the "old South" were yoked together in the same provincial governments; but in other respects they were far apart. The back-country people had more in common with those of their own kind who lived to the northward or southward than with their fellow citizens on the eastern seaboard. From now on this east-and-west sectionalism appears in almost every phase of southern history. *Sectionalism in the South.*

The increasing supply of negroes helped to fix the system of large plantations, and though there were still small farmers in the tidewater, they were relatively unimportant. Other influences were at work in the same direction. Land could now be taken up without the actual importation of new settlers, on payment of five shillings per hundred acres. There were also irregular practices *Characteristics of the tidewater.* *Landed estates.*

which enabled influential men to secure land on even easier terms. One third of the land recorded in 1704 on the rent roll of Henrico County, Virginia, on the edge of the tide-water, was held by four persons, — in all nearly 56,000 acres. One of these four persons was William Byrd of West-over, the founder of a notable landowning family, who bequeathed to his son, the second William Byrd, 26,000 acres, which the son increased before he died to nearly 180,000. This was exceptional, but a careful student has estimated that the "average well-to-do Virginian of the period owned as much as three thousand acres." These great estates descended to the eldest sons on the death of the owners, according to the English rule of primogeniture, and were preserved intact by entail.

Quitrent troubles.

The quitrent system made trouble everywhere. In Mary-land these payments were due to the proprietors; in Vir-ginia and the Carolinas, most of them went to the King, but there were troublesome exceptions. The "Northern Neck" in Virginia had been given away to Lord Culpeper, and was held in the eighteenth century by Lord Fairfax. Another strip in North Carolina was held by Lord Gran-ville, the one Carolina proprietor who had reserved his title to the land. Both these noblemen had their own rent rolls and their own collectors. Quitrents were somewhat better collected in Maryland and Virginia than in the Carolinas; in North Carolina only a small amount was ever paid up.

Products of the tidewater; tobacco, rice, and indigo.

The southern plantations still concentrated largely on a few staples. For Maryland, Virginia, and a part of North Carolina the staple was tobacco; for South Carolina and Georgia it was rice, with the addition later of indigo. The tobacco planters had their fair share of difficulties. Waste-ful methods of agriculture wore out the soil and many planters became land poor. Fluctuations in price were also trying, especially when the long wars interfered with shipping and brought prices down. People then began to talk about other industries, though without much permanent effect. The South Carolinians had similar troubles with rice. Production had barely begun on a considerable scale when Parliament put rice in the list of enumerated articles which had to be shipped to England before its exportation to any other European ports. The effect on the trade was so disastrous that Parliament later allowed rice to be shipped to European countries south of Cape Finisterre. Even then, however, the South Carolinians complained that in the Mediterranean countries they had to meet foreign competition, while their best market was really in northern Europe. Important as these staples were, even the lowland South was not wholly given over to their production. North Carolina had its "naval stores" — pitch, tar, and turpentine — from the pine forests. Lumber was cut for export and some of it was used for shipbuilding, though on a smaller scale than in the North. Cattle raising was important in the Carolinas and some provisions were exported from the southern colonies.

Other exports.

Though the plentiful supply of negroes established slavery as the prevailing labor system of the tidewater, white servants continued to come in. The importation of convicts, promoted by act of Parliament, was fairly large, especially in Maryland, and colonial laws restricting it were disallowed by the King. "The Lads of Virginia," a popular eighteenth-century English ballad, pictures the unhappy fate of a young offender, "sold for a slave in Virginia"; but many white servants were of a better sort and fared more comfortably, as, for instance, John Harrower, who, "being reduced to the last shilling," went to Virginia as a schoolmaster for bed, board, washing, and five pounds for his full term of four years. He was presently put in charge of a school on a Rappahannock plantation, where he taught his master's children and those of neighbor-

The labor system. White service.

ing planters. There were some skilled workmen among the white servants, the best of whom subsequently acquired land for themselves.

Slavery.   There were some misgivings about negro slavery. Peter Fontaine, an Anglican clergyman of Huguenot stock, spoke of it as the "original sin and curse of the country," but urged that when the colonists tried to restrict importation, their acts were commonly disapproved in England. Besides, he argued, the negroes had been first enslaved in Africa by men of their own color; and in any case, "to live in Virginia without slaves" was "morally impossible." Few people were much troubled by this ethical problem; but many realized that it might be unsafe to have too many of these half-savage people. It is this anxiety chiefly which explains the restrictive laws just mentioned as well as the elaborate "patrol" systems adopted to control the negro population. South Carolina was especially troubled, not only because of its large proportion of negroes but also because it was close to the Spanish border. In 1739 the colony was alarmed by a negro insurrection which was said to have been instigated by the Spaniards. The proportion of negroes to whites was never so great in the continental colonies as in the West Indies. In South Carolina thirty slaves to a plantation was considered normal. In Virginia there were some large holdings; but the average was lower and there was more human contact between master and slave than in South Carolina, where many negroes remained in a savage state. Efforts were made to Christianize and educate the negroes, and the Anglican missionaries were expected to make this part of their work. The results were comparatively small, however, except for such discipline as seemed necessary to effective service in the fields and in the household.

There was still much talk about establishing towns and concentrating trade at certain ports; but though some laws

were passed, little was accomplished.   Transatlantic as well Slight im-
as coastwise commerce was still carried on at widely dis- portance
tributed points on the coast and on the chief navigable of the
rivers.   Until the latter half of the eighteenth century, towns.
there was no considerable town in Maryland, Virginia, or
North Carolina.   Their provincial capitals — Annapolis,
Williamsburg, and Wilmington — were hardly larger
than country villages, though dignified by the official resi-
dences of the governors and filled up temporarily by the
people who attended meetings of the colonial assembly or
sessions of the provincial courts.   The county seats were
more insignificant still, except when elections were held or
the county court was sitting.   Norfolk, at the entrance of
Chesapeake Bay, was said to have more "the air of a town"
than any other place in Virginia, but it could not be compared with any one of half a dozen northern towns.   The
development of Baltimore had barely begun and its later
prosperity was due more to the wheat farmers of Maryland and Pennsylvania than to the plantations of the tidewater.   Charleston had a unique place in the South.   It Exceptional
was not only a political capital but the center of almost position of
every kind of provincial activity.   Here there was a sub- Charleston.
stantial class of merchants with intercolonial and international relations comparable with those of Boston, New
York, and Philadelphia.   Many planters also had town
houses in Charleston.   As one able student of southern
history has put it, "Charleston was so complete a focus of
commerce, politics, and society, that South Carolina was
in a sense a city-state."

In the broad strip of scattered settlements beyond the Character-
"fall line," there was room for many phases of economic istics of
development.   On its outer edges in close contact with the the back
Indians, hunting and fur trading went on side by side with country.
cattle raising and the clearing of small fields for cultivation.
Here there was no question of slaves, white or black;

it was a society of freemen, developing on lines of equal opportunity. In some counties of the piedmont a good deal of pioneer simplicity existed side by side with farms of moderate size employing, as Patrick Henry did in his early married life, half a dozen negro slaves. The most efficient agriculture of the South was to be found among the Scotch-Irish and German farmers of the Great Valley. Here, as in Pennsylvania, the Germans distinguished themselves by their selection of the most productive lands, their capacity for hard work, and their consequent prosperity. Many settlements were made in a quite individualistic and isolated fashion; but throughout this region there were also groups of pioneers who settled together for common defense or on the basis of common religious interests. Community settlements were especially characteristic of such German sects as the Mennonites and Moravians. One such Moravian community was Wachovia, founded in 1753 in the back country of North Carolina.

Separated by long distances from the seaboard, these interior settlements were forced to make the necessaries of life for themselves. Their chief business was the raising of foodstuffs — cattle and grain, especially wheat. By the middle of the eighteenth century, the wheat production of the back country was gaining rapidly on the tobacco of the tidewater. The frontier had not only to raise its own food, but also to engage in the simpler forms of manufacture. Flour mills were set up; homespun clothing was prepared at home; in the villages of the Great Valley, there were wagonmakers, shoemakers, gunsmiths, and artisans of other essential trades. As the new settlements prospered they felt more and more the need of outlets for their surplus products. Cattle could be driven to market, but the transportation of wheat and flour was more difficult. Nevertheless, these products were hauled to the seaboard in considerable quantities for consumption there or for

Products of the back country.

Economic problems of the back country.

export. The Shenandoah valley traded more with Baltimore and Philadelphia than with tidewater Virginia; but in South Carolina the Charleston district began, after a time, to get from the back country foodstuffs previously imported from New York and Philadelphia. Naturally the upland farmer had a keen interest in internal improvements, such as the building of bridges and roads in place of Indian trails.

While the back country was laying the economic foundations of future power, it was leaving politics largely to the tidewater planters and merchants. The monarchical principle was stronger in the southern governments than in the North. In Maryland, the proprietor and his governor had, in spite of many vigorous controversies, much more power than Penn and his agents in Pennsylvania. From the imperial point of view, Virginia probably came nearer to being a model province than any other on the continent. The consent of the assembly was necessary for new laws or taxes; but the governor was the real, as well as the nominal, chief executive. While the governors of New York and Massachusetts were dependent on temporary votes of the assembly for their salaries and other ordinary charges, the Virginia governor drew his salary, by royal order, from a permanent fund which the assembly had set apart for this purpose. The quitrents formed another permanent fund, controlled not by the assembly but by the Crown. While Maryland was under royal government, her assembly also established a permanent fund and, in spite of protests from the assembly, the governor's salary was paid from it even after the proprietor had been restored.

In the Carolinas, the governor was less fortunate. In North Carolina, his salary was supposed to be paid from the quitrents; but the coöperation of the assembly was necessary in order to collect them, and this coöperation was not forthcoming, so the governor's income was quite precarious. In South Carolina the governor was as badly off as in New York. He had to take what the assembly saw fit to give him from year to year and was often forced to accept measures which encroached upon his legitimate authority. Governor Glen declared in 1748 that executive power was largely in the hands of commissioners appointed by the assembly. Yet the difference between a strong royal government like Virginia and a weak one like South Carolina was only one of degree. Even in Virginia the governor had to go to the assembly (House of Burgesses) for supplies to meet emergencies and had to make concessions in return. Even there, the provincial treasurer was appointed not by the governor, according to the official theory, but by act of assembly. For many years this office was combined with that of speaker of the House of Burgesses.

The councilors and the local aristocracy.

In the South, as in the North, the governor could not always count upon the support of the councilors, even though they were appointed by the Crown. Especially influential were the Virginia councilors. Chosen as they usually were from the principal landowning families and having also influential connections with British officials and merchants, it was not easy for the governor to manage them. An energetic governor sometimes undertook to reform abuses in which councilors had a direct interest; but such efforts were often unsuccessful. More easy-going officials secured smooth administration by yielding to the wishes of the provincial politicians. In South Carolina, where politics turned largely on the conflict of interests between planters and merchants, councilors were frequently chosen from the latter class, which was naturally more conservative on such questions as the issue of paper money.

Character of the lower house.

To what extent the representative house, variously known as burgesses, commons, or simply assembly, can be regarded as really democratic is not an altogether simple question.

Though the suffrage was limited by property qualifications, the proportion of actual voters in the white population seems to have been as large as in the North, if not larger. This is not surprising since the white total for the South included a much smaller proportion of the working class, which was there composed largely of negro slaves. To a conservative gentleman like Governor Spotswood, the Virginia House of Burgesses seemed at times much too democratic, being chosen "from the meaner sort of people." Similar complaints were made elsewhere. The suffrage.

The efficiency of popular control varied according to the personal qualities of the governor, the leading councilors, and the popular leaders. Spotswood, in spite of his remarks about the "meaner sort of people," had previously prided himself on his ability to manage an assembly. Hostile critics also complained that governors could bear down opposition through their control of the patronage and their right to prorogue and dissolve assemblies. Conflicts between the council and the lower house were frequent here as elsewhere, the latter especially insisting on its right to frame money bills without amendment by the council. Nevertheless, the leading families, which were represented in the council, undoubtedly had great influence also in the lower house. Extent of popular control.

It is not worth while to dwell on minor politicians and the details of provincial politics. A few southern leaders, however, deserve notice either for what they did or because they illustrate important phases of colonial life. Of the southern governors during the first half of the eighteenth century, Alexander Spotswood seems to deserve the leading place usually assigned to him. A Scotchman by birth, like his two immediate successors, he came to Virginia in 1710 to begin his twelve years' service as lieutenant governor. In his time, as during the next half century, the lieutenant governor was the resident head of the administration, the nominal governor being a distinguished British noble, who Southern leaders.
Governor Spotswood.

drew a considerable salary but did not think it necessary to live in the province. Unlike many other governors, Spotswood did not leave the province after his removal from office and may be considered a real Virginian. A sturdy fighter himself, he had to face councilors who were equally determined; but in spite of their opposition he managed to reform some abuses in land administration. He was an active promoter of William and Mary College, then a young, struggling institution; coöperated with other governments in breaking up piracy; and took an active interest in westward expansion, personally leading an expedition over the Blue Ridge. Unfortunately, he antagonized so many influential men, including the Bishop of London's commissary, James Blair, that he was finally removed from office. This was not, however, the end of Spotswood's public service. He interested himself in the manufacture of iron and in 1730 he was made deputy postmaster-general for America. Just before his death in 1740, he was busy helping to organize a military expedition against the Spaniards.

William Byrd II.

One of Spotswood's chief opponents was William Byrd II, who belonged to a great landowning family which kept its place in the council for three generations. William Byrd II was a councilor for thirty-seven years and for a short time president of the council. Like his father before him, he held also for several years the office of receiver-general of quitrents. A strenuous defender of his personal and class interests, he was also a man of cultivated tastes. He had been educated in England, was a member of the Royal Society, and gathered at his beautiful estate of Westover on the James one of the largest and best-selected libraries in America. His best monument, however, is the collection of his *Writings*, published long after his death and containing among other things a charming description of his friendly visit to the plantation of his former antagonist, Governor Spotswood. Most familiar of all is his picturesque, if unfair, description of the North Carolina countrymen. "They keep," he said, "so many sabbaths every week that their disregard of the seventh day has no manner of cruelty in it either to servants or cattle."

Among the ablest leaders of popular parties in the provincial assemblies two men may be mentioned as fairly typical: Daniel Dulany, the elder, of Maryland, and Charles Pinckney of South Carolina. Dulany, beginning as a poor immigrant from Ireland, became a large landowner, as well as a leader at the bar. Though he held office as attorney-general under the proprietor, he led the lower house in a memorable fight to secure for Maryland certain advantages of the English statute law. Pinckney, unlike Dulany, was born into an influential family, and his wife, Eliza Lucas, was not only a fine personality but a capable plantation manager. He, too, rose to high office, serving first as attorney-general and then as chief justice. He was also for a time speaker of the lower house and a strenuous defender of its privileges, including the exclusive control of money bills. Having been educated in England, Pinckney emphasized English precedents. The South Carolinians, he argued, were entitled to all the rights of Englishmen, and their representative house had the same rights in this respect as the House of Commons in England. Both these American defenders of the "rights of Englishmen" gave their sons a legal education in the famous "Middle Temple" in London. It is worth noting that Dulany's son argued against the Stamp Act and that one of the younger Pinckneys helped to frame the Federal Constitution of 1787.

During most of this period, the older settlements controlled provincial politics without serious difficulty. When new counties were formed and their population grew, the seaboard districts insisted on more than a fair share of the representation. Because of this under-representation of the interior counties, their special interests were naturally

Popular leaders.

Dulany.

Pinckney.

Sectionalism in politics.

neglected. Insufficient provision was often made for local government, the administration of justice, and public improvements of special importance to the frontiersmen. In the next generation, this conflict between tidewater and back country, and the effort of the latter, under the leadership of men like Patrick Henry and Thomas Jefferson, to break the exclusive control of the old ruling class, had an important relation to the struggle with the mother country.

Established churches. The Church of England still had an important part in southern society. Its status as a state church entitled to public support was recognized in all the colonies from Maryland to South Carolina; and, except in North Carolina, the establishment was fairly effective. In the Carolinas, this official support was supplemented by the missionary work of the Society for Propagating the Gospel. Taking the period as a whole, however, the established church lost ground as compared with the dissenters; so much so that when the Revolution of 1776 cut off the support of the British government, the separation of church and state became comparatively easy.

Anglican Church in Virginia. Of all the colonies, Virginia seemed most thoroughly grounded in Anglican principles. In 1699, when the assembly passed its first toleration act, there were only a few dissenters, chiefly Quakers and Presbyterians. Here as in other colonies, however, the colonial church suffered by not having its normal organization. The Bishop of London's commissary had little authority and was involved in frequent disputes with the governor and with the planters who formed the parish vestries. The status of the ministers, who, instead of being permanently inducted were commonly "hired" from year to year, was far from dignified. Many of the clergy did good work, even under this lax system, but others neglected their duties and thus weakened the influence of the church.

Dissenters. Meantime the dissenters were becoming more numerous, partly because the government itself made concessions to prospective settlers, especially on the frontier. In the Great Valley, as a result of Scotch-Irish and German immigration, the Anglican churchmen found themselves in a minority among the Presbyterians, Lutherans, and other sects. To encourage the Presbyterians, Governor Gooch not only promised the restricted toleration recognized by law but in practice went even farther. So the religious life of the Valley was guided by a great variety of preachers, some of whom took long missionary journeys through the frontier settlements from Pennsylvania to the Carolinas. From the Anglican point of view, this was undesirable; but, just as the English government had been willing to allow overseas a degree of religious toleration not considered safe at home, so many Virginia churchmen did not mind having their frontiers secured by people whose religious ideas were not entirely orthodox.

Presently, however, dissent began to grow nearer home. Some of the northern immigrants moved into the piedmont and so came in contact with Anglicans who had moved up from the tidewater. About the same time, echoes of the Great Awakening began to reach these middle counties and create a demand for a different kind of religious teaching from that furnished by the established church. These conditions, together with increasing friction between the Anglican clergy and laity, gave the Presbyterians especially an opportunity of which they quickly took advantage, to the annoyance of the Anglican party. The latter now demanded a stricter enforcement of the law requiring ministers and places of worship to be licensed by the civil authorities and thus restricting considerably the traveling preachers. Dissenters who failed to observe these rules were fined for nonattendance at church and ministers were sometimes refused licenses. Under the able leadership of Samuel Davies, afterwards president of Princeton, the Presbyterian clergy appealed to

The Great Awakening and the fight for toleration.

the home government, which declared in favor of a more liberal policy. Meantime the need of coöperation against the French, together with the militant patriotism of the Presbyterians, turned public opinion toward a more liberal policy. The fight for simple toleration was now practically won and before the Revolution the dissenters outnumbered the adherents of the established church. Complete separation of church and state and the abolition of church taxes did not come, however, until after the Revolution.

Church and state in Maryland and the Carolinas.

In Maryland also, the Anglican establishment was fairly strong at the close of the seventeenth century, though dissenters were more numerous than in Virginia. The Catholics, though only a persecuted minority, had a social prestige out of proportion to their numbers. The Quakers kept up a persistent fight against church taxes and there was always a strong Puritan element, later reënforced, as in Virginia, by Germans and Scotch-Irish Presbyterians. Here, too, the unfortunate character of some of the clergy weakened the establishment and prepared the way for its final overthrow. In North Carolina, the Quakers were first in the field and the dissenters gained a lead which was confirmed by later immigration. In South Carolina, Anglicans and dissenters were for a time more nearly equal, especially since the Huguenots were inclined to sympathize with the Anglicans. Here also, however, the up-country population ultimately gave the dissenters a decided majority.

Preponderance of the dissenters.

So before the Revolution the religious complexion of the South was radically changed. The Anglican Church had the greatest prestige in the tidewater; but in the back country it was overshadowed by the dissenters, of whom the strongest and most aggressive were the Presbyterians. These Puritans of the South looked for inspiration and leadership, not to the older settlements of their own provinces or to England, but to the northern presbyteries of New York and Philadelphia, or, going still farther back, to those of Scotland and Ulster. They were often quite as intense in their ecclesiastical partisanship as the Anglicans; but contact with men of different faiths gradually developed among the frontier people a spirit of mutual toleration. In this respect the South drifted much farther from seventeenth-century conditions than Puritan New England.

Educational development in the South differed from that of New England chiefly in the fact that the former section, because of its scattered and largely rural population, could not establish effective state systems of elementary education and consequently depended more largely on private initiative, combined with the efforts of the clergy. Regarding the actual progress of education in the two sections, extreme claims have been made on both sides and more scientific study of the subject is necessary before a just statement can be made. It is certain, however, that this period in southern history is marked by some notable advances in education. *Educational development.*

The only institution of collegiate grade was William and Mary College, founded, after a long period of preliminary discussion, largely through the efforts of that energetic Scottish churchman, Commissary James Blair, who secured the royal charter in 1693. Blair himself was president for fifty years, his associates were generally clergymen, and religious training was emphasized. The college was supported by quitrents, provincial appropriations, and private gifts; but many years passed before it gave anything more than the most elementary instruction; and even after 1729, when its faculty consisted of President Blair and six professors, it resembled other colonial colleges in being little more than an academy. It had, however, some able English and Scotch teachers, who trained many of the future leaders in Virginia politics. *William and Mary College.*

Some well-to-do Southerners sent their sons abroad. In the first three quarters of the eighteenth century, fourteen Virginians went to Oxford and eight to Cambridge. Others *Education abroad.*

studied in such famous English "public schools" as Eton
and Harrow. South Carolina, which had no college of its
own, probably sent a larger proportion of its young men
to England than any other province. A fair number of
Southerners got their legal training in the English Inns
of Court. Of the seventy colonials who entered the
Middle Temple before 1760, more than half came from
Virginia and Maryland. If all the entries down to 1775 are
included, the South furnished more than two thirds, with
South Carolina in the lead. The intellectual training of the
educated leaders was distinctly English, whether received in
England or through Oxford and Cambridge graduates in
America. How important this influence was may be seen
by studying the representative Virginians and South Caro-
linians of the Revolutionary era. Of the seven Virginians
who signed the Declaration of Independence, four had been
students at William and Mary, one at Cambridge University,
and another at an English academy. Four "Middle
Templars" signed the Declaration of Independence for
South Carolina and three were members of the Federal
Convention from that state.

Elementary
education.

Elementary education was provided in various ways.
There were some endowed schools in every colony. Many
of the Anglican clergy kept schools in connection with their
parish work and some of them were real scholars. Sometimes groups of planters combined to build schoolhouses
and provide masters for their children. Private tutors were
also employed, especially by the wealthier families. No
exact statement can be made as to the amount of education
thus furnished; but a careful study of the advertisements
in the *South Carolina Gazette* indicates that there were in
that colony between 1733 and 1774, nearly two hundred
persons engaged as tutors, schoolmasters, or schoolmistresses.
Among the subjects taught were French, Latin, and Greek.
There were schools for girls as well as boys. Provision was

also made in the South, as elsewhere, for training children of the poorer classes, especially in connection with apprenticeship to a trade.

The first southern newspaper was the *Maryland Gazette*, founded in 1727; then came the *South Carolina Gazette* in 1732 and the *Virginian Gazette* in 1736. The first and last were founded by William Parks, who, in 1741, added to his printing shop at Williamsburg a bookstore with an assortment of ancient and modern classics. There were some large private libraries, such as the Byrds' at Westover. Rev. Thomas Bray, a founder of the Society for Propagating the Gospel, established a number of small lending libraries for the clergy, and in 1743 a few book-lovers founded the Charleston Library Society.[1] *Newspapers.*

The chief intellectual centers of the South were Williamsburg and Charleston. Williamsburg was the residence of the Virginia governors, who were, sometimes at least, men of cultivated tastes and broad interests, like Spotswood, or Fauquier, who half a century later stimulated, if he did not altogether improve, young Virginians of Jefferson's time. Here also were the provincial printing press, the principal book shop, and the College of William and Mary with its faculty recruited from the British universities. The drama, too, had its place; the Williamsburg theater, built about 1716, was probably the first in America. Charleston had no college, but it was a real city, with perhaps the most cultivated society to be found anywhere in America. Here in the middle years of the eighteenth century the South Carolinians had a chance to hear scientific lectures, good concerts, and some English plays. *Intellectual centers of the South.*

Intellectual interests of the kind just described were confined to a small class, even in the tidewater. In the newer *Education in the new settlements.*

[1] Other important colonial libraries were those of the Library Company of Philadelphia (1731), the Redwood Library of Newport (1747), and the New York Society Library (1754).

settlements educational opportunities were naturally more limited and progress, when it came, was on quite different lines. Here, too, religion and education were closely associated; but the dissenting ministers took the place of the Anglican clergy; especially significant was the work of the Scotch and Irish Presbyterians. After the establishment of Princeton College its graduates took an active part in the education of the "new South," though their influence was not strongly felt until just before the Revolution. By that time Princeton was attracting southern students, among them James Madison, who helped to frame the Virginia constitution of 1776 and the Federal Constitution of 1787.

BIBLIOGRAPHICAL NOTES

General.   Chapters on this section in Osgood, *18th Cent.*, I–IV.

Sources, general.   Hart, *Contemporaries*, II, chs. V, VI, XI, nos. 82, 83, 106. Burnaby, A., *Travels* (ed. by R. R. Wilson). Quincy, J., *Journal* (1773) (Mass. Hist. Soc., *Proceedings*, XLIX).

Virginia.   Bassett, J. S., *Writings of Colonel William Byrd*, Introduction. Meade, W., *Old Churches, Ministers, and Families of Virginia.* Stanard, M. N., *Colonial Virginia.* Ford, W. C., *Washington*, I, ch. VII. Rowland, K. M., *George Mason*, I, chs. II, III. Tyler, L. G., *Williamsburg.* Beveridge, A. J., *John Marshall*, I, 19–60. Dodson, L., *Alexander Spotswood.* Detailed study of political institutions by P. S. Flippin in *Columbia Univ. Studies.*

Sources.   Byrd's *Writings.* Maury, A., *Huguenot Family.* Fithian, P. V., *Journal and Letters.* Harrower, J., "Diary," *A.H.R.*, VI, 65–107. Jones, H., *Present State of Virginia* (1724; partial reprint in Stedman and Hutchinson, *Library of American Literature*, II, 279–287). Spotswood, A., *Official Letters* (Virginia Hist. Soc.).

Maryland.   Mereness, *Maryland as a Proprietary Province.* Articles by Sioussat, in *Johns Hopkins Studies*, XXI, nos. VI, VII, XI, XII.

The Carolinas.   Channing, *United States*, II, ch. XII. Ashe, S. A., *North Carolina.* McCrady, *South Carolina, 1670–1719*, and *South Carolina, 1719–1775.* Hughson, S. C., *Carolina Pirates (Johns Hopkins Studies).* Ravenel, H. H., *Charleston*, chs. IV–X. Sellers, L. S., *Charleston Business on the Eve of the Revolution.*

Wallace, D. D., *Henry Laurens.* Schaper, W. A., *Sectionalism and Representation in South Carolina.* Coulter, E. M., "The Granville District," *James Sprunt Hist. Publications,* XII, 36–56. For governments, see Smith, W., *South Carolina,* and Raper, C. L., *North Carolina.*

Salley, A. S., *Narratives of Early Carolina,* 211–373. Glen. J., "Description of South Carolina," in Carroll, *Collections of South Carolina,* II. "Some 18th Century Tracts concerning N. C.," N. C. Hist. Comm., *Publications,* XVIII. — Sources.

Greene, *Provincial America,* ch. XV. Jones, C. C., *Georgia,* I. Biographies of Oglethorpe. For government, see McCain, J. R., *Georgia as a Proprietary Province.* Macdonald, *Select Charters,* no. 49. — Founding of Georgia.

Channing, *United States,* II, 376–398. Wertenbaker, T. J., *Planters of Col. Virginia.* Phillips, U. B., *American Negro Slavery,* chs. I–V, and *Plantation and Frontier.* Donnan, E. C., *Documents . . . of the Slave Trade to America,* and her "Slave Trade into S. C. before the Revolution," *A.H.R.* (1927), XXXIII, 804–828. — Slavery.

Faust, *German Element,* I, chs. VI–IX. Ford, *Scotch-Irish.* Hirsch, A. H., *Huguenots of Colonial South Carolina.* Turner, *Frontier in American History,* ch. III. *Records of the Moravians of N. C.* (N. C. Hist. Comm., *Pubs.*). Crane, V., *Southern Frontier, 1670–1732.* — Immigration, expansion, and frontier society.

Gewehr, W. M., *Great Awakening in Virginia.* Guilday, P., *John Carroll.* Perry, W. S., *American Episcopal Church,* I. McIlwaine, H. R., *Struggle of the Protestant Dissenters (Johns Hopkins Studies).* Good studies of religion in North Carolina by S. B. Weeks in *Johns Hopkins Studies,* X, XI. McLaughlin, A. C., *et al., Source Problems in U. S. History,* 183–235. — Religion.

Jernegan, M. W., *Laboring and Dependent Classes,* 131–175. Heatwole, C. J., *Education in Virginia.* Tyler, L. G., "Education in Colonial Virginia," *William and Mary College Qly.,* V–VII. McCrady, E., "Education in South Carolina," S. C. Hist., *Collections,* IV; Raper, C. L., *Church and Private Schools in North Carolina.* Motley, *James Blair (Johns Hopkins Studies).* Steiner, B. C., "Thomas Bray and His Libraries," *A.H.R.,* II, 59–75. — Education and libraries.

Tyler, *Amer. Literature,* II, ch. XVII. Cook, *Literary Influences in Colonial Newspapers,* chs. VI–VIII. Wroth, L. C., *Printing in Col. Maryland.* Weeks, S. B., *Press of N. C. in 18th Century.* — Southern press.

CHAPTER XV

ENGLISH AND AMERICAN WAYS

"We hope to plant a nation
Where none before hath stood."

THESE lines, written by one of the Virginia pioneers, of 1610, perhaps express the feeling of his more thoughtful comrades, at a time when the fate of the young colony still hung in the balance. What kind of nation he was dreaming of one can only guess, but it was certainly nothing remotely resembling the American nation of the twentieth century. It is interesting, however, for the moment to place ourselves midway between these two points in time and see what elements of a new nationality can be traced after a century and a half of colonial development.

The thirteen colonies and their neighbors. It must be remembered, first, that the thirteen colonies which were to become the nucleus of a new American nation were closely associated with other English provinces which have had quite a different history. To think of the "thirteen" as having a clear group consciousness, marking them off sharply from all other settlements and uniting them to each other, would be to read back into the past the thought of later generations. With the fishing stations of Newfoundland and the sugar islands of the West Indies, the continental colonies had relations too close to be broken without serious inconvenience. Politically also the mainland colonies had much in common with the West Indies. The constitutional controversies of Barbados and Jamaica were often much like those of the continental colonies. It is equally true that within the traditional group of thirteen there were sharp

338

conflicts of interest and radically different traditions. A
South Carolina planter of 1750 would probably have felt
himself more at home in Barbados than in Boston.

Nevertheless, the developments of the eighteenth century
were gradually bringing the continental colonies closer to
each other and giving them some common interests which
were not so fully shared by the island settlements. One of
these developments was the improvement of land communications. In the seventeenth century, nearly all intercolonial
trade was carried on by sea. In those days Charleston was
for practical purposes not much farther from the West
Indies than from New England. In the eighteenth century,
this sea trade was still most important; but with the development of the interior more attention was paid to roads and
bridges. By 1739, a complete series of post routes had
been established from Portsmouth, New Hampshire, to
Charleston, South Carolina; and, with increasing population,
the wilderness intervals between successive stations were
gradually getting shorter. Meantime Indian trails were
taking shape as recognized highways through the upland
country from New York and Pennsylvania to Georgia.
All along this north-and-south line were settlers, to whom the
island colonies were far off indeed, but who had much in
common with their fellow landsmen in other provinces.
To the twentieth-century man with his railroads and motor
cars, his telegraph and telephone, these primitive beginnings
of colonial intercourse seem poor indeed. Roads were bad,
almost impassable rivers often blocked the way, and even
tolerable lodgings were quite uncertain. Journeys now
counted in hours then took as many days. Yet an increasing
number of travelers were braving the hardships and dangers
of the road, letters were passing to and fro, and newspapers
were beginning to bring the inhabitants of each colony some
information at least about the business and politics of their
fellow provincials.

*Common
interests.*

*Communi-
cations.*

Conflict
with insular
interests.

While intercolonial barriers were thus becoming less formidable on the continent, the northern colonies especially were keenly conscious of a conflict of interests between themselves and the British West Indies. So far, the latter were still the favorite children of the imperial family, as Parliament showed when it passed the Molasses Act of 1733; but the continental group with its expanding population, territory, and wealth was getting a new sense of its own importance. On the eve of the last French War, the population of the continental colonies was rapidly approaching a million and a half, a small figure as compared with the national states of the present day, but enough to make a respectable political community when judged by eighteenth-century standards. It seems worth while, therefore, to ask whether there were among these provincial Americans any common elements of a new civilization sufficiently differentiated from that of England to justify us in calling it American rather than English.

Elements
of unity.
The English
language.

In race and language, the Americans of 1750 were of course predominantly British. So far as language was concerned the predominance was overwhelming. In New England, the non-English element was weakest and racial consciousness was felt, even when the people were most resentful of British policies. The same John Adams who led the fight for the Declaration of Independence wrote only a few months earlier that among the chief advantages of his own New England was its "purer English blood," less "mixed" than any other. Elsewhere the problem was

Dutch and
German ele-
ments.

not so simple. In New York, the traveler of 1750 found Dutch still the prevailing language of Albany and some of the smaller villages, though in the province as a whole English was increasing its lead as the younger generation of Dutchmen gradually gave up the mother tongue. In New York, also, was the northern end of an important series of German settlements, extending southward through Pennsylvania and the Shenandoah valley to the new colony of Georgia. Here were communities taught by German-trained clergy, speaking the German language, reading the Bible in Luther's translation instead of the King James version, depending for information on German newspapers and German calendars. Only in Pennsylvania, however, was the German stock more than a small minority before the Revolution. The proportion in Pennsylvania was perhaps a third of the total population; in the thirteen colonies as a whole, the proportion was perhaps a little over one in ten. The only other non-English stocks which came in large numbers before 1750 were the Scotch and the Scotch-Irish, both for the most part English-speaking though with distinct national or racial feelings of their own. In politics and the shaping of political institutions, the men of English speech, and even of English descent, had a greater advantage than statistics indicate, because the non-English people were largely newcomers, who had scarcely found their bearings. They were also, except in New York, largely massed in the interior counties, which were not fully represented in the colonial assemblies.

Through their common language, educated Americans shared with other Englishmen of their day a common literature and the traditional ideals which that literature expressed. Easily first in this common literature was the King James version of the Bible, the one great book of the "plain people" of English speech on both sides of the Atlantic. Shakespeare and other classics of the sixteenth and seventeenth centuries were neglected in America, as indeed they were by Englishmen at home; but there was an educated class which read, and was influenced by, contemporary English essayists, novelists, and playwriters. Some continental writers, like the Dutch publicist Grotius, the German Pufendorf, and the later French thinkers Voltaire and Montesquieu, were known to a few Americans in their original texts or in English translations; but English books on theology and politics

Common traditions in literature.

were the most familiar of all to the educated leaders of
provincial society.   Hundreds of young Americans formed
their ideas upon, or adapted to their purposes, the political
philosophies of Richard Hooker, Algernon Sidney, and John

*English
fashions.*

Locke.

Well-to-do merchants and planters built Georgian houses,
imported Chippendale furniture, used London silver and
Wedgwood china at table, adopted London fashions of
dress, perhaps a trifle out-of-style, and reflected prevailing
English standards of eighteenth-century elegance.   The
landed gentry of Virginia and New York cultivated the sports
of country squires on the other side, even importing English
foxes for the purpose.   In short, as one Englishman said,
in 1771, there seemed to be little difference in the "manner
of a wealthy colonist and a wealthy Briton."

*English
traditions in
government.*

In more important matters, most Americans believed
themselves to be following the substance, if not the letter,
of English tradition.   As one colonial government after
another was remodeled, the people who lived under it came
to regard it as a miniature copy of the English constitution.
The governor was not a hereditary monarch; but, theoretically at least, the prerogatives which he defended with more
or less success were those of the King whom he represented.
The councilors who formed the upper house had no such
independent status as the nobles and bishops who sat in the
House of Lords; but in New York and Virginia especially
they represented to a considerable extent the leading families of the province.   Above all, the assembly stood for the
English principle of representation, a kind of representation
enjoyed in those days by none of the great nations of continental Europe.

*English
precedents
in the
colonial
assemblies.*

Under various names,—burgesses, commons, or representatives,— the members of these provincial assemblies regarded
themselves as legitimate heirs, within their limited field,
to the great traditions of the English House of Commons.

Even in formal procedure, English parliamentary practice was closely followed. At Williamsburg and New York, as at Westminster, the representatives of the property holders were summoned or dismissed by the King or his representative, but while in session they chose their own speakers, claimed the same privilege of free debate, and administered similar rules of procedure. Messages and addresses passed between governor and assembly, or assembly and council, much as they did between Commons and King, or Commons and Lords. Doubtless colonial advocates were not always consistent. They could find reasons why the governor should not exercise all the prerogatives of the Crown and they sometimes denounced councilors for claiming the privileges of the House of Lords; but they were practically unanimous in insisting that English precedents held good on their own side of the argument. Above all, they asserted their exclusive right to grant the people's money and determine how it should be spent. In matters like this, Massachusetts, New York, and South Carolina, with all their differences, were substantially agreed. Orthodox English lawyers did not accept this reasoning and insisted that a colonial assembly was scarcely more than a municipal corporation; but this official theory did not appeal to the colonists.

Local government, which came much closer to daily life, was naturally more influenced by the special needs of a new country and the particular needs of each section — its physical environment, its economic development, or the distinctive ideals of its founders. Massachusetts, New York, Pennsylvania, and Virginia worked out four quite different systems of county government. Yet in all these colonies the English county reappeared in some form. Boroughs organized on the English model were not so common; but, nearly everywhere, under different names and varying forms, there was something corresponding roughly to the English parish. Justices of the peace, sheriffs, and con-

Local government.

stables were equally familiar to Englishmen on both sides of the water. Virginia with its county courts and parish vestries came closest to the old model; but everywhere the Americans of 1750 cherished the English tradition of local self-government, controlled by general laws yet ready to assert itself on occasion against the central authority.

English traditions of personal liberty.

More vital to the ordinary man than governmental forms was the protection of individual liberty against arbitrary interference. In defending this liberty, eighteenth-century Americans generally used English precedents, putting into them much that would have seemed strange to their medieval authors. This reading of new ideas into old documents was, however, a well-recognized English habit on both sides of the Atlantic. When, therefore, the Massachusetts representatives claimed to find in Magna Carta a good argument against giving their governor a permanent salary, they were certainly twisting that famous document, but doing it in quite the traditional English manner. Long before the Revolution, Americans had learned to talk also of natural rights, again with good English authorities, like Hooker and Locke, to support them; but their most confident appeal was to the "rights of Englishmen." Old John Wise of Ipswich made himself obnoxious to His Majesty's government of New England in 1687, but in 1710 he founded his opposition to absolutism, partly, at least, on English traditions. The English people, he said, had been "through immemorial ages" "the owner of very fair enfranchisements and liberties"; "Englishmen hate an arbitrary power (politically considered) as they hate the devil."

The common law in the colonies.

For enforcing the "rights of Englishmen," the colonists depended largely on the common law as administered through the courts of justice. Their claim to share in this inheritance was based in part upon such royal declarations as that made in the Virginia charter of 1606, that English

subjects born in the proposed new settlements should "enjoy
all Liberties, Franchises, and Immunities" "as if they had
been abiding and born, within this our Realm of England."
They could strengthen this argument by British legal opinions
like that of Richard West, counsel to the Board of Trade,
who declared in 1720 that wherever an Englishman went he
took "as much of law and liberty with him as the nature of
things will bear." In the application of this principle, however, the colonists differed widely among themselves. In
the early days of New England, when the Puritan leaders had
a clear field for their theories, with almost no external
authority over them, common-law principles were repeatedly
set aside in order to meet local requirements or in favor of
English local customs and Biblical law. Quaker theories had
a similar effect in Pennsylvania. Indeed, there was no colony
in which the common law was universally or rigidly followed.
A system of law which had grown up gradually in an old
country plainly could not be applied mechanically in a new
community constantly facing problems quite unfamiliar to
English jurists.

In the eighteenth century, this tendency to modify the
common law in accordance with local conditions was counteracted by two important influences. During this period
strong pressure was brought to bear by the British government, which was now more careful to appoint provincial
judges and attorneys-general who knew something about the
common law and could be counted on to apply it so far as
possible. The royal disallowance of colonial laws and the
appeal from provincial courts to the Privy Council were also
used for the same purpose. Meantime, entirely different motives were helping to popularize the common law among
the colonists. With the overthrow of the old charters,
the problem of defending English liberty against abuse of
the royal prerogative became more nearly like what it had
been in England. More attention was, therefore, paid to

*Increasing
influence
of the com-
mon law.*

those provisions of the common law which had proved useful for this purpose in the past. Meantime, the lawyer class, at first weak and discredited, gradually increased in numbers and prestige. Many lawyers, especially in Pennsylvania and the South, were trained in the English Inns of Court; others came indirectly under the same influence. Those lawyers who took the popular side were soon making effective use of English law in defense of colonial rights.

According to the orthodox theory, the only English law which took effect in any particular colony was the common law, so far as it was applicable to local conditions, and such statute law, chiefly for the enforcement or development of common-law principles, as had been enacted before the colony was founded. There were, however, some later English statutes, notably the Habeas Corpus Act of 1679 establishing new safeguards against arbitrary arrest, of which Americans were anxious to take advantage even though they were not strictly applicable in the colonies. Some of this legislation was reproduced in acts of the various colonial assemblies, though such acts were sometimes defeated by the royal veto. Sometimes colonial judges put English statutes into effect without waiting for a specific provincial statute. In Maryland, particularly, the assembly insisted that the provincial judges should give the people the benefits of such English statutes as seemed applicable to local conditions.

A friendly British critic declared in 1758 that the Americans went too far in their acceptance of the English law, much of which was adapted to a past age or to England alone. "Certainly," he said, "our American brethren might have carried with them the privileges which make the glory and happiness of Englishmen" without burdening themselves unnecessarily with so much that was useless or harmful in a new society. Judges also found it

The lawyer class.

Influence of English statutes.

Difficulties in administration.

difficult to say what parts of the English law were applicable to colonial conditions and should therefore take effect in any particular case. On some common-law rights, however, American opinion was practically unanimous. One was the right of trial by jury both in civil and in criminal cases.[1] Another was the privilege of securing a writ of *habeas corpus* to prevent arbitrary imprisonment. A third was the right of every subject not to be deprived of his property without some regular legal process.

Accepted principles.

Thus in many aspects of American life, — in language, government, and law, — colonial theory and practice were largely English. Yet Americans were after all developing something quite different from the prevailing English type. Even when inherited forms were preserved, their real meaning was often changed. How did this come about?

New American ideas.

First of all, there is the familiar fact that a large proportion of those who went from the Old World to the New did so because they were dissatisfied with the institutions — economic, political, religious — which they left behind. More or less consciously, many of them tried to establish the social order which they were setting up in America on new, and, as they thought, better, principles. Many political experiments, of course, proved disappointing. New England Puritans and Pennsylvania Quakers had to adjust themselves more or less to the old traditions which they had tried to escape. Meantime, however, they had built into the foundations of American society some elements which resisted the unifying influence of imperial policies.

Desire for a different social order.

The second, and perhaps most important, influence making for differentiation grew out of the practical problems of colonization. Colonial promoters in England often had to establish in America, not the arrangements to which they were accustomed in England or which they personally

Influence of American environment.

[1] In petty civil suits, however, the jury was often dispensed with; in Maryland criminal cases were tried, at the election of the accused, without juries.

preferred, but rather those which would be most attractive to settlers. When colonial assemblies began legislating about frontier conditions they often found little help in ancient precedents and so developed a new common law of their own. Again, some allowance must be made for the influence on American practices or ideals of the non-English immigrants from Scotland, Ireland, and the Continent, whose traditions were of quite a different sort. Finally, it must be remembered that, when English and American ways diverged, it was not always the American that moved farthest from the older English practice. So, for instance, obsolete forms of English speech have sometimes survived longer here than in England.

The suffrage. "Americanizing" influences may be seen in almost every phase of provincial life, either producing new institutions or modifying old ones. Representative government, for instance, did not work out in America quite as it did in England. In both cases, the suffrage was limited to the property-holding class, but the practical difference was very great. In an old English county, where estates were concentrated in a few hands, the limitation of suffrage to freeholders was a serious matter. In a new country, the opportunity to qualify as a freeholder was open to a much larger proportion of the population. So in spite of some **Weakening of class distinctions.** class distinctions, a country in which almost any industrious white man could hope to own land tended to become democratic both socially and politically. Every colony had its "gentry," but they had no such prestige as the landed aristocracy in England.

New theory of representation. The relations between a representative and his constituents were also closer in America than in England, where a member of the House of Commons was not required to be a resident of the district which elected him. An English west-country constituency may still be represented by a London lawyer, or a great seaport by some country gentleman. For better or worse, Americans have come to think differently and the beginnings of the change go back to colonial times. In Massachusetts representatives had to be residents of the towns from which they were elected, and a Virginia burgess had at least to hold property in the county which he represented. Elsewhere the practice varied, but the tendency was to associate representatives with their constituencies by requiring them to be either residents or property owners. So, for most Americans, the representation of the voters in a given district came to mean their choice of one of themselves to speak for them in matters of taxation and public policy. The English theory, that any group of people could be "virtually" represented by some outsider in whose selection they might have had no part, naturally did not appeal to Americans when it was urged a little later in support of parliamentary taxation for the colonies.

It has already been pointed out that, while English constitutional law was more and more emphasizing the absolute authority of Parliament and getting away from the idea of constitutional limitations binding even upon Parliament itself, Americans were moving in the opposite direction. From the beginning they had been accustomed to legislatures which were limited in various ways, — sometimes by the charters, sometimes by the necessity of conforming to particular rules of English law. Such limitations were not merely theoretical; they were enforced by decisions of the Privy Council, which acted on appeals from colonial courts. Whether there were similar limitations on Parliament itself was a question not yet clearly thought out by most Americans. Some of them, however, had more or less definite notions of the empire as a quasi-federal system with a rough boundary line separating the legitimate authority of Parliament from that of the colonial legislatures.

American ideas about constitutional limitations.

American local government.

In local government, similar transforming influences were at work, though the results varied widely from one colony to another, Virginia, for instance, keeping most closely to the English model. The New England town meeting went far beyond the English parish both in the free handling of local business and in its power to influence or check the policies of the central government. In the middle provinces, county administration was brought more fully under popular control. In New York the justices had to share their authority with supervisors elected by the inhabitants of each township. In Pennsylvania, the voters of each county elected or nominated not only members of the assembly but also such officers as sheriff, coroner, and county commissioners.

Modifications of the common law.

In the matter of personal and property rights also, American thought drifted from the old moorings. Even when claiming for themselves all possible benefits of the common law, they also discarded much which did not appeal to them or seemed unsuited to local needs. The New Englanders, for instance, decided that the prosperity of their settlements would be secured best by a wide distribution of property in land. Accordingly, when a landowner died without leaving a will, the law did not, as in England, give all the real estate to the eldest son, but divided it among the children, the eldest son receiving only a double portion. In the case of *Winthrop* v. *Lechmere*, decided in 1728, the English Privy Council set aside the Connecticut law on this subject, on the ground that it was contrary to the law of England, and if this action had been taken generally, New England land titles would have been thrown into confusion. Fortunately this policy was not carried out and later decisions practically gave the New Englanders a free hand in this respect. Another example of more or less radical departure from English models is to be found in the penal codes of the colonies. Though harsh enough, from a modern point of view, they were generally less so than the contemporary English practice, which still imposed the death penalty for various minor offenses. Something was done to simplify legal procedure and make justice less expensive for the poor man. New Englanders especially prided themselves on certain improvements, such as public registration of land titles, the use of English in all proceedings, and in general making justice "easy, quick, and cheap."

In the matter of safeguards for free speech and a free press, progress was made on both sides of the Atlantic. The policy of requiring books to be licensed before publication was given up both in England and in America. In one important matter, however, American practice anticipated that of England. In the Zenger case, already described, a New York jury attracted attention by asserting its right to decide whether the publication was false and malicious instead of merely accepting the judge's decision. This was in 1735. In 1784, the great English lawyer, Erskine, defended substantially this doctrine in a famous libel suit, though it was not until 1792 that it was definitely established by act of Parliament. *Freedom of the press.*

One feature of American society which has always interested foreign observers is the status of religion and more particularly of religion in its relation to the state. The development of American thought on this subject was gradual and there was no generally accepted theory before the Revolution. Nevertheless, the tendency was certainly against state control. Even in New England and Virginia, where such control was most effective, it was clearly growing weaker. The various influences at work to bring about religious liberty and the separation of church and state have been noted in the history of particular colonies or groups of colonies; but the main features of the development may be recalled briefly. *American thought on church and state.*

Tendency
toward
religious
liberty.

Sometimes religious liberty was advanced because leaders like Roger Williams and William Penn thought out a definite theory of freedom and applied it in the colonies which they founded or helped to found. Elsewhere, as in most of the proprietary provinces, a more or less liberal policy toward religious dissenters was adopted because it was "good business"; land was worthless without people to work it and the promise of religious liberty was likely to attract some particularly solid and hard-working immigrants. So also the Anglican authorities of the South found it worth while to allow a larger religious liberty to the dissenters whose settlements guarded their Indian frontiers. Sometimes the ruling element in a colony had ecclesiastical views opposed to those of the home government. In such cases dissatisfied groups could often make trouble in England. The Catholic Lord Baltimore might have pursued a tolerant policy in any case; but in 1648, with an ultra-Protestant government in England, he could hardly have done anything else. Certainly the appeals of Anglicans and Quakers to the authorities in London helped to break down the rigid Puritan systems of Massachusetts and Connecticut. Practical expediency was probably more decisive than theory in the progress of religious freedom

Conditions
at the close
of the
colonial era.

The outcome, at any rate, is clear. Actual persecution for religious opinion almost disappeared. The one group which still remained under the ban was the Catholics, and some of the legislation against them was extremely harsh, notably in New York and Maryland, but it was probably less so in practice than on paper and the number actually interfered with was comparatively small. Furthermore, there were several provinces with no state church at all, including Rhode Island and all the middle provinces except part of New York. In these colonies, with their great variety of religious sects, men were gradually accepting the now familiar American philosophy that the state should be neutral in its attitude toward competing religious bodies. Their example also helped dissenters in those provinces which still clung to the state-church idea.

Scarcely less significant than this drift away from church establishments was the relative weakness in America of the churches whose evolution was most closely associated with the older society of Europe. The Church of England, as well as the Catholics and to a lesser extent the Lutherans, cherished institutions and forms of worship which preserved the sense of continuity in the organized life of the church. So far as these institutions were transplanted to America, they carried with them something of the old soil; modes of thought and feeling which kept men more conscious than they might otherwise have been of their kinship with European civilization. Respect for authority, deference to what Edmund Burke called the "early received and uniformly continued sense of mankind," — these were mental attitudes which some men, at any rate, were likely to carry over from religion into their political and social philosophy. *Relative weakness of the older churches.*

The position of the radical Protestants — such as the Congregationalists, Quakers, Baptists, and the minor German sects — was quite different. In Europe they were protesting minorities, fighting for life, with the main forces of national life against them. Their peculiar ideals were indeed born in Europe; but they found in America a more congenial soil and the European background meant much less to them. They cared little for venerable liturgies, or established orders, or divine right in kings and bishops. In America, many of these sects now had a free field for experimentation. Their pet theories were transmuted into the working philosophy of men who shaped public opinion and sometimes, as in New England and Pennsylvania, controlled the government. By 1776 there was not a single one of the old thirteen colonies in which a combination of *Strength of the dissenting spirit.*

these groups could not claim a majority of the population. Such conditions certainly helped to make American ideals different from those prevailing in Europe, not only in religion but in other phases of popular philosophy.

Effect of westward expansion. Obviously the differentiation of Americans from Englishmen went on much faster in certain regions and in certain social groups than in others. A Virginia planter, educated in religion and letters by Anglican clergymen, corresponding with relatives and business agents in the old country, and priding himself on his broad acres, was much nearer to his English contemporaries than the heterogeneous population of the middle region, or the Puritan farmers of Massachusetts and Connecticut who had not quite forgotten the republican spirit of the Cromwellian era. Most American of all in our modern sense were the newer communities of the interior. As the seaboard settlements developed with age a new conservatism of their own, the pioneering spirit had found its outlet on the westward-moving frontier. Here again there was land to be had almost for the asking; capital was useful, but individual energy and courage were less handicapped in competition with inherited wealth and social status. Here also, sometimes for better but sometimes also for worse, men lost touch with the traditions and conventions of an older society. Separated from their neighbors on the seaboard, they were still further removed from their cousins across the sea. Finally, it was in the back country that men of purely English stock found themselves most generally outnumbered by new immigrants from Scotland, Ireland, and the Continent, with their varied religious and social traditions.

The making of an American. On the eve of the Revolution an able observer, himself a recent immigrant, wrote a well-known book, called *Letters from an American Farmer*, in which he tried to show what it was that made an American different from a European. What struck him particularly was the tendency of American life to break down old distinctions of class, nationality, and religion. He noted the "pleasing uniformity of decent competence" which prevailed here, contrasting it with a European society made up of landlords and tenants. "This fair country alone is settled by freeholders, the possessors of the soil they cultivate, members of the government they obey." Coming as a poor immigrant, the European peasant found his labor in demand and was able before long to buy land on his own account. Ownership of land and a liberal rule of naturalization transformed him into a self-respecting citizen and voter. Mutual tolerance also developed through contact with men of widely different conditions. "If they are peaceable subjects, and are industrious, what is it to their neighbors how and in what manner they think fit to address their prayers to the Supreme Being?" In this atmosphere of economic, political, and religious freedom, the European became an American, "a new man, who acts upon new principles." For provincial America as a whole this picture was overoptimistic. It does not, for instance, take into account the very different outlook of a conservative Puritan merchant in Boston or a typical slave-owning planter on the James. It does, however, fairly represent the new America which was everywhere beginning to assert itself against the more conservative spirit of the seaboard.

BIBLIOGRAPHICAL NOTES

Beard and Beard, ch. IV. Andrews, *Colonial Period*, chs. VII, IX. Greene, *Provincial America*, chs. V, XII, XIII, XVIII. Lecky, W. E. H., *England in the Eighteenth Century*, III, 294–324. Trevelyan, G. O., *American Revolution*, I, 12–56, 63–69. *General discussions.*

Turner, *Frontier in American History*, chs. I, III. Roosevelt, *Winning of the West*, I, ch. V. Semple, E. C., *American History and Its Geographic Conditions*, chs. III, IV. St. John de Crève- *Geographic influences. The frontier.*

cœur, H., *Letters from an American Farmer* (convenient *Everyman* edition).   Thwaites, R. G., *Early Western Travels*, I.

Political theory and practice.

Channing, *United States*, III, 74–76, and his *Town and County Government* (*Johns Hopkins Studies*, II, no. 10).   Cheyney, *European Background*, 313–315.   Frothingham, R., *Rise of the Republic*, chs. I–IV.   Greene, E. B., *Provincial Governor*, chs. VIII–X. Labaree, L. W., *Royal Government in America*.   Howard, G. E., *Local Constitutional History of the United States*, I.   McIlwain, C. H., *High Court of Parliament*, chs. IV, V.   McKinley, A. E., *Suffrage Franchise in the English Colonies* (summary in ch. XV). Merriam, C. E., *American Political Theories*, ch. I.   Foster, H. D., "International Calvinism through Locke and the Revolution of 1689," *A.H.R.*, XXXII, 475–499.   Mullett, *Fundamental Law and the American Revolution*.

English law in America.

Morris, R. B., *Studies in the History of American Law*, ch. I. *Select Essays in Anglo-American Legal History*, I (articles by Reinsch, Sioussat, and Andrews).   Chalmers, G., *Opinions of Eminent Lawyers* (see index under *Common Law*).   On lawyers and their training, see Warren, C. W., *History of the American Bar*, pt. I; Stillé, C. J., *John Dickinson*, ch. II; and Jones, E. A., *American Members of the Inns of Court*.

Architecture. Interior decoration. Silver.

Kimball, F., *Domestic Architecture of the American Colonies and of the Early Republic*.   Lockwood, L. V., *Colonial Furniture in America*, 2 vols.   Avery, C. L., *Early American Silver*.

Provincial theater.

Quinn, A. H., *A History of the American Drama*, chs. I, II. Odell, G. C. D., *Annals of the New York Stage*, I.

Post office, roads, and travel.

Dunbar, S., *Hist. of Travel in America*, I.   Smith, W., *Hist. of the Post-Office in British North America*, chs. I–II.   Rich, W. E., *Hist. of the U. S. Post-Office to the Year 1829*, pp. 3–60.

Nation in embryo.

Kraus, M., *Intercolonial Aspects of American Culture*, ch. X. Schouler, J., *Americans of 1776*.

CHAPTER XVI

THE STRUGGLE FOR THE WEST AND THE PASSING OF NEW FRANCE

THE great fact of American history during the first half of the eighteenth century is the process of expansion, by which the British provinces preëmpted not only the seaboard from Nova Scotia to Georgia but also the eastern slopes of the Appalachian system. With the exception of two struggling settlements, Nova Scotia in the north and Georgia in the south, this expansion had come about through the development of older provinces rather than the organization of new ones. The work could not have been done, however, without the help of many thousand new immigrants, who found on these upland frontiers opportunities no longer open to them in the region occupied by the seventeenth-century pioneers. *British expansion.*

Along with this solid colonization of the "Old West," as Turner has called it to distinguish it from the newer West beyond the mountains, there was a more adventurous and picturesque kind of enterprise which broke through or passed around the mountain barrier to the "western waters" of the Mississippi valley. Before the end of the seventeenth century, a few daring spirits among the English colonists had ventured into the great "hinterland" to trade with the Indians in the Lake region and in the valleys of the Ohio and its southern tributaries. Then and for the next half century, these English hunters, trappers, and traders, though active enough to disturb their French and Spanish rivals, were still quite insignificant in numbers and worked at a great disadvantage, often separated from *English enterprise beyond the Alleghenies.*

their bases of supplies by several hundred miles of wilderness. Gradually, however, the pioneer settlements of western Pennsylvania, Virginia, and the Carolinas were putting another face on the situation. Here were new and more convenient points of approach to the trans-Allegheny region, and here also were trained, in large part, the men who were to form the skirmish line of the English advance into the Mississippi valley. So the process of expansion already described leads naturally to the next and most dramatic chapter in colonial history, the decisive struggle of the English-speaking people with their two great Latin rivals for predominance in North America.

The French colonists.   The more formidable of these two antagonists was, of course, France, whose pioneers had been active in the trans-Allegheny country since the days of La Salle, Marquette, and Iberville. In the north were the Lake posts — Fort Frontenac at the outlet of Lake Ontario, Niagara, Detroit, Mackinaw, Green Bay. The western line was held by New Orleans and a few struggling settlements farther up the Mississippi, including the villages of the Illinois country and a post on the Wabash. On the Gulf, facing the Spaniards in Florida, was the French outpost of Mobile. The white population of this vast region was still insignificant. There were certainly fewer white people between the Alleghenies and the Mississippi in 1750 than in one of the smaller English colonies. Even in this meager population many were not real home makers, but more or less temporary occupants — officials, traders, soldiers, and missionaries. White women were scarce and many of the younger generation in the French villages were the children of Indian mothers. A few farmers in the Illinois country were raising wheat and shipping flour down the river to New Orleans; but the dominating interest of this western country was the fur trade. It was the fur trade also in which the English adventurers beyond the mountains were chiefly interested.

Gradually a larger issue dawned upon Englishmen and Frenchmen alike. From the French point of view, the Ohio valley was an essential link between the colonies on the St. Lawrence and those on the Mississippi; the loss of that link would be a serious blow to the integrity of their North American empire. The English were equally sure that French settlements on the western rivers which rose on the Appalachian plateau would hem in their natural advance from the seaboard. Thus, as so often happens in history, both sides had aggressive plans for expansion; but each declared with more or less sincerity that its own aims were primarily defensive, the securing of legitimate interests against unjust aggression.

French and English points of view.

Important as this western problem was from an American point of view, it is necessary to remember always that, for the rulers of the British Empire, it was only one of many threads in the complicated web of world politics. Still, as in the era of the Restoration, the first object of British foreign policy was the advancement of sea power and the promotion of commerce. In the first half of the seventeenth century, the leaders in the race for commercial supremacy were the Dutch, who had destroyed the old Portuguese monopoly of Asiatic commerce and won also a large share in the carrying trade, of both the European nations and their American dependencies. These achievements naturally excited the jealousy of the other two great maritime powers of western Europe. France and England still had much to learn from the Dutch; but their superiority in population, territory, and other physical resources, if properly organized, was bound to tell in the end. To provide such organization through governmental action became, therefore, a prime object of British and French statesmanship. Trade was to be developed not merely by individual initiative, but through protective legislation, diplomacy, and even war. A commerce thus built up by the

The western problem and world politics.

Struggle for commercial supremacy.

state was expected also to work for the state. Trade properly controlled would bring revenue to the Crown; revenue would support armies and navies; and, to close the circle of commercial imperialism, armies and navies could be used in defending and promoting trade. Of course this reasoning practically carried with it the notion, unfortunately not yet dead, of international trade as a kind of warfare rather than a mutually helpful exchange of services.

In this kind of international competition, England and France soon set a pace with which a small country like the Netherlands could hardly keep up, and the Dutch gradually lost ground. Meantime, the conflict between the two leading powers became more intense and far-reaching. In India, English and French companies set up "factories," or agencies, through which they tried to control the European trade in Eastern wares. The African coast furnished ports of call on the way to the Indies and above all a field for strenuous competition in the slave trade. From the governmental point of view even America was primarily worth while, not because it furnished territory for European settlements but because political control of territory would carry with it control of certain American products: fish, fur, and naval stores from the North; tobacco, sugar, and dyestuffs from the South. Finally, sea power was

essential to protect these distant trade routes, and this meant not only expanding navies, but naval stations at strategic points like Gibraltar on the Mediterranean, Louisburg on the Canadian coast, and certain ports in the West Indies.

Notwithstanding these intense rivalries, actual warfare was avoided for a quarter century after the peace of Utrecht. Both the French and British governments had been heavily burdened by the War of the Spanish Succession and both were made cautious by internal difficulties. France had an infant king and was troubled by endless court intrigues, while in England the Whigs were trying to avoid foreign complications and keep down taxes until their new German dynasty could be domesticated. So both parties were willing to postpone the conflict, though each kept a jealous eye upon the other.

Meantime, Spain still played an important, though secondary, part in the game of world politics. After a long war in which the Spanish crown and its dependencies in three continents had been fought over by the rival powers of Europe, the spoils had been divided between the contending parties. So far as trade and colonies were concerned, England reaped the chief advantage; but a younger branch of the French Bourbon monarchy was established in Spain. Though Frenchmen and Spaniards were not always sympathetic, they were drawn together by this dynastic relation and by their common hostility towards England, their most dangerous rival. *Position of Spain in world politics.*

In the century and a half which ended with the treaty of Utrecht, Spain had accumulated a long list of grievances against the English. The freebooting expeditions of Hawkins and Drake, the conquest of Jamaica, and finally the humiliating loss of Gibraltar — these were a few of the old scores which the rulers of Spain would have been glad to pay off. Even since the peace, they had much to complain of; British seamen were not content with the trading privileges given them by the treaty and were constantly colliding with the customs officials in the Spanish colonies. On the North American mainland, the whole process of English colonization, especially in the South, seemed nothing less than a series of encroachments on Spanish territory; and the occupation of Georgia threatened to crowd Spain altogether from the Atlantic seaboard. Spain also had its grievances against the French, who occupied the Gulf coast at New Orleans and Mobile; but these were not sufficient to prevent the two powers from drawing together at certain *Spanish grievances against England.*

The Family Compact.

times for defense against a common enemy. So it came about that the Bourbon governments of France and Spain united in the Family Compact of 1733, which was aimed primarily at England.

Anglo-Spanish War of 1739.

Six years later the friction between British seamen and the Spanish customs guards caused so much excitement in Great Britain that the peace-loving ministry of Walpole was pushed reluctantly into a new war with Spain. Even before the declaration was known in America, Admiral Vernon had attacked and captured Porto Bello on the northern side of the Isthmus of Panama. Reënforcements were sent him at once and plans made for an extensive campaign against Spanish America. The outcome was disappointing, but there was one notable achievement worthy of the Elizabethan seamen, — the voyage of Captain Anson in the *Centurion*. Like Drake, Anson sailed up the Pacific coast of South America, preying upon the enemy's commerce as he went, and then crossed the Pacific Ocean. After spending several months in Chinese waters and capturing one of the great Spanish treasure ships, he returned to England in 1744. He brought back only a fraction of his original force, but he had dealt Spain a serious blow. The North American colonies also had a part in this war. The British in Georgia under Oglethorpe made an unsuccessful expedition against St. Augustine; and in 1742 the Spaniards landed a force on the Georgia coast, which was repulsed after hard fighting. The northern colonies were called on to furnish men and supplies for the campaigns in Central and South America; and in New England, at least, they responded with some enthusiasm. Privateering, through its combination of business with war, was especially attractive to colonial capitalists and seamen.

Spain joined by France.

The Spanish war was, however, soon overshadowed by the conflict with France, which had already been helping her ally so far as she could without being technically

at war. The French declaration of war in 1744 was hastened
by events in Europe which seemed to have little relation to
the New World. The Anglo-Spanish War had hardly begun,
when Frederick the Great, the ambitious young King of
Prussia, seized the Austrian province of Silesia. The integrity
of the Austrian dominions had been guaranteed by the European powers, including France, Great Britain, and Prussia
herself; but France had her eye on the Austrian Netherlands,
and soon allied herself with Prussia. For England, it was not
merely a question of observing her treaty obligations; her
own interests were directly affected. She could not afford
to have an aggressive maritime power like France establishing its hold on the coast provinces of the Netherlands.
So the conflict both in Europe and in America was largely
one of sea power. No one understood this more clearly than
Frederick himself, who was not only a great soldier but a
keen student of politics. He saw in this persistent antagonism of the two rival maritime powers the controlling factor in European politics, on which he could count with
confidence to prevent united action in defense of Austria.

In this European War of the Austrian Succession, the com- **War of the**
bination to which England belonged met with serious reverses. **Austrian**
Succession.
Prussia kept its grip on Silesia and the French armies advanced into the Netherlands. In 1745 the uprising of the
Jacobites under the "Young Pretender" gave the British
government some anxious moments, though the rebels were
defeated in the battle of Culloden. At sea, the British gradually established their superiority over the French; but they
failed to use this advantage for large enterprises in America. There both sides made extravagant claims, but neither
was quite ready to force the issue.

The outstanding event of the war in America was the **The war in**
New England expedition against Louisburg, the fortress **America.**
Louisburg.
on Cape Breton Island, built by the French after the surrender
of Acadia. Louisburg was the most important French post

on the seaboard, both for the defense of the St. Lawrence gateway, and for more aggressive purposes. Under its shelter, the French fisheries developed so fast as to arouse the anxiety of the New Englanders, and connections were kept up with the Acadians in Nova Scotia which were quite inconsistent with their new English allegiance. In time of war, Louisburg became more formidable still. From its safe harbor, French privateers sailed out from time to time with disastrous results to New England traders and fishermen. It was also a convenient base for military and naval expeditions against the neighboring colonies. To get rid of this "thorn in the flesh," Governor William Shirley of Massachusetts proposed to the House of Representatives in secret session a plan for the capture of the fortress. The assembly hesitated but the plan was finally approved. With some difficulty, Shirley secured the coöperation of Commodore Warren of the British navy with a few ships from the West Indies. New England, however, made the largest contribution, including the commander of the expedition, William Pepperell of Kittery, Maine. Pepperell was a man of varied experience and good sense, but, like most of his associates, without much military experience. From the point of view of a military expert, this amateur enterprise was quite reckless, and it would doubtless have failed if the French commander and his men had done their duty. Actually, however, Yankee energy, aided by sheer good luck, won in spite of all the rules, and on June 17, 1745, Louisburg was taken.

Indecisive operations.

Inspired by this achievement, Shirley now urged upon the British ministry a much more ambitious project for the complete conquest of Canada. Unfortunately his correspondent, Newcastle, was too much occupied with other matters and lacked the imagination which a few years later made Pitt the great imperial statesman of his time. So the last years of "King George's War" passed with no events of real importance. The French attempted to avenge the blow at Louisburg, but their fleets were baffled, first by storms and later by the British navy. In the Mohawk valley the French agent, Joncaire, and the British agent, William Johnson, were playing a close game for the support of the Iroquois. On the New England frontiers there was the old dismal story of French and Indian raids, inflicting much distress but producing little permanent effect.

By 1748 nearly everybody was tired of the war. Frederick the Great was content with peace and Silesia, while France and England had fought so evenly that both were ready to go back to the conditions before the war. This meant the return of Louisburg, to the great disgust of the New England people, who saw all their efforts go for nothing. A serious effort was made by the British government to keep it, but France was equally determined and had, besides, a strong position in the Netherlands which she would not give up without compensation. For British sea power, the exclusion of France from the Netherlands seemed even more important than the keeping of Louisburg; incidentally also, the British East India Company recovered Madras, which had been taken by the French. So far as America was concerned, the war settled nothing.

Treaty of Aix-la-Chapelle, 1748.

The diplomatists next took up the task of trying to settle the conflicting claims of the two nations in the West, and on the Acadian frontier. Commissioners appointed for this purpose met in Paris, among them Governor Shirley, who could give first-hand information on American conditions and the American point of view. There was another battle of the maps; extravagant claims were made on both sides, and the spirit of compromise was utterly lacking. So the negotiations came to nothing. Colonial officials on both sides urged thoroughgoing measures, but their home governments were more conservative and the decisive struggle approached without effective preparation

Diplomacy, 1748-1754. The battle of the maps.

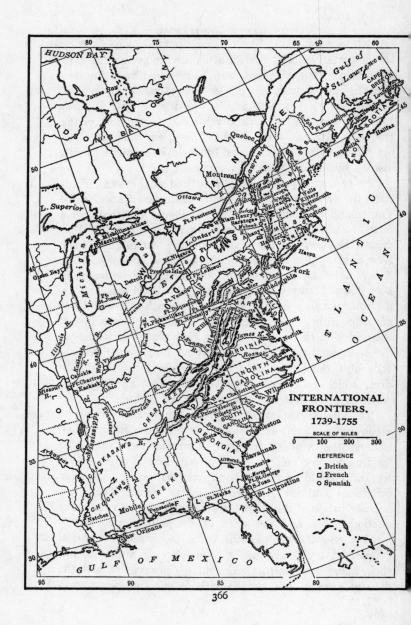

INTERNATIONAL
FRONTIERS,
1739-1755

SCALE OF MILES

0   100   200   300

REFERENCE
• British
□ French
○ Spanish

on either side. When war came, the opening scenes were overseas in India and America.

The points of hostile contact, where the territorial claims and trading interests of the French and English met, were many. Four were especially important on the North American continent. The first was on the seaboard, where the English at Halifax were watching the French at Louisburg. That Acadia had been duly ceded by Louis XIV in the treaty of Utrecht was one of the few English claims which France was willing to concede, but what was Acadia? To England it meant not only the present peninsular province of Nova Scotia, but also much additional territory stretching northward and westward to the St. Lawrence basin. The French, on the contrary, proposed to confine Acadia to a small tract on the peninsula. Both sides took steps to enforce their theories. The British began in earnest the long-neglected colonization of Nova Scotia, and by 1752 the new town of Halifax had about four thousand people, though this British element was still outnumbered by the Acadian French. Meantime, the French not only kept up their religious and political connections with the Acadians, but established the fort of Beauséjour on the narrow neck of the peninsula. The British, equally determined, fortified Beaubassin, only a few miles away, making at the same time new efforts to secure the allegiance of the Acadian farmers.

A second debatable region lay along the waterway which connects New York with Montreal. The southern part of that line, formed by the Hudson River, was definitely British for a short distance above Albany. Its northern section, the Richelieu River, was quite as definitely French. Between these two sections was the disputed area, the portage from the Hudson to Lake George and the region about that lake and Lake Champlain. The French had an outpost at Crown Point on Lake Champlain;

Points of hostile contact. Acadia and Nova Scotia.

The Hudson-St. Lawrence waterway.

but the New Yorkers were less enterprising and a fort built at Saratoga was abandoned in 1747. The French advance on this line was a serious matter for the New Englanders, whose pioneer settlements on the upper Connecticut could easily be reached by raiding expeditions from Crown Point.

The Great Lakes. Oswego and Niagara.

The third field of international rivalry, the Great Lakes basin, with its rich fur trade, was approached by the two competing nations on converging lines. The French had taken the lead by way of the St. Lawrence and Ottawa rivers; their strategic points were Fort Frontenac, Niagara, and Detroit. The English moved somewhat later by the Mohawk valley to Oswego on Lake Ontario; but in the second quarter of the eighteenth century they gained distinctly on the French. The treaty of Utrecht recognized British suzerainty over the Iroquois, which was exploited for more than it was worth, as a basis for British claims to the West. The post at Oswego soon did a more thriving business than that at Niagara. Yet the French always regarded the Oswego traders as trespassers and still hoped to bring the Iroquois over to their side.

The Ohio valley.

The youngest, but soon to become the most urgent, of these frontier issues turned on the control of the Ohio valley. A century and more of western enterprise gave the French a fair claim by right of occupation to the upper Lakes and the line of the Mississippi; but, when peace was made in 1748, the only safe communication between Canada and Louisiana was the long and difficult northern route. The shorter and easier thoroughfare of the Ohio was blocked at its eastern end; for the portages connecting that river with the lower Lake region and the St. Lawrence were dominated by the Iroquois. This difficulty became more serious as new English pioneers pressed forward into the Mississippi basin. In Pennsylvania and Virginia especially, men of wealth and influence were planning systematically for the exploitation of western trade and western lands.

The forks of the Ohio, where the Monongahela from the south and the Allegheny from the north join their forces, lay within the charter lines of Pennsylvania; but the Virginians, remembering the "west and northwest" clause in their charter of 1609, put in a counterclaim. Though these dissensions hurt the British cause, enough was being done on that side to cause the French serious anxiety.

The Canadian governor at this critical moment was the Marquis de la Galissonière, a distinguished naval officer, but also a statesman, clear-sighted and capable of large views. While the diplomatists were discussing documents in Paris, Galissonière was doing what he could to strengthen the French case. It was by his orders that Céloron de Bienville (or Blainville) made a celebrated journey from Lake Erie to the Allegheny River, then down the Allegheny and Ohio to the Miami, then up the Miami and down the Maumee to Lake Erie again. The lead plates which he left at various points in this long circuit, setting forth the French title to the valley, hardly affected the course of history; but the information which he brought back was discouraging and called for speedy action. Everywhere Céloron found English traders or evidences of their activity and influence among the Indians; but his force was too weak for anything more than a protest. *French expedition to the Ohio.*

Meantime new forward moves were being made by the British. In 1749 the Ohio Company, a group of influential Virginians, obtained from the King a grant of half a million acres on the Ohio, where they were to plant a colony. The next year they sent out a seasoned pioneer, Christopher Gist, who was able to get the coöperation of George Croghan, the ablest of the Pennsylvania traders. On the Ohio and the Miami these agents were well received. Especially encouraging was the development about Pickawillany, on the Miami, where the great chief of the Miami tribe, a firm friend of the British, ruled over a population of five *The Ohio Company.*

thousand Indians. Here the British had a fort, the center of a rapidly growing trade. Before long, however, the tide began to run against them, and in the next five years disaster followed disaster, largely because mutual jealousies and a generally provincial outlook prevented the British colonies from acting effectively together.

New French forts.

In 1752 the French dealt a severe blow at British influence when a party of western Indians, led by a French trader from Wisconsin, broke up the post at Pickawillany. The next year the new French governor, Duquesne, took up the task of securing the northern approach to the Ohio from Lake Erie. Forts were built at Presque Isle, now Erie, Pennsylvania, and on French Creek, a tributary of the Allegheny. Here the work was interrupted by disease and the approach of winter, just as the English began to wake up to the new danger.

Instructions to colonial governors.

Late in the summer of 1753, Lord Holdernesse, the secretary of state specially responsible for the colonies, sent a circular to the colonial governors warning them of French encroachments. They were not to take the offensive, but if the enemy invaded territory "within the undoubted limits" of the British dominions, they must "repell force by force." This continued to be the official theory of the British government during the next two years. The French position was essentially the same in principle, but the "undoubted limits" asserted by one nation were quite as confidently denied by the other. Of the governors to whom this message came, the most alert and aggressive were William Shirley in Massachusetts, Horatio Sharpe in Maryland, and Robert Dinwiddie in Virginia. Dinwiddie was a Scotchman, ardently patriotic, with plenty of fighting spirit, though not always a skillful politician. The lack of enterprise displayed by the Pennsylvania government gave Dinwiddie his opportunity, and he determined on a mission to warn the French out of the Ohio country.

The agent selected for this difficult task was George Washington, then a young man of twenty-one. Though his family was connected with the Virginia gentry, he was already familiar with the hardships of the wilderness, and accustomed to dealing with the Indians. He was also associated with the group of men who had organized the Ohio Company and were interested in the occupation of western lands. In the late autumn of 1753, Washington set out on his long journey. At the trading post of Wills Creek on the Potomac he was joined by Christopher Gist, with whom he pushed on to the forks of the Ohio. After conferences on the way with the Indians and with the French agent, Joncaire, he delivered his message to the commandant at Fort Le Boeuf, only to be answered by a flat defiance.

Washington's mission to the Ohio.

Diplomacy had failed, and prompt action was necessary if the British were to keep a foothold in the Ohio valley. Preparations were, therefore, made for a British fort at the forks; but the small detachment sent to hold the position had to give way before a superior French force, which proceeded to establish its own post of Fort Duquesne. The main body of the Virginians, under Washington, moved forward to recover the lost ground and on the way fell in with a French reconnoitering party. A skirmish followed in which the French commander was killed, but before long Washington's party was attacked and defeated by a stronger detachment from Fort Duquesne. For the time being, the British had to withdraw from the disputed region.

Fort Duquesne. French and Indian War begun.

By October, 1754, the news of this frontier skirmish and its results had reached the British government. The Newcastle ministry, representing the old Whig traditions, was disposed to uphold British claims at the various points in dispute, but had strong reasons for not beginning a European war. George II had territory in Hanover which lay between two hostile neighbors, France and Prussia, and

British policy in 1754.

there was also danger that if Great Britain appeared to be the aggressor, Spain might be drawn into the fight on the French side. The British game, therefore, was to treat the fighting in America as a local affair, which might still be settled without actual war between the two sovereign governments. If, however, war could not be averted, then, if possible, the odium of beginning it must be thrown on the French. Meantime, the American representatives of the British Crown must be supported by military force against alleged encroachments, and a strong force of regular soldiers was, therefore, sent to America under the command of General Braddock. The lost ground on the Ohio was to be recovered by the capture of Fort Duquesne and in the Lake region there was to be an attack on Niagara. On the Nova Scotia border, the French were to be driven from Fort Beauséjour and the King's rebellious Acadian subjects reduced to submission. The danger of incursions from the north was to be guarded against by the seizure of Crown Point.

The French plan. Unfortunately for this program, the French government felt itself equally entitled to use military force in support of its claims and prepared a counter expedition of regular troops. To permit this reënforcement of the French in America was to neutralize the whole British plan of operations. Therefore, in spite of the nominal peace between the two nations, the British fleet under Boscawen was ordered to intercept the French transports on their way across the Atlantic. This plan miscarried, however, and the main French fleet reached Canada safely. All the British commander could do was to engage and defeat a few detached vessels.

British reverses in 1755. The failure of this naval campaign opened a year of almost continuous defeat for the British arms in America. Braddock met the colonial governors in conference and worked out the details of the general plan agreed upon in

England. The one entirely successful operation was the capture of Beauséjour, followed by the tragic removal of the so-called "neutral French" from Acadia, where, with all their virtues, they were a constant menace to the British colonists. On the Hudson-Champlain line, the Indian agent William Johnson, and the New England colonel Phineas Lyman, commanded the English forces, which established new posts at Fort Edward on the Hudson and Fort William Henry on Lake George. In the battle of Lake George, the British colonials repulsed the French attack, but failed to follow up their victory. The French still held Crown Point and their general position on this front was not seriously weakened.

The most disastrous and humiliating event of the year was the defeat of Braddock's expedition against Fort Duquesne. Matters went badly from the beginning. Braddock was a brave man, but like many other British officers he did not know how to bring out the hearty coöperation of his American associates, who were doubtless more or less at fault themselves. The Pennsylvania government especially tried his patience, though Franklin was able to give substantial help. At last the preparations were completed and the long march through the mountains and forests began. On July 9, as the expedition was nearing Fort Duquesne, it was suddenly attacked by a force of French and Indians. The British officers fought bravely, but Braddock refused to modify his tactics to meet the requirements of Indian fighting in the woods. He himself was mortally wounded and his regulars were badly demoralized. Washington, who served on Braddock's staff, did good service with the Virginia provincials during and after the battle; but the defeat was overwhelming. The last reverse of this unlucky year was the abandonment of the expedition against Niagara, undertaken in person by Shirley, who succeeded Braddock as commander in chief of the American forces.

Braddock's defeat.

Loss of
British
prestige in
the West.

Following upon Braddock's defeat in the Ohio valley, this failure on the Lakes meant an almost complete collapse of British influence in the West. The whole frontier was now attacked by the most appalling border warfare, and the line of British occupation, which had been advancing westward before the war, was forced suddenly back.

The war in
Europe.

All these operations took place before either party had definitely declared war; but the pretense of peace could not be kept up much longer. Great Britain postponed formal action until the French attacked the British post on the island of Minorca in the Mediterranean, and then put forward this operation as the technical ground for a declaration of war. This technicality probably helped to keep Spain neutral for a time and so postponed a dangerous combination of the French and Spanish fleets. Meantime, the so-called "diplomatic revolution" had taken place in Europe with momentous consequences for America as well. The Austrian government, abandoning its traditional policy of working with England to preserve the balance of power against France, entered a new combination with its old enemy, France, and Russia, in order to check the rising power of Prussia. The natural result was to put England, with Hanover, in the opposite camp. An alliance was made between Great Britain and Prussia which proved to be one of the essential factors determining the outcome of the American conflict. So the Seven Years' War began, more distinctly a world war than any before in human history.

Sea power in
the Seven
Years' War.

For England the great stake in this war was her sea power and the interests which sea power was intended to protect, her commerce and her colonies. For France, also, these were vital issues, but she was deeply concerned with continental politics, and the new alliance with Austria involved her much further than her real interests required. Thus France was heavily burdened by expensive military operations in Germany and consequently less able to provide for her navy and the defense of her overseas interests. At the beginning of the war, the difference between the two navies was not so great; but it was steadily increased, and in the critical years of the conflict British domination of the ocean routes to America was decisive. All this, however, could not have been known beforehand and when the war broke out numerous complicating factors made the outcome far from certain.

In America the British had one immense advantage in a colonial population perhaps fifteen times larger than their opponents. Equally evident was the superiority of the British colonists in wealth, in agriculture, in commerce, and in a generally self-reliant economic life. In the long run, the same self-reliant, independent spirit in their politics would doubtless also have counted in their favor. Success in international conflict does not, however, depend on number and wealth alone, but often quite as much on the intelligence and efficiency with which these resources are organized. In this respect the British colonies often fell short of their rivals. French authority in North America was largely concentrated at Quebec; and, though the Canadian governor had troubles of his own, he was not dependent for men or money on popular assemblies, which could give or refuse as they saw fit and on their own terms. The British authorities, on the contrary, had to deal with a dozen different governors and as many different assemblies, with quite uncertain and uneven results. In this final struggle with France, the New Englanders did fairly well because they appreciated their direct interest in the outcome and also because their governors, first Shirley and then Pownall, knew how to work with high-spirited popular assemblies. Provinces less directly affected at any given time were likely to hold back or use some time of special danger to secure political concessions from their governors. In Pennsylvania Quaker theories of nonresistance were

Opposing forces in America. British resources.

Weakness of the British organization.

embarrassing until the Quakers decided to withdraw temporarily from the assembly and leave the responsibility to men who had no scruples about war.

Plans for intercolonial union.

The need of some intercolonial organization for the management of Indian relations and military affairs was realized by far-sighted men on both sides of the water, but it was hard to agree on concrete propositions. Royal officials were usually most interested in the centralization of military power, with a governor-general commanding the militia of all the colonies. The funds needed for military purposes might then be raised by an imperial assessment on all the provinces, perhaps taking the form of taxation by Parliament. Even so popular a governor as Shirley favored such a parliamentary tax, because it seemed the only way of distributing the burden fairly on all the colonies, instead of leaving a few to carry more than their fair share. On the other hand, Franklin saw little chance of an effective organization unless the Americans were given a hand in it, and therefore favored a conference of representative men from the various colonies to form a voluntary union.

The Albany Plan.

The most notable effort to realize Franklin's ideal of coöperation was made by the Albany Congress of 1754, which was called by order of the home government for the purpose of strengthening the English hold upon the Indians, more particularly the Iroquois. Seven colonies sent commissioners to the congress, and Franklin was one of the active members. The plan finally agreed upon by the congress included a president-general appointed by the King, and a council consisting of representatives chosen by the colonial assemblies. This federal council was to provide for the common defense, control Indian relations, and levy taxes for these purposes, subject always to the veto of the president-general. It was a statesmanlike plan, too much so for the politicians on either side of the Atlantic. Royal officials preferred a union of a less popular sort and the colonial assemblies were jealous of their independence. Few Americans were capable of rising, as Franklin did, to a statesmanship at once imperial and liberal. So the plan was given up and the war had to be fought, in the main, with the old machinery, though something was done to secure more unified treatment of Indian affairs by the appointment of two general superintendents, one in the North and another in the South. The former post was given to Sir William Johnson, the most successful of the British agents among the Iroquois.

British management of the war suffered not only from poor coöperation, but also at first from poor leadership. The British officers sent to America were often ignorant of colonial conditions and points of view. Quite legitimate demands for quarters and supplies were often presented so tactlessly as to cause unnecessary irritation. Rules of military precedence also made trouble and provincial officers complained that their rank was not properly recognized. Washington, for instance, colonel in the Virginia militia and already an outstanding figure among the American defenders of the western frontier, ranked no higher than a simple captain of regulars. Doubtless most militia officers were poorly trained, but the failure of routine officials to discriminate in such matters had a depressing effect on some of the very men whose larger vision and true patriotism especially fitted them for leadership among their more provincial neighbors. *British blunders.*

Canada escaped some of these problems but not all of them. The center of power at Quebec was undoubtedly well placed for defense even against great superiority in numbers; and in the West the French had more than recovered their old prestige among the Indians. Before the war ended, however, it became clear that the autocratic administration of New France had serious defects of its *French difficulties.*

The
Canadian
government.

own. Of the three important offices in the Canadian government — those of the governor, the intendant, and the general in command of the royal forces — two were in bad hands. The governor, Vaudreuil, was a Canadian by birth, with some experience as governor of Louisiana; but he lacked force, was easily used by corrupt associates, and in the supreme crisis of his career allowed petty personal views to interfere with his devotion to the public service. A more positive and dangerous personality was Bigot, the intendant, who used his position as the head of the financial administration to enrich himself and his accomplices with disastrous consequences for his country. In sharp contrast to Vaudreuil and Bigot stands the fine figure of the

Montcalm.

commanding general, the Marquis of Montcalm, who was not only a brave soldier but a gentleman and a real student of military science. The corrupt administration with which he had to work filled him with disgust, though he could do little to improve it. His position was especially awkward because in the last resort he was subject to the orders of the governor, who also kept the direct command of the Canadian militia. New France was also troubled by the same jealousy between provincial and regular officers which appeared on the British side.

The outcome
uncertain.

So far as American conditions were concerned they did not point clearly towards a decisive victory for either side. It was scarcely conceivable that the French should actually conquer the rich and populous British colonies; but it was doubtful whether the latter could coöperate sufficiently to break down the strong French defensive or even to secure, in the near future, the control of the great interior valleys. Evidently the final outcome would depend largely upon the relative strength of the two home countries.

The French
and British
governments.

The French monarchy under Louis XV was still formidable, though it had lost something of its efficiency. The King was weak and there was no dominating personality, like

Richelieu, among the ministers. The King's mistress, Madame de Pompadour, had great political influence, which she often used to advance incompetent favorites, and she was partly responsible for the disastrous diplomacy of the war. There were many able and patriotic men in the French service; but first-rate national leadership was certainly lacking. The British were not much better off at first. Their German King, George II, was a soldier himself and was deeply interested in foreign politics; but the real power was exercised by the ministry, representing the majority in the House of Commons, which in turn was largely controlled by a group of influential Whig families. Newcastle, the prime minister, and other leaders of this inner group were fairly skillful politicians, but they were too much occupied with distributing patronage to give proper attention to larger problems. Here, as in France, favoritism rather than merit too often determined important appointments in the army and navy as well as in the civil service. Thus both governments began without competent leadership, and at first England made a poorer showing than France.

In the Mediterranean, the French scored a decided triumph by the capture of Minorca. In America, also, the year 1756 went badly for the English. Under Montcalm's leadership, the French took the offensive and captured Oswego, which in spite of its importance for the western trade was not prepared for a serious attack. The new British commander, Lord Loudoun, was clumsy in dealing with the provincial governments, whose coöperation was essential to his success, and the British fleet, though superior in power, was not sufficiently so to cut French communications with the colonies or cope with the commerce-destroying of enemy privateers. The one big personality on the English side of the war at first was not an Englishman at all, but Frederick of Prussia, who was making a

Events of 1756.

gallant fight against the French and their allies on the
Continent.

William
Pitt.By the autumn of 1756 most intelligent Englishmen
realized that a new leadership was needed. The most effective critic of the existing political machine was William
Pitt, long a conspicuous member of the House of Commons
but as yet without a cabinet appointment. Impatient of
mere partisanship and keenly interested in the larger problems of the empire, Pitt had the kind of self-confidence
that inspires confidence in others. Above all he knew how
to inspire the loyalty of the English middle class, as yet
imperfectly represented in the House of Commons. A great
national crisis now gave him his first opportunity for constructive statesmanship. The Newcastle ministry was forced
to resign and a new one was formed with Pitt as its real,
though not its nominal, head. Pitt soon found, however,
that the old leaders were still formidable, and a few months
later he was forced to retire. Fortunately for the country
Pitt and his opponents now saw the necessity of coöperation, and so the two elements presently came together in
a powerful combination which lasted four years — long
enough to decide the main issues of the war. During this
period, from 1757 to 1761, Newcastle looked after "practical politics" and Pitt kept himself comparatively free
for vital issues of imperial statesmanship. As secretary
of state he was primarily responsible for the colonies and
for international diplomacy; but he also kept his hand
on the military and naval services, thus helping to insure
effective coöperation between them. In both the fighting
services, Pitt had able technical advisers who carried out
his plans loyally; but the "grand strategy" of the war was
largely his own.

Development
of Pitt's
strategy.When Pitt took the helm the outlook was not encouraging. The navy could not prevent the French fleets from
getting across the Atlantic in sufficient force to block the

British operations in America, including a proposed attack on Louisburg. In 1757 Montcalm once more took the offensive, this time on the line of Lake Champlain and Lake George, where he captured the British post of Fort William Henry. During the next few months, however, Pitt worked out his strategy for the coming year, in which the American campaigns took the first place. To keep France busy in Europe, Frederick the Great was supported by British subsidies, with some Hanoverian troops; and some expeditions were sent against the French coast. Meantime, England's main strength was free for decisive operations overseas. Pitt had now got beyond the boundary disputes with which the war began and was planning for the conquest of New France.

These were great designs, and Pitt's next task was to find men capable of carrying them out. Incompetent officers had to be set aside and younger men who had shown ability were brought to the front. "Politics" still made trouble and Pitt was not infallible; but there was soon a decided toning up in the military service. The clumsy and ineffective General Loudoun was recalled, and though Abercrombie, the new general in chief, was little if any better, two of the junior officers soon justified Pitt's confidence. Jeffrey Amherst was a solid, though not brilliant, officer just transferred from Germany to the American service, and Brigadier-General James Wolfe, though still a young man in the early thirties, was a thorough student of military science. These two men were chosen for the important task of taking Louisburg from the French. The coöperating naval force was commanded by Admiral Boscawen, one of the ablest officers of his day. *New appointments in the army and navy.* *Wolfe.*

The main responsibility for this year's American campaigns fell on the navy and the British regulars; but Pitt also understood the importance of colonial coöperation. In December, 1757, he sent a spirited circular to the colonial *Pitt's appeal to the colonies.*

governors which helps us to understand his unique success in winning American confidence and good will. He began with a stirring appeal for help in "carrying war into the heart of the enemy's possessions." The King, he said, would not limit the zeal of any province by fixing the exact quota of troops, but all were urged to do their utmost for the common cause. Provincial military officers were to receive more favorable ranking than before; arms and provisions were to be paid for from the imperial treasury; and Parliament was to be asked to compensate the colonial governments for war expenses. Most of the colonial assemblies responded loyally and the prospect soon grew brighter.

The victories of 1758. Louisburg. In the summer of 1758, the army and navy under Amherst, Wolfe, and Boscawen brought the siege of Louisburg to a successful close. Wolfe was now eager to go on with Pitt's more ambitious project for the taking of Quebec; but he was overruled, partly because of the lateness of the season, and partly because of bad news from the Lake Champlain region, where Abercrombie had been repulsed in a badly managed attack on Ticonderoga. The casualties were serious, including Lord Howe, Abercrombie's second in command, who was not only an able officer but unusually successful in winning the confidence of the provincial militia. This reverse at the center was offset by notable victories in the West. First came the capture Fort Frontenac. of Fort Frontenac by a force composed mainly of provincials under the command of a New England officer, Lieutenant-Colonel Bradstreet. The fall of Fort Frontenac carried with it the French vessels on Lake Ontario and broke the main line of communication between Canada and the western posts. The final event of the year was Fort Duquesne. the taking of Fort Duquesne by General Forbes, another of Pitt's fortunate appointments, after a painful march in late autumn through the forests of western Pennsylvania.

The French, discouraged by the fall of Fort Frontenac, did not wait for Forbes's arrival. The British commander, who had been seriously handicapped by illness during the campaign, died soon after; but before the end came, he reported to the great war minister in England that he had given the captured fort the new name of Pittsburgh, "as I hope it was in some measure the being actuated by your spirits that now makes us masters of the place."

Thus in a single year the American situation had completely changed. Pitt and his advisers now looked forward to the crowning enterprise — the seizure of Quebec and the conquest of Canada. By this time, British naval superiority was much more evident than in the early years of the war; though a few French ships managed to slip across to the St. Lawrence, they were not strong enough to interrupt the British transport service or relieve the besieged garrison of Quebec. The general strategy adopted for the new campaign against Canada was substantially the old plan of a double attack, one by way of the ocean and the lower St. Lawrence and the other by land from the Hudson valley. The latter movement, with the general command of the land forces, was entrusted to Amherst.

The attack on Quebec was led by Admiral Saunders and General Wolfe, both admirably fitted for the task in hand. First came the difficult operation of getting the fleet safely up the St. Lawrence. This was accomplished by the end of June, when the expedition came to anchor off Quebec. Then followed two months of hard and anxious work with the outcome quite uncertain until the very end. It was Montcalm's policy to take full advantage of his strong defensive position at Quebec by avoiding a decisive encounter with the British on anything like equal terms. He did not have to defeat Wolfe's army; for if he could only hold his ground until winter, the invaders would have to give up the attack. It was Wolfe's game, on the contrary,

The outlook in 1759.

The plan of campaign.

Capture of Quebec. Wolfe and Montcalm.

to tempt Montcalm into taking the offensive. One plan after another failed, however; for the "wary old fellow," as Wolfe called his opponent, steadily refused to take chances. So, as the summer passed and the first week of September, it began to look as if Montcalm would win. Wolfe was handicapped by his own illness and seemed for a time to have lost the confidence of his subordinates; but he finally decided to take a desperate chance. In the dark morning hours of September 13, 1759, he landed his troops on the northern shore of the river above Quebec, scaled the difficult cliffs and won a position on the Plains of Abraham, which so commanded the city that Montcalm was at last forced to a decisive engagement. Wolfe fell leading his victorious forces, and Montcalm soon after. The young English general was not quite thirty-three years old, but he had lived long enough to associate his name forever with the final predominance, on this continent, of English-speaking people.

A year of victories.

The taking of Quebec was the chief but not the only important result of the year's work in America. In the center, Amherst advanced far enough to occupy the abandoned French positions at Ticonderoga and Crown Point; but the proposed advance on Montreal was postponed. On the Great Lakes, the British captured the French post of Niagara. Another substantial achievement was the capture of Guadeloupe in the West Indies. It was a great year for Pitt, full of anxieties, — as when England's ally, Frederick the Great, was almost overwhelmed by the Russians and Austrians, — yet finally crowned with victory almost everywhere.

The conquest of Canada completed.

The fall of Quebec was not completely decisive. Governor Vaudreuil still held Montreal, and in the early months of 1760 the French came dangerously near recovering Quebec. A few months later, however, Amherst's carefully prepared and well-executed plans resulted in the taking of

Montreal and the surrender of Canada to the British forces. So far as North America was concerned, the primary object of the war had been won; but Pitt was not satisfied. In the West Indies, Guadeloupe was already taken and he was planning expeditions against the other French islands. There was also talk of expeditions against New Orleans and Mobile. Above all, Pitt hoped to weaken the national power of France to the point where she would accept a "dictated peace."

Now, however, a new danger appeared above the horizon. Spain, which had so far been kept neutral, was finally led by fear of English domination into a new Family Compact with France. Convinced that this treaty of 1761 would bring Spain into the war, Pitt proposed to anticipate the danger by attacking the Spanish treasure fleet from America. His colleagues, who had so far accepted his leadership, — not to say dictation, — now refused to follow him. Meantime the new King, George III, and his favorite new minister, Lord Bute, were working for peace. Thus blocked on what he considered a vital matter, Pitt resigned. "I will be responsible," he declared, "for nothing that I do not direct." *Spain and the Family Compact.* *Pitt resigns.*

Spain did come in as Pitt predicted, but too late to save her ally from defeat. West and east, England kept her supremacy on the sea. In 1762, Martinique was taken from the French and Cuba from the Spaniards. In the Far East, there was another notable victory when the British captured Manila. Notwithstanding these victories, Pitt's successors would not stand for his extreme terms, and peace negotiations were pushed forward at Paris. On the British side there was a long and interesting debate on the desirability of keeping Canada after all. It was said by some writers to be a barren and unprofitable country, whose occupation by the French would serve to remind the British colonies of their need for protection by the mother coun- *New British victories.* *Peace negotiations.*

try. From this point of view, the sugar island of Guadeloupe seemed a more valuable acquisition. Others, including Benjamin Franklin, described in glowing colors the prospective development of the continental colonies, giving new strength to the empire and an expanding market for British manufacture. Incidentally also, the owners of sugar plantations in the British islands were not eager for new competitors in the empire. So in the final treaty of 1763 Guadeloupe and Martinique were given up and Canada was held. To Spain the British restored Manila, and also Cuba; but for this they received the cession of Florida, and thus North America became British from the Atlantic to the Mississippi, with the exception of New Orleans, which, with all of Louisiana west of the Mississippi, went to Spain as an offset for the loss of Florida. All that remained of the great French dominion in North America was a pair of little islands, St. Pierre and Miquelon, with some privileges for French fishermen on the coast of Newfoundland.

The treaty of Paris.

Results to England and the colonies.

With these conquests in America and the establishment at the same time of British predominance in India, England for the first time became the unquestioned leader among the maritime and colonial powers of the world. To the people of the British continental colonies, the Paris treaty of 1763 meant the removal of a constant menace to their peaceful development and the breaking of the barriers which checked their westward expansion.

BIBLIOGRAPHICAL NOTES

General references.

Bolton and Marshall, *North America*, ch. XX. Channing, *United States*, II, chs. XVIII, XIX. Osgood, *18th Cent.*, III, pt. III, ch. III; IV, chs. XII–XVII. Lucas, *Historical Geography of the British Empire, Canada*, pt. I, chs. VII–XI. Thwaites, *France in America*, chs. V–XVIII. Winsor, *America*, V, chs. I, VII, VIII. Wrong, G. M., *Conquest of New France*, chs. IV–XI. *Rise and Fall of New France*, 2 vols.

Hart, *Contemporaries*, II, pt. V. Macdonald, *Select Charters*, nos. 51, 52, 54. Selected sources.

Abbott, W. C., *Expansion of Europe*, II, chs. XXX, XXXII. Andrews, "Anglo-French Rivalry, 1700–1750," *A.H.R.*, XX, 539–556, 761–780. *Cambridge Modern History*, VI, chs. V, VI, XIII. Mahan, *Influence of Sea Power, 1660–1783*, chs. VI–VIII. Background of world politics.

Pargellis, S. M., *Lord Loudoun in North America*. Mayo, L. S., *Jeffery Amherst*, chs. III–IX. Whitton, F. E., *Wolfe and North America*. Casgrain, H. R., *Wolfe and Montcalm* (French-Canadian writer). Corbett, J., *England in the Seven Years' War*. Parkman, F., *Montcalm and Wolfe*. Wood, W., *The Fight for Canada*. Doughty, A. G., and Parmelee, G. W., *Siege of Quebec* (leading authority but too detailed for most readers). Baker-Crothers, H., *Virginia and the French and Indian War*. Jameson, J. F., *Privateering and Piracy in the Colonial Period*. The last French war.

Hertz, G. B., *Old Colonial System*, chs. I, II. Biographies of Pitt by W. D. Green, von Ruville, and B. Williams. Hotblack, K., *Chatham's Colonial Policy*, especially chs. VIII–XII. Kimball, G. S., ed., *Correspondence of William Pitt with Colonial Governors*. Pitt's leadership.

Correspondence of William Shirley, 2 vols., ed. by C. H. Lincoln. Biographies of Washington by Fitzpatrick, Hughes, and Sears. See also Washington's *Journal* and letters in *Writings* (edited by Fitzpatrick), I. Franklin, B., *Autobiography* in *Writings* (edited by Smyth), I, and letters *ibid.*, III. Pound, A., *Johnson of the Mohawks*. See also correspondence of Governors Dinwiddie (Virginia Historical Society) and Sharpe (*Maryland Archives*). American leaders.

Alvord, C. W., *Illinois Centennial History*, I, chs. VIII–XI. Henderson, A., *Conquest of the Old Southwest*, chs. III–VI. Thwaites, *Early Western Travels*, I (Weiser, Croghan). Volwiler, *George Croghan*. Winsor, J., *Mississippi Basin* (cartography and trade movements). Hulbert, A. B., *Historic Highways*, III–V. Hanna, C. A., *Wilderness Trail*, and *Scotch-Irish*. Western phases.

Beer, G. L., *British Colonial Policy*, chs. I–VIII. Alvord, C. W., *Mississippi Valley in British Politics*, I, ch. II. Franklin, *Writings* (edited by Smyth), IV. Foster, W. E., *Stephen Hopkins* (Rhode Island Historical Tracts). Pitman, F. W., *British West Indies*, ch. XIV. McCormac, I. E., *Colonial Opposition to Imperial Authority during the French and Indian War*. British colonial policy in the war and the peace.

CHAPTER XVII

IMPERIAL PROBLEMS AND POLICIES, 1760 TO 1766

New imperial problems.

IN the great struggle with France for colonial empire, England's resources and her statesmanship were severely taxed; but peace brought problems not less serious, demanding an even higher type of leadership if the empire was to be held together. These problems were of many different kinds. In Asia, for instance, the British East India Company was no longer a mere trading corporation but had to assume responsibility for the government of alien peoples. For nearly a century more, British statesmen wrestled with the problem of ruling India through a commercial company in such a way as to secure decent administration as well as a profitable income to the stockholders. A significant fact for the American colonies was the East India Company's monopoly of the China trade, including tea, an increasingly popular beverage on both sides of the water.

New provinces of Canada and Florida.

In America old difficulties remained and new ones were added. In the north was Canada with perhaps eighty thousand people of alien race, religion, and law. These "new subjects" of the King had to be protected in the rights guaranteed to them by treaty; but the government also had to consider the "old subjects," from Great Britain and the older colonies, who, though few in numbers, were pushing aggressively into the conquered territory, chiefly for purposes of trade. Along the Gulf coast from the Atlantic to the Mississippi was another conquered territory, consisting of Spanish Florida and the eastern section of French Louisiana. Here also there was the double duty

388

of governing the conquered inhabitants and regulating the activities of British traders and land speculators.

An even more important and interesting problem was the management of the great western domain lying south of the Great Lakes between the Alleghenies and the Mississippi. The interests to be considered were many and conflicting. First, there were the Indians, whose use of the country had been comparatively little affected by the few French posts scattered through the wilderness but who now feared a more serious invasion by British pioneers. Then there were the English fur traders, some working for themselves, others for companies great and small, financed by American and British capital and eager to develop the trade which they had begun before the war. Finally, there were the pioneer colonists, colony promoters, and land speculators, who hoped to establish new settlements beyond the mountains. Within each group there were numerous conflicting interests. Pennsylvanians and Virginians came to blows, literally as well as figuratively, over land and trade in the upper Ohio valley. Well-to-do land speculators, some with dreams of proprietary colonies like those of Baltimore and Penn, were eager for royal grants which would enable them to forestall the squatters now fast pushing through the mountains. Some of these questions could wait, but others pressed for immediate action. Especially urgent was the Indian problem forced on the attention of the British government by the Conspiracy of Pontiac in 1763.

At the outbreak of the French war the King had tried to regulate Indian relations by appointing two superintendents of Indian affairs, one for the North and one for the South. These officials did some useful work; but they could not manage the scattered traders of the western country, and intercolonial jealousies interfered with cooperation. Naturally these conditions led to great abuses,

Western problems.

Indian problems. Conspiracy of Pontiac.

and the Indians were often treated quite unfairly. At this critical moment of increasing hostility between the races, the Indians found an able leader in the Ottawa chieftain, Pontiac, through whose efforts a great combination was formed against the English. At first this "conspiracy" was remarkably successful. The British could not take possession of their new territory on the Mississippi; many of their western posts fell into the hands of the Indians; and there were destructive raids along the whole frontier. The ultimate failure of the uprising was inevitable; but it emphasized the need of more unified and effective control of Indian affairs.

The Proclamation of 1763.

The British government tried to gain time for the study of western problems by a temporary arrangement, which was embodied in the royal Proclamation of 1763. This order provided, first, for the organization of three new royal provinces out of the conquered territory on the continent: Quebec, which was limited to the St. Lawrence valley; East Florida; and West Florida. Most of the trans-Allegheny territory between the thirty-first parallel and the Great Lakes was treated as an Indian reservation, in which the seaboard governors were forbidden to make any further grants; settlers who had already entered it were required to withdraw. The Proclamation of 1763 was a natural and not unreasonable attempt to deal temporarily with a pressing problem, whose permanent solution would require further consideration; but it had to meet an equally natural and almost irresistible westward movement from the older colonies.

Colonial administration inadequate.

It was not only the newly conquered territory which required attention from British statesmen. The whole machinery for colonial administration was felt to be quite inadequate. During the war the colonies, stimulated by Pitt's leadership, had done fairly well in furnishing soldiers and supplies, so well indeed that Parliament appropriated money to reimburse them for some of their expenses. Nevertheless the burden had been unevenly distributed and some provinces failed to do their part. The recent wars had also shown more clearly than ever the weakness of the colonial customs service. The trade with the foreign West Indies which Parliament tried to check by the Molasses Act was continued on a large scale even with French and Spanish enemy ports. This commerce, covered by fraudulent practices, such as the use of "flags of truce," was profitable to the individual traders engaged in it; but from an imperial, or even broadly patriotic, point of view, it was highly objectionable because it helped the enemy islands to hold out against the British navy. Even so good a friend of the colonies as Pitt was exasperated by these irregular practices and tried to stop them by drastic methods, including the use of naval vessels. This use of the navy continued after the war ended and was very unpopular.

In general, then, British statesmen were led by the war, and the resulting expansion of the empire, to consider more seriously the problems of colonial administration. They were becoming more and more convinced that there should be a tightening of the bonds which united the colonies with the mother country, in order that the empire as a whole might act efficiently, whether for economic purposes or for common defense. This movement for a more efficient imperial system was natural enough, and to a great extent legitimate. It came, however, at a time when equally natural and legitimate forces were making themselves felt in America in the direction of greater freedom from external control. *Plans for reorganization.*

For one thing, the continental colonies were growing so rapidly that they felt, more confidently than ever before, their own strength and importance. Immigration was going on steadily and the natural increase in population was also large; for cheap land and a brisk demand for labor made *Growth of the colonies. A new self-confidence.*

possible early marriages and large families. A few Americans, including Franklin, looked forward to a time when the population of the colonies would be larger than that of the mother country. No wonder that European observers began to doubt whether British America would always be content to remain a subordinate part of the empire. The French war and its results also stimulated American self-consciousness and self-confidence. In its beginning the war was largely an affair of the colonists themselves, and though British regulars afterwards played the more important part, the final victory could hardly have been won without provincial coöperation on a large scale. None of the great commanders were colonials, but some provincial officers made excellent records and won a continental reputation. One New England colonel, Phineas Lyman, deserved the chief credit for the repulse of the French army in the battle of Lake George. Another Yankee officer, Bradstreet, commanded the attack on Fort Frontenac, one of the best-managed expeditions of the war. In the terrible months of border warfare after Braddock's defeat, Washington won an enviable reputation which went far beyond the limits of Virginia. There were a few civilians also whose leadership expanded beyond provincial limits. Chief among them was Franklin, who, in the midst of general inefficiency, rendered substantial service to the unlucky Braddock, and whose opinions on the difficult problem of colonial union were sought and respected even by royal officials who did not agree with him.

American feeling about the empire.

On the whole and for the time being, the achievements of the war stimulated the patriotic pride of Americans in the great empire to which they belonged. The heroes of the war were gratefully remembered. To General Howe, who fell at Ticonderoga, Massachusetts set up a monument in Westminster Abbey, and Pitt had a unique place in the affections of his American fellow subjects. In this growing empire, however, Americans were demanding more liberal recognition. Their leaders were sensitive to slights, and tact was not the strong point of most British officials in America, or of their superiors at home. Even such an admirable officer as Wolfe shared the expert's impatience with the provincial militiamen, — their slackness in discipline and their ignorance of military technique. In the early years of the war, no provincial commission above the grade of captain was formally recognized by the British military authorities.

Few Americans of that time were more attached to England and the English people than Franklin; but he wrote to one of his friends in Scotland that "the foundations of the future grandeur and stability of the British Empire lie in America." He complained that heretofore "a petty corporation" or a "particular set of artificers or traders in England" had sometimes "been more regarded than all the colonies." British statesmen, he thought, should get over the idea of discriminating in favor of a particular group of their fellow subjects. What difference did it make from a truly imperial point of view "whether a merchant, a smith, or a hatter" grew rich in "Old or New England"? If there were to be any partiality at all, should it not be shown to those who worked for the good of the empire "at the risk of their own lives and private fortunes in new and strange countries"? Back of these opinions, too, was the personality of a man who in spirit at least was no longer provincial, who felt himself at ease in the best intellectual company of Europe. Franklin was an exceptional American, of course; but there were also young men coming forward, like John Adams, in Massachusetts, and Thomas Jefferson in Virginia, whose thinking, in some respects at least, was outgrowing provincial limitations.

Opinions of Franklin.

With Americans of this sort to deal with, it was not easy to maintain even the existing system of control, not to speak of that "closer dependence" which was the constant

New friction over old issues.

aim of imperialist officials on both sides of the Atlantic. In one colony after another, there was new friction over old issues. Colonial assemblies had used the necessities of the war as a means of extorting concessions from their governors, who complained bitterly of encroachments on their own prerogatives and those of the Crown. The old dispute whether judges should be removable at discretion or serve as in England during good behavior loomed up again, and a New Jersey governor who yielded to local pressure on this question was disciplined by dismissal from his office. In Maryland and Pennsylvania the provincial assemblies were exasperated by the stubborn insistence of the proprietors on having their lands exempted from taxation; and when the war ended, the Pennsylvania assembly sent Franklin to England to work for the overthrow of the proprietary rule and the establishment of a royal government in its place.

Outstanding controversies, 1761–1763.

Among the provincial controversies which disturbed the harmony between the colonies and the mother country during the closing years of the war period, two have always had a prominent place in the story of the Revolution. These were the "Parson's Cause" in Virginia and the case of the "writs of assistance" in Massachusetts. Neither affair involved any new principle of British policy, but they are significant because of the fundamental issues discussed, the character of the men thus brought to the front as leaders of the American opposition, and their effect on public opinion in these two important colonies.

The Parson's Cause, 1763.

The Parson's Cause had its starting point in the Virginia system under which the salaries of clergymen as well as of civil officers were provided by public taxation; thus the annual salary of a minister was fixed at sixteen thousand pounds of tobacco. Unfortunately tobacco was constantly fluctuating in value; when the price went up the parishioners thought the clergy were getting too much. During the war crops were poor, prices rose, and the planters complained that the clergy were profiting by the necessities of the people. So in 1755 and 1758 the assembly ordered the payment of the church tax in money instead of tobacco, at the rate of two pence a pound, considerably below the market rate. The clergy protested against this legislation, pointing out that in the past they had not been compensated for falling prices; but public opinion was against them.

Failing to get relief in Virginia, the clergy appealed to the King and in 1759 secured an order in council annulling the objectionable law. In this again there was nothing new, for colonial statutes had often been vetoed by the Crown. The question now arose, however, whether this royal order was retroactive, so as to affect salaries payable between the passage of the act and its repeal by the Crown. To determine this point, suits were brought by several of the clergy, and in one case the magistrates of Hanover County ruled that the act of 1758 was void. In order, however, to determine the payment due under the old law, a jury verdict was required, with unexpected results.

Appeal to the King.

The parishioners engaged the services of Patrick Henry, a young lawyer of twenty-seven, who, though of a good family, sympathized with the small farmers of the upland districts rather than with the planter aristocracy. One of Henry's uncles was an Anglican clergyman and he himself belonged to that church; but his mother was a Presbyterian and the young man had inherited a certain sympathy for the dissenters. In his argument on the case Henry refused to recognize the royal veto as final, denounced it as tyrannical, and made a violent attack on the established clergy. The jury, which included some dissenters, listened with approval, and their verdict of only one penny damages for the plaintiff practically nullified the former decision of the court on the question of principle.

Patrick Henry.

Other cases came up and the issue was taken to the Privy
Council in England; but the clergy could not secure any
practical redress. Thus an obscure provincial lawyer,
supported by strong popular feeling, had successfully
attacked a recognized prerogative of the crown. Incidentally, also, the democracy of the back country had found
an eloquent spokesman.

"Writs of
assistance,"
1761.

Two years before Henry's notable speech, a Massachusetts lawyer had questioned the validity of an act of
Parliament. In this case also there was an economic grievance. The Massachusetts merchants were disturbed because stricter enforcement of customs regulations was cutting into their business, especially with the foreign West
Indies. They now objected strenuously to the use, for
this purpose, of the so-called "writs of assistance," or general search warrants, differing from the ordinary variety
in not specifying the premises to be searched. These writs
were offensive both because they were used to enforce
unpopular duties and because they might cause annoyance
to innocent persons; but they were authorized by act of
Parliament and there were precedents for them in America
as well as in England. When, therefore, the death of George
II made it necessary to secure new writs in the name of
his successor, the judges were apparently bound to issue
them as a matter of course. The merchants, however,
determined to make a stand, and engaged as their counsel

James Otis.

James Otis, a rising lawyer, who resigned his royal commission as advocate-general in order to take the case. Refusing to confine himself to the technical points immediately involved, Otis raised a much larger issue. Relying on
certain English opinions of the early seventeenth century,
he argued that Parliament was limited by the fundamental
principles of the common law. General warrants, he held,
were contrary to these principles and therefore illegal, acts
of Parliament to the contrary notwithstanding. Otis's

argument made enough impression to delay action, but in the end his clients were defeated and the writs were issued. Meantime Otis had made his reputation as a defender of colonial rights, and got before his fellow provincials the doctrine that even the power of Parliament had its constitutional limitations.

Such incidents as the Parson's Cause and the fight over writs of assistance were not of course sufficient in themselves to endanger the union of Great Britain and her colonies. Yet they developed a sensitive public opinion which could easily be aroused against any attempt to extend the field of parliamentary action beyond the customary limits. Under these circumstances, the task of reconciling imperial efficiency with American ideas of self-government certainly demanded statesmanship of the highest order. Unfortunately, such statesmanship was painfully rare among those who then shaped the policies of the British government. *The need of imperial statesmanship.*

The beginning of a new reign is not always very important; but the succession of George III in 1760 was a momentous event for the British Empire. Certainly the new king began his reign in a very different spirit from that of his immediate predecessors and with strong convictions about his constitutional rights. Under the first two Hanoverian kings the actual government of Great Britain was mainly controlled by the Whigs, though their organization had been weakened of late by the independent leadership of Pitt. The nucleus of this "Old Whig" organization was a group of great noble families who professed a kind of aristocratic liberalism. More particularly they advocated the constitutional principles of the "glorious revolution" of 1688, including the sovereignty of Parliament as against the personal will of the King. Their power rested partly on their wealth and social prestige, which gave them great influence in the choice of members of the House of Commons; but they could also count on the merchant class *British politics in 1760.*

and the dissenters, who for various reasons joined the
Whigs in supporting the Protestant succession against the
Stuart pretenders. Meantime, the old Tory party, discredited by its Jacobite members, almost disappeared and
politics degenerated into factional contests between Whigs
in office and Whigs out of office. Under this system the
King had little to say except sometimes about military
matters or continental foreign policy, in which as Elector
of Hanover he had a special interest. Nearly everything
was decided by the ministry, which once in power dominated the House of Commons through a majority largely
composed of officeholders. All this could be done without
much difficulty when the king was a foreigner, ill informed
about English politics and quite aware that too much
interference on his part might cost him his throne. With
the accession of George III, however, the situation was
radically changed.

For one thing, the Hanoverian dynasty, after two reigns
covering about half a century, was at last securely established. Except for a handful of enthusiasts no one took the
claims of the Stuarts seriously. Even conservative country
gentlemen of Tory antecedents could now promise unre-
served loyalty to the new king, who, unlike his predecessors,
was born in England and in his first speech gloried "in
the name of Britain." In matters of personal decency,
too, George III was infinitely superior to his immediate
predecessors. These were great advantages and George was
determined to use them in order to secure for himself a position of real dignity and power. His political theories were
not those of the Whigs, who asserted the complete supremacy
of Parliament over the Crown, but rather those of the Tory
philosopher-statesman, Lord Bolingbroke. The "patriot
king," according to Bolingbroke, should be no puppet carrying out the will of this or that group of party politicians,
but a real leader rising above parties to speak for the nation

The Hano-
verian kings.

George III
and his po-
litical ideas.

as a whole. That was the kind of king George III meant to be if he could, and he nearly succeeded. Of the stubborn determination necessary for such a program, he had more than enough; but he lacked the breadth of intelligence and sympathy necessary to the government of a world-wide empire.

The King's first move was fairly successful. His peace policy, developed under the influence of his Scotch tutor, Lord Bute, soon brought him into conflict with Pitt, who sympathized with the King in his dislike of party government but was too proud to remain in a cabinet which he could not control. Bute became secretary of state and soon crowded out Newcastle, the chief of the Whig politicians. Thus within two years of his accession George was able to put his personal representative and favorite into the position hitherto held by the leader of the dominant party. The new ministry was also able, partly at least through corruption, to secure the election of a compliant Parliament. In his conflict with the old Whig machine, George III had some support from liberal-minded men. Even some Americans, like Franklin, believed in his patriotism and sympathized with his fight against the old-line politicians. Unfortunately for the King's policy, Lord Bute's personality was not popular; he was not an Englishman but a Scotchman and was believed to owe his position to backstairs influence with the Queen Mother and the King. The French treaty also was highly unpopular. So Bute, who had taken office reluctantly, was glad to retire, though he still had great influence over the King.

The fall of Pitt; the Bute ministry.

The break-up of the Whig party into warring factions, which had begun in the last years of George II, now seemed complete. Some of these factions professed more or less definite principles; but in the main they were dominated by personal ambitions and interests, some of which affected directly the management of colonial affairs. One of these

The Whig factions.

The "Old Whigs."

groups, known as the "Old Whigs," was led at first by the veteran politician, Newcastle, and later by the Marquis of Rockingham, a wealthy and public-spirited, but intellectually second-rate nobleman. The best mind in this party was Edmund Burke, a young and comparatively obscure Irishman, who made himself an expert on American affairs, served for a time as a colonial agent, and later, as member of Parliament for Bristol, made some famous speeches on conciliation with America. A second group was led by William Pitt. Though Pitt was not fond of the "Old Whigs" and disliked their whole system of party government, he was too masterful a personality and too liberal in some

The "Pittites."

respects to work steadily with the King. The "Pittites" took a keen interest in overseas problems and may fairly be called "liberal imperialists." Pitt was in office very little after 1761; but he was a great figure in Parliament until his death in 1778. His ablest follower was the young Earl of Shelburne, who as president of the Board of Trade and secretary of state had a good deal to do with American affairs. During the next twenty years it was these two groups, the "Old Whigs" and the "Pittites," which on the whole were most sympathetic toward America, though neither was able to work out a really constructive policy.

George Grenville.

There were two other groups, led respectively by George Grenville and the Duke of Bedford, whose attitude toward America was much less friendly. Grenville, who was connected with Pitt by marriage but did not act with him politically, became a member of the Bute ministry and was selected as Bute's successor when the latter retired. Grenville thus became officially responsible for the new policy of colonial taxation. The followers of Bedford, commonly

The "Bloomsbury gang."

called the "Bloomsbury gang" were on the whole conservative, though without very definite principles. The Duke himself was one of the chief landed magnates of the kingdom and his followers were notorious for a particularly cynical kind of politics even in a time of generally low standards.

Cutting across these factional lines to a certain extent were other divisions based on economic interests. The county members, who represented the landed gentry in the House of Commons, were a conservative but comparatively uncorrupt element. They kept a sharp eye on any proposal which might require more taxes from them and took kindly to the idea of getting some revenue out of the colonies. A new element, especially obnoxious to the country gentlemen, were the "nabobs," who had made fortunes in the East India trade and, like some present-day American millionaires, were ready to spend money freely for political honors, thus raising uncomfortably the market prices for seats in the House of Commons. Then there were the merchants of London, Bristol, and other important ports, who stood for the enforcement of the acts of trade, but sometimes raised their voices against measures which might provoke American retaliation and so interfere with their colonial business.

Other influences in Parliament.

In this chaos of factions, it was almost impossible to form party cabinets capable of carrying out any well-considered and continuous policy. Ministries were therefore generally made up of men belonging to different factions and holding quite different opinions on the leading issues of the day. To speak of Whig and Tory parties during this period is quite misleading. No such definite party division existed during the whole period of the American Revolution. In these troubled waters George III found his opportunity. He played off one faction against another and did not scruple to use public funds either to buy elections or to buy members after election. So there came to be a group of men in Parliament whose votes the King could control, sometimes even against the ministry. These "King's Friends," or court party, became increasingly in-

The "King's Friends."

fluential, so much so as to endanger the whole principle of parliamentary government.

Grenville and his administration.

When George Grenville became prime minister, in 1763, he had already learned as secretary of state something about American business, and now for the next two years he became the chief exponent of British policy in America. Grenville has not an enviable place in American history but he had some good qualities; he was honest, he had the courage of his convictions, and he was a real reformer. Some years later he secured the passage of a bill which made it possible to decide contested elections on some other basis than favoritism or partisan advantage. In the same spirit he now insisted that men who held colonial offices should actually administer them, instead of merely drawing salaries in England and getting cheap substitutes to do the real work. It is a picturesque exaggeration to say that Grenville was the first secretary to read the American dispatches and discover how far the actual management of colonial business was from the theory; that had been pretty well understood in official circles for some time. He was, however, particularly conscientious in this respect. Unfortunately all his information about irregularities in colonial trade never gave him any real insight into the colonial point of view, which he considered quite unreasonable and perverse.

Readjustment of the acts of trade.

The first result of Grenville's studies and those of his advisers on the Board of Trade was a conviction that the customs administration in America needed to be tightened up and adjusted to new conditions. Not all of the changes which he carried through Parliament were injurious to the colonies; old bounties on the importation of American hemp were revived, and the reduction of duties on whale fins put the New England whalers on a better footing in the English market. Nevertheless, the main features of the old legislation were retained and more stringent measures taken for their enforcement. The use of the navy for this purpose was authorized by law; the jurisdiction of the courts of admiralty in revenue cases was enlarged; and governors were urged to keep a sharp lookout for illegal trade. Grenville faced a particularly knotty problem when he took up the Molasses Act of 1733, which had run so squarely against the normal course of American trade that no serious effort was made to enforce it. He now decided to substitute for the old molasses duty of sixpence per gallon, which, if enforced, would have stopped the trade with the foreign West Indies altogether and therefore yielded no revenue, a lower duty of threepence per gallon which was really to be collected. This change was accordingly made in the Sugar Act of 1764, and it began to look as if the northern merchants in particular would lose a large share of the profits which they had made in the old easy-going days. Disturbing as this was in itself, there were other features of the Sugar Act which indicated a new and unlucky turn in British colonial policy.

The idea of raising a revenue in America by act of Parliament had occurred to many people during the first half of the eighteenth century, but cautious statesmen like Walpole and Pitt fought shy of it. Now, however, the temptation was stronger than ever. The country gentlemen were anxious to get rid of war taxes, but there was a heavy war debt and the new territories in America seemed to demand more expensive machinery for defense and for the regulation of Indian affairs. What, it was said, could be fairer than to require the colonists to contribute their share, and how could they be made to do so regularly without an act of Parliament? That was probably the most common argument back of the demand for American taxation. Another idea, somewhat in the background, was quite familiar to a group of men who had studied colonial problems in the Board of Trade. How, they argued, could England control

American taxation.

her colonial governments properly so long as the royal governors and other officials were dependent on temporary grants of provincial assemblies, when governors and judges could be coerced by reducing their salaries or cutting them off altogether? Why not, then, establish a parliamentary revenue which should be raised in America but determined in England, thus securing governments independent of local pressure, more fully controlled by the Crown, and more faithful in the enforcement of British statutes?

The Sugar Act, 1764.

So the Sugar Act of 1764 began with a memorable preamble, declaring it "just and necessary that a revenue be raised" in the King's "dominions in America," now "happily enlarged," "for defraying the expences of defending, protecting, and securing the same." For this purpose, duties were levied not only on molasses and sugar imported from the foreign plantations, but also on coffee, wines, East India goods, and other foreign commodities. The colonial merchants were much disturbed by this act, especially in the matter of the West Indian trade; but the importance of the revenue feature was not fully realized, partly because some external duties had long been levied in connection with the Navigation Acts. The great issue of taxation without representation was not clearly defined until the passage of the Stamp Act, which was proposed by Grenville in 1764 but not actually adopted until the following

Need of more revenue.

year. It was known that the revenue provided by the act of 1764 was only about one seventh of the amount needed to support the army in America. The government, therefore, looked about for other American sources of revenue, and concluded that the simplest method was a stamp tax, requiring the use of stamps on a great variety of official and legal documents, which were necessary or desirable for the orderly transaction of public and private business.

Before putting the Stamp Act through the House of

Commons, Grenville asked the colonial assemblies to suggest alternative methods of securing a steady revenue; but they had nothing to propose except a continuance of the old requisition system. Petitions sent from America against the new tax were not taken seriously; for, as Grenville said, "all men wished not to be taxed." So in the early months of 1765 the Stamp Act was passed with little opposition. Franklin, then in England as agent for Pennsylvania, was chiefly interested in trying to have that colony made into a royal province. A few years before he had argued against parliamentary taxation; but he does not seem to have been much excited about the question at this time. In one of his arguments in favor of a royal government in Pennsylvania, he said that the British authorities might think it necessary to secure "some revenue" from the American trade for the purpose of supporting the troops and that his fellow provincials might be reconciled to it "after a few years' experience." Franklin opposed the act, noting provisions which he thought particularly hard on lawyers and on his fellow craftsmen, the printers; but he thought it no more practicable to defeat the bill than to prevent "the sun's setting." He even secured a collector's commission for one of his Pennsylvania friends, and suggested that tactful management of that office might "by degrees" lessen its unpopularity.

The Stamp Act passed.

Franklin's attitude.

While this momentous business was being done in England, a storm was fast gathering in America. The stricter enforcement of the acts of trade was cutting the profits of colonial merchants, especially in the West India trade, which supplied the northern colonies not only with sugar and molasses but also with hard money. Attempts to make up the shortage of specie by the issue of legal-tender paper money were blocked, for New England, by the British law of 1751; and the Currency Act of 1764 applied this restriction to all the colonies. To these grievances there

Sources of colonial discontent.

were now added the new duties imposed by the Sugar Act
and the Stamp Act. It is to be remembered, too, that while
some of the earlier measures had comparatively little effect
on the southern planters, the Stamp Act, establishing for
the first time a direct internal tax, created a new issue
which could be presented to merchants, planters, and
farmers alike.

Statements
of the
American
case. Otis.
The debate in the colonies began even before the Stamp
Act was passed, with some vigorous pamphlets setting forth
the American point of view. One of the most aggressive was
James Otis's *Rights of the British Colonies Asserted and Proved.*
Otis now applied to the Stamp Act his theory that Parliament
was limited by a fundamental law and that even acts approved
by King, Lords, and Commons might be unconstitutional
and invalid. To levy taxes on the colonies without their
consent or that of persons definitely selected by them was
"absolutely irreconcilable" with their rights as "British
subjects and as men." What then was the remedy? Here
Otis shrank from the extreme application of his principles.
Though he seemed to believe that unconstitutional legislation could be corrected by the courts, his practical conclusion in this case was that the power of Parliament was
"uncontroulable, but by themselves, and we must obey,"
trusting that Parliament itself would reconsider its decision.

In the preliminary fight against the passage of the Stamp
Act, Northerners like Otis of Massachusetts and Stephen
Hopkins of Rhode Island were probably the most conspicuous. After it became law, the leadership in resistance
Patrick
Henry.
was taken by Virginia. By this time Patrick Henry had
become a member of the House of Burgesses and was gathering a group of radical members, some, like himself, from the
western counties, and others, largely young men, who belonged to the planter class, but were dissatisfied with the
older leaders. This radical element took up the issue of
parliamentary taxation and forced through some vigorous

resolutions, asserting the right of the Virginians to be governed by their own assembly in matters of taxation and "internal police." The fiery speech of Henry in support of these resolutions has not come down to us in any accurate form; but it certainly made a strong impression on friends and enemies alike, with its daring comparison of George III with Caesar and Charles I. To Governor Fauquier writing home to England, Henry's language appeared "very indecent"; but Thomas Jefferson, a young law student in Williamsburg, listened with admiration to an orator who seemed "to speak as Homer wrote."

Virginia had gone on record, and in other colonies, where men were hesitating and final submission to the Stamp Act seemed quite possible, the news from the Old Dominion proved an "alarm bell to the disaffected." Numerous pamphlets were issued, setting forth a great variety of arguments. Efforts were made to convince Parliament that the new taxes were unjust because the colonies were already contributing liberally to the royal treasury through their commerce, which had to pass largely through British ports and was there subject to British customs. It was also argued that the new policies were bad for British as well as American interests. Taxation and new trade restrictions were making it harder for Americans to spend money on English goods. To press this argument home, the colonists were urged to cut down their purchases of imported articles. Sometimes special emphasis was laid on the constitutional argument, denying the right, as well as the justice and expediency, of colonial taxation. Nearly all admitted the general legislative authority of Parliament over the whole empire; but there were a few exceptions. Richard Bland, whose learning was much admired by his Virginia neighbors, wrote a pamphlet asserting in substance that the existing union of England and the colonies was simply a personal union like that between England and Scotland under the Stuart kings. He agreed that Virginians and New Englanders owed allegiance to George III, but denied that Parliament had any real authority over them. In 1766, when Bland's pamphlet appeared, few Americans were quite so radical as this, but in later years the doctrine became more popular.

The
Stamp Act
Congress.
Differing as they did in their modes of attack, the sober judgment of the Americans was best expressed by the Stamp Act Congress, which met in New York in October, 1765. Only nine colonies were represented, and one of the assemblies which had no chance to choose delegates was Virginia; but the Congress was fairly representative of the colonies as a whole, including not only radicals but moderates and conservatives as well. Even Massachusetts sent with Otis two conservatives, one of whom was chosen president of the Congress. Nevertheless the resolutions adopted were strongly, though cautiously, worded. The delegates were doubtless quite sincere in expressing their loyalty to the King. They were even ready to admit "all due subordination to that august body the parliament of Great Britain"; but "due subordination" did not include taxation because the colonists were not and could not be represented in Parliament. The Congress had its own theory of representation; no one could represent the American colonies except "persons chosen therein by themselves." The resolutions also objected to the provision recently made for more general use of admiralty courts, without juries, in the trial of revenue cases.

Appeal to
force.
Pamphlets and resolutions helped to rally American opinion against "taxation without representation" and against the new restrictions on trade; but they were not the most effective arguments. Whether the Stamp Act was right or wrong, the tax evidently could not be collected without the greatest difficulty. The lives of stamp distributors were made miserable by their neighbors and most of them were glad to resign. Newspapers were published and ship's papers

issued without the prescribed stamps; after a time the courts
began to do business in similar disregard of the law.   Here
and there, occurred outrageous acts of violence against
unpopular officials, of which the colonists themselves were
soon ashamed, as when a Boston mob attacked the house of
Chief-Justice Thomas Hutchinson.   In fact, the opposition
which the northern merchants had done so much to stir up
was getting beyond their control and falling under the
influence of more radical leaders.   Probably the most successful argument against the tax was its effect on British
trade.   Already American purchases from England had fallen
off and one colony after another was adopting nonimportation agreements which seemed likely to hurt the trade still
more.   Many of the English merchants, therefore, began to
throw their influence in favor of repealing the Stamp Act.

Meantime, the Grenville ministry had gone out of office.
The King was troubled by the American disturbances; but
he had other reasons for the change, not the least of which
was his personal dislike of Grenville, whom he considered
too independent and something of a bore.   The King was
ready to take Pitt again; but a satisfactory combination
could not be made and he therefore had to accept a cabinet
made up mainly of the " Old Whigs," with the young Marquis of Rockingham as prime minister, but including some
members from other factions.   The King, however, liked
the new ministers no better than their predecessors, and
their failure to secure Pitt's coöperation left them without
first-rate leadership.   It was this comparatively weak government which in the winter of 1765–1766 had to face the
American uprising against the Stamp Act.

*English
politics
again. The
Rockingham
ministry.*

The ministry was certainly in a trying position.   Something had to be done to restore order in America and revive
colonial commerce; but it was not easy to repeal the Stamp
Act without seeming to countenance colonial arguments
against the authority of Parliament.   In this dilemma, three

*Debate on
taxation.*

possible policies were proposed by representative leaders.

The Grenville-Mansfield theory.

Grenville and his friends stood firmly for the absolute sovereignty of Parliament. They were equally certain that this authority had been rightly exercised in the passage of the Stamp Act and that its repeal would be a humiliating and disastrous surrender to rebellious subjects. Grenville was supported by Chief-Justice Mansfield, the greatest lawyer of the time, who made a strong legal argument against the American doctrine of representation. Parliament, he said, was the sovereign authority for the whole empire. In the House of Commons were represented not only the small fraction of the English people who actually voted for members, but the whole nation, including the dominions beyond the sea. When, therefore, the colonists claimed that Parliament represented only those who elected its members, their argument went squarely against the orthodox English theory of representation. The colonists had repeatedly submitted to acts of Parliament, and the distinction which they now made between external duties and internal taxes was, in his opinion, quite illogical.

Pitt's views.

The Grenville-Mansfield doctrine was vigorously attacked by Pitt and he, too, was supported by a distinguished lawyer, Lord Camden. Pitt believed as strongly as Mansfield in the lawmaking power of Parliament over the whole empire; but he insisted that taxation was something quite distinct from legislation. The House of Commons could rightly grant the money of English subjects at home because it was chosen by the substantial landowners of England, who "virtually represent the rest of the inhabitants"; but to extend this notion of "virtual representation" to America was "the most contemptible idea that ever entered into the head of a man." Like the Americans, Pitt distinguished between taxes levied for revenue and duties for the regulation of trade, even though the latter might incidentally bring in revenue. The latter were justifiable, the former were not.   So Pitt said, "I rejoice that America has resisted."

Powerful as Pitt still was, responsiblility for leadership rested with the Rockingham ministry, which finally decided to take a somewhat different position from that of either Grenville or Pitt.   The ministers did not deny the Mansfield theory of the absolute sovereignty of Parliament; but as a practical matter, they decided against the stamp tax because it was unfair, contrary to the spirit of English liberty, and likely to do more harm than good. So they proposed to repeal the Stamp Act; but also to adopt a resolution asserting that Parliament might at its discretion bind the colonies "in all cases whatsoever."

Policy of the Rockingham ministry.

On the same day that Lord Mansfield made his memorable speech, the House of Commons ordered Franklin to appear before it for examination.   Franklin now declared emphatically that the Americans would resist all internal taxes. So far, he said, they had been entirely loyal, accepting even the duties which had been laid on their external trade; but, if the discussion continued, they might forget that distinction and reject any kind of tax or duty.   Already, he thought, the feeling of Americans toward England had been changed for the worse.   Formerly they had been proud to "indulge in the fashions and manufactures of Great Britain"; now it was their pride to "wear their old clothes over again till they can make new ones."   The Stamp Act could not be enforced by the British army; if troops were used for this purpose, they would not find a revolution, but they might make one.

Franklin before the House of Commons.

In March, 1766, Parliament voted by a decisive majority in favor of repeal.   At the same time, however, the Declaratory Act was passed, condemning the American doctrine that Parliament could not legally tax the colonies and asserting in the most sweeping language that Parliament had and "ought to have" authority to "bind the colonies

Stamp Act repealed. Declaratory Act.

and people of America, subjects of the crown of Great Britain, in all cases whatsoever."

BIBLIOGRAPHICAL NOTES

General references.

Beard and Beard, I, ch. V. Andrews, *Colonial Period*, ch. X, and his *Colonial Background of the American Revolution*. Becker, C. L., *Eve of the American Revolution*, 1–115. Channing, *United States*, III, chs. I–III. Fisher, S. G., *Struggle for American Independence*, I, chs. I–VIII (iconoclastic). Van Tyne, C. H., *Causes of the War of Independence*. Adams, J. T., *Revolutionary New England*, chs. XII–XV. Howard, G. E., *Preliminaries of the Revolution*, chs. I–IX. Lecky, W. E. H., *England in the Eighteenth Century*, III (fair-minded British statement; same material in Lecky, *American Revolution*). Winsor, *America*, VI, 1–34. Bancroft, *United States* (author's last revision), III, chs. I–XVI, and Beer, G. L., *British Colonial Policy, 1754–1765*, chs. IX–XIV, illustrate the difference between older and later views.

Collected sources.

Macdonald, *Select Charters*, nos. 53, 55–60. Hart, *Contemporaries*, II, chs. XXI, XXIII, especially no. 143 (Franklin's examination). Hart and Channing, *American History Leaflets*, no. 33 (Writs of Assistance). McLaughlin *et al.*, *Source Problems in U. S. History*, Problem II. Morison, *Sources and Documents*.

English politics.

Alvord, *Mississippi Valley in British Politics*, I, chs. I–IX. Namier, L. B., *The Structure of Politics at the Accession of George III*, 2 vols. *England in the Age of the American Revolution*. Coupland, R., *American Revolution and the British Empire*. Fitzmaurice, E., *Shelburne*, I, especially chs. IV–VII. Hunt, W., *Political History of England, 1760–1801*, 1–72. Von Ruville, *Pitt*, III, ch. VIII. Williams, B., *Chatham*, ch. XXI.

English economic and social life.

Mantoux, P., *Industrial Revolution in the 18th Century*. Hammond, J. L. and B., *Skilled Labourer, 1760–1832; Town Labourer, 1760–1832; Village Labourer, 1760–1832*.

English sources.

Annual Register. Cobbett, W., *Parliamentary History*, XVI, especially 97–181 (including speeches by Pitt, Grenville, and Mansfield), 137–161 (Franklin's examination). Grenville, G., *Papers*. Jenyns, S., *Objections to the Taxation of Our American Colonies Briefly Considered* (1765; also in his *Works*, II). Hertz,

G. B., *Old Colonial System*, ch. IV, and Holland, B., *Imperium et Libertas*, pt. I, give recent English views.

Henry, W. W., *Patrick Henry*, I, chs. I–IV. Tyler, M. C., *Patrick Henry*, chs. I–V. Hosmer, J. K., *S. Adams*, chs. I–VI. Gipson, L. H., *Jared Ingersoll*. Lincoln, C. H., *Revolutionary Movement in Pennsylvania*, chs. I–VII. McCrady, *South Carolina, 1719–1776*, chs. XXVII, XXVIII. Tyler, M. C., *Literary History of the American Revolution*, I, chs. I–V. Adams, R. G., *Political Ideas of the American Revolution*. Mullett, *Fundamental Law and the American Revolution*. — Controversy in America.

Important pamphlets by R. Bland, S. Hopkins, J. Otis, D. Dulany, and J. Dickinson. See also writings of Franklin (Smyth edition, IV; or *Life Written by Himself*, edited by Bigelow), S. Adams, and J. Adams (Diary in *Works*, II). Morison, S. E., *Sources and Documents Illustrating the American Revolution*, 14–54. Pease and Roberts, *Readings*, 83–94. — American sources.

Andrews, C. M., "The Boston Merchants and the Non-Importation Movement," Col. Soc. of Mass., *Publications*, XIX (1917). Schlesinger, A. M., *Colonial Merchants and the American Revolution (Columbia Studies)*. Weeden, W. B., *Economic and Social History of N. E.*, chs. XVIII, XIX. Wiener, F. B., "Rhode Island Merchants and the Sugar Act," *N.E.Q.* (1930), III, 464–500. Laprade, W. T., "Stamp Act in British Politics," *A.H.R.* (1930), XXXV, 735–757. Keith, A. B., *Constitutional History of the First British Empire*, 337–358. — Sugar Act, Stamp Act, and the merchants.

Alvord, *Mississippi Valley in British Politics*, I, and his *Illinois Centennial History*, I, chs. XII, XIII. — Western policy.

Commager, *Documents*, 47–49. Pease and Roberts, *Readings*, 75–78. Morison, *Sources and Documents*, 1–4, 9–14. Callender, *Selections from Economic History of the U. S.*, 122–148. Bogart and Thompson, *Readings in Economic History of U. S.*, 143–169. Hart, *Contemporaries*, II, ch. XXII. — Sources.

CHAPTER XVIII

THE EVE OF REVOLUTION, 1766 TO 1774

The taxation issue unsettled.

THE repeal of the Stamp Act did not settle the issue of taxation without representation; for Parliament had expressly asserted its absolute sovereignty over the colonies, and the revenue duties laid by the Sugar Act were still in force. On the specific issue of the stamp tax, however, the Americans had won a notable victory and for the moment they were too enthusiastic about that to think much about the theory of the Declaratory Act. So Pitt and other friends in Parliament were gratefully remembered and George III came in for his share of the general good feeling.

Lack of constructive statesmanship.

It is easy to see now that no progress had been made toward a constructive policy which should safeguard the common interests of the empire, including America, and yet harmonize with traditional ideals of liberty and self-government. Among those common interests was the working out of an effective and liberal plan for the management of the great undeveloped country beyond the mountains. The revenue policy, which was intended to finance the administration of the western territory, had broken down; but no other solution had been worked out. A few men in England and in America were thinking about these matters in a statesmanlike spirit, but they were rare exceptions. Franklin was

Franklin on the constitution of the empire.

one of those exceptional men and for many years had given serious thought to the constitutional relations of the colonies with the mother country. At one time he thought that a legislative union was desirable, with American representatives sitting side by side with those of England, Wales, and

Scotland in the Parliament at Westminster. He concluded,
however, that British pride would stand in the way. "Every
man in England," he said, "seems to consider himself a
piece of a sovereign over America." Meantime, most
Americans were too much absorbed by local interests and in
warding off real or supposed encroachments on their rights
to do any important constructive thinking. So the common
interests of the English-speaking peoples were largely at
the mercy of shortsighted politicians.

About four months after the repeal of the Stamp Act,
the Rockingham ministry fell and once more Pitt was called
in to form a cabinet, this time with the Duke of Grafton,
an able young nobleman with some statesmanlike ideals,
but an unfortunate personal reputation. Following Pitt's
theories, the new ministry was made up of men from different groups, so much so that it could not act harmoniously.
With Pitt at his best the discordant elements might have
been pulled together; but this was not the case. His promotion to the House of Lords, as Earl of Chatham, was described with some truth as a "fall upstairs" for the "great
commoner." Poor health not only robbed him of that extraordinary vigor which had carried him through his great war
ministry, but also made it harder for others to work with
him. After a few months of service, Pitt broke down and
retired to the country, leaving a practically headless government behind him.

The Chatham-Grafton ministry.

Two of Pitt's colleagues are especially important for
their part in American affairs. One was the Earl of Shelburne, who, as secretary of state for the Southern Department, was chiefly responsible for American affairs. Three
years before, as president of the Board of Trade, he had
taken a leading part in the discussion which led up to
the Proclamation of 1763. The reservation of the western
territory to the Indians was in his mind only a temporary
policy, to be followed by more constructive measures.

Shelburne and the problems of the West.

After careful study he now favored a policy of westward expansion, including land cessions from the Indians, which would open up the territory to new settlers, and the formation of new governments on liberal principles. He hoped to secure the revenue necessary for a progressive policy by more businesslike administration of the crown lands in America. One of Shelburne's chief advisers was Franklin, who, with several prominent associates in England and in America, was working for a new colony on the Ohio. Franklin argued that the establishment of such colonies would be a comparatively cheap way of defending the new territories, which might even be made a base for military expeditions against the Spaniards in Cuba or Mexico. So, for a time, it looked as if British officials might coöperate with representative Americans in promoting a vigorous expansionist policy. Perhaps the most tangible outcome of this discussion was the treaty of Fort Stanwix, negotiated by Sir William Johnson in 1768, by which the Iroquois opened up to white settlement a large area extending from western New York southward to eastern Kentucky. Shelburne was not long in office, however, before the American business was taken from him and given to Lord Hillsborough, who received the new office of secretary of state for the colonies. Under Hillsborough's shortsighted management, the opportunity for harmonious coöperation was thrown away.

Charles Townshend. Meantime, another member of the cabinet was committing it to an American policy directly opposed to that advocated by Pitt in 1766. This was Charles Townshend, who, like Shelburne, had presided over the Board of Trade and was interested in American problems, but had a very different point of view. Though a member of the Rockingham ministry, Townshend had previously declared himself in favor of parliamentary taxation and close control of the colonial governments. Now, in 1767, as chancellor of the exchequer, this clever but irresponsible politician was suddenly put in a position to shape the revenue policy of the government.

Since more money was needed and the country gentle-men were anxious to keep their own taxes down, Townshend suddenly, without consulting his colleagues, pledged him-self to find a new revenue in America. The result was the fatal Townshend Duty Act, imposing import duties payable in the colonies on tea, paper, glass, and painters' colors. In establishing "external duties," Parliament seemed to be keeping in mind the distinction made in 1765 by most of the American leaders; it was also following a precedent set by the Sugar Act of 1764. The preamble was, however, distinctly a challenge to the colonies since it declared not only that the duties were for revenue, rather than for the purpose of reg-ulating commerce, but also that this revenue should be used "where it shall be found necessary" to support the pro-vincial governments and in particular the courts of law. So far as this policy could be made to work, the Americans would still support their own governments; but the levying of the tax and the use to be made of the money would be determined not by the colonial assemblies, but by the Brit-ish government. Unfortunately the seriousness of this issue was not generally appreciated and the bill went through without much opposition.

Townshend Duty Act.

The Duty Act was not the only challenge to American opinion. The customs service was to be stiffened; the writs of assistance attacked by Otis in 1761 were specifically approved and a new customs board was organized for America. Hardly less important as a matter of principle was the act suspending the legislative power of the New York assembly because it had failed to supply certain articles required for the soldiers stationed there. If a colonial legislature could be ordered to make appropriations and punished for not doing so, what became of the American doctrine that each assembly was, in its own sphere, a kind

The new commis-sioners of customs.

New York assembly suspended.

of parliament? If Parliament could suspend one provincial legislature for a limited time, what was to prevent the same sovereign power from abolishing such legislatures altogether? These were serious questions, to be raised in such a light-hearted fashion.

American opposition. Dickinson.

The ablest American critic of the Townshend Acts was John Dickinson of Pennsylvania, who set forth his views in the *Letters from a Farmer*. Dickinson was a native of Pennsylvania, but received his legal training in the English "Inns of Court," where he learned more than most Americans about the history and spirit of the common law. In characteristic English fashion, he laid more stress on precedents than on theories of abstract right. For him the new acts of Parliament, including the suspension of the New York legislature, were dangerous innovations, contrary to the principles of political liberty which Englishmen had claimed for themselves and had embodied also in the government of their colonies. Dickinson did not dispute the legislative supremacy of Parliament, nor attack the general system of the Navigation Acts. He did not even condemn the restrictions on colonial manufactures, since they were part of a large imperial policy. Like Pitt, however, Dickinson denied that the right to tax was a necessary part of the sovereign authority of Parliament over the colonies. He also discarded the distinction between external and internal taxes, so long as either was laid for the purpose of raising revenue. Finally he pointed out that if colonial governments could be supported without grants from their assemblies, the latter would soon cease to have any real power. Dickinson was by no means a violent radical. He tried rather to persuade Englishmen that the new policies were unjust, un-English, and contrary to their own permanent interests. At the same time, he urged Americans to refrain from violent methods. They should begin with petitions and remonstrances, he said; then they could use economic pressure by refusing to buy

British goods; only if these failed, would it be right to use force.

When the *Letters from a Farmer* were published in London, Lord Hillsborough called them "extremely wild"; but he soon received news from Massachusetts which made Dickinson's articles seem quite tame. In that province, the short-lived peace after the repeal of the Stamp Act had been broken by disagreeable controversies between the governor and the assembly. The Massachusetts people were, therefore, already irritated, when they were suddenly brought into uncomfortably close contact with Townshend's reorganized customs service, of which Boston became the American headquarters. Influential merchants, who were used to bringing in Madeira wine without paying duties, began to find the business somewhat less safe. One such merchant was John Hancock, whose sloop *Liberty* was seized by the customs officials and later condemned by the admiralty court, not, however, before some of the wine had been landed and several officers roughly handled. Troubles in Massachusetts.

The people who watched these proceedings with more or less active resentment were not all of one mind. Many of the well-to-do merchants were much less interested in constitutional theories than in preventing awkward interference with their trade. They had gone very far in stirring opposition to recent measures of the British government, but they were certainly not aiming at revolution. Another and more radical group, whose help the merchants sometimes found convenient, included many of the smaller business men and farmers. These people were jealous of the ruling class among their neighbors and they disliked some imperial measures which the merchants found quite satisfactory, as, for instance, restrictions on the issue of paper money. The old Puritan traditions were also much stronger with these men than with the social leaders of the seaboard towns, and this aggressive Puritan spirit had just been stirred by a renewal of the old Conservatives and radicals.

proposal to establish Anglican bishoprics in the colonies. Doubtless this religious issue helped to put most of the Congregational ministers on the radical side in the whole political controversy with the mother country; and they were quite willing to take their politics into the pulpit.

Samuel Adams.

The chief leader of the Massachusetts radicals was Samuel Adams, who first dominated the Boston town meeting and later became the most influential member of the House of Representatives. The loyalist politician and historian, Thomas Hutchinson, denounced Adams as a demagogue, who as town collector had misused public funds and was now playing recklessly on the passions of the mob. Hutchinson was deeply prejudiced, however, and his statement can hardly be taken at its face value. Doubtless Adams was unsuccessful in business and careless in his public accounts; but it is equally certain that most of his fellow citizens believed in his integrity and that he did not make money in politics. Even hostile critics admitted his skill as a political organizer, and he was successful, partly at least, because he shared the views of his followers.

Adams's political theories.

Adams's political theories are set forth in a large number of papers drafted by him and adopted by the Massachusetts House under his influence. Like Dickinson, he appealed to the English constitution; but he emphasized the "natural rights" of the colonists, as well as the doubtful theory that colonial governments rested on a compact or agreement between the King and the first colonists. The Massachusetts radicals still denied that they were working for independence; and the House of Representatives still acknowledged that Parliament was the supreme legislature of the empire They insisted, however, that in the British Empire, as in "all free states" there was a "fixed," if not a written, "constitution" which "neither the supreme legislature nor the supreme executive can alter."

Of all the Massachusetts documents, the most obnoxious

to the home government was the *Circular Letter* sent by the House of Representatives to the other colonial assemblies, urging them to coöperate against the policies of the ministry. To avert this danger, Lord Hillsborough, as secretary of state for the colonies, ordered the Massachusetts House to rescind the circular; but the demand was rejected by an overwhelming majority. Thereupon Governor Bernard obeyed his instructions and dissolved the assembly. The other assemblies answered Massachusetts with sympathetic resolutions, which were backed up by more or less effective nonimportation agreements against British goods. The most important provincial resolutions of this period were the "Virginia Resolves" of 1769, introduced by George Washington, now a prosperous planter and by no means a radical democrat. Even he, however, was now writing impatiently about "our lordly masters in Great Britain" and proposing to boycott British trade and manufactures. In the last resort he thought an appeal to arms would be justifiable.

The Massachusetts Circular Letter.

The Virginia Resolves, 1769.

One measure especially attacked by the Virginians was the joint address of the two houses of Parliament asking the King to apply in the colonies an old statute of Henry VIII, authorizing the trial in England of persons who had committed crimes outside of the "realm." This proposal was aimed chiefly at the Massachusetts leaders, who were held responsible for the rebellious attitude of that colony. Another measure, not altogether unnatural in view of the violent resistance offered to the commissioners of customs, was the sending of two regiments of British regulars from Halifax to Boston. It was equally natural, however, that the presence of these redcoats should be resented by the Bostonians and that the rougher elements should go farther in expressing their dislike than the more cautious leaders. Out of this strained situation came the so-called "Boston Massacre" of March 5, 1770, when some soldiers, under

New coercive measures.

"Boston Massacre."

considerable provocation, fired on their assailants and killed four of the citizens. Samuel Adams now came to the front again and with the Boston populace behind him forced the governor to transfer the soldiers to Castle William, outside the town. A more difficult but highly creditable stand was taken by John Adams, who helped to prevent injustice by acting as legal counsel for the British officer in command and securing his acquittal on the charge of murder.

Effects of colonial opposition.

The methods used against the Townshend duties were like those which had proved successful against the Stamp Act. Again there was a steady flow of pamphlets and resolutions; the commercial boycotts cut down imports from England; and again there were numerous acts of violence. Once more, too, colonial opposition, combined with other forces, brought a partial reversal of policy. It happened just then that business conditions in England lessened somewhat the damage done by the American boycotts; but English politicians and business men realized that the Townshend duties were working against the very interests which the old commercial system was intended to promote.

Reorganization of the British ministry. Lord North.

Meantime, British politics had changed in some respects for the worse since 1766. After an unusually corrupt and disorderly campaign, a new Parliament was elected in 1768. Franklin, who watched the political game with much interest, thought the prospect for any statesmanlike handling of American affairs was very black. By 1769 there were radical changes in the ministry. Chatham and Shelburne were now out and politicians less sympathetic with America were gaining strength, including the "King's Friends," or court party, and the "Bloomsbury gang," or Bedford faction. The latter were especially sharp in their criticism of the Americans and the King himself now took a similar attitude. The man who was coming to the front in these cabinet changes was Lord North, who succeeded Townshend as Chancellor of the Exchequer and finally in 1770 became prime minister. North was an able parliamentary leader and was personally more liberal than some of his associates; his worst fault was that he yielded to the King's desires to an extent quite inconsistent with his duty as a responsible minister. So it came about that his name is linked with that of George III in the measures which finally split the old empire in two.

North realized that the Townshend Duty Act was costing more than it brought into the treasury and was also unsound as a commercial measure, since it imposed duties on British manufactures. Accordingly it was decided to repeal all these duties except that on tea, about which George III later said that there must "always be one tax to keep up the right." With the tea duty there remained the offensive preamble declaring it expedient to raise a revenue in America. In the end this "preambulary tax," as Burke contemptuously called it, proved disastrous; but for the present no such outcome was in sight. In fact, many of the merchants lost their enthusiasm for continued opposition and in one colony after another the nonimportation agreements were relaxed. So far as tea was concerned, the matter was not of much practical importance, since large quantities were smuggled in from Holland. It looked, therefore, as if the storm might blow over.

Townshend duties abandoned except on tea.

The responsibility for renewing the controversy rested about equally with the extremists on both sides. The radicals did what they could to keep the fires burning, and on the other side there were tactless officials who played into the hands of their opponents by inconsiderate acts or too much talking. In Massachusetts these two elements are best represented by Samuel Adams and Thomas Hutchinson, who usually managed between them to set the political pot boiling whenever it showed any signs of cooling off.

Controversy revived by extremists.

Hutchinson, who became governor in 1770, belonged
to an old Massachusetts family and had served many
years in the legislature, where he did some excellent work,
especially in helping to put the Massachusetts currency on
a sound basis. He was also a real scholar, as may be seen
in his *History of Massachusetts Bay.* Hutchinson did not
approve of the Stamp Act but he disliked the radical leaders and, like many other well-to-do people, regarded the
connection with the mother country as a valuable conservative influence. This conservative spirit was naturally
strengthened by his career as an officeholder under the
Crown, — as chief justice, lieutenant governor, and governor. So he became more and more a defender of the
imperial government against colonial opposition. Unfortunately for him, he was quite overmatched as a politician by the opposition leaders, especially by Samuel
Adams, who was quick to take advantage of the governor's
mistakes. Hutchinson was not long in office before he got
into a series of debates on the sovereignty of Parliament.
The radical leaders were glad of the chance to publish
their views, and so popular feeling, which had seemed to be
quieting down, was again stirred up. In the heat of controversy each side naturally became more aggressive; and
moderate men were gradually, often reluctantly, forced
to take sides with one set of extremists or the other.

In the neighboring colony of Rhode Island there was
no royal governor, but here too there were imperial officials,
— customs collectors, naval commanders, and an admiralty
court, — all trying to see that duties were collected and
the Navigation Acts enforced. These royal agents were
worse off in Rhode Island than in Massachusetts because
the colony government was entirely in the hands of elective
officers, whose coöperation in enforcing unpopular measures

could not be expected. Even acts of violence could not be
prevented or punished. When, for instance, a mob de-

stroyed the *Gaspee*, a royal vessel employed in the revenue service, no responsible person would inform against the offenders. The *Gaspee* affair and certain proposals made by the British authorities in this connection, including the transportation of suspected persons to England for trial, had a marked effect outside of Rhode Island and stimulated the radical party to more effective organization. In 1772 Samuel Adams organized for Massachusetts an elaborate system of town "Committees of Correspondence," which served to keep the radicals in touch with each other, and in 1773 the Virginians took the initiative in a still more important movement.

Committees of Correspondence.

In Virginia, as in New England, friction had developed in many different ways. Even in the Old Dominion, the proposal of a colonial bishop was warmly debated by the House of Burgesses, which passed a resolution against it. There were economic issues, also, such as the perennial friction between the planters and their British creditors, which were made more acute by a period of "hard times." The Virginia planters also took a keen interest in strictly constitutional matters and in safeguarding colonial self-government against imperialistic and centralizing tendencies. Thus the spirit of discontent was fairly general. Under these circumstances some of the younger Virginians, including Patrick Henry, Richard Henry Lee, and Thomas Jefferson, decided, as Jefferson wrote many years later, that the older members were not "up to the point of forwardness and zeal which the times required." This radical group now persuaded the House of Burgesses to appoint a provincial committee of correspondence to keep in touch with similar committees in other provinces. The Virginia plan was heartily approved by radicals elsewhere and was gradually adopted in other colonies.

Unrest in Virginia.

Virginia radicals.

Notwithstanding all this organized agitation, the radicals were for a time disappointed with the results. Many

Conservative influences.

of the "best people" held themselves aloof; they could get tea from smugglers and they were tired of denying themselves conveniences or losing business profits in order to protest against the tea duty. The wealthier merchants, especially, now realized that when the populace had once been stirred up to violent measures, it could not easily be kept in hand. Again, however, the radicals received valuable assistance from the home government. In May, 1773, Parliament passed a new measure which for the time being brought radicals and moderates together.

The Tea Act of 1773.   The Tea Act of 1773 had two principal objects. The first was to help the East India Company, which controlled the Asiatic tea trade and was then financially embarrassed, by giving it a larger market in the colonies. This object was to be accomplished, without lowering the duty paid in America, by refunding to the company all import duties collected in England on teas which were afterwards shipped to the colonies. The company was also given the new privilege of engaging directly in the American tea trade, through its own agencies. The American consumer could now buy tea at a price lower than that charged in England, and the company could compete successfully in the American market not only with the private merchants who had previously carried on the business but even with the dealers in smuggled tea. The other object of the act was, of course, to accustom the colonists to paying the duty, even though the amount collected was almost negligible.

Colonial resistance.   The action of Parliament on the tea duty soon brought together in opposition some of the most influential elements in American society. The private merchants and even the smugglers feared the competition of a powerful corporate monopoly, while leaders like Samuel Adams were determined to resist this new effort to establish the taxing power of Parliament. So when the East India Company's ships arrived in American ports, they found a formidable

combination organized against them. Once more men of
large interests and social prominence were working with
radicals who had no such interests at stake, and much less
respect for vested rights. The measures adopted varied
according to local conditions. In New York and Philadelphia the masters of tea ships were persuaded to turn back
without unloading the tea. At Charleston cargoes were
landed only to repose harmlessly in the government ware-
house. In Boston the proceedings were more spectacular
because the tea ships, having once entered the harbor, were
held there by Governor Hutchinson's refusal to issue clear- **Boston Tea Party.**
ance papers for their return. The result was the famous
Boston Tea Party, in which the objectionable cargoes were
thrown into the sea. In these various ways the opposition
leaders accomplished the same essential object of preventing the sale of the company's tea; but in England the
Boston proceedings, with their wholesale destruction of
property, naturally attracted special attention.

To moderate Englishmen, and even to a man like Frank- **Coercive acts of 1774.**
lin, who kept in touch with English public opinion, the
Boston Tea Party seemed a serious blunder. The whole
proceeding was not only a deliberate defiance of Parliament,
the most powerful legislature in the world; it showed also
reckless disregard of property rights. "I suppose," said
Franklin, "we never had, since we were a people, so few
friends in Britain." When the news reached London, about
the end of January, the ministry decided to take drastic
action. Early in March the King reported to Parliament
the "unwarrantable practices" in America and more
particularly "the violent and outrageous proceedings" in
Boston. The speech was followed by a series of coercive
bills which were pushed through Parliament rapidly and
by large majorities. The first of the coercive acts was
the Boston Port Bill, closing that port to commerce until **Boston Port Bill.**
the Bostonians should compensate the owners of the tea

and give assurance of future good behavior; this was a punitive measure pure and simple. Another law, the Massachusetts Government Act, raised a more serious issue, since it made permanent changes in the constitution of a chartered colony.

Massachusetts Government Act.

The idea of reconstructing the chartered colonies, so as to bring them more completely under royal control, had been discussed for a hundred years; but most of the older Whig leaders hesitated about carrying the policy to its logical conclusion. Now, however, the feeling against the New Englanders was so intense that even the most extreme measures could be ·carried through. Some of the liberals tried to stem the tide, notably Edmund Burke, who declared that the ministry had been thinking too much about theories of sovereignty and not enough about the best way to secure harmonious coöperation. Under the old system Parliament had regulated colonial trade but had refrained from taxing the Americans. Why should this policy, under which the empire had prospered, be changed to satisfy a theory which, whether right or wrong, was bound to cause serious friction? It is doubtful whether this negative policy was really adequate; at any rate, it was too tame for the politicians who controlled Parliament. So, in direct contravention of the royal charter, the government of Massachusetts was radically changed. Councilors were not to be elected, but appointed by the King; judges were brought more fully under the control of the governor; and juries were no longer to be elected by the people but chosen by the sheriffs. The town meetings, which had been resolving freely on imperial problems, were to be kept strictly to local business, transacted, except by special permission of the governor, only at certain fixed times. To the Massachusetts theory that "in all free states the constitution is fixed" the answer was now given that the Massachusetts constitution was what Parliament chose to make it.

So far as constitutional principles were concerned, the Other coercive measures. Massachusetts Government Act was the most important of the coercive measures. Two other acts intended to strengthen the government in its dealings with the rebellious colonists were the Act for the Impartial Administration of Justice and a new Quartering Act. The former law enabled royal officials, who thought they could not get a fair trial on charges brought against them in the courts of any colony, to transfer their cases either to some other colony or to England. Probably this was not unreasonable in a time of so much excitement; but two years later the Declaration of Independence asserted that its purpose was to protect lawless officials by "mock" trials.

Quite different from these coercive acts, though generally associated with them, was the Quebec Act, whose The Quebec Act. Liberal features. main object was to correct certain defects in the government of that province which had developed since its organization under the Proclamation of 1763. Evidently a colony inhabited mostly by Frenchmen could not be governed on strictly English lines. It did not seem practicable, for instance, to install at once a system of representative government among people who had never been accustomed to anything of the kind. Again, the treaty by which the British acquired Canada promised that the religious and legal institutions of the French settlers should be respected, and it seemed desirable that these pledges should be carried out by legislation, not only as a matter of justice but in order to secure the loyalty of the Canadian population. For the present, therefore, Quebec was to be governed without a representative assembly; English law was to apply in criminal cases, but in civil cases the old French customs were continued, including the trial of such cases without a jury; the customary rights of the Catholic clergy were recognized, including that of collecting tithes. So far as the Canadian population was concerned, these were the important matters.

Objections
to the
Quebec Act.

During the debate on this bill, there was some sharp criticism. Ministers were accused of setting up an arbitrary government, depriving Englishmen of trial by jury, and being too liberal with the Catholics. These objections were also urged in America, but the chief grievance of the English colonists was that the boundaries of Quebec were extended south and west to the Ohio and the Mississippi, thus including a region covered by several of the old sea-

The West.

to-sea charters, in which traders, land speculators, and colony promoters were keenly interested. Some Americans looked for the extension of the existing colonies westward; others, with some encouragement from the British ministry, planned to establish new colonies. Treaties had also been made with the Indians opening up new lands for settlement. Now this land of promise was annexed to a province inhabited mainly by aliens and governed on principles radically different from those prevailing in the older English commonwealths. As a measure for the government of Canada, the law was on the whole just and fair; but Americans generally saw in it only one more example of unreasonable opposition to the westward expansion of their settlements and their free institutions.

Franklin and
the Hutchinson letters.

The same ministry which put through the coercive acts also alienated the most statesmanlike representative of American public opinion in England. Benjamin Franklin was an effective colonial agent, but he was quite capable of rising above provincial prejudices. As deputy postmaster-general for the colonies, he held office under the Crown and was on friendly terms with some of the leading ministers. It became known, however, that he had secured and sent back to Massachusetts private letters written from that province by Governor Hutchinson and other loyalist leaders. The ideas expressed by Hutchinson in these letters were partly those which he had stated publicly; the point most emphasized was the need of vigorous measures to curb the radical element. Having received the correspondence, the Massachusetts leaders proceeded to publish it for the purpose of breaking down Hutchinson's influence. Franklin was sharply criticized for such use of this correspondence and, on January 29, 1774, when he appeared before a committee of the Privy Council to urge Hutchinson's removal from office, he was savagely attacked by Solicitor-General Wedderburn. This meeting was largely attended by councilors and others, who, as Franklin grimly remarked, seemed "to enjoy highly the entertainment," frequently breaking out in loud applause. This humiliating experience was immediately followed by Franklin's dismissal from the postal service. His conduct was not above criticism, but the attack upon him went beyond the bounds of decency and proved a serious blunder. *Franklin disciplined.*

By the summer of 1774, the new ministerial policies were being inaugurated in Massachusetts. In place of Hutchinson, who now sailed for England, the governorship was given to a military man, General Gage, who had been for some time the commander in chief of the British regulars in America. The Boston Port Bill was no idle threat but a stern reality and presently there came royal commissions for the new "mandamus councilors," marking the end of the old constitution. Meantime, the radical leaders had gone too far to draw back and soon took up the challenge, declaring that the new government was founded on a plain usurpation of power by Parliament. Under the leadership of Boston, the towns of Suffolk County worked out a plan of resistance, which was summed up in the "Suffolk Resolves" of September, 1774. The "mandamus councilors" were set aside and those who were not already frightened into resigning were warned to do so at once. Sheriffs and other officers were told to ignore the judges appointed under the new law, and town collectors were advised to hold back taxes from the provincial treasury. *Resistance of Massachusetts.* *The Suffolk Resolves.*

A provincial congress was elected as the central agency for this organized resistance and plans were set on foot for a popular militia independent of the governor. So, over against Gage's establishment in Boston, a new government was gradually taking shape, quite irregular, no doubt, but no more so, according to the popular leaders, than the rival organization.

Attitude of the middle colonies.

The success of this experiment in revolutionary government depended largely on the attitude of the other colonies; and that was still uncertain. Sympathy for the hardships of Boston was widespread; but many moderate people thought Massachusetts had been overradical. The Puritan traditions of New England and its supposed "leveling spirit" were not popular with the merchants and gentry of New York, who feared that a break with England would mean civil war among themselves. In Pennsylvania, the old Quaker ruling class, though ready at times to defend its own rights, was afraid of violent methods. The Pennsylvania conservatives were ably led by Joseph Galloway, then speaker of the House of Representatives; even Dickinson, the writer of the *Farmer's Letters*, feared that Massachusetts had gone too far. Even in the middle colonies, however, the radicals were gaining ground. In Pennsylvania, for instance, the workmen and small traders of Philadelphia were combining with the back-country people to demand a larger share in the provincial government as well as more decided opposition to the policies of the British ministry. These radical elements now organized local committees and a provincial convention which, though without any legal authority, could bring pressure to bear upon the more conservative members of the regular assembly.

Virginia and the first Continental Congress.

While the middle colonies wavered, the radicals were encouraged by the attitude of Virginia, which had somewhat more prestige than the New England group. Here too there were radicals and conservatives; but the two elements were less irreconcilable than in Massachusetts and among the "Whigs" there were many substantial landowners. So it came about that in May, 1774, the Virginia burgesses agreed to call a provincial congress, which in turn was to choose delegates to a "Continental Congress," for the purpose of taking counsel with the "Whigs" in other colonies. These Virginia delegates were a strong and representative group. Radical agitators, like Patrick Henry and Richard Henry Lee, were included; but Washington was also among them and the delegation was headed by Peyton Randolph, one of the "old guard" whose power Henry and his friends had been trying to curb. One colony after another fell in line and in September, 1774, when the Congress assembled in Carpenter's Hall, Philadelphia, every colony except Georgia was represented. The delegates were chosen in various ways, sometimes by colonial assemblies, sometimes by unofficial conventions, and sometimes by local authorities. It is quite misleading, however, to speak of these people as irresponsible and impecunious agitators. Many were prosperous merchants and landowners; in the elegant mansions of some of the Philadelphia Whigs, visiting delegates were entertained with "sinful" feasts, which John Adams describes with evident pleasure.

The members of this truly "continental" assembly could see, as few of them had seen before, the varied elements of which America was composed. Anglicans and Puritans, Quakers, and even the much-distrusted Catholics, all saw the necessity of mutual understanding and coöperation. John Adams, who was a conscientious churchgoer, visited Moravian, Methodist, and Baptist meetings and was impressed by the stately ritual of the Catholic Church. His "old Puritan" cousin, Samuel Adams, was less liberal, but he too could sometimes sacrifice his prejudices, as when he proposed that an Episcopal clergyman should offer prayer before the Congress.

The problem of mutual understanding.

Radical and conservative parties.

Not only were there old prejudices to be removed; there were also sharp differences of opinion on current issues. Sherman of Connecticut denied altogether the legislative authority of Parliament. According to Patrick Henry, the old governments were already dissolved and the Congress should work out a new system. Alarmed by such radical ideas, the conservatives felt the necessity of offering some constructive plan. Their chief spokesman was Joseph Galloway of Pennsylvania, who with the support of some New York and South Carolina delegates, proposed a kind of imperial constitution, establishing a general legislative authority which could regulate American affairs without violating the principles of English liberty as commonly understood in America. This authority he proposed to divide between Parliament and an American legislature consisting of representatives from the colonial assemblies, the consent of both these bodies being required for imperial legislation affecting America. In time of war the American legislature could levy taxes independently. The Galloway plan, which was somewhat similar to the Albany plan of 1754, was supported not only by loyalists, or Tories, but by men like John Jay and Edward Rutledge, who afterwards worked for American independence. The radicals were able, however, to discredit the proposal as a loyalist scheme to prevent effective action in defense of American interests.

Galloway and his plan of union.

The Declaration and Resolves.

Compromises.

Gradually differences of opinion were overcome and a substantial majority of the delegates met on common ground. The New England radicals gained a clear victory when Congress approved the revolutionary program set forth in the Suffolk Resolves. In discussing the basis of American rights, some emphasized "natural rights," while others regarded the English constitution and the colonial charters as more important. On these and similar questions compromise was necessary; in the "Declaration and Resolves" as finally adopted, "natural rights," the British constitution, and the charters were all given a place. As to the theory of parliamentary sovereignty, the delegates were of different minds; but the Congress, while denying the right of Parliament to tax the colonies, made no objection to laws which were clearly limited to the regulation of commerce. Some questions were also avoided by limiting the list of grievances to those which had arisen since 1763.

More important than this statement of principles was the plan for carrying them into effect. In general this was the old method of boycotting English trade and manufactures. By the "Continental Association" the delegates bound themselves and, so far as possible, their constituents not to import or use British goods or other articles on which duties had been levied. The slave trade was to be discontinued and, unless Parliament came to terms within a year, exports to the British Isles and the West Indies were also to be stopped. Experience showed the difficulty of enforcing such boycotts, and Congress, therefore, recommended an elaborate machinery of provincial and local committees, chosen by the people, to watch over suspicious persons and make life hard for those who refused to conform. Out of this network of committees there gradually developed something like a revolutionary government, often better able to enforce its will than the regularly constituted authorities. The idea of a central assembly to coördinate all these local agencies was kept alive by calling a second Continental Congress to meet in May, 1775. Thus the coercive acts, instead of restoring law and order in the colonies, produced exactly the opposite result and played directly into the hands of the radicals.

The "Continental Association."

BIBLIOGRAPHICAL NOTES

Becker, *Eve of the American Revolution*, 115–220. Channing, *United States*, III, chs. IV–V. Fisher, *Struggle for American In-*

General references.

dependence, I, chs. IX–XX.   Frothingham, R., *Rise of the Republic*.
Howard, *Preliminaries*, chs. X–XVI.   Lecky, *England in the
Eighteenth Century*, III, 344–447 (or his *American Revolution*).
Trevelyan, G. O., *American Revolution*, I, chs. I–V (liberal English
view).   Van Tyne, C. H., *Causes of the War of Independence*.

Collected sources.   Macdonald, *Select Charters*, nos. 61, 64–73.   Hart, *Contemporaries*, II, ch. XXIV, and no. 153.   Callender, *Selections from
Eco. Hist. of U. S.*, 148–159.   Pease and Roberts, *Readings*, 75–96.

English politics   Fitzmaurice, *Shelburne*, II, ch. I.   Ruville, A. von, *Pitt*, III,
chs. IX–XII.   Williams, B., *Chatham*, ch. XXII.   Detailed dis-
cussion in Alvord, *Mississippi Valley in British Politics*.

English sources.   Burke on American Taxation, April, 1774, in *Works* and else-
where.   Cobbett's *Parliamentary History*, XVII (debates 1774).
Mumby, F. A., *George III and the American Revolution*.   Donne,
W. B., *Correspondence of George III and Lord North*.   Knox, W.,
Controversy between Great Britain and Her Colonies Reviewed (1769).

The Ameri- can opposi- tion.   Henry, *Patrick Henry*, I, chs. VI–X.   Tyler, *Patrick Henry*,
chs. VII–VIII.   Hosmer, J. K., *S. Adams*, 81–289.   Harlow, R. V.,
Samuel Adams.   Adams, J. T., *Revolutionary N. E.*, chs. XV, XVI.
Baldwin, A. M., *N. E. Clergy and the American Revolution*.   Morris,
R. B., "Legalism vs. Revolutionary Doctrine in N. E.," *N.E.Q.*
(1931), IV, 195–215.   Brown, E. F., *Joseph Hawley*.   C. Becker
and W. E. Dodd in *The Spirit of '76*.   Schlesinger, *Colonial Merchants*, chs. III–X.   Lincoln, C. H., *Revolutionary Movement in
Pennsylvania*, chs. VIII–X.   McCrady, *South Carolina, 1719–
1776*, chs. XXX–XXXIX.   Stillé, C. J., *John Dickinson*, 79–149.

American sources.   Dickinson, J., *Letters of a Farmer* (Various Editions).
Franklin, *Writings* (Smyth edition), V, VI.   Hutchinson, T.,
Massachusetts, III, ch. III (loyalist view).   Jefferson, T., *Writ-
ings* (Ford edition), I (including autobiography).   For Conti-
nental Congress, see *Journals*, I (Library of Congress edition);
Burnett, *Letters of Members of the Continental Congress*, I; and
Adams, J., *Works*, II, 340–402 (diary and notes).   Morison,
Sources and Documents, 104–124.

Canada and the West.   Alvord, *Centennial History of Illinois*, I, ch. XIV, and his *Mis-
sissippi Valley in British Politics*.   Coupland, R., *The Quebec Act: a
Study in Statesmanship*.   Wrong, G. M., *Canada and the American
Revolution*.   Keith, A. B., *First British Empire* 386–391.

CHAPTER XIX

REVOLUTION, 1774 TO 1776

IN England a few friends of the colonies, including Chatham, were impressed by the ability and self-control shown in the published statements of the Continental Congress. Another group, made up largely of merchants and manufacturers, was anxious about the effect of the "Association" on business. During the summer there had even been some talk of a change in the ministry which might bring in a more liberal element and so make possible a different American policy, perhaps some "great constitutional charter to be confirmed by King, Lords, and Commons." Unfortunately the new parliamentary elections strengthened those elements which followed the ministry and had little sympathy for the American point of view.

Not only were the liberals in a minority; they were also unable to agree on a constructive policy. The "Old Whig" view, best expressed by Burke, was to put Anglo-American relations back where they were before 1763. This could be done by repealing the coercive acts and leaving the taxing power with the separate colonial assemblies; also there should be as little talk as possible about legal theories of Parliamentary sovereignty. Chatham favored a constitutional agreement defining both the rights of Parliament and those of the colonies. The colonies, he thought, should acknowledge their dependence on the "imperial crown of Great Britain" and the supreme legislative authority of Parliament. In return for this acknowledgment, Parliament should expressly renounce any authority to tax the colonies.

English opinion.

Conciliatory proposals. Burke and Chatham.

Instead of treating the Continental Congress as a group of rebels, Chatham accepted it as a fair representation of American opinion, entitled to join with Parliament as a party to this proposed agreement. The American Whigs were not quite satisfied with this plan, but they were willing to accept it as a basis for discussion. The ministry, however, regarded it as impossible and it was rejected in the House of Lords by a vote of nearly two to one.

New measures of coercion.

Among the ministers, even, there were differences of opinion. They had to take into account the British trading interests which might be injured by a purely repressive policy. In London, large meetings were held by merchants who had business interests in the continental colonies, and petitions were sent to Parliament from the leading commercial and manufacturing centers asking the government to reconsider its American policy. Nevertheless, the King and the factions which supported him were determined not to yield. Some merchants also believed that they would gain more in the end by the enforcement of parliamentary authority than by an immediate reopening of trade through concessions which later might be awkward. So the appeals of the Continental Congress were rejected and the policy of coercion was continued.

North's "Conciliatory Proposition."

The New England Restraining Act restricted still further the trade of that section and votes were taken for increasing the military and naval forces in America. The only offset to the coercive policy was the "Conciliatory Proposition" of Lord North, offering to exempt from parliamentary taxes any colony whose assembly would guarantee a definite sum for imperial purposes. Whatever its purpose may have been, this proposal proved futile. The Americans and their English sympathizers generally regarded it as a trick to divide the colonies; but before the latter had time to act on it, war began at Lexington and Concord.

Though the serious fighting began in Massachusetts,

similar conditions existed elsewhere. From New Hampshire Enforcing the "Continental Association." to Georgia, the radicals organized committees to enforce the "Continental Association." These committees had no legal authority, but they had more real power than many of the regular governments. Those who violated the "nonimportation" and "nonconsumption" agreements were punished by social ostracism, by trade boycotts, and by physical violence. In order that the colonies might be more independent economically, home industries were encouraged and people were urged to produce more wool for domestic manufactures. More ominous still was the attention given to military preparations. Munitions were collected, plans were made for a larger production of them, and independent military companies were formed.

Virginia illustrates admirably the way in which revolutionary methods were undermining the regular provincial governments. In the summer of 1774 the Virginians, especially the frontiersmen and others who were interested in western lands, were much occupied with Indian affairs. The movement of new settlers into the Ohio valley had brought on a new conflict with the Indians, generally known as Lord Dunmore's War, which for a time brought governor and people together in defense of their common interests. But the Indians were soon defeated and the men who fought the victorious campaign emerged from the wilderness with ideas quite different from those of their governor. Even a disagreeable boundary controversy between Pennsylvania and Virginia did not prevent the radicals in both colonies from working together. By the end of 1774, Dunmore had to report that his authority had almost disappeared. The courts could not transact business and militia companies were taking orders not from him but from revolutionary committees. In the following spring, these military preparations, in which Washington took an active part, were vigorously pushed and Virginia came near having an armed

Revolutionary methods in Virginia.

encounter between the governor and the colonial volunteers similar to that which actually occurred about the same time in Massachusetts.

The loyalists.   Meantime, the Whigs were confronted in every colony by a more or less influential "loyalist," or Tory, element, which felt that the Continental Congress and the various revolutionary committees had gone dangerously far. These men were not all thick-and-thin defenders of the British government. Some of them had not only criticized the Stamp Act and other revenue measures but had done what they could to secure their repeal. Now, however, it seemed to them that Whig measures were leading directly to disruption of the empire. All this they dreaded not merely because they were loyal to the King and the mother country, but because they needed the help of the home government to protect them against aggressively democratic neighbors. Besides the out-and-out loyalists, there were many others who disliked Whig methods and shrank from the idea of armed conflict. To a certain extent and in a negative way, such men coöperated with the real loyalists; but in general they tried to steer a safe middle course. Such people were not willing to make sacrifices for the loyalist cause and were often intimidated by their radical neighbors.

Social factors in the loyalist party.   The loyalists did not belong to any one class in society, though they were most numerous among the naturally conservative people of wealth, social standing, and education. In Massachusetts, for instance, the old office-holding class, and many of the leading merchants, the Anglican clergy, and the college graduates were loyalists. In New York and Philadelphia, many of the merchants took a similar stand. The loyalists counted on the conservatism of the old Quaker families and strong resolutions were passed by the Quaker meetings against violent resistance to the civil authorities. In Virginia, moderates and radicals worked together better than in most colonies and thus checked the development of the loyalist party except among the Scotch and other merchants. Farther south, in the Carolinas and Georgia, the Tories were numerous and active. The loyalists laid much stress on the hardships resulting from the "Association." Some kinds of legitimate business undoubtedly suffered and poor people complained of the high prices which they had to pay because "nonimportation" cut down the available supply of goods. The local committees were also accused of showing favoritism, making concessions to influential people while others were held up more strictly. Much was made of the undoubted fact that loyalists were not allowed to write or speak their opinions; from their point of view Whig interference with personal liberty was more serious than that of the British government. *The loyalist argument.*

The net result, then, of the Continental Congress and of the program carried out in accordance with its directions by the local committees, was to bring about a clearer alignment between radicals and conservatives, — between the old provincial governments which rested on royal authority and the more or less revolutionary organizations which were gradually getting the real power. Evidently this state of things could not go on indefinitely. The radicals could not easily draw back and some of them were now ready to secede from the empire. *Transfer of power to revolutionary organizations.*

For various reasons the crisis was first reached in Massachusetts, which was most directly affected by the coercive acts. From the Whig point of view, Parliament itself had inaugurated a revolution by arbitrarily destroying the old provincial constitution. The opponents of General Gage argued with some show of reason, that they, rather than he, were standing for the "good old ways." The Massachusetts Whigs also had a group of skillful leaders who knew just what they wanted and had developed an unusually effective organization. By the beginning of 1775 military *The outbreak in Massachusetts.*

preparations were well advanced on both sides. "Minute-men" were drilling and munitions were being gathered; but each side preferred to put on the other the responsibility for striking the first blow. Gage's government in Boston was getting to be little more than a besieged garrison and he could hardly afford to let matters drift much longer. So it came about that on April 19, 1775, a few British regulars, sent to seize military supplies accumulated at Concord by the revolutionary government, clashed with a handful of militiamen on Lexington Common, marched on to Concord, where they met more serious resistance from the "em-battled farmers," and finally had to make a humiliating retreat back to Boston.

Lexington and Concord.

The question of coöperation.

So far, the conflict was primarily a Massachusetts affair. Already, however, there was a general understanding be-tween the Massachusetts Whigs and their neighbors in the other New England colonies. Within a few weeks of the affair at Lexington and Concord, all the colonies of this group were represented in the numerous, but poorly organ-ized and equipped, army which had assembled at Cambridge, only a few miles from Gage's headquarters in Boston. This coöperation of the New England colonies was, of course, only the first step; the enterprise could not possibly succeed without active support from the middle and south-ern provinces. Whether that support was to be given was the great question to be decided by the Second Continental Congress in May, 1775.

The second Continental Congress.

The new Congress, like its predecessor of 1774, included men of various opinions, — radical, moderate, and conserv-ative. The conservatives were, however, much weaker than before and they had no such aggressive leader as Joseph Galloway. The radicals were correspondingly stronger, but they had to move slowly in order to keep in touch with their more cautious associates. Hancock of Massachusetts was chosen president, and radicals and moderates agreed that Congress should assume responsibility for the army in Cambridge, of which Washington was presently made commander in chief. Even cautious people like Dickinson believed there were good English precedents for military resistance to unconstitutional measures.

The choice of Washington as commander in chief was a notable event. He was selected partly because he was a Virginian, but also because none of the other Whig leaders had any general reputation as a soldier. Even Washington had never commanded more than a few hundred men nor seen a battle between two disciplined armies. Fortunately the technical preparation which he lacked was not indispensable. There was no battle of the Revolutionary War in which either side had more than a few thousand men, and the commanders in chief on the other side were second-rate. The qualities most needed, Washington had in extraordinary measure: capacity for leadership, persistent courage during long periods of defeat and general discouragement, sturdy common sense, and a personal character which, in spite of some jealousy and even disloyalty in Congress and in the army, won for him the confidence of the people whom he served.

Washington as commander in chief.

The war in which Washington now engaged was not conceived by him or most of his comrades as a struggle for national independence; it was hardly even a revolt against the King, but rather armed resistance to the group of ministers then advising the King and guiding Parliament. During the early months of the war, Washington referred to the British army as the "ministerial troops" and Americans were still appealing from the King "badly advised" to the King "better advised." Yet every month made more difficult this attempt to reconcile a theoretical loyalty to the King with the actual fact of armed resistance to his agents in America.

The American cause in 1775.

The British government was now preparing for a real

British
preparations.

war. This took time, however, and for about a year no important offensive movement was undertaken by the British. Great Britain had no large standing army and even in the Seve. Years' War had never called more than a small fraction of her able-bodied men into military service; she depended rather on her navy and the wealth which enabled her to subsidize her European allies. Even now, in a conflict with his own subjects, the head of a great world power felt obliged to make up for the lack of English recruits by buying soldiers from the Landgrave of Hesse and other minor German princes. The British government also counted heavily on the American loyalists, and to a less extent on Indian allies, who had been attached to the British cause by skillful agents like the Johnson family in New York, and Stuart, the superintendent of Indian affairs in the South. Both the loyalists and the Indians were disappointing. Though the loyalists were numerous, the superior aggressiveness and organizing ability of the Whig element prevented them from getting effectively together. The Indians could do a good deal of damage by raiding frontier settlements, but could not be relied on in a complicated campaign.

Bunker Hill
and the siege
of Boston.

The military history of the year which began with Washington's appointment may be briefly told. First came the battle of Bunker Hill, fought before Washington's arrival by New England volunteers, who had tried to make the British position in Boston untenable by fortifying certain heights in the neighboring village of Charlestown. In this battle the colonials twice repulsed the advancing British under General Howe, but were defeated in the third attack, after their ammunition was exhausted. They had, however, inflicted heavy losses on the enemy and shown that they could use both spade and rifle to good advantage. During the next few months there was not much change in the situation. The British and their loyalist supporters were cooped up in Boston while the revolutionary party was

terrorizing the Tories outside of the British lines and per-
fecting its organization. In the autumn Gage gave up his
unpleasant task and sailed home. A few months later,
Washington's fortification of Dorchester Heights made
Howe's position so precarious that he decided to leave
Boston, taking with him more than a thousand loyalists.
Within a year after Gage's unlucky expedition to Concord,
royal authority had practically disappeared in New England.

Evacuation
of Boston.

American success up to this point was due largely to
British incompetence rather than to American efficiency.
To a man of soldierly instincts and training, the army at
Cambridge was discouraging. During the summer of 1775
several thousand New England volunteers came in; there
were also some riflemen recruited from the frontier districts
of Pennsylvania and the South, of whom the best known
were the Virginians under the capable Daniel Morgan.
New England ideas about discipline were free and easy, and
mistaken notions of democracy prevented officers from getting proper respect from their men. Stern discipline was
sometimes necessary under these circumstances and Washington was not afraid to apply it, to officers as well as men.
Munitions and other equipment were also quite insufficient.

Washing-
ton's army.

Much of Washington's trouble came from the fact that the
civilian chiefs of the insurgent government in Philadelphia
also had pioneer work to do in organizing a central war office.
There were good men engaged on this task — John Adams
of Massachusetts, Sherman of Connecticut, Wilson of Pennsylvania, and Rutledge of South Carolina; but they were
quite inexperienced in such matters. All things considered,
they probably did as well as could reasonably be expected.

Congress and
the army.

With this hastily improvised organization, Congress
undertook at the end of 1775 a new and difficult offensive
movement against the British forces in Canada. So far the
revolutionary spirit had been almost wholly limited to the

Other
British
colonies.

"old thirteen" colonies. The British West Indies grumbled somewhat about parliamentary taxation; but for them resistance to British sea power was almost inconceivable. In the new provinces of East and West Florida, British and colonial land speculators were already at work; but English settlers were few and the scattered Spanish and French population was not good material for a revolutionary party. In the north, Nova Scotia was equally unpromising. The French peasantry took little interest in politics and the small English population was out of touch with movements to the southward. About Canada, however, the Whigs were for a time more hopeful. This newly conquered province could hardly be expected to show any real loyalty to the British Crown, or toward the English ruling class, from whom they differed in nationality, language, and religion. On the other hand, these differences separated the Canadians even more from the American Whigs than from the imperial government. Under the Quebec Act the rights of their church were now fully recognized and their old civil law reëstablished; but the Continental Congress of 1774 had denounced these very concessions and had used the prevailing anti-Catholic feeling of the older colonies as "campaign material" against the British. In undertaking after this to enlist the Canadians as allies, on issues which meant little to them, the Whigs were playing a difficult game. Yet the chance seemed to be worth trying and so the Congress of 1775 published an appeal to the Canadian people. The delegates also overcame their Protestant prejudices sufficiently to send the Catholic, John Carroll, from Maryland, along with Franklin to plead the Whig cause in Canada. This diplomatic move was to be supported by a military expedition.

Canada and the Revolution.

In May, 1775, the frontiersmen of Vermont, led by the strenuous Ethan Allen, gained an important advantage by seizing Ticonderoga and Crown Point, which controlled an

The Canadian campaign of 1775–1776.

important section of the historic waterway between the
Hudson and the St. Lawrence. Soon afterwards Congress
determined to attempt the invasion of Canada, and in the
autumn of 1775 two coöperating expeditions were on their
way. One, under the young Irish officer, Richard Montgomery, followed the Lake Champlain route and in November
captured Montreal. The other, commanded by Benedict
Arnold, an energetic officer from Connecticut, made a heroic winter march through the wilds of Maine. The two
forces united before Quebec; but on the last day of the old
year the American assault was beaten back and Montgomery
was killed. The siege continued for several months and
Congress sent reënforcements; but the British were ably
led by Sir Guy Carleton and the French showed little
interest. By the summer of 1776 the Americans had fallen
back to Crown Point.

Though the immediate object of the Quebec expedition
was not realized, it did some good by weakening the British
offensive. Three months passed after the occupation of
Boston before Howe was ready to begin his attack on New
York. There were attacks on seaboard towns like Falmouth
in Maine and Norfolk in Virginia, but they accomplished
little; their chief result was to exasperate the Americans
and help the radical agitation for independence. The only
important offensive movement of the British before the
summer of 1776 was the southern campaign, which aimed
at the capture of Charleston, and a loyalist uprising to
detach the southern colonies from the Continental Congress.
This campaign failed, partly because the up-country loyalists of the Carolinas were poorly organized and did not
come out in sufficient numbers. Before they were ready
to coöperate with the British landing force, they were overwhelmed by the Whigs at Moores Creek Bridge, North
Carolina. In spite of this disappointment, the British
commander, General Clinton, with the coöperation of the

The British
offensive
of 1776
delayed.

Defense of
Charleston.

fleet, attacked Charleston in June, 1776; but the South Carolinians, led by President Rutledge and William Moultrie, made a brave defense and Charleston was saved. After fourteen months of fighting the British had no solid foothold in any of the thirteen colonies.

The drift
toward in-
dependence.

As the summer came on, it was evident that the whole character of the conflict had changed. In June, 1775, the colonists still professed to be merely British subjects defending themselves against unconstitutional measures. However reasonable that theory may have been in the beginning, it was fast becoming untenable. Americans could not go on indefinitely professing loyalty to a King whose fleets were attacking their coasts and whose armies they were doing their best to destroy. In other ways, too, the struggle had ceased to be a mere family quarrel. George III was calling in German mercenaries and the colonists were beginning to think seriously of foreign help. Already the French had sent agents to study the situation, and in November, 1775, the Continental Congress appointed a committee to correspond " with our friends in Great Britain, Ireland, and other parts of the world." After some violent protests against negotiations with foreign powers, Congress finally, in March, 1776, appointed Silas Deane as its agent in Paris. If the colonists were still British subjects, this was nothing less than treason.

Breakdown
of the
provincial
governments.

Another factor which helped the advocates of independence was the gradual disappearance of the old governments. In the early months of 1776, a few royal governors were still trying to preserve some shreds of authority. Governor Tryon of New York and Lord Dunmore of Virginia took refuge on British vessels, from which they tried to organize the loyalists against the revolutionary forces. Generally speaking, however, the royal and proprietary governments had given way to provincial congresses and committees. These revolutionary organizations were well enough for temporary purposes but they could not meet the permanent needs of the community. They had been chosen in irregular ways and their powers were not clearly defined; in short, they had no legal status. The old constitutions of the colonies rested largely on royal charters or commissions, and officeholders had to swear allegiance to the King. These foundations were crumbling and a new public law would have to be developed, or the country would drift toward anarchy. Loyalists regarded these destructive tendencies as the natural result of Whig teaching; even thoroughgoing Whigs were alarmed by the growing spirit of lawlessness.

The problem of reconstruction was comparatively simple in Connecticut and Rhode Island, because their governments, though based on royal charters, consisted wholly of officials chosen directly or indirectly by the people. Even Massachusetts kept up as much of its old government as it could, after eliminating the royal governor. In the ordinary royal and proprietary governments no such arrangement was practicable. So, from one province after another, came appeals to Congress for advice. In November, Congress answered an inquiry from New Hampshire by advising the formation of a temporary government based on the authority of the people. Similar advice was given to South Carolina, which adopted a temporary constitution early in 1776. All these developments made compromise more difficult and forced Americans to choose squarely between going back to the old loyalty or pressing resolutely forward toward independence. *The problem of reconstruction.*

During the last months of 1775, radicals like John Adams and Richard Henry Lee grew more and more impatient with halfway measures, and Washington's influence was presently felt in the same direction. Between Virginia and New England, however, — in New York, New Jersey, Pennsylvania, and Maryland, — the loyalists were powerful, *Failure of the conciliation policy.*

as they were also in the Carolinas and Georgia. Franklin, back at home once more, was now definitely on the radical side; but the moderate Whigs, led by John Jay of New York, James Wilson and John Dickinson of Pennsylvania, and the Rutledges of South Carolina, still hoped against hope for reconciliation. Unfortunately for them, the conciliatory documents which Congress adopted under their influence in the summer of 1775 were not well received in England. New legislation cut off intercourse with the rebellious colonies and negotiations for German mercenaries were continued.

Public
opinion.
Paine's
*Common
Sense.*
In these trying months, when perhaps half of the American people were wavering between the hope of reconciliation and the radical proposal of absolute independence, a young man named Thomas Paine published a small pamphlet entitled *Common Sense*. Paine, who had lived in America only a few months, was not a great thinker; but he could write vigorously and knew how to influence the average man. He now argued that the time had come for breaking away from old traditions; "a new method of thinking hath arisen." He answered the appeal for loyalty to the mother country by saying that America was the child not of England only but of Europe. There was "something absurd," he said, "in supposing a continent to be perpetually governed by an island." There was some language in the pamphlet which, as John Adams said, was "suitable for an emigrant from Newgate"; as, for instance, his reference to George III as the "royal Brute" of England. With all its coarseness and declamation, *Common Sense* was a great book. It did popularize a new and less provincial "method of thinking." In a remarkable way, Paine touched the imagination of Americans with his vision of a new, independent, and democratic nationality. Many of them disapproved of his ultraradical philosophy; but there was a driving force in it which no one was more ready to recognize than

the hard-headed, somewhat aristocratic, gentleman who commanded the Continental army.

Early in 1776, the moderate Whigs were forced into a series of measures which, taken together, made independence almost inevitable. Especially important was the decision to break away from the old commercial system which excluded foreign ships from American ports. The Association of 1774, the retaliatory measures of Parliament, and the outbreak of hostilities made impossible most of the old trade within the empire, though some exceptions were made on both sides, as when Congress permitted South Carolina to export rice and the British allowed trade with certain colonies in the hope of winning them over. In short, the old system had broken down; but there was no clean-cut uniform policy to put in its place, and the result was much misunderstanding and friction among the colonies. Especially urgent just then was the need of importing military supplies from continental Europe; in spite of strenuous efforts to stimulate American production, it was impossible to get on without foreign help, not only in selling supplies but in transporting them across the ocean. So after long debates and strenuous opposition from conservative members, Congress voted in April, 1776, a kind of commercial declaration of independence. In flat defiance of the Navigation Acts, American ports, hitherto open only to British and colonial vessels, were thrown open to the trade of all nations except Great Britain.

Congress opens ports to foreign shipping.

Meantime, Congress was also discussing the difficult problem of the loyalists, who still upheld the old government and even though temporarily overawed were likely at any time to coöperate actively with the British army. The Whig party everywhere acted on the theory that, for the time being at any rate, a new authority had been created and intrusted to the revolutionary government, Continental, provincial, and local. Those who accepted this new order

Disarming of the loyalists.

were good citizens; all others were to be regarded as enemies. As the war went on it became increasingly necessary to draw this clean-cut line between enemies and friends; but to a large extent the problem was dealt with independently by the revolutionary organization in each province. Everywhere it became harder for men to be neutral, and persons suspected of having Tory sympathies were persecuted, required to take various tests, and often driven into exile. Effective as this local action often was, it seemed desirable that Congress should adopt a general policy. Accordingly, in the spring and winter of 1776, Congress passed resolutions urging the government of each colony to disarm all persons who were "notoriously disaffected" or who refused to help in defending the country against the British forces.

Resolution of May, 1776.

This virtual assertion of a new allegiance replacing the old one led naturally to another forward step which made the formal declaration of independence almost superfluous. By resolution of May 10, adopted on the initiative of John Adams, Congress recommended all the colonies to form such governments "as shall, in the opinion of the representatives of the people, best conduce to the happiness and safety of their constituents in particular and America in general." Especially significant was the preamble, published with the resolution though adopted five days later. The taking of an oath to support government under the Crown was declared to be contrary to reason and conscience; and all authority under the Crown was held to be "totally suppressed." Governmental powers should now be exercised "under the authority of the people of the colonies, for the preservation of internal peace, virtue, and good order."

Victory of the radicals.

This was not done without a vigorous protest. Wilson of Pennsylvania admitted the need of new organizations to preserve order but feared the resolution would make trouble in his own colony, where the regular provincial assembly was having a hard struggle with radical elements in Philadelphia, as well as in the up-country districts. If the preamble were adopted, Pennsylvania might fall into a state of confusion. Why such haste? Wilson asked. "Before we are prepared to build the new house, why should we pull down the old one?" But Adams and his supporters were determined and this time they had the votes.

This same month of May saw the Virginians hard at work putting the new theory into practice. The blundering violence of Governor Dunmore, his attempts to excite a slave insurrection, and the intrigues of some of his associates had discredited the loyalists and consolidated sentiment in favor of decisive measures. The provincial convention now committed itself to the principle of independence and began forming a state constitution. A resolution was also adopted instructing the Virginia delegates in Congress to move for independence, confederation, and foreign alliances. Such a motion was accordingly made on June 7, by Richard Henry Lee, appropriately seconded by John Adams. *Action of Virginia.*

Virginia and Massachusetts were now standing together for independence; but Congress still hesitated. Men like Jay and Duane in New York, or Dickinson and Wilson in Pennsylvania, were placed between two fires. As Whigs they had gone too far for their conservative neighbors; but they were alarmed by the radical democratic forces which the revolution had developed. So they pleaded for delay, and the radicals waited in the hope of getting united action later. On June 10, the vote on independence was postponed for three weeks to give the delegates another opportunity to get the opinions of their constituents. Meantime, the advocates of independence, anxious to lose as little time as possible, secured the appointment of three important committees. The committee to draft a declaration of independence included four radicals, Jefferson, Franklin, Adams, and Sherman, with one moderate, Livingston of New York. *The issue postponed.*

Committees on independence, etc.

The two other committees were to consider confederation
and foreign alliances, and on these the moderates were
liberally recognized. Dickinson was a member of both and
chairman of the former; his equally cautious colleague,
Robert Morris, served on the committee to consider
foreign alliances.

During the next three weeks the radicals were hard at
work bringing the doubtful colonies into line. In the
middle group the conventions of New Jersey and Maryland
voted for independence. In Pennsylvania the assembly
hesitated, but a conference of revolutionary committees
declared for independence. The South Carolina delegates
found it hard to reach a decision, because their instructions
were indefinite and they were too far away to keep in touch
with their constituents. When, on July 1, the debate was
resumed in Congress there was a clear majority for independence; but the conservatives were still asking for more
time. Dickinson argued that the colonies should form an
effective federal union before committing themselves to
permanent separation from the empire. He was vigorously
answered by John Adams, and on the same day a vote was
taken in committee of the whole, showing nine colonies
for independence — the four New England colonies, New
Jersey, Maryland, Virginia, North Carolina, Georgia; of
the remaining four, the New York delegates refused to vote
at all and Delaware's vote was divided, while Pennsylvania
and South Carolina voted against independence. The
formal vote was then postponed until the next day, July 2,
and a great effort was made to secure unanimous
action.

Before the vote was taken, the arrival of an absent
member gave the radicals a majority from Delaware, and
the South Carolinians decided to take the chance of voting
for independence and getting the approval of their constituents later. The Pennsylvania delegation was still divided;

but its members were under heavy pressure from impatient radicals in their own colony, and when the final vote was taken only two voted definitely against independence. Two others, Dickinson and Morris, stayed away, and Wilson went with the majority. So on July 2 the great decision was made with twelve colonies voting aye. New York still refrained from voting, but a week later the provincial convention gave its formal assent. The same day, the committee appointed to draft a declaration made its report. This draft was almost wholly the work of the chairman, Thomas Jefferson, and in some passages the document reflected the individuality of the writer. There were, for instance, extreme views about colonial independence of Parliament which were certainly not shared by all his colleagues. There was also a passage denouncing the King for his part in the introduction of slavery into the colonies, which offended some of the delegates who were interested in the slave trade, and was accordingly struck out. Congress made other minor changes and then formally adopted the text of the Declaration on July 4. Some time afterwards, Congress voted that the Declaration should be signed by all the members, and signatures were accordingly attached at different dates during the next few months.

The Declaration of Independence.

The political theory of the Declaration was not new. John Adams, who, with all his great qualities, was not always magnanimous, complained of its lack of originality; but in such a document originality was not desirable. What the occasion required, and what Jefferson actually did, for the most part, was to put together, in effective literary form, ideas and language familiar to all who had followed the discussions of the past fifteen years: All men are created equal; being naturally free, they have established governments for the purpose of securing their inalienable rights; all just governments rest on the consent of the governed and can be dissolved when they fail to serve the fundamental

Political philosophy of the Declaration.

purposes for which the compact was made, — all these doctrines Americans had learned from John Locke, Algernon Sidney, and other seventeenth-century English writers. Locke had used them to defend the English Revolution of 1688, which established the sovereignty of Parliament as against the claims of the Stuart kings; but now they were used against Parliament itself.

The list of grievances.

The Declaration of 1776 resembled the Whig documents of 1765 and 1774 in denouncing acts of Parliament which were held to be unconstitutional, especially those imposing taxes and the Coercive Acts of 1774. Unlike the older statements, however, the Declaration of Independence directed its main attack against the King himself. Even acts of Parliament were treated as the result of a conspiracy for which George III was held largely responsible. Striking also is the long list of grievances, which included not merely

The real cause of the Revolution.

those of recent years but reached back to the old colonial system. More fundamental, however, to an understanding of the American Revolution than any mere list of grievances, new or old, was the inevitable difficulty of reconciling imperial authority exercised across three thousand miles of ocean, with traditional English ideals of self-government, developed and made more aggressive by the stimulating atmosphere of the American frontier.

An American civil war.

Finally, it must be remembered that, though the Declaration was officially described as "unanimous," it did not express the unanimous opinion of the American people, even after its tardy ratification by New York. In New England and Virginia there was a decided preponderance of opinion in its favor; but elsewhere the opposing forces were strong and many people asked only to be let alone. So the great war for independence was not simply a conflict between the imperial government and a group of revolting colonies, but almost as truly a civil war between two American parties, one standing for an old allegiance and an old patriotism, the other looking forward hopefully to the establishment of a new order.

BIBLIOGRAPHICAL NOTES

Becker, C., *Eve of the American Revolution*, 220–256. Channing, *United States*, III, chs. VI, VII. French, A., *First Year of the American Revolution*. Fisher, *Struggle for American Independence*, chs. XXI–XLI. Howard, *Preliminaries*, chs. XVII, XVIII; with Van Tyne, C. H., *American Revolution*, chs. II–VI, and his *War of Independence*, chs. I–XII. Lecky, *England in the Eighteenth Century*, III, 456–499. Trevelyan, G. O., *American Revolution*, I, chs. VII–XI; II, chs. XII–XVI. Winsor, *America*, chs. II, III. Bancroft, *United States*, IV (author's last revision). *{General references.}*

Morison, S. E., *Sources and Documents Illustrating the American Revolution*, 125–161. Macdonald, *Select Charters*, nos. 74–80. Hart, *Contemporaries*, II, nos. 154–161, 184–188 (illustrating public opinion). Very extensive collections, worth sampling even by the general reader, are Burnett, E. C., *Letters of the Members of the Continental Congress*, I; Force, P., *American Archives;* and Moore, F., *Diary of the American Revolution* (newspaper material). Willard, M. W., *Letters on the American Revolution*. *{Collected sources.}*

Hinkhouse, F. J., *Preliminaries of the American Revolution as Seen in the English Press*. Clark, D. M., *British Opinion and the American Revolution*. Guttridge, G. H., "Adam Smith on the American Revolution," *A.H.R.* (1933), XXXVIII, 714–720. Schuyler, R. L., *Josiah Tucker*. *{English opinion.}*

Biographies of J. Adams by J. T. Morse, M. Chamberlain, and G. Chinard; Washington, by J. C. Fitzpatrick, L. M. Sears, and R. Hughes; Henry, by Henry and Tyler; Dickinson, by C. J. Stillé; Paine, by Conway; Jefferson, by Chinard. *{American leaders. Whigs.}*

Adams, J., Diary, etc. in *Works*, II, 405–417, III, 3–59 (debates on independence, 44–59). Franklin, B., *Writings* (VI in Smyth edition). Paine, T., *Common Sense* in *Works* (Conway edition), I. Washington, *Writings* (Ford, or Fitzpatrick, edition), II. *{Writings of Whig leaders.}*

Tyler, M. C., "The Loyalists," *A.H.R.*, I, 24–45; more fully in his *Literary History of the American Revolution*, II. Van Tyne, C. H., *Loyalists in the American Revolution*, chs. I–V. Schlesinger, *{Loyalist elements.}*

Colonial Merchants and the American Revolution, chs. XI–XV. Hosmer, J. K., *Thomas Hutchinson*. Gipson, *Jared Ingersoll*. Batchelder, S. F., *Bits of Cambridge History*. Flick, A. C., *Loyalism in New York during the American Revolution*. Harrell, I. S., *Loyalism in Virginia*.

Loyalist writings. Hutchinson, T., *Diary* and *Letters*, I. Eddis, W., *Letters from America*. Whig-Tory debate in J. Adams and [D. Leonard], *Novanglus and Massachusettensis*. Summaries in Tyler, *Literary History of the American Revolution*.

Local conditions. Becker, *Political Parties in the Province of New York*. Eckenrode, H. J., *Revolution in Virginia*, chs. I–V. Lincoln, *Revolutionary Movement in Pennsylvania*, chs. XI–XIII. McCrady, *South Carolina, 1719–1776*, chs. XXXIX–XLI, and his *South Carolina in the Revolution*, chs. I–VIII. Sharpless, *Quaker Government*, II, ch. V.

Mass action in the Revolution. Longley, R. S., "Mobs in the Revolution," *N.E.Q.* (1933), VI, 98–130.

Constitutionality of the Whig position. McIlwain, C. H., *The American Revolution: A Constitutional Interpretation;* disputed by Schuyler, R. L., *Parliament and the British Empire*, chs. 1, 2.

Declaration of Independence. Sources and text. Merriam, C. E., *American Political Theories*, ch. II. Dunning, W. A., *Political Theory, Luther to Montesquieu*, ch. X (Locke). Mullett, *Fundamental Law*. Locke, J., *Two Treatises of Civil Government*. Jefferson, *Writings* (Ford edition), II, 42–58. *American History Leaflets*, no. 11. Fuller discussion in Hazelton, G. H., *Declaration of Independence*, and in Becker, C., *Declaration of Independence*. See also Smith, T. V., *American Philosophy of Equality*.

CHAPTER XX

THE OPPOSING FORCES

WHILE Congress was debating the subject of independence, the first installment of Howe's army was arriving in New York harbor, and on the day after the decisive vote was taken, British troops landed on Staten Island. The Whig section of the American people, speaking through their delegates in Congress assembled, had declared that "these united colonies are and of right ought to be free and independent states." Now the hard practical question was whether they could make that declaration good against Great Britain and their own conservative neighbors. *Making the Declaration good.*

To many a hard-headed American who had got along comfortably under British sovereignty, this attempt to break up the greatest empire of modern times seemed utterly reckless. The British advantage in population, perhaps about three to one if Ireland is left out of the account, was not so serious, considering the distance at which British operations had to be carried on. More important was the disparity in wealth. America was rich in unused and largely unknown natural resources; but it was still largely dependent on European capital, which so far had come almost entirely from England, and it was especially lacking in facilities for the manufacture of military supplies. England, on the contrary, though much smaller than France in population, was the strongest commercial nation in the world. *British advantages.*

For military campaigns carried on across three thousand miles of ocean and along a great stretch of coast line, naval power was vital, and here again the British position seemed *Naval and land forces.*

unusually strong. The Seven Years' War had shown the superiority of England's navy, even to a combination of her two most formidable rivals, France and Spain. In land forces England was as usual much weaker, but it was not unreasonable to suppose that even a small disciplined army, with officers and men like those who fought under Amherst and Wolfe in Canada, could defeat the inexperienced commanders and hastily improvised armies of the American rebels. Besides, British money could be used to pay for foreign soldiers, as it had been in the last war with France and was to be again in the Napoleonic Wars. The American loyalists could also be used; though disappointing in some respects, they probably furnished something like 50,000 soldiers to the British army, and they were active in other ways, open or secret, which were scarcely less dangerous to the American cause.

America poorly organized.

A most serious handicap on the American side was the lack of an adequate organization to use such resources as were available for the common cause. At the head of the revolutionary movement was the Continental Congress, a convention of party leaders suddenly called on to perform some of the most important and difficult functions of government; to maintain an army and a navy, to initiate diplomatic intercourse with foreign governments, and to find the money necessary for these expensive operations. The American leaders were like manufacturers trying to turn out finished products while the factory was still being built and the machinery still in process of installation. That was an enormous handicap which can hardly be overemphasized in trying to form a fair judgment of the revolutionary leaders. This disadvantage continued throughout the war, which was nearly over before the states could be persuaded to confer formally upon Congress even the limited authority allowed by the Articles of Confederation.

In certain great crises Congress acted vigorously as a

de facto government, in something like a national character, as may be seen in the extraordinary powers given to Washington in December, 1776, and in the French alliance of 1778; but generally the local politicians regarded Congress merely as a coöperative agency for thirteen sovereign states, with no claim on the direct allegiance of any citizen. In that spirit a New Jersey politician complained of Washington for trying to distinguish between friends and enemies by demanding an oath of allegiance to the United States. In this matter of organization, the seceding Americans of 1776 were very different from the southern secessionists of 1861. When the Civil War began, the South had a federal government with a definite constitution, a recognized legislature, a president with real power, and responsible heads of several executive departments. The leaders of the American Revolution had no such advantages at any time during the eight years between the outbreak at Lexington and the peace treaty of 1783.

The troubles of Congress were not due wholly to the grudging attitude of the states. Few of its members had ever held any important executive office, and there were important principles of governmental efficiency which they had to learn by slow and painful experience. They did not realize, for example, the advantage of concentrating responsibility. On the contrary, their colonial experience had developed extreme jealousy of one-man power. So Congress tried to handle an impossible amount of detail in general meeting. When they could not do that, they organized numerous committees for administrative as well as legislative work. It was not until June, 1776, after nearly a year of fighting, that Congress organized a War Office, in the charge of a board of which John Adams was chairman. Able men served on this committee, but most of them belonged also to many other committees, some of which were scarcely less important. The wonder is not that men so

The Continental Congress.

Congressional methods.

The War Office.

heavily loaded with unfamiliar duties should often have blundered, but rather that they accomplished as much as they did. In 1777 Congress appointed a new Board of War, with General Gates, then very popular on account of his victory at Saratoga, as one of its members; but this also proved disappointing. Not until 1781, when the war was nearly over, did Congress see the necessity of appointing a single executive head for this department. Other important departments were similarly managed by committees without sufficient power or responsibility, though they also were served by some able men. In finance the chief figure was Robert Morris, perhaps the ablest business man of his day. With great energy and public spirit, he gave to Congress at a critical time the advantage of his own prestige. When in 1781 Congress finally decided on a single head for this department, Morris was naturally chosen. Of those best qualified for handling foreign relations, several were naturally drafted for service abroad, — Franklin, in 1776, and later John Adams and John Jay. The first Secretary of State for Foreign Affairs, also appointed in 1781, was Robert R. Livingston of New York, better known now for his part, thirty years later, in the Louisiana purchase.

Committees on finance and foreign affairs.

The state governments.

Poor organization and inefficiency were conspicuous not only in the federal government but also in the states, most of which had to go through the process of transformation from revolutionary conventions and committees to orderly constitutional governments. Only Connecticut and Rhode Island, with their exceptionally liberal charters, could continue the old machinery without material change. Massachusetts tried to keep up some features of its charter government without a royal governor; but elsewhere new governments had to be built up almost from the ground. Virginia framed a permanent constitution in 1776, but other colonies were less fortunate; the Massachusetts constitution was not adopted until 1780. Meanwhile, the legal authority of these new organizations was disputed by the large part of the population which still professed allegiance to the King. Much of the ordinary business of government, including the administration of justice, was performed with great difficulty and sometimes suspended altogether.

The character of the new constitutions also made trouble. The same distrust of executive authority which weakened the federal government showed itself in the state governments also. So the early state constitutions weakened the executive and made it subordinate to the legislature. The Virginians, for example, had been accustomed to a strong royal governor, appointed for an indefinite term, with a veto on colonial laws and a liberal appointing power; but now they went to the opposite extreme. The governor became a mere creature of the legislature, chosen by it for one year only, with no right of veto and little authority of any sort. Pennsylvania preferred to have no governor at all and put the executive power in the hands of a council. As the war went on, some people realized that this weakening of the executive was dangerous; and under the leadership of John Adams, the Massachusetts constitution of 1780 made the governor more independent of the legislature. Quite aside from any mistakes in the constitutions, both state and federal governments suffered from that lessening of respect for constituted authority which naturally results from a great political upheaval. The lawless element did not object to this; but responsible leaders had unpleasant visions of the country drifting into a state of anarchy. No one suffered more from these conditions than the Continental army, and especially its great commander, who saw his followers exposed to unnecessary hardships, and their cause endangered, by weak administration.

New constitutions. Weak executives.

Nowhere was governmental weakness more apparent than in dealing with economic problems. War is a great financial enterprise, requiring not only brave and disciplined

Economic problems.

soldiers led by trained officers, but a large number of strictly business operations. Food, clothing, and munitions must be bought and distributed; means of transportation must be provided by land and water; officers and men must be regularly paid. Congress had to meet these needs with no effective means of raising money except loans or requisitions. The states, which alone possessed the taxing power, were afraid to use it vigorously, partly because such action was bound to be unpopular. Whatever justification there may have been for this policy, it is certain that the Americans of 1776 did not throw their economic resources into the struggle to any such extent as, for instance, the Southern Confederates of 1861, or the belligerent nations in the recent World War. As Washington said, the country lacked not so much resources as the means of drawing them out. Meantime, the army complained bitterly of the civilians who clung to their money when the soldiers were giving up their lives.

Paper money.

One way of keeping down taxes to which most of the colonies were accustomed before the Revolution, was the free use of paper money. This practice had been checked by the British government; but with this check removed, Congress and the state legislatures vied with each other in reckless issues of currency, which naturally sank lower and lower in value, until the Continental money was worth only

Loans.

a small fraction of its face value. The issue of paper currency was, of course, one way of borrowing money. Loans were also made in more businesslike ways from the French and Spanish governments and from private capitalists in those countries. One of John Adams's most important services was the securing of loans from the Dutch; in fact, the American envoys abroad were largely occupied with efforts of this kind, and sometimes the efforts of the United States to shift the burden from their own shoulders to those of foreign governments were embarrassing to their representatives.

The financial weakness of the government naturally showed itself in the management of the army. Because of it Congress could not long support more than a handful of real Continental troops, as distinguished from the state militia; and the state militia could not be counted on for steady service. Now and then, as at Saratoga, the militia helped to hem in an enemy force which had got too far from its base; but they were likely to weaken in a pitched battle or when anything began to go wrong. At certain critical moments Washington's main army had less than three thousand men, and in the decisive Yorktown campaign he had no more than six thousand Continental troops. Since the terms of enlistment were short, the army was constantly on the verge of disintegration. It was, of course, hard to recruit men for an army in which they could not count on getting their pay regularly, and officers resented the unnecessary hardships imposed on them and their families. Even when money was available, it was often ineffectively used. The terrible sufferings of the army at Valley Forge, in the winter of 1777–1778, were due partly to difficulties of transportation and the preference of some Pennsylvania farmers for British gold over Continental paper; but bad management in the offices of the quartermaster-general and commissary-general was also largely to blame. In 1778 General Greene was persuaded to serve as quartermaster-general and did excellent work; but in 1780, when Congress tried the plan of getting the states to furnish specific supplies instead of money, there was another period of unsatisfactory administration, for which the soldiers had to suffer. Naturally the morale of the army was lowered and there were some serious mutinies.

Problems of the kind described were particularly trying when so many of the officers were comparatively inexpert. The first four major generals under Washington were mediocre or worse, and one of them, Charles Lee, was quite

Management of the army.

Inexperience of American officers.

erratic and untrustworthy. Of the men who came to the front later a few had real military ability. Conspicuous among them was Benedict Arnold, who showed great daring and initiative in the naval campaigns on Lake Champlain in 1776; Daniel Morgan of Virginia, an effective leader of the frontiersmen; and finally Nathanael Greene, the ablest of them all. With no military experience before the war, Greene soon won Washington's confidence, and in the southern campaigns of 1781 fairly earned a place second only to his commander in chief among the soldiers of the Revolution.

Foreign officers.

Besides the American officers, there were many Europeans who were willing to practice their profession in America for what they considered proper rewards in rank and pay. Comparatively few, however, were really useful; even the best of them were hampered by imperfect knowledge of English and the common prejudice against outsiders. Of the foreigners who gave valuable expert service, the first place undoubtedly belongs to the German, Steuben, who as inspector-general gave America the benefit of his experience in the army of Frederick the Great. With him should be mentioned Kalb, a German officer in French employ. Among those who combined professional skill with real enthusiasm for the American cause were two Poles, Kosciusko and Pulaski, representatives of a nation whose independence was already threatened by unscrupulous neighbors. Both were good soldiers and Kosciusko did effective work as an

Lafayette.

engineer. Quite unique among the foreign officers was the Marquis de Lafayette. Coming to America as a young man just under twenty, he was presently given a commission as major general, for which he certainly was not qualified at that time. He did some good work later; but his chief claim to the gratitude of the American people was his steady loyalty to their cause and the influence of his personality in establishing a lasting bond of sympathy between his own country and the struggling young republic.

As commander in chief Washington was much harassed by political interference with military appointments. Individual states tried to push the promotion of local favorites. At the beginning, the South complained that New England had too many of the higher commissions and there was similar feeling in the Middle States. Some New England leaders were very critical of Washington and inclined to push Gates at his expense. Even in Washington's own state, Richard Henry Lee sympathized with the malcontents.

Politics and the army.

Sea power played an important part in the winning of independence, but the direct contributions of the American navy were of minor importance. There was never any considerable American fleet and the fighting marine consisted largely of privateers, who devoted themselves mainly to commerce destroying. The profits were so attractive, both to officers and men, that they interfered at times with recruiting for the army and the regular navy. First and last, much damage was done to British trade, and there were some brilliant exploits, notably those of Paul Jones, best remembered for the naval duel between his ship, the *Bonhomme Richard*, and the British frigate *Serapis*. With a worn-out French ship and a heterogeneous crew, of whom scarcely more than a third were Americans, Jones won his victory by fine seamanship combined with almost reckless courage. Incidents like these deserve to be remembered; but the navy which counted most heavily in the fight against British sea power was that of France.

Beginnings of the American navy.

In spite of all these evidences of weakness on the American side, the great fact which has to be accounted for is that, after all, independence was won. What, then, were the forces that made victory possible? Clearly one of these factors was the personal contribution of certain great leaders. Washington doubtless made many mistakes between his defeat on Long Island and the final victory at Yorktown; but he held Americans together under conditions which

American assets. Great leaders. Washington.

would have discouraged a mere military expert. He did
not win many battles; but, like William of Orange in
the wars against Louis XIV, he could save the day even
after some apparently irretrievable disaster. John Adams

Civilian
leaders.

had his foibles, — his vanity, his jealousy of colleagues who
seemed to have more than their share of recognition, and
his amateur notions of war, — all these were a part of the
man; but they were the least important part. It is much
more worth while to remember his administrative service
in the Continental Congress, under most discouraging conditions, and his solid work for America in France and Holland.
Surely, too, there were few statesmen in any country at
that time who could compare in diplomatic skill and solid
good sense with Benjamin Franklin. There were followers,
too, who should not be forgotten. If then, as always, there
were profiteers and slackers, there were also the loyal officers
and men who stood by Washington through the discouraging
autumn of 1776 and the even more tragic winter at Valley
Forge.

Geographic
factors.

With these great human assets, America had also certain
great natural advantages. Even for a first-class naval power
like Great Britain, the conduct of military operations on a
distant continent was a serious matter, so serious that some
of the King's advisers thought it almost hopeless. Until the
American army could be finally disposed of, the holding of
more than a few points on the seaboard would require a
much larger army than the British government could send.
Therefore the expeditionary forces were largely dependent
on supplies from England. Though the little American navy
played a minor part in the strategy of the war, it could now
and then cut off British supplies. Distance also complicated the planning of military operations to an extent that
can hardly be appreciated in these days of cable and wireless
communication. Plans made in London, on the basis of
advice from returned officers or dispatches from generals

in the field, were several months old before they could be effectively acted upon. In 1777 the three men most directly responsible for the Saratoga campaign were Lord Germain in England, General Burgoyne, who led the invading army through the wildernesses between Montreal and Albany, and General Howe at New York, who was planning his attack on Philadelphia. The failure of these men to act effectively together was due partly to personal reasons, but partly also to the distances which separated them.

Finally, it must be remembered that the war was won almost as truly in Europe as in America. Even during the first three years, when the colonies were nominally fighting alone, the British government was handicapped by the unfriendly attitude of the continental powers, — France, Spain, Holland, and even Prussia, England's recent ally. They were all nominally neutral at first; but neutrality was often strained to the breaking point in the interest of the American rebels. Both France and Spain gave substantial assistance through individuals, acting with the connivance and often the secret coöperation of their governments. European factors. English isolation.

England also had difficulties nearer home, particularly in Ireland. Some Irishmen served in the British army, but of the recent Irish emigrants to America a considerable number entered the American service. Franklin, who visited Ireland shortly before his return home in 1775, found a good deal of sympathy for the American cause, and suggested that Irishmen and Americans might combine to secure "more equitable treatment," "for them as well as for us." Interest in the American cause was especially noted among the Scotch-Irish Presbyterians of Ulster, so many of whose neighbors had already crossed the Atlantic. Disturbance of trade resulting from the war increased Irish discontent, and after France came in, in 1778, the armed Volunteers used their organization to secure concessions from the British government, including the removal of old Ireland.

restrictions on the legislative freedom of the Irish parliament.

The attitude of Englishmen toward the war cannot be stated in a few simple generalizations. This is partly because Parliament did not fairly reflect public opinion. The various districts were allotted representation with little reference to population, and in many boroughs the handful of voters could easily be managed by local magnates or by court politicians who could distribute offices, pensions, and secret-service money. This was an old game which the Whig politicians had played with great success; but now the King was using the same methods to promote his policies. The King also got fairly steady support from the Scotch members, who had been chosen under a system even more unrepresentative than that of England. The country gentry who came up from the comparatively honest county constituencies also at first generally supported the government. Even the merchants, though reluctant to disturb friendly and profitable business relations with the colonies, were offended by such disregard of property rights as that shown in the Boston Tea Party and were encouraged for a time by a new development of trade nearer home. In almost every class, there were honest and otherwise intelligent men, like Samuel Johnson, whose fighting spirit was stirred by deliberate defiance of King and Parliament. Johnson's tract against the colonies entitled *Taxation No Tyranny* was done over for popular consumption by no less a person than John Wesley, the great leader of the Methodist movement. For a time, therefore, English support of the war was fairly general.

Throughout the war, however, there was a considerable element which strongly condemned the whole policy. This discontent was perhaps most general among the middle classes, and in the manufacturing centers the loss of American trade was soon keenly felt. There were mutterings even in the army and navy. Admiral Keppel, one of the great naval commanders of the time, refused to take service "in the line of America" and General Conway declared that there were limits to the principle of military obedience in a civil war. Apparently neither of these men lost much popularity by statements which would ordinarily be regarded as flagrantly disloyal. Several prominent newspapers in London and elsewhere opposed the government's American policy, and though they were often extremely violent the government rarely ventured to interfere with them.

The opposition in Parliament was at first ineffective. Lord Rockingham, the leader of the "Old Whigs," was an honorable man but he lacked energy, and Burke, though a great political thinker, was not then an important party leader. Pitt made impressive speeches in the House of Lords, expressing his sympathy with American complaints; but he was opposed to American independence and did not get on well with the Rockingham Whigs. Before long, however, the opponents of Lord North found a most effective leader in Charles James Fox. This young man entered Parliament at about the age of an American college sophomore and made his mark before he was twenty-seven. In spite of this precocious political activity he was not a model youth. He had already wasted a great deal of money in gambling, and his political ideals did not, at first, seem more promising than his private conduct. Yet he was a man of generous spirit and soon developed a keen interest not only in the political game but in real public service. During the latter years of the war, Fox's vigorous and picturesque personality was the rallying point of the steadily growing opposition.

The opposition in Parliament.

Fox.

Nevertheless, Lord North, the Bedford faction, and the "King's Friends" had so strong a hold on the political machine that the parliamentary opposition would have been comparatively helpless if the government had really managed the war efficiently. That, however, they could not do,

Weakness of the government. George III and Lord North.

largely because they had filled the important government offices with a view to winning the support of this or that group of politicians, rather than securing high-class service. For this, as well as for the war policy itself, the King was partly responsible. A hard worker with an intelligent personal interest in military matters, George III was too much involved in "machine politics." Perhaps his greatest offense was his refusal in certain great crises to call in the most competent men, without regard to factional or personal differences. Lord North was in some respects a capable leader and in his personal views on American questions was more liberal than some of his associates. On one occasion, at least, he was ready to resign in order to escape responsibility for measures which he could not approve. He was not, however, strong enough either to control the government or to break away from it.

Departmental inefficiency. Germain and Sandwich. Nowhere was the ministry weaker than in the departments directly responsible for the conduct of the war. The secretary of state for the colonies, who directed the army in America, was Lord George Germain, a thoroughly unfortunate choice. During the Seven Years' War, he had been cashiered for disobedience to orders on the field of battle, a fact which certainly embarrassed his relations with officers who had to serve under his direction in America. He lacked also the executive ability and understanding of "grand strategy" which made Pitt a great war minister. In naval administration, the falling off since Pitt's time was even worse. At the head of the administration was Lord Sandwich, a disreputable character, under whose administration the Admiralty reached perhaps its lowest level of corruption.

The fighting services. The demoralizing influence of corrupt and factional politics at headquarters made itself felt in the fighting personnel. Admirals complained of being sent to sea in ships that were unprepared, and there was some serious friction between officers who belonged to different political factions.

When France came into the war and the danger to the British Empire became more serious, the British navy pulled itself together and, after missing one great opportunity in 1781, established once more its superiority on the sea. With the army in America it was different. The two commanders in chief, Howe and Clinton, were both second-rate men. Howe had some tactical skill; but he was dilatory and failed to get out of a victory the results which might reasonably have been expected. Though allowances must be made for earlier failures which made Clinton's work more difficult, he also was certainly not a military genius.

It is, of course, impossible to say how far the outcome of the war was determined by any particular group of influences. There can be no doubt, however, that the American cause was powerfully aided by the internal troubles of the mother country as well as by the peculiar condition of international politics which enabled the colonies to secure support from England's enemies in continental Europe. *Importance of European factors.*

BIBLIOGRAPHICAL NOTES

Channing, *United States*, III, 210–225, 388–408. Van Tyne, C. H., *War of Independence, American Phase.* Fisher, S. G., *Struggle for American Independence*, I, chs. XXXI, XLII. Trevelyan, G. O., *American Revolution*, II, ch. XVII; III, chs. XXIV–XXVI; IV, ch. XXVIII. Strongly British view in Belcher, J., *First American Civil War*, I, chs. VII, VIII; II, chs. IX, X. Collected sources in Hart, *Contemporaries*, II, pts. VII, VIII. *General references.*

Winsor, *America*, VII, ch. I. Trevelyan as above, and his *George III and Charles Fox.* Hertz, G. B., *Old Colonial System*, chs. V–IX. Clark, D. M., *British Opinion and the American Revolution.* Hinkhouse, F. J., *Preliminaries of the American Revolution as Seen in the English Press.* (See also references in ch. XXI.) *European conditions: English opposition.*

Guttridge, G. H., "Lord George Germain in Office," *A.H.R.* (1927), XXXIII, 23–43. *British departmental inefficiency.*

Civilian management.

Oberholtzer, E. P., *Robert Morris*, chs. I, II. Sumner, W. G., *Financier and Finances of the Revolution*, I and II, especially chs. XXIII, XXIV; also his *Hamilton*, chs. IV–VII. Dewey, D. R., *Financial History of the U. S.* Bullock, C. J., *Finances from 1775 to 1789.* Harlow, R. V., "Aspects of Revolutionary Finance, 1775–1783," *A.H.R.* (1929), XXXV, 46–68. Van Tyne, C. H., *American Revolution*, chs. IX, XI, XIV. Eckenrode, H. J., *Revolution in Virginia*, chs. VII–XI. (See also references in ch. XXV.) Flügel and Faulkner, *Readings in Economic and Social Hist. of U. S.*, 9–22.

Sources.

Burnett, *Letters of Members of the Continental Congress*, I, II. Continental Congress, *Journals* (Library of Congress edition; may be sampled for illustrations of business). Adams, J., *Autobiography* in *Works*, III, 59–93; and *Familiar Letters* of John and Abigail Adams. *Warren-Adams Letters* (Mass. Hist. Soc.).

Loyalists and pacifists.

Van Tyne, *Loyalists*, chs. VI–XII. Sharpless, *Quaker Government*, II, chs. VI–VIII. Harrell, I. S., *Loyalism in Virginia*.

Geographic and economic conditions.

Callender, *Selections from the Economic History of the U. S.*, 159–168. Weeden, *New England*, II, chs. XX, XXI. Semple, E. C., *American History and Its Geographic Conditions*, ch. IV.

The army.

Hatch, L. C., *Administration of the American Revolutionary Army*. Bolton, C. K., *Private Soldier under Washington*. Thacher, J., *Military Journal*. Beveridge, A. J., *John Marshall*, I, chs. III–IV (army conditions). See also chapters in Belcher, Fisher, and Trevelyan and for the British army, Fortescue, J. W., *History of the British Army*, III, and Curtis, E. E., *Organization of the British Army in American Revolution*.

Washington.

Ford, P. L., *The True George Washington*, chs. IX–XI. Read as many as possible of his letters in *Writings* (Fitzpatrick edition; also short collections by C. B. Evans and J. Viles), and biographies by L. M. Sears, J. C. Fitzpatrick, and R. Hughes (vol. III).

Naval warfare.

Clowes, W. L., *History of the Royal Navy*, III, ch. XXXI (Mahan). Fuller narrative in Allen, G. W., *Naval History of the American Revolution;* James, W. M., *The British Navy in Adversity*.

Early state governments.

Nevins, A., *American States during and after the Revolution*. (See also references in ch. XXV).

CHAPTER XXI

EUROPE AND AMERICA, 1776 TO 1780

CONSIDERING the immense political importance of the American Revolution, the military operations of the war were on a surprisingly small scale. During a considerable part of the war, Washington's main army hardly reached the size of a modern brigade, and in the march to Yorktown in 1781 he took with him only about two thousand American regulars, or roughly the equivalent of a present-day regiment. Compared with the European and American armies of the World War, the forces on both sides seem infinitesimal. *Operations on a small scale.*

Up to the end of June, 1776, the military results were fairly satisfactory from the American point of view. The expedition against Canada had failed, but the British had withdrawn from Boston and their attack on the Carolinas had broken down. For the moment no territory in any of the thirteen colonies was held by the British, though their navy enabled them to control New York harbor and keep in touch with the strong loyalist element in that state. Now, however, the Americans had to face two invading armies, striking at opposite ends of the Hudson-Champlain waterway and threatening to isolate New England from the southern colonies. One of these expeditions, commanded by Sir Guy Carleton, the efficient governor of Quebec, gradually pushed the Americans back from Canadian territory and organized a naval force for the control of Lake Champlain. Fortunately the Americans had in Benedict Arnold a resourceful leader who knew something about ships. *The military situation in 1776.*

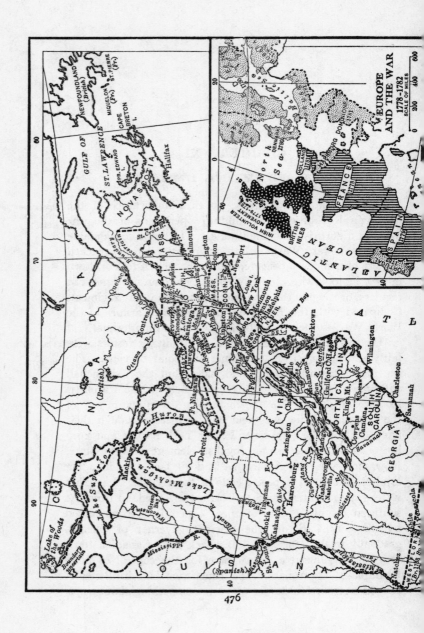

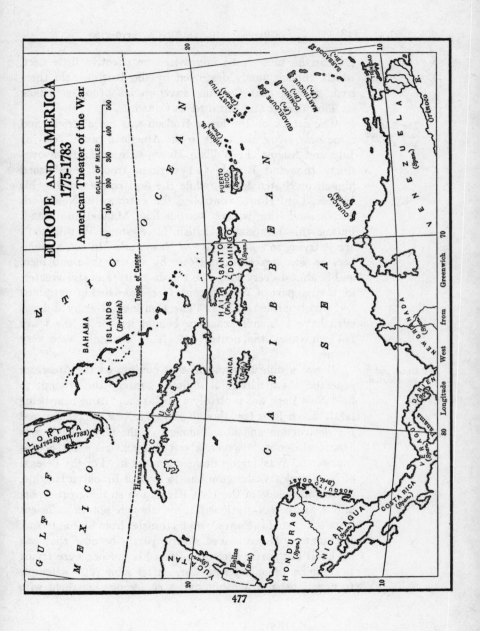

EUROPE AND AMERICA
1775-1783
American Theater of the War

SCALE OF MILES

0   100   200   300   400   500

NORTH ATLANTIC OCEAN

GULF OF MEXICO

FLORIDA
Brit. 1763 Span. 1783

BAHAMA ISLANDS (British)

Tropic of Cancer

Havana

CUBA (Span.)

JAMAICA (Brit.)

YUCATAN (Span.)

Belize (Brit.)

HONDURAS (Span.)

MOSQUITO COAST (Brit.)

NICARAGUA (Span.)

COSTA RICA (Span.)

VERAGUA (Span.)

DARIEN (Span.)

HAITI (Fr.)

SANTO DOMINGO (Span.)

PUERTO RICO

VIRGIN Is. (Dan.)

CURAÇAO (Dutch)

NEW GRENADA (Span.)

VENEZUELA (Span.)

Orinoco R.

TRINIDAD

BARBADOS (Br.)

MARTINIQUE (Fr.)

DOMINICA (Br.)

GUADELOUPE (Fr.)

ST. EUSTATIUS (Dutch)

CARIBBEAN SEA

Longitude West from Greenwich

80   70

20

10

80

10

During the summer he improvised an effective little fleet, which, though finally destroyed by the British, held them back so long that Carleton gave up his proposed attack on Ticonderoga and returned to Canada.

The British in New York harbor.

The attack on the lower Hudson was more serious and came near being disastrous to the American cause. During July and August Sir William Howe, with an army of over thirty thousand British and German troops, established himself on Staten Island, while the fleet commanded by his brother, Lord Howe, controlled the entrance to New York harbor and the waters surrounding Manhattan Island. Facing this formidable British force stood Washington's army, trying to hold the city of New York. In actual numbers he was weaker than Howe by several thousand men, and in almost everything else the disparity was still greater; for a large part of Washington's force consisted of untrained and poorly armed militia. The Continental army did not even have a friendly country behind it; for in the lower Hudson valley the neutral and Tory elements were very strong.

Howe and Washington.

It was a difficult problem that confronted the American generals. As a matter of military strategy the attempt to hold New York was probably a mistake and came near being fatal. Even John Jay, though himself a New Yorker, favored the destruction and abandonment of the city. There was a natural doubt, however, about the political effect of this course, and Washington decided against it. For the defense of New York, Washington had to control Brooklyn Heights, on the other side of the East River, and so the greater part of his army was stationed there, though not in sufficient force to resist Howe's army on its transfer from Staten Island. Fortunately, Howe moved slowly, partly because that was his habit but partly because he and his brother were trying to combine diplomacy with war. After some futile attempts to negotiate with Washington, a conference was held with some of the leaders of the Continental Congress; but it came to nothing. Meanwhile General Howe proceeded with his military plan.

Almost two months after the first landing on Staten Island, the British crossed the bay to Long Island, and on August 27 fought the battle of Brooklyn Heights. The American army was defeated, lost many of its best troops, and probably could have been almost destroyed if Howe had followed up his advantage quickly. The delay gave Washington his chance and on the night of August 29 he ferried his troops across to New York. In September Howe also landed on Manhattan, but again missed an opportunity to destroy the American army, which gradually fell back to White Plains, and finally crossed the Hudson into New Jersey. Battle of Long Island; evacuation of New York.

Washington had saved his main army, but his fighting strength had fallen very low. Before long he had to leave northern New Jersey to the enemy and take refuge across the Delaware in Pennsylvania. The New Jersey Tories received the British with open arms, garrisons were posted across the state, and as winter came on the American cause seemed almost hopeless. Once more, however, Howe's lack of energy saved the day and Washington took full advantage of it. Washington's retreat.

By December, 1776, Howe had withdrawn most of his army to comfortable winter quarters at New York. One of his chief lieutenants, Lord Cornwallis, was ready to take a furlough in England, and the few thousand men left in New Jersey, chiefly Germans, were widely scattered, the outposts on the Delaware being dangerously far from their base at New York. The depredations of the German troops had also weakened the loyalist feeling in the neighborhood, and though the Hessian commander at Trenton had been warned, he failed to take proper precautions. It was a great opportunity for Washington; but he had to act quickly, for most of his soldiers had enlisted for short terms and were Trenton and Princeton.

likely to leave him in a few days. So, crossing the Delaware and catching the enemy off his guard, Washington struck hard at the Trenton garrison and broke it up, taking many prisoners. This unceremonious interference with Howe's plans for a quiet winter forced Cornwallis to give up his proposed holiday and take the field against the rebels. His forces were superior to those of his enemy; but Washington, avoiding a general engagement, managed to defeat a detached portion of the British army at Princeton. Howe thereupon drew in his garrisons to the vicinity of New York, leaving the Tories to the vengeance of their Whig neighbors. Coming after a period of great discouragement, the victories of Trenton and Princeton gave the army new confidence in itself and in its commander.

The new year.

At the beginning of the new year the British held, in addition to the city of New York and its environs, the town of Newport, which had been taken a few weeks before. The control of these two harbors was an important advantage, secured largely through the coöperation of the navy; but in view of the great superiority of Howe's army, the results of his campaign seem hardly sufficient to justify the Order of the Bath conferred on him in recognition of his "abilities and activity."

British strategy.

In working out the British strategy for 1777, four men were principally concerned: Lord George Germain, in London; Howe, at New York; Carleton, at Quebec; and General Sir John Burgoyne, who, after serving under Howe at Boston, had gone home to offer advice and criticism to his superiors there. Howe was then planning an extensive campaign, aimed primarily at Philadelphia, the seat of the "rebel" government. This plan was approved in general; but the government could give him only a small part of the 15,000 troops which he considered necessary for his purpose. Meantime, the way seemed open for another advance from the north against the American positions on the upper

Hudson, and for reënforcing Howe's army with some of the British troops then stationed in Canada. So a northern army of invasion was formed, of which Burgoyne was made commander. Unfortunately for Burgoyne, especially, there was no proper coördination of his enterprise with that of Howe; the result was a humiliating defeat in one case, and, in the other, apparent success which had little strategic value.

For some months Washington was in doubt as to Howe's plans; but at last the British transports entered Chesapeake Bay, having taken that route to avoid the American defenses on the Delaware. From the head of the bay, Howe's army moved northward overland toward Philadelphia, while the navy, after convoying the troopships, began clearing obstructions in the Delaware River. Thereupon, in September, 1777, Washington's army moved southward to block Howe's advance. With a force decidedly inferior to Howe's, especially in discipline, Washington engaged the enemy at Chads Ford on the Brandywine, but had to fall back with heavy losses. About three weeks later the British entered Philadelphia. Whatever may be said about Washington's strategy in this campaign, he had improved the fighting spirit of his army and he now made a determined attack on a British detachment at Germantown, only to suffer another defeat. Weakened by these reverses, Washington could not support the garrisons on the Delaware and by the end of the year the British navy had complete control of that river and the bay.

Howe's Philadelphia campaign.

Chads Ford and Germantown.

In a superficial sense, Howe's capture of the rebel capital was a great stroke and the loyalists of the neighborhood were in high spirits. Local business men enjoyed a profitable trade with the British army and Howe settled down for another comfortable winter. It is doubtful, however, whether the British gained any solid advantage by this campaign. Once more Howe contented himself with merely defeating

Howe at Philadelphia.

his enemy when he might have crushed him. It was a question whether Howe had taken Philadelphia or, as Franklin said, Philadelphia had taken Howe. The army which before had been concentrated at New York was now divided; and, with the American army still in the field, land communication between these divided forces was at best difficult and might become almost impossible.

Burgoyne's expedition.

Meantime, Burgoyne's invasion had ended in absolute disaster. The general plan of the northern expedition was apparently to strengthen Howe's army by bringing to its support some of the best English and German troops in Carleton's contingent, now reasonably secure against an American attack. Unfortunately for Burgoyne, the instructions given by Lord Germain left Howe free to follow out his original plan of attacking Philadelphia and so prevented any effective coöperation between the two commanders.

St. Leger in the Mohawk valley.

It was also expected that Burgoyne's southward expedition would be supported by a secondary movement from the Mohawk valley under the command of Colonel St. Leger, who was expected to rally the loyalists and their friends among the Iroquois. Sir William Johnson, the famous Indian superintendent, was dead, but his son and nephew inherited some of his prestige with the Indians. In the early months of the war, the Johnsons, with many other Tories, had been driven from their homes by a combination of the German frontiersmen with the Albany Whigs under General Philip Schuyler. Now these loyalist exiles were organized in military companies, with whose help and that of the Indians St. Leger was expected to crush the Mohawk valley Whigs, and then join Burgoyne at Albany. The plan seemed promising; but it was held up by the stubborn resistance of the American garrison at Fort Stanwix, or Fort Schuyler, which controlled the portage between Lake Ontario and the Mohawk. The Mohawk valley Germans now came to the rescue, under the command of General

Herkimer. At Oriskany the Americans were caught in an Oriskany. ambush in which Herkimer was fatally wounded; but they were finally victorious. The Indians soon deserted their British allies; by the end of August, St. Leger had to give up the siege of Fort Schuyler and return to Canada.

Burgoyne's main expedition began fairly well. The Burgoyne's campaign of 1776 had left the British in control of the Lake army on the upper Champlain waterway as far as the neighborhood of Ticonder- Hudson. oga, and the Americans soon gave up that post also. From this point on, however, Burgoyne's troubles became serious. First came a slow march through the wilderness to Fort Edward on the Hudson, — with an excessive pro- portion of noncombatants, including women and children, and much superfluous baggage. Fort Edward was reached by the end of July but Burgoyne was now uncomfortably far from his base and he had been obliged to weaken his effective force by detaching part of it to secure his com- munications. The army now had to get what supplies it could from the surrounding country; but a detachment of Germans sent into Vermont for this purpose was over- whelmed at Bennington by the New England militia under Bennington. Captain John Stark and lost several hundred men, a serious matter for an army already too small for the work in hand. Further advance into the enemy's country was evidently dangerous; but Burgoyne felt bound by his instructions and pushed on along the western bank of the Hudson.

Meantime, the American forces had occupied a good American position at Bemis Heights, commanding the river road toward forces under Gates. Albany. Here and in the adjacent country there were already twenty thousand fighting men, some of them regu- lars, but a much larger number militia and other more or less temporary recruits, drawn chiefly from New England. The command of such an army was not easy, and General Schuyler, who had been in charge, did not get on well with the New Englanders. Through their influence in Congress,

Schuyler was superseded by Horatio Gates, whose experience in the British army had given him a certain prestige. The position which Gates held was naturally strong and was scientifically fortified by Kosciusko, the Polish volunteer.

Burgoyne's surrender at Saratoga.

On September 19, the British moved forward again and a sharp engagement followed, which is known sometimes as the battle of Stillwater and sometimes as the first battle of Freeman's Farm. Though not a clean-cut victory for either side, it had serious consequences for Burgoyne. His advance was stopped and he lost another large fraction of his effective force. His one hope was a strong coöperating expedition from New York; but no such expedition was undertaken until two weeks after the battle of Stillwater, and then it did not get beyond Kingston, fifty miles south of Albany. Meantime, Burgoyne made another attempt to break through, but was repulsed with heavy losses in the second battle of Freeman's Farm. He could not go forward, and, with the enemy closing in on all sides, it was soon too late to retreat. On October 17, 1777, the northern invasion came to a disastrous end with the surrender of Burgoyne's army at Saratoga.

Valley Forge.

Important as this victory was for the American cause, the next few months were in many respects discouraging. Just before Christmas, Washington's army went into winter quarters at Valley Forge. The record of that winter will always stand as one of the most painful in American history, not only because of the terrible hardships suffered by the army but even more so because those hardships were unnecessary. There was, said Washington, "an eternal round of the most stupid management," by which "the public treasure is expended to no kind of purpose, while the men have been left to perish by inches with cold and nakedness." The American camp was surrounded by a rich countryside; but even men who were not loyalists sold their produce for Howe's hard money rather than take the almost worthless paper of the Continental Congress.

The man who bore the brunt of these troubles could not even count on the hearty support of those he served. Congress and the army itself were divided into hostile factions and many believed that Washington was not equal to his great task. Gates, who after his victory at Saratoga was transferred to the newly organized Board of War, became the nucleus of a discontented faction among the officers. Conspicuous among these malcontents was Thomas Conway, an Irish officer who had been a colonel in the French service and was now anxious for a high command in the American army. This faction gained a point when Conway was made inspector-general of the army; but public opinion on the whole supported Washington and in the spring of 1778 the "Conway cabal" collapsed. *Intrigues against Washington.*

To the men who suffered at Valley Forge and to their friends, the prospect must have seemed dark indeed. Fortunately, however, events were then taking place in Europe which changed the whole character of the war and made the ultimate victory of the American cause almost inevitable. The British government was willing to offer new concessions in the hope of securing peace without the final disruption of the empire; but the time for compromises of this kind had long passed. Much more important were the developments in France and in Spain. For more than two years, these two great continental powers had followed with keen interest the widening breach between the two divisions of the English-speaking people. The French government had helped the United States so far as it could without getting into a direct conflict with England. In Spain there were divided counsels and some misgivings about encouraging rebel colonies who might become dangerous rivals on the Gulf coast and in the Mississippi valley; but in general the Spaniards followed the French policy of furnishing money *European developments.*

The attitude of France and Spain, 1775–1777.

and supplies to the Americans. Until the autumn of 1777, this cautious policy seemed to work fairly well from the standpoint of the Bourbon governments. It was weakening the British on both sides of the Atlantic, and accomplishing this result without involving either France or Spain in the heavy cost of another world war. Now, however, the news of Burgoyne's surrender at Saratoga forced the diplomatists of Paris and Madrid to reconsider the whole problem in the light of this new fact.

Conditions in France.

It was a complicated diplomatic game in which the young republic was just beginning to take a hand. The center of interest was the French government, whose nominal head since 1774 was Louis XVI. This well-meaning but mediocre gentleman inherited the autocratic traditions of his great ancestor, Louis XIV; but the real strength of the French monarchy had been seriously impaired. The civil government was corrupt and its finances were badly demoralized by reckless extravagance at court and a vicious revenue system. The national wealth was also diminished by antiquated restrictions on industry and commerce. Altogether the times were "out of joint" and Louis XVI was clearly not the man to set them right, though he had some able advisers, like the great economist, Turgot, who attempted thorough-going reforms in finance, commerce, and industry, only to be driven from office through the influence of those who profited by the old abuses.

Vergennes.

Of the French ministers during this period, the most significant for American history was Charles, Count of Vergennes, the minister for foreign affairs. Vergennes was an experienced diplomat, thoroughly imbued with the traditions of French foreign policy and determined to reëstablish French leadership in European politics. To him the American revolt was interesting chiefly because it weakened England, thus readjusting the balance of power and improving the relative position of France. From this point of view,

Vergennes wished to encourage the Americans and help them as much as possible without involving France prematurely in war. On this point, however, there were sharp differences of opinion at the court. Among liberal Frenchmen there was some real sympathy for the American cause, but this sentiment did not at first have much effect on the government. Others, including the King himself, disliked the idea of aiding rebels against a legitimate sovereign, and conservative financiers wished to avoid policies which might lead to an expensive war. In the end, however, Vergennes carried his point. With the coöperation of Beaumarchais, a versatile playwright and politician, substantial help was given to the Americans through various agencies, including a commercial company, promoted by Beaumarchais, which shipped large quantities of munitions and other supplies to the American rebels. *The policy of secret aid.*

Under ordinary conditions such a policy could not long be followed by a nominally neutral government without bringing it into the war. For the present, however, England preferred to avoid a complete break, and Lord Stormont, the British ambassador in Paris, limited himself to protests against unneutral acts. Vergennes also kept up the outward forms of neutrality, avoiding, for instance, any official recognition of the American union or its representatives in Paris. Before throwing off the mask and entering the war directly, he needed certain assurances, including a reasonable probability that the Americans would see the war through to the point of absolute independence. Another very desirable, if not essential, condition was the coöperation of Spain. *A waiting policy.*

So far as secret support of the rebels was concerned, Spanish and French policies were similar; but the problem of the Madrid government was more complicated. For Vergennes, intervention was primarily a question of European politics and the balance of power. Having little interest in the revival of French colonial power in America, the devel- *French and Spanish points of view.*

opment of a new nation across the Atlantic meant for him chiefly a check upon the British Empire. For Spain, colonial issues were more important, and she was anxious about the expansion of British naval and military forces which might endanger her own colonies. The Spanish government was also annoyed because England seemed to be supporting Portugal in a South American boundary dispute. If war developed out of these issues, Florida might be recovered from Great Britain, and perhaps even Cromwell's old conquest of Jamaica. Of course Spain also had important European interests at stake. There was always the hope of getting the British out of Gibraltar, and weakening their hold on the Mediterranean. Possibly Portugal might again be brought under Spanish control. Attractive as these prospects were, the Spanish government was not sure that they were sufficiently so to justify another serious war. It seemed quite possible, indeed, that England might give up something to her old rival as the price of Spanish neutrality. In spite of these doubts, the early autumn of 1776 found both the Bourbon governments on the verge of war. The Declaration of Independence seemed to prove that the British colonies could no longer be satisfied within the empire, and Count Aranda, the Spanish ambassador at Paris, joined Vergennes in support of the war policy. Presently, however, came the news of Washington's defeat on Long Island and his retreat before Howe's advancing army. Vergennes therefore decided to wait.

Franklin in France.

Under these somewhat discouraging circumstances Benjamin Franklin began his long and distinguished service as the American envoy at Paris. He was then seventy years old, and there was something heroic in his willingness to take not only the ordinary risks of an ocean voyage, but also the chance of falling into the hands of the enemy. Technically, Franklin was one of three commissioners chosen by Congress to negotiate with France and other friendly powers;

but his associates, Silas Deane and Arthur Lee, were not very helpful to him. Unlike either of those men, Franklin brought to his work an established reputation and an extraordinarily attractive personality. He liked the French people and they were enthusiastic about him. He had enough worldly wisdom to appreciate the importance of social conventions and yet enough independence about his own speech and conduct to give him a kind of picturesque interest as the representative of a younger and simpler society. Settling down at Passy, in the suburbs of Paris, he soon led an active social life, dining out "six days in seven" and "being treated with all the politeness of France and the apparent respect and esteem of all ranks from the highest to the lowest." At a time when even the aristocracy was beginning to feel the influence of liberal, not to say revolutionary, ideas, Franklin's personality established a new contact between the liberalism of the Old World and that of the New.

Much of Franklin's energy went into a kind of propaganda which contrasted the sins of the British with the virtues of his own countrymen. British credit, he said, was crumbling; but the Americans were frugal, honest people who could be trusted to pay their debts. Of course one great object of this propaganda was to secure loans, but it was also important to secure definite recognition from the French government. Such recognition Vergennes was not yet ready to give, but in an interview with the American commissioners soon after Franklin's arrival the French minister was as sympathetic as could reasonably be expected. Franklin also had some difficult negotiations with the Spanish ambassador, Count Aranda. The Americans were willing to help Spain recover Florida and even to coöperate in an attack on the British West Indies; but there was one issue on which the two nations could not agree. That was the free navigation of the Mississippi, a matter of special importance to those Americans who, like Franklin, were deeply

Propaganda for funds and recognition.

Spain and the United States.

interested in the settlement of the West. By urging this point, the United States was virtually announcing a policy of expansion which was almost certain to conflict with the colonial ambitions of Spain on the Gulf coast and in the Mississippi valley.

Influence of Burgoyne's surrender.

So matters stood until, in the last weeks of 1777, the news of Burgoyne's surrender convinced Vergennes that "watchful waiting" was no longer sufficient. The Americans seemed to have at least a good chance of winning their independence. Now or never was the time for France and Spain to strike the decisive blow which should break up the British Empire and secure the gratitude of the American people. "We must now," Vergennes argued, "either support the colonies or abandon them." If the alliance were not formed before England offered independence, France and Spain would lose the benefit to be derived from America and England could still control its commerce. In spite of Vergennes's arguments, the controlling influences at Madrid were now too cautious to follow his lead. So he had to get on for a time without Spanish coöperation.

The Franco-American alliance.

Vergennes's negotiations with the American commissioners were now pushed forward rapidly and on February 6, 1778, two treaties were signed, one a general treaty of amity and commerce between France and the United States, and the other a formal alliance. A year later Spain decided to enter the war as an ally of France; but the Spaniards could never bring themselves to a direct alliance with the United States. Considering all the circumstances, the French treaties were liberal. Neither party was to make peace without the consent of the other, and for both parties the absolute independence of the United States was an indispensable condition. The French expressly gave up any claim to their former possessions in North America and agreed to coöperate in the defense of any territory secured by the United States as a result of the war. In return the United

States made a similar promise regarding the French possessions in the West Indies. On this understanding the two powers agreed to act together both in the war and in the negotiations for peace.

The real importance of the alliance cannot be measured by the military and naval forces which France sent across the Atlantic, though these were considerable. The great fact was that the British government now had to face a serious danger near the very heart of the empire. The commerce-destroying operations of the American navy and American privateers could now be carried on freely from French ports, unhampered by neutrality regulations. Once more British supremacy in home waters was menaced by the French fleet, soon to be reënforced by that of Spain. All in all, this was one of the great crises in the history of the British Empire. Naturally the opposition leaders were bitter in their denunciation of the ministry which, having brought the country into the war, seemed so incompetent to carry it on. Some of the Whigs were already convinced that American independence was inevitable. *Effect on the British government.*

Grave as the danger was, there were compensations. It was easier to rouse enthusiasm for a war with a rival European power than for the uninspiring struggle with revolted colonists who, in the opinion of many Englishmen, had some right on their side. Pitt now made a dramatic appeal to his countrymen for a great patriotic effort to hold the empire together, and there was some talk of getting him to form another war ministry; but he died almost immediately afterwards. Even without first-rate leadership, the English nation braced itself for a supreme effort and in the end came out better than could reasonably have been expected. It was too late, however, to avoid a long series of reverses or to realize Pitt's ideal of a reunited empire. *Pitt's last appeal for the empire.*

The new drain on England's resources resulting from

the war in Europe seriously handicapped British operations
in America and this was perhaps the most important contribution made by France to the winning of American
independence. At the same time the direct intervention
of the French navy in American waters brought some notable
results. In the spring of 1778, a French fleet under Admiral
d'Estaing sailed for America and the British soon had to
take this new factor into account. Hitherto British command
of the sea had been fairly complete; but now their West
Indian colonies were threatened and troops had to be withdrawn from the continent for service in the islands. It
was also more difficult to insure regular communications
by sea between the British armies at New York and Philadelphia. Accordingly, Sir Henry Clinton, who succeeded
Howe as commander in chief, was ordered to concentrate
his forces by evacuating Philadelphia and transferring that
part of the army to New York. In June, 1778, the order
was carried out, to the great disappointment of the Pennsylvania loyalists, a large number of whom decided to
take refuge with the British army in New York rather than
remain at the mercy of their Whig countrymen.

As Clinton marched across New Jersey, Washington
prepared for another trial of strength. The discipline and
morale of the army had been much improved, particularly
through the efforts of Steuben, the new inspector-general,
and Washington could attack with some prospect of success.
On June 28, he fell upon Clinton's army at Monmouth;
but the attack miscarried, largely through the misconduct
of General Charles Lee, and Clinton got safely into New
York.

During this summer, the arrival of d'Estaing's fleet
gave the Americans their first experience of joint action,
and it was disappointing. Though his fleet was superior
to that of Lord Howe, then holding New York harbor,
d'Estaing decided not to risk an attack there. He agreed,

Marginal notes:

Effect of the alliance on British strategy.

Battle of Monmouth.

The French fleet in American waters.

however, to coöperate with an American land force in an attack on the British post at Newport. The plan failed, partly because of the superior skill and aggressiveness of Lord Howe, who followed d'Estaing to Newport. Before a decisive engagement was fought, a storm came up in which both fleets were badly damaged. Thereupon the French admiral withdrew his fleet to Boston for repairs and the expedition was abandoned. Whatever may be said for d'Estaing's course, it certainly made him unpopular with his American allies, especially with the New Englanders. Notwithstanding this fiasco, British strategy was still much influenced by the presence of the French fleet, and when d'Estaing, after some months in the West Indies, came north again in 1779, the British garrison at Newport was withdrawn.

Evacuation of Newport.

After Burgoyne's defeat no important offensive operations were undertaken by the British in the northern states, though the coast towns suffered from naval and military raids. They kept their grip on the city of New York and the lower Hudson, but the significant movements of the later years were in the South. Here the British relied largely on the loyalists, who were especially strong in the Carolinas and Georgia, and hoped with their help to detach those states from the Union. For a time the new British policy was apparently successful. In December, 1778, Savannah was captured and, with the help of a detachment which came up from the new British province of East Florida, Georgia was conquered. In 1779 the Americans, with the aid of the French fleet, tried to recover Savannah; but once more a promising plan of coöperation broke down, and shortly afterwards d'Estaing sailed for Europe. With the French fleet out of the way, the British could move their troops more freely by sea, and in 1779 Clinton took seven thousand men from New York to Charleston, then held by a comparatively weak American force under General Lincoln.

British operations in the South.

Capture of Savannah and Charleston.

In May, 1780, Charleston was taken, together with Lincoln's army, and for the next two years the most important town on the southern seaboard was held by the British.

A few weeks after the surrender of Charleston, Clinton returned to New York, but the British campaign for the conquest of South Carolina went forward under Cornwallis. Almost everywhere the loyalists were triumphant and the Whigs discouraged. The state government almost ceased to exist and some of the Whigs were ready to take a neutral position for the remainder of the war. The Continental Congress sent reënforcements from the North under General Gates, but, though he had an able lieutenant in General Kalb, he was overmatched by Cornwallis. In August, 1780, the two armies met near Camden, South Carolina, after night marches in which each hoped to surprise the other, and the Americans were badly beaten.

Battle of Camden. The Continental regulars fought well under their brave commander, Kalb, who was fatally wounded during the battle; but the militiamen, with Gates, took refuge in headlong flight. This disaster left the Americans with no real army in the Carolinas. The blunders of the British authorities at Charleston fortunately revived the Whig feeling, and there were able guerrilla leaders, like Marion, Sumter, and Pickens, who sometimes made life uncomfortable for the British and their loyalist allies; but the British also had some capable officers for such work, notably Colonel Tarleton and Major Ferguson, the commander of a well-known regiment of loyalist volunteers. Altogether these were dark days for the southern Whigs.

Partisan warfare.

The turn of the tide. It was at this critical moment, when the Carolina seaboard seemed hopelessly lost, that the West took up the fight and revived the failing courage of the Whigs by striking one of the most effective blows in the whole history of the Revolution. How this came about is a story which must be reserved for the next chapter.

BIBLIOGRAPHICAL NOTES

Channing, *United States*, III, 229–320. Van Tyne, *American Revolution*, chs. VII–XIII, XVI; and his *England and America, Rivals in the American Revolution*. Fisher, *Struggle for American Independence*, I, chs. XLIII–LII; II, chs. LIII–LXXXIV. Lecky, *American Revolution*. `General references.`

Hart, *Contemporaries*, II, chs. XXXI–XXXIII. Moore, *Diary of the American Revolution*. `Collected sources.`

References on Washington in ch. XX. Adams, C. F., *Studies, Military and Diplomatic*, chs. II–IV. Avery, E. M., *United States*, V, VI (excellent illustrations). Ford, W. C., *Washington*, I, chs. XII–XVI; II, chs. I, II. Fortescue, J. W., *History of the British Army*, III, chs. VIII–XVII. Greene, F. V., *Revolutionary War*, chs. II–VI. Winsor, *America*, VI, chs. IV, V. `Military history.`

Barck, O. T., *New York City during the War for Independence*. Johnston, H. B., *Battle of Harlem Heights*. `British army in New York.`

Nickerson, H., *The Turning Point of the Revolution*. Clark, J., "Responsibility for the Failure of the Burgoyne Campaign," *A.H.R.* (1930), XXXV, 542–549. `Burgoyne's campaign.`

Mahan, A. T., *Influence of Sea Power, 1660–1783*, 330–376, and his *Major Operations of the Navies in the War of American Independence*, chs. I–VI. Paullin, C. O., *The Navy of the American Revolution*. `Naval operations.`

Bancroft, *United States* (author's last revision), especially V, pt. IV, chs. X, XVI–XXI. Corwin, E. S., *French Policy and the American Alliance* (excellent; cf. Van Tyne in *A.H.R.*, XXI, 528–541). Perkins, J. B., *France in the American Revolution*. Hale, E. E., *Franklin in France*. Tower, C., *Lafayette in the American Revolution* (detailed narrative). Whitlock, B., *Lafayette*, I. Hazard, B., *Beaumarchais and the American Revolution*. Faÿ, B., *The Revolutionary Spirit in France and the U. S.* French accounts in Lavisse, E., *Histoire de France*, IX, bk. II, pp. 91–126, and Doniol, H., *Participation de la France à l'établissement des États Unis*. Bemis, S. F., *Diplomacy of American Revolution*, chs. I–V. `European conditions and the French Alliance.`

Franklin's letters in *Writings* (Smyth edition), VII, VIII; very readable. Wharton, F., *Revolutionary Diplomatic Correspondence*, II. `Sources.`

CHAPTER XXII

INDEPENDENCE WON

Western
phases of the
Revolution.

WHEN the Revolution broke out, it was mainly the work of men who lived within a hundred miles of the coast, and the number of permanent settlers who had actually crossed the mountains was insignificant. Before the war ended, however, the frontiersmen on the eastern and western slopes of the Appalachians made some real contributions to the American cause, and even the Mississippi valley was the scene of some notable events.

Frontier
communities.
Vermont.

When actual fighting began, in 1775, the air was full of plans for new colonies, or commonwealths, independent of the existing colonial governments. In the north, the Vermont frontiersmen who helped to defeat Burgoyne's army were troubled by the conflicting claims of New York and New Hampshire, and tried to solve the problem by organizing a state government of their own. In 1778 they adopted their first state constitution, though they had to wait thirteen years before they were admitted to the Union. The German settlers on the Mohawk seem to have had no such aspirations; but in Pennsylvania new settlements were forming around Fort Pitt, which it was proposed to combine with others in the present limits of West Virginia and eastern Kentucky, in order to form the new colony of Westsylvania. In central Kentucky was the colony of Transylvania, promoted by the North Carolina speculator, Richard Henderson, with the coöperation of Daniel Boone, the most notable figure among the pioneers and trail makers of his day. The Kentuckians gave up for a time their hope

The South-
west. Ken-
tucky.

of a separate government and in 1777 were organized as a county of Virginia, which claimed this territory under the charter of 1609. It was difficult, however, for the Virginia government to keep in touch with these outlying settlements and to protect them against the Indians. In the north-eastern corner of what is now Tennessee, near the head-waters of the Tennessee River, a handful of frontiersmen from Virginia and North Carolina adopted, just before the Revolution, the so-called "Watauga Compact" and, like the early New Englanders, based upon it a rudimentary kind of self-government. Migration was not stopped by the war, and in 1780 a new and quite isolated settlement was formed on the Cumberland River, the beginning of what is now Nashville. These Tennessee settlements were within the charter limits of North Carolina and were brought under the jurisdiction of that state, though here, as in Kentucky, the relation was not wholly satisfactory.

Beginnings of Tennessee.

The frontiersmen differed among themselves about the issues of the Revolution. All along the line from New York to South Carolina, Georgia, and the Floridas, British agents, like the Johnsons in New York and Stuart in the South, had built up a strong loyalist influence among the traders and the Indians. Tories were especially numerous among the recent Scotch immigrants, particularly the Highlanders. Over against these Tory frontiersmen may be set such Whig groups as the Green Mountain pioneers in Vermont, the Germans of the Mohawk valley, and a large proportion of the Irish and Scotch-Irish from Pennsylvania southward. Nowhere was the feeling between Whig and Tory so bitter or the fighting so savage as among these border people.

Whigs and Tories on the border.

In dealing with the Indians the Americans were handi-capped in various ways. It took time to build up an organ-ization as effective as that developed by some of the British agents. In some respects, too, the attitude of the Indians reminds one of that taken by them during the last French

The Indian problem.

war. In that conflict the Indians had rightly regarded the French, whose interests were chiefly in trading or missions, as less objectionable than the English, who began with hunting and trading but were more likely to develop permanent settlements and gradually crowd the Indians out.

Now the rôle of the French was partly taken over by the British; in fact, many old Canadian *voyageurs* were working for British companies. It was the American frontiersmen, on the contrary, who now represented the slow but sure advance of white settlements into the old Indian hunting grounds. The Montreal merchants, protected by the British navy, could bring in a steady supply of European goods, including arms and ammunition, to be exchanged for peltries; for the Americans this was much less easy. So the bulk of the Indian trade was held by the British merchants, and with trade went a large amount of political influence. From Montreal this influence reached out far to the westward, with garrisons and trading posts at Oswego, Niagara, Detroit, and Mackinaw, on the Great Lakes; also at Vincennes, Kaskaskia, and Natchez, in the Mississippi valley. The

Iroquois of the North, the Cherokees of the South, and most of the western tribes, thus kept within the British sphere of influence, were constantly raiding the pioneer settlements, from the Mohawk valley to the lonely clearings of Kentucky and Tennessee. Among the British officers most active in promoting this border warfare was Henry Hamilton, commander of the post at Detroit.

Many Americans, not only frontiersmen and land speculators but also seaboard merchants, were eager to curb British influence in the West and protect American interests in the fur trade; but the problem was far from simple. After all, independence had to be won, if at all, on the eastern side of the Alleghenies, and it was impossible to detach large forces for the conquest of the West. Now and then, however, some tragic incident occurred which made strenuous action necessary; as, for instance, the terrible massacre of 1778 in the Wyoming valley of Pennsylvania. The next year Washington sent into the Iroquois country a retaliatory expedition which was fairly effective; but it was not the end of border warfare.

Meantime, notable events were taking place in the Mississippi valley. In 1777, the Kentuckians, who had suffered severely from Indian raids, for which they held the British largely responsible, were eager to strike back at the British posts in the Northwest. Accordingly one of their ablest and most daring leaders, George Rogers Clark, went to Virginia and secured the backing of that government. In the spring of 1778 he led some of his fellow backwoodsmen down the Ohio to the eastern edge of the Illinois country, and then overland to the old French settlement of Kaskaskia. The regular garrisons had been withdrawn from this neighborhood; but Kaskaskia, then held with a few militia by a French officer in the British service, was still an important center of British influence. This post was easily captured by Clark on the night of July 4, 1778, and this stroke was soon followed by the taking of Vincennes on the Wabash. *Clark's expedition to the Illinois country.*

Clark's daring move naturally provoked retaliation, and in the winter of 1778–1779 a British expedition from Detroit, commanded by Colonel Hamilton, recovered Vincennes and threatened the Virginians at Kaskaskia. Clark determined to strike first, and in February, 1779, made a heroic march across the flooded prairies to Vincennes. Taken off his guard, Hamilton was forced to surrender and was presently sent to Virginia as a prisoner of war. These conquests had been made, not strictly for the United States, but for Virginia, which now claimed jurisdiction under its charter of 1609 and organized the new "county of Illinois." *The capture of Vincennes*

American activities in the Mississippi valley naturally brought out the complicated problem of relations with Spain. In 1778 the Spaniards held the west bank of the Mississippi *Spanish activities in the Southwest.*

from St. Louis to New Orleans. East of New Orleans along the Gulf were the British provinces of West and East Florida, acquired from France and Spain during the last war. Resenting this British occupation of the Gulf coast, the Spaniards were willing to help the rebellious colonies by shipping military supplies up the Mississippi, from which they could go on up the Ohio as far as Fort Pitt. On the outbreak of war between Great Britain and Spain, in 1779, the Spaniards, under the command of Galvez, their governor at New Orleans, attacked the posts in West Florida, taking first those on the lower Mississippi, then Mobile, and finally, in 1781, Pensacola. The successes of the Americans in the Mississippi valley and of the Spaniards on the Gulf coast weakened British prestige; but they also made more evident the real conflict of interests between Spain and the United States.

These developments in the West seem to have little to do with the movements of British and American forces on the Atlantic seaboard; but in the southern campaigns of 1780 the "men of the western waters" were brought into closer touch with the main operations of the war. In the early autumn of that year these sturdy pioneers were able to strike a blow which, coming as it did soon after the disaster of Camden, proved to be a kind of turning point in the whole history of the war in the South.

When Cornwallis had disposed of Gates's army and was moving on to the conquest of North Carolina, he felt the need of larger forces. Accordingly he sent Major Patrick Ferguson, one of his best officers, to gather up recruits among the loyalist mountaineers. Ferguson was fairly successful in drawing the Tories; but he also aroused the antagonism of the Whig frontiersmen and soon found that he had blundered

into a kind of hornets' nest. At Kings Mountain, on the eastern edge of the mountain country, he was surrounded by a swarm of backwoodsmen, many of whom had come from the new settlements in Tennessee. Ferguson and his loyalist supporters fought bravely, but he himself was killed and his command practically destroyed. The numbers engaged in this battle — not far from a thousand on each side — were quite out of proportion to its real importance. Cornwallis's plan for the North Carolina campaign had to be held up and the Whigs got a chance to rally for a new stand under more effective leadership.

This ray of light came in one of the darkest moments of the war. The most startling event of the year 1780 was, perhaps, the success of the British in corrupting Benedict Arnold, previously regarded by Washington as one of his best officers. Arnold's plot to surrender the fortress of West Point on the Hudson fortunately failed, though he himself escaped and soon began fighting his old friends. The execution of Major André, the unlucky British agent in this ugly transaction, has always excited sympathy; but it was strictly in accordance with the rules of war. More serious than this spectacular incident was the increasing weakness of the revolutionary government. It was during this year that Washington wrote some of his most pessimistic letters. "I see," he wrote, "one head gradually changing into thirteen . . . one army branching into thirteen." The Articles of Confederation were not yet ratified and Congress was still clinging to unbusinesslike methods. The army, poorly fed and clothed, was in an ugly mood and in the following winter there was a serious mutiny among the Pennsylvania troops.

A critical time. Arnold's treason.

Weakness of the Confederation.

Gradually, however, the skies began to clear. In March, 1781, the Articles of Confederation were adopted through the ratifying act of Maryland, which had hitherto held off because of the fear that Virginia and a few other states would monopolize the western lands. The adoption of the Articles changed very little the practical working of the Continental government but at least gave it a kind of legal basis. More important in its immediate results was the

Progress in 1781. Confederation adopted.

tardy decision of Congress to reorganize the chief executive departments — war, treasury, foreign affairs — each with a single responsible officer at its head. The ablest of these department heads was undoubtedly Robert Morris, who was able to make at least some improvements in the finances.

The war in the South.

The chief military developments during the first six months of 1781 were in the South, where Cornwallis was getting ready to resume his advance into North Carolina. The American army now gathering to oppose him was not an altogether hopeful organization, composed as it was of a few hundred regulars and a rather uncertain militia; but it had one great asset in the person of its new general, Nathanael Greene.

Nathanael Greene.

For many months Greene had served loyally and efficiently as the quartermaster-general of the Continental army; but he was too much of a fighter to like such work indefinitely, and he took up energetically the southern command, for which he was chosen by Washington. His chief lieutenant was Daniel Morgan, one of the best officers in the Continental army; but he also had the coöperation of several successful partisan leaders, and the cavalry, though small in numbers, had an important part in the campaign. Though Cornwallis's army was stronger, he had one serious handicap: almost every forward move increased the difficulty of keeping up communications with the seaboard, on which he was largely dependent for supplies. Greene understood very well the enemy's weakness in this respect, and he made the most of it.

The Carolina campaigns of 1781.

On the opening of the new year Greene's little army was in two main sections, both near the boundary between North and South Carolina. The main army, under his own command, was at Cheraw, South Carolina, on the Great Pedee River, a few miles south of the state line. The other division under Morgan, was over a hundred miles to the westward looking after some British posts in that neighborhood.

Here, at a place called the Cowpens, Morgan was attacked in January, 1781, by Colonel Tarleton, the ablest and most ruthless of the British cavalry commanders in the South. Fortunately Morgan was equal to the emergency, and Tarleton's force was almost annihilated. Having disposed of Tarleton, Morgan now fell back before Cornwallis's army to join General Greene; but their combined forces were insufficient to cope with the British and so they steadily retreated northward, drawing Cornwallis after them. By the middle of February this retreat had carried the two armies across North Carolina to the Virginia border, where Greene took up his position behind the Dan River and Cornwallis gave up the pursuit.

The Cowpens.

Greene's retreat.

Though Cornwallis had temporarily driven the Americans out of North Carolina and might claim in a sense to have conquered the state, his position was not at all satisfactory. By persistent running away, Greene had drawn the British far from their base and consolidated his own scattered forces. Now he was ready to change his tactics and take the offensive. Returning to North Carolina, he met Cornwallis at Guilford Courthouse, and though the battle taken by itself may be called a victory for the British, their loss was so heavy and their whole position after it so precarious that Cornwallis retired to the seaboard at Wilmington. Shortly afterwards he left the Carolinas, in order to join Arnold's small British army in Virginia. With Cornwallis out of the way, Greene returned to South Carolina, where Lord Rawdon, with Charleston as his principal base, was trying to hold a few rallying points for the loyalists of the back country. Between May and September there were several engagements in this region, most of them either British victories or drawn battles; but the net result was that the British left the upcountry loyalists to their fate and contented themselves with holding Charleston. Except for the Charleston garrison and that of Wilmington, the

Later campaigns of 1781.

British retirement to the seaboard.

Carolinas were practically freed from British control. Considered in relation to the world war of which they formed a part, these encounters, in which the aggregate numbers engaged rarely exceeded five thousand men, seem petty enough; but they helped to cloud still further the gloomy prospect then unfolding before the British public.

Great Britain's isolation. In Europe there was growing antagonism between Great Britain and the continental powers which had so far remained neutral. With the belligerents on both sides doing their best to destroy enemy commerce, it was almost inevitable that neutrals also should suffer. There was no clear agreement about neutral rights and duties, and this led to many complaints, especially against the British navy, which generally kept the upper hand in European waters. The complaints were not, however, all on one side. England was annoyed by the sheltering of American war vessels in Dutch ports and the development of an immense munition trade between the Dutch West Indies and the United States. **Armed neutrality.** In these controversies nearly all the European powers became involved in one way or another. Finally, under the leadership of the great Russian empress, Catherine II, a formidable group of neutral governments, including the Scandinavian countries, Prussia, and the German Empire, organized a league called the "Armed Neutrality." Though the league was formed to defend neutral rights against belligerents generally, it was aimed chiefly at Great Britain, principally because France was willing to accept the principle that "free ships make free goods," while the British insisted on their right to seize enemy property even under neutral flags. In the case of the Dutch Republic, the trouble **War with the Dutch.** with Great Britain developed by 1781 into open war. Thus Great Britain was almost isolated, with the three chief maritime powers of Europe against her and most of the others more or less unfriendly.

In this dangerous isolation England's chief reliance as

usual was on her navy; but even this was seriously chal- Naval operations, 1779-1780. lenged. In 1779 the French and Spanish fleets appeared in force off the British Isles and for a time there was real fear of an invasion. From this particular danger, England was saved largely by the mismanagement of the allied fleets; but the destruction of British shipping sent up the rates of marine insurance. In the work of commerce destroying the Americans had a large part. In 1779 Franklin wrote of one privateer which in three months had taken, ransomed, burned, or destroyed more than thirty British vessels. It was in this year also that Paul Jones won his famous fight with the *Serapis*. The next year was one of alternate victory and defeat for the British navy. It began with the successful campaign of Admiral Rodney on the coast of Spain, where he defeated the Spanish fleet off Cape Vincent, besides relieving the besieged British garrison at Gibraltar. Later in the year Rodney took his fleet to the West Indies, but failed to bring on a decisive engagement with the cautious French admiral. Meantime the enemy had succeeded in capturing a great transport fleet bound for the West Indies with British troops and supplies for the island garrisons. The naval historian, Mahan, describes this as "the greatest single blow that British commerce had received in war during the memory of men then living."

The entry of Holland into the war, though adding to In the West Indies, 1781. the number of England's enemies, gave Rodney's West Indian fleet a new opportunity. The Dutch West Indies were no longer protected by a neutral flag and in February, 1781, the island of St. Eustatius, described as practically "a military and naval arsenal for the American revolutionists and their allies," was taken by the British. A few months later, however, this victory was partly offset by the French seizing one of the smaller British islands, and the summer passed without a real test of strength between the opposing fleets. So matters stood when Admiral de Grasse, the new commander in chief of the French fleets in American waters, was called to coöperate with the allied armies in what proved to be the last important operation of the Revolutionary War.

During the spring of 1781, Washington's main army was on the upper Hudson, watching the British in the city of New York. The American outlook was still clouded. The French general, Rochambeau, wrote as late as June, 1781, that Washington had "but a handful of men"; that America had "been driven to bay" and all her resources were "giving out at once." So far as direct participation in the continental campaigns was concerned, the French alliance had been disappointing and the French government, already embarrassed by its financial contributions to the American cause, felt that the United States was not carrying its fair share of the burden. Fortunately, this mutual irritation was overcome, largely through the steady good sense of Franklin and the efforts of Lafayette, who made a long visit to France in 1779. New grants were made to the United States from the French treasury, and in the early summer of 1780 five thousand French regulars landed at Newport under the command of Count Rochambeau, a veteran of the Seven Years' War and one of the most distinguished officers of the French army.

More than a year passed, however, before the French troops were effectively used. For most of that time the British kept their superiority in American waters and were able to blockade the French at Newport harbor. Meantime the American and French commanders were exchanging ideas. Washington wished to attack New York, where Clinton's army had been weakened by the sending of troops to the southward. In July, 1781, the main body of the French army joined the Americans on the Hudson; but it was doubtful whether the allies were strong enough to dislodge Clinton from his strong position.

At this critical moment, the allied commanders found a new opportunity in Virginia, where small British detachments under Generals Arnold and Phillips had just been reënforced by the arrival of Cornwallis. For a time this shifting of the British strategy from the Carolinas to Virginia seemed to work fairly well. The Americans under Lafayette were not strong enough to face Cornwallis, who was sure the "boy" could not long escape him. In June, 1781, Tarleton broke up the state legislature, then sitting at Charlottesville, on the eastern slope of the Blue Ridge, compelling Governor Thomas Jefferson to beat a hasty retreat from his neighboring estate of Monticello. Humiliating as this experience was to the Virginians, Cornwallis soon found that he had really gained very little. Lafayette was hard pushed at times but always managed to get away. Finally, in accordance with instructions from Clinton at New York, Cornwallis retired to the peninsula between the York and the James rivers. On the northern side of this narrow strip, at the little village of Yorktown, Cornwallis settled down, fortifying himself from attack by land and counting on the navy to keep open his communications by sea. Here he was fairly safe so long as his friends controlled the sea. If, however, that control were interrupted, his position might become very dangerous.

A new opportunity in Virginia.

Cornwallis at Yorktown.

It was on this famous old Virginia peninsula that Washington, after long years of patient waiting, found at last his supreme opportunity. Fortunately also Admiral de Grasse, in response to urgent appeals from Washington and Rochambeau, had just decided to bring his fleet north to Chesapeake Bay. Whatever was done, however, had to be done quickly, for De Grasse explained that his stay would be short and the troops which he was to bring with him would be needed for other service during the winter. So in the latter part of August, with a warning to Lafayette not to let Cornwallis escape from the trap in which he had placed himself,

The Yorktown campaign.

Washington began a rapid overland march from the Hudson valley to Virginia. He had with him a handful of Continental troops, about two thousand in all, and four thousand French regulars under Rochambeau. About a month later the allied armies were closing in upon the British lines at Yorktown.

Victory of the French fleet.

On August 30, a few days after Washington left for the South, De Grasse's fleet anchored within the capes of Chesapeake Bay. A week later, a British fleet under Admiral Graves appeared off the Capes, but after a sharp engagement was forced to withdraw. So the French kept their station, hemming in the British army by sea as the allied armies were about to close in by land. In the last days of September, the allies began their attack on the British lines, and on October 19, after a siege of about three weeks, Cornwallis surrendered his whole command. Two days later Graves's fleet again appeared, this time bringing General Clinton with reënforcements for the besieged army; but they were too late to prevent the greatest disaster which had come to the British cause since Burgoyne's defeat at Saratoga. For this crowning victory, the Americans were largely indebted to the French alliance. Not to speak of the financial support which kept the American armies in the field, about two thirds of the regular troops engaged in the siege were French, and without the coöperation of the French fleet the whole operation would have been impossible.

Surrender of Cornwallis.

The war not yet over.

In Europe and America the effect of the surrender at Yorktown was generally recognized as decisive; but the war was not yet over and there were many anxious months ahead. More than thirty thousand British soldiers still remained in the United States, chiefly at New York with smaller garrisons at Charleston and Savannah. Even in this hour of victory the American government seemed almost at the end of its resources. Although Washington urged the need of continued effort in order to secure a satisfactory peace, it was hard to overcome the general weariness and apathy. Notwithstanding the ratification of the Articles of Confederation, supplies of money and men still depended on the good will of individual states and only a fraction of the money called for was actually paid in.

Fortunately, the English people also were tired of the war, and the disaster at Yorktown convinced nearly everyone that there was no chance of subduing the colonies. The King was stubborn and the North ministry was held together for a few months longer; but the logic of events was too much, even for George III. For six months after Yorktown the tide continued to run strongly against the British. In the West Indies they lost not only their recent conquest of St. Eustatius, but even some of their own islands. Across the Atlantic, British prestige in the Mediterranean was weakened by the loss of Minorca. Economic developments were also discouraging; shipping was still being destroyed on a large scale, expenditures were steadily rising, new loans were needed, and the public credit was shaken. All these things naturally strengthened the opposition party. Even former supporters of the ministry had been turned against it by increasing evidences of corrupt and inefficient administration. Long before Yorktown, the government majorities had begun to go down; as early as 1780 the House of Commons passed an often-quoted resolution, declaring that the power of the Crown had increased, was increasing, and ought to be diminished. After Yorktown the attack was pushed with new vigor, and by March, 1782, the House of Commons had committed itself squarely against the continuance of the war. Lord North gave up the fight and the King had to accept his resignation.

English opinion turning against the war.

Fall of the North ministry.

The new ministry was headed by the same Lord Rockingham who had proposed the repeal of the Stamp Act; several of his associates were also known for their liberal

Liberal elements in the new ministry.

ideas on American questions. Among them were such men as Burke, the eloquent advocate of conciliation in 1774 and 1775; Charles James Fox, who had gone to great lengths in expressing his sympathy with the American revolutionists; and Lord Shelburne, the ablest member of the little group that followed the elder Pitt. With such a government Americans could negotiate with some chance of mutual understanding. It was also fortunate for the new ministry that the naval war began to turn in favor of the British. In April, 1782, a French fleet which was expected to combine with the Spaniards in an attack on Jamaica was beaten by Admiral Rodney, whose victory restored British superiority in the West Indies. The thirteen colonies were indeed lost; but so far as her European enemies were concerned, England could look forward to peace terms more favorable than had seemed probable only a few months before.

BIBLIOGRAPHICAL NOTES

General references. Channing, *United States*, III, 300–342. Van Tyne, *American Revolution*, chs. XV, XVII. Winsor, *America*, VI, 447–467, and chs. VI–IX. Fisher, *Struggle for American Independence*, II, chs. LXXXIV–CV. Bancroft, *United States*, V, pt. IV, chs. XXII–XXIII, XXVI–XXVIII; pt. V, chs. I–IV. Lecky, *American Revolution*.

Sources. Hart, *Contemporaries*, II, ch. XXXIV. Moore, *Diary of the American Revolution*. Washington, *Writings* (Ford edition), IX. Franklin, *Writings* (Smyth edition), VIII.

The last campaigns. Fortescue, J. W., *History of the British Army*, III, chs. XVII–XX. Ford, W. C., *Washington*, II, chs. I–III. Greene, F. V., *Revolutionary War*, chs. VII–VIII. Greene, G. W., *Nathanael Greene*. (See also references for ch. XX.)

French co-operation. European politics and the world war. Corwin, *French Policy and the American Alliance*. Bemis, S. F., *The Diplomacy of the American Revolution*, 3–171. Jusserand, J. J., *With Americans of Past and Present Days* (essays on Rochambeau and Washington). Tower, C., *Lafayette*. Trevelyan, G. O.,

George III and Charles Fox (Whig view of English politics).
Mahan, *Influence of Sea Power on History, 1660–1783*, chs. X, XI.
Jameson, J. F., "St. Eustatius in the American Revolution"
(*A.H.R.*, VIII, 683–708).

Mahan, *Major Operations*, especially chs. VII–X. Allen, G. *Naval
W., Naval History*, II. De Koven, A. F., *Paul Jones*, especially I, *warfare.*
ch. X–XIV. Maclay, E. S., *A History of American Privateers.*
Howe, O. T., "Beverly Privateers in American Revolution,"
Col. Soc. of Mass., *Publications*, XXIV, 318–435.

James, J. A., *Life of George Rogers Clark.* Alvord, C. W., *The West.*
"Virginia and the West," *M.V.H.R.*, III, 19–39, and his *Centennial History of Illinois*, I, chs. XV, XVI. Henderson, A., "Crea-
tive Forces in Western Expansion," *A.H.R.*, XX, 86–107, and his
Conquest of the Old Southwest, chs. XI–XVIII. Roosevelt, *Winning of the West.* Thwaites, *Daniel Boone.* Turner, "Western
State Making in the Revolutionary Era," *A.H.R.*, I, 70–87.

Swiggett, H., *War out of Niagara; Walter Butler and the Tory Whig and
Rangers.* Siebert, W. H., "Loyalists in West Florida and the *Tory on the
Natchez District," *M.V.H.R.*, II, 465–484; "Kentucky's Struggle frontier.*
with its Loyalist Proprietors," *M.V.H.R.*, VII, 113–127. Mc-
Crady, *South Carolina in the Revolution*, I, II (detailed accounts of
partisan warfare; cf. Channing, *United States*, III, 343).

Thwaites, R. G., and Kellogg, L. P., *Revolution on the Upper Sources on
Ohio* and *Frontier Defence on the Upper Ohio.* J. A. James, *Clark the West.*
Papers* (Illinois State Historical Library, *Collections*).

CHAPTER XXIII

REPUBLICAN DIPLOMACY, 1779 TO 1784

Informal
negotiations;
Hartley and
Franklin.

BEFORE the fall of the North ministry, the British government had made several proposals looking towards peace with the colonies on some basis short of complete independence. There were also a few English liberals who hoped and worked for reconciliation throughout the war, among them David Hartley, a member of Parliament and an old friend of Franklin's. Hartley visited Paris in 1778 and tried to interest the American envoy in his peace plans; but Franklin pointed out that Congress, having committed itself to common action with the French, could not desert its new allies or make any terms short of independence. Notwithstanding this disappointment, Hartley continued his friendly efforts and, during the winter of 1781–1782, after a conference with Lord North, he suggested a kind of armistice for a term of years. This suspension of hostilities he proposed to use for friendly conferences about the future relations of the two countries. Of course, Franklin's original objection applied equally well to this new proposal.

The
Rockingham
ministry.
Shelburne's
overtures.

Even after the Rockingham ministry came in, there were difficulties to be overcome; but the conditions were much more favorable. In March, 1782, Burke wrote to Franklin expressing his hope of a "speedy peace between the two branches of the English nation." A little later Franklin, having been told that Shelburne would be glad to hear from him, sent a courteous note recalling their old acquaintance and expressing his satisfaction with Shelburne's recent appointment. Starting with this informal correspondence,

512

Shelburne, who was now secretary of state for the colonies, gradually prepared the way for more regular diplomatic intercourse.

Meantime, the Continental Congress had opened the way for negotiations by appointing commissioners and formulating peace terms. In 1779 John Adams was sent abroad with definite instructions as to certain points which were regarded as essential. This first mission did not make much headway, however, partly because there was then no prospect of the British granting independence, and partly because Adams did not get on well with the French. Vergennes and his associates thought the Americans were asking too much and considered Adams too aggressive in his attitude toward their own government. So in 1781 the French minister at Philadelphia persuaded Congress to change its action in three important particulars. First, Adams was to share his authority with four other commissioners — Franklin, John Jay of New York, Henry Laurens, a South Carolinian who was for a time president of the Continental Congress, and Thomas Jefferson; secondly, the commissioners, though still required to insist on independence, were given more discretion in other respects; thirdly, they were to make "the most candid and confidential communications upon all subjects" with the French ministers, taking no step in the negotiations "without their knowledge and concurrence." *American commissioners and their instructions.*

Of the five men named by Congress, Jefferson declined the appointment, and Laurens, then a prisoner in London, arrived in Paris too late to have much influence on the negotiations. The three who really counted, therefore, were Franklin, Adams, and Jay. Of these three men, Franklin undoubtedly stood first in experience, in tact, and in appreciation of European and especially French points of view. More than twenty years of his long life had been spent in Europe, where he had a prestige and a wide *Franklin.*

personal acquaintance which were most useful to his country. Realizing more keenly than his colleagues how much his country had depended on French support, he was more anxious to maintain relations of mutual confidence between the two nations. He was now seventy-six years old and not so active as his younger colleagues; but even his critics had to admit that his mind was keen and vigorous.

John Adams. In the spring of 1782, John Adams was nearing the end of a successful campaign for financial support and diplomatic recognition from the Dutch government. Before he left the Hague to join Franklin in Paris, he had got from the Dutch not only considerable loans, but also the first American treaty with any European government since the French alliance of 1778. Adams was justly proud of this achievement, all the more because his methods were not those recommended to him by the French government. He believed that his success was a striking vindication of independent American diplomacy. Unfortunately, Adams was too much inclined to emphasize his own achievements and not always generous in his references to his older colleague. If Franklin was too optimistic about French diplomacy, Adams was at times oversuspicious, and tact was

John Jay. certainly not his strong point. John Jay, the youngest of these three colleagues, was first known as a moderate leader of the New York Whigs; but for several years he had taken special interest in foreign affairs, first in Congress and then, since 1779, as American envoy to Spain. There he spent two exasperating years without securing even dignified recognition as the representative of an independent government. This humiliating experience gave Jay a pessimistic view of Bourbon diplomacy in general. Unlike Franklin, he did not like the French people, agreeing with Adams that the commissioners should emancipate themselves as much as possible from French tutelage.

From the French point of view there was some question

just how independent the United States had a right to be at that time. The war was, after all, not merely an affair between Great Britain and the United States. To the success of her ally France had made large contributions in sea power, in soldiers, and in money lent or given outright. Even now Robert Morris was asking France for new loans, which in his opinion were made necessary not so much by the poverty of the American people as by their unwillingness to shoulder a fair share of the burden. This demand, too, was made at a time when the desperate condition of the French treasury had become generally known. So far, the United States seemed to be the chief beneficiary of the alliance; was it not fair, then, that America should pay some attention to French interests and the French point of view?

Unfortunately the problem was still further complicated by the fact that France, the ally of the United States, was also the ally of Spain; and this latter alliance, in which the United States had no direct part, was nevertheless also a factor in the winning of American independence. To secure the Spanish alliance, Vergennes had made promises which had to be considered in the final settlement. Though the terms of the treaties which the French had made with the United States and with Spain were not necessarily incompatible, there was a real conflict of interests between Spain and the United States, especially in the Mississippi valley. Vergennes probably meant to keep faith with both his allies; but, in view of the moderate demands made by his own country, he also felt justified in trying to check what he considered the unreasonable pretensions of either Spain or the United States. The Spaniards were indifferent and at times hostile to the United States, and the Americans felt similarly toward Spain; but Vergennes had to think of both.

So matters stood when the overtures of the British government were clearing the way for formal negotiations. These negotiations were, however, delayed by differences of opinion inside the British government. Within the Rockingham ministry there were then two distinct groups, headed respectively by Shelburne, secretary of state for the colonies, and Fox, secretary for foreign affairs. Of these two men Shelburne was undoubtedly much the better informed about America; but, like his old leader, Pitt, he was deeply interested in preserving the empire and hoped almost to the last that the colonies might accept something less than absolute separation. Shelburne was undoubtedly a very able man, who as the French diplomatist, Rayneval, once said, took " a broad view of affairs "; but he had a certain reserve which led many of his contemporaries, both European and American, to doubt his sincerity.

Shelburne now saw that American independence would probably have to be conceded in the end, but he still thought of the Americans as colonists and wished to keep the negotiations in his own colonial office. He also hoped for close trade relations with the United States. A few weeks after he took office, he followed up his first approaches to Franklin by sending to Paris a confidential agent, named Richard Oswald. Oswald was a Scotch merchant, who had been in America and had some business interests there; he was not a professional diplomat and was sometimes surprisingly frank in acknowledging the strength of his opponents' case. He found Franklin willing to talk and got from him a plan of settlement, which included, among other things, the cession of Canada to the United States.

Meantime, the British government as a whole had no definite program. Parliament was considering a bill to authorize negotiations with the revolted colonies, and there were also some strenuous debates in the cabinet. Unlike Shelburne, Fox took independence for granted and thought that negotiations with the United States, as with any foreign government, should be handled by him as foreign secretary. Accordingly he too had his agent in Paris, who, though primarily concerned with the French government, also conferred with Franklin. Thus the rivalry of the two secretaries was reflected in their agents at Paris. Evidently these two departments could not be allowed to work indefinitely at cross purposes and Fox finally brought the issue to a head in the cabinet meeting by proposing the immediate recognition of American independence. This proposal, which would have taken the American negotiations out of Shelburne's hands, was defeated. Shortly afterwards Rockingham died, the ministry was reorganized with Shelburne as its head, and Fox resigned. So the deadlock ended with Shelburne in control. Meanwhile Parliament authorized negotiations with the colonies, and Oswald was commissioned for that purpose. Another agent, Fitzherbert, was appointed to negotiate with France; but the two men were now working under the same general direction.

Shelburne in control.

Now that the British cabinet had settled its internal differences another difficulty developed. Jay, who had recently joined Franklin in Paris, objected to Oswald's commission because it spoke simply of "colonies" and did not formally recognize the United States as independent. Vergennes thought this was making too much of a formality, but Jay persisted and Shelburne decided to accept the situation, without haggling over technical points. On September 21, Oswald received a commission authorizing him to negotiate with the "Thirteen United States of North America." The vital question of independence was now disposed of; but there were still difficult and far-reaching issues to be decided, and more than two months passed before the preliminary treaty was signed.

The question of immediate recognition.

First of all, it was necessary to define the territory of the United States. So far as the coast line was concerned, the question was comparatively simple. Notwithstanding Franklin's suggestion to Oswald, Congress did not expect to get Canada, and on the northeastern border it was a

Territorial boundaries.

question of detail as to the exact line between Maine and Nova Scotia. So, on the south, it was easily agreed that the United States would not claim Florida or the Gulf coast. The important and difficult question was the fate of the territory between the Alleghenies and the Mississippi. In 1779, Congress had insisted on the line of the Mississippi; but the instructions of 1781 did not make this an ultimatum and there was room for difference of opinion about the justice of the American claim.

American claims to the trans-Allegheny country.

American arguments on this subject began with certain colonial charters, particularly those of Massachusetts, Connecticut, Virginia, the Carolinas, and Georgia, all of which contained sea-to-sea clauses, covering in the aggregate, the whole trans-Allegheny territory from the Great Lakes to the Floridas. The clause in the royal Proclamation of 1763, forbidding grants beyond the mountains, was correctly held to be only temporary; as for the Quebec Act, extending the boundaries of that province to the Ohio and the Mississippi, that was dismissed as one of those encroachments on American rights which had brought on the Revolution. These paper claims were now supported by the actual movement of population into the West. The growth of pioneer settlements in Kentucky and Tennessee, the activity of Virginia and Pennsylvania traders in the Mississippi valley, and Clark's operations in the Illinois country, all served to stimulate American interest in the West. Not all Americans, however, were equally interested. Some delegates from states which had no sea-to-sea charters were comparatively indifferent on western questions.

The views of France and Spain.

The most serious objection to the American claim came not from Great Britain but from Spain, whose hopes of controlling the trade of the Gulf and the Mississippi were threatened by the American westward movement. On this point the French government could not satisfy one ally without disappointing the other, and though Vergennes stood by the guarantee of American independence, he questioned whether the United States had a fair claim to the country beyond the mountains. In September, 1782, Rayneval, Vergennes's secretary, proposed to Jay a plan which showed plainly the influence of Spanish ideas. The territory south of the Ohio between the Alleghenies and the Mississippi was to be a vast Indian reservation, the western part being placed within the Spanish "sphere of influence" and the eastern within that of the United States. The fate of the country north of the Ohio was to be "regulated" by the court of London.

Much troubled by the attitude of the French government and especially by a visit of Rayneval to London, Jay sent a confidential messenger to Shelburne. Fortunately Jay's effort to secure a more direct and independent understanding with the British government harmonized with the policy of Shelburne, who, having once agreed to recognize American independence, was anxious to establish friendly relations with the new government, incidentally detaching it, so far as possible, from France. Perhaps Shelburne's study of American problems before the war showed him the futility of trying to check the western expansion of the seaboard colonies. So before long the British and American commissioners came together on the general outlines of the territorial settlement. With slight regard for Spanish claims, it was agreed that the United States should extend to the Mississippi, sharing the free navigation of that river with the British. *Shelburne accepts the American claim.*

In working out these articles, Jay and Adams, with the reluctant consent of Franklin, not only ignored their instructions, which required them to consult the French ministers at every point, but they also agreed on a secret article about the Floridas which gave the British a distinct preference over the Spaniards. If at the close of the war the Floridas were held by Spain, the northern boundary of *Action of the American envoys. The secret article.*

West Florida was to be the thirty-first parallel; but if Great Britain kept these provinces, then the boundary was to be drawn somewhat farther north, beginning with the mouth of the Yazoo River. When the final treaty was made, Spanish possession of the Floridas was assured, and the line was therefore drawn at the thirty-first parallel; but for many years afterwards the Spaniards were, quite naturally, unwilling to accept a boundary line about which they had not been consulted.

The northern boundary.

In discussing the northern boundary one plan proposed was the extension of the forty-fifth parallel, now the northern boundary of New York, straight west to the Mississippi. This would have given the United States a large part of the present province of Ontario: but Lake Superior would have become wholly British, and with it the rich mineral resources of northern Michigan, Wisconsin, and Minnesota. On the whole, therefore, it was fortunate that the present water boundary through the upper St. Lawrence and the Great Lakes was finally adopted.

The fisheries.

Other questions, then discussed at great length, are now of less general interest. One was the question of the northern fisheries, for which John Adams, the New England member of the commission, felt himself particularly responsible. His theory was that the fisheries, not only on the high seas but even in the territorial waters of Newfoundland and other parts of British America, were part of a joint stock acquired by the colonies with the mother country while still partners in the same empire. The partnership was now dissolved; but the United States was still entitled to share in this joint interest, even within British jurisdiction. This was an extreme position, not only from the British point of view but from that of the French also, who had certain claims on the Newfoundland fisheries. Adams was stubborn, however, and won a substantial victory.

On the questions of territorial boundaries and the fisheries, the American commissioners did remarkably well. Of **British debts.** the other issues discussed, two proved particularly difficult. These were the question of American debts to British creditors and the complicated problem of the loyalists. For Scotch and English business men the first question was vitally important, since the balances due by American planters and merchants to their correspondents in London were very large. The outbreak of war seemed to Americans an excellent opportunity for canceling these debts and that was done in one state after another. Now, however, the British government demanded that such obligations should be recognized as still binding. Franklin questioned whether the commissioners or Congress had a right to bind the States in this matter, but Adams declared that he had no intention of cheating anybody, and so made possible a mutual agreement that there should be no interference with the collection of just debts due by citizens of either country to those of the other.

Still more troublesome was the problem of the loyalists. **The problem of the loyalists.** The British position in relation to their American supporters was very difficult. Though one of the principal parties to the war, the loyalists had no voice in the final settlement. Some were exiles in England or within the British lines in America and others clung to their old homes; their property had been confiscated and many had suffered untold hardships. For all this distress little sympathy was felt either by the Whigs in the United States or by the commissioners in Paris. From their point of view the Tories were traitors to America, who by their advice to the British government had been largely responsible for bringing on the conflict. Having chosen their part, they must now take the consequences. This attitude was natural enough after a civil war marked by harshness and brutality on both sides; but it was equally natural that the British should feel differently. For them it was clearly a debt of honor to protect those who had sacrificed so much in their devotion to the ideal of a united empire. If at any time British statesmen were inclined to forget these obligations, they were painfully reminded of them by the throng of exiles in London. At times the deadlock seemed almost hopeless, but a compromise was finally reached. It was agreed, first, that Congress should recommend to the states some concession, especially to those loyalists who had not taken up arms on the British side; and secondly, that there should be no further proceedings against anyone because of his part in the war. The promise to make recommendations to the states was fulfilled, but proved to be of little value because of the intense popular feeling against the Tories. Taken together, however, these two measures enabled the ministry to "save its face" to some extent at least.

Compromise on the loyalists.

The document finally signed by Oswald and the American commissioners, on November 30, 1782, was not strictly a treaty, but an agreement on certain articles which were to be incorporated in a formal treaty after Great Britain had come to terms with France. In this way the formal requirements of the French alliance were satisfied, though the proceedings as a whole hardly showed the spirit which might have been expected between allies. At last, in January, 1783, preliminary articles of peace were signed by France and Spain, by which the Bourbon powers recovered some of the ground lost in 1763. France made a slight gain in the West Indies and Spain secured not only her old colony of Florida but also that part of the Gulf coast east of New Orleans which had been a part of French Louisiana. Though Great Britain had to reconcile herself to the loss of the thirteen colonies, she got through the war with less damage than might have been expected, considering the combination of forces against her. Of all the powers, America was the only one to gain any great advantage from the war. The French monarchy had won a supposed advantage by weakening

Preliminary treaty of 1782.

International results of the war.

England, but paid for it by a burdensome debt. Spain failed to shake England's hold on Gibraltar, and though she held more territory in North America than ever before, she had to face a new rival in the young American republic, whose hopes of western expansion conflicted with her own.

During the peace negotiations, the American commissioners were acting with little opportunity to consult their constituents. They were subject to instructions of which they did not wholly approve but which could not be changed without long and perhaps disastrous delays. When the work was at last done, they were naturally anxious about the impression it would make in America. Congress was finally convinced that the commissioners had on the whole made a satisfactory bargain; but on some points there was sharp criticism. The articles on the loyalists were unsatisfactory; there was no arrangement for the reopening of commercial relations with the West Indies; finally, the commissioners had failed to obey their instructions in the matter of consulting with the French government. Special point was given to this last criticism by a communication from Vergennes, and his resentment was embarrassing because Congress was then making fresh demands on the French treasury. Before long, however, the controversy died down and the articles were accepted. Meantime, Franklin undertook the task of pacifying Vergennes, who was persuaded to accept the situation, and the French government made a new loan of six million livres to the United States.[1]

French and American criticism of the treaty.

Hostilities were suspended in February, 1783, but more than six months passed before the final treaty was signed. In the British Parliament the treaty and the ministry which made it were vigorously attacked, partly at least for factional reasons. Shelburne had to resign and a new ministry was formed by a curious alliance between the followers of Fox

English criticism.

---

[1] The total loans from France to the United States, 1777–1783, amounted to $6,352,500.

Last stages
of the
negotiations. and North.   So, after all, it was Fox who directed the negotiations for the final treaty of peace.   His agent in Paris
was David Hartley, who had corresponded with Franklin
during the war, and whose friendly feeling for the Americans
now led him to propose concessions which would have cut
deep into the old British commercial system.   Fox himself
was, of course, friendly to the Americans, and many of the
London merchants were interested in plans for the reopening of American trade.   Unfortunately there were also
strong interests on the other side, including the shipowners and the merchants trading to the West Indies, who
were afraid of American competition.   So the hope of a
commercial understanding came to nothing, and a great
opportunity for promoting international good will was lost.

The defini-
tive treaty
and its
ratification. It was not possible now to do more than incorporate the
preliminary articles in the definitive treaty of peace, which
was duly signed on September 3, 1783.   Even yet the business was not completed, for the treaty had to be ratified
by both governments, and it took a long time for the Congress to get a quorum for this purpose.   Finally, however, in
May, 1784, ratifications were exchanged in London and the
work was done.

It was nine years since the war began and nearly eight
since the thirteen colonies first asserted their right to "assume
among the powers of the earth" their "separate and equal
station."   Now this right had been formally recognized by
the mother country and the American people were at last
free to work out more adequately the difficult problems of
economic, political, and social reconstruction.

BIBLIOGRAPHICAL NOTES

General
references. Channing, *United States*, III, ch. XII.   Fish, C. R., *American
Diplomacy*, chs. IV, V.   Bemis, *Diplomacy of the American
Revolution*, 172–256.   McLaughlin, A. C., *Confederation and Con-
stitution*, chs. I, II.   Winsor, *America*, VII, ch. II.   Bancroft,
United States, V, pt. V. chs. I–VII.

Hart, *Contemporaries*, II, ch. XXXV. Treaty in Macdonald, *Select Documents*, no. 3. — Collected sources.

Morse, J. T., *John Adams*, chs. VIII–IX. Chinard, G., *Honest John Adams*, bk. II. Pellew, G., *John Jay*, chs. VI–VIII. Various biographies of Franklin. — American negotiators.

Adams, J., Diary in *Works*, III, 298–383. Franklin, *Writings* (Smyth edition), VIII. Wharton, F., *Revolutionary Diplomatic Correspondence*, especially V, VI. — Sources.

Corwin, *French Policy and the American Alliance*. Phillips, P. C., *The West in the Diplomacy of the American Revolution* (University of Illinois, *Studies*), especially 203–227. Faÿ, B., *The Revolutionary Spirit in France and the U. S.* Winsor, J., *Westward Movement*, ch. XII. — Relations with France and Spain. The West.

Fitzmaurice, *Shelburne*, III, chs. III–VI. Wead, E., "British Public Opinion of the Peace with America in 1782," *A.H.R.* (1929), XXXIV, 513–531. (For the British peace proposals of 1778, see Guttridge, G. H., *David Hartley*, and Morison, *Sources and Documents*, 186–203.) — British policy and opinion.

CHAPTER XXIV

INDEPENDENT AMERICA

The new era. In his "Farewell Orders" to the American armies, Washington expressed the mingled hope and anxiety with which thoughtful Americans looked forward to the new era of independence. There were indeed unique opportunities, "enlarged prospects of happiness," almost exceeding "the power of description." It seemed, not only to Americans but to liberal Europeans in England and on the Continent, that here, unfettered by the traditions of the Old World, there was a chance to work out a new kind of politics and a new social order for the enlightenment of mankind. The French economist, Turgot, spoke of American independence as the most important event since the discovery of the New World. "New-born Republics of America," he wrote, "I salute you as the hope of mankind, to which you open a refuge, and promise great and happy examples."

Advice and criticism. But Washington had also his word of warning. In the "Farewell Orders" and elsewhere, he put the serious question, whether the American people would be equal to their great task. Independence was won but "unless the principles of the federal government were properly supported, and the powers of the Union increased, the honor, dignity, and justice of the nation would be lost forever." Nor was the possibility of failure overlooked by friends and enemies abroad. The same Turgot who greeted the new republics with so much enthusiasm felt also the seriousness of the issue. Fifty years from now the world would have learned "whether modern peoples can preserve republican constitutions, whether morals are compatible with the great progress of civilization, and whether America is meant to improve or to aggravate the fate of humanity." Some Englishmen shared this sympathetic interest, as, for instance, Hartley, negotiator of the peace treaty, and Richard Price, one of the best-known political philosophers of his time, whose advice on American problems was welcomed by Franklin and John Adams. Other critics were not so friendly. Franklin complained that American prospects were disparaged in the British press, which was filled with "strange accounts of anarchy and confusion," and there was much skepticism in Europe about the permanence of this republican confederation. It is easy to smile at these doubts, but they were not wholly unreasonable in view of the previous history of republics and federations.

The territorial extent of the Union was a great permanent asset, but it furnished also many serious problems. Much of the territory allotted to the United States by the peace treaty was not really brought under American control until the following decade. The British continued to hold posts beyond the line at Oswego, Niagara, Detroit, Mackinaw, Green Bay, and a few other points south of the Lakes. In western New York, in the present areas of Michigan and Wisconsin, and in a considerable stretch of territory across what is now northern Ohio, Indiana, and Illinois, it was the British flag that counted most during the next decade. Farther south the situation was similarly confused. The handful of American citizens in Illinois looked across the Mississippi to a Spanish province. Whether that river should be an international waterway as well as a boundary was a question still to be thrashed out with the Spaniards, who controlled not only the whole western bank but also the eastern side for more than two hundred miles from the Gulf. Spain also refused to accept the Anglo-American agreement fixing the southern boundary of the United

Resources and problems. Territory.

British posts.

Spanish claims.

States at the thirty-first parallel. Whether this contention
was right or wrong, the advantage of actual possession
was with the Spaniards, who had a military post at Natchez
well above that boundary and could block the passage of
American ships to the Gulf.

The Indians. The Indians also had to be considered; they had no pleni-
potentiary at Paris, but they were still the chief occupants
of the trans-Allegheny country. It was an interesting
question which Aranda, the Spanish ambassador, put to Jay
in August, 1782. "What right," he asked, had the Americans to "territories which manifestly belong to free and
independent nations of Indians." The solution then proposed by the French secretary, Rayneval, was the recognition of Spanish, British, and American "spheres of
influence," or protectorates. The British decided at that
time in favor of the American rather than the Spanish
contention, and by agreeing to surrender the western
posts seemed to have committed themselves against the
theory of a buffer territory under Indian sovereignty; but
the notion was not quite dead. London and Montreal
merchants interested in the fur trade of the Great Lakes
region were not reconciled to the surrender of the western
posts. Though they could not keep this article out of the
definitive treaty, they did delay its execution. Unfortunately the American state legislatures played into the hands
of this British group by violating other articles of the treaty,
so providing an argument against the surrender of the posts.
A large proportion of the northwestern Indians consequently
remained under British influence and were encouraged to
hold out against the claims of the United States, thus checking the progress of white occupation. In the southern section
of the Ohio valley the settlements of Kentucky and Tennessee
were now numerous enough to insure their permanence; but
farther south the boundary dispute with Spain created an
Indian problem much like that of the Northwest.

Interstate boundary questions also made trouble. At the close of the Revolution congressional arbitration decided one such dispute by giving Pennsylvania jurisdiction over the Wyoming valley, which had been claimed by Connecticut. A similar dispute between New York and Massachusetts over the territory south of Lake Ontario was still undecided in 1783; Massachusetts did not give up her claim until three years later. In New England Maine still belonged to Massachusetts, but the status of Vermont was uncertain; its new government was not yet recognized by Congress, and New York still claimed jurisdiction. In the south, Kentucky remained under the government of Virginia, and though the liberals of the mother state soon conceded Kentucky's claim to statehood, the terms of separation were not so easily arranged. Feeling that in this period of uncertainty their interests were neglected, some of the frontier leaders were seriously discontented. North Carolina also had an embryo commonwealth to deal with in the Tennessee country, where an attempt was made to form the new state of Franklin; it failed, however, to get congressional approval and the authority of North Carolina was reëstablished.

As to the rest of the western country, north of the Ohio and south of Tennessee, there were differences of another sort. Should the sea-to-sea charters of Virginia, Massachusetts, and the rest be recognized as still valid, or should this territory be treated as a federal domain? Some of the states were not ready to give up without a struggle. Virginia, for instance, reasserted her charter claims in the constitution of 1776, and after Clark's expedition to Kaskaskia she organized a large part of the "old Northwest" into the "county of Illinois." The American arguments at the peace conference also assumed the validity of the old charters. On the other hand there were strong arguments against these state claims. For one thing, they conflicted with each other.

Against the vague "west and northwest" clause of the Virginia charter there were overlapping claims of Massachusetts and Connecticut, not to mention the pretensions of New York, based on its alleged suzerainty over the Iroquois and their western tributaries. Furthermore, states which had no western claims thought it quite unfair that territory won by the common efforts of thirteen commonwealths should be monopolized by a bare majority of them. On this ground Maryland stubbornly refused to ratify the Articles of Confederation until convinced that Virginia would give up her jurisdiction, at least north of the Ohio.

State cessions.

In 1780 Congress urged the states to surrender their western claims, agreeing, if that were done, to hold the territory for the common benefit of all, with the understanding that out of it new states should be developed. In 1781 New York cleared the way by transferring to Congress her shadowy Iroquois title. Virginia, after some controversy about details, gave in 1784 a formal deed of cession covering the territory northwest of the Ohio, and during the next three years Massachusetts and Connecticut followed suit. By 1787, federal jurisdiction was established over the whole "Northwest" except the "Connecticut Reserve" in northern Ohio. South of the Ohio the state claims were still kept up until after 1789, except for a narrow strip ceded by South Carolina in 1787.

Physical resources.

Making all possible allowance for disputed boundaries, the new republic was already more fortunate in physical endowment than any European nation. Its territory was many times greater than that of any except Russia, and the enormous extent of that empire was offset by the long water frontage of the United States on a temperate ocean, giving facilities for international commerce quite beyond the dreams of the most hopeful Russian patriot. Without being fanciful the comparison may be carried a little farther. Neither people had more than scratched the surface of their great landed inheritance and both had great opportunities for colonization over contiguous territory, with only moderate mountain barriers to delay their progress. Probably no American of that day appreciated the economic resources of his country better than Washington. In a letter to a French friend he told of a recent tour in the back country, dwelling with special enthusiasm on " the vast inland navigation of these United States."

Within this "new empire," as Washington called it, there were probably about three million people, not counting the Indian tribes. After the war, immigration set in on a large scale and by 1790 the population had risen to about four million. All estimates for this period, even the first federal census, are quite imperfect; but it is probable that the American population was at least doubled in the quarter century which followed the passage of the Stamp Act. But there were only about half as many Americans in the whole country as now live in New York City alone. *Population.*

Somewhat less than half these people lived in the states from Maryland southward and the northerners were about equally divided between New England and the middle group, though the latter soon forged ahead. If, however, the whites only are counted, the two northern sections would outnumber the South nearly two to one. We can only make rough guesses about the distribution of population between East and West, partly because there was not then and is not now any agreement as to the meaning of those terms. If we classify as eastern all the people living within the present limits of the original thirteen states, the westerners would scarcely exceed one in thirty. If we take the crest of the Appalachian watershed as the dividing line, even this would probably leave nineteen twentieths of the American people on the eastern side. If, however, we include also the hill-country farmers from New England southward to Georgia who were still struggling with frontier *Distribution of population.*

problems, we get several hundred thousand more Western-ers, — still a small minority but a vigorous and rapidly ex-panding one. Even the oldest colonies had plenty of elbow room. The entire population of the four middle states in 1783 was probably about one tenth of the number now living within the continuous urban area of which the city of New York is the center. The largest city in the country was Philadelphia, with something over 30,000 inhabitants. In 1790, the number of people living under urban conditions as now defined by the Bureau of the Census was less than one in thirty.

A rural people.

The constituent elements of the American people did not change much during the three decades from 1760 to 1790. The English stock still largely outnumbered all the others in New England and in the southern tidewater. New immi-gration strengthened the Irish, Scotch-Irish, and German elements; but the growth of the German element was offset by the steady assimilation of older non-English elements, especially the Dutch, with their English neighbors. Such representative New Yorkers as John Jay and Gouverneur Morris represented the mingling of French blood with Dutch and English, but their social outlook was not essentially different from that of men whose descent was wholly English.

Racial elements.

Many of the older German immigrants retained their distinctive traditions and their community life; and in this respect their churches exerted a strong conservative influence. Their language persisted not only in common speech but also in their own press. Yet they too were beginning to share in the more general interests of their adopted country. While mercenaries from Brunswick and Hesse fought on the British side, sturdy German colonials like Herkimer and his Mohawk valley neighbors played their part in the winning of inde-pendence. In the decade following the Revolution, some of the Germans held positions of leadership in state and federal politics. Frederick Muhlenberg, son of the famous Lutheran

The German element.

pioneer, served successively as speaker of the Pennsylvania assembly, president of the state convention which ratified the Federal Constitution, and finally as the first Speaker of the United States House of Representatives.

When all is said, however, there were comparatively few of the governing class whose ancestry was not traceable to some part of the British Isles. The signers of the great historic documents of this period — the Declaration of Independence, the Articles of Confederation, and the Constitution of 1787 — were nearly all of English, Scotch, or Irish descent. *Predominance of English-speaking people.*

Religious distinctions were not yet negligible. The Anglican (or Episcopal) Church suffered most from the Revolution, because of its connection with the British government and the strength of the loyalist element among its members. Even after the first American bishopric was established in Connecticut, the prejudice against that church persisted, especially in New England. In Virginia there were sharp conflicts between Episcopalians and Presbyterians, though at times conservatives in both groups combined against more radical elements like the Baptists and the "New Lights." Most Americans who made any religious profession at all called themselves Christians and Protestants; the only state in which Catholics were influential was Maryland. Even the Episcopalians decided to call their church "Protestant Episcopal." This Protestant feeling showed itself in several of the early state constitutions, which excluded Catholics from certain offices. On the whole, however, religious partisanship counted much less in politics than it had in colonial days. *Religion.*

Compared with Europe, American society seemed to most observers distinctly democratic; but there was one class distinction more radical than any then existing in western or central Europe. That was the distinction between white masters and their black slaves. This servile class *Social distinctions. Slavery.*

not only furnished the South with most of its unskilled labor but formed about one fifth of the whole American population. Though tending to disappear in the North, slavery was so deeply involved in the social structure of the South that even men like Jefferson, who hated the institution, emphasized the difficulty of blacks and whites living together on any other basis. Nevertheless, the border states of Virginia and Maryland were beginning to realize the economic disadvantages of slavery, and by 1783 both governments had prohibited the importation of negro slaves.

No formal aristocracy.

Other class distinctions were much less serious. A few titled personages had lived in America, but most of them considered the old country as their permanent home. Attempts to organize an American nobility had broken down; a few Americans had been knighted for special services, as, for instance, Sir William Pepperell of Massachusetts and Sir William Johnson of New York, but these were rare exceptions. Formal aristocracy quickly disappeared from American life. Titles of nobility were condemned in several of the early state constitutions and the feeling was so strong that the association of Revolutionary officers known as the Cincinnati was sharply attacked because the privilege of membership was made hereditary. It is true that independent America had not quite forgotten the distinction between "gentle" and "simple." The Pinckneys of South Carolina, the Randolphs of Virginia, and the Livingstons of New York were still looked up to by their fellow citizens. The older American gentry was considerably weakened by the Revolution, but many of the "new men" who came to the front gained a similar prestige. In Virginia, Washington and Jefferson enjoyed on their landed estates a kind of life not unlike that of well-to-do English country gentlemen. Pennsylvania had in John Dickinson a good example of the rich "gentleman-farmer" who could afford the luxury of a town house, and in Robert Morris an equally notable

Persistence of other social distinctions.

example of the merchant prince. John Adams, no longer quite so insurgent as in his early days, believed that the "well born" should have some recognition even in a republic. The essential fact, however, is that such class distinctions were, even in the older settlements, far less rigid than in Europe. The aristocracy of an undeveloped country is one which almost any man of force may hope to enter. The French writer, Ségur, describing society in Rhode Island during the war, said that he had seen nowhere "a more complete mingling of persons of all classes, between whom an equal decency allowed no untoward difference to be seen."

The small farmers, who formed the largest single element in American society, had not changed radically since colonial times. Though much better off than the typical European peasant, their intellectual outlook, as well as their commercial intercourse, was much restricted. Their supply of ready money was small and they complained that too much of it went to the commercial and creditor class. They believed with some justice that taxes were inequitably levied; also that if lawyers were fewer and paper money plentiful, a more equitable distribution of wealth might be secured. In some of these demands the farmers were supported by the small shopkeepers of the towns. *The small farmers.*

Leaving the negroes out of account, the landless laboring class was much smaller than it now is. At its lower level were the white indentured servants, or redemptioners, who were still imported from abroad and could still be bought and sold. A little higher in the scale were the hired men on the northern farms, the free servants in well-to-do households, and some of the poorer mechanics. Such people commonly did not have the right to vote and the labor unions of later years had not as yet developed for their protection. Even in these groups, however, extreme poverty was comparatively rare. Food was abundant and cheap, *Labor and wages.*

and the chance of free or practically free land on the frontier tended to pull wages up. Americans like Franklin and Jay, returning from long periods of absence abroad, were impressed by the high cost of labor. In a few of the larger towns the mechanics were beginning to make a stir in politics, as in Philadelphia, where they combined with the back-country farmers against the old ruling class.

Sectionalism. Sectionalism played an even larger part in the early days of the American Union than it now does. There were conflicts of interests between groups of states, between sections within a given state, and between sectional areas which cut across state boundaries. All these divisions were accentuated by difficulties of communication. It took more time and trouble to go from Boston to New York in 1783 than it now takes to go from either to San Francisco. Exchanges of information now possible in a few minutes by telephone often took many days. Slow and expensive transportation produced great differences in price levels, which were aggravated by the failure of the Confederation to provide a standard coinage, so that different localities had different rates of exchange for English shillings and Spanish dollars.

New England after the Revolution. New England was still the most closely knit of all the sections, with definite common traditions in manners, politics, and religion. Its most characteristic economic activities were, as in colonial times, connected with the sea. New England's interest in the northern fisheries had been guarded in the treaty of 1783; but there was some anxiety about the foreign markets, in which a large part of each season's catch had formerly been sold. Royal orders closed the British West Indies to American fish, and Yankee ships in the Mediterranean were no longer protected by the British navy against the Barbary pirates. The fisheries and the **Commercial problems.** shipping interest suffered from the uncertainties of this period of readjustment. Under the English Navigation Acts New England vessels were now foreign, and though some new lines of foreign trade were opened up during the war, Frenchmen and Spaniards were about as reluctant as the English to relax their old commercial systems. Imports from England came in freely, so freely, indeed, as to overload the market; but the export trade was thrown out of gear. So, after a period of abnormal war risks, with correspondingly high prices, New Englanders whose capital was invested in shipping and foreign commerce were for a time much depressed.

It was not long, however, before Yankee ingenuity found new opportunities. The open ports of the Danish and Dutch West Indies furnished one way of evading British colonial regulations; the use of fraudulent British papers was another. The French made some concessions in their islands, which helped the American export trade in lumber and breadstuffs. During this decade came also the modest beginnings of New England commerce with China, and before long the American share in the Canton trade was second only to that of the British. In 1789 four ships belonging to a single Salem family were at that port at one time. Still, as in colonial times, important branches of foreign trade were carried on not only from Boston but from minor ports like Newport and Salem. Newport business men were getting letters from English correspondents looking toward the revival of old business relations. One such correspondent in Manchester presented an *ante-bellum* bill for payment and invited orders for British manufactures. There were Irish merchants, too, who hoped for some New England business and were ready with advice. One of them suggested that the "general run of New England rum" was too "weak and ill-flavored for this market." Other places in which Newport merchants then had correspondents were Portugal, Hamburg, the Netherlands, and the Scandinavian countries.

The interruption of trade during the earlier years of

Revival of trade.

Home
manufac-
tures.
the Revolution stimulated home manufactures; but peace brought back the old trade with the mother country before they could compete effectively with British goods. Though New Englanders followed with interest recent improvements in the British textile industry, the development of such manufactures in New England, except of a rudimentary kind and for a limited market, had to wait until the next Agricultural
and com-
mercial
interests. generation. More New Englanders were still engaged in farming than in any other single occupation, and when well organized the farmers could outvote the merchants. Even in a small area like Rhode Island, the rural population dominated politics for a large part of this period. Nevertheless, New England was generally thought of as the distinctively commercial section of the country. Politically, also, the commercial interest, supported by the professional classes, had an influence out of all proportion to its numbers and was usually able to speak for New England in the councils of the Union.

New York.
In New York, the conflict of commercial and agricultural interests was complicated by the bitter antagonism between the Whigs who came back to the city at the end of the British occupation and their Tory neighbors who had remained at home. For several years, the city of New York had been cut off from other parts of the Union; it had also suffered from extensive fires, and the uncertainties of the Commerce. time delayed the work of restoration. These disadvantages, however, were only temporary and could not long prevent the city from exploiting its position as the market and outlet not only for up-state New York but for much of Connecticut and New Jersey as well. In fact, the New York legislature sometimes took unfair advantage of this situation by levying duties on the trade of its neighbors. In the export trade of New York, furs had lost much of their former importance, partly because British occupation of the Lake posts, including Oswego, discouraged the American traders.

Naturally the merchants were all the more anxious for the reopening of the West Indian trade.

The landed interest was relatively more important in New York than in New England, and for several years such leaders as Governor Clinton kept themselves in power by skillful appeals to the rural voters against the moneyed interests of the city of New York. In opposition to John Jay, and later Alexander Hamilton, the up-state political machine went in for paper money and for shifting taxation as far as possible from land to commerce, by means of customs duties. Naturally the New Yorkers were not anxious to see this revenue transferred from the state to the federal government. *The landed interest.*

In Pennsylvania there was a similar balancing of rural and commercial interests. Philadelphia was the chief financial center in the country and the great merchants of that city were important factors in the national life, notably Robert Morris, the most conspicuous representative in his day of "big business" in politics. Genuinely patriotic, he was also deeply involved in speculative enterprises of every kind — trade with the East Indies, the development of iron manufactures, and investments in western lands. In Philadelphia, as in Boston, trade suffered from international complications. One merchant wrote in 1783 to a Newport correspondent that till a commercial treaty could be made with England, it was impossible to tell "what to carry or where to go." Meantime, however, the European demand for American foodstuffs was growing and much of it was supplied by the Pennsylvanians, who, like the New Englanders, were finding back doors to the British West Indies. By 1786, Franklin could write optimistically about business conditions in Philadelphia. Improved real estate had trebled in value since the Revolution, new buildings were going up fast, and European goods could be had on easy terms. *Pennsylvania, Philadelphia merchants.*

The Philadelphia magnates had, however, to reckon with strong opposition elements. They could count generally *Democratic forces.*

on the older and wealthier landowning communities; but in the city itself a radical democracy was taking shape. The old antagonism between the eastern and western sections, which had been so important a factor in the Revolution, was very much alive. The up-country farmers counted for more than in colonial days; but they were scattered over a wider area and it was hard for them to organize against the more compact communities of the East. It is worth noting, for instance, that all the Pennsylvania delegates to the Federal Convention of 1787 were chosen from Philadelphia.

East and West.

In the Chesapeake country the growth of Baltimore was striking. Though far behind Philadelphia, New York, and Boston, it had already a merchant class of some importance, buying and selling the products of Maryland and the neighboring states. The tobacco trade went on about as in colonial times, with the planters selling to British merchants or to "factors" on this side of the water. Jefferson pointed out, in his *Notes on Virginia*, that the planters still had trade brought up the rivers to their "doors," with the result that Virginia even now had "no towns of any consequence," though he had some hope of Norfolk's becoming the "emporium" for Chesapeake Bay. On the other hand, Jefferson was pleased to note that wheat production was rapidly gaining on tobacco; the latter, with its impoverishment of the soil, seemed to him a "culture productive of infinite wretchedness." With this decline in tobacco cultivation went other important changes: the shifting of power from the tidewater to the interior and growing doubts about the efficiency of slave labor.

Growth of Baltimore.

Virginia planters and farmers.

During the later years of the war the Virginians suffered considerably from hostile armies and their old dependence on English shipping made the interruption of trade with the mother country more inconvenient than it was for most of the northerners. Here also there was some attempt to

Economic difficulties.

develop home manufactures; but Jefferson thought his fellow citizens would go back as soon as they could to the business of exchanging raw materials "for finer manufactures than they are able to execute themselves." Meantime, the planters were burdened with debts and therefore reluctant to carry out the clause of the peace treaty regarding the rights of British creditors. For similar reasons there was a good deal of paper-money sentiment, though not enough to overcome the opposition of the more conservative leaders.

In both the Chesapeake colonies there was consider- Internal im-
able interest in constructive projects. Both wanted a better provements.
regulation of trade on the Potomac and in the Bay; there was also a strong movement for coöperation in the improvement of interior waterways, especially for the purpose of developing trade with the West. By canals and the removal of obstructions, the James and the Potomac might be connected with the Ohio, and Virginia thus enabled to compete more effectively with Pennsylvania. Washington and other prominent Virginians who held western lands naturally had a special interest in such plans. The North Carolinians also were North
deeply interested in the development of the West, whether Carolina.
as land speculators, like Richard Henderson, the founder of Kentucky, or as trail makers and pioneers.

In South Carolina political power was still held by the South
rice and indigo planters in combination with the leading Carolina and
Charleston merchants. The conspicuous people in this state Georgia.
were generally great planters, or lawyers with large plantation interests. Much Charleston money was, however, invested in foreign commerce. While the Virginians were becoming dubious about slavery, South Carolina believed that economic salvation depended upon continuing that system. The older settlements of Georgia resembled those of South Carolina; but the most striking characteristic of this frontier state during the next few decades was its potential wealth in unoccupied lands.

Westward
expansion.
New Eng-
land's part
in the
movement.

This survey of the sections would be quite incomplete without some account of the people who were laying the foundations of new commonwealths in the West. So far as the trans-Allegheny region was concerned, the part taken by New Englanders in this movement was negligible. New England's pioneering was at that time mainly "down East," in Maine, or in Vermont, which was then growing rapidly. According to the census of 1790, Vermont ranked higher in population than three of the original thirteen states. These new settlements were less compact than those of seventeenth-century New England and somewhat more democratic; yet they reproduced to a considerable extent the Puritan spirit of the Massachusetts and Connecticut towns from which the founders came. As in earlier times, some New Englanders migrated to other sections. Before the Wyoming valley dispute was settled in favor of Pennsylvania, a few Connecticut people moved into that region. Disappointed in the outcome of that controversy, Connecticut began to plan seriously for the exploitation of its charter claims in northern Ohio. During this period pioneer settlements were made by New Englanders in central and western New York, and a few adventurous spirits began to think of the Ohio country.

Ohio valley
pioneers.

The real pioneers of the Ohio valley, however, were not the New Englanders, but the men who pushed through the Appalachian passes from Pennsylvania southward. The most common northern route to the valley then ran from Philadelphia through the old German town of Lancaster and across the mountains to Pittsburgh. Every spring and summer a great stream of colonists made their way along this road and then floated down the river on flatboats.

Movement
along the
southern
rivers.

Even more important at first was the movement which followed the great southern tributaries of the Ohio. The Monongahela and Kanawha furnished convenient approaches from Virginia. Farther south, where the present states of

Virginia, North Carolina, Kentucky, and Tennessee come together, are the sources of the Cumberland and the Tennessee. The latter, rising among the Virginia mountains, flows southwestwardly across Tennessee into northern Alabama and Mississippi; here it takes a sharp turn to the northwest, flowing across Tennessee again and through Kentucky into the Ohio. To-day a steamboat can make its way up the Tennessee as far as Alabama with less risk of grounding than on the Mississippi between St. Louis and Cairo. For the flatboats and other small craft used by the pioneers, the upper reaches of the river were also navigable, though the difficulties were great, including not only rapids and snags, but also the possibility of Indian attacks. *The Tennessee valley.*

On the upper courses of these southern rivers were planted the first settlements of West Virginia and eastern Tennessee; later and more adventurous pioneers went on to lonely outposts still farther west. The early settlers of Nashville, for instance, followed the Tennessee to the Ohio, the Ohio to the Cumberland and up that river to the site of the present city. Until 1789 most of these Ohio valley settlements were in Kentucky and Tennessee. North of the Ohio there were only a few Anglo-American pioneers interspersed among the old French settlements, at such widely scattered points as Vincennes and Kaskaskia.

Many of these frontier people were still chiefly occupied with hunting and Indian trading; but there were farmers, too, with surplus products to exchange for clothing, household goods, and tools. Since it was difficult for these frontier farmers to move their wheat, flour, and pork up the rivers to the East, they were deeply interested in getting an outlet through the Mississippi to the Gulf. Unfortunately Spain's exclusive policy interfered with this movement of trade. Now and then river cargoes were held up by Spanish officials, and impatient frontiersmen, like George Rogers *Problems of the West.* *The Mississippi question.*

Clark, were ready to retaliate without waiting for Congress to act.

Not all Americans were sympathetic toward this colonization of the West. John Jay, for instance, feared it would not be easy to manage the western people and doubted whether they would be "fit to govern themselves" even "after two or three generations." Even Washington thought the western movement might go too fast and that it would be better to fill in first the region adjoining the old colonies. In general, however, the South was more sympathetic than the northeastern states.

Characteristics of the western settlers.

Generalizations about the western people have always been popular and usually one-sided. Eastern contemporaries often overemphasized the lawless and even vicious characters who found their way to the border country. On the other hand, many writers, including some able students of western history, tend to idealize the frontiersmen and assume that they represented a natural selection of the most vigorous people in the older settlements, leaving behind men of less force and initiative. As a matter of fact, many kinds of people were represented among the western settlers as well as among those who remained at home. Some of those who felt the fascination of the wilderness were fine types of self-reliant manhood, like Daniel Boone, the pathfinder of Kentucky. Others slipped into savage ways and became much like the Indians with whom they fought or trafficked. Most of the pioneers, however, were plain, practical people, who, were tired of working for wages or making a meager living out of poor land and were attracted by the free lands of the West. The moneyed class also had a part in the movement, sometimes as land speculators, sometimes by furnishing colonists with the necessary capital. Now and then such men went with their capital to the new country.

The attractive qualities of the frontiersmen were their courage, the self-reliance and resourcefulness called out by the isolated life of the wilderness, and the democratic spirit which developed as men got away from the inherited distinctions of an older society. There were losses, however, as well as gains. As Jay said, somewhat stiffly, the "progress of civilization and the means of information" were "very tardy" in "separate settlements." With boundless resources to draw upon, the pioneers naturally used them wastefully and established habits which a later generation, forced to conserve its resources, cannot easily shake off.

The older colonial churches had comparatively little influence in the early development of the trans-Allegheny region. The Scotch-Irish Presbyterian clergy tried to care for their own people, who formed a large proportion of the western pioneers. But in this sparsely settled region it was hard to form churches and give them educated ministers. This left a wide field for service, in which important work was soon being done by two comparatively new churches, the Baptists and the Methodists. Their traveling preachers laid little stress on the formalities of worship, but their zeal made a deep impression. The Methodists, in particular, were soon able to conserve the results of this emotional preaching by an effective central organization, especially well adapted to the work of an expanding church. The field was too vast, however, for the forces then available and large populations grew up with an absence of educational and religious opportunities which scandalized the home missionaries of the next generation. *Religion in the West.*

BIBLIOGRAPHICAL NOTES

Jameson, F. J., *American Revolution Considered as a Social Movement*. Nevins, A., *American States*. McMaster, *History of the People of the United States*, I, ch. I. *General survey.*

Channing, *United States*, III, 408–427. Callender, *Selections from the Economic History of the U. S.*, 168–177. Weeden, W. B., *New England*, chs. XXII, XXIII. Morison, S. E., *Maritime History of Massachusetts*, chs. III, IV. *Economic conditions.*

Expansion and the West.

Paxson, F. L., *History of the American Frontier.* Semple, E. C., *American History and Its Geographic Conditions*, ch. V. Henderson, *Conquest of the Old Southwest*, ch. XIX. Hulbert, A. B., *Washington and the West.* Matthews, L. K., *Expansion of New England.* Whitaker, A. P., "The Muscle Shoals Speculation, 1783–1789," *M.V.H.R.*, XIII, 365–387. For the secession of Vermont, see Flick, A. C., *History of the State of N. Y.*, V, ch. I.

Frontier leaders.

Pell, John, *Ethan Allen.* Turner, F. M., *Life of Sevier.* Kenton, E., *Simon Kenton.* Thwaites, R. G., *Daniel Boone.* Savelle, M., *George Morgan, Colony Builder.*

Western state governments.

Turner, F. J., *Western State Making in the American Revolution*, II (*A.H.R.*, I, 251–269). Alden, G. H., *New Governments West of the Alleghenies.* Williams, S. C., *History of the Lost State of Franklin*, and his *Beginnings of West Tennessee.* Abernethy, T. P., *From Frontier to Plantation in Tennessee.*

Sources.

Writings of Washington (Ford edition, X), Franklin, and Jefferson (including his *Notes on Virginia*). Chastellux, J. F. de, *Travels in North America* (1780–1782). Schoepf, J. D., *Travels in the Confederation* (translated by Morrison). Quotations from French visitors in Jusserand, *With Americans of Past and Present Days*, and in Sherrill, C. H., *French Memories of Eighteenth Century America.* Hart and Channing, *American Historical Leaflets*, no. 22 (State land claims and cessions).

See also references for ch. XXVI.

CHAPTER XXV

REPUBLICAN PRINCIPLES IN RECONSTRUCTION

THE American commonwealths began their independent existence with great natural resources; but their prosperous development still depended in part on the kind of political institutions they could establish to replace the old colonial system. In the storm and stress of the Revolution, one state after another expressed its ideals and tried to provide for its own special needs by the adoption of a state constitution. Imperfect as these early experiments in self-government were, they were notable contributions to the science and art of politics. As such they attracted attention abroad, especially in France, where they were translated and widely read. *Constitution making in the states.*

The new state constitutions began with the principle that all just governments rest on the consent of the governed and that the permanent will of the people should be expressed in a fundamental written law. These constitutions were adopted in various ways, sometimes as in Virginia by a revolutionary assembly originally chosen for a very different purpose. In 1780, however, Massachusetts inaugurated substantially the method now prevailing of having the constitution framed by a convention chosen for that specific purpose by the voters themselves, to whom it was submitted for their approval. These constitutions generally took for granted certain fundamental rights which could not be abridged or taken away even by the lawmaking power. In colonial times Americans had been accustomed to having acts of their assemblies annulled by the English Privy Council on the *Methods of adoption.* *Unconstitutional legislation and the courts.*

547

ground that they were contrary to their charters, or to the principles of common law. Now the new state courts began to exercise a similar authority. In the New Jersey case of *Holmes* v. *Walton*, the judges declared an act of the legislature null and void because it authorized a jury of less than twelve men to try certain criminal cases. There were some protests against such action; but by 1787 the principle that judges might declare laws invalid seemed to be supported by the best legal opinion.

Suffrage qualifications.

Nearly everybody agreed that ultimate sovereignty rested with the people; but just who were the "people" in the political meaning of that term? In this respect the first state constitutions were conservative. The Virginia Declaration of Rights declared that all men should vote who could offer "sufficient evidence of permanent common interest with, and attachment to, the community"; but the old property qualifications were retained and Jefferson declared that this meant the disfranchisement of more than half the men who paid taxes or were enrolled in the state militia. With variations in detail, the precedent set by Virginia was followed by the other states. Even with these restrictions, however, the American system entrusted political power to a much larger proportion of the population than was thought desirable in any European country.

Republican ideals.

Though not strictly democratic from a twentieth-century point of view, the constitution makers of that day were committed to republican ideals and against any kind of hereditary rule. In Virginia, for instance, the most conservative leaders did not apparently propose anything more monarchical than a governor serving during good behavior, and even that does not seem to have been seriously considered. The whole structure of American society was against the hereditary principle. Besides, many Americans were familiar with republican theories, especially those of seventeenth century English Puritans; in two of the chartered colonies, they had seen practically republican governments at work.

Notwithstanding their rejection of the hereditary principle, the American constitutions were much influenced by English and colonial theory, though sometimes mistaken in their interpretation of the former. Following the French writer, Montesquieu, in his interpretation of the English system, Americans accepted the theory of the separation of powers, or "checks and balances." This required the differentiation of three departments of government: the legislative, to make the laws; the executive, to enforce them; and the judiciary, to apply them in individual disputes. These three departments were perfectly familiar, both in English practice and in the American colonial governments. It was, therefore, primarily a question of how to get a better balance between the executive, on the one side, and the legislature and the judiciary on the other.

Quite in accordance with English and colonial precedents, all the new legislatures except that of Pennsylvania consisted of two houses. It was believed that bills would be more carefully considered under this plan than if one assembly were given full power, and many thought an upper house was needed to protect property rights against radical legislation. On this theory senators sometimes had to have higher property qualifications than were required of representatives; in New York and North Carolina they were chosen by a more limited group of voters. Efforts were made to secure a fairer representation of districts and sections than had existed before the Revolution. John Adams believed that the assembly should be "in miniature an exact portrait of the people at large" and in the Massachusetts lower house representation was in fair proportion to population; but the senate appointment was based on property. Elsewhere too the results were unsatisfactory, and Jefferson complained that the Virginia apportionment was

Sources of political theory.

"Separation of powers."

State legislatures; bicameral system.

Problems of apportionment.

decidedly unfair. In 1782, he calculated that the tidewater districts had seventy-one members of the lower house as against forty-six for the piedmont area with substantially the same number of fighting men.

The question of veto power.

To secure a more complete separation of powers, the executive functions of the old provincial councils were given not to the senate but to a distinct executive council. On the question of giving the governor a veto there was a decided difference of opinion. The Virginia constitution rejected the idea, and this example was followed by most of the other states. It was a natural result of popular feeling against the abuse of this power by the royal governors; but cautious thinkers like John Adams thought the executive needed some such protection against encroachments by the legislature. In 1780 Massachusetts worked out a compromise, giving the governor a suspensive veto which could be overruled by a two-thirds majority in both houses of the legislature. New York tried the experiment of giving this power to a council of revision consisting of the governor and a group of judges. This latter plan was popular for a time and as late as 1818 was incorporated in the constitution of Illinois; but the Massachusetts idea has finally prevailed in nearly all the states, as well as in the federal Constitution.

Extent of legislative power. Bills of rights.

Notwithstanding the theory that the legislature was bound by a fundamental law, specific limitations on its power were largely confined to the so-called "bill of rights," which was chiefly designed to prevent arbitrary interference with individual liberty. These rights were largely drawn from English sources, but some ideas like freedom of the press and religious liberty were more fully developed. Except for these safeguards, the powers of the legislature were broadly stated. The long list of things which a twentieth-century legislature is forbidden to do was conspicuously absent.

Weak executives.

The executive, on the other hand, was treated with great suspicion. Pennsylvania preferred to have no governor at all, but only an executive board. In New England governors were chosen annually by the qualified voters, and in New York the election was intrusted to a select group of large freeholders; elsewhere the governor was chosen by the legislature and usually for one year only. Jefferson was not an ardent believer in one-man power; but even he objected to this excessive dependence of the executive on the legislature. Jealousy of the governor showed itself also in other ways. In Virginia, for instance, he could not adjourn or prorogue the legislature as the royal governors had done; the appointment of judges and other important officers was taken from him; and he could not establish his authority in any matter " by virtue of any law, statute, or custom of England." The executive council, already mentioned, also limited the governor's power.

There was a general desire to make the judiciary more independent than in colonial times, and in a majority of the states judges were appointed to serve during good behavior; two other constitutions fixed terms of five and seven years. In Massachusetts the judges were chosen by the executive, but in several states this power was given to the legislature. Direct choice by the people was not approved anywhere. An independent judiciary.

These changes in the mechanism of government did not satisfy the radicals, who valued them largely as means to the establishment of a freer and more democratic society. In the matter of religious liberty, for example, great progress had been made; but liberals like Franklin and Jefferson believed there was still much to be done. Religious discrimination of one kind or another was quite general. In Massachusetts, for instance, the governor had to declare himself a supporter of the Christian religion, and though every citizen could claim the right to worship God in the way "most agreeable to the dictates of his own conscience," another clause promising equal protection under the law was Religious tests.

apparently limited to Christian denominations. Massachusetts practically excluded Catholics by requiring every officeholder to declare on oath that no "foreign prince, person, prelate, state, or potentate" had any authority "in any matter civil, ecclesiastical, or spiritual, within this commonwealth." In New York, a similar oath was required for naturalization. In several other states Catholics were specifically excluded from office. Even in Pennsylvania, Franklin had to apologize for a clause in the constitution requiring legislators to declare their belief in the divine inspiration of the Old and New Testaments.

Church and state relations.

The Revolution did not at once do away with state churches, whether in New England or in Virginia. The Massachusetts constitution declared that each town must be required by law to support "public Protestant teachers of piety, religion, and morality." Individuals might be compelled to attend religious services, if there were any which they could "conscientiously and conveniently attend," and to pay taxes for the support of some kind of Protestant service. Though some concessions were made to Baptists and other dissenters from the Congregational system, complete separation of church and state did not come either in Massachusetts or Connecticut until the nineteenth century. The

Separation of church and state in Virginia.

change came more easily in Virginia, because the Anglican establishment had depended partly on the support of the British government, which was now withdrawn. The Virginia bill of rights contained an eloquent declaration in favor of religious liberty, but left the question of a church establishment still open. A strong party, composed largely of Episcopalians but including some Presbyterians, favored an "assessment" law which would secure public support for some kind of Protestant worship. Patrick Henry favored this measure; but Madison and Jefferson opposed any kind of state support, and it was defeated by a narrow majority. In 1785 Jefferson's bill for absolute religious liberty was passed by the legislature. No Virginian could thenceforth be compelled to attend or support any form of religious worship or be discriminated against in any other way because of his religious opinions.

The constitutional changes of the Revolution affected the American churches in various ways. For the Episcopalians, political separation from the mother country carried with it also separation from the state church of England. Because of technical difficulties resulting from parliamentary control of the English church, the first American bishop was consecrated by bishops of the Scottish Episcopal Church, which was not restricted by any state connection. Before long, bishops were chosen in other states, and by 1789 the American branch of the Anglican communion was reorganized as the Protestant Episcopal Church of the United States. About the same time the Roman Catholics also adjusted themselves to the new political situation. Some of the Maryland Catholics had taken an active part in the Revolution, and one of their number, Charles Carroll of Carrollton, signed the Declaration of Independence. They now got rid of the harsh legislation from which they had suffered before the Revolution, and presently took the lead in securing from the Pope an organization independent of the Vicar-Apostolic in London. In 1789 a papal bull authorized the consecration of John Carroll, a cousin of Charles, as the first bishop of this church in the new republic. Other churches also were forming national organizations. In 1788 the Presbyterians organized a general assembly, and in 1784 John Wesley took the first steps leading to the formation of the Methodist Episcopal Church in the United States. By 1789 these reorganized churches and several others were ready to coöperate in the great American experiment of "free churches in a free state."

Important as it was to establish the principles of political liberty in statutes and constitutions, some Americans at

Reorganization of American churches.

The struggle for a democratic society.

least realized that political democracy could not be maintained without a democratic society. No one felt more strongly than Jefferson how much needed to be done in this direction, especially in his own state of Virginia. One of the first measures of this kind which he advocated and carried through was a law abolishing primogeniture in order to make possible a wider distribution of landed property. In this way he hoped to reduce the influence of the great landowning families.

Primogeniture abolished.

Antislavery movement.

Another subject which troubled many Americans was slavery. When Granville Sharp, a well-known leader of the English antislavery movement, suggested that this institution could hardly be reconciled with American professions about the rights of man, John Jay, then president of an antislavery society in New York, could only reply that American opinion was moving in the right direction. Some Virginians also were embarrassed by this anomaly, and Jefferson actually prepared a plan for gradual emancipation. Realizing, however, that emancipation alone would not solve the race problem, he favored colonizing the negroes in some other country. Measured by actual numbers, the results of this humanitarian philosophy were disappointing. In New England, where the number of negroes had always been small, emancipation was easily accomplished within a few years after the Revolution, and Pennsylvania passed a gradual emancipation act in 1780; but none of the other middle states took decisive action before 1789, and south of Mason and Dixon's line, the realization of Jefferson's ideal was postponed to a distant future.

State encouragement of education.

In the republican philosophy of this period, state encouragement of education had an important place; for if the people were to be sovereign, they must be educated to carry this new responsibility. Among the state constitutions, that of Massachusetts was the first to give education a prominent place among the duties of the state. A remarkable clause, drafted by John Adams, set forth the dependence of free government upon the general diffusion of "wisdom and knowledge"; legislators and magistrates must therefore "cherish the influence of literature and the sciences, and all seminaries of them." Jefferson was equally interested in education and he proposed a series of public institutions extending from elementary schools to a much improved and enlarged William and Mary College.   Elementary instruction was to be free and the best pupils were then to be selected for higher education.   Once more, however, Jefferson's ideas were too advanced for his fellow citizens and many years passed before his plan of higher education was partly realized in the new University of Virginia. Yet some real progress was made during this period.   State funds, especially revenues from public lands, were set aside for educational purposes.   The North with its more fully developed town life still led in systematized public education; but North Carolina and Georgia took their first steps toward the establishment of state institutions of higher learning, a policy afterwards developed more fully in the state universities of the West.

The work of these early conventions and legislatures was marked by many inconsistencies; and yet, taken as a whole, it makes a remarkable record of constructive statesmanship.   Each state had, of course, its own problems which it was free to solve in its own way; but underlying all differences there was a common body of political doctrine which, though drawn from various sources, may fairly be called American.

A record of constructive statesmanship.

The making of an adequate federal union was more difficult and took more time; but even here the experimental stage was short and the whole process of construction surprisingly brief when judged in the light of previous human experience.   It was less than thirteen years after the Declaration of Independence when George Washington took his

The making of a federal union.

place as the head of a new government which has now been tested longer than any other constitutional government in the world except that of Great Britain.

Colonial
precedents.
The British
Empire. In federal as well as state organization the American people profited largely by their experience in the British Empire. Under that system the self-governing colonies of Rhode Island and Connecticut could determine more matters for themselves than they now can as states of the American Union. In the proprietary colonies the inhabitants had less power; but here also the actual control of colonial business by the imperial government was comparatively limited. Even in a royal province the representative assemblies could go very far in the practical exercise of self-government. So Jefferson and some other radical thinkers came to regard the old empire as a kind of federal system. Virginia, according to Jefferson's theory, was a free commonwealth united to the commonwealth of England by a common king and not legally subject to the British Parliament. Jefferson was exceptional among the revolutionary leaders in the extreme to which he pushed this theory, but others were more or less consciously moving in the same direction, and the idea of some roughly defined boundary between the legitimate authority of Parliament and that of a colonial assembly was fairly general.

Distribution
of govern-
mental
powers. The actual distribution of business between imperial and colonial governments also had some significance for later American history. Generally speaking, foreign affairs, the regulation of commerce either with foreign countries or between different jurisdictions within the empire, the regulation of coinage, and the establishment of postal facilities, were all generally regarded as proper business for the imperial government, however unpopular its action might be in any particular case. On the other hand, certain functions now exercised by the federal government were left mainly to the colonial assemblies. With some exceptions

customs duties were fixed by colonial statutes rather than by acts of Parliament. Of course such action was not entirely uncontrolled; each colony was expected to conform to its charter, to certain royal instructions, and to the general principles of English law. If these limitations were ignored, a provincial law might either be disallowed or declared invalid by the English Privy Council in its capacity as a court of appeals.

Aside from such precedents as could be drawn from the British imperial system, American statesmen were doubtless influenced by some of the earlier projects for colonial union, not so much by the rather limited New England confederation of 1643 as by the discussion which went on during the last quarter century of British rule. It was then that the conflict with France and the new problems resulting from the expansion of the empire led men to think more seriously of some political organization which might act for America as a whole. Most Americans, however, were then too intent on preserving their local independence, and so the Albany plan of 1754 proved no more acceptable in the colonies than it did in England. The taxation controversy also revived interest in some sort of federation, through which America might contribute its share of imperial revenue instead of acting only through a large number of provincial assemblies. Franklin's correspondence with Galloway and others shows a steady interest in this subject until he finally became convinced that such a constitutional adjustment within the empire was impracticable. Even after Franklin had given up hope, Galloway urged an American federation as the best means of holding the empire together, and his plan of 1774, which was rejected by the First Continental Congress, contained some features of the Albany plan.

As the prospect of federation within the empire faded away the Whig leaders set to work on plans of their own. Even in the First Continental Congress, Patrick Henry

Colonial experiments and projects for union.

Franklin and Galloway.

Discussion in the Continental Congress.

seemed to favor a permanent union with proportionate representation. In the early days of the Second Continental Congress Franklin presented a plan of his own, based on the idea of proportional representation and giving Congress fairly liberal powers. A year passed, however, before the subject was taken up seriously and, though a committee was then appointed to draft a plan of confederation, the war was nearly over before any federal constitution was adopted.

State sovereignty, 1775–1781.

The actual government of the United States from 1775 to 1781 was, therefore, in the Continental Congress, whose only political authority consisted of the credentials given by each state to its delegates; these were not only extremely indefinite, but could be changed or revoked at will, so that Congress was wholly dependent upon the coöperative spirit of the individual states. Even in matters of general interest like the conduct of the war and negotiations with foreign powers, the states sometimes acted quite independently. So far, therefore, as legal theory is concerned, the case for state sovereignty seems to be complete and the Continental Congress appears as a merely diplomatic body, consisting of representatives from independent states which found it convenient to act together for the time being.

The Continental Congress as a government.

It is equally clear, however, that no mere diplomatic body had ever exercised such a wide range of functions as were actually performed by the Continental Congress. It maintained a Continental army, appointed the commander in chief, issued a Continental currency, incurred debts for the Union without consulting the states, and finally, in 1778, ratified a treaty with a foreign power. Virginia may also have thought it necessary to ratify the treaty; but this was an exceptional proceeding. Certainly the American negotiators of that treaty were acting on the general authority of Congress and not on the instructions of thirteen different states. Without a formal constitution, Congress managed to organize executive departments for war, foreign affairs, and finance, as well as a general postal service. It even organized a court for the trial of appeals in prize cases. From this practical point of view, it can hardly be denied that the Continental Congress, with all its obvious limitations, was a *de facto* federal government, acting for a real political entity known to the outside world as the United States of America.

All this time, however, the need of a more tangible constitution was fully recognized. The committee on confederation, of which Dickinson was chairman, reported to Congress about a week after the Declaration of Independence was adopted. There was some debate then; but it was not until November 15, 1777, that Congress agreed on a document to be recommended to the states. Within a year ten states ratified; but three held out, and it was March, 1781, before the consent of Maryland made it possible to put the new constitution into effect.

Framing of the Articles of Confederation.

The failure to reach an agreement earlier was due partly to the pressure of war business, but chiefly to serious differences of opinion about certain provisions of the Articles of Confederation. The delegates from Massachusetts, Pennsylvania and Virginia were anxious to have in the new government a representation proportional not only to their population but to the financial and military burdens which they had to bear. The drafting committee, however, yielded to the demand of the smaller states for equal representation and after a vigorous debate that plan was finally adopted.

Question of representation.

The debate on the powers of Congress was less important; for there was then little sentiment in favor of a strong federal government. On one issue, however, the smaller states took a somewhat nationalistic attitude. That was the question of the western lands. The states which claimed this territory were determined to have their titles recognized; and the Articles of Confederation as finally adopted declared

Question of western lands.

that no state should be deprived of territory for the benefit of the United States. Interpreting this statement in the light of Virginia's recent reassertion of her sea-to-sea claim, the non-claimant states objected strenuously. From any point of view, a union in which a single state controlled such a vast territory would certainly be quite unequal in fact, whatever the machinery of government might be. The most persistent champion of the non-claimant states was Maryland, which, though voted down in Congress, kept up the fight by refusing to ratify the Articles and so helped toward a reconsideration of the whole question. The Articles were allowed to stand as they were, but with the definite expectation that Virginia would give up her claims to land north of the Ohio River.

The Articles compared with other federations.

It is not quite fair to the Articles of Confederation to compare them always with the riper federal systems of the present time — the present Constitution of the United States, the Canadian and Australian federations, or the reorganized republic of Switzerland. Compared with any of these the Confederation of 1781 was feeble enough, but comparison with previous experiments in federal government gives a different impression. In delegating to Congress exclusive jurisdiction over foreign relations, however ineffective that jurisdiction may have been, the Articles of Confederation went farther than the Holy Roman Empire, or the German confederation of 1815. The Dutch and Swiss unions were both very loose and they had much smaller areas to deal with. With all its faults, this first constitution of the United States was a serious contribution to the art of federal government.

State "sovereignty" asserted.

The governmental machinery of the Confederation was substantially that worked out by Congress before the Articles were adopted. The division of functions between Congress and the states also remained practically the same. What the written document did, in the main, was to state more definitely both the underlying theory of the system and certain methods of doing business. The authors of this constitution took infinite pains to secure what they called the "sovereignty" of the states, though some of them would probably have defined that word in a less absolute sense than that later assumed either by nationalists or by advocates of "state rights." Undoubtedly the Articles were made by states and for states. Like a treaty made by a group of nations, its provisions could not be changed except by unanimous consent. The Confederation was a "league of friendship" in which each member retained its "sovereignty, freedom, and independence," with "every power, jurisdiction and right" not "expressly delegated to the United States." As in a diplomatic congress, each member state voted as a unit and had an equal vote; delegates, though annually elected, could be recalled at any time by the state which chose them and supported them.

The general principle governing the division of powers between the federal and state governments was that Congress was responsible for the external relations of the United States and to a very limited extent for interstate relations. So far as foreign relations were concerned, the Articles were fairly consistent in delegating power to Congress and withholding it from the states. No state could, without the consent of Congress, make a treaty, send or receive diplomatic agents, or engage in war except in case of actual invasion. Without the approval of Congress no state could keep a standing army or navy, or even make an agreement with another member of the Union. In this respect, then, Congress took the place of the British imperial government. Other imperial precedents were followed in giving Congress power to regulate the value of coins, establish a postal service, and deal with Indian affairs. Unfortunately the weak features of the old system were also taken over. The federal army was to be secured by requisitions on the states, similar

Federal and state functions.

Imperial precedents.

to those made by the British government on the provincial assemblies; the taxing power which the colonists denied to Parliament they also denied to their own Congress. In the matter of commerce Congress was worse off than Parliament. Not only could each state establish its own tariff and tonnage duties, as in colonial times, but Congress had no general authority to regulate either foreign or interstate commerce, except to a limited extent by means of commercial treaties.

Citizenship and inter-state comity. One constructive feature of the Articles which has not been sufficiently appreciated is the clause which guarantees to citizens going from one state to another the privilege of citizenship in the latter. This may be considered the first step in the direction of a really national citizenship. A similar spirit was shown in the agreement that the records and judicial proceedings of one state should receive full credit in the others.

Defects of organization. The deficiencies of the Confederation are well known. Not only was the authority of Congress closely limited, but it did not have the organization necessary for doing effectively the work assigned. The rule requiring nine states to approve all important measures often amounted practically to a requirement of unanimous consent; for there were often only nine or ten states present. Equally vicious was the giving of executive as well as legislative authority to Congress. Notwithstanding the demonstrated weakness of committee management, no provision was made for a central executive which should leave Congress free for strictly legislative business.

Question of a federal judiciary. A few timid steps were taken toward a federal judiciary; Congress might establish courts for trying crimes committed on the high seas and for hearing appeals in prize cases; there was also a plan for the arbitration of interstate disputes in land cases. Little use, however, was made of these powers, and the appellate court for prize cases disappeared after the war. The arbitration machinery was indeed used to settle the long-standing controversy between Pennsylvania and Connecticut about the Wyoming valley, and Livingston wrote of this to Lafayette as a model for some future international court, where "all disputes in the great republic of Europe will be tried in the same way." In no other case, however, was such a decision actually rendered under the Confederation. The absence of a federal judiciary made Congress dependent on the state courts for the enforcement of its will on individual citizens, and this illustrates the fundamental weakness of the Confederation. So far as the individual was concerned, his primary allegiance was to the state in which he lived and the federal government could not reach him directly. Congress could make a treaty, but its enforcement depended on the efficiency and good will of state governments.

Even after the adoption of the Articles, men differed as to the kind of government they had established. John Adams called Congress a " diplomatic assembly " and Livingston, in a circular letter to the governors, spoke of "independent states, united not by the power of a sovereign but by their common interest." Yet Livingston spoke in the same letter of "national objects" for which all should work together, and a committee of which Jefferson was chairman declared in 1784 that the states were "consolidated in one federal republic." In a similar spirit, Congress declared in its instructions to Jefferson and other ministers about commercial treaties, that "these United States" should be considered "as one nation, upon the principles of the Federal Constitution." Even in 1787, the members of the Federal Convention disagreed about the nature of the Confederation. In short, the Union of 1781 was of such a kind that men found it hard to speak consistently, thinking of it in one aspect as a league of "independent states" and in another as "one federal republic."

Nature of the system. Contemporary views.

BIBLIOGRAPHICAL NOTES

General accounts.
: Channing, *United· States*, III, chs. XIV, XVIII. Van Tyne, C. H., *American Revolution*, chs. IX, XI; with McLaughlin, *Confederation and Constitution*, ch. III. Nevins, A., *American States*.

Collected sources.
: Johnson, A., *Readings in American Constitutional History*, nos. 17–27. Morison, *Sources and Documents*.

Political theory.
: Merriam, C. E., *American Political Theories*, 74–95. Dunning, W. A., *Political Theories from Luther to Montesquieu*, chs. X, XII, and his *Political Theories, Rousseau to Spencer*, 91–99.

Reconstruction in the states.
: Beard, C. A., *Economic Interpretation of the Constitution*, ch. IV. Dealey, J. Q., *Growth of American State Constitutions*. Dodd, W. F., *Revision and Amendment of State Constitutions*. Cushing, H. A., *Transition from Provincial to Commonwealth Gov't. in Mass.*, esp. chs. VI–IX. Morison, S. E., "Adoption of Constitution of Mass" (Mass. Hist. Soc., *Proceedings*, I, 353). Adams, J. T., *N. E. in the Republic*. Purcell, R. J., *Conn. in Transition*. Bates, F. G., *R. I. and the Formation of the Union*. Flick, A. C., *Hist. of State of N. Y.*, IV, ch. V. Lincoln, *Revolutionary Movement in Penn.*, ch. XIV. Eckenrode, H. J., *Revolution in Va.*, chs. VI, XII. Lingley, C. R., *Transition in Va. from Colony to Commonwealth*. Henry, *Patrick Henry*, I, ch. XVII. Rowland, *George Mason*, I, chs. V–VII. Biographies of Jefferson by G. Chinard and W. E. Dodd. Hunt, G., *Madison*.

Sources on the states.
: State constitutions in Poore, B. P., *Charters and Constitutions*, and Thorpe, F. M., *Colonial and State Constitutions*. Adams, J., *Works*, IV, esp. 185–267, 283–298. Jefferson, *Writings* (Ford ed.), II, III, esp. *Notes on Virginia*, queries, XIII–XIX. Madison, *Writings* (Hunt ed.), I, II. McLaughlin *et al.*, *Source Problems in U. S. Hist.*, Problems III, IV.

Beginnings of federal government.
: Jameson, J. F., *Essays in the Constitutional History of the U. S.*, chs. I, III. Small, A. W., *Beginnings of American Nationality* (*Johns Hopkins Studies*, VIII, nos. I, II). Van Tyne, "Sovereignty in the American Revolution," *A.H.R.*, XII, 529–545.

Sources.
: Hart and Channing, *American History Leaflets*, nos. 14 (Plans of Union, 1690–1776) and 20 (Art. of Confed., etc.) Debates in Continental Congress, *Journals*, VI, 1076–1083, 1098–1106 (Lib. of Cong. ed.).

CHAPTER XXVI

FEDERAL PROBLEMS, 1783 TO 1787

So far as the conduct of the Revolutionary War was concerned, the adoption of the Articles of Confederation seemed to make little difference. The real test came afterwards, when the states were no longer held together by the necessity of defending themselves against foreign armies. Congress could not go on indefinitely borrowing from France, creditors were pressing for the settlement of their accounts, and every department seemed to bristle with difficult, almost insoluble, problems. *The problems of peace.*

In the organization of executive departments Congress made no substantial advance. The disbanding of the Revolutionary army lessened the importance of the war department and for a time there was no secretary in charge; in 1785, however, General Henry Knox was appointed to that office. In the management of the finances, Congress actually took a step backward. In 1784 Robert Morris, disgusted with his thankless task of staving off creditors and writing futile appeals to the state governments, resigned his post as superintendent. His place was never filled, but Congress appointed instead a treasury board of three members. In foreign affairs, Congress did somewhat better. Shortly after Livingston's resignation from the secretaryship, he was succeeded by John Jay, who, fresh from his experience abroad, might fairly be called an expert diplomatist. One point which Jay insisted on was that all foreign correspondence must pass through his hands before going to Congress. *Executive departments.* *John Jay.*

The personnel of the Confederation Congress was stronger

Personnel
of the Con-
federation
Congress.

than has commonly been supposed, though it suffers from comparison with the signers of the Declaration or the members of the Constitutional Convention. There were other posts more attractive to able men than a seat in a body which had little real authority and where experience was so much disparaged that members could not serve more than three consecutive years. Of the men who stood out at the beginning of the Revolution few took part in the Confederation Congress. Washington was enjoying his retirement at Mount Vernon, though his correspondence kept him in touch with leaders in other states. Franklin was abroad at first and later was made president of his state council. Samuel Adams and Patrick Henry devoted themselves chiefly to state politics, and John Adams spent the whole period in the diplomatic service abroad. Not all the delegates, however, were second-rate politicians. Virginia sent Jefferson, Madison, and Monroe, all three of whom were active members and left their mark on some important measures. Among the New England members were Roger Sherman, Oliver Ellsworth, and Rufus King; Hamilton sat for New York, and Charles Pinckney, later an influential member of the Federal Convention, represented South Carolina. In fact, a large proportion of the members of that convention profited by more or less experience in the Confederation Congress.

Irregular
attendance.

Congress was, however, badly hampered by its constitution and the negligence of the states. An attendance of eleven states was unusually good, and under the nine-state rule two or three obstinate individuals could often prevent the passage of important measures. The Congress which was to ratify the peace treaty was supposed to meet at Annapolis in November, 1783; but more than a fortnight later only six states were represented, and only seven were present to receive Washington's impressive resignation of his commission as commander in chief.

The new year began without a quorum to act upon the treaty, and it was not until January 14, with barely nine states present, that this important transaction was completed. This discreditable incident was fairly typical. Some months earlier, Congress had an even more humiliating experience, when it was forced by the mutiny of a few Pennsylvania troops to leave Philadelphia and take refuge at Princeton, New Jersey. Later it migrated in succession to Annapolis, Trenton, and finally New York. It was with such handicaps that Congress had to take up a whole series of complicated problems.

A peripatetic Congress.

One urgent matter was the disbanding of the army, always a difficult problem for the leaders of a successful revolution. Almost from the beginning it had been hard for the politicians and their constituents to appreciate the point of view of the army and its officers. During the war officers and men had been poorly and irregularly paid, and when peace arrived they faced the prospect of going back to civil life without adequate security for the settlement of their just claims. When the preliminary treaty was signed the officers had a general promise that they should receive half pay for life; but in the Confederation Congress, with its nine-state rule, it seemed impossible to carry out this agreement. Aside from the desperate condition of the finances, there were many who had what Madison called "a penurious spirit" about their obligations to the army.

Settling with the army.

Washington was especially troubled because he sympathized with the officers and yet could appreciate the difficulties of Congress. While he was doing his best to keep the army from violent measures, others were not so scrupulous. In the autumn of 1782 Washington wrote that the patience of the army was almost exhausted and that there was danger of serious trouble. Already he had found it necessary to rebuke an officer who suggested the desirability of a monarchy, with Washington himself as king. The

Washington and the army.

crisis came in March, 1783, when some discontented officers at Newburg, New York, proposed a meeting to discuss the pay question, declaring that the time for moderate measures had passed. Fortunately Washington took the matter promptly in hand. Meeting the officers himself he urged them not to mar the patriotic record made in their years of service together; at the same time he promised to support their legitimate demands. A committee of officers was accordingly appointed to take the matter up with Congress, which now realized the necessity of doing something and finally agreed to full pay for five years instead of half pay for life. This was at least a definite acknowledgment of obligation and in 1783 the army was peacefully disbanded.

The chief reason for this and other embarrassments was of course the lack of a proper financial system. The requisition method worked no better for Congress than it had for the British government, notwithstanding the solemn promise that all such obligations would be "inviolably observed." The amount of money required to meet the running expenses of government at that time would now seem quite insignificant, averaging $400,000 a year for the first five years of peace; but considerably larger amounts were needed to make the necessary payments on the public debt. Accordingly, Congress asked the states for $8,000,000 for the year 1782 and for an additional $2,000,000 for 1783. Of these amounts, however, only about $1,500,000 was actually paid up to the end of 1783.

Even before the Articles went into effect, their weakness was recognized by some of the leaders, and in 1781 Congress proposed an amendment authorizing a federal duty of five per cent on imports, to pay the interest on the public debt. Modest as this proposal was, it did involve a real change in the character of the Union; for if it had been adopted federal agents would have collected money directly from individual citizens within the states. So it is on the whole less strange that the amendment was defeated than that it should actually have been ratified by all the states except Rhode Island. To the stubborn Rhode Islanders a congressional collector seemed almost as objectionable as his British predecessors. To meet this objection, Congress proposed in 1783 the "revenue amendment," authorizing, for twenty-five years, certain duties to be levied by Congress through collectors named by the states. This would provide only a part of the revenue needed; for the rest Congress would depend on requisitions, with the understanding that each state would set apart certain revenues for the purpose. This amendment was discussed at intervals for four years but received even less support than the five-per-cent scheme. Congress also considered the possibility of some compulsory process for collecting requisitions, but never got so far as to propose a formal amendment for this purpose.

A government which could not pay its current expenses or the interest on its debts was not likely to meet other responsibilities, and it was certain to have a depressing effect on private business. Especially demoralizing was the depreciated paper money, issued both by Congress and by the states, and the absence of any uniform standard of values. The Spanish dollar, still the most important metallic coin, passed in various ratios to the English pounds, shillings, and pence in which business transactions were ordinarily calculated. To these uncertainties must be added the widespread debasement of the coinage, through clipping or otherwise. For any merchant who tried to do business outside of his own neighborhood this confusion of values was, of course, a very serious matter. Among those who realized the urgent need of reform in this respect were Gouverneur Morris, a clever young New Yorker, who served under Robert Morris in the department of finance, and Thomas Jefferson. Both worked out plans for a decimal system, which was

Coinage and currency.

finally agreed upon, with the Spanish dollar as the unit. The new plan was not, however, put into effect under the Confederation.

There was similar uncertainty about foreign and inter-state commerce. Whatever might be said against the British colonial policy, it did establish a system of known rules. Under that system, American ships were limited in their trade with foreign countries; but in the ports of England and her colonies they shared the privileges of the British merchant marine. In 1783, no one knew what to expect. There were, indeed, some Englishmen who were willing to go far in promoting trade relations with the colonies. Adam Smith's *Wealth of Nations*, published in 1776, stimulated liberal thinking about international trade, among statesmen as well as among political philosophers. A strong American government might perhaps have secured more concessions; but the conservative forces in England soon reasserted themselves, and orders in council were issued which, among other things, excluded American shipping from the West Indies.

To offset the loss of former commercial privileges within the British Empire, Congress hoped for concessions from other nations. Franklin, Adams, and Jefferson were appointed commissioners to negotiate treaties for this purpose and a few were actually secured, including one with Prussia in 1785 and a consular convention with France in 1788. In general, however, the results were disappointing. After all it was harder to develop trade with continental Europe than with English merchants, who spoke the same language and whose business methods had long been familiar. So

the great bulk of American foreign trade was carried on with England, and English statesmen concluded that they could get what they wanted without making substantial concessions in return. This attitude was naturally annoying to the Americans, and John Adams, the first American minister in London, did his best to change it, both by diplomatic methods and by trying to persuade his countrymen to adopt retaliatory measures. Some such legislation was attempted by individual states without much effect but Congress could do nothing without an amendment to the Articles, which the states refused to adopt.

In the matter of interstate commerce, Congress was even worse off, since the subject was reserved exclusively to the states. Virginia, for instance, in levying tonnage duties, discriminated in favor of its own shipping as against that of its neighbors, and states which controlled important harbors or access to interior waterways sometimes made unfair use of these advantages. New York's discriminatory duties exasperated New Jersey to such an extent that the latter state proceeded to tax a lighthouse built by the New Yorkers on Sandy Hook. Scarcely less serious than these irritating controversies was the inability of the states to get together in constructive plans for the improvement of waterways and similar enterprises. *Interstate commerce.*

Domestic policies were complicated by international disputes, expecially with the British and the Spaniards. In 1784, when Jay took charge of foreign affairs, no progress had been made in settling any of the outstanding issues. In the following year, however, a step of some importance was taken when John Adams appeared at London as the first of a long series of distinguished Americans who have represented the United States at the British court. The reception of this arch-rebel by his former sovereign was a striking event, and the bearing of both men was worthy of the occasion. Adams expressed his desire to help restore "the old good humor between people who, though separated by an ocean, and under different governments, have the same language, a similar religion, and kindred blood." King George answered in a similar spirit, but little was done to give the sentiment practical effect. *Foreign affairs.* *John Adams at the British court.*

The new prime minister, William Pitt the younger,

British
policy under
the younger
Pitt.

was a great man with liberal views on many questions; but, so far as Anglo-American relations are concerned, he missed a great opportunity. For several years his government failed to send any regular minister to the United States, and those who later were chosen for that post were quite unfit for so difficult a service. In the absence of a minister, British interests were largely in the hands of consular agents at New York and Philadelphia, who sent home dismal accounts of the American situation. Meantime, Adams in London was discouraged by his inability to make any real headway or even to secure punctual observance of the peace treaty.

Western
posts and
British debts.

In the matter of the western posts, the British ministry was influenced by the powerful fur-trading interest and by Canadian officials in sympathy with that interest; but the American case also suffered because the states did not keep their agreements about the loyalists and the British debts, a fact of which Adams was duly reminded when he made his formal demand for the surrender of the posts. Jay investigated the subject carefully and concluded that, so far as many of the states were concerned, the British contention was well founded. He therefore proposed that Congress should pass a resolution denying the right of any state to construe, limit, or obstruct a treaty; each state was also asked to pass a general law repealing all acts in conflict with the peace treaty. Such a resolution was accordingly passed by Congress and some of the objectionable legislation was actually repealed.

*Rutgers v.
Waddington.*

One state law mentioned by Jay was the New York Trespass Act, which permitted Whigs, whose property had been held by Tory occupants under the orders of the British military authorities, to recover damages. In the case of *Rutgers* v. *Waddington*, the Tory defendant, represented by Alexander Hamilton, questioned the validity of the state law on the ground that it was in conflict with the treaty and with international law. In spite of the intense anti-Tory feeling, the court ruled in favor of the defendant on the ground that his occupation of the property under military orders was in accordance with international law, and that state legislation must be so construed as not to conflict with that principle. In short, the Trespass Act, though not definitely declared invalid, was practically set aside. The decision was unpopular and the legislature denounced it; but it attracted attention outside of New York and Washington expressed his hearty approval. Generally speaking, however, state legislatures, in New York or elsewhere, were quite free to violate treaties if they pleased. Under such circumstances, foreign governments could hardly be blamed for wondering whether they were dealing with one government or with thirteen.

Though the settlement of Indian affairs and the colonization of the Northwest were held back by the failure of the United States to take over the western posts, these complications were just then less dangerous than the failure to reach an agreement with Spain. With this subject Jay was quite familiar through his long experience abroad. His first business was to get Spain to accept the clauses of the Anglo-American treaty, fixing the southern boundary of the United States and guaranteeing the free navigation of the Mississippi; he wished also to make favorable trade arrangements with Spain and her colonies. On the first two points, the Spaniards were stubborn. They knew that the United States had agreed in 1782 to accept somewhat less territory if Florida remained in British hands and they insisted that the lower Mississippi must be regarded as a strictly Spanish river. *Spanish-American complications.*

Florida and the Mississippi.

Confronted with an apparently hopeless deadlock and realizing the interest of the seaboard states in a general commercial treaty, Jay was willing to give up temporarily the free navigation of the Mississippi in return for other *Jay's policy.*

concessions. A majority of the states were apparently willing to make the proposed concession but not enough to make the nine votes required, and the feeling ran high. The Kentuckians were so angered by this supposed betrayal of their interests that some of their leaders were ready to deal directly with the Spaniards. The air was full of intrigues and at any moment the government was likely to have its hand forced by some hot-headed frontiersman. The southerners also, especially the Virginians, were deeply concerned, financially and otherwise, with the future of the West. Patrick Henry was particularly violent in his denunciation of Jay's proposal, and Madison, who had been trying to get his fellow Virginians into a more helpful attitude towards Congress, was much discouraged by the effect of this discussion in exciting sectional feeling against the northeastern states.

Ineffective as the federal government was, in most respects, there is one great achievement which goes far to redeem it, namely, the inauguration of a unique and admirable colonial policy. The underlying principle of this new policy was taken by the Confederation from its revolutionary predecessor, the Continental Congress, which had declared as early as 1780 that any western lands ceded by the states should be held temporarily as federal domain, but ultimately formed into self-governing members of the Union. Nevertheless, when the Articles of Confederation went into effect, in 1781, there was not an acre of territory to which the United States had a perfectly clear title. The Virginia cession of that year made so many reservations that Congress refused to accept it, and three years passed before a satisfactory deed was executed. The Virginia deed of 1784 marks the real beginning of a federal domain, and during the next two years the title to the Northwest was further cleared by the surrender of the Massachusetts strip in 1785 and the partial Connecticut cession of 1786. Here at last was the

Opposition of the West and South.

Beginnings of American colonial policy.

opportunity to work out a definitely American colonial policy.

In the administration of the new federal territory, two distinct problems had to be solved. There was, first, the question of the land itself. How was it to be managed while in the possession of the government and on what conditions should it be turned over to actual settlers? The second and equally important question was that of government for the present and future inhabitants of the district.

In considering both these questions, and especially the first, the impecunious Confederation Congress was naturally anxious to use the public lands either to bring in revenue directly or to satisfy the claims of the army and other public creditors. For this purpose it was important to adopt an orderly system of land surveys, which would enable both the government and the purchaser of land to know just where they stood. The New England people had been accustomed to township grants; but, so far, the western lands, more particularly in Kentucky and Tennessee, had been taken up in a very unsystematic fashion. North of the Ohio, however, where very little land had been occupied, there was a chance to develop a well-considered permanent policy. Among the members of Congress most interested in this subject was Jefferson, who had a plan by which the western lands were to be marked out in "hundreds," each ten miles square. After his withdrawal from Congress, the plan was finally developed into the Land Ordinance of 1785, which provided for rectangular surveys but substituted for Jefferson's hundreds the township unit of thirty-six square miles, marked off by north and south meridians and by intersecting lines running east and west. The immediate practical results were slight; but this general plan of land registration became a permanent feature of national policy.

Genesis of a public land system.

The Land Ordinance of 1785.

The question of governments for the western country

Genesis of
territorial
government.

was also much discussed during the whole period from 1781 to 1787, and numerous projects were considered. In 1783, the Virginia delegate, Richard Bland, proposed a scheme for territories, or colonies, each covering two degrees of latitude and three of longitude. As soon as any colony had 20,000 male inhabitants it was to enter the Union on equal terms with the original states. The best known of these earlier plans was drafted by Jefferson, reported by him from a committee of which he was chairman, and finally adopted by Congress with important amendments in April, 1784. The committee report, which covered all territory then under federal control and any other which might subsequently be acquired, divided the whole region into "states," arranged in tiers from north to south, each state covering two degrees of latitude. In each "state" the free male adults could organize a temporary government; when the number reached 20,000 they might form a permanent constitution; and when the population was equal to that of the smallest of the original thirteen states, they would be eligible for admission to the Union. A striking feature of this plan was the proposed "compact," embodying certain fundamental principles: republican government, the exclusion of hereditary titles, and the prohibition of slavery after 1800. Congress struck out the antislavery clause and the ordinance as a whole was never put in force; but it shows the gradual crystallization of public opinion on certain broad principles of colonial policy.

The
Ordinance
of 1784.

The Ohio
Company.

Meantime, representative men in the various states were planning for actual colonization. Conspicuous among these promoters was an organization composed largely of New England army officers, which called itself the Ohio Company. Through their agent, Manasseh Cutler, a versatile clergyman, these people took the matter up with Congress and offered, if they could make satisfactory terms, to buy a large tract of land in the Northwest. Such a business

proposal naturally gave the subject a new practical importance, and Cutler was a skillful lobbyist. A bargain was
accordingly made for the sale of a large tract to Cutler's
associates. About the same time the long discussion about
territorial government came to an end with the adoption of
a definite constitution for the "territory of the United States
northwest of the river Ohio."

This Ordinance of 1787 was not the work of a moment *Ordinance
but the outcome of long discussion, and it was based to a *of 1787.*
considerable extent on experience within the British Empire.
This is especially evident in the provisions for colonial,
or, as Americans prefer to call it, territorial government.
After a preliminary stage, in which the business of the district *Colonial
was managed by federal officials, there was to be a government *precedents.*
closely resembling that of an English royal province, more
particularly that of Massachusetts under the charter of
1691, with Congress taking the place of the King. In both
cases, the governor was appointed by the federal, or imperial,
government, and in both there was a representative assembly
chosen by the property holders. In the Northwest Territory, as in provincial Massachusetts, both the central
government and the colonial assembly had a share in the
choice of councilors, though in somewhat different ways.
The American governor, like his British predecessor, had
a considerable appointing power and a veto on acts of the
assembly. The framers of the ordinance were evidently not
radical democrats, for they insisted on property qualifications — fifty acres for voters, two hundred for representatives, and five hundred for councilors. Suggestive also is
the clause prohibiting interference with private contracts,
which was evidently intended to protect creditors against
radical economic legislation. So far, then, as strictly colonial
government is concerned, the ordinance was not strikingly
original.

The most significant features of the Ordinance of 1787

Articles of
Compact.

were contained in the "Articles of Compact," which were declared to be perpetually binding both on Congress and on the people of the territory. Most memorable of all was Article V, which provided for the ultimate transformation of this American province into self-governing states, not less than three nor more than five in number. When any of these subdivisions had 60,000 free inhabitants, it could become a member of the Union with its own constitution "on an equal footing with the original states in all respects whatever." The policy laid down in this article and since carried out in the admission of more than thirty states represents a new conception of the relation which ought to exist between colonies and the parent state. In all former systems, colonies had either become quite independent or had remained subordinate to the mother country. The American system makes possible permanent union, on the basis of political equality, between the new commonwealth and the original members.

Organization
of new states.

A new
conception of
colonial
policy.

Other pro-
visions of the
"Compact."

The "Compact" also guaranteed certain common-law rights, such as trial by jury and the writ of *habeas corpus*. Religious liberty was recognized; but church establishments were not definitely forbidden, and one of the chief reasons for maintaining schools was declared to be the promotion of religion. The clause on education should be interpreted in the light of a provision in the Land Ordinance of 1785, setting apart the sixteenth section of every township for the support of schools. The humanitarian spirit of the time also found expression in a clause prescribing fair treatment of the Indians, and in the sixth article, prohibiting slavery. This article, though not strictly enforced for several years, certainly helped to check the westward extension of that institution.

Colonization
under federal
supervision.

Colonization was delayed by Indian troubles; but in 1788 the New England promoters of the Ohio Company planted their first settlement at Marietta, on the Ohio, under the protection of a federal fort. This federal protection was significant of a new era in the westward movement. There was still plenty of room for individual initiative and self-help; but the colonization of the West was henceforth more largely under the supervision and control of the Union. These new commonwealths, at any rate, were never "sovereign" and "independent"; for they developed under a central government which assumed for them a distinctly national character. All this, however, was hardly appreciated by the men who were responsible for this great achievement. When the ordinance was voted, in July, 1787, Congress could hardly keep a quorum; public interest was turning to the more important gathering at Philadelphia, which was then hammering into shape a radical reconstruction of the whole federal system.

The movement for a more effective union was partly the work of far-sighted and broad-minded leaders who could look beyond state boundaries to the larger interests of the country as a whole, who saw things needing to be done which could not be accomplished without a strong federal or national organization. Such men, however, were few in any community. Before the movement could succeed it had to win support from another group, who could not take the larger view but were beginning to see that the weakness of Congress might have something to do with troubles nearer home. *The movement for a more effective union.*

It was quite evident that many people were dissatisfied with what had so far been done in the matter of political and social reconstruction. They believed that the early state constitutions gave the property-holding class an influence quite inconsistent with real democracy. The farmers of the interior were especially convinced that, by unfair apportionments or otherwise, the commercial and financial interests of the seaboard had secured more than their share of political power. So far, there were no formal party organizations, but *Economic and social discontent.*

there was a tendency toward political divisions based on economic interests. On one side there was a compact group of merchants and professional men, lenders of capital, men of education and social prestige, who felt that the revolutionary spirit was in danger of going too far. To this class belonged also many of the wealthier southern planters. On the opposite side were the farmers, the less prosperous elements in the towns, the men who depended on borrowed capital and felt that they were not fairly treated by their creditors.

Economic grievances. These class conflicts were embittered by special conditions growing out of the war. Many people everywhere suffered either from the burden of war expenses or from the necessity of sudden adjustment to new conditions after the peace. With scientific taxation, the financial load might have been carried more easily; but the taxes of that day were even less scientific than those of the present time. The New England farmer, for example, believed that the merchants were not paying their share of the cost of government. Interruption of certain lines of trade, especially with the West Indies, lessened the supply of specie; but at the same time there was an abnormal demand for money to settle old obligations and pay for European goods. Creditors, British and American, were pressing for payment; courts were again enforcing old claims; and lawyers seemed to be profiting by the troubles of their country neighbors. So there came a demand for legislation to help the debtor class; stay laws, deferring the payment of interest or principal, and "tender" laws providing various substitutes for specie payments.

Paper money. The most popular remedy was the free issue of paper money; but the success of this movement varied widely. In Virginia it was strong enough to trouble the conservatives but was finally defeated; and in Pennsylvania the issues were comparatively moderate. In New England the paper-money party was formidable, especially in Rhode Island, which in spite of two important commercial towns was then controlled by the rural voters. There, as elsewhere, excessive issues of paper money caused rapid depreciation, and attempts to prevent this result by compelling people to take it under penalty made matters worse. A striking incident of this long controversy was the case of *Trevett* v. *Weeden*, in which a Newport butcher was sued for refusing to accept paper money in payment of a bill. The plaintiff's lawyer relied on a state law authorizing the court to act in such a case without a jury trial. Thereupon Weeden's lawyer argued that the law itself was unconstitutional, null, and void; the judges did not technically commit themselves to this doctrine, but they refused to take jurisdiction, with much the same practical result. The legislature denounced the judges but left them in office until their terms expired. *Trevett* v. *Weeden.*

In the interior of Massachusetts the feeling was about as intense as in Rhode Island; but the conservatives were stronger and better organized, with an able leader in the person of Governor James Bowdoin. Unable to get the legislation it desired, the paper-money party turned against the government — the legislature, the judges, and the lawyers. Radical conventions were held; rioters obstructed the courts; and at the end of 1786 the movement culminated in the Shays rebellion led by a revolutionary veteran. Though the federal arsenal at Springfield was in danger, Congress seemed almost helpless. Some federal guns were actually used against the insurgents; but the suppression of the revolt was chiefly due to the energy of Governor Bowdoin and his associates, who financed the state campaign against the rebels by contributions from the wealthy citizens, telling them that it was a question of giving up part of their property to save the rest. The Shays rebellion.

A serious danger had been averted for the time being; but

there were sympathetic movements in other New England states and conservative people were still anxious. Even in Massachusetts, the rebels and their sympathizers were strong enough to prevent the reëlection of Governor Bowdoin. Outside of New England, also, these events were followed with interest. Jefferson took the situation rather lightly, and Franklin, with his usual optimism, thought the disturbances were not very important. Others were less cheerful. Edward Rutledge of South Carolina feared that "liberty" was degenerating into "licentiousness" and called upon "men of virtue" to keep up the fight for "good government." Jay complained that the masses were carried away by "a desire of equality in all things" and were being played upon by unscrupulous leaders. Meantime, the fear of radicalism seemed likely to produce a reaction to the opposite extreme, until, as Jay put it, "the more sober part of the people" might "even think of a king." Washington in his retreat at Mount Vernon was also much disturbed. Even more significant was the fact that all over the country many conservative people of less intelligence began to favor a new federal system in the hope that it would counteract radical tendencies within the states.

BIBLIOGRAPHICAL NOTES

General accounts.

Channing, *United States*, III, chs. XV, XVII. Nevins, A., *American States*. McLaughlin, *Confederation and Constitution*, chs. IV–XI. McMaster, *People of the U. S.*, I, chs. II–IV.

Sources.

Bogart and Thompson, *Readings in the Economic History of the U. S.*, 185–205. "London Merchants on American Trade, 1783," *A.H.R.*, XVIII, 769–780. Callender, *Selections from the Economic History of the U. S.*, ch. V. Franklin, *Writings* (Smyth edition), IX. Jay, *Correspondence, etc.*, III. Hamilton, *Writings* (Lodge edition), I, especially 203–228 (letter to Duane, 1780), and VIII (private correspondence). Jefferson, *Writings* (Ford ed.), III. Madison, *Writings* (Hunt ed.), II.

Ford, W. C., *Washington*, II, chs. V, VI. Hunt, *Madison*, Biographies.
chs. V–IX. Oberholtzer, *Robert Morris*, especially chs. III–V.
Oliver, F. S., *Hamilton*, bk. II, chs. III, IV.

Bullock, C. J., *Finances of the U. S.*, *1775–1789.* Sumner, Finance.
W. G., *Financier and Finances of the Revolution*, especially II, chs.
XVI–XXIII.

Hertz, G. B., *Old Colonial System*, chs. X, XI. Fish, C. R., Commerce
American Diplomacy, chs. VI–VII. Hunt, G., *Department of* and diplo-
macy.
State, chs. II, III. Pellew, G., *John Jay*, ch. IX. Bemis, S. F.,
Jay's Treaty. McLaughlin, A. C., "The Western Posts and the
British Debts," Amer. Hist. Assoc., *Reports*, 1894. Whitaker,
A. B., *The Spanish-American Frontier*.

Adams, J. T., *N. E. in the Republic*. Bates, F. G., *Rhode Island* Economic
and the Formation of the Union (*Columbia Studies*), chs. III, IV. and social
unrest.
Warren, J. P., "Confederation and the Shays's Rebellion," *A.H.R.*,
XI, 42–67. Spaulding, E. W., *New York in the Critical Period*.

Flick, A. C., *Loyalism in N. Y.* Boucher, J., *Reminiscences of* Loyalists
an American Loyalist, *1738–1789*. Einstein, L. D., *Divided* after the
Revolution.
Loyalties. Siebert, W. H., "Dispersion of the American Tories,"
M. V. H. R., I, 185–197. Morris, R. B., *Select Cases of the Mayor's
Court of New York City*, 57–59, 302–327. Egerton, H. E., *Royal
Commission on the Losses and Services of American Loyalists*, *1783–
1785*. Van Tyne, C. H., *Loyalists and the American Revolution*.
Wrong, G. M., *Canada and the American Revolution*.

Corwin, E. S., *The Doctrine of Judicial Review*, 70–75. Boudin, The courts
L., *Government by Judiciary*, I. and social
unrest.

Henderson, *Conquest of the Old Southwest*, ch. XX. Hinsdale, Western
B. A., *Old Northwest*, chs. XI–XV. Alvord, C. W., *Centennial* problems
and the
History of Illinois, I, chs. XVII–XVIII. Treat, P. J., *National* Northwest
Land System, chs. I–III. Barrett, J. A., *Evolution of the Ordinance* Ordinance.
of 1787 (University of Nebraska Seminary, *Papers*). Cutler,
W. P., and J. P., *Manasseh Cutler*. Bond, B. W., Jr., "An Experi-
ment in Colonial Government," *M.V.H.R.*, XV, 221–309.

Macdonald, *Select Documents*, no. 4. Hart and Channing, Documents.
American History Leaflets, no. 32. Morison, *Sources and Documents*, 208–232. Pease and Roberts, *Readings*, 166–175. Commager, *Documents*, 126–132.

CHAPTER XXVII

THE GREAT CONVENTION

Plans for revising the Articles. THE movement to revise the Articles of Confederation began even before they were finally adopted. The need of such revision was strongly felt by Washington and in 1780 his young secretary, Alexander Hamilton, wrote a striking letter in which he boldly suggested that Congress should assume the necessary powers by a sort of peaceful revolution. If it had not the courage to do that, then a federal convention should be called to reorganize the government. In 1781 Congress discussed several amendments, but the only one actually recommended to the states was that authorizing the five-per-cent impost. The failure of this and other amendments proposed during the next three years showed that there was little chance of carrying through any measure **The idea of a convention.** which required unanimous consent. Meantime, the idea of something more serious than merely patching up the Articles was spreading. One of the more advanced thinkers on this subject was Pelatiah Webster, of Philadelphia, who published a pamphlet proposing a new federal constitution, with a Congress of two houses which could levy taxes independently of the state governments. By 1785 the plan of a federal convention was very much in the air. It was proposed by New York in 1782 and by Massachusetts in 1785, though the congressional delegates from the latter state threw cold water on the plan.

Virginia and Maryland conferences. The convention idea harmonized well with a movement then under way in Virginia to secure coöperation on certain questions of interstate commerce. Such men as Washington and Madison felt especially the need of coöperation with the neighboring state of Maryland. The first tangible result of their efforts was a meeting of Virginia and Maryland commissioners, held first at Alexandria and then at Mount Vernon; but it was soon evident that their problems were too large to be solved without bringing in representatives from other states. Accordingly Virginia invited all the states to join in a convention at Annapolis. The response was disappointing, since only Virginia and the four middle states were represented, and decisive action was clearly impossible. Fortunately, the leading spirits, especially Madison and Hamilton, were determined not to adjourn without taking some forward step and they put through a resolution in favor of a new convention at Philadelphia. Without going into details that might provoke antagonism, it was proposed that this Philadelphia convention should study the defects of the existing government and recommend such "further provisions" as they might think necessary "to render the constitution of the federal government adequate to the exigencies of the Union"; this recommendation was accordingly sent to the state governments. Congress finally indorsed the proposed convention, and by persistent efforts on the part of a few leaders all the states except Rhode Island were at last represented. *Annapolis Convention. The Federal Convention of 1787.*

Virginia, which had taken such an active part in the movement, also set a high standard in its choice of delegates. Some revolutionary leaders, including Patrick Henry, Richard Henry Lee, and Jefferson, were conspicuously absent, but more significant was the fact that Washington consented to serve. Among his older colleagues was George Mason, author of the Virginia bill of rights; from the younger men, Governor Edmund Randolph was chosen, together with James Madison. Madison, though not a spectacular person, was a hard worker, a solid thinker, and already at thirty-six an experienced legislator. All in all, he was *Delegates. Virginia.*

probably the most steadily efficient worker in the convention.

Pennsyl-
vania.

Next in dignity and importance was the Pennsylvania delegation. When the convention met, Franklin was over eighty years old and his tangible contributions to the Constitution were not important; but his conciliatory spirit was helpful in holding the convention together. When the work was done, probably no signature except that of Washington did so much as Franklin's to win popular confidence. With Franklin sat three other signers of the Declaration of Independence: Robert Morris, the chief representative of "big business" in the convention; James Wilson, perhaps its ablest lawyer; and George Clymer, a rich Philadelphia merchant. A younger man but already experienced in public service was Gouverneur Morris. Belonging to an old New York family, his outlook was aristocratic and rather cynical; but he was a keen thinker and a real patriot.

Massachu-
setts.

The Massachusetts delegation was less conspicuous than it had been in the old Continental Congress. Neither John nor Samuel Adams, the two radical leaders of 1776, was there, though John Adams probably had some indirect influence in the convention through his writings on government and his part in framing the Massachusetts constitution of 1780. Perhaps the ablest member from the old

Connecticut.

"Bay State" was young Rufus King. On the whole, Connecticut was more strongly represented, and its senior delegate, Roger Sherman, had the advantage of long experience in public service, both state and federal. He had sat in the first Continental Congress, signed the Declaration of Independence, and helped to frame the Articles of Confederation. A practical business man and a sensible rather than an eloquent speaker, he was perhaps the most typical product of New England republican politics. Sherman's colleagues were younger men of conspicuous ability, notably Oliver Ellsworth, later Chief Justice of the United States.

The most brilliant among the middle state delegates New York. was Alexander Hamilton; but he was outvoted by his two New York colleagues, and though he made some striking contributions to the debate, his advanced ideas of centralization and strong government were not popular. In marked contrast to Hamilton was the veteran John Dickinson, who, as a member from Delaware, showed something of the Delaware. same cautious temper which made him an appropriate draftsman for the Articles of Confederation. New Jersey New Jersey. sent some able lawyers, including her governor, chief justice, and attorney-general.

Next to Virginia among the southern delegations was South Carolina. South Carolina, with a group of rich planters and lawyers, two of them from one influential family. First in previous reputation was John Rutledge, a leader in the first Continental Congress and war governor of his state. Important younger colleagues were Charles Cotesworth Pinckney, an officer in the Revolution, and his cousin Charles Pinckney, who though only twenty-nine years old had been active in Congress and had some definite ideas about a new constitution. The most interesting of the Maryland members Maryland. was Luther Martin, a vigorous defender of state rights.

A few members of the convention were careful students Experience of history and politics, notably Madison, Wilson, and in public and private Hamilton; more characteristic of them as a whole was their business. experience in public and private business. About three fourths of them had been in Congress and seven had signed the Declaration of Independence. More than half the states were represented by men who had served as governor or president, and several members had held high judicial office. Others had served in the Revolutionary army; the two Morrises, Hamilton, and Madison were well informed about federal finances; and the diplomatic service was represented by Franklin, its most distinguished member. Well-to-do merchants from New England and Pennsylvania could speak with authority about foreign and domestic commerce. Closely associated with these business interests were the lawyers, who made up a large part of the membership. There were also rich planters from Virginia and the Carolinas, land speculators on a large scale, and promoters of roads and canals.

Outlook on public affairs.

The convention as a whole undoubtedly represented the prosperous property-holding class. Many of its members were creditors of the state and federal governments, and therefore had a direct interest in the permanence of the Union. The influence of such personal and class interests in comparison with more altruistic motives undoubtedly varied with individual members. Washington, for instance, had given abundant proof of his willingness to sacrifice his personal interests to the welfare of the country at large. All in all, the most striking difference between the men who sat in the convention and those outsiders who remained indifferent or suspicious about the whole enterprise was that the former group had got from their experience a broader horizon, a better appreciation of general, as distinguished from purely local, interests.

Convention procedure.

On May 25, the convention chose Washington as its president and settled down to its work. The sessions were held behind closed doors, the members were pledged to secrecy, and every effort was made to encourage full and frank discussion. There was no rule for cutting off debate by moving the previous question, and after the fullest discussion actual voting could be deferred if any delegation so desired. Votes were taken by states, each state casting a single vote regardless of the number of its delegates. This disturbed some of the large-state delegates; but it was probably good politics, because in the end the individual states would have to pass on the finished work.

Generally speaking, the members of the convention agreed that the federal government should be made much stronger. The most conservative plan proposed during the debates went much further in this direction than would have been thought possible five or six years before. Starting with this fundamental agreement, the chief difference which developed at the outset was whether the convention should try to strengthen the existing congressional system or should form a new government on different principles. This central issue was, however, complicated by special interests of various kinds so that the alignment of members was at times rather confused.

There was, first, a group of nationalist leaders who stood for what were called "high-toned" principles. Realizing for the most part that the state governments must be preserved, this group wished to make them clearly subordinate to the federal government, which should rest not on the states but directly on the people. Governmental efficiency was to be gained not only by giving Congress more power but by creating a strong executive. Some members of this group were even accused of being monarchists. The most influential of the nationalist leaders was Washington, who seldom spoke but whose opinions on fundamental issues were generally known. Other consistent advocates of this policy were Madison of Virginia, Wilson and the Morrises of Pennsylvania, Hamilton of New York, and Rufus King of Massachusetts. Their ideas were somewhat imperfectly expressed in the so-called Virginia plan, which probably represents more nearly the views of Madison than those of any other single person, though it was presented to the convention by Governor Randolph.

This Virginia, or Randolph, plan proposed an entirely new government with distinct legislative, executive, and judicial departments. The legislature was to have two houses, and the states were to have proportional rather than equal representation. One house was to be elected directly by the people; and in the choice of the other the state governments were to have partial but not complete control. **The general spirit of the plan is fairly expressed by the introductory resolution, added in committee of the whole, though afterwards eliminated to save the feelings of the state-rights men, that a "national government ought to be established."** The issue between nationalism and state rights was, however, complicated by the conflict between the large and the small states. Some delegates from Virginia, for instance, who were not at all "high-toned," supported the original Randolph plan because it gave their own state a fuller representation in Congress. On the other hand, some delegates from the small states were willing to strengthen the federal government but feared that without equal representation their special interests would not be protected. In the early stages of the convention, the large-state group had the advantage, since the four leading states — Massachusetts, Pennsylvania, Virginia, and North Carolina — could usually count on the support of South Carolina and Georgia. The New Hampshire delegates were not present at first and Maryland was frequently divided; so the normal majority of the large-state group was six to four.

The opposition, though in a minority, was too strong to be disregarded. There were keen debaters as well as shrewd politicians in the Connecticut and New Jersey delegations and Martin of Maryland fought hard on the same side. These men regarded the Virginia plan as revolutionary. They believed the Confederation was formed by a compact between the states, much as the state governments were supposed to be based on the "social compact" between individual citizens. Some of them argued that to base the new constitution directly on the people would be not only a violation of the federal compact but also a radical change in the relation of the state governments to their own citizens. The states were equally sovereign and, therefore, should be represented equally. The nationalist answer to this argu-

Large and small states.

The opposition.

ment was that it was more important to think of individuals
than of "imaginary beings called states"; it was grossly
unfair to give an individual who happened to live in a small
state several times as much influence as if he lived in a large
one.

During the early weeks of June the debate went on not in
formal sessions but more freely in committee of the whole,
until the Virginia plan, with amendments, was provisionally
approved. Meanwhile the opposition had been working out
a rival plan, which was submitted on June 15 by Paterson of
New Jersey. This was not a purely negative proposal, for
it recommended additions to the powers of Congress, including
a limited taxing power and the regulation of commerce; it
also proposed distinct executive and judicial departments
and a method of coercing delinquent states. The vital
difference between the Virginia and New Jersey plans was
that the latter proposed no change in the organization of
Congress, which would still act as the agent of "sovereign"
and "equal" states. Again there was a warm debate, en-
livened by some daring proposals of Hamilton which went
much farther toward centralization than anything so far
presented. He proposed that the state governors should
be appointed by the federal government and that the chief
executive of the United States should be a powerful officer
serving during good behavior. This was much too "high-
toned" to please any except a few extremists, and the
"committee of the whole" presently renewed its indorsement of the amended Virginia plan, which now went before
the convention to be thrashed out in detail. It was not
yet even a draft of a constitution, but merely a rough outline.

The crisis on the question of representation came at the
end of June. On June 29 the convention decided, six to
four, in favor of proportionate representation in one house,
and some of the small-state men began to think of compromise. Ellsworth said that, assuming the Union to be "partly

The New Jersey plan.

The Hamilton plan.

The question of representation.

national" and "partly federal," he would be satisfied if the "federal" or state-sovereignty idea could be recognized in the "second branch," or Senate. Accordingly he made a motion for equal representation in that house; but the large-state men were not yet ready to yield, and the motion resulted in a tie. The feeling during this debate was intense; a Delaware representative even suggested that if the old Confederation was abandoned the small states might have to find "some foreign ally" to "do them justice."

Deadlock and compromise.
The convention was now, as Sherman said, "at a full stop"; it was therefore agreed to refer the question of representation to a committee consisting of one member from each state. Not one of the aggressive nationalists was chosen for this committee, while the small states were represented by their most strenuous champions. Quite naturally, the committee adopted substantially Ellsworth's suggestion of equal representation in one house to offset proportionate representation in the other, with the unimportant concession that the "first branch" alone could originate money bills. Madison and Wilson tried to defeat this compromise; but on July 16 it was adopted, five to four. Even with equal representation the Senate was made far less dependent on the states than the old Congress had been. Each senator, though chosen by his state legislature, was to sit for a six-year term, during which his salary was to be paid from the federal treasury, and he could vote independently without being subject to recall.

The federal executive.
Scarcely less difficult than the problem of representation was that of the federal executive. All the plans agreed on the need of a distinct executive department, but they differed radically as to its organization and powers. At one extreme was Hamilton's plan for a single executive, chosen indirectly by the people, holding office during good behavior, and exercising great powers. At the opposite extreme were those who feared that a single executive would sooner or

later become a monarch. On the question whether there should be an executive board or a single head, the Virginia plan was noncommittal and Randolph himself urged a plural executive; but the convention was against him by a decided majority. It was also hard to decide how the President should be chosen. The Virginia and New Jersey plans favored election by Congress and the convention seemed at first in favor of that plan. The great objection to this method was that it would make the executive too dependent on the legislature. It was therefore proposed that the President should be chosen for the fairly long term of seven years and made ineligible for reëlection. It was finally agreed, however, that he should get his authority from some source outside of Congress. Direct election by the people was regarded as visionary even by ardent republicans, and so it was agreed that the President should be chosen indirectly by electors, the precise method of choosing electors in each state being left to the state legislatures. The question of the President's tenure of office was decided in favor of a four-year term, with no restrictions on his reëlection.

Election and tenure of office.

After adopting the principle of a single head, efforts were made to limit his power through some kind of council; but, in the end, executive power and responsibility were concentrated in the President, except that the consent of the Senate was made necessary for treaties and for certain appointments. The Constitution refers to "heads of departments," and they have since been formed by the President into a "cabinet"; but their advice is not binding and the President could not share his constitutional responsibility with them even if he wished to do so. This independent status of the President is to-day one of the striking differences between the American government and the parliamentary systems of Great Britain and France, in which executive power is exercised by a ministry responsible not to king or president but to the legislature.

Concentration of executive responsibility.

Checks and balances.

The idea of "checks and balances" runs through the whole work of the convention. The executive is checked by the Senate in the matter of treaties and appointments. The legislative department is checked by its division into two houses and by the President's veto, which was finally agreed upon instead of giving this power to a "council of revision," composed of the executive and the judges.

The judiciary.

Even more important, perhaps, was the "check" imposed upon both these departments through the judiciary. Practically everyone agreed on the need of a strong and independent federal judiciary; but some members wished to limit it to a supreme tribunal hearing appeals from the state courts. They feared that inferior federal courts with original jurisdiction would interfere with the state judiciary. The national view prevailed, however, and Congress was authorized to establish such courts. Federal judges were to be appointed by the President with the advice and consent of the Senate; but they were to serve during good behavior and could be removed only by the difficult process of impeachment.

The "supreme law" and its enforcement in the states.

A most difficult problem was that of harmonizing federal and state authority. How could the federal government compel individuals within the states to obey the provisions of a treaty? How could a state legislature be prevented from taking action in conflict with the constitutional authority of the United States? The Virginia plan proposed two methods of dealing with this problem. One method, suggested by the King's disallowance of colonial legislation, was to give Congress a veto on state laws. Madison advocated this method and was much disappointed when it was rejected. The other method, proposed in both the Virginia and New Jersey plans, was to give Congress power to use force against a delinquent state. Unfortunately this plan implied a Union based upon states rather than upon individuals and seemed more likely to provoke antagonism than to lessen it. On July 16, when the congressional veto was being discussed, it was suggested that a better way would be to have unconstitutional legislation dealt with by the judges, as had already been done in some of the state courts. Thereupon the convention rejected the veto plan and, on the motion of Luther Martin, declared that the laws and treaties of the United States, made in accordance with the Constitution, should be the "supreme law" of the states, whose judges should be bound by them, any state law to the contrary notwithstanding. Out of this resolution there developed a far more sweeping statement, quite beyond Martin's intention but finally embodied in Article VI of the Constitution, by which the Constitution itself, together with laws and treaties made in accordance with it, was made "the supreme law of the land," binding on the judges not only as against state laws but against state constitutions as well. It was also agreed that in such cases federal courts should have original as well as appellate jurisdiction.

Enforcement by the judiciary.

The federal judiciary was expected to exercise a similar check upon Congress. This is evident from the discussion about the desirability of making federal judges members of the council of revision. In opposition to that plan it was argued that the judges could more properly act on legislation in their strictly judicial capacity, as individual cases came before them; that some state courts had declared state laws unconstitutional and federal judges could do the same thing for acts of Congress which did not conform to the "supreme law." Not all the members of the Convention accepted this view, but the weight of evidence seems to indicate that the framers of the Constitution meant the judges not only to interpret the statute law but also to determine whether it was in harmony with the higher law embodied in the Constitution.

Unconstitutional legislation by Congress.

So far as the framework of the new government was

concerned, the convention had departed radically from the Articles of Confederation. Though almost everything in it was based on previous experience in the British government, in colonial practice, or in the state constitutions, the total effect was distinctly original. In sharp contrast to the old Congress, the new government was to stand squarely on its own feet, depending as little as possible on the state governments, and acting everywhere, through its own agents, upon the individual citizen. In all these matters, the Articles of Confederation were of little use except by way of warning. When, however, the convention came to the task of dividing the field of government between federal and state authorities, the existing powers of Congress were the natural starting point. In foreign affairs the nominal jurisdiction of the old Congress had been fairly complete; what was mainly needed now was to provide more effective means of exercising such authority. To a greater or less extent this principle applies also to such matters as the war power, the postal service, the regulation of weights and measures, and the coinage system, though as regards this last item the Constitution took a long step forward by forbidding the states to issue any kind of money — gold, silver, or paper.

The most important additions to the powers of Congress were those relating to finance and commerce. In these matters the state legislatures were subordinated to an extent to which they had never been accustomed before, even in colonial times. After stubbornly denying the taxing power to Parliament and to their own existing Congress, the states were now asked to give the new federal legislature general authority to "lay and collect taxes, duties, imposts, and excises"; subject, of course, to a few restrictions, which, though not unimportant in themselves, were relatively so in comparison with the powers given. While the federal government got these new sources of revenue, the states had to give up the right, always enjoyed before, of levying customs duties. Radical, also, was the change in the matter of commerce. The control of foreign trade exercised by the imperial Parliament had, for the most part, been withheld from the Confederation Congress; but it was now made the exclusive business of the federal government. In the field of interstate commerce, the states lost even the limited freedom of colonial days. This exclusive control of interstate commerce by Congress is even more important from an economic than from a constitutional point of view; for it established the principle of free trade within a wider area than that of western Europe. In this case, however, the victory was not easily won; for a time the task of reconciling the opposing interests seemed almost hopeless.

Regulation of commerce.

In general, the commercial states of the Northeast wished to give Congress liberal powers for the encouragement of their special interests. In particular, they wished to protect their shipping from foreign competition, somewhat as it had been protected under the English Navigation Acts. In opposition to this view, the staple-export states of the South feared that sectional legislation might sacrifice the interests of the South and West to those of the Northeast. The attitude of Jay and his supporters on the Mississippi question had intensified this sectional feeling among the southern members, and they proposed to protect themselves by requiring a two-thirds majority to pass a navigation act.

Commercial and agricultural interests. Sectionalism.

About one kind of commerce the southerners could not agree among themselves. Since the outbreak of the Revolution, the movement for the suppression of the foreign slave trade had made considerable progress through the action of individual states, even in the South. In the convention, this traffic was vigorously denounced by Mason of Virginia and Martin of Maryland; but the planters of South Carolina and Georgia believed that continued importation of negroes was still desirable and they threatened to

The slave trade and sectional representation.

reject the Constitution unless the slave trade were secured against congressional interference. This question was complicated by that of sectional representation. If negro population was to be counted in determining the representation of a state in Congress, northern members objected to the indefinite expansion of that element through fresh importations. Both issues were finally settled by compromise. For purposes of apportionment, negroes were to count only to the extent of three fifths of their total number. On the question of the slave trade the planters of South Carolina and Georgia struck a bargain with the northern merchants. Congress was authorized to regulate commerce by a simple majority vote; but the planting interests were protected by a clause prohibiting duties on exports, and the special demands of the lower South were partly met by forbidding Congress to abolish the slave trade before the year eighteen hundred and eight.

The compromises.

There was some genuine antislavery feeling in the convention; but it was impossible to establish the Union on any other condition than that of recognizing slavery as a matter to be dealt with by the individual states. Meantime, the use of the word slave was carefully avoided. Fugitive slaves were referred to only as "persons held to service or labor"; the slave trade was covered by a phrase about the "migration of such persons" as the states might wish to admit; representation was to be based on free whites and three fifths of all "other persons."

The Constitution and slavery.

Scarcely less significant than the feeling between the North and the South was another kind of sectionalism between East and West. The difference of opinion on the Mississippi question was mentioned in this connection also, and some members, southern as well as northern, feared that the future western states might come to have too much power. A North Carolina member, for instance, was opposed to paying the salaries of congressmen from the

Sectionalism between East and West.

federal treasury, for fear that the old states might some day have to support representatives from the supposedly poorer states of the West, who would be employed in "thwarting" the "measures and interests" of the East. Just as individual colonies and states had kept down the representation of their western counties, so it was proposed to base federal representation, partly at least, on property, in order that the western states might not be too strong in Congress. Gouverneur Morris argued that the "back members" in the state legislatures were always against the "best measures." "If the western people," he said, "get the power into their hands, they will ruin the Atlantic interests."

Fortunately the West also had able champions. Wilson declared that a narrow attitude toward westward expansion would be disastrous to the United States, as it had been to the British Empire. Madison also urged the duty of treating the prospective western states as equals in the Union. This broader view prevailed and no restrictions were imposed on the representation of the West. The advocates of restriction did, however, succeed so far as to strike out of the paragraph on the admission of new states, the words "on the same terms with the original states." This was apparently done in order that Congress might be free to impose conditions. Morris explained that he did not mean to discourage the growth of the western country, but was unwilling to "throw the power into their hands." Actually, however, no conditions of the particular kind then suggested have ever been imposed. *Champions of the West.*

This discussion about the West was closely connected with the idea of protecting the property-holding class against radical legislation. No property qualifications were specifically required either of officers or of voters; but since the suffrage for federal elections in any particular state was to be that prescribed for elections to the lower house of the state legislature, property qualifications were *Protection of property.*

practically required for congressmen also, at least for the
time being.   The conservative business point of view is
also illustrated by the clauses of the Constitution which
prohibit the states from impairing the obligation of contracts, issuing paper money, or making anything except
gold and silver a legal tender.   There was little opposition
to these clauses in the convention, and they undoubtedly
helped to make the Constitution attractive to conservative
people.

Committees on Detail and on Style.   After agreeing on principles, there was still the slow and
difficult process of working up details; much of this work
was left to the Committee of Detail and the Committee
of Style.   The former committee followed in the main
the principles of the amended Virginia plan but it also used
other plans, including that of New Jersey and one prepared
by Charles Pinckney.   The Articles of Confederation and
some of the state constitutions were also drawn upon.   After
the report of the Committee of Detail had been thoroughly
debated, the actual phrasing of the Constitution was intrusted
to the Committee of Style, consisting of five of the ablest
delegates.   Since the choice of particular words and phrases
was often much more than a mere matter of literary taste,
it is worth noting that four of the five members of this
committee — Hamilton, Madison, King, and Gouverneur
Morris, the chairman — had taken the national side in the
convention debates.

The finished work.   When the Committee of Style finally reported to the
convention, on September 12, the members were evidently
impatient of further debate.   On September 15 the Constitution was agreed to by all the states then present and
two days later the engrossed copy was signed by one or
more members from each of them.   A few dissatisfied delegates had previously left the convention, and of those who
remained three refused to sign.

In framing the Constitution, the members of the convention realized that they were simply draftsmen and that their work would go for nothing unless ratified by the states. Much, however, depended on the method of ratification, and in this matter the convention took a revolutionary step. Since the new Constitution was technically an amendment or a series of amendments to the Articles of Confederation, it should have been first acted upon by Congress and then ratified by the unanimous vote of the thirteen states. It was doubtful, however, whether such unanimous consent could be secured and the convention therefore determined that if nine states ratified the Constitution it should go into effect between those states, without waiting for the others. Scarcely less revolutionary was the decision to have the states act not through their legislatures but through conventions chosen by the people for that specific purpose. With this understanding, then, the Constitution was sent to Congress, which, with little enthusiasm and no indorsement, favorable or otherwise, submitted it to the states.

The plan of ratification. Revolutionary features.

BIBLIOGRAPHICAL NOTES

Channing, *United States*, III, 469–481, 494–517. McLaughlin, *Confederation and Constitution*, chs. XI–XVI, and his *Foundations of American Constitutionalism*. Farrand, M., *Making of the Constitution; Framing of the Constitution; Fathers of the Constitution.* Schuyler, R. L., *The Constitution of the United States.* Comprehensive older accounts in Bancroft, *United States*, VI (author's last revision), and Curtis, G. T., *History of the Constitution* (or *Constitutional History of the United States*, I).

Accounts of the convention.

Beard, C. A., *Economic Interpretation of the Constitution*, chs. I–VII (similarly in Schlesinger, A. M., *New Viewpoints in American History*, ch. VIII, and Smith, J. A., *The Spirit of American Government*). Compare Merriam, *American Political Theories*, ch. III, McLaughlin, *Steps in the Development of American Democracy*, ch. III, and Warren, C., *The Making of the Constitution.*

Economic interpretation.

Special
topics.
Meigs, W. M., *Growth of the Constitution in the Federal Convention* (traces the development of particular clauses). Beard, C. A., *The Supreme Court and the Constitution*, ch. II. Biographies of Madison by Hunt, Ellsworth by W. G. Brown, Sherman by L. H. Boutell, Mason by K. M. Rowland, bring out different views.

Sources.
Farrand, M., *Records of the Federal Convention* (comprehensive collection of sources for the convention, including its journal, Madison's notes, and fragmentary notes of other members). Madison's notes also in Elliott's *Debates*, V ; *Documentary History of the Constitution* (U. S. State Department publication) ; and in his *Writings* (this part of Hunt's edition also published separately). Selections from Madison's notes, *e.g.*, from the debates on representation, June, 1787, make excellent supplementary reading. For selections from the debates in the federal convention, see Morison, *Sources and Documents*, 233–292. See also McLaughlin and others, *Source Problems*, Problem III.

CHAPTER XXVIII

THE NEW UNION

THE friends of the Constitution began their fight for ratification with one great advantage. Several of their leaders, having sat in the convention, had become thoroughly familiar with most of the questions which were likely to be discussed. There were also many other men who had taken an active part in the movement for a stronger Union; they knew what they wanted and felt that the new Constitution, though not perfect, was a long step in the right direction. So in most of the states this "Federal" party was well organized and equipped for the struggle. On the "Anti-Federalist" side, organization and leadership were less effective. A few dissatisfied members of the convention, like Martin of Maryland and Mason of Virginia, were ready to carry the fight into the states, and they could count on the help of some veteran revolutionists like Patrick Henry; Samuel Adams also, though finally won over to the Federal cause, was dubious at first. On the whole, however, the Anti-Federalist leaders were comparatively obscure and second-rate men. Furthermore, the working up of a political campaign on short notice was slower and more difficult in the Anti-Federalist areas of the interior than in the more compact communities of the seaboard, which generally took the Federal side.

The Federal party and its opponents.

The advantage of an early start was soon apparent. Within less than four months after the close of the Federal Convention, the Constitution was ratified by five states, a majority of the nine required to put the system into effect. Four of these five belonged to the "small-state" group in

Early ratifications.

603

the convention; but their delegates had been satisfied with the compromise on representation and had gone home to work for ratification. In Delaware, New Jersey, and Georgia, the state conventions voted unanimously for ratification, and in Connecticut the majority was more than three to one. In Pennsylvania, the first large state to ratify, there was more of a fight, and in some respects the situation there was fairly typical of the country at large.

Pennsylvania. The fight in the legislature.

The Federal leaders in Pennsylvania worked hard for an early decision, and within two weeks after the Federal Convention adjourned, a motion was made in the legislature for calling a state convention. The legislature was about to adjourn and the Anti-Federalists made desperate attempts to break the quorum; but local opinion in Philadelphia was strongly against them and absentee members were forcibly brought back to their seats. Having secured a quorum, the Federal leaders put through their motion; about a month was allowed before the election of delegates and the convention was to assemble two weeks later. This was certainly moving fast, so much so as to justify the protests of the opposition.

Philadelphia and the back country.

When the elections were held, early in November, the eastern section, and especially Philadelphia with its large business interests, chose Federal delegates by a decided majority. In the interior counties, the current ran in the opposite direction. These back-country farmers, especially the Scotch-Irish Presbyterians, had waged a long fight against the conservatives of the seaboard; in 1776 they had put Pennsylvania on the side of independence and had forced through a comparatively democratic state constitution. The new federal system now looked to them like an attempt of the "moneyed interests" in Philadelphia to weaken their cherished state government by transferring much of its power to a central authority, less responsive to the will of the people.

The convention which met in Philadelphia in November, 1787, illustrated very well the various elements of which the state was composed. The Scotch-Irish delegates were numerous and furnished the chief opponents of ratification. The Germans were also strongly represented, and one of their number, Frederick Muhlenberg, was elected president. On the Federal side the outstanding figure was James Wilson, but he was ably supported by Chief-Justice McKean. The recognized leaders of the opposition were William Findley, John Smilie, and Robert Whitehill; the first two born in the north of Ireland and the third of Scotch-Irish parentage. They were evidently able men, and all of them subsequently represented Pennsylvania in the new federal Congress; but none of them ever won a really national reputation. *The Pennsylvania convention.* *Opposition leaders.*

The opponents of ratification argued that the framers of the Constitution had exceeded their authority, organized a consolidated rather than a truly federal government, and undertaken to secure its adoption by a method not authorized in the Articles of Confederation. Wilson answered with a frankly nationalistic argument. There was no question, he said, of transferring sovereignty from the states to the federal government; for real sovereignty belonged only to the people, who, by ratifying this Constitution, would simply transfer certain powers and duties from one of their agents to another. The Anti-Federalists objected to the taxing power, which they thought might be used to cripple the state governments, and complained that there was no bill of rights to protect personal liberty, more particularly freedom of speech and of the press. The suspicious attitude of the rural population toward the "moneyed interests" was quite evident and the Senate was considered especially dangerous from this point of view. On the other hand, Wilson and his associates argued that the new system was not less democratic than the state governments and that a federal bill of rights was unnecessary because the *The issues defined.*

new government was limited to certain enumerated powers. While the Anti-Federalists urged the necessity of distrusting authority, the advocates of ratification pleaded for governmental efficiency. The new government, they said, would protect American commerce, provide for national defense against enemies abroad or at home, and prevent vicious legislation, particularly in the matter of paper money. In short, the adoption of the Constitution would "make us a nation."

Ratification.

Notwithstanding the strenuous efforts made on both sides, the outcome of the Pennsylvania convention was practically certain from the beginning. Under the existing apportionment the Anti-Federalist voters were not fairly represented; on test questions they were outnumbered two to one, and the final vote was forty-six to twenty-three in favor of ratification. This result undoubtedly encouraged the friends of the Constitution in other states, but the methods used by the victorious party were sharply criticized. It was even charged with obstructing the circulation of Anti-Federalist papers.

The fight in Massachusetts.

The second of the larger states to act was Massachusetts. All but one of the delegates from this state to the Federal Convention came back to fight for ratification, and they had with them most of the merchants and professional men, especially in the coast towns and in the Connecticut valley. In the state convention, they were superior to their opponents in parliamentary tactics and debate; but the numerical advantage was probably at first on the other side.

The opposition. Economic factors.

The opponents of the Constitution were especially strong in the frontier district of Maine and in the interior counties of Massachusetts, where the insurgents of 1786 and their sympathizers were most numerous. These people took little interest in foreign commerce and were much afraid of the supposed machinations of the creditor class. Indeed, the fact that lawyers and moneyed men favored the Constitution seemed to some of these rural voters a good reason for voting against it.

What counted most heavily against the Constitution, here as in Pennsylvania, was the feeling of many plain people that to go into the new Union would be to move, to some extent at least, away from democratic control of their own affairs. The only man of much prominence who sided definitely with the opposition was Elbridge Gerry, a member of the Federal Convention, who, curiously enough, was himself a large holder of government securities and a prosperous merchant; but for some time it seemed possible that Hancock and Samuel Adams might throw the great weight of their revolutionary prestige on the same side. In the end, however, both these men were won over by the skillful tactics of the Federal leaders, who flattered Hancock by helping to make him president of the convention. Realizing that an early vote would probably go against them, the friends of the Constitution insisted on having it first thoroughly discussed, paragraph by paragraph. Finally, they also persuaded some doubtful members, including Adams, to vote for unconditional ratification, with the understanding that certain amendments would be recommended. Even with this clever management, the victory was won only by the narrow margin of 19 in a total vote of 355. Probably a direct vote of the people would have gone against the Constitution.

Superiority of Federal leadership.

Close vote for ratification.

In the spring of 1788 two more southern states ratified the Constitution. In Maryland, Luther Martin tried hard to convince his fellow citizens that the Constitution would lead straight towards centralized, and perhaps even monarchical, government; but the prevailing sentiment was decidedly against him. In South Carolina, the opposition was more serious. The merchants and planters of the seaboard were fairly content with the concessions which had been made to them; but there was strong opposition

Maryland and South Carolina.

New
Hampshire,
the ninth
state.

in the back country, and nearly a third of the delegates voted against ratification. Eight states had now ratified, and in June New Hampshire came in by a close vote to fill out the minimum requirement of nine states; but three of the five largest still wavered.

New York.

In New York, the enemies of the Constitution were better organized than in Massachusetts. At their head was George Clinton, the popular war governor and the manager of a strong political "machine." Back of him were a majority of the Hudson River landowners, who were jealous of the city merchants and especially anxious to save the revenue from import duties, which the new Constitution would take from them. On the same side were Yates and Lansing, Hamilton's state-rights colleagues at the Philadelphia convention, with other able politicians and lawyers. The stronghold of the Federal party was the city of New York, whose business and professional men, like the corresponding class elsewhere, wanted a strong government, capable of regulating and protecting commerce. They were ably led by Jay and Hamilton, but at first were evidently in a minority. Their final victory by the narrow margin of three votes was due partly to skillful management and partly to the fact that the Clinton party hesitated to hold out against the nine states which had already adopted the Constitution. This ratification was unconditional; but some votes were secured by agreeing to recommend a new convention to revise the Constitution.

The contest
in Virginia.

While the debate was going on in New York an even more important contest was taking place in Virginia. Both sides had great names to conjure with. On the Federal side Washington was of course the outstanding figure; but with him were Madison and a young lawyer named John Marshall, who was destined to become famous as Chief Justice of the United States. After some wavering, Governor Randolph also decided to support the Constitution, and

Jefferson from his diplomatic post at Paris agreed that it was safer to accept the new plan with all its faults than to reject it. Meantime the opposition had on its side three conspicuous leaders of the Revolution: Richard Henry Lee, who in the Continental Congress had moved the memorable resolution in favor of independence, confederation, and foreign alliances; George Mason, chief author of the Virginia Declaration of Rights; and Patrick Henry. This was a hard combination to beat, and it came near winning.

Many of the arguments presented by the opposition were like those in other states. Henry objected to such phrases as, "We the people, of the United States," "ordain and establish this constitution," which seemed to transfer sovereignty from the states to the Union and establish a "consolidated," or national, government. The President might easily become a King and Congress might also abuse its power unless held in by a bill of rights. In all this there was comparatively little new matter. The great difficulty in Virginia was the fear that in the regulation of commerce Congress might sacrifice the agricultural interests of the South in order to promote northern manufactures and shipping. Jay's Mississippi proposal was again brought up in this connection. On such issues Henry was able to carry with him the great majority of his neighbors in the piedmont district. *Henry's arguments.*

On the other hand, Washington and Madison were supported by a majority of the tidewater planters and merchants, whose experience was such as to emphasize the need of strong government. The Virginia system of representation gave the planters an unfair advantage; but even so the Constitution would probably have been beaten if many of the Scotch-Irish and Germans in the Great Valley had not broken away from their neighbors in the piedmont and voted with the Federal party. These valley people were probably influenced partly by friendliness toward Madison, *Sectional aspects of the contest.*

who had successfully defended their dissenting sects against the established church. When the convention finally voted for ratification by a narrow majority, that result was said to have been made possible by the action of certain delegates who acted against the known wishes of their constituents.

The action of New York and Virginia practically ended the fight. Neither of the two states which still held out was important enough to cause much anxiety. In North Carolina, opposition elements, much like those in Virginia, prevented ratification until the following year. As for Rhode Island, then discredited by the excesses of the paper-money party, it was only a question of time when she would be forced to come in. For the present, however, both these States lost the distinction of being original members of the new union, which was formed by the revolutionary secession of eleven states from the old Confederation.

In September the Confederation Congress recognized this revolution as an accomplished fact by asking the states to choose presidential electors and members of the new Congress. In some states the opponents of the Constitution made serious efforts to send to Congress men of their own way of thinking. Occasionally they were successful, as in the election of the first two senators from Virginia; Madison had to content himself with a seat in the lower house. In most cases, however, men of Federal sympathies were elected. The unanimous vote of the presidential electors for Washington cannot of course be credited to any particular party; but he was the most influential leader of the Federal group. In short, the great experiment was to be conducted by men who wished it to succeed.

On one important point the critics of the Constitution were successful. In one state after another they had demanded a federal bill of rights, and in some cases the ratifying conventions had recommended amendments for this purpose. There was even some talk of a second convention,

Victory for the Constitution.

North Carolina and Rhode Island.

The new government organized by its friends.

The first ten amendments.

which might have reopened many trying questions. Finally the moderates on both sides combined to secure action by the first Congress under the new Constitution, recommending certain amendments, of which ten were ratified. These first ten amendments constituted substantially a bill of rights of the kind demanded by the moderate Anti-Federalists. Whether necessary or not, these formal declarations appealed to most men at that time as desirable guarantees against federal interference with religious liberty, freedom of the press, trial by jury, and other cherished rights. Many people also felt safer when the tenth amendment set down in black and white the principle that all rights not delegated to the federal government or prohibited to the states were reserved to the states or to the people.

One advantage of the controversy over ratification was that, along with a great mass of unimportant speeches and pamphlets, it left behind a few really important essays on the science and art of government. Of these the most famous is *The Federalist*, a series of newspaper articles which appeared over the signature of Publius. A considerable majority of these were written by Hamilton; but several important ones were contributed by Madison, and a few by John Jay. It is hard to say how far *The Federalist* made votes for the Constitution; but it is permanently valuable because it illustrates the political philosophy of the day and shows how the Constitution was interpreted by some of the men most responsible for its adoption. Very suggestive also are the principal publications on the opposite side. Luther Martin's essay called *Genuine Information*, which was intended primarily for the enlightenment of his neighbors in Maryland, brings out many objections to the Constitution and helps to show why it was unsatisfactory to a large part, perhaps a majority, of the American people. In Pennsylvania, the *Centinel* essays tried to do for the Anti-Federalists what

The Federalist.

Anti-Federalist publications.

Hamilton and Madison did for the friends of the Constitution.

Contemporary interpretation of Constitution.

A study of this contemporary literature shows that men were already divided, somewhat as they were in the next century, about the nature of the government which was being established. Its opponents generally claimed that it was a centralized, or centralizing, system; a dangerous departure from the sacred principle of state sovereignty; a national, rather than a truly federal, government. Some friends of the Constitution, like Wilson for instance, frankly declared that the Constitution was intended to create a national government and that state sovereignty was an idle phrase. More cautious members of that party tried to disarm criticism by showing that the change in principle from the Articles of Confederation was less revolutionary than it seemed. In general, such men seemed to regard sovereignty as divided between the states and the Union. They undoubtedly spoke of the federal Constitution as a "compact"; but they often used the same word in speaking of the state constitutions. When, in one of his best-known *Federalist* essays, Madison described the proposed new government as neither wholly federal nor wholly national, but a composite of both principles, he was of course emphasizing the element of compromise in the system; but his statements also suggest that many of the people who adopted the Constitution did not have precise notions about the meaning of such words as nationality and state sovereignty. It has therefore always been possible for extreme advocates of nationalism on one side, or of states rights on the other, to find material for their arguments in the writings of the founders.

The Constitution in relation to democratic ideals.

Careful study of contemporary literature also shows that, though the radical democracy of the time was generally against the Constitution, there was no clean-cut issue of this kind between the friends and enemies of the

Constitution. Speeches on both sides show much more emphasis on property rights than would now be regarded as democratic, as well as a keen interest in devices for curbing popular majorities. Some of Luther Martin's articles indicate real democratic feeling and so do those of some other less conspicuous Anti-Federalists; but it would be hard to prove that such opponents of the Constitution as George Mason, Richard Henry Lee, or Elbridge Gerry, were really more democratic than James Madison or James Wilson. It was Mason who said that the people could no more choose a President intelligently than a blind man could choose colors. It was Gerry, one of the chief opponents of the Constitution in Massachusetts, who declared that the evils of the time came "from the excess of democracy" and added in the same speech that though he was still a republican he "had been taught by experience the danger of the levilling spirit." In short, the evolution of American democracy, as well as of American nationality, was incomplete.

When all is said, however, the inauguration of Washington as the first President of the United States does indeed mark the end of a great historic process, which began in 1607 with the landing of the first English settlers at Jamestown. The struggling and dependent colonies of a European nation had at last grown into self-reliant commonwealths capable of winning their independence from the mother country, of reorganizing their institutions on republican principles, and finally of establishing a federal system different from, and in advance of, any previous experiment of that kind. Whether the American people of 1789 were already a nation or not, whether their Union was a national government or a federation of sovereign states, it is quite certain that they had established the foundations upon which American nationality has been built. They had also determined to a large extent the political framework within which a great nation is still able to live and work.

American achievements, 1607-1789.

BIBLIOGRAPHICAL NOTES

General
accounts.

Channing, *United States*, III, 515–524. Beveridge, A. J., *Life of John Marshall*, I. McLaughlin, *Confederation and Constitution*, chs. XVII–XVIII. McMaster, *People of the United States*, I, 454–502.

Contempo-
rary argu-
ments.

Elliott, J., *Debates*, II–IV (state conventions, etc.; selections in Morison, S. E., *Sources and Documents*, 307–362). Farrand, *Records of the Federal Convention*, III. *The Federalist* (editions by H. B. Dawson, E. G. Bourne, W. C. Ford, and others; selections by W. B. Munro). Representative Hamiltonian essays are nos. 15, 16, 21–23, 27, 70; see also 10 and 39 (Ford edition, 38 in some others; *The Constitution Strictly Republican*), by Madison. *Writings* of Washington, Hamilton, Madison. For opposition arguments see *Centinel* essays in McMaster and Stone, *Pennsylvania and the Federal Constitution*, and Luther Martin's *Genuine Information* in Farrand, *Records*, III, 172–232.

Special
topics.

Beard, *Economic Interpretation of the Constitution*, chs. VIII–XI; also his *Economic Interpretation of Jeffersonian Democracy*, ch. III, and his *Supreme Court and the Constitution*, chs. III–V. Libby, O. G., *Geographical Distribution of the Vote of the Thirteen States on the Federal Constitution*. McLaughlin, A. C., *The Courts, the Constitution and Parties*, 189–242.

Penn-
sylvania.

McMaster, J. B., and Stone, F. D., *Pennsylvania and the Federal Constitution* (with sources).

Massachu-
setts.

Harding, S. B., *Ratification of the Constitution in Massachusetts*. Morse, A. E., *Federalist Party in Massachusetts*, chs. I–IV.

New York.

Spaulding, E. W., *New York in the Critical Period*, chs. X–XIV. Biographies of Hamilton by Morse, Oliver, and Hamilton.

Virginia.

Ambler, C. H., *Sectionalism in Virginia*, 53–60. Beveridge, A. J., *John Marshall*, I, chs. IX–XII. Henry, *Patrick Henry*, II, especially chs. XXXVI, XXXVIII. Hunt, *Madison*, chs. XV–XVII. Rowland, *George Mason*, II, chs. V–VII. Tyler, *Patrick Henry*, chs. XVIII, XIX.

Rhode
Island.

Bates, F. G., *Rhode Island and the Union*, especially ch. V.

INDEX

Abercrombie, General, in French and Indian War, 381, 382.

Acadia, French colony established. 25, 212; under Cromwell. 133; character. 212; taken by English (1690) and recovered. 219; British attack and conquest. 222, 223; cession by France to Great Britain, 224; French influence over Acadians, 364, 367; dispute as to extent, 367; removal of Acadians, 373.

Act for the Impartial Administration of Justice, 429.

Act of Settlement. 194; protected judges, 232.

Act of Union, 226.

Acts of trade. 178, 182–184; protective principle, 184; problem of enforcement. 184; effect of Revolution of 1688, 205; readjusted by Grenville. 402–403.

Adams, John, influenced by European writers, 255; broad thinking, 393; counsel for British officer, 422; in first Continental Congress, visits churches in Philadelphia, 433; War Office, 445, 461; favors independence, 449; opinion of Paine's *Common Sense*, 450; resolution of May, 1776, 452; moves for American independence, 453; committee on Declaration of Independence, 453; argues for independence, 454; comment on Declaration, 455; chairman of War Office, 461; influence on Massachusetts constitution, 463; secures loans from Dutch, 464; character and contribution to victory, 468; peace commissioner, 513; envoy to Holland, 514; attitude as peace commissioner, 514; ignores instructions, 519; negotiates for fisheries, 520; negotiates concerning private debts, 521; advice by Price, 527; belief in class distinctions, 535; view on apportionment, 549; on veto power, 550, drafts clause on public education in Massachusetts constitution, 555; on nature of Confederation, 563; commissioner to negotiate commercial treaties, 570; tries to secure commercial concessions from England, 570; minister to Great Britain, 570, 571, 572; influence on constitutional convention, 586; cited, 340, 433.

Adams, Samuel, character and political theories, 420; forces transfer of soldiers, 422; opposes Hutchinson, 423, 424; Committees of Correspondence 425; opposes tea tax, 426; in first Continental Congress, proposes Episcopal chaplain. 433; state politics, 566; favors federal Constitution, 607.

Addison, *Spectator* essays, influence on America, 254.

Admiralty, courts of, 241; jurisdiction, 403.

"Adventurers," in Maryland. 71.

Agriculture, in England, 3–5; of Indians, 50; in New England, 101, 102; in middle colonies, 292; in the South, 320, 324.

Aix-la-Chapelle, treaty, 365.

Albany, originally Fort Orange, 146, 157; fur trade, 146, 161; government, 158; opposes Leisler. 197; Dutch language, 284, 340.

Albany Congress of 1754, 376.

Albany Plan, 376; unacceptable to colonies, 377, 557.

Albemarle, Duke of, friend of Charles II, 134; Carolina proprietor, 136.

Albemarle settlements, 138–139.

Aldermen, in England, 9.

Alexander, Sir William, colonizer, 42.

Algonquian Indians, political organization, 50.

Allegheny River, Céloron's journey, 369.

Allen, Ethan, takes Ticonderoga and Crown Point, 446.

Amboina massacre, 125.

Amendments, to Articles of Confederation, defeated, 568, 569, 571, 584; to Constitution, first ten, 610–611.

American nationality, English and other contributions, 1, 130, 131, 532, 533; in 1750, 338–355; elements of unity, 340; English influences, 340–347; new American ideas, 347–355; religious tendency, 351–354; effect of westward expansion, 354; the making of an American, 354–355; feeling about the empire, 392–393; English predominate, 532, 533; common body of political doctrine, 555; evolution incomplete, 613; foundations established, 613.

American Philosophical Society, 309.

Americanizing influences, 347–348.

Amherst, Jeffrey, takes Louisburg, 381, 382; takes Montreal, 383, 384.

Amory, Thomas, Boston merchant, career, 263.

Anarchy, threatened during Revolution, 463.

André, Major, execution, 501.

Andros, Edmund, character, 158, 189; governor of New York, 158, 160; attempted control of New Jersey, 162; governor of New England, 189–192; relations with Indians, 190; character, 191; disregard of Puritan traditions, 192; deposed, 195.

Anglican Church, 11; in Virginia, 56, 61, 77, 330, 331, 552; high church party, 96; in North Carolina, 137, 250; in South Carolina, 142, 248, 250, 332; in New York, 159, 248, 303, 304; in Pennsylvania, 171, 175, 304; in New England, 192, 248, 250, 276; in Ireland, 227; position in the colonies, 248–250; bishops proposed for America, 249, 420; in Philadelphia and Burlington, 304; schools in middle colonies, 306; in Maryland, 332; in Thirteen Colonies, conservatism, 353; in United States, 533, 553.

Anglo-Spanish War of 1739, 362.

Annapolis (Md.), founded, 72; capital Maryland, 323; Confederation Congress at, 566, 567.

Annapolis Convention, 585.

Anne, Queen, 220; reduction of power, 228; death, 249.

Anson, Captain, voyage of, 362.
Anti-Federalist party, 603; in Pennsylvania, 604–606; in Massachusetts, 606; in New York, 608; in Virginia, 609; leaders elected to First Congress, 610; publications opposing the Constitution, 611; democratic feeling, 613.
Antinomians, in Massachusetts, 114.
Antislavery movement, after the Revolution, 554.
Apportionment, in states, problems of, 549.
Aquidneck, settled, 117.
Aranda, Count, war policy, 488; negotiation with Franklin, 489; questions United States claim to West, 528.
Architecture, colonial, 265; in New England, 265–266; in New York and Philadelphia, 294.
Argall, Captain, attacks French colonies, 216.
Aristocracy, in England, 9; in Carolina, 137, 140; in New York, 160, 196, 297; in Great Britain, 228; in the South, 326; in Thirteen Colonies, 348; conditions after the revolution, 534.
Arizona, Coronado in, 24.
Arkansas, De Soto in, 23.
Arlington, Lord, Virginia grant, 81.
Armada, Spanish, 15, 30.
"Armed Neutrality," in Revolutionary War, 504.
Arminian teaching, in New England, 277.
Army, beginnings at Cambridge, 442, 445; lack of discipline and equipment, 445; control by Congress, 445; suffers from weak administration, 463; management, 465; mutinies, 465, 501; inexperience of American officers, 465; foreign officers, 466; political interference, 467; Conway Cabal, 485; in 1780, 501; disbanding, 567–568; officers threaten revolt, 568.
Arnold, Benedict, Canadian expedition, 447; military ability, 466; on Lake Champlain, 475, 477; treason, 501; British officer in Virginia, 503, 507.
"Articles of Compact," in Ordinance of 1787, 578.
Articles of Confederation, adopted, 501; nationality of signers, 533; framed and adopted, 559; delayed by question of western lands, 560; compared with other federations, 560; provisions, 560–563; citizenship and interstate comity, 562; deficiencies, 562, 563; proposed amendments, 568, 569, 571, 584; movement to revise, 584; relation to new Constitution, 596, 600.
Ashley, Lord, Earl of Shaftesbury, friend of Charles II, 134; Carolina proprietor, 136; leadership, 140; interest in trade expansion, 181.
Asiento agreement, 316.
Assembly, colonial, in Virginia, 57, 59, 60; in Maryland, 72; British and American points of view, 234, 343; freedom limited by royal instructions to governors, 238; control over governor, in colonies generally, 241; conflict with governor in Massachusetts, 270–271; gains control in New York, 297–299; in Pennsylvania, 299–300; in South Carolina, 326; follows traditions of the English House of Commons, 342–343; view of English lawyers, 343; New York assembly suspended by Parliament, 417.
Assistants, or council, of Massachusetts, 103, 104, 105.
Assizes, court of, New York, 158.
"Association." See "Continental Association."
Austria, in Seven Years' War, 374, 384.
Austrian Netherlands, in War of the Austrian Succession, 363, 365.

Austrian Succession, War of, 363–365.
Autocracy, in New Netherland, 147; in New York, 157; in New France, 210.
Avalon colony, 42.
Ayllon, in North Carolina, 23.

Back country, physical features, 49; led by Bacon, 82; characteristics, 319, 323–325; products, 324; under-representation, 329–330; conflict with tidewater, 330; education, 335; Americanism, 354, 355; opposes Constitution (in Pennsylvania) 604, (in South Carolina) 608, (in Virginia) 609.
Backwoodsmen, at Kings Mountain, 500.
Bacon, Nathaniel, Virginia leader, 82; Rebellion, 82–84.
Bacon, Sir Francis, in Virginia Company, 55.
Bacon's Rebellion, 82–84.
Balboa, explorer, 21.
Baltimore, sphere of influence, 282; trade center of wheat farmers, 323; trade, 540; conditions after the Revolution, 540.
Baltimore, Lord, 67. See Calvert.
Banking, regulated by Parliament, 237.
Baptists, in Massachusetts, 114; in Boston, 273; in New England, 277, 552; in Thirteen Colonies, radicalism, 353; in Virginia, 533; in West, 545.
Barbados, English colony, 40, 43; trade ordinance (1650), 75; in 1660, 130; emigrants from, 139, 141; constitutional controversies, 338.
Barbary pirates, attack American ships, 536.
Bard, Samuel, physician, 309.
Bartram, John, botanist, 308.
Baxter, Richard, theological writings, 250.
Bayard, Nicholas, aristocratic leader, 196.
Beaubassin, fort established, 367.
Beaumarchais, aids United States, 487.
Beauséjour, fort established, 367; captured, 373.
Bedford, Duke of, 400; gains power in 1769, 422; faction in power during Revolution, 471.
Belcher, governor of Massachusetts, 266, 272.
Bellomont, governor of New York, cited, 296.
Bemis Heights, American forces at, 483.
Bennett, Richard, commissioner, 75.
Bennington, battle, 483.
Berkeley, Dean, philosopher, influence on America, 254; visits Rhode Island, 278.
Berkeley, Lord, Carolina proprietor, 136; proprietor New Jersey, 162, 164.
Berkeley, Sir William, governor of Virginia, 60, 65; deposed (1652), 75; restored (1660), 77; opposes Navigation Acts, 81; misgovernment, 81–82; war with Bacon, 83; recall, 83; character, 84; Carolina proprietor, 136.
Berkshire region, settled, 259.
Bermudas, English colony, 40.
Bernard, Governor, dissolves Massachusetts assembly, 421.
Bible, importance in colonial literature, 341.
Bible Commonwealth, in Massachusetts, 103, 105; in New Haven, 122.
Biblical Christianity, advocated by Puritans, 89.
Bicameral system, in Virginia, 59; in Massachusetts, 105; in state legislatures, 549.
Bienville, Céloron de, claims Ohio valley, 369.
Bigot, intendant of New France, 378.
Bill of Rights, English, 194, 205.
Bill of rights, in state constitutions, 550; in federal Constitution, 610–611.
Biloxi, founded, 212, 221.

Bishop of London, authority in colonies, 249; member of S. P. G., 250.
Bishops of the Church of England, 10, 11; proposed for America, 249, 420.
Blainville, claims Ohio valley, 369.
Blair, James, opposes Spotswood, 328; president of William and Mary College, 333.
Bland, John, opposes Navigation Acts, 81.
Bland, Richard, denies authority of Parliament, 407; plan for territories, 576.
Blathwayt, William, member Board of Trade, 231.
Bloomsbury gang, defined, 400; gains power in 1769, 422.
Board of Admiralty, British, 229, 232.
Board of Trade, organization and functions, 230; members, 231; defects, 231; disallowance of colonial laws, 238; indicts chartered colonies, 268; reports against New York, 298.
Board of War, appointed by Congress, 462.
Body of Liberties, in Massachusetts, 106.
Bolingbroke, Lord, political theories, 398.
Bombay, acquired by Charles II, 134.
Bonhomme Richard, victory, 467.
Boone, Daniel, promotes colonization of Kentucky, 496; character, 544.
Borough, in England, 9; American like English, 343.
Boscawen, attempt against French fleet, 372; takes Louisburg, 381, 382.
Boston, named, 100; under Andros, 192, 195; slave trade, 247; population, 259; shipping and trade, 261, 262; merchants, 263; houses and dress, 266; *Newsletter*, 278; mob attacks Hutchinson house, 409; headquarters of Townshend's customs service, 419; "Massacre," 421; Tea Party, 427; Port Bill, 427; siege, 444–445; foreign trade, 537.
Boston "Massacre," 421.
Boston Newsletter, 278.
Boston Port Bill, 427, 431.
Boston Tea Party, 427.
Boundary controversies, colonial, 169–170, 295–296; over forks of the Ohio, 369, 389; in United States, 529; dispute with Spain, 573.
Bourbons, claim to Spain, 219, 220; in France and Spain, 361.
Bowdoin, James, governor of Massachusetts, puts down the Shays rebellion, 581; fails of reëlection, 582.
Boycott, in opposition to Townshend Acts, 422; in 1774, 435.
Braddock, General, sent to America, 372; defeat, 373.
Bradford, William, governor of Plymouth, 95.
Bradford, William, printer, 295.
Bradstreet, Lieutenant-Colonel, takes Fort Frontenac, 382, 392.
Brandywine, battle, 481.
Bray, Rev. Thomas, establishes libraries, 335.
Brazil, becomes Portuguese, 21; French colony in, 25; visited by English, 26.
Bread colonies, 247, 292.
Breda, treaty of, 153.
Breton fishermen, visit Newfoundland, 24.
Brewster, William, Separatist leader, education, 91.
Bristol, importance in 1606, 4; voyages to Newfoundland, 26.
British creditors and American debtors, 237, 246, 247; after the Revolution, 521.

British Empire, lack of an imperial constitution, 233; authority of Parliament, 234, 237; government, 234–242; menaced by French alliance with United States, 491; as a quasi-federal system, 556.
Brooklyn Heights, Washington's army at, 478; battle, 479.
Bryn Mawr (Pa.), Welsh name, 175.
Buckingham, Duke of, colonizer, 41.
Bunker Hill, battle, 444.
Bunyan, John, dissenter, 132.
Burgesses of Virginia, 57, 59.
Burgoyne, Sir John, lack of support in Saratoga campaign, 469; plan for 1777, 480; expedition, 481, 482–484; surrender, 484; effect of surrender on diplomacy, 486, 490.
Burke, Edmund, leader of "Old Whigs," 400; on tea tax, 423; opposes coercion of Massachusetts, 428; conciliatory proposals, 437; opposition ineffective, 471; in ministry of 1782, 510; letter to Franklin (1782), 512; cited, 353, 423.
Burlington (N. J.), settled, 164; trade, 294.
Burnaby, English writer, cited, 294.
Burnet, William, governor of Massachusetts, 270; governor of New York, opposes exports to Canada, 293; intellectual character, 307.
Bute, Lord, ministry, 385, 399.
Byles, Mather, Boston clergyman and poet, 254.
Byllinge, proprietor West New Jersey, 164.
Byrd, William, fur trade, 80; large estate, 320.
Byrd, William, II, Royal Society, 253; large estate, 320; character and career, 328.
Byrds, library, 328, 335.

Cabinet, British, 229; in United States, 593.
Cabot, John, explorer, 26.
Cacique, title in Carolina, 137.
Cadillac, founds Detroit, 221.
California, visited by Drake, 30.
Calvert, Cecilius, founds Maryland, 67, 69–72; religious problem, 70, 73, 74, 75, 352; loses and regains control, 76, 77.
Calvert, Protestant, reclaims Maryland, 312.
Calvert, Sir George, colonizer, 39, 42, 67; Avalon colony, 42; career, 67, 68.
Calvin, John, influence on English, 11, 89; on Dutch, 18; doctrines, 89, 90.
Calvinism, 89, 90; expounded by Jonathan Edwards, 276.
Calvinistic churches in middle colonies, 305.
Calvinists in Germany, 286; in Pennsylvania, 305. *See* Presbyterians, and Puritans.
Cambridge (Eng.), University of, 13.
Cambridge Agreement, 98.
Cambridge (Mass.), army at, 442, 443, 445.
Camden, battle, 494.
Camden, Lord, denies power of Parliament to tax America, 410.
Canada, French colony, *see* New France; in French and Indian War, 375, 382–384; taken by British, 385; decision to hold, 385–386; ceded, 386, 429; new and old subjects, 388; Quebec Act of 1774, 429–430; religious toleration, 429; no revolutionary spirit, 446.
Canals, proposed by Chesapeake states, 541.
Canton trade, American ships in, 537.
Cape Breton Island, fortress of Louisburg, 363.
Cape Fear River, colony on, 139.
Cape Vincent, battle, 505.

Carleton, Sir Guy, defends Quebec, 447; in campaign of 1776, 475, 477; plan for 1777, 480.

Carlisle, Earl of, colonizer, 39, 40.

Carolina, patent to Heath, 41, 136; English colony, 136–142; charters, 136, 137, 185; boundaries, 137; government, 137, 140, 142; toleration, 137; aims of promoters, 138, 139; northern settlements, 138–139; Fundamental Constitutions, 140; South Carolina, 140–143; slow development before 1689, 311; complaints of the home government, 312; friction with proprietors, 313; proprietors give up, 314. *See* Carolinas, North Carolina, and South Carolina.

Carolinas, fur trade, 215, 221; Anglican Church in, 250; population, 311; piracy, 312; Indian wars, 313.

Carroll, Charles, of Carrollton, signed Declaration of Independence, 553.

Carroll, John, envoy of Congress to Canada, 446; first Roman Catholic bishop, 553.

Cartagena, sacked by Drake, 30.

Carteret, governor of New Jersey, 162.

Carteret, Sir George, Carolina proprietor, 136; proprietor New Jersey, 162; takes East New Jersey, 164; death, 164.

Cartier, Jacques, explorer, 25.

Castle William, British soldiers transferred to, 422.

Catharine II, armed neutrality, 504.

Catholic Church, 10. *See* Roman Catholics.

Cattle, in South Carolina, 141; in Carolinas, 321; in back country, 324.

Cavaliers, in Virginia, 62, 75.

Céloron de Bienville, claims Ohio valley, 369.

Centinel essays, 611.

Central America, Spanish in, 21, 22.

Centurion, voyage of, 362.

Chads Ford, battle, 481.

Champlain, Lake, under British control, 475, 483.

Champlain, Samuel de, founds Quebec, 207, 208.

Charles I, conflict with Parliament, 6, 74, 97; grants colonies, 40, 41; charters Maryland, 67; execution, 74; church policy, 96; attempted control of American colonies, 109.

Charles II, ascends throne, 77; grants in Virginia, 81; Connecticut charter, 123; policies and character, 131, 132, 133, 134; marriage, 134; patent for New Netherland, 152; grant to Penn, 168–169; colonial policy, 181, 185; pension from Louis XIV, 216.

Charleston (S. C.), founded, 141; importance, 142; in Queen Anne's War, 221; in 1689, 311; center of provincial activity, 323; foodstuffs from back country, 325; intellectual center, 335; Library Society, 335; tea landed, 427; attacked in 1776, 447–448; taken by British, 493, 494; British base, 503; held by British after Yorktown, 508; conditions after the Revolution, 541.

Charleston Library Society, founded, 335.

Charlottesville, British at, 507.

Charter of Freedoms and Exemptions, in New Netherland, 145.

Charter of Liberties and Privileges, in New York, 159.

Charter of Privileges, in Pennsylvania, 172.

Chatham, Earl of, 415, *see* Pitt; out of power, 422; opinion of Continental Congress, 437; proposal to define colonial rights, 437–438.

Chatham-Grafton ministry, 415.

"Checks and balances," in state constitutions, 549–551; in federal constitutional convention, 594.

Cheraw, Greene's army at, 502.

Cherokee country, Virginians trade with, 80.

Cherokees, raids in Revolution, 498.

Chesapeake Bay, description, 48.

Chesapeake colonies. *See* Virginia, and Maryland.

Chesapeake country, physical features, 48.

China, New England commerce with, 537.

Church, established, in England, 10–12; in Virginia, 61, 248, 394–396 (Parson's Cause), 552; in Massachusetts, 107, 552; in New Netherland, 149; in West Indies, 248; in New York, 248; in New England, 273; in South Carolina, 313; in South, 330; in Thirteen Colonies, 352–353.

Church of England, 10–12. *See* Anglican Church.

Church of Ireland, Anglican, 290.

Churches, reorganized after Revolution, 553. *See* names of churches and sects.

Cincinnati order, membership hereditary, 534.

Circular Letter, Massachusetts, 421.

Citizenship, national, under Articles of Confederation, 562.

Civil War, in England, 7, 74; effect on colonization, 42; effect on Virginia, 62.

Claiborne, William, opposes Lord Baltimore, 70; commissioner, 75, 76.

Clarendon, Earl of, friend of Charles II, 134; Carolina proprietor, 136; interest in trade expansion, 181; cited, 43.

Clark, George Rogers, conquers the Illinois country, 499; opposition to Spain, 544.

Class conflicts, after the Revolution, 580.

Class distinctions, weakened in America, 348, 355.

Classes, social, in England, 3–5, 9; in Virginia, 62; in New England, 266; American tendency to break down, 348, 355; in United States, 534–535; conflicts after the Revolution, 580.

Clinton, General Sir Henry, attacks Charleston, 447; military ability, 473; British commander in chief, 492; battle of Monmouth, 492; takes Charleston, 493, 494; defends New York, 506; orders to Cornwallis, 507; reënforcements to Cornwallis, 508.

Clinton, George, governor of New York, appeals to rural voters, 539; opposes Constitution, 608.

Clymer, George, delegate in constitutional convention, 586.

Coercive Acts of 1774, 427–430; effect of, 435; of 1775, 438.

Coinage, regulated by Parliament, 237; debasement of, 569.

Colbert, Jean Baptiste, policies, 208.

Colden, Cadwallader, physician and author, 307.

Coligny, promotes colonies, 25.

College of New Jersey, founded, 307.

Colleges, Harvard, 109, 275, 277; Yale, 277; in Middle Colonies, 307, 309; William and Mary, 333.

Colleton, Sir John, Carolina proprietor, 136.

Colonial agents, 242.

Colonial Duty Act of 1673, 182, 185.

Colonial government, development of self-government, 43, 109, 195–200, 267–268, 556; government in Virginia, 59, 60; in Massachusetts, 103–110; reorganization 1685–1688, 188–192; after 1688, 200–204; influence of Board of

Trade, 230, 231, 238; control by Parliament, 234–238; levies customs duties, 237, 557; control by Privy Council, 238–239; imperial agencies, 239–242; difficulties of overseas administration, 242; colonial agents, 242; English traditions, 342–347; new ideas, 348–350; powers, 556. *See* Assembly, Council, Governor, Representative government, and names of colonies.

Colonial merchants. *See* Merchants.

Colonial policy, new conception in Ordinance of 1787, 578.

Colonial trade (in general), seventeenth century, 179–185; in English ships, 182; supervised by Board of Trade, 230; regulated by Parliament, 234–236; trade with England, 243; articles and conditions of commerce, 243–247; map, 244.

Colonies. *See* names of colonies; *also* Colonial, Colonization, Thirteen Colonies.

Colonists, rights of, 234, 344; proposed trial in England, 421.

Colonization, motives of, 31–34, 42–43, 88, 92, 100, 133–136; public interest, 37; promoters of, 38, 87, 134; methods of promoting, 39, 135; English colonies in 1660, 130; new phases, 131; in Restoration era, 133–135; aims and methods, 135.

Columbus, Christopher, discoverer, 20.

Commerce, English, 4, 32, 33, 132–135, 179–185, 243–247; West Indies, 40, 235, 247, 261, 264, 403, 405, 537, 539, 570; of New England, 103, 138, 139, 151, 183, 236, 246–247, 261–264, 536–538; in Restoration era, 132–135; of colonies in general, 179–185, 234, 243–247, *see* Colonial trade; of New York, 160, 247, 292; of Virginia, 180, 183, 246; French, under Colbert, 208; supervised by Board of Trade, 230; colonial commerce with England, 243–247; of Pennsylvania, 247; of middle colonies, 293; importance in British foreign policy, 451; regulated by Continental Congress, 451; American, after the Revolution, 536–537, 539, 540; controlled by states, 562; under Confederation, 570, 571; Congress given power to regulate, 597.

Commissary-general, bad management, 465.

Commissioners of Customs, British, 229, 232; new, 417.

Committee of Detail, in constitutional convention, 600.

Committee of Style, in constitutional convention, 600.

Committee on Trade and Plantations, 185; opposes Massachusetts charter, 186–187; replaced by Board of Trade, 230.

"Committees of Correspondence," organized, 425.

Common lands, in England, 5; in Massachusetts, 102.

Common law, in England, 7; in Massachusetts, 105; in the colonies, 344–346; American modifications, 350.

Common Pleas, court in England, 7.

Common Sense, by Thomas Paine, 450.

Commons, House of, in 1606, 6; gains control of executive, 228; unrepresentative character, 228, 398, 470.

Commonwealth in England, 74.

Communal system, in Virginia, 57; in Plymouth, 93, 94.

Communication, slowness, 536.

Community spirit, in New England, 102.

Concession and Agreement, New Jersey, 163.

"Conciliatory Proposition," of Lord North, 438.

Concord, battle, 442.

Confederates of 1861, use of economic resources, 464.

Confederation, adopted, 501, 559; weakness, 501; state sovereignty under, 561; deficiencies, 562, 563; nature of, 563; problems of peace, 565; colonial policy, 574–579; secession of eleven states from, 610.

Confederation Congress, equal representation, 559; functions, 560, 561, 562; control of foreign relations, 561; no power to tax, 562; nine-state rule, 562, 566; organization of executive departments, 565; personnel, 565–566; irregular attendance, 566; ratifies treaty with Great Britain, 524, 567; migrations, 567; settling with the army, 567–568; finances, 568, 569; proposes amendments, 568, 569, 571; resolution denying right of states to interfere with treaties, 572; public land policy, 575; proposes convention at Philadelphia, 585; submits Constitution to states, 601; asks for elections under the Constitution, 610.

Congregational organization of Separatists, 91.

Congregational system, in Plymouth, 95; in Massachusetts, 107; in New England, 273–275.

Congregationalists, in South Carolina, 142; in New Netherland, 149; relation with English Independents, 250; in Thirteen Colonies, radicalism, 353. *See* Puritans.

Congress, Albany, 376.

Congress, Confederation. *See* Confederation Congress.

Congress, Continental. *See* Continental Congress.

Congress, provincial. *See* Provincial congress.

Congress, Stamp Act, 408.

Congress, under the Constitution, made up of two houses, 592; unconstitutional legislation by, 595; powers, 596–598.

Connecticut, Plymouth fur trade, 94; colony founded, 120–122; Dutch in, 120, 146; Fundamental Orders, 121; population, 121, 122; charter, 123, 185; Pequot War, 123; in New England Confederation, 126, 127; dispute with Massachusetts, 127; treaty with Stuyvesant, 151; western boundary, 156; merged in New England, 189; separate government resumed, 195; resumes charter, 203; about 1690, 258; self-government, 267; churches in, 273, 275; church and state relations, 276, 552; education, 277, 278; boundary disputes, 295; religious toleration, 352; independent government, 449; state constitution, 462, 463; loses Wyoming valley, 529, 563; claims Northwest, 530; yields claim to Northwest, 530, 574; first American bishopric, 533; trade through New York city, 538; westward movement of Connecticut pioneers, 542; extent of power as colony, 556; Wyoming valley dispute settled by arbitration, 563; delegates in constitutional convention, 586; in small-state group, 590; ratifies federal Constitution, 604. *See* New England, and Thirteen Colonies.

"Connecticut Reserve," 530.

Connecticut River, fertile valley, 101; Dutch settlers on, 146; English settlements about 1690, 257, 258, 259.

Conservative provisions in Constitution, 600.

Conservatives, in Massachusetts, 272, 274, 419; in first Continental Congress, 434. *See* Loyalists.

Consociation, in Connecticut, 275.

Conspiracy of Pontiac, 389–390.

Constables, in England, 8; American like English, 343–344.

Constitution, federal, nationality of the signers, 533; framework of the government, 592–595; compromises, 592, 598; relation to the Articles of Confederation, 596, 600; powers of Congress, 596–598; provisions concerning slavery, 598; conservative provisions, 600; committees on detail and on style, 600; signed, 600; plan of ratification, 601; ratified, 603–610; by Pennsylvania, 604–606; by Massachusetts, 606–607; by New York, 608; by Virginia, 608–610; arguments for and against, in Pennsylvania, 605–606; Henry's arguments against, 609; first ten amendments, 610–611; contemporary interpretation of, 611–612; relation to democratic ideals, 612.

Constitutional limitations, American ideas, 349.

Constitutions, state, 547–551.

Continental army, 465.

"Continental Association," of 1774, 435; enforcement, 439; loyalist argument against, 441.

Continental Congress, first, 433–435; appeals rejected, 438; net result, 441.

Continental Congress, second, call for, 435; members, 442; appoints Washington commander, 443; control of army, 445, 465; appeal to Canadians, 446; approaches foreign powers, 448; advises formation of temporary governments, 449; opens ports to foreign shipping, 451; advises independent governments, 452; adopts Declaration of Independence, 453–455; functions, 460; character, 461; methods, 461–462; economic problems, paper money, 464; management of army, 465; Conway Cabal, 485; Articles of Confederation adopted, 501; reorganizes executive departments, 502; appoints peace commissioners, 513; political authority, 558; governmental functions, 558; a *de facto* federal government, 559; colonial policy, 574.

Continental money, 464.

Convention, Annapolis, 585.

Convention, constitutional (of 1787), first suggested, 584; delegates, 585–588; procedure, 588; nationalist leaders, 589; large and small states, 590; question of representation, 591–592, 598; federal executive, 592–593; checks and balances, 594; the judiciary, 594–595; powers of Congress, 596–598; slave trade and slavery, 597–598; sectionalism, 598; committees on detail and style, 600; the finished work, 600.

Convicts, importation, 33, 62, 321.

Conway, General Henry, on service in America, 471.

Conway, Thomas, inspector-general, 485.

Conway Cabal, 485.

Coode, John, Protestant leader in Maryland, 199, 200.

Corn, cultivated by Indians, 50; in Virginia, 57, 64; in New England, 101; in North Carolina, 138; in South Carolina, 141.

Cornbury, Lord, misgovernment in New York, 297.

Cornwallis, Lord, in New Jersey, 479, 480; war in South, 494; campaign in North Carolina, 500; campaign in the Carolinas, 502–503; retires to Virginia, 503; campaign in Virginia, 507; **at** Yorktown, 507; surrenders, 508.

Coronado, explorer, 24.

Cortes, conquest of Mexico, 22, 24.

Cosby, governor of New York, Zenger case, 299.

Cotton, John, minister in Massachusetts, 99, 105; code of laws, 106; plan of church government, 107; friendly to Mrs. Hutchinson, 114.

Council, English, powers, 6, 7, 8, *see* Privy Council; colonial, in Virginia, 59, 60, 326, 342; in Pennsylvania, 173; in colonies generally, 240 (powers), 342 (comparison with House of Lords); in Massachusetts, 269, 271, 428, 431; in New York, 298 (power to amend money bills), 342; in the South, power, 327; comparison with House of Lords, 342; under act of 1774 in Massachusetts, 428, 431; in state constitutions, 550.

Council for Foreign Plantations, appointed by Charles II, 185.

Council for New England, 88; grant to Pilgrims, 94; grants in Massachusetts, 95; grant to Massachusetts Bay Company, 97; Saybrook grant, 121.

Country party, in England, 6; in Massachusetts, 272.

County, in England, 8; in Virginia, 60, 61, 82; in Massachusetts, 106; in New York, 157.

County government, American like English, 343; new American ideas, 350.

Coureurs de bois, in fur trade, 215.

Court of assizes, in New York, 158.

Courten, Sir William, colonizer, 38.

Courts, in England, 7, 232; in the colonies, appointment, 240; power to declare laws unconstitutional, 548, 595; under Articles of Confederation, 562, 563; federal, 594. *See* Judges.

Courts of admiralty, 241; jurisdiction, 403.

Cowpens, battle, 503.

Coxe, Daniel, sends vessel to the Mississippi, 220.

Cranston, Samuel, governor of Rhode Island, 268.

Craven, Lord, Carolina proprietor, 136.

Criminals, transported, 33, 321; in Virginia, 62.

Croghan, George, backwoods leader, 293; agent of Ohio Company, 360.

Cromwell, Oliver, rules England, 74, 132, 133; policy in Maryland, 77; administration, 132, 133; takes Acadia and Jamaica, 133; plans against New Netherland, 133, 152; policy toward Dutch, 152, 180; cited, 9.

Crown Point, French outpost, 367, 368, 373; abandoned by French, 384; taken by Allen, 446.

Cuba, Spanish colony, 21; taken by British, 385; restored, 386.

Culloden, battle, 363.

Culpeper, Lord, Virginia grant, 81; governor of Virginia, 84; grant of Northern Neck, 320.

Cumberland valley, Scotch-Irish in, 291.

Currency, regulated by Parliament, 237, 405; under Confederation, 569.

Currency Act of 1764, 405.

Customs duties, levied by Parliament, 183, 403, 417, 423; by colonial legislatures, 237, 557; controlled by states, 562.

Cutler, Manasseh, agent of Ohio Company, 576, 577.

Cutler, Timothy, president of Yale College, converted to Anglican Church, 277.

Dale, Sir Thomas, governor of Virginia, 56.
Davenport, John, founder of New Haven, 122.
Davies, Samuel, appeals for religious toleration, 331.
Deane, Silas, agent of Congress in Paris, 448; commissioner to France, 489.
Debtor class, 247; after the Revolution, 580.
Debts, in peace negotiations, 521.
"Declaration and Resolves" of first Continental Congress, 434.
Declaration of Independence, influence of Revolution of 1688, 194; on disallowance of colonial laws, 239; adopted, 455; political philosophy, 455; list of grievances, 456; nationality of signers, 533.
Declaratory Act of 1766, 411.
De Grasse, Admiral, commander of French fleet, 505; Yorktown campaign, 507, 508.
De Lanceys, in New York, intermarriages, 284.
Delaware, Dutch and Swedes in, 146, 150, 151; claimed by Duke of York, 155; grant to Penn, 169, 170; government, 173; population, 174–175, 281; manufactures, 294; attitude on independence, 454, 455; state constitution, 462–463, 547–551; delegates in constitutional convention, 587; in small-state group, 592; ratifies federal Constitution, 604.
Delaware, Lord, governor of Virginia, 56.
Delaware River and valley, importance, 143; Dutch settlers, 146; Swedish settlement, 150; Scotch-Irish settlers, 291; controlled by British navy, 481.
De Leon, Ponce, explorer, 22.
Demarcation, papal line of, 20.
Democracy, advocated by John Wise, 275; influence of frontier conditions, 348, 354, 355; in United States, 547, 548, 551; struggle for, 554; in relation to the Constitution, 612.
Denmark, in seventeenth century, 17.
De Soto, explorer, 23.
d'Estaing, Admiral, commands fleet, 492; attempt on Newport, 493; leaves Savannah, 493.
Detroit, founded, 221; French post, 358, 368; British trading post, 498; held by British, 527.
d'Iberville, Le Moyne, founds Biloxi, 211, 220.
Dickinson, John, criticizes the Townshend Acts, 418; character and views, 418; attitude toward Massachusetts in 1774, 432; opinion of military resistance, 443; hopes for reconciliation, 450; pleads for delay, 453; committees on confederation and foreign alliances, 454; opposes immediate declaration of independence, 454, 455; gentleman-farmer, 534; committee on confederation, 559; in constitutional convention, 587.
Dinwiddie, Robert, governor of Virginia, sends mission to Ohio country, 370–371.
Disallowance of colonial laws, 238.
Divine right, theory of, 7.
Dominion of New England, 189; ended, 195.
Dongan, Thomas, governor of New York, 161, 196; wins Iroquois, 216.
Dorchester Heights, fortified, 445.
Downing, Sir George, career and influence, 181, 182.
Drake, Francis, exploits, 15, 27, 30.
Dress, colonial, 266, 342.
Duane, pleads for delay, 453.
Dublin, Anglican Archbishop of, cited, 290.
Dudley, Joseph, president of New England, 187; associated with Andros, 190, 191; governor of

Massachusetts, 253, 269; visits to England, 253; speakership question, 271.
Dudley, Thomas, colonizer, 98.
Duke's Laws, in New York, 158.
Dulany, Daniel, of Maryland, career, 329.
Dummer, Jeremiah, defends New England charters, 268.
Dunk, George, president of the Board of Trade, 231.
Dunmore, Lord, governor of Virginia, 439; opposes revolution, 448; violence, 453.
Duquesne, Governor, builds forts, 370.
Durham, palatinate of, 68.
Dutch, rebellion against Philip II, 14; relations with England, 14, 18, 125, 216; in seventeenth century, 17; Eastern trade, 32, 144; in Connecticut, 120, 146; in New Netherland, 144–153; alliance with Iroquois, 150; alliance of 1668, 216; commercial rivalry, 359, 360; loans to United States, 464; relations with Great Britain, 504; aid in Revolution, 504; treaty with United States, 514.
Dutch colonists, in New Netherland, 144, 145, 146; in New Sweden, 151; in New York, 156, 157, 160, 284, 294, 340; in New Jersey, 163; in Pennsylvania and Delaware, 174; in Berkshire region, 259; in New York city, 294.
Dutch East India Company, exploration, 144.
Dutch Guiana, English colony, 41.
Dutch language in New York, 284, 340.
Dutch Protestants, rebellion, 14; some go to England, 3, 18, 91.
Dutch Reformed Church, in New Netherland, 148; in New York, 159, 305; connection with Netherlands, 251.
Dutch Republic, war with Great Britain (1781), 504.
Dutch West India Company, aims, 144; organization, 147.

East Florida, British province, 390.
East India Company (English), chartered, 4; control in India and China, 233; recovers Madras, 365; government of India, 388; monopoly of the China trade, 388; Tea Act of 1773, 426; tea ships, 426–427.
East New Jersey, 164, 165; reunited, 204; conflicting grants, 283.
Eastland Company, chartered, 4.
Eaton, Theophilus, founder of New Haven, 122.
Economic theories, seveateenth-century, 32, 178–179; in Restoration era, 132, 135.
Education, in England, 13; in Massachusetts, 108; in New Netherland, 149; in New England, 277; in middle colonies, 306; in South, 333–335; in states, 554–555; in Ordinance of 1787, 578.
Edwards, Jonathan, character and achievements, 276, 277; writings, 278.
Eliot, John, missionary, 125.
Elizabeth, Queen, increases royal power, 6; relations with Spain, 14, 15; aids Huguenots, 15; colonial enterprise, 34, 35.
Elizabethan seamen, 27.
Ellsworth, Oliver, member Confederation Congress, 566; delegate in constitutional convention, 586; urges equal representation in Senate, 591–592.
Emancipation movement, after the Revolution, 554.

England, mother country, 1; in 1606, 2; dominions, 2; relations with Scotland, 2, 226; relations with Ireland, 2, 182, 227; population, 2; economic interests, 3–5; landlords, 4; social classes, 3–5, 9; trade, 4, 32, 33, 132–135, 179–185, 243–247, 261; government, 6–9, 227–232; churches, 10–12; civilization in 1606, 12; education, 13; international relations in seventeenth century, 13–18; relations with Spain, 14, 15, 27–28, 133, 142, 361; with France, 15, 18, 133, 207, 208, 216–224, 360–367; with Russia, 17; with Denmark, 17; with Sweden, 17, 216; with Holland, or Netherlands, 18, 125, 133, 152–153, 216; sea power founded, 15; chief rivals, 18, 207; outlook on America, 20; claim to North America, 26; early slave trade, 27; motives of colonization, 31–34, 42–43, 88, 92, 100, 133–136; early colonies, 34–42; island colonies, 39–40; under Cromwell, 74; in Restoration era, 131–134; sea power increased, 132–133; colonial policies of the Restoration, 135, 181–185; war with Holland (1652), 152; imperialism, seventeenth-century, 178–191; colonial trade regulations, 179–185; Revolution of 1688, 192–205 (see Revolution of 1688); alliance of 1668, 216; King William's War, 217–219; Queen Anne's War, 220–224; Act of Union, 226; constitutional changes after 1688, 227–229, 232; colonial empire, 233–242; difficulties of overseas administration, 242; trade with colonies, 243–247; church influence on colonies, 248–252; intellectual relations with colonies, 252–255; Protestant refugees in, 286, 287; German refugees near London, 287; claims Ohio valley, 359. See Parliament, and Great Britain.

English and American ways, chapter on conditions in 1750, 338–355.

English colonists, predominant race in Thirteen Colonies, 130, 131, 340, 341; in Pennsylvania, 174–175; majority not in Anglican Church, 248; predominant in New York, 284; in the South, 318, 319; in trans-Allegheny trade, 357, 369, 389; in United States, 532, 533. See name of each colony.

English fashions, followed, 266, 342.

English language, in Thirteen Colonies, 340, 341; survival of obsolete forms in America, 348.

English law, in America, 344–347.

English literature in America, 254, 341.

English merchants. See Merchants.

English population, predominates in United States, 532, 533. See English colonists.

English ships, defined, 182.

English traders, in the West, 80, 161, 293, 315, 357, 369, 389.

Englishmen, rights of, 7, 46; attitude toward Revolution, 470–471; opinion after Yorktown, 509.

Enumerated articles, in Navigation Acts, 182, 183; list extended, 235; modified, 236.

Episcopal Church, in United States, 533, 553. See Anglican Church.

Episcopal system, 11.

Episcopalians, in Boston, 273; reorganized, 553; first American bishop, 553.

Erie (Pa.), French fort, 370.

Erskine, on law of libel, 351.

Eugene, Prince, in Queen Anne's War, 221.

European background of American history, 1.

Executive authority, weakened in new governments, 463; provisions concerning in constitutional convention, 592–593. See Governor.

Executive council, in state constitutions, 550.

Executive departments, under Confederation, 565.

Factors, defined, 246.

Fairfax, Lord, landed proprietor, 320.

Falmouth (Maine), attacked in 1776, 447.

Family Compact, of 1733, 362; of 1761, 385.

Faneuil, Peter, Boston merchant, 263.

Faneuil Hall, gift of Peter Faneuil, 263.

Farmers, in England, 3, 5; status in United States, 535; in New England, 538; in the West, 543; in the interior, discontent after the Revolution, 579, 580. See Agriculture.

Fashions, influence of English, 266, 342.

Fauquier, governor of Virginia, intellectual influence, 335; opinion of Patrick Henry, 407.

Federal Convention of 1787, 584–600. See Convention.

Federal domain, 574.

Federal party, 603; in Pennsylvania, 604–606; in Massachusetts, 607; in New York, 608; in Virginia, 608–609; in First Congress, 610.

Federal union, development, 555–563.

Federalist, The, essays, 611.

Fenwick, proprietor West New Jersey, 164.

Ferdinand of Spain, 14.

Ferguson, Major Patrick, guerrilla leader, 494; Kings Mountain campaign, 500.

Finance, colonial 241.

Finance committee of Congress, 462.

Finances of United States, controlled by Congress, 460, 462, 502, 565; paper money, 464, 569; loans, 464, 515, 523; requisition system, 568.

Findley, William, Anti-Federalist leader, 605.

Finns, in New Sweden, 151; in Pennsylvania and Delaware, 174.

Fisheries, importance to England, 32, 33; of New England, 101, 102–103, 260; French, near Louisburg, 364; in peace negotiations, 520; after the Revolution, 536.

Fishermen visit Newfoundland, 24, 26.

Fitzherbert, peace commissioner, 517.

Fitzhugh, William, a typical planter, 79.

Five Nations, 150. See Iroquois.

Fletcher, Benjamin, governor of New York, 218.

Florida, explored, 21, 22; colonized, 24; fur trade, 215; in Queen Anne's War, 222; ceded to British, 386; under British rule, 388, 390; no revolutionary spirit, 446; secret agreement concerning, 519; regained by Spain, 520, 522.

Fontaine, Peter, views on slavery, 322.

Forbes, General, takes Fort Duquesne, 382, 383.

Foreign affairs department, with single head, 502.

Foreign officers in the Revolution, 466.

Fort Casimir, Dutch post, 151.

Fort Duquesne, built, 371; Braddock's expedition, 373; taken by British, 382.

Fort Edward, established, 373; taken by British in 1777, 483.

Fort Frontenac, French post, 358, 368; taken by British, 382, 383.

Fort Le Bœuf, Washington at, 371.

Fort Orange, Dutch settlement, 146; Iroquois fur trade, 146, 156; renamed Albany, 157.

Fort Pitt, settlements near, 496.

Fort St. Louis, in Illinois, 211.

Fort Schuyler, siege in 1777, 482, 483.

Fort Stanwix, treaty, 416; siege in 1777, 482.
Fort William Henry, established, 373; captured, 381.
Fox, Charles James, character and leadership, 471; in ministry of 1782, 510; foreign secretary, attitude in peace negotiations, 516; resigns, 517; in power, directs treaty of peace, 524.
Fox, George, dissenter, 132; founder of Quakers, 167, 168.
Frame of Government, Pennsylvania, 172.
France, power, 15–16; relations with England, 15, 18, 133, 207, 208, 216–224, 360–367; explorations in North America, 24–25; American colonies, 25, 207–215, see New France, etc.; colonial policy, 212–215; King William's War, 217–219; Spanish succession, 220; Queen Anne's War, 220–224; relations with Germany, 285; pioneers in trans-Allegheny region, 358; claims Ohio valley, 359, 369; Family Compact, 362, 385; War of the Austrian Succession, 362–365; points in dispute with the British, 367–371; French and Indian War with the British, 372–386; loans to United States, 464; other aid to America, 467, 469, 485, 487, 490, 491; relations with Great Britain, 469; first aid to United States, 485; conditions in 1777, 486; policy of secret aid, 487; alliance with United States, 490, 491; fleet at Yorktown, 507, 508; attitude in peace negotiations, 515; attitude on claims to West, 518–519; treaty of peace with Great Britain (1783), 522; new loan to United States, 523; interested in state constitutions, 547; consular convention with United States, 570.
Francis I of France, 25.
Frankfort Land Company, 174, 175.
Franklin, proposed state, 529.
Franklin, Benjamin, training as colonial agent, 243; Royal Society, 253; influenced by European writers, 254, 255; early career in Philadelphia, 254; fears establishment of German language, 288; printer, 295; opposes proprietary rule and tries to secure royal government for Pennsylvania, 301, 394; founds University of Pennsylvania, 307; intellectual achievements, 308; helps Braddock, 373; Albany plan of Union, 376; confidence in colonial growth, 392; leadership, 392; opinion concerning America's place in British Empire, 393; opinion of George III, 399; attitude on Stamp Act, 405; testimony before the House of Commons, 411; on the constitution of the empire, 414; new colony on the Ohio, 416; opinion on prospects in 1768, 422; opinion of Boston Tea Party, 427; deputy postmaster-general for the colonies, 430, 431; Hutchinson letters, 430–431; envoy of Congress to Canada, 446; favors independence, 450; committee on Declaration of Independence, 453; character and contribution to victory, 468, 489; suggests combination of Irishmen and Americans, 469; envoy at Paris, 488–489; propaganda for funds and recognition, 489; allays French irritation, 506; negotiations with Hartley, 512; with Shelburne, 512; peace commissioner, 513; proposes cession of Canada to United States, 516; ignores instructions, 519; negotiates concerning private debts, 521; pacifies Vergennes, 523; advice by Price, 527; favors religious liberty, 551, 552; interest in colonial federation, 557; new plan of Union,

558; president of Pennsylvania council, 566; commissioner to negotiate commercial treaties, 570; opinion of the Shays rebellion, 582; delegate in constitutional convention, influence, 586, 587; cited, 393, 414–415, 427, 431, 482, 505, 527, 539.
Franklin, Governor, cited, 294.
Frederick the Great, in War of the Austrian Succession, 363, 365; in Seven Years' War, 379, 381, 384.
Freedom of the press, Zenger case, 299; in England and America, 351; in state constitutions, 550; in federal constitution, 611.
Freeman's Farm, battles, 484.
Freemen, or voters, of Massachusetts, 103, 104, 105; in Connecticut, 122; in Pennsylvania, 172.
French and Indian War, 371–386; opposing forces, 375; events of 1756, 379; of 1757, 381; of 1758, 382; of 1759, 383–384; of 1760–1762, 384–385; treaty of peace, 386.
French colonists, in New Amsterdam, 145; in Pennsylvania, 175; in New York city, 294; in Virginia, 317. See Huguenots.
French Creek, French fort, 370.
French Protestants. See Huguenots.
Friends, Society of, 167.
Frontenac, Count, governor of New France, 209, 211; and Iroquois, 215; second governorship, 218; policy, 218; defends Quebec, 219; attacks Iroquois, 219.
Frontier, influence of, 282, 319, 324, 354, 355.
Frontiersmen, in the Revolution, 497; at Kings Mountain, 500; western, 544–545. See Back country.
Fundamental Constitutions of Carolina, 140.
Fundamental law, English and American ideas, 232.
Fundamental Orders of Connecticut, 121.
Fur trade, in Virginia, 80, 215, 221; in Plymouth, 94; in South Carolina, 141; in New Netherland, 145, 146; in New York, 160–161, 293, 538; Iroquois, 161, 215, 368; English and French rivalry, 161, 215, 293, 315, 368; of New France, 209, 210, 215; in South, 215; of Pennsylvania, 293; in Southwest, 315; in West, 358, 368, 498.

Gage, General, governor of Massachusetts, 431; government opposed, 442; retires, 445.
Galissonière, Marquis de la, claims Ohio valley, 369.
Galloway, Joseph, Pennsylvania conservative, 432; in first Continental Congress, proposes imperial constitution, 434; interest in colonial federation, 557; plan of Union, 557.
Galvez, conquests in Southwest, 500.
Gaspee affair, 425.
Gates, Gen. Horatio, member Board of War, 462, 485; rival of Washington, 467; Saratoga campaign, 484; at Camden, 494.
Gates, Sir Thomas, governor of Virginia, 56.
General Court, legislature of Massachusetts, 102, 103.
Gentlemen, social class in England, 3, 9; in America, 62, 342, 348, 534.
Genuine Information, Martin's essay, 611.
George I, reduction of power, 228.
George II, reduction of power, 228, 379; territory in Hanover, 371; interests, 379.
George III, accession, 385, 397; character and political theories, 398–399; conflict with the

old Whig machine, 399; builds up party of "King's Friends," 401; repeal of Stamp Act, 414; cited on tea tax, 423; attacks colonies, 448; attacked by Declaration of Independence, 456; responsibility for weakness of British government, 472; after Yorktown, 509; receives John Adams as minister, 571.

Georgetown (S. C.), settled, 315.

Georgia, founded, 315; slavery, 316; products, 320; war with Spain, 362; loyalists, 441; state constitution, 462–463, 547–551; conquered by British, 493; conditions after the Revolution, 541; state institution of higher learning, 555; in large-state group, 590; favors slave trade, 508; ratifies federal Constitution, 604. See South, and Thirteen Colonies.

Germain, Lord George, part in the Saratoga campaign, 469, 482; character and control of British army, 472; plan for 1777, 480.

German colonists, in Pennsylvania, 175, 176, 288, 293, 303, 305, 341; sects in America, 251, 305, 353; in Newport, 263; motives for emigration, 285–287; in England, 287; in New York, 287, 482, 496, 497; in North Carolina, 287, 319; in New Jersey, 288; in Maryland, 288, 319; in Virginia, 288, 317, 319, 609; influence in America, 288; buffer communities, 291; prosperous farmers, 293, 323; manufactures, 294; printers, 295; churches, 305; education, 306; in Georgia, 315; in South Carolina, 318, 319; in Thirteen Colonies, 341; in Mohawk valley, 287, 482, 496, 497; immigrants in United States, 532; in Pennsylvania convention, 605; attitude toward federal Constitution (in Virginia), 609.

German confederation of 1815, compared with Articles of Confederation, 560.

German Empire, armed neutrality, 504.

German language, in colonies, 288, 341; in the states, 532.

German Reformed Churches, in middle colonies, 305.

German sects, in American colonies, 251, 305, 353; radical Protestantism, 353.

German soldiers supplied to British, 444; in New Jersey, 479; with Burgoyne, 482, 483; on the American side, 482, 497.

Germanna (Va.), founded, 317.

Germantown (Pa.), founded, 175; manufactures, 294; battle, 481.

Germany, in seventeenth century, 16; in seventeenth and eighteenth centuries, 285; suffering from war, 285; relations with France, 285; religious troubles, 286; the great migration, 286.

Gerry, Elbridge, opposes Constitution, 607; opposes "excess of democracy," 613.

Gibraltar, acquired by Great Britain, 223, 361; importance in control of trade routes, 360.

Gilbert, Raleigh, in Plymouth Company, 45.

Gilbert, Sir Humphrey, colonizer, 34.

Gist, Christopher, agent of Ohio Company, 369; travels with Washington, 371.

Glen, governor of South Carolina, cited, 326.

Gold, from Spanish America, 22; English search for, 32.

Gooch, governor of Virginia, religious policy, 331.

Gorges, Sir Ferdinando, colonizer, 38, 39, 41, 42; Council for New England, 87–88; Maine, 88; criticizes Massachusetts, 110.

Gorton, Samuel, founds Warwick, 118.

Government, of England, 6–9, 227–232; of Great Britain, 228–232, 379, 397–398; of New France, 209; of the colonies, see Colonial government; of the states, 547–551; of the United States, see Continental Congress, Confederation, and Constitution; territorial, 576–578. See Autocracy, Democracy, Representative, Local government, etc.

Governor, in Virginia, 59, 60, 325, 326; in Plymouth, 94; in Massachusetts, 103, 269–272; expected to enforce Acts of Trade, 184, 235; royal instructions to, 238; imperial agent, 240; veto power, 240; control by colonies, salary, 241, see Governor's salary; in Connecticut and Rhode Island, 267–268; in Maryland, 325; in the South, 327; representative of the king, 342; in states, authority weakened, 463; in state constitutions, 550–551; election, 551; of Northwest Territory, 577.

Governor's salary, 241; in Massachusetts, 270; New York, 298; Pennsylvania, 300; Virginia, Maryland, and the Carolinas, 325, 326; proposal to pay by parliamentary tax, 404.

Grafton, Duke of, ministry, 415.

Granville, Lord, landed proprietor, 320.

Grasse, Admiral De, commander of French fleet, 505; Yorktown campaign, 507, 508.

Graves, Admiral, fights De Grasse, 508.

Great Awakening, influence of Whitefield, 252; main account, 276, 277; Presbyterians, 306; in Virginia, 331.

Great Britain, in Queen Anne's War, 222–224; created by Act of Union, 226; government, 228–232, 379, 397–398; overseas empire, 233; control of colonies, 233–242, 391; policy as to commerce and sea power, 359–360; relations with Spain, 361, 362, 374, 385, 469, 488; Anglo-Spanish War of 1739, 362; war with France, 363–365; claims Ohio valley, 368–371; policy in 1754, 371; French and Indian War, 372–386; alliance with Prussia, 374; treaty of 1763, 386; imperial problems and policies (1760–1766), 388–412; Proclamation of 1763, 390; plans for colonial reorganization, 391; old causes of friction with colonies, 393; government under Hanoverian kings, 397–398; politics under George III, 398–401; new American policies, 402–412; Stamp Act, 404–411; lack of constructive statesmanship, 414; Townshend Acts, 417; Coercive Acts, 427–430, 438; American Revolution, 437–524, see Revolution; no large army, 444; advantages in Revolutionary War, 459; handicapped by opposition of European powers, 469; British opposition to policy of coercing colonies, 470–471; governmental weakness, 471–472; the fighting services in Revolutionary War, 472; effect of French alliance with United States, 492; war with Spain (1779), 500; opposed by neutral powers, 504; war with the Dutch, 504; peace with United States, 512, 515–524; treaties of 1782 and 1783, 522–524; holds posts in northern United States, 527; relations with United States, 571–572. See England, and Parliament.

Great Case of Liberty of Conscience, 168.

"Great commoner," 415. See Pitt.

Great Lakes, in dispute between France and Great Britain, 368.

Great migration, to New England, 98; from Germany, 286.

Great Valley of Virginia, defined, 49; settled, 318, 324; churches and missionary preachers, 331; attitude toward Constitution, 609.

Green Bay, French post, 358; held by British, 527.

Green Mountain pioneers, Whigs, 497.

Greene, Gen. Nathanael, quartermaster-general, 465; military ability, 466; campaign in the South, 502–503.

Grenville, George, factional leader, 400; character and policy, 402; Stamp Act, 405; ministry ends, 409; argues for sovereignty of Parliament, 410.

Grenville, Sir Richard, exploits, 35, 36.

Grotius, Hugo, Dutch author, 17; read by Americans, 341.

Guadeloupe, taken by British, 384; restored, 386.

Guerrilla leaders, in South, 494.

Guiana, English colony, 40–41.

Guild system, breakdown, 4.

Guilford Courthouse, battle, 503.

Habeas Corpus Act, 346, 347; in Ordinance of 1787, 578.

Habitants, in New France, 214.

Haiti, Spanish colony, 21.

Hakluyt, Richard, geographer, influence, 31; map, 28–29; member Virginia Company, 45; cited, 26, 31.

Half-Way Covenant, adopted, 273.

Halifax, founded, 367.

Halifax, Earl of, president Board of Trade, 231.

Hals, Dutch painter, 17.

Hamilton, Alexander, opposition to up-state political machine, 539; member Confederation Congress, 566; opposes New York Trespass Act, 572; urges revision of Articles of Confederation, 584; proposes convention at Philadelphia, 585; delegate in constitutional convention, 587; 'nationalist leader, 589; plan of constitution, 591; plan for a single executive, 592; Committee on Style, 600; Federal leader, 608; author of The Federalist, 611.

Hamilton, Andrew, defends Zenger, 299; speaker Pennsylvania assembly, 300; cited, 300.

Hamilton, Col. Henry, promotes border warfare, 498; contest with Clark, 499.

Hancock, John, sloop Liberty seized, 419; president second Continental Congress, 442; president Massachusetts state convention, attitude toward Constitution, 607.

Hanover, under George II, 371; in Seven Years' War, 374, 381.

Hanoverian kings, government, 397, 398.

Hapsburg claim to Spain, 219, 220.

Harcourt, Robert, colonizer, 41.

Harrower, John, indentured servant, 321.

Hartford, founded, 121.

Hartley, David, negotiations for peace, 512; peace commissioner under Fox, 524; interest in American problems, 527.

Harvard, John, gift to college, 109.

Harvard College, 109; under liberal control, 275; protest against Great Awakening, 277; development, 278.

Harvey, Capt. John, governor of Virginia, 60.

Hat manufacture, restricted in colonies, 236.

Hawkins, Capt. John, exploits, 15, 27.

Hawkins, William, visits Brazil, 26.

Haynes, John, founder of Connecticut, 120.

Head right system, 63.

Heath, Sir Robert, patent or charter for Carolina, 41, 136.

Hemp, bounties, 402.

Henderson, Richard, founder of Kentucky, 496, 541.

Henrico County (Va.), large estates, 320.

Henry, Patrick, back-country farm, 324; leader of back-country party, 330; Parson's Cause, 395; opposes Stamp Act, 406–407; advocates committee of correspondence, 425; in first Continental Congress, 433, 434; favors state support of church, 552; plan of Union, 557; state politics, 566; opposes Jay's Spanish policy, 574; Anti-Federalist, 603, 609; arguments against Constitution, 609.

Henry VII, sends out Cabot, 26.

Henry VIII, increases royal power, 6; relations with Spain, 14.

Henry IV of France, 16, 207.

Herkimer, General, at Oriskany, 483; a German Whig, 532.

Hesse, Landgrave of, supplies soldiers to British, 444.

High church party, in Anglican Church, 96; in South Carolina, 313.

Hillsborough, Lord, colonial secretary, 416; opinion of Letters from a Farmer, 419; contest with Massachusetts assembly, 421.

Hispaniola, Spanish colony, 21.

Hobbes, Thomas, philosopher, 132.

Holdernesse, Lord, circular to governors, 370.

Holland, or the Netherlands, under Philip II, 14; in seventeenth century, 17; relations with England, 18, 133, 152, 153; Pilgrims in, 92; in America, 144; war with England (1652), 152; relations with Great Britain, 469. See Dutch.

Holmes v. Walton, cited, 548.

Holt, Chief-Justice, decision on Maryland, 202.

Holy Roman Empire of the German Nation, disrupted, 285; compared with Articles of Confederation, 560.

Honduras, English colony, 41.

Hooker, Richard, influence, 342, 344.

Hooker, Thomas, founder of Connecticut, 120.

Hopkins, Stephen, opposes Stamp Act, 406.

Housatonic valley, settled, 259.

House. See Commons, Lords, Burgesses, Assembly, etc.

House of Hope, Dutch colony, 120, 146.

Howard of Effingham, Lord, governor of Virginia, 84.

Howe, General (Lord), killed at Ticonderoga, 382; monument by Massachusetts, 392.

Howe, General Sir William, at Bunker Hill, 44; leaves Boston, 445; failure to coöperate in Saratoga campaign, 469; military ability, 473; campaign of 1776, 478–480; attempted diplomacy, 478; campaign of 1777, 480–482; retires, 492.

Howe, Lord, naval commander, 478; attempted diplomacy, 478; at Newport, 493.

Hudson, Henry, explorer, 144.

Hudson Bay, explored by Hudson, 144; French interests, 212; cession by France to Great Britain, 224.

Hudson River and valley, importance, 143; explored by Hudson, 144; Dutch settlers, 146; campaign of 1776, 478; campaign of 1777, 483–484.

Hudson's Bay Company, formed, 134.

Huguenots, or French Protestants, in France, 15–16, 96; in Florida, 24; in Carolina, 25; in South Carolina, 141, 317, 332; excluded from French colonies, 213; churches in America, 251; in Newport, 263; in Virginia, 317.

Hundred Associates, of New France, 207, 209.

Hunter, Robert, governor of New York, promotes immigration of Germans, 287; proposes taxation by Parliament, 298; intellectual character, 307; appoints Colden, 308.

Hutchinson, Anne, in Massachusetts, 113; banished, 114; followers in Portsmouth and Newport, 117, 118.

Hutchinson, Thomas, house attacked, 409; view of Adams, 420; governor of Massachusetts, 424; character, career, and political views, 424; tea ships, 427; letters secured by Franklin, 430; opposed by Franklin, 431; goes to England, 431; cited, 258.

Hyde, Edward. See Clarendon.

Hyde, Lawrence, colonizer, 41.

Iberville, Le Moyne d', founds Biloxi, 211, 220.

Illinois, veto power in council of revision, 550.

Illinois country, French in, 211, 358; conquered by Clark, 499; British influence in, 527.

Immigration, 292; see German, Scotch-Irish, etc.

Imperialism, English, seventeenth-century, 182–191; development, 185; principles, 187; reorganization of colonial governments 1685–1688, 188–192; reorganization after 1688, 200–204; eighteenth-century, 226, 233–242, 388–412; in 1760–1766, 388–412; plans for colonial reorganization, 391; friction with colonies, 393; need of imperial statesmanship, 397; Grenville's policy, 402–405; Stamp Act, 404–412.

Indentured servants, in Virginia, 62; in Maryland, 71; in Pennsylvania, 172; in New England, 266; in middle colonies, 292; in the tidewater, 321; in United States, 535.

India, English and French "factories" in, 360; British predominance, 386; governed by East India Company, 388.

Indiana, British influence in, 527.

Indians, under Spanish rule, 22; English missionary activity, 34, 125; in Virginia, 49–51, 58, 62, 63, 82, 439; political organization, 49, 50; customs, 50; agriculture, 50; in Maryland, 70; Pequot War, 123; in New England, 123, 124, 128; King Philip's War, 128; in New Netherland, 150; influence of Andros, 190; La Salle's plans, 211; French brandy, 212; fur trade, 215, 293, see Fur trade; under Frontenac, 218; in Maine, 258; in the Carolinas, 313; transAllegheny trade, 357, 369; in French and Indian War, 373, 376; in the West, 389, 390, 528; Pontiac's War, 390; Lord Dunmore's War, 439; aid to British in Revolutionary War, 444, 483, 497, 498; under St. Leger, 483; policy in Revolution, 497; Indian problem under the Confederation, 528. See Iroquois.

Indigo, in South Carolina and Georgia, 320.

Inflation, in New England, 265; in Massachusetts, 272; Continental currency, 464; under the Confederation, 569, 581.

Inns of Court, American lawyers trained in, 253, 334, 346.

Intendant, officer of New France, 209.

Interstate commerce, under Confederation, 571; Congress given power to regulate, 597.

Invincible Armada, 15, 30.

Ipswich, opposes Andros taxation, 191.

Ireland, colonized, 2, 289; relation to England, 2, 182, 227; Irish ships not foreign, 182; regulation of trade with colonies, 183; war between James II and William III, 217; export of woolens prohibited, 227; trade with New England, 262; German refugees, 287; economic grievances, 290; influence on American practices and ideals, 348; assistance to America, 469; relations with Great Britain, 469; invites New England trade, 537.

Irish colonists, in Virginia, 77; in American colonies, 135, 251, 252; in South Carolina, 141; in Pennsylvania, 175; in Newport, 263; causes of emigration, 289; in Revolutionary army, 469; frontier Whigs, 497; immigrants in United States, 532. See Scotch-Irish.

Iron manufacture, restricted in colonies, 236.

Iroquois, alliance with Dutch, 150; under English influence, 156, 161; fur trade, 161, 215, 368; war with New France, 208, 209; French attempts to win, 215, 216, 221; massacre of La Chine, 216; treaty with French, 221; British protectorate recognized, 224; in King George's War, 363–365; in dispute between France and Great Britain, 368; dominate Ohio valley, 368; treaty of Fort Stanwix, 416; raids in Revolution, 498; retaliation by Washington, 499.

Isabella of Spain, 14.

Island colonies, 39–40; in 1660, 130. See West Indies.

Italy, in seventeenth century, 16.

Jacobites, in 1745, 363.

Jamaica, Spanish colony, 21; taken by English, 133; constitutional controversies, 338; proposed attack (1782), 510.

James, Duke of York, activities, 134; extent of patent, 155; government of New York, 157, 158, 159. See James II.

James I King of England, 2, 37; conflict with Parliament, 6; church policy, 12, 91; Spanish policy, 15, 45; marriage, 17; Guiana patent, 41; patent for Nova Scotia, 42; Virginia charters, 45, 54, 59; policy toward Pilgrims, 93.

James II, Duke of York, 134, 155–159; becomes king, 159; Roman Catholic, 159, 193; grant to Penn, 168–169; religious policy, 192, 193; Revolution of 1688, 192–193; pension from Louis XIV, 216; tries to regain throne, 217; death, 220; supported by Catholic Irish, 289.

James VI of Scotland. See James I, King of England.

James River, navigable, 48; settlements on, 51, 61; proposal to connect with the Ohio, 541.

Jamestown settlement, 51.

Jay, John, in first Continental Congress, 434; hopes for reconciliation, 450; pleads for delay, 453; favors abandonment of New York city to Howe, 478; peace commissioner, 513, 514; envoy to Spain, 514; negotiations for West, 519; ignores instructions, 519; mixed ancestry, 532; opposition to up-state political machine, 539; opposes colonization of the West, 544; antislavery leader, 554; Secretary of Foreign Affairs, 565; secures resolution denying right of state to obstruct a treaty, 572; policy towards Spain, 573; opinion of the Shays rebellion, 582;

Federal leader, 608; author of *The Federalist*, 610; cited, 544, 545, 582.

Jefferson, Thomas, influenced by European writers, 255; leader of back-country party, 330; broad thinking, 393; opinion of Patrick Henry, 407; advocates committee of correspondence, 425; Declaration of Independence, 453, 455; governor of Virginia, retreats from British, 507; declines peace commission, 513; typical country gentleman, 534; *Notes on Virginia*, 540; opinion of tobacco culture, 540; opinion of manufactures, 541; on the suffrage in Virginia, 548; on apportionment, 549–550; on election of governor, 551; favors religious liberty, 551, 552; law abolishing primogeniture, 554; favors emancipation and colonization of negroes, 554; proposals for public education, 555; theory of British Empire as a federation, 556; on nature of Confederation, 563; member Confederation Congress, 566; devises decimal system of currency, 569; commissioner to negotiate commercial treaties, 570; proposes public land system, 575; plan for territories, 576; opinion of the Shays rebellion, 582; favors Constitution, 609; cited, 407, 425, 540, 541.

Jesuits, in Maryland, 70, 73, 74; missions to Indians, 208, 211, 212; in New France, 213; colony on Maine coast, 216.

Jesus, Hawkins's ship, 27.

Jews, in New Netherland, 146; in Pennsylvania, 173; in Newport, 263; in New York, 304.

Johnson, Edward, Massachusetts author, 100.

Johnson, Samuel, president of King's College, 254, 307; influence of Berkeley, 254.

Johnson, Samuel, tract against colonies, 470.

Johnson, Sir Nathaniel, governor of South Carolina, 222.

Johnson, Sir William, in King George's War, 365; in French and Indian War, 373; superintendent of Indian affairs, 377; treaty of Fort Stanwix, 416; son and nephew, 482; knighted, 534.

Johnsons, attach Indians to British cause, 444; in Revolution, 482; loyalist influence, 497.

Joint-stock companies before 1606, 4.

Joliet, Louis, explorer, 210.

Joncaire, in King George's War, 365; meets Washington, 371.

Jones, Paul, victory over *Serapis*, 467.

Judges, in England, 7; colonial, dispute as to tenure of office, 394; power to declare laws unconstitutional, 548; state, 551; federal, 594; control over unconstitutional legislation, 595.

Judiciary, state, 551; under Articles of Confederation, 562, 563; federal, 594.

Juniata valley, Scotch-Irish in, 291.

Jury trial, in England, 7; in America, 347.

Justices of the peace, in England, 8; in Virginia, 60; in Massachusetts, 106; in New York, 158; American like English, 343.

Kalb, General, valuable service, 466; at Camden, 494.

Kalm, Swedish writer, cited, 294.

Kanawha River, route to West, 542.

Kansas, Coronado in, 24.

Kaskaskia, British trading post, 498; taken by Clark, 499.

Keith, George, Quaker leader, 304.

Kennebec River colony, 47, 87.

Kent Island, in Maryland, 70, 72.

Kentucky, colonized, 496; county of Virginia, 497; Indian raids, 498, 499; Clark's expedition, 499; claim to statehood, 529; opposes Jay's Spanish policy, 574.

Keppel, Admiral, refuses service in America, 471.

Kidnaped white servants, in Virginia, 62.

King, of England, powers, 6, 7, 227–228; head of church, 10; governs Virginia, 46, 54, 59; title to land, 63; control of colonies, 180; reduction of power, 227–228; in Council, 228–229. *See* Privy Council.

King, Rufus, member Confederation Congress, 566; delegate in constitutional convention, 586; nationalist leader, 589; Committee on Style, 600.

King George's War, 364.

King Philip's War, 128.

King William's War, 217–219.

King's Bench, Court of, 7.

King's College, founded, 307, 309.

"King's Friends," party in Parliament, 401; in power, 422, 471.

Kings Mountain, battle, 500.

Knox, General Henry, Secretary of War, 565.

Kocherthal, Joshua, promotes colonization, 286.

Kosciusko, valuable service, 466; fortifies Bemis Heights, 484.

Laborers, in England, 3–5; in the middle colonies, 292; in the tidewater, 321; in United States, 535–536. *See* Indentured servants, and Slavery.

La Chine, massacre, 216.

Lafayette, Marquis de, valuable service, 466; allays French irritation, 506; campaign in Virginia, 507.

Lake Champlain, in dispute between France and Great Britain, 367.

Lake George, in dispute between France and Great Britain, 367; battle, 373, 392.

Lancaster (Pa.), settled, 282; Germans and Swiss in, 288, 293; fine farms, 293; manufactures, 295; on route to West, 542.

Land bank, in Massachusetts, 237, 272.

Land Ordinance of 1785, 575, 578.

Land system, of United States, 575.

Land tenure, in Virginia, 63; in Maryland, 71; in New England, 101, 350; in New Netherland, 145; in New York, 160, 283; in New France, 171, 283–284; in middle colonies, 282; in New Jersey, 283; inheritance in New England, 350; in Virginia, 554. *See* Quitrents.

Landgrave, title in Carolina, 137.

Landlords, in England, 4, 5; in middle colonies, 283; in Ireland, 290. *See* Land tenure.

Lansing (of N. Y.), opposes Constitution, 608.

La Salle, achievements, 211.

Laud, Bishop, church policy, 96; supports autocratic rule, 97; commissioner for the colonies, 109.

Laurens, peace commissioner, 513.

Lawyers, American, trained in Inns of Court, 253, 334, 346; influence, 346.

Lee, Arthur, commissioner to France, 489.

Lee, Gen. Charles, character, 465; battle of Monmouth, 492.

Lee, Richard Henry, advocates committee of correspondence, 425; in first Continental Congress, 433; favors independence, 449; moves for American independence, 453; opposed to Washington, 467; opposes Constitution, 609.

Leeward Islands, English colony, 130.
Legislature, state, 549, 550; elects governor and judges, 551.
Leisler, Jacob, party leader, 196; revolt, 197–198; character, 197; fall, 198.
Leisler's revolt, 196–198.
Letters from a Farmer, Dickinson's, 418, 419.
Letters from an American Farmer, cited, 354.
Lexington, battle, 442.
Leyden, Pilgrims in, 92.
Libel law, English and American, 351.
Liberty, Hancock's sloop seized, 419.
Libraries, 335.
Lincoln, Earl of, Puritan leader, 98.
Lincoln, General, loses Charleston, 493, 494.
Lindsay, Capt. David, in slave trade, 262.
Lining, John, Royal Society, 253.
Literature, English, in America, 254, 341; New England, 278; in 1750, 341.
Livingston, Robert R., committee on Declaration of Independence, 453; Secretary of State for Foreign Affairs, 462; on Wyoming valley dispute, 563; on nature of Confederation, 563.
Livingstons, Scotch family in New York, 161; intermarriages, 284; typical American gentry, 534.
Loans, from foreign countries, 464.
Local government, in England, 8; in Virginia, 60; in Massachusetts, 106; in New Netherland, 148; in New England, 267; American-like English, 343–344; new American ideas, 350.
Locke, John, philosopher, 132; member Board of Trade, 231; influence on American thought, 255, 342; *Two Treatises of Government*, 194; influence on Americans, 342; authority on natural rights, 344; defends English Revolution of 1688, 456.
Logan, James, complains of Scotch-Irish in Pennsylvania, 291; scientist and man of affairs, 308.
London, importance in 1606, 4; trade with plantations, 246; German refugees, 287; attitude of merchants in 1775, 438.
London Company, for settling Virginia, 46, 47.
Long Island, Dutch settlers, 146; English settlers, 146, 148, 149; divided between Dutch and English, 151; patent to Duke of York, 155; made part of New York, 156; influence of New England, 157; discontent, 158; large land grants, 283; battle, 479.
Long Parliament, 74.
Lord Dunmore's War, 439.
Lord lieutenant, in England, 8.
Lords, House of, in 1606, 6; reduction of power, 228.
Lords Commissioners for Trade and Plantations, 230. *See* Board of Trade.
Loudoun, Lord, in French and Indian War, 379, 381.
Louis XI of France, 15.
Louis XIV, promotes French expansion, 208; colonial policy, 213; aids James II, 217; in King William's War, 217; Spanish succession, 220; in Queen Anne's War, 220, 221; wars against German states, 285.
Louis XV, weakness, 378.
Louis XVI, character, 486; policy toward United States, 487.
Louisburg, importance in control of trade routes, 360; main account, 363–364; taken in 1745,

364; return of, 365; saved from attack, 381; taken in 1758, 381, 382.
Louisiana, colony begun by Iberville, 221; ceded to Spain, 386.
Loyalists, or Tories, in first Continental Congress, 434; views, 440; social factors, 440; argument, 441; deprived of liberty of speech, 441; aid to British in Revolutionary War, 444, 460, etc.; defeat at Moores Creek Bridge, 447; oppose independence, 449; persecuted and disarmed, 451–452; in New York, 475, 482; in New Jersey, 479, 480; in Pennsylvania, 402; in South Carolina, 493, 494; in North Carolina, 493; in Georgia, 493; on the frontier, 497; problem in peace negotiations, 521; hardships, 521, 522; compromise, 522; states do not keep agreements concerning, 572.
Lucas, Eliza, wife of Charles Pinckney, 329.
Lumber, in New England, 102; in South Carolina, 141; trade, 247, 294.
Lutherans, in New Netherland, 149; in Pennsylvania, 175, 305; first American synod, 305; in Virginia, 331; in Thirteen Colonies, conservatism, 353.
Lyman, Phineas, in French and Indian War, 373, 392.

McKean, Chief-Justice, Federal leader in Pennsylvania, 605.
Mackinaw, French post, 358; British trading post, 498; held by British, 527.
Madison, James, educated at Princeton, 336; opposes state support of church, 552; on nature of Confederation, 563; member of Confederation Congress, 566; on obligations to army, 567; discouraged by sectional feeling over Mississippi question, 574; favors coöperation of Virginia and Maryland, 585; proposes convention at Philadelphia, 585; character, delegate in constitutional convention, 585, 587; nationalist leader, 589; opposes compromise on representation, 592; advocates congressional veto on state laws, 594; favors West, 599; Committee on Style, 600; favors Constitution, 608, 609; elected to First Congress, 610; author of *The Federalist*, 611; interpretation of the Constitution, 612.
Madras, recovered from French, 365.
Magellan, explorer, 21.
Magna Carta, argument against governor's salary, 344.
Magnalia Christi, Mather's book, 274.
Mahan, cited, 505.
Maine, first English colony in, 37, 47; proprietary government, 88; Plymouth fur trade, 94; Puritan settlers, 117; absorbed by Massachusetts, 117; patent to Duke of York, 155; merged in New England, 187; joined with Massachusetts (1691), 203; Jesuit colony on the coast, 216; in King William's War, 218, 219; Queen Anne's War, 221; about 1690, 257; Indian wars, 258, 259; remains part of Massachusetts, 529; settled by New Englanders, 542; opponents of the federal Constitution in, 606.
Makemie, Francis, Presbyterian leader, 251, 306.
Malaria, in Virginia, 49.
Mandamus councilors, in Massachusetts, 431.
Manhattan Island, Dutch settlers, 144, 145, 146.
Manila, taken by British, 385; restored, 386.
Manorial estates, in England, 5; in Maryland, 71.
Manorial system, in Carolina, 137; in New Netherland, 145; in New York, 160, 283.

Mansfield, Chief-Justice, argues for sovereignty of Parliament, 410.

Manufactures, in England, 4; in Pennsylvania, 176; English policy, 179; Board of Trade, 230, 232; colonial, restricted by Parliament, 236; development, 243; in New England, 264; in Ulster, 289, 290; in middle colonies, 294; of United States, 538, 541.

Marcos, Friar, explorer, 24.

Marietta, founded, 578.

Marion, guerrilla leader, 494.

Marlborough, Duke of, in Queen Anne's War, 221.

Marquette, Father Jacques, explorer, 210.

Marshall, John, favors Constitution, 608.

Marthas Vineyard, patent to Duke of York, 155.

Martin, Luther, delegate in constitutional convention, 587; leader of small-state group, 590; provision concerning enforcement of laws and treaties of the United States, 595; denounces slave trade, 597; Anti-Federalist, 603; opposes Constitution in Maryland, 607; essay *Genuine Information*, 611; democratic feeling, 613.

Martinique, taken by British, 386; restored, 386.

Mary, Queen of England, 14.

Mary, Queen of Scots, 14.

Mary II, accession, 194.

Maryland, charter, 67–69; boundaries, 68; early settlers, 69–72; religious toleration, 70, 73, 76, 77; Claiborne, 70, 75, 76; manors, 71; tobacco, 72, 320; government, 72; parliamentary commissioners, 75, 76; Toleration Act, 76, 77; Puritan revolt, 76–77; conditions in 1688, 84–85; controversy with Pennsylvania, 169–170, 296; friction with imperial collectors, 185; Revolution of 1688, 198–200; discontent, 199; Protestant Association 199; royal province, 202, 312; trade with England, 246; Anglican Church, 248, 332; Germans in 288, 319; dispute with Pennsylvania settled, 296; securely established before 1700, 311; royal government, and again proprietary, 312; growth of population, 314–315; slavery in, 317; Germans and Scotch-Irish in, 319; quitrent troubles, 320; governor's power, 325; churches, 332; claims benefit of English statutes, 346; laws against Catholics, 352; proprietors exempt from taxation, 394; votes for independence, 454; state constitution, 462–463, 547–551; ratifies Articles of Confederation, 501; opposes state claims to West, 530; prohibits importation of slaves, 534; western land question, 560; conference with Virginia, 585; delegates in constitutional convention, 587; in small-state group, 590; ratifies federal Constitution, 607. See South, and Thirteen Colonies.

Maryland Gazette, newspaper founded, 335.

Mason, Capt. John, proprietor New Hampshire, 88.

Mason, George, delegate in constitutional convention, 585; denounces slave trade, 597; Anti-Federalist, 603, 609; opposes popular election of President, 613.

Mason and Dixon's line, 296.

Massachusetts, early settlements, 95; Massachusetts Bay Company, 95, 97; original boundaries, 97; charter of 1629, 98, 103, 187; Cambridge Agreement, 98; leaders, 98–100; motives of colonization, 100; population, 100, 258; rapid development, 100; physical features, 101; land tenure, 101; industries, 102; government, 103–110, 269–272; voters, 103, 104, 274; Puritan oligarchy, 104; Body of Liberties, 106; town

meeting, 106; church organization, 107; union of church and state, 107; religious intolerance, 108, 113–116; importance of church, 108; education, 108, 278, 554; practical independence, 109, 127; dissenters, 109, 112–115; persecution, 115–116; in New England Confederation, 126, 127; dispute with Connecticut, 127; independence threatened, 128; lands claimed by Duke of York, 155; relations with Charles II, 186; charter annulled, 187; merged in New England, 187; land titles and taxes under Andros, 190, 191; separate government resumed, 195; charter of 1691, 202–204; Queen Anne's War, 221; land bank, 237, 272; royal collector, 241; trade, 247; about 1690, 257, 258; expansion westward, 259; paper money, 265; government under second charter, 269–272; constitutional conflicts, 270–272; explanatory charter of 1725, 271; military policy, 271; party politics, 272; churches in, 273–277; witchcraft epidemic, 274; separation of church and state, 276, 552; boundary dispute, 295; religious toleration, 352; writs of assistance, 396; customs disputes, 419; *Circular Letter*, 421; controversy revived by extremists, 423; Government Act passed by Parliament in 1774, 428; resistance to Coercive Acts, 431; provincial congress, 432; loyalists, 440; outbreak of Revolution, 441; independent government, 449; state constitution, 462, 463, 547–551; claim to western New York, 529; claims Northwest, 530; yields claim to Northwest, 530, 574; method of adopting state constitution, 547; apportionment, 549; suspensive veto, 550; choice of judges, 551; religious discriminations, 551–552; provision for public education, 554; Shays rebellion, 581; proposes federal convention, 584; delegates in constitutional convention, 586; in large-state group, 590; ratifies federal Constitution, 606–607. See New England, and Thirteen Colonies.

Massachusetts Government Act, 428.

Massasoit, Indian chief, 128.

Mather, Cotton, writings. 250, 274, 278; Royal Society, 253; recommends Dudley, 270; character, 274; church policy, 275.

Mather, Increase, mission to England, 192, 253, works for Massachusetts charter, 202; theological writings, 250; visits England, 253; colonial agent, 253; character, 274; church policy, 275.

Mathers, writings, 250; church policy, 275.

Maumee River, Céloron's journey, 369.

Mayflower, voyage, 93.

Mayflower Compact, 94.

Mayor, in England, 9.

Mechanics, in United States, 535, 536.

Medical science, 309.

Menendez, in Florida, 24.

Mennonites, in Pennsylvania, 175, 288, 305; in Switzerland, 286; community settlements, 324.

Mercantile theory of economics, 178–179.

Merchants, Canadian, on Indian trade, 498; oppose surrender of the West to United States, 528.

Merchants, colonial, in New England, 263, 265, oppose writs of assistance in Massachusetts, 396; customs disputes in Massachusetts, 419; tea tax, 426; loyalists, 440, 441.

Merchants, English, social class, 3, 9; development, 4, 5; promote colonies, 37, 38, 45; in Restoration era, 132, 133; influence on colonial policy, 181, 182; War of the Spanish Succession,

220; object to colonial currency, 237; relations with planters, 246; relations with colonies, 247; influence in Parliament, 401; favor repeal of Stamp Act, 409; attitude concerning Coercive Acts, 438; attitude toward Revolution, 470; influence on treaty with United States, 524; oppose surrender of West to United States, 528.

Merchants, Irish, invite New England trade, 537.
Merchants, Scotch, influence for Union, 226.
Merion (Pa.), 175.
Merrimac valley, in dispute, 257; settled, 259.
Methodist Episcopal Church, national organization, 553.
Methodists, in West, 545.
Mexico, Spanish colony, 22, 24.
Miami Indians, friendly to British, 369.
Miami River, Céloron's journey, 369.
Michigan, held in part by British, 527.
Middle colonies, beginnings, 143–177; chapter on period 1689–1760, 281–309; rapid expansion, 281; land policies, 282–284; immigration, 284–292; industries, 292–295; religion, 303–305; education, 306; religious toleration, 352; attitude toward Massachusetts in 1774, 432. See names of colonies.
Middle Temple, colonials in, 334.
Milborne, son-in-law of Leisler, 198.
Military service, question of, in Pennsylvania, 302.
Militia, character, 465.
Minorca, attacked by French, 374; captured, 379; lost by British, 509.
"Minutemen," in Massachusetts, 442.
Miquelon, retained by France, 386.
Missionaries to Indians, Spanish, 22, 24; English, 33–34, 125; French, 208, 210, 211, 212; Moravian, 305.
Mississippi River, discovered by De Soto, 23; explored by Joliet and Marquette, 210; explored by La Salle, 211; English on (1699), 220; free navigation question, 489, 519, 543, 573.
Mississippi valley, French occupation, 211; English traders in, 357; in the Revolution, 499, 500.
Mobile, French post, 358; taken by Spain, 500.
"Mock" trials, clause in Declaration of Independence, 429.
Mohawk valley, settled, 282; German colonists, 287, 482, 496, 497; military operations in 1777, 482; Whigs, 497; Indian raids, 498.
Mohegans, Indian tribe, 123.
Molasses, trade restricted, 235.
Molasses Act, 235, 236; American objections, 247; evaded, 391; not enforced, 403.
Money, provisions in Constitution, 596. See Paper money.
Monk, General, friend of Charles II, 134.
Monmouth, battle, 492.
Monongahela River, route to West, 542.
Monroe, member Confederation Congress, 566.
Montcalm, Marquis of, character, 378; takes Oswego, 379; takes Fort William Henry, 381; defends Quebec, 383–384; death, 384.
Montesquieu, read by Americans, 341; influence on American constitutions, 549.
Montgomery, Richard, Canadian expedition, 447.
Montreal, French at, 25; taken by Amherst, 385; taken by Montgomery, 447; Indian trade, 498.
Moores Creek Bridge, battle, 447.
Moravians, in Pennsylvania, 305; community settlements, 324.

Morgan, Daniel, commands Virginians at Cambridge, 445; military ability, 466; service with Greene, 502; battle of the Cowpens, 503.
Morgan, Dr. John, physician, 309.
Morris, Gouverneur, mixed ancestry, 532; devises decimal system of currency, 569; character, delegate in constitutional convention, 586, 587; nationalist leader, 589; opposes West, 599; Committee on Style, 600.
Morris, Robert, committee on foreign alliances, 454; committee on finance, 462; head of finance department, 502; asks French loan, 515; typical merchant prince, 534; "big business" in politics, 539 resigns as superintendent of finances, 565; delegate in constitutional convention, 586, 587; nationalist leader, 589.
Morrises, in New York, intermarriages, 284; nationalist leaders, 589.
Mosquito Coast, English colony, 41.
Moultrie, William, defends Charleston, 448.
Muhlenberg, Frederick, political positions, 532–533; president Pennsylvania state convention, 532–533, 605.
Muhlenberg, Heinrich, Lutheran leader, 305.
Muscovy Company, chartered, 4.
Mutinies, in the army, 465, 501.

Nabobs, in Parliament, 401.
Nantucket, patent to Duke of York, 155; whalers, 260.
Narragansett planters, 266.
Narragansett settlements, 117–119.
Narragansetts, Indian tribe, 123.
Narvaez, explorer, 23.
Nashville, founded, 497; route of first settlers, 543.
Natchez, British trading post, 498; held by Spain, 528.
Naturalization Act, British, 286.
Naval stores, importance to England, 32, 33, 179; in South Carolina, 141; trade restricted, 235; bounties, 236; in North Carolina, 321.
Navigation Act of 1651, 75; full account, 180.
Navigation Act of 1660, 182.
Navigation Act of 1696, 234.
Navigation Acts, provisions, 80, 180; dependent on colonial governments, 170, influence for union of Scotland and England, 226; defied by Congress, 451. See Acts of Trade.
Navy, American, beginnings of, 467; contributions to victory, 467, 468; advantage of French alliance, 491.
Negroes, Spanish slavery, 22; in Virginia, 62, 77, 78; increase in southern colonies, 131, 135, 316–318; in South Carolina, 141, 322; in New York, 160, 292; in New England, 266; negro plots in New York, 292; increase in the South, 316–317; few in piedmont, 318; negro insurrection in South Carolina, 322; three-fifths rule, 598. See Slavery, and Slave trade.
Netherlands. See Dutch, and Holland.
Neutral rights, dispute during Revolutionary War, 504.
New Amsterdam, founded, 145; municipal government, 148; attacked by the Indians, 150; named New York, 157.
New England, pioneers, 87; explored by Smith, 87; Council for, 88, 94, 95, 97, 121; motives for colonization, 88; Plymouth founded, 93; great migration to Massachusetts, 98; physical features, 101; agriculture, 101, 102; land system, 101;

community spirit, 102; industries, 102; commerce, 103, 138, 139, 151, 183, 236, 246–247, 261–264, 536–538; town meeting, 106, 350; union of church and state, 107; Indians in, 123, 124, 128; summary of Puritan enterprise, 124; effect of English Civil War, 124; relations with French and Dutch, 125, 126; Confederation, 125–127; English government (Restoration) unfriendly, 127–128; emigrants from, 136, *see* New Englanders; trade with North Carolina, 138, 139; trade with New Netherland, 151; salt for fisheries, 183; trade in tobacco, 183; friction with imperial collectors, 185; imperial control, 186–192; the "Greater New England," 187–189; under Andros, 189–192, 195; land system attacked, 190; Anglican Church, 192, 248, 250, 276; Revolution of 1688, 195; reorganization, 201–204; King William's War, 218, 219; Queen Anne's War, 221–224; trade with West Indies, 235, 236, 261; distilleries, 247; aided by English dissenters, 250; chapter on period 1690–1760, 257–279; sectional individuality, 257; population, 258, 259; causes of slow growth, 258; expansion, 259; fisheries, main account, 260; shipbuilding, 260; trade, main account, 261–264; manufactures, 264, 538; currency problem, 264, 265; common political problems, 267; charters threatened, 268; churches in, 273–277, 351; separation of church and state, 276, 552; Great Awakening, 276; education, 277; literature, 278; provincialism, 278; Scotch-Irish in, 291; racial character, 340; common law modified, 345; inheritance of land, 350; improvements in court procedure, 351; Anglo-Spanish War of 1739, 362; King George's War, 363–365; French and Indian War, 375; Restraining Act, 438; coöperation in opposing Gage, 442; volunteers at Cambridge, 445; troops in Saratoga campaign, 483; English population predominates, 532; conditions after the Revolution, 536–538; emancipation, 554; paper-money movement, 580. *See* names of colonies.

New England Confederation, 125–127.

New England Restraining Act, 438.

New Englanders, special characteristics, 131; in South Carolina, 141; in New Netherland, 148, 151; in New Jersey, 163–165; westward movement, 542.

New France (Canada), beginnings, 207; war with Iroquois, 208; population, 209, 210; government, 209; autocracy, 210; paternalism, 213, 214; influence of the church, 213; feudalism, 214; fur trade, 215; in French and Indian War, 375, 377, 382–386; taken by British, 385–386. *See* Canada.

New Hampshire, proprietary government, 88; Puritan settlers, 117; absorbed by Massachusetts, 117; separated from Massachusetts and reunited in New England, 187; separate royal province (1691), 203; King William's War, 218, 219; Queen Anne's War, 221; about 1690, 257; expansion northward, 259; government, 272; dispute with New York, 295; independent government, 449; state constitution, 462–463, 547–551; claims Vermont, 496; ratifies federal Constitution, 608. *See* New England, and Thirteen Colonies.

New Haven, founded, 122; united with Connecticut, 123; in New England Confederation, 126, 127; treaty with Stuyvesant, 151; profit from commerce, 259.

New Jersey, beginnings, 162; boundaries, 162; disputed government, 162; physical features, 163; early settlers, 163; East New Jersey and West New Jersey, 164–165; population, 165, 281; added to New England, 189; restored to proprietors, 202; royal province, 204; rent riots, 283; landlords, 283; Germans in, 288; commerce, 294; manufactures, 294; boundary dispute, 295; political connections with New York and Pennsylvania, 296; votes for independence, 454; state constitution, 462–463, 547–551; military operations, 479–480, 492; trade through New York city, 538; judges annul act of legislature, in *Holmes* v. *Walton*, 548; taxes Sandy Hook lighthouse, 571; delegates in constitutional convention, 587; in small-state group, 590; ratifies federal Constitution, 604. *See* Thirteen Colonies.

New Jersey plan of constitution, 591; executive, 593; power of Congress over states, 594; influence on details, 600.

"New Lights," in New England, 277; in Virginia, 533.

New London, profit from commerce, 259.

New Mexico, Spanish colony, 24.

New Netherland, founded, 145; land tenure, 145; fur trade, 145, 146; population, 146; government, 146–148; churches, 149; education, 149; Indians, 150; conquest of New Sweden, 151; English rivalry, 151; conquest by England, 152, 153.

New Orleans, ceded to Spain, 386.

New Plymouth, 94, 95. *See* Plymouth.

New South, development, 318, 319.

New Sweden, founded, 150; conquest, 151.

New World, discovered and named, 20.

New York, English colony, originally New Netherland, 153, 155; boundaries, 156; government, 157–159, 297, 549–552; English institutions introduced, 157–158; Duke's Laws, 158; churches, 159, 248, 303–305; land tenure, 160, 283; aristocracy, 160, 196, 297; slavery, 160, 292; commerce, 160, 247, 292; fur trade, 160–161, 293, 538; Governor Dongan, 161; imperialism in charter, 185; added to New England, 189; anti-Catholic spirit, 196, 352, 552; Leisler's revolt, 196–198; separate royal province, 202; Queen Anne's War, 221–222; population, 281; expansion, 281–282; large land grants, 283; fusion of Dutch and English, 284; German colonists, 287; Scotch Irish in, 291; flour exports, 292; boundary disputes, 295, 496, 529; strategic importance, 296; politics, 297; voters, 297; constitutional conflicts, 297–299; education, 306; language in 1750, 340; English sports, 342; local government, 350; laws against Catholics, 352; assembly is suspended by Parliament, 417; attitude toward Massachusetts in 1774, 432; attitude on independence, 454, 455; state constitution, 462–463, 547–551; claims Vermont, 496, 529; held in part by British, 527; claim of Massachusetts to western New York, 529; yields claim to Northwest, 530; conditions after the Revolution, 538–539; duties on trade of New Jersey and Connecticut, 538, 571; landed interest, 539; western New York settled by New Englanders, 542; state senate, 549; veto power in council of revision, 550; election of governor, 551; excludes Catholics from naturalization, 552; discriminatory duties, 571; Trespass Act,

572–573; proposes federal convention, 584; delegates in constitutional convention, 587; ratifies federal Constitution, 608. *See* Thirteen Colonies.

New York Bay, explored by Hudson, 144.

New York city, originally New Amsterdam, 157; center of population, 281, 282; commerce, 293, 538; society and houses, 294; Stamp Act Congress, 408; tea ships, 427; loyalists, 440; harbor under British, 475, 477; taken by British, 479; British retain control, 493; after Yorktown, 508; during and after the Revolution, 538; Confederation Congress at, 567; favors Constitution, 608.

Newburg Addresses, 568.

Newcastle, Duke of, colonial administrator, 230; prevents parliamentary duties on the colonies, 237; in King George's War, 364; policy in 1754, 371; politician, 379; resigns, 380; alliance with Pitt, 380; crowded out by Bute, 399; leader of "Old Whigs," 400.

Newfoundland, fishing grounds, 24, 26, 103; visited by English, 26; Gilbert's colony, 35; Avalon colony, 42; Banks, visited by New England fishermen, 103; French in, 212; cession by France to Great Britain, 224; relations with Thirteen Colonies, 338; French fishing rights, 386; fisheries in peace negotiations of 1782, 520.

Newport (R. I.), founded, 118; slave trade, 247; profit from commerce, 259; trade, 262, 263, 537; merchants, 263; liberal society, 279; taken by British, 480; attack planned in 1778, 493; evacuation, 493; French troops at, 506.

Newport, Capt. Christopher, commands fleet to Virginia, 47; councilor, 51.

Newspapers, Colonial, 254; New England, 278; middle colonies, 299, 300; in the South, 335; intercolonial interests, 339; German, 289, 341.

Niagara, French post, 358, 368; unsuccessful expedition against, 373; taken by British, 384; British trading post, 498; held by British, 527.

Nicholson, lieutenant-governor of New York, 196; retires, 197.

Nicolls, Richard, becomes governor of New York, 152, 153; guarantees to Dutch, 156; administration and character, 157–158; grants in New Jersey, 163.

Nine-state rule, 562, 566.

Nobility, no formal nobility in United States, 534. *See* Aristocracy.

Noell, Martin, consulted on colonial policy, 181.

Nombre de Dios, raided by Drake, 30.

"Nonconsumption" agreement, enforcement, 439.

Nonimportation, in opposition to Stamp Act, 409; in 1769, 421; in opposition to Townshend Acts, 422, 423; in 1774, 435; enforcement, 439; loyalist argument against, 441.

Norfolk, chief town of Virginia, 323; attacked in 1776, 447; Jefferson's expectation, 540.

North, Lord, character and ministry, 422–423, 472; "Conciliatory Proposition," 438; in power, 471, 472; resigns, 509; conference with Hartley, 512.

North America, early colonies, 22–25; passage through, 32, 144.

North Carolina, Spanish colony in, 23; Raleigh's colony, 35, 36; included in Virginia, 136; churches, 137, 139, 250, 232; pioneers, 138; character, 138–139; Cape Fear River colony, 139; friction with imperial collectors, 185; insurrections, 198, 313; before 1689, 311; becomes separate royal province, 314; growth of

population, 314–315; slavery in, 317; Germans and Scotch-Irish in, 319; back country settled, 319; quitrent troubles, 320; products, 320, 321; governor's salary, 325; loyalists, 441; loyalists defeated in 1776, 447; state constitution, 462–463, 547–551; Tennessee settlements, 497; battle of Kings Mountain, 500; military operations in 1781, 502–504; authority over Tennessee, 529; interest in the West, 541; state senate, 549; state institution of higher learning, 555; in large-state group, 590; delays ratification of federal Constitution, 610. *See* Carolina, South, and Thirteen Colonies.

Northampton (Mass.), Great Awakening, 276.

Northern Neck, in Virginia, 81, 320.

Northwest, state claims and cessions, 529, 530, 574.

Northwest Territory, creation and government, 577–578.

Norwich (Eng.), Separatists, 91.

Nova Scotia, French colony, 25; patent to Sterling, 42; under Cromwell, 133; joined with Massachusetts (1691), 203; ceded by France, 224; royal government, 240; English colonization, 367; no revolutionary spirit, 446.

Oath of supremacy, 67.

Oaths, question of, in Pennsylvania, 301–302.

Oglethorpe, James, founds Georgia, 315; war with Spain, 362.

Ohio, held in part by British, 527; Connecticut Reserve, 530.

Ohio Company, before the French and Indian War, 369.

Ohio Company, formed by New England army officers, 576; plants settlement at Marietta, 578.

Ohio River, Céloron's journey, 369.

Ohio valley, English traders in, 357; claimed by French and by English, 359; in dispute between France and Great Britain, 368–371; in dispute between Pennsylvania and Virginia, 369, 389; pioneers, 542, 543.

Old Dominion, 62–63. *See* Virginia.

Old South, defined, 318.

"Old Whigs," defined, 400; attitude toward America, 400; conciliatory proposals, 437; opposition ineffective, 471.

Olive oil, hopes of, in Carolina, 138; in Virginia, 179.

Orange County (N. Y.), Scotch-Irish, 291.

Orangemen, bitterness against Catholics, 289.

Ordinance of 1784, 576.

Ordinance of 1787, 577–578, 579.

Oriskany, battle, 483.

Oswald, Richard, negotiations with Franklin, 516; peace commissioner, 517; new commission, 517; signs treaty, 522.

Oswego, English trading post established, 293, 368; taken by Montcalm, 379; British trading post, 498; held by British, 527; effect of British occupation, 538.

Otis, James, opposes writs of assistance, 396; opposes Stamp Act, 406; questions power of Parliament, 306, 406; in Stamp Act Congress, 408.

Oxford, University of, 13, 333, 334.

Paine, Thomas, *Common Sense*, 450; cited, 2.

Palatinate (Germany), suffering from war, 285; colonists in England and America, 287.

Palatinate of Durham, 68.

Panama, Spanish colony, 21; raided by Drake, 30.

Paper money, regulated by British government, 237, 238, 239, 265, 405; differing views, 247, 272; in New England, 265; restricted by Parliament, 265, 405; issued by Congress and by states, 464, 569; movement after the Revolution, 580–581; the case of *Trevett* v. *Weeden*, 581.

Paris, treaty (1763), 386, 429.

Parish, in England, 8, 10; in Virginia, 60, 61, 82; American like English, 343.

Parks, William, newspaper publisher, 335.

Parliament, English, in 1606, 2, 6; sovereignty established, 7, 194, 205, 228; governs church, 10; Long Parliament, 74; conflict with Charles I, 74, 97; right of taxation in Pennsylvania charter, 171; control of colonies, 180, 205, 234; British, 227; sovereignty established, 228; unrepresentative character, 228, 470; not controlled by any fundamental law, 232; control of colonial legislatures, 234; legislature for the empire, 237; restricts paper money, 265, 405; proposed revocation of colonial charters, 268; proposed taxation of colonies, 298; absolute authority of, 349; reimburses colonies after French and Indian War, 390; powers questioned by Otis, 396, 406; under George III, 401; proposed American taxation, 403; authority denied by Bland, 408; by Stamp Act Congress, 408; debate on taxation and authority, 409–411; declares its authority over colonies, 411; power to tax denied by Dickinson, 418; Tea Act of 1773, 426; changes government of Massachusetts, 428, 441; authority denied in first Continental Congress, 434, 435; Chatham's views, 437; Jefferson's theory as to authority, 556.

Parliamentary government established, 228.

Parson's Cause, in Virginia, 394.

Partisan warfare, in Revolution, 494.

Pastorius, Francis Daniel, leader in Pennsylvania, 175.

Paterson, proposes New Jersey plan in constitutional convention, 591.

Patroons, in New Netherland, 145, 149.

Patuxent River, navigable, 48.

Pauperism, in England, 5.

Peckham, Sir George, cited, 2.

Pemaquid, fort, 271.

Penn, Sir William, father of William Penn, 166.

Penn, William, proprietor New Jersey, 164; character and early life, 165–167; as a Quaker, 167, 168; defense of religious liberty, 168, 173; grant of Pennsylvania and Delaware, 168–169; controversy with Maryland, 170; as proprietor of Pennsylvania, 170–171, 175, 176; holy experiment, 171; land policy, 171–172, 284; constitutional experiments, 172–173; Indian policy, 174; stays in Pennsylvania, 174, 176; promotes settlement of Pennsylvania, 174; trials, 176, 301; loses and regains Pennsylvania, 204; religious policy, 352; cited, 167, 172.

Penn family, as landlords in Pennsylvania, 300–301.

Pennsylvania, charter, 169, 170–171, 185–186; boundaries, 169, 295; controversy with Maryland, 169–170, 296; government, 170–171, 549–552; religious freedom, 173; population, 174–175, 281; churches, 175, 304–306; industries, 176, 294; friction with Penn, 176, 283; influence of imperialism on charter, 186; temporarily a royal province, 204; trade, 247, 293; expansion, 281, 282; large-scale immigration,

284; Germans in, 288, 303, 305, 341; Swiss in, 288, 305; influence of the German element, 288; Scotch-Irish in, 291, 303; slavery, 292; chief granary of the continent, 293; fur trade, 293; manufactures, 294; boundary disputes, 295, 369, 389, 529, 563; politics, 299–303; taxing of the proprietary estates, 301; laws disallowed, 301, 302; question of oaths, 301–302; question of military service, 302; Quaker control, 302, 303; education, 306; common law modified, 345; local government, 350; claims upper Ohio, 369, 389; hinders Braddock, 373; French and Indian War, 375; opposes proprietary rule, 394; attitude toward Massachusetts in 1774, 432; radicals in 1774, 432; riflemen in army at Cambridge, 445; attitude on independence, 453, 454; state constitution, 462–463, 547–551; governor replaced by council, 463; settlements near Fort Pitt, 496; gains Wyoming valley, 529, 563; conditions after the Revolution, 539–540; on route to West, 542; one-house legislature, 549; no governor, 550; religious test for legislators, 552; emancipation act, 554; Wyoming valley dispute settled by arbitration, 563; paper money issued, 580; delegates in constitutional convention, 586; in large-state group, 590; ratifies federal Constitution, 604–606. *See* Thirteen Colonies.

Pennsylvania Gazette, Franklin's paper, 254.

Pensacola, taken by Spain, 500.

Pepperell, William, takes Louisburg, 364; knighted, 534.

Pepys, Samuel, naval adviser, 134; cited, 166.

Pequot War, 123.

Persecution, theory of, 116.

Personal liberty, protection of, 344.

Perth Amboy, port of East New Jersey, 165; trade, 294.

Peru, Spanish colony, 22.

Petition of Right, 97.

Philadelphia, founded, 176; Catholic church in, 252; center of population, 281, 282; main gateway of immigration, 284; commerce, 293; first among American cities, 294; society and houses, 294; manufactures, 294; medical science, 309; tea ships, 427; radicals in 1774, 432; first Continental Congress, 433; loyalists, 440; taken by British, 481, 482; evacuated, 492; largest city in United States, population, 532; mechanics in politics, 536; conditions after the Revolution, 539–540; political conditions, 539–540; Confederation Congress, 567; convention, 585–600, *see* Convention; favors federal Constitution, 604; state convention, 605.

Philip II, tyranny in Netherlands, 2, 14; relations with England, 14–15; wife, 14; controls Portugal, 17.

Philip V, 220.

Philippines, Magellan in, 21; in war, 385, 386.

Phillips, General, in Virginia, 507.

Phillipse family, in New York, 160.

Philosophical Society, 309.

Phips, Sir William, in King William's War, 219; governor of Massachusetts, 269.

Pickawillany, British post, 369; broken up, 370.

Pickens, guerrilla leader, 494.

Pieces of eight, 264.

Piedmont, colonization, 49, 318; characteristics, 323–325; in Virginia, opposes Constitution, 609. *See* Back country.

Pilgrims, in Holland, 92; found Plymouth, 92-95; influence, 95.

Pinckney, Charles, of South Carolina, career, 329; member Confederation Congress, 566; delegate in constitutional convention, 587; influence on details, 600.

Pinckney, Charles Cotesworth, delegate in constitutional convention, 587.

Pinckneys, typical American gentry, 534.

Piracy, act of Parliament against, 237; broken up by Spotswood, 328.

Piracy courts, 242.

Pirates, in North Carolina, 139, 312; in Pennsylvania, 176, 204; Newport, 262; in the Carolinas, 312.

Piscataqua, shipyards, 261.

Pitt, William, the elder, character, 380; ministry, 380; strategy, 381; appointments, 381, 382; appeal to the colonies, 381; plans for 1759, 383; for 1761, 385; resigns, 385, 399; uses navy to enforce Molasses Act, 391; American affection, 392; independence of Whig organization, 397; leader of Pittites, 400; declines office in 1765, 409; denies power of Parliament to tax America, 410; repeal of Stamp Act, 414; ministry with Grafton, 415; becomes Earl of Chatham, 415; out of power, 422; opposition ineffective, 491; last appeal for the empire, 491; cited, 410, 411. See Chatham.

Pitt, William, the younger, attitude toward United States, 571-572.

"Pittites," defined, 400; attitude toward America, 400.

Pittsburgh, named, 383; on route to West, 542.

Pizarro, conquest of Peru, 22.

Plains of Abraham, battle, 384.

Plantation colonies, commerce, 246.

Plantations, in Virginia, 63, 64, 79, 319; in South Carolina, 141, 316, 319, 541; in Georgia, 316, 541; in tidewater, 319; products, 320.

Planters, relations with English merchants, 246.

Plymouth (Eng.), importance in 1606, 4.

Plymouth (Mass.), founded, 93; business basis, 93, 94; fur trade, 94; government, 94; church organization, 95; influence, 95; in New England Confederation, 126, 127; merged in New England, 189; separate government resumed, 195; united with Massachusetts, 203.

Plymouth Company, for settling Virginia, 46, 47, 87.

Pompadour, Madame de, 379.

Ponce de Leon, in Florida, 22.

Pontiac, Indian chief, war, 390.

Poor Richard's Almanac, Franklin's, 308.

Pope, poet, influence on America, 254.

Pope's line of demarcation, 20.

Popham, Sir John, colonizer, 38, 45.

Population, Colonial, 340, see also particular colonies; of United States, 531.

Port Royal (Acadia), French colony, 25, 212; attacked by Argall, 216; taken by Phips, 219.

Port Royal (S. C.), French colony, 25.

Port Royal (S. C.), Scotch settlement, 143.

Porto Bello, captured, 362.

Porto Rico, or Puerto Rico, 21.

Portsmouth (R. I.), founded, 117.

Portsmouth (N. H.), profit from commerce, 259.

Portugal, temporary union with Spain, 15, 17; American possessions, 21; trade in East, 32, 144; supported by England in South American boundary dispute, 488.

Post office, colonial, established by Parliament, 237.

Post routes, colonial, 339.

Potomac River, navigable, 48; proposal to connect with the Ohio, 541.

Poverty, rare in United States, 535.

Povey, Thomas, consulted on colonial policy, 181.

Powhatan, Indian chief, 49, 50.

Pownall, governor of Pennsylvania, 293, 375; cited, 293.

Prerogative, royal, in England, 6, 7; in control of colonies, 238, 239; weakening, 241.

Presbyterians, in Massachusetts, 114; in South Carolina, 142; in East New Jersey, 165; in American colonies, 251, 305, 306; organization, 251; in Ulster, 290; first American presbytery and synod, 306; in middle colonies, 305, 306; in Virginia, 330, 331, 332, 533; in Maryland, 332; in back country, 332, 336; education in the back country, 336; in West, 545; national organization, 553; in Pennsylvania, oppose Constitution, 604.

President, provisions in constitutional convention, 593, 594; independent status, 593.

Presque Isle, French fort, 370.

Price, Richard, interest in American problems, 527.

Prime minister, British, 229.

Primogeniture, 320; abolished in Virginia, 554.

Princeton, battle, 480; Confederation Congress, 567.

Princeton College and University, founded, 307; intellectual center of Scotch-Irish, 307; influence on New South, 336.

Privateers, in Queen Anne's War, 222; relation to piracy, 262; in Revolution, 467, 491, 505; advantage of French alliance, 491.

Privy Council, committees on colonial affairs, 185; control over colonial laws, 203, 238, 349; court of appeals from colonial courts, 203, 239, 349; powers, 228; judicial authority, 232; disallowance of colonial laws, 238.

Proclamation of 1763, 390; Shelburne's view, 415–416.

Proprietary provinces, Maryland, 69; in New England, 88; Carolina, 136-137; New York, 157; New Jersey, 162; Pennsylvania, 170-173; British policy on, 184-186, 204, 240.

Protective principle in acts of trade, 184.

Protestant Association, Maryland, 199-200.

Protestant Episcopal Church, in United States, 533; national organization, 553.

Protestant Reformation, 10, 11, 16.

Protestants. See Dutch Protestants, Huguenots, Puritans, Presbyterians, etc.

Providence, colony in the Caribbean, 41.

Providence, settlement in Maryland, 72.

Providence (R. I.), founded, 117; profit from commerce, 259.

Provincetown, Pilgrims at, 93.

Provincial congress, of Massachusetts, 432; in Virginia, 433; in colonies generally, gains power, 448.

Prussia, War of the Austrian Succession, 363, 365; Seven Years' War, 374, 384; alliance with Great Britain, 374; favorable to American rebels, 460; armed neutrality, 504; commercial treaty with United States, 570.

Public lands system, 575. See also Land.

Puerto Rico, Spanish colony, 21.

Pufendorf, read by Americans, 341.

Pulaski, valuable service, 466.

Puritanism, defined, 89; doctrines, 89-90.
Puritans, in England, 11, 12, 74, 89, 90, 96, 131; Dutch influence, 18; in Maryland, 65, 74, 75-77; control England, under Cromwell, 74; doctrines, 89-90; kinds of, 90; outlook in England in 1629, 96-97; oppose Laud, 96; intolerance, 96, 108, 116; found Massachusetts, 97-99; oligarchy in Massachusetts, 104-105; churches in Massachusetts, 107-108; in Connecticut, 121; in New Haven, 122; results of 50 years enterprise, 124; in New York, 159; in New Jersey, 163-165; offended by Andros, 192; weakening of the Puritan tradition in New England, 273; Consociation, 275. See Congregationalists.
Pym, John, colonizer, 41, 42.

Quakers, doctrines, 115, 167, 168; persecuted in Massachusetts, 115; in Rhode Island, 120; in American colonies in general, 135, 250, 353; in North Carolina, 139, 332; in New Netherland, 149; control New Jersey, 164-165; persecution in England, 168; control of Pennsylvania, 168, 171, 173, 301-303; settlers in Pennsylvania, 175, 301-305; connection between American and English organizations, 250; in Boston, 273; in New England, 276; slave owners, 292, 305; antislavery, 292, 304-305; question of oaths, 301-302; question of military service, 302; differences, 304; schools, 306; in Virginia, 330; in Maryland, 332; in Thirteen Colonies, radicalism, 353; in French and Indian War, 376; in the Revolution, 440.
Quarter sessions, court in England, 8.
Quartering Act of 1774, 429.
Quartermaster-general, bad management, 465.
Quary, Robert, cited, 246.
Quebec, founded, 207; taken by English (1629), 208; renewed growth under French, 208; attacked in King William's War, 219; threatened in Queen Anne's War, 222, 223; well placed for defense, 377; siege (1759), 383; taken, 384; attacked in 1775-1776, 447.
Quebec, British province, 390; boundaries extended, 430.
Quebec Act of 1774, 429-430.
Queen Anne's War, 220-224.
Quitrents, in Virginia, 63, 320, 325; in New Jersey, 164, 283; in Pennsylvania, 171, 283, 292, 300, 301; under Andros, 190; in middle colonies, 283; in Maryland, North Carolina, and South Carolina, 320, 325.

Radicals, in Massachusetts, 419-420, 431; in Virginia, 425, 432; in middle colonies, 432; in first Continental Congress, 434; propose independence, 449, 450; win Declaration of Independence, 453-455; in the United States, 579-582, 613.
Radnor (Pa.), 175.
Raleigh, Sir Walter, colonizer, 35-36, 40; death, 36.
Randolph, Edmund, governor of Virginia, delegate in constitutional convention, 585; plan of Constitution, 589; urges plural executive, 593; favors adoption of Constitution, 608.
Randolph, Edward, collector, 185; evidence against Massachusetts, 187; in government of New England, 189, 190; deposed, 195.
Randolph, Peyton, in first Continental Congress, 433.
Randolphs, typical American gentry, 534.

Rappahannock River, navigable, 48.
Rawdon, Lord, campaign in South Carolina, 503.
Rayneval, proposal concerning the West, 519, 528; cited, 516.
Redemptioners, in Pennsylvania (Germans), 288. in United States, 535. See Indentured servants;
Redwood, Abraham, Newport merchant, career, 264.
Regicides, in New England, 127.
Religion, in England, 10-12; in Thirteen Colonies, 351-354; in United States, 533, 545. See Church, Anglican, Roman Catholics, Puritanism, Religious toleration, etc.
Religious intolerance, in Virginia, 65, 331; in England, 96; in Massachusetts, 108, 113-116; in New York, 149, 303; in the colonies, 352; in the United States, 551, 552.
Religious liberty, Penn's defense, 168, 173; in state constitutions, 550; in Virginia, 552; in Ordinance of 1787, 578.
Religious tests, in states, 551.
Religious toleration, in Maryland, 70, 73, 76; in Rhode Island, 119, 120; in Carolina, 137; in South Carolina, 142; in New Netherland, 149; in New York, 159, 303-304; in Pennsylvania, 173, 303-304; in Massachusetts, 273, 275-276; in New Hampshire, 273; in Connecticut, 275-276; in Germany, 286; in middle colonies, 303-304; in Virginia, 330-332, 552; in Thirteen Colonies, 351-354; in Canada, 429; in states, 550; in Ordinance of 1787, 578.
Rembrandt, Dutch painter, 17.
Renaissance, 13.
Rensselaer, Killian Van, patroon, 145.
Representation, new theory, 348-349; theory of Stamp Act Congress, 408; theory of Mansfield, 410; theory of Pitt, 410; in Congress of Confederation, 559; in Congress of the Constitution, 591-592, 598.
Representative government, established in Virginia, 57; in Maryland, 72; in Massachusetts, 104, 203; in North Carolina, 138; in South Carolina, 142; in New Netherland, 147-148; in New York, 157, 158-159; in New Jersey, 163; in Pennsylvania, 172-173; subverted by imperialism, 187, 189; reëstablished by William and Mary, 200; in the South, 326; American and English compared, 342, 343, 348, 349; in Canada, 429.
Republican ideals, in state constitutions, 548.
Requisition system, under Confederation Congress, 568-569.
Restoration, 77, 131-135; colonial policy, 135, 181-185.
Restoration era, characteristics, 131-135.
Revenge, Grenville's ship, 35.
Revolution of 1688, 7; main account, 192; results in England, 193-194; in America, 194-200; colonial policy of new government, 200-204; significance in American history, 205.
Revolution of 1775-1783, eve of (proximate causes), 414-435; revolutionary government developed, 435; proposals of Burke and Chatham, 437; fighting begun, 438, 441-442; the American cause in 1775, 443; British preparations, 444; attitude of other British colonies, 446; drift toward independence, 448-452; resolution of May, 1776, 452; Declaration of Independence, 453-456; real cause, 456; an American civil war, 456; the opposing forces, 459-473;

naval forces and land forces, 459; America poorly organized, 460–463; economic problems 463; finances, 464; management of the American army and navy, 465–467; reasons for American victory, 467–473; geographic factors, 468; European factors, 468–473; operations on a small scale, 475; campaign of 1776, 475–479; of 1777, 480–484: attitude of France and Spain, 485–491; campaign of 1778, 492–493; of 1779, 493; of 1780, 494; partisan warfare, 494; Indians in, 497–498; war in the West, 498–500; war in the South, 500, 502–504, 507–508; campaign of 1781, 502–508; armed neutrality, 504; naval operations, 505, 508; treaties of peace, 517–524; hostilities ended, 523; effect on churches, 533, 553; adoption of state constitutions, 547–551.

Rhode Island, founded, 117–119; parliamentary patent, 118; religious toleration, 119, 120, 352; charter of 1663, 119, 185; merged in New England, 189; separate government resumed, 195; resumes charter, 203; paper money, 265, 581; slaves, 266; self-government, 267; charter threatened (1701), 268; education, 278; Dean Berkeley's visit, 278; the *Gaspee* affair, 423–424; independent government, 449; state constitution, 462, 463; absence of class barriers, 535; rural population predominant, 538; extent of power as colony, 556; defeats amendment of Articles of Confederation, 569; delays ratification of federal Constitution, 610. *See* New England and Thirteen Colonies.

Rice, trade restricted, 235, 236; in South Carolina, 246, 317, 320, 321; in list of enumerated articles, 321.

Richelieu, French statesman, 16; crushes Huguenots, 96; colonizer, 207.

Richelieu River, military colony, 214.

Rights of Englishmen, 7, 46; claimed by colonists, 46, 344.

Rights of the British Colonies Asserted and Proved, pamphlet by Otis, 406.

Rights of the colonists, 46, 234, 344.

Roads, colonial, 325, 339.

Roanoke colony, 36.

Roberval, plants colony, 25.

Robinson, John, character, 91; in Leyden, 92.

Rochambeau, Count, at Newport, 506; at Yorktown, 507, 508; cited, 506.

Rockingham, Marquis of, leader of "Old Whigs," 400; ministry, 409, 411, 415; opposition ineffective, 471; again minister in 1782, 509; death, 517.

Rockingham ministry, 409; policy as to Stamp Act, 411; fall, 415.

Rodney, Admiral, operations in Revolutionary War, 505; victory in West Indies in 1782, 510.

Rodrigue, Admiral, operations in Revolutionary War, 505; victory in West Indies in 1782, 510.

Roman Catholics, in England, 10, 11, 12, 69; excluded from Virginia, 56; in Maryland, 69, 70, 73, 332; in New York, 159, 196, 303; in Pennsylvania, 173; under James II, 192; after Revolution of 1688, 194; suspicion in New York, 196; in Ireland, 227, 289; in American colonies, 251–252, 352, 353; organization, 252; persecution in New York, 303; discrimination against in Pennsylvania, 304; persecuted in Thirteen Colonies, 352; in Thirteen Colonies, conservatism, 353; in Canada, 429–430; excluded from office in United States, 533, 552; American organization after Revolution, 553.

Royal African Company, chartered, 78, 135; share of slave trade, 233.

Royal province, government, 59; in the eighteenth century, 239–242. *See* Colonial government.

Royal Society, founded, 132; American members, 253.

Rum, made in New England, 247, 264; in slave trade, 262.

Rupert, Prince, interest in trade, 134.

Russia, in seventeenth century, 17; in Seven Years' War, 374, 384; United States compared with, 530.

Rutgers v. Waddington, cited, 572.

Rutledge, Edward, in first Continental Congress, 434; war office, 445; opinion of the Shays rebellion, 582.

Rutledge, John, president of South Carolina, defends Charleston, 448; delegate in constitutional convention, 587.

Rutledges, hope for reconciliation, 450.

Ryswick, peace of, 219.

Sabbath, Puritan, 90, 108.

St. Augustine, founded, 24; broken up by Drake, 30; ravaged by English, 222; attacked by English, 362.

St. Christopher, English colony, 40; ceded by France, 224.

St. Croix, French colony, 25.

St. Eustatius, taken by British, 505; lost by British, 509.

St. Johns River, French colony on, 24.

St. Lawrence, explored, 25.

St. Leger, Colonel, in Mohawk valley, 482, 483.

St. Lusson, takes possession of Great Lakes region, 210.

St. Marys, settled, 70, 71.

St. Pierre, retained by France, 386.

Salem (Mass.), founded, 98; profit from commerce, 259, 263; witchcraft, 274; foreign trade, 537.

Salem (N. J.), settled, 164.

Salisbury, Earl of, in Virginia Company, 55.

Saltonstall, Sir Richard, colonizer, 99.

Salzburg, colonists from, 315.

Sandwich, Lord, in charge of British navy, 472.

Sandy Hook lighthouse, 571.

Sandys, Sir Edwin, colonizer, 38, 54; influence on Virginia, 54, 58; friendly to Puritans, 91, 93.

San Miguel, colony, 23.

Santo Domingo, taken by Drake, 30.

Saratoga, fort abandoned (1747), 368; campaign, cause of British failure, 469; Burgoyne's surrender, 484; effect on diplomacy, 486, 490.

Sauer, Christopher, printer, 295.

Sault Ste. Marie, St. Lusson at, 210.

Saunders, Admiral, capture of Quebec, 383–384.

Savannah, taken in 1778, 493; attempt to retake, 493; held by British after Yorktown, 508.

Saybrook, founded, 121.

Schenectady, massacre, 218.

Schlatter, Rev. Michael, leader of the German Reformed Church, 305.

Schoharie valley, settled, 282.

Schools, in England, 13; in Massachusetts, 109. *See* Education.

Schooner, devised, 260.

Schuyler, Peter, aristocratic leader, 196; opposes Leisler, 197; influence over Iroquois, 218.

Schuyler, Gen. Philip, attacks loyalists, 482; in command against Burgoyne, 483–484.

Schuylers, family in New York, 161; inter-marriages, 284.
Scotch, in Virginia, 77; in American colonies generally, 135, 251, 341; in South Carolina, 142, 143, 318; in East New Jersey, 165; "factors" in America, 246; in Newport, 263; in Ulster, 289; in New York city, 294; frontier loyalists, 497. See Scotch-Irish.
Scotch seamen, counted as English, 182.
Scotch-Irish, oppression in Ireland, 227, 290; immigration, effect on church, 251; colonists in Maine, 258; in Massachusetts, 258; in New Hampshire, 258; in Pennsylvania, 282, 291, 303, 604; defined, 289; in Ulster, 289–290; religious grievances, 290; motives for emigration 290; in New England and New York, 291; buffer communities, 291; occupy land without legal title, 291, 292; aggressiveness in Pennsylvania, 303; Presbyterians, 305, 306; intellectual center at Princeton, 307; in Virginia, Maryland, North Carolina, and South Carolina, 319, 609; in Thirteen Colonies, 341; frontier Whigs, 497; immigrants in United States, 532; characteristics, 532; in West, 545; oppose the federal Constitution, 604, 609; favor Constitution, 609.
Scotland, relation to England, 2, 182, 226; Scotch ships foreign, 182; influence on southern Presbyterians, 333; influence on American practices and ideals, 348.
Scrooby congregation, 91.
Sea power, of England, founded, 15; importance in British foreign policy, 359, 360; in the Seven Years' War, 374, 383, 385; in Revolution, 467, 473.
Secretaries of state, British, 229.
Secretary of state for the colonies, new office, 416.
Sectionalism, in Virginia, 82; in the colonies, 257; in the South, 319, 329; in politics, 329; in United States, 536; in the constitutional convention, 598.
Ségur, French writer, cited, 535.
Seigneurs, in New France, 214; military leaders, 218.
Selectmen, in Massachusetts, 106.
Self-government, of colonies, 43, 109, 348, 556; after the Revolution of 1688, 195–200; in Connecticut and Rhode Island, 267–268, 556.
Senate, representation in, 592.
Separation of powers, in Virginia, 60; in state constitutions, 549–551.
Separatists, in England, 12, 89–90; defined, 89; in Holland, 92. See Pilgrims.
Serapis, capture, 467.
Seven Years' War, 374–386.
Sewall, Samuel, typical Puritan, 253.
Shaftesbury, Earl of. See Ashley.
Shakespeare, popularity, 13; neglected in America, 341.
Sharp, Granville, antislavery leader, 554.
Sharpe, Horatio, governor of Maryland, 370.
Shays rebellion, 581.
Shelburne, Earl of, leader of "Pittites," 400; problems of the West, 415–416; out of power, 422; in ministry of 1782, 510; colonial secretary, correspondence with Franklin, 512–513; character, attitude in peace negotiations, 516; prime minister, 517; negotiations for West, 519; resigns, 523.

Shenandoah valley, trade with Baltimore and Philadelphia, 325; Germans in, 341. See Great Valley of Virginia.
Sheriff, in England, 8; in Virginia, 60; in Massachusetts, 106; American like English, 343.
Sherman, Roger, in first Continental Congress, 434; war office, 445; committee on Declaration of Independence, 453; member Confederation Congress, 566; political career, delegate in constitutional convention, 586; cited, 592.
Shipbuilding, in New England, 103, 260, 261, 264; in New York, 160, 293; in Pennsylvania, 176, 293.
Ships, provisions of Navigation Act, 182.
Shirley, William, governor of Massachusetts, in King George's War, 364, 365; character, 370, 375; in French and Indian War, 373; favors parliamentary tax, 376.
Sidney, Algernon, philosopher, 132; influence on Americans, 255, 342.
Silesia, seized by Prussia, 363.
Silk, in Virginia, 57, 64, 78, 179; in Carolina, 138.
Silver, from Spanish America, 22; English search for, 32.
Slaughter, governor of New York, 198.
Slave trade, English, 27, 78; interest of royal family, 134; why favored, 135; Dutch rivalry, 152; French, 208; British 223, 233, 316; New England, 247, 262; Newport, 262; Captain Lindsay's voyage, 262; importation of slaves prohibited by Virginia and Maryland, 533; movement for suppressing, 597–598.
Slavery, in Spanish colonies, 22; development in Virginia, 78; in South Carolina, 141; in New York, 160, 292; in West New Jersey, 165; in New England, 266; in Pennsylvania, 292; in Georgia, 316; responsibility for, 316; increase in the South, 316–317; conditions in the South, 322; status in United States after Revolution, 533; prohibited in Ordinance of 1787, 578; in the Constitution, 598.
Smilie, John, Anti-Federalist leader in Pennsylvania, 605.
Smith, Adam, Wealth of Nations, influence, 570.
Smith, Capt. John, in Virginia, 52; explores New England, 87; cited, 48, 49, 50.
Smith, Sir Thomas, colonizer, 38, 45, 52; character, 52–54; influence on Virginia, 52, 54, 55, 58; portrait, 53.
Smith, William, historian, on toleration, 304.
Smuggling, 243; Liberty seized, 419; tea, 423.
Social scale in 1606, 3. See Classes.
Society for Propagating the Gospel in Foreign Parts, 249; work in New England, 250; work in middle colonies, 250, 304; work in Carolinas, 250, 330.
Society of Friends, 115. See Quakers.
South, colonies in 1660, 130; fur trade, 215; in Queen Anne's War, 222; chapter on period 1689–1760, 311–336; political readjustment, 312; growth of population, 314; development of negro slavery, 316–317; colonization of the uplands, 318; immigrants from the North, 318; sectionalism, 319, 329; few towns, 322–323; voters, 327; churches, 330–333; education, 333–335; intellectual centers, 335; newspapers, 335; Revolutionary War, 500, 502–504, 507–508; after the Revolution, 540, 541; opposes Jay's Spanish policy, 574. See names of colonies.
South America, colonized, 20–22.

South Carolina, French colony in, 25; English colony, founded, 140–143; population, 141, 314–315; plantation system, 141; products and trade, 141; churches, 142, 248, 250, 313, 332; opposed by Spain, 143; Queen Anne's War, 222; rice, 246, 317, 320, 321; uprising of 1719, 312–314; Church Acts of 1704, 313; election law of 1716, 314; becomes separate royal province, 314; growth of population, 314–315; slavery in, 317, 322; Germans and Scotch-Irish in, 319; quitrent troubles, 320; importance of Charleston, 323; governor curbed, 326; council, 326; education abroad, 334; schools, 334; similarity to Barbados, 339; loyalists in, 441; loyalists defeated in 1776, 447; independent government, 449; attitude on independence, 454; state constitution, 462–463, 547–551; in Revolutionary War, 494, 502–504; yields claim to Western lands, 530; conditions after the Revolution, 541; opinion as to slavery, 541; delegates in Constitutional Convention, 587; in large-state group, 590; favors slave trade, 598; ratifies federal Constitution, 607. See Carolina, South, and Thirteen Colonies.
South Carolina Gazette, newspaper founded, 335.
Southern secessionists of 1861, organization, 461.
Sovereignty, See States.
Spain, power, 14; relations with England, 14–15, 27, 30, 133, 220–224, 361; and the New World, 20; colonies, 21–24; treatment of Indians, 22; exclusive trade policy, 27; opposes Virginia, 45, 56; opposes South Carolina, 143; Spanish succession, 219–220; alliance with France, 220–223; Queen Anne's War, 221–224; relations with Great Britain, 361, 374, 385, 469, 488, 500, 522; results of the War of the Spanish Succession, 361; grievances against England, 361; the Family Compact, 362; Anglo-Spanish War of 1739, 362; alliance with France (1761), 385; results of Seven Years' War, 386; loans and aid to United States, 464, 469, 485; policy in 1777, 488; relations with United States, 489, 515, 573; question of free navigation of the Mississippi, 489–490; enters war as an ally of France, 490; activities in the Southwest, 490; war with Great Britain (1779), 500; attitude toward United States, 515; claims in West, 518–519; regains Floridas, 520, 522; treaty of peace with Great Britain (1783), 522.
Spanish Netherlands, attacked by Louis XIV, 216, 220.
Spanish Succession, War of the, 220, 361.
Speakership question, in Massachusetts, 271.
Spectator essays, influence on America, 254.
S. P. G., defined, 249.
Spotswood, Alexander, governor of Virginia, career, 327–328; cited, 327.
Springfield (Mass.) founded, 121.
Stamp Act, passed, 404–405; opposition, 406; Stamp Act Congress, 408; appeal to force, 408; repealed, 411, 414.
Stamp Act Congress, 408.
Staple Act of 1663, 182, 183.
Star Chamber, court in England, 7.
Stark, Capt. John, battle of Bennington, 483.
State rights, basis of New England confederation, 126. See States.
Staten Island, Dutch settlers, 146; British troops on, 459, 478.
States, declaration of Congress, 459; grudging attitude toward Congress, 461; poor organization, 462; character of the new constitutions, 463; taxing power, paper money, 464; militia, character, 465; claims to western lands, 529, 530; constitution making, 547–551; suffrage qualifications, 548; veto power, 550; religious tests, 551; encouragement of education, 554; sovereignty under Continental Congress, 558; sovereignty under Confederation, 561; violate treaties, 572–573; provision for new states in Ordinance of 1787, 578; sovereignty under the Constitution, 612.
States-General, of Netherlands, 144.
Staves, in trade of New England, 181.
Stay laws, demanded by debtor class, 580.
Steele, Richard, essayist, friend of Joseph Dudley, 253; Spectator essays, influence on America, 254.
Steuben, inspector-general, 466, 492; valuable service, 466.
Stillwater, battle, 484.
Stirling, Earl of, colonizer, 42.
Stone, governor of Maryland, 76, 77.
Stormont, Lord, ambassador in Paris, 487.
Strafford, Earl of, supports autocratic rule, 97.
Stuart, superintendent of Indian affairs in the South, 444; loyalist influence, 497.
Stuarts, royal family, 133. See Charles I, Charles II, James I, James II.
Stuyvesant, Peter, governor of New Netherland, 147; autocratic government, 148; church policy, 149; opposes Swedes and English, 151, 152.
"Suffolk Resolves" of 1774, 431; approved by Congress, 434.
Suffrage, in Massachusetts, 103, 104, 274; in Connecticut and Rhode Island, 267; in New York, 297; in the South, 327; in Thirteen Colonies, 348; in the states, 548; for federal elections, 599.
Sugar, in English West Indies, 40; trade regulated, 182, 183; duty, 235, 403, 404.
Sugar Act of 1764, 403, 404; effects of, 405–406.
Sumter, guerrilla leader, 494.
Supreme law, and its enforcement, 594–595.
Surinam, English colony 41.
Susquehanna River, navigable, 48.
Susquehanna valley, early settlers, 282; Scotch-Irish in, 291; Connecticut settlers in Wyoming Valley, 295, 542.
Susquehannocks, Indian tribe, 49, 70.
Sweden, in seventeenth century, 17; alliance of 1668, 216.
Swedes, in New Sweden, 150–151; in New Jersey, 163; in Pennsylvania and Delaware, 174.
Swiss colonists, motives for emigration, 285; in North Carolina, 287, 317; in Pennsylvania, 288, 305; churches, 305; in South Carolina, 318.
Switzerland, in seventeenth and eighteenth centuries, 285; emigration, 286.

Talon, Jean, intendant of New France, 210.
Tangiers, acquired by Charles II, 134.
Tarleton, Colonel, guerrilla leader, 494; battle of the Cowpens, 503; campaign in Virginia, 507.
Taxation, in Virginia, 59, 60; in charter of Pennsylvania, 171; in the colonies, 237, 343; arguments for tax by Parliament, 403, 404; Sugar Act, 404; Stamp Act, 404–412; issue unsettled, 414; Townshend Duty Act, 417; taxing power given to Congress, 596.

Taxation No Tyranny, Johnson's tract, 470.

Taxation without representation, under Andros, 191; argument against Stamp Act, 408.

Tea, trade, 388; tax, 417; retained, 423; Act of 1773, 426; colonial resistance, 426; Boston Tea Party, 427.

Tenants, in England in 1606, 5; in middle colonies, 283. *See* Land tenure.

"Tender" laws, demanded by debtor class, 580.

Tenison, Thomas, head of S. P. G., 250.

Tennessee, De Soto in, 23; early settlements, 497, 543; Indian raids, 498; frontiersmen in battle of Kings Mountain, 500; proposed state of Franklin, 529.

Tennessee River, route to West, 543.

Tennyson, cited, 35.

Territorial government, genesis of, 576–578.

Territories on the Delaware, 169, 170. *See* Delaware.

Texas, Spanish missionaries in, 24.

Theater, first in America, 335.

Thirteen Colonies, control and influence by England, 229–255; common interests, 339; conflict with insular interests, 340; population, 340; race and language, 340–341; government, 342–350; law, 344–347; churches, 351–354; in French and Indian War, 375, 377, 382, 390, 392; plans for intercolonial union, 376; reimbursed, 391; growth, 391; self-confidence, 392; friction with British government, 393–397, 402–408; eve of Revolution, 414–435; breakdown of provincial governments, 448–449; distribution of powers between colonial and imperial governments, 556. *See* Revolution, and names of colonies.

Thirty Years' War, 16; effects on colonization, 17, 151, 174, 285; destructiveness, 285.

Ticonderoga, battle (1758), 382; abandoned by French, 384; taken by Allen, 446; taken by British in 1777, 483.

Tidewater region, physical features, 48, 49; dominated by English, 318; characteristics, 319–323; products, 320; labor system, 321; Anglican Church, 332; in Virginia, favors Constitution, 609.

Timber trade restricted, 235.

Tithes, in England, 10.

Titles of nobility, in Carolina, 137; condemned in state constitutions, 534.

Tobacco, cultivated by Indians, 50; in Virginia, 57, 64, 78, 540; the plantation system, 64, 320; production in England prohibited, 64; trade regulated, 64, 81, 180, 182–184; in Maryland, 72; in North Carolina, 138; extent of trade (1706), 246; planters' difficulties, 320; used as money, 394; conditions of trade after the Revolution, 540.

Toleration. *See* Religious toleration.

Toleration Act, Maryland, 76, 77.

Toleration Act of 1689 in England, 194, 205.

Tories, in America, 434, 440. *See* Loyalists.

Tory party, in Great Britain, discredited by Jacobites, 398; in reign of George III, 401.

Town meeting, in New England, 106, 267; powers, 106, 350; under Andros, 191: restricted by Massachusetts Government Act, 428.

Towns, New England, 102; few in the South, 323.

Townshend, Charles, character and policy, 416; Townshend Acts, 417.

Townshend Acts, 417; American opposition, 418–422; duties abandoned, 423.

Township system of public land surveys, 575.

Trans-Allegheny country, 518. *See* West.

Transatlantic travel in seventeenth century, 47; communications in the eighteenth century, 242.

Transportation, seventeenth-century ocean vessels, 47; rivers in Virginia, 48; in Pennsylvania, 293; in the South, 324–325, colonial roads, 325, 339; slowness, 536; proposed canals, 541; western pioneers, 542–543.

Transylvania, colony, 496.

Treasurer, colonial, 241.

Treasurer, provincial, 241; in New York, 298; in Pennsylvania, 300; in Virginia, 326.

Treasury Board, British, 229, 232.

Treasury department, with single head, 502.

Treaties, Westphalia, 151, 286; Breda, 153; Ryswick, 219; Utrecht, 223–224; Aix-la-Chapelle, 365; Paris (1763), 386; Fort Stanwix, 416, 429; treaty of 1782, 512–522; treaty of Paris, 1783, 524; commercial treaties, 570; treaties violated by states, 572–573; enforcement of treaties, 594–595.

Trenton, battle, 479–480; Confederation Congress at, 567.

Trespass Act, in New York, 572–573.

Trevett v. *Weeden*, cited, 581.

Trial by jury, in colonies, 347; in Ordinance of 1787, 578.

Trial in England of colonists who had committed crimes, proposed, 421, 425.

Triple Alliance of 1668, 216.

Tryon, governor of New York, opposes Revolution, 448.

Tudor kings, 6, 14.

Turgot, minister of Louis XVI, 486; on American independence, 526; on American problem of government, 526; cited, 526.

Turkey Company, chartered, 4.

Turner, cited, 357.

Tuscaroras, war, 313.

Ulster, settled by Scotchmen and Englishmen, 2; colonists from, 289; colonists in, 289; economic grievances, 290; influence on southern Presbyterians, 333; assistance to America, 469.

Ulster County, N. Y., Scotch-Irish, 291.

Uncas, Mohegan chieftain, 126.

Unconstitutional legislation, and the courts, 547; controlled by judges, 595.

Union, Albany plan, 376; Galloway plan, 434; development of, 555–563.

Unitarian movement, in New England, 277.

United Colonies of New England, 126.

United Kingdom of Great Britain, created, 226.

United States, Declaration of Independence, 455; financing the Revolution, 464; alliance with France, 490, 497; peace negotiations, 512–524; attitude toward Spain, 515; independence conceded, 517; territorial boundaries, 517–520; fisheries, 520; preliminary treaty of 1782, 522; treaty of 1783, 524; doubtful prospects, 526–527; British posts, 527; Spanish claims, 528; Indians in West, 528; interstate boundary questions, 529; physical resources, 530; population, 531; distribution, 531–532; racial elements, 532; churches, 533, 545; social distinctions, 534–535; sectionalism,

536; commercial problems, 536; internal improvements, 541; development of federal union, 555–563; powers of the Continental Congress, 558; federal problems, 1783–1787, 565–582; beginnings of colonial policy, 574–579; movement for a more effective union, 579–582; economic and social discontent, 579–581; economic grievances, 580; nature of union, 612. *See* Revolution, Congress, Constitution, etc.

Universities, in England, 13.

University of Pennsylvania, founded by Franklin, 307.

University of Virginia, inspired by Jefferson, 555.

Usselinx, Willem, colonizer, 150.

Utrecht, treaty of, 223–224.

Valley Forge, cause of sufferings, 465; American army at, 484.

Van Cortlandt, Stephen, aristocratic leader, 196.

Van Cortlandt family, in New York, 160.

Vane, Henry, governor of Massachusetts, 114.

Van Rensselaer, Killian, patroon, 145.

Van Rensselaers, in New York, intermarriages, 284.

Vaudreuil, governor of New France, 378, 384.

Vera Cruz, Captain Hawkins at, 27.

Vergennes, Count of, policy toward United States, 486, 487, 488; negotiation with Franklin, 489; alliance with United States, 490; opinion of Adams, 513; attitude in peace negotiations, 515; opinion of Oswald's commission, 517; attitude on claims to West, 518–519; communication to Congress, 523; pacified by Franklin, 523.

Vermont, first settlements, 259; taking of Ticonderoga and Crown Point, 446; becomes a state, 496; claimed by New York, 496, 529; Whigs in, 497; settled by New Englanders, 542; population, 542.

Vernon, Admiral, takes Porto Bello, 362.

Verrazano, explorer, 24.

Vespucius, Americus, explorer, 20.

Vestry, Virginia, 60.

Vetch, Samuel, in Queen Anne's War, 222.

Veto power, of provincial governor, 238; in state constitutions, 550; President's, 594.

Vincennes, British trading post, 498; taken by Clark, 499.

Virginia, Spanish claim, 22; name, 37; charter of 1606, 37, 45; opposition of Spain, 45; expedition of 1606, 47; instructions to colonists, 47, 51; physical features, 48, 49; Indians 49–52, 58, 62, 63, 82; Jamestown settlement, 51; near failure, 52, 56; population, 52, 56, 62, 77, 314, 315; charter of 1609, 54; of 1612, 55; churches, 56, 61, 77, 248, 330–332, 351, 533, 552; tobacco, 57, 64, 78, 79, 320, 540; first legislature, 57; royal province, 59–61; social classes, 62; servants, 62, 77; land system, 63; plantations, 63, 64, 79, 319; loyalists, 65, 74, 77; emigrants from, 65, 136, 138; opposes Lord Baltimore, 68; Commonwealth government, 75; Restoration, 77; negro slavery, 77–78, 317, 322; early westward movement, 80; fur trade, 80, 215, 221; grievances, 80–82; Bacon's Rebellion, 82–84; conditions in 1688, 84–85; trade, 151, 180, 183, 246; friction with imperial collectors, 185; unrest in 1689, 198; Germans in, 288, 317, 319; securely established in 1700, 311; growth of population, 314–315; Scotch-Irish in, 319;

large estates, 320; quitrent troubles, 320; governor's power, 325; model imperial province, 325; council influential, 326; education abroad, 333, 334; English sports, 342; local government much like English, 344, 350; similarity to England, 354; claims upper Ohio 369, 389; Parson's Cause, 394; opposes Stamp Act, 406–408; Resolves of 1769, 421; friction before the Revolution, 425; radicals and conservatives, 425–426, 432; committee of correspondence, 425; Lord Dunmore's War, 439; revolutionary methods, 439; loyalists (Tories), 440–441; riflemen in the army at Cambridge, 445; independent government, 453; state constitution, 462, 463, 547–551; Kentucky county, 497; Clark expedition, 499; county of Illinois, 499; military operations, 507–508; Kentucky claims statehood, 529; claims Northwest, 529, 530; yields claim to Northwest, 530, 574; prohibits importation of slaves, 534; conditions after the Revolution, 540; interest in the West, 541; method of adopting state constitution, 547; suffrage qualifications, 548; apportionment, 549–551; no veto power, 550; state governor, 551; complete religious liberty 552; primogeniture abolished, 554; public education, 555; discriminatory duties, 571; paper-money movement defeated, 580; conference with Maryland, 585; Annapolis Convention, 585; delegates in constitutional convention, 585; in large-state group, 590; ratifies federal Constitution, 608–610. *See* South, and Thirteen Colonies.

Virginia Company, members, 38, 39, 45, 55; aims and methods, 56; internal troubles, 58; fall, 59; relation to Pilgrims, 92, 94.

Virginia Gazette, newspaper founded, 335.

Virginia plan of constitution, 589; approved, 591; executive, 593; power of Congress over states, 594; influence on details, 600.

Virginia Resolves of 1769, 421.

Voltaire, read by Americans, 341.

"Volunteers," of Ireland, 469.

Voyageurs, work for British, 498.

Wachovia (N. C.), founded, 324.

Wages, in United States, 536.

Wall Street, compared with England, 247.

Walloons, in New Netherland, 145.

Walpole, Sir Robert, prime minister, 229; against parliamentary duties on the colonies, 237; war with Spain, 362.

War department, or War Office, organized by Congress, 461; with single head, 502; under Confederation, 565.

War of the Austrian Succession, 363–365.

War Office, organized by Congress, 461.

Warren, Commodore, takes Louisburg, 364.

Warwick (R. I.), founded, 118.

Warwick, Robert Rich, Earl of, colonizer, 39, 41, 42; commissioner, 74; Council for New England, 88.

Washington, George, mission to Ohio country, 371; skirmish with French, 371; aide to Braddock, 373; military rank, 377; reputation, 392; Virginia Resolves of 1769, 421; in first Continental Congress, 433; revolutionary activity, 439; appointed commander in chief, 443; character, 443, 467, 534, 588; takes Boston, 445; favors independence, 449; oath of allegiance to the United States, 461; hampered by governmental weakness, 463–465; hampered by political interference, 467; contribution to victory, 467; tries to defend New York, 478–479; battle of Long Island, 479; retreat across New Jersey, 479; Trenton and Princeton, 479–480; Chads Ford and Germantown, 481; Valley Forge, 484; Conway Cabal, 485; battle of Monmouth, 492; expedition against Iroquois, 499; on weakness of government, 501; chooses Greene for southern command, 502; plans to attack New York, 506; Yorktown campaign, 507; "Farewell Orders," 526; warning as to federal government, 526; appreciation of American economic resources, 531; typical country gentleman, 534; interest in canals, 541; conservative Western policy, 544; retirement at Mount Vernon, 566; pacifies army officers, 567–568; offer of kingship, 567; Newburg addresses, 568; approves annulment of Trespass Act, 573; opinion of the Shays rebellion, 582; favors revision of Articles of Confederation, 584; favors coöperation of Virginia and Maryland, 584; delegate in constitutional convention, 585; public spirit, 588; president of the convention, 588; nationalist leader, 589; favors adoption of Constitution, 608; Federal leader, 610; first President of the United States, 610, 613; cited, 464, 484, 501, 526, 531.

Watauga settlement, 497.

Webster, Pelatiah, proposes new federal constitution, 584.

Wedderburn, Solicitor-General, attacks Franklin, 431.

Weiser, Conrad, backwoods leader, 293.

Welsh, in American colonies, 135; in Pennsylvania, 175; in South Carolina, 318.

Wentworth, Sir Thomas, supports autocratic rule, 97.

Wesley, John, publishes tract against colonies, 470; leads to formation of Methodist Episcopal Church in United States, 553.

West, French in, 212, 357–386; old and new distinguished, 357; struggle for, 357–386; loss of British prestige, 374; under British rule, 389; Shelburne's policy, 415–416; added to Quebec, 430; Mississippi question, 489, 519, 543, 573; frontier communities, 496–497; British influence, 498; in Revolution, 498–500; in peace negotiations, 518–519; occupation delayed by British and Spanish claims, 528; conflicting state claims, 529, 559; state cessions, 530; population, 531; conditions after the Revolution, 542–545; characteristics of the western settlers, 544–545; religion, 545; provision in Articles of Confederation concerning state claims, 559; opposes Jay's Spanish policy, 574; land system, 575; genesis of territorial government, 576–578; colonization under federal protection, 579; proposed restrictions in Constitution, 599.

West, Richard, cited on rights of Englishmen, 345.

West Florida, British province, 390; taken by Spain, 500; secret agreement concerning boundary, 520.

West Indians, in Newport, 263.

West Indies, Spanish colonization, 21; English colonies, 40; trade, 40, 235, 247, 261, 264, 403, 405, 537, 539, 570; in 1660, 130; French, 209; Queen Anne's War, 221; influence in Parliament, 228, 235, 340; relations with Thirteen Colonies, 338; favored colonies, 340; Molasses Act evaded, 391; trade affected by Sugar Act, 403, 405; no revolutionary spirit, 446; operations in Revolutionary War, 505, 509, 510; trade after the Revolution, 537, 539; American shipping excluded, 570.

West New Jersey, 164, 165; reunited, 204.

West Point, Arnold's plot, 501.

West Virginia, colonized, 496; early settlements, 543.

Westchester County, large land grants, 283.

Westover estate of William Byrd, 320, 328, 335.

Westphalia, peace of, effect on New Sweden, 151; religious settlement, 286.

Westsylvania, proposed colony, 496.

Wethersfield (Conn.), founded, 121.

Whaling industry, 260; favored by Grenville, 402.

Wheat, in Virginia, 49, 540; in New England, 101; in South Carolina, 141; in New York, 160; in Pennsylvania, 176; in middle colonies, 292, 293; in back country, 324; in Illinois country, 358.

Whig party in England, decides against American bishops, 249; in power under George I and George II, 379, 397; principles, 397; factional contests, 398, 399–400.

"Whigs," American, in Virginia and the Continental Congress, 433; attitude toward Chatham's proposal, 438; in Massachusetts, 441–442; appeal to Canadians, 446; victory at Moores Creek Bridge, 447; moderate Whigs, 450, 451; theory of governmental authority, 451; on the frontier, 497; attitude toward loyalists, 521.

White, Father, in Maryland, 70.

White, John, at Roanoke, 36.

White Plains, American army at, 479.

Whitefield, George, Great Awakening, 252; main account, 276, 277.

Whitehill, Robert, Anti-Federalist leader in Pennsylvania, 605.

Wilkinson and Ayrault, in slave trade, 262.

William III, accession, 194; colonial policy, 200–203; opposes France, 216, 217; controls Ireland, 217; Spanish succession, 220; power as King, 227; supported by Scotch-Irish Orangemen, 289.

William and Mary College, founded, character, 333; at Williamsburg, 335; Jefferson's plan, 555.

William the Silent, Dutch leader, 18.

Williams, Roger, views, 112; banished, 113; founds Providence, 117; secures patent, 118; policy toward Quakers, 120; religious policy, 325.

Williamsburg, capital of Virginia, 323; intellectual center, 335.

Willoughby, Lord, colonizer, 41.

Wills Creek, trading post, Washington at, 371.

Wilmington (Del.), Swedish fort, 150.

Wilmington (N. C.) settled, 315; capital, 323; British base, 503.

Wilson, James, War Office, 445; hopes for reconciliation, 450; opposes proposal for independent governments, 452; delegate in constitutional convention, 586, 587; nationalist leader, 589; opposes compromise on representation, 592; favors West, 599; Federal leader, 605; interpretation of the Constitution, 612.

Windsor (Conn.), founded, 121.

Wine, in Virginia, 57, 179; in Carolina, 138.
Winthrop, John, governor, voyage to Massachusetts, 47, 98; character, 99; president of New England Confederation, 126; cited, 113.
Winthrop, John, Jr., founds Saybrook, 121; governor of Connecticut, secures charter, 123.
Winthrop, John, professor in Harvard, 278.
Winthrop v. *Lechmere*, cited, 350.
Wisconsin, held in part by British, 527.
Wise, John, opposes Andros taxation, 191; on democracy, 275; opposes absolutism, 344; cited, 344.
Witchcraft, Salem, 274.
Wolfe, James, takes Louisburg, 381, 382; capture of Quebec, 383–384; death, 384; impatience with militia, 393.
Women, in Virginia, 57; Anne Hutchinson in Massachusetts and Rhode Island, 113, 114, 117, 118; girls educated in England, 253; ladies in New England, 266; schools in the South, 334.
Wood, Capt. Abraham, explorer, 80.
Woolen manufactures, in England, 4; in Ireland, 227, 290, 291; restricted in colonies, 236, 264.

Woolens Act of 1699, 236, 264, 290.
World War, use of economic resources, 464.
Writs of assistance, in Massachusetts, 396; approved by Parliament, 417.
Wyoming valley, settled by Connecticut colonists, 295, 542; massacre, 499; awarded to Pennsylvania, 529; dispute settled by arbitration, 563.

Yale College, founded, 277; protest against Great Awakening, 277.
Yates (of N. Y.), opposes Constitution, 608.
Yemassees, war, 313.
Yeomen, English social class, 3, 9.
York, Duke of. *See* James II.
York River, navigable, 48.
Yorktown campaign, 507; effect on English opinion, 509.

Zenger, John Peter, libel case, 299.
Zenger case, 299; significance, 351.
Zuñiga, cited, 55.